Praise for Speak Softly and Carry a Big Stick

"Broadcasters have always been coddled by politicians, and "Speak Softly…" explains how and why. J.H. Snider tells the story with the rigor of a scholar, the doggedness of an investigative reporter and the zeal of a reformer."

—Paul Taylor, Executive Vice President, Pew Research Center

"J.H. Snider offers an extremely comprehensive and well-documented look "behind the curtain" at how the National Association of Broadcasters drives its national legislative agenda. This is must reading for not only political scientists but for all who are interested in media policy and how it gets made in Washington."

—Chellie Pingree, President and CEO, Common Cause

"This astute book is a first-rate work of original scholarship. It also provides an unsettling description of broadcasters' policy influence. When their own interests are involved, broadcasters cannot be trusted to act in the way they demand of all others in society. Readers will no doubt question whether J.H. Snider's recommended solution is a practical one. But no reader will question his call for new measures."

—Thomas E. Patterson, Bradlee Professor of Government and the Press, Harvard University

"Having played a role in the mad-cap drama of telecommunications legislation Snider documents, I can tell you he has captured the essence of the machinations, strange bedfellows, and almost single-minded, righteous self-interest that drives the telecommunications debate. Like it or not, this is how the power game is really played."

—Stephen R. Effros, Former President (1976–1999), Cable Telecommunications Association

"Speak Softly documents the broadcast industry's striking influence on public policy, including the landmark Telecommunications Act of 1996. As Congress gears up to re-write the Act, J.H. Snider's analysis is particularly timely."

—Kevin Werbach, Professor, The Wharton School, University of Pennsylvania

"This is a theoretically rigorous and meticulously researched examination of the growing conflicts of interest embedded in our communications policymakers and the media institutions that cover them. Snider's documentation of the various means by which broadcasters can influence policymakers—and the extent to which they use such influence—on behalf of their own economic self-interest is a wake-up call to any citizen concerned about the future of our media system and our democracy."

—Philip Napoli, Professor and Director, Donald McGannon Communication Research Center, Fordham University

"This lucid work, based on extensive research and insightful analysis, demonstrates the "low visibility" but effective influence local TV stations have to promote their industry interests at the expense of the public interest; it illustrates this with the 1996 Congressional spectrum "giveaway" to the broadcasters and shows the damage to the nation."

—Henry Geller, former Chief Counsel, FCC

"This is an indispensable resource for anyone seeking to understand the mechanics of broadcaster bias in the mass-media age. J.H. Snider peers into the files of powerful corporate lobbyists in Washington to shed light on one of the worst cases of industry-government collusion in the last twenty years, involving the wholesale handover to private interests of one of the American public's most valuable assets—the broadcast spectrum."

—Tim Karr, Executive Director, Media Channel

"A fascinating and perceptive look at the politics behind the biggest grant of public property to private parties in the 20th Century."

—Blair Levin, former Chief of Staff, FCC Chair Reed Hundt

"A meticulously researched case study illustrating why 'public interest' regulation of local TV broadcasting has been a cruel charade."

—Adam Thierer, Director of Telecommunications Studies,
Cato Institute

"J.H. Snider lifts up the veil of secrecy to reveal the inner workings of one of the most powerful political lobbying groups in the U.S. Through ground-breaking research, this book documents how the National Association of Broadcasters and local TV station owners have set the policy agenda for Congress and the FCC. "Speak Softly" will become the key source for those who desire to understand how decisions about TV and spectrum policy are really made in Washington. An important contribution to our understanding of the critical issues affecting the future of U.S. media and our democracy."

—Jeffrey Chester, Executive Director, Center for
Digital Democracy

"This book marks a major conceptual advance in the surprisingly under-developed study of media bias. Deploying sophisticated analyses that draw widely from sources as diverse as public choice theory and Plato, J.H. Snider demonstrates the implausibility of broadcast news organizations' claims to act consistently as agents guarding the public's interest in responsive, democratic government. Instead he shows how when it comes to public policy decisions that directly affect them, broadcasters—quite rationally and predictably—use their control over news coverage, and thus their power over politicians, to advance their own welfare at the expense of the public's. Scholars and citizens concerned with the clash between democratic ideals and political realities, and those seeking to understand the dilemmas that confront the news business in an era of growing market-driven pressures upon journalistic ideals, should read this important book."

—Robert M. Entman, Author, Projections of Power: News,
Public Opinion, and U.S. Foreign Policy

"In a democracy, public policies toward the media carry unusual importance, since they shape the amount and direction of information on which the people make their decisions. J.H. Snider's diligent research and keen intelligence has produced one of the most revealing studies of this poorly understood but vital topic. By examining the remarkably secretive but powerful lobby, the National Association of Broadcasters, and how it worked to ensure that the Telecommunication Act of 1996 gave sweeping grants of free television spectrum to local stations, Snider has given us a eye-opening and indispensable account of how and why the media do what they do."

—Timothy Cook, Reilly Chair in Political Communication,
Manship School of Mass Communication,
Louisiana State University

"J.H. Snider's Speak Softly and Carry a Big Stick is one of the most important books on media policy and governance that I have read in years. With rare thoughtfulness, Snider combines a rigorous and detailed examination of how policy making works in the United States with a provocative and intellectually imaginative proposal for reform. This book not only deserves, it demands, the attention of policy makers and concerned citizens who wish to see a free press and a free society."

—Robert W. McChesney, Author, *The Problem of the Media*

"A thorough and insightful look at the subtle ways in which TV broadcasters exert a great deal of political power."

—Benjamin I. Page, Gordon Scott Professor of Decision Making,
Northwestern University

"J.H. Snider's book provides a well-reasoned case for the view that broadcasters' wield undue political influence over communications policy in the United States. His in-depth theoretical and empirical substantiation of his arguments make this important reading for practitioners and academics involved on all sides of the debate over broadcast regulation, spectrum policy, and media bias."

—William Lehr, Associate Director, Internet and Telecoms
Convergence Consortium, MIT

"Speak Softly and Carry A Big Stick, by J.H. Snider, addresses an important and understudied aspect of Washington politics: the formidable influence wielded by television broadcasters on public policy and public perception—with consequences worth tens of billions of dollars. Snider, a nationally recognized expert on telecommunications policy trained in political science, has written an elegant, well-informed, and well-documented account of the often hidden influence of television broadcasters not only over communications policy that affect virtually all Americans, but on the quality and fundamental fairness of electoral democracy itself. Here is a political scientist who deals directly with the logic and reality of political power in the nation's capital."

—Bartholomew Sparrow, Professor of Government, University of
Texas at Austin

"Local TV stations' Washington lobbyists prefer their tactics to be essentially invisible to public scrutiny, so they won't like 'Speak Softly.' But you will—if you care about the accountability of media power."

—Martin Kaplan, Professor and Director, The Norman Lear Center
at the USC Annenberg School for Communication

"A good policy-maker seriously considers the interests of every stakeholder. Speak Softly shows how hard it is for a spectrum policy-maker to do that when the best organized stakeholders of today eloquently present their case, there is little analysis of the complex technical issues from disinterested experts, and no one is speaking for the potential stakeholders of tomorrow."

—Jon M. Peha, Professor and Associate Director, Carnegie Mellon
University Center for Wireless and Broadband Networking

"The regime adopted to regulate radio broadcasting in 1927 is still, waves of technology later, with us today. The political stability of this regulatory structure is not well understood, however, and it confuses much analysis in telecommunications policy. J.H. Snider's ambitious book offers fascinating detail of the relationship between interests and outcomes, free speech and spectrum allocation. This research constitutes an impressive advance in our study of American media and the institutions that govern them."

—Thomas W. Hazlett, Senior Fellow, Manhattan Institute
for Policy Research

Speak Softly and Carry A Big Stick

Speak Softly and Carry A Big Stick

How Local TV Broadcasters Exert Political Power

J.H. Snider

iUniverse, Inc.
New York   Lincoln   Shanghai

Speak Softly and Carry A Big Stick
How Local TV Broadcasters Exert Political Power

iUniverse books may be ordered through booksellers or by contacting:

iUniverse
2021 Pine Lake Road, Suite 100
Lincoln, NE 68512
www.iuniverse.com
1-800-Authors (1-800-288-4677)

Cover Photo: President Clinton signing the Telecommunication Act of 1996 in the Library of Congress before approximately 400 invited guests. Photo provided courtesy of the Library of Congress.

ISBN-13: 978-0-595-34704-9 (pbk)
ISBN-13: 978-0-595-79448-5 (ebk)
ISBN-10: 0-595-34704-5 (pbk)
ISBN-10: 0-595-79448-3 (ebk)

Printed in the United States of America

In memory of FM radio pioneer
Edwin Howard Armstrong
(1890–1954)

CONTENTS

PREFACE

"[Broadcasters] are the most powerful lobby I have encountered in Washington."

—Senator John McCain, Chair, Senate Commerce Committee[1]

"[T]he most successful lobbying has traditionally been that which is least overt...."

—Schlozman and Tierney, Organized Interests and American Democracy[2]

The title of this book, "Speak Softly and Carry a Big Stick," is derived from an African proverb made famous by President Theodore Roosevelt.[3] I apply it here in the context of local broadcast TV lobbying. All rational lobbyists pursuing an unpopular cause will seek to exert power below the public radar. But few have been as successful in that effort as local TV broadcasters. The distinctive genius of the local TV broadcast industry lobby is that it carries an extremely powerful stick—control of the most influential public affairs medium in America—yet, when lobbying for its industry interests, can wield that resource without leaving a verifiable trace.

A secondary meaning of the title has to do with the idiosyncratic broadcast industry definition of the term "stick," which is used as a synonym for an FCC licensed broadcast tower. An FCC license grants a broadcaster the exclusive right to transmit information from a tower (which from a distance looks like a stick) of a specific height at a specific longitude and latitude, so tower and spectrum rights are inextricably linked. The big stick the broadcaster wields is thus literally his broadcast license.

The challenge for the broadcaster is that overtly wielding the stick for political gain is self-defeating. Viewers tune in information sources they trust and

---

[1] Paul Farhi, "Their Reception's Great," *Washington Post*. 16 February 1997, p. H1.

[2] Kay Lehman Schlozman and John T. Tierney, *Organized Interests and American Democracy* (New York: Harper & Row, 1986), p. 153.

[3] Seward W. Livermore, "The American Navy as a Factor in World Politics, 1903–1913," *American Historical Review* 63, no. 4 (1958): p. 864.

tune out the rest. So if the stick is to be used, it must be used quietly, out of the public eye. Surprisingly for such a visible stick, it turns out that discreet, unverifiable uses are eminently feasible.

This book's cover photo symbolizes the discrepancy between broadcasters' private and public communications. In private, broadcasting executives lobbied the Telecommunications Act of 1996 as if their life depended on it (see Chapter 15). In public, however, they sought to appear above the fray. Journalistic credibility, after all, depends on media organizations not appearing to be part of the stories they cover. So when President Clinton signed the Telecommunications Act of 1996 on network TV before an audience of prominent telecommunications CEOs, it was no surprise that the broadcasting executives refused an invitation to attend. The interest of the photo, therefore, lies not in what's in it but what is missing. See page 279 for a more detailed description of this historic and symbol laden bill signing.

The idea for this book came during my second year in graduate school in the Political Science Department at Northwestern University. I was taking Professor Benjamin I. Page's course on Mass Media and Public Opinion when the TV broadcasters' quest for a windfall of tens of billions of dollars worth of free spectrum rights was briefly front page newspaper news. The course looked at a number of different types of alleged media bias, notably partisan bias (favoring the interests of tens of millions of people across many industries) and company bias (favoring the interests of a single company within an industry). What was missing was a study of industry bias (favoring the interests of all companies within a single industry), which was the type of bias potentially involved here.

Evidence of partisan bias is the holy grail of political communication scholars. But for me, a finding of industry bias would be a very important finding. The broadcast industry is at the center of the information revolution; it controls much of the "beachfront" spectrum ideal for anytime, anywhere communications; and through its influence on both telecommunications and copyright law, has a profound impact on the structure of the media and with that the possibilities for democratic deliberation and accountability.

Professor Page, one of the country's leading scholars on media as a political actor, encouraged me to do my Ph.D. dissertation on this set of topics. And out of that dissertation came this book.

In pursuing this project, I was infused with Professor Stephen Jay Gould's advice to his graduate students. As an undergraduate at Harvard, I audited his graduate course on evolutionary biology. He advised his students that if they wanted to do grand theory they should first start, like he did, by studying something mundane such as snails. Through the study of such narrow phenomena, the great laws of nature would make themselves manifest.

I contend that the broadcast industry's extraordinary resources for pursuing industry bias without public detection makes it an excellent case study to illustrate the logic of low visibility politics. In addition, since First Amendment values are paradoxically a leading contributor to this darkness, this case also illustrates one of the most intractable failures of our democracy: politicians' intrinsic conflict of interest when they are given control of the systems, including media, that directly affect their re-election prospects. Unlike non-political information providers such as stock brokers, accountants, and investment analysts—which all have legally enforceable government mandated codes of conduct to deter economic bias—politicians have a direct conflict of interest regulating political information providers. Given First Amendment considerations, then, any conventional government remedy to industry bias would appear to be worse than the problem.

This book took some 8 years from conception to completion. Early parts won first and third place awards at the Telecommunications Policy Research Conference for best graduate student paper on Telecommunications Policy, and a Goldsmith Research Award from the Harvard Kennedy School of Government's Joan Shorenstein Center on the Press, Politics, and Public Policy. These and other related papers were cited in scholarly publications by political communication scholars Alger,[4] Arnold,[5] Gilens,[6] Sparrow,[7] and

---

[4] Dean Alger, *Megamedia: How Giant Corporations Dominate Mass Media, Distort Competition, and Endanger Democracy* (Lanham: Rowman & Littlefield, 1998), pp. 98, 100, 09, 10, 11.

[5] R. Douglas Arnold, *Congress, the Press, and Political Accountability* (Princeton, N.J.: Princeton University Press, 2004), p. 25.

[6] Martin Gilens and Craig Hertzman, "Corporate Ownership and News Bias: Newspaper Coverage of the 1996 Telecommunications Act," *Journal of Politics* 62, no. 2 (2000).

[7] Bartholomew H. Sparrow , *Uncertain Guardians: The News Media as a Political Institution, Interpreting American Politics* (Baltimore: Johns Hopkins University Press, 1999), pp. 91, 129.

[8] Darrell M. West and Burdett A. Loomis, *The Sound of Money: How Political Interests Get What They Want* (New York: W.W. Norton, 1998), p.155.

West,[8] and by an article in the *American Journalism Review*.[9] One section was published in a book containing the research of twenty-two "of the best young minds on political communications."[10] Rick Ducey, Senior Vice President of the National Association of Broadcasters' Research and Information Group, had the opportunity to critique some of the key findings of Chapter 15 when he was the discussant at a Telecommunications Policy Research Conference panel including myself. Much to my surprise, he had nothing negative (nor much at all) to say, which I took as a backhanded compliment. He reserved his criticism for the other panelists. Senator McCain, Chair of the Senate Commerce Committee, waved an early version of Chapter 15 at a Senate Commerce Committee hearing, and this incident was later reported in the *Washington Post*[11] and *Los Angeles Times*.[12] The New America Foundation published a series of my working papers and issue briefs seeking to reform use of the spectrum assigned to local TV broadcasters, issues covered in Chapter 12.

The information policy component of this book goes back more than 15 years. By 1996, when I finally embarked on this project to merge my interest in information policy with political science, I had already been studying the broadcasters' quest for a spectrum windfall for close to ten years. In 1989 and 1990, I co-authored a book with my wife titled *Future Shop*.[13] That book argued for new policies to transform America's information infrastructure so that e-commerce could thrive. The core policy recommendation, labeled "The New Consumerism," involved bringing information disclosure laws for products and services into the information age. But one chapter recommended creating a high speed, affordable telecommunications network, the last link of which would be wireless. The high speed would allow for high

---

[9] Charles Layton, "Lobbying Juggernaut," *American Journalism Review*, October/November 2004.

[10] Roderick P. Hart and Bartholomew H. Sparrow, *Politics, Discourse, and American Society: New Agendas* (Lanham, Md.: Rowman & Littlefield, 2001), back cover.

[11] Frank Ahrens, "FCC Sees Local Gain to Age of Max Media," *Washington Post*, 16 May 2003, p. E1.

[12] Jube Shiver Jr., "Focus of Media Debate Turns to Congress," *Los Angeles Times*, 28 July 2003, business section, p. 1.

[13] Jim Snider and Terra Diane Ziporyn, *Future Shop: How New Technologies Will Change the Way We Shop and What We Buy*, 1st ed. (New York: St. Martin's Press, 1992); reprinted as J.H. Snider and Terra Ziporyn, *Information Age Consumerism*, 2nd ed. (New York: iUniverse, forthcoming 2005).

fidelity communications, and the wireless last leg would allow for anytime, anywhere communications.[14]

In the late 1980s, one of the hottest issues of the day was what to do with the unused spectrum in the TV band. The broadcasters argued that they should get that spectrum to transition to high fidelity TV (known as "high definition TV" or "HDTV"). HDTV, we were told by Congress and broadcasters alike, would save America's economy and its tradition of local, free TV. Moreover, only currently licensed FCC broadcasters could speedily bring the benefits of HDTV to America.

However, as much as I loved the idea of high resolution, high fidelity images to enhance online shopping for goods and services, I hated the use of the country's "beachfront" spectrum to prop up the increasingly inefficient and archaic terrestrial broadcast system. Strongly influenced by the ideas developed at MIT's Media Lab,[15] I lamented that broadcast TV—whether in

---

[14] The information policy problem addressed in this book was summarized on page 241:

> "Of the special-interest groups opposing smart TV, perhaps the most influential is the television broadcasters. As Ernest Hollings, chairman of the U.S. Senate Commerce, Science, and Transportation Committee, put it: 'Our broadcast friends are the most powerful I know.... They can change votes right and left, and that is quite understandable. We live and breathe by TV, and that is our reelection. If the local broadcaster calls, you are going to do him a favor.'
>
> 'I am worried that what we are seeing on this panel are three very large, very powerful dinosaurs [the three major networks] who are protecting their feeding grounds," observed Representative Jim Cooper in the 1988 hearings on HDTV before the House Subcommittee on Telecommunications and Finance, one of the few politicians who directly challenged the broadcasters' arguments.... George Gilder, in his book *Microcosm*, agreed: "[P]oliticians around the world are propping up this obsolete system in the name of progress."
>
> Even the FCC grudgingly recognizes the obsolescence of terrestrial broadcasting, which it has so long defended against all opposition. As one senior official there admitted: "Ultimately, everything below a gigahertz will be mobile in nature.... We cannot tell the broadcasters about this: they would be furious.'"

Unfortunately, this description is as apt today as it was more than fifteen years ago—despite dozens of Congressional hearings, tens of thousands of pages of FCC comments, hundreds of millions of dollars of lobbying expense, and tens of billions of dollars of public subsidies to the broadcast industry.

[15] E.g., Stewart Brand, *The Media Lab: Inventing the Future at Mit* (New York, N.Y.: Viking, 1987).

high or standard definition—was a gross misuse of that spectrum[16] and that it would be much better used for either mobile higher powered licensed services[17] or lower powered unlicensed services.[18]

Alas, Congress, the FCC, and broadcasters had no interest in such arguments. The broadcasters were interested in receiving a spectrum windfall. Congress was interested in getting re-elected. If the facts collided with the interests of a powerful constituency, the facts would just have to take a backseat.[19] No wonder I became a political scientist. Politics seemed to trump policy analysis as the fundamental explanation for what I was observing.

I have dedicated this book to Edwin Armstrong, who committed suicide more than 50 years ago, because he personifies the tragic consequences of U.S. spectrum/media politics and the systematic failure of our democratic institutions to reform themselves. Armstrong is widely credited as the inventor of FM radio, but the government refused Armstrong access to the spectrum necessary to deploy his invention until the incumbent AM spectrum licensees and radio manufacturers could control FM technology and reap the profits from its invention.[20] Although many details vary, a similar type of injustice and social welfare loss has played out with the TV broadcasting spectrum. The major difference is that with TV the scale and duration of the injustice and social welfare loss has been much greater. TV broadcasting is allocated more than twenty times the amount of spectrum allocated to FM broadcasting. Like FM broadcasting, it also occupies the "beachfront" spectrum because this spectrum can send information through obstacles such as trees, walls, and precipitation. This spectrum, in short, is the crown jewel of the Information Age.[21] And for more than twenty years now the local TV broadcast industry has been warehousing

---

[16] Snider and Ziporyn, *Future Shop*, pp. 240-2.

[17] Ibid., p. 236.

[18] Ibid., pp. 237-8. E.g., "Each home ultimately will need to have its own personal communications cell. Already all of our homes have some personal spectrum allocated for such things as baby monitors, cordless telephones, wireless alarm systems, wireless camcorder microphones, garage-door openers, and TV remote controls. But this amount of spectrum—less than 2 megahertz (2 MHz)—cannot satisfy the needs of the future."

[19] Ibid., pp. 245-6.

[20] For a history of Armstrong, see Lewis, T.S., *Empire of the Air: The Men Who Made Radio* (New York, HarperCollins, 1991), chapters 10-12.

[21] See Chapters 3 and 12 and, for the latest installment of this saga, FCC comments of NAB and NAF et al. in the matter of *Unlicensed Operation in the TV Broadcast Bands*, Dockets 04-186 and 02-380.

its unused portions with the goal of keeping them out of the hands of competitors, holding them hostage as negotiating leverage for government subsidies, and ultimately acquiring them for itself—all through the industry's extraordinary lobbying prowess.

I would like to thank Professor Page for his words of wisdom and early encouragement of this project; Northwestern University for giving me a University Fellowship and then a Dissertation Year Fellowship, without which this book would not have been written; Newton Minow, former FCC Chair and Northwestern University Professor of Communications Policy and Law, who wrote a recommendation helping me get an American Political Science Association Congressional Fellowship; Jeffrey Biggs for selecting me as an American Political Science Association Congressional Fellow in Communications and Public Policy, which gave me an opportunity to work in the U.S. Senate and observe information policy politics up close; Gordon Silverstein, the New America Foundation's Program Director (now returned to academia), for selecting me as a New America Markle Fellow to work on information policy issues while finishing my dissertation on spectrum policy politics; Michael Calabrese, New America's Vice President, for the opportunity to co-found New America's spectrum policy program, turn my ideas into action, and exploit his fundraising, political, and PR skills; and the Ford Foundation's Becky Lentz for funding and enthusiastically supporting my reform efforts, especially my oddball proposals to create a concise visual language to help rectify some of the low visibility spectrum policy politics described in this book.[22]

Professor Page co-authored with me four papers that later became the foundation of this book. A separate related paper on methodology was co-authored with Northwestern Professor Kenneth Janda. Various other faculty who gave me helpful advice early in this project include Timothy Cook, Henry Geller, Roderick Hart, Lawrence Lichty, Jane Mansbridge, Newton Minow, Bartholomew Sparrow, Scott Althaus, Susan Herbst, and Thomas Patterson. More than 100 Congressional aides, FCC staffers, and telecom/broadcast industry lobbyists also volunteered their valuable time to educate me, often on the condition that I would not identify them by name. I would especially like

---

[22] J.H. Snider and Nigel Holmes, *Citizen's Guide to the Airwaves*, (Washington, DC: New America Foundation, 2003), and J.H. Snider, *Explanation of the Citizen's Guide to the Airwaves* (Washington, DC: New America Foundation, 2003). See also J.H. Snider and Nigel Holmes, *The Cartoon Guide to Federal Spectrum Policy: What If the Government Regulated Spoken Words the Way It Regulates the Airwaves?*, (Washington, DC: New America Foundation, 2004).

to thank David Wilson, Senator Dole's former telecom aide, for providing me with a copy of the Nick Evans letter (see Chapter 15) and facilitating key Hill interviews during 1996 and 1997.

Lastly, for tolerating a husband and father both holding a job and trying to finish this manuscript during his "non-work" time, I thank my wife Terra and children Pallas, Sage, and Solon. David Squire, a family friend and lifelong activist in pursuit of good causes, also deserves thanks for his confidence in me.

In an ideal world, I would have spent more time converting this from a dissertation into a trade book. But my priority is speed. Congress and the FCC are currently debating many important information policy issues, including the future of the broadcast band and a rewrite of the Telecommunications Act of 1996. Going through the conventional editing and publishing process would undoubtedly have improved this book, but possibly at the expense of policy relevance.

Needless to say, I take responsibility for any errors in this book.

Book Outline

This book is divided into three main parts: I) Theory, II) Case Study, and III) Policy Recommendations. The parts need not be read in sequence, and many less devoted readers will want to skip the first part altogether. Readers who are interested in the most direct (but not necessarily the best) evidence of industry broadcast media bias may want to start with Chapters 14 and 15 and then backtrack to earlier chapters. The chapters in Part II are ordered roughly from less to more direct types of evidence, with Part I providing only a theoretical basis to expect certain types of media bias.

Chapter 1 explains the basic logic of principal-agent behavior, including bias, and the special methodological difficulties of studying a type of behavior that is effective only to the extent it is unverifiable. Chapter 2 places the type of bias analyzed here—industry policy media bias—in the larger universe of potential media biases. Chapter 3 looks at the range of interests that might motivate broadcasters to pursue industry policy media bias. Chapters 4 to 6 develop a model of rational bias across all political actors, arguing that broadcasters have at least on occasion conformed to this model of rationality. Chapter 7 closes the section with a discussion of what makes broadcasters special: their resources, not their strategies.

Part II argues that the broadcasters' political success in winning a spectrum giveaway in the Telecommunications Act of 1996 was at least partly due to media bias.

It focuses on the indirect circumstantial evidence ("information short-cuts") that politicians and others dependent on the broadcast media can use to assess the likelihood of information policy media bias and that, conversely, broadcast media can use to intimidate potential opponents without leaving a smoking gun.

Chapter 8 provides an overview of the argument that rational legislators had reasonable grounds to anticipate media bias based on their support of the spectrum giveaway. Chapter 9 presents media claims to always act in the interests of audiences—even at the expense of profits. Chapters 10 to 15 present four complementary types of argument why it was reasonable for legislators to treat those claims as "cheap talk" and anticipate broadcast TV media bias based on their actions on the spectrum giveaway. Chapters 14 and 15 contain the best evidence of smoking guns I was able to find.

Part III, Chapter 16, concludes with a set of recommendations to remedy the type of media bias described here. It turns out that the remedy to this particular case of democratic failure can also be used to remedy a much larger class of democratic failures.

Note that some examples are used more than once: in the theory driven and case study parts, or in the chapters in Part II that provide complementary types of evidence. If a fact could illustrate more than one concept, I used it multiple times—e.g., in a chronological account (Chapters 14 and 15) and cost-benefit analysis (Chapters 12 and 13).

For those interested in the public policy implications of this analysis, I suggest jumping to Chapter 16. The Citizens' Committee proposal in Chapter 16 is my solution to the fundamental cause of the ills described in this book and, more generally, the fundamental cause of America's failure to strengthen and modernize its democratic institutions. That fundamental cause is that elected officials have a conflict of interest when they exercise any control over their means of re-election, including not only media but also redistricting, ethics enforcement, campaign finance, and voting systems.

Here are a few other suggestions to jump to relevant sections:

For those who want to get a quick glimpse of why the broadcasters are so powerful, see Chapters 7 and 14.

For those interested in the Machiavellian logic of special interest groups in general, see Chapter 5; for public, reporter, and legislator opinion survey data on whether broadcast industry behavior conforms to this logic, see the second half of Chapter 11; and for Machiavellian type arguments used by the broadcast industry, see the second half of Chapter 12.

For those interested in the handouts the government has given the broadcast industry, See Chapter 3, the first half of Chapter 12, and Appendices C and D.

For those interested in the contrast between journalistic ethics claims and actual incentives, see Chapters 9 and 13.

For those interested in understanding the role of media content in lobbying for specific information policies, see Chapter 14 (the must-carry and retransmission consent provisions of the Cable Act of 1992), and Chapter 15 (the spectrum provisions of the Telecommunications Act of 1996).

Research Sources

The documentary evidence for this book comes from a mix of published and unpublished sources. Unpublished documents include transcripts of interviews with dozens of broadcast executives, lobbyists (for both broadcasters and their competitors), journalists, FCC commissioners, and Capitol Hill staff; notes from attending broadcaster conventions; and internal lobbying publications of the National Association of Broadcasters such as *TV Today* (a weekly), *Congressional Contact* (a monthly), *Telejournal* (a monthly), *Leaders of the PAC* (a monthly), irregular fax alerts to broadcasters (now done via e-mail), and miscellaneous grassroots lobbying toolkits.[23] Published documents include academic works; newspapers such as the *New York Times, Wall Street Journal,* and *Washington Post*; popular journals of media criticism such as the *American Journalism Review, Columbia Journalism Review,* and *Brill's Content* (now defunct); and trade association publications such as *Broadcasting & Cable, Electronic Media* (now *Television Week*), *Communications Daily, Communicator* (a publication of the Radio-Television News Directors Association), and *The Financial Manager* (a publication of the Broadcast Cable Financial Management Association).

Informal field research also was an important source of information. As a telecom policy analyst at a major DC think tank, the New America Foundation, I am immersed in information policy politics. This includes regularly attending Congressional and FCC hearings; working with Congressional

---

[23] Some NAB periodicals have changed their names and formats subsequent to the periods covered in this dissertation. For example, in October 2003 NAB shifted delivery of *Telejournal* from satellite to Internet. In general, there has been a shift to Internet document delivery.

and FCC staff; hosting and participating in events with senior policy lobbyists from major trade associations and companies; and fielding calls from the trade and national press. I have had extensive informal contact with many of the Washington players involved with the telecom and media politics described here.[24]

Complementing my telecom policy work at the New America Foundation, I spent eight months working as a Congressional Fellow in the U.S. Senate, more than half of that time covering telecom policy for a member of the U.S. Senate Commerce Committee.

Various interactions with the press also influenced my thinking. As a politician, legislative aide, and candidate for public office, I have had substantial dealings with the press and the lust for favorable press coverage. In addition to serving in the U.S. Senate as an American Political Science Association Congressional Fellow, I have served as a school board member in a small urban school district and won a Democratic nomination to the Maryland House of Delegates. In all these situations, I was forced to look at the press through the eyes of a politician.

I have also looked at the press through the eyes of journalists. Over the years, I have been a member of the Society of Professional Journalists, The Radio-Television News Directors Association, the National Press Club, and the Authors Guild. I am married to a former journalist (and author or co-author of 8 books) and have worked side-by-side with some of the nation's top journalists and commentators as a senior research fellow at the New America Foundation.[25]

Northwestern University media and telecom resources helped me get started on this project. This included the Medill School of Journalism (one of the county's top rated journalism schools), the Newspaper Management Center at the Kellogg Graduate School of Management (a leading research center on media management), the Communications Studies Department (one of the country's top-rated communications departments), the Radio/Television/Film Department (a leading training institution for future broadcasters), former Northwestern University trustees (some of whom have been prominent broadcast executives), and the Northwestern University Library (one of the best media/telecom libraries in the world).

—J.H. Snider, Washington, DC, April 2, 2005

---

[24] See www.spectrumpolicy.net.

[25] For a list of fellows, see www.newamerica.net.

Part I:

Broadcasters as Information Agents

CHAPTER 1:

A Principal-Agent Theory of Broadcaster Bias

"Perhaps the greatest internal threat to democracy arises from the possibility that those who exercise power can deceive those upon whose authority they act."

—Arthur Lupia and Mathew D. McCubbins, *The Democratic Dilemma*[1]

"Lying and cheating are facts of life. They pervade all aspects of human existence. Books, TV shows, films and newspapers thrive on stories of deception and betrayal. Pop songs are full of tales of broken-hearted lovers who have been taken in by their partners. Half-lies and downright falsehoods are the stock-in-trade of politicians, diplomats, business executives, lawyers, accountants and ordinary everyday people. A glance through the pages of the Bible would be enough to show that this state of affairs goes back to time immemorial...."

—Ian Molho, The Economics of Information[2]

Division of labor is a defining attribute of modern societies. No individual can efficiently produce the millions of different products found in a modern economy. Therefore, people specialize in different tasks and depend on others to produce the goods and services they need. Specialization is also necessary for democratic governance. Direct democracy is not practical in a country with

---

[1] Arthur Lupia and Mathew D. McCubbins, *The Democratic Dilemma: Can Citizens Learn What They Need to Know?*, *Political Economy of Institutions and Decisions* (New York: Cambridge University Press, 1998), p. 70.

[2] Ian Molho, *The Economics of Information: Lying and Cheating in Markets and Organizations* (Malden, Massachusetts: Blackwell, 1997), p. 1.

3

hundreds of millions of citizens and tens of millions of government employees. So voters delegate political decision-making to elected representatives.

But the division of political labor does not stop there. It is not practical for
voters to monitor their elected officials directly. In the United States, there are
more than 500,000 elected officials. Each citizen is responsible for electing
dozens of officials from the local to the national level. These officials are scattered across thousands of miles, work in physical spaces not suitable for millions or even thousands of onlookers, and make decisions about complex,
technical matters that require substantial amounts of time and other resources
to master. If citizens attempted to monitor their representatives directly—
assuming such an endeavor were even possible—they would not have time to
do anything else. Cars would not be produced. Kids would not be taken to soc-
cer practice. Civilization would return to the dark ages.

Therefore, voters delegate the task of monitoring their elected representatives to various political intermediaries. These political intermediaries include
the mass media, interest groups, political parties, opposition candidates, think
tanks, and informal opinion leaders. Figure 1-1 depicts the two categories of
delegations, to elected officials and political intermediaries.

Figure 1-1. Voters delegating the task of monitoring elected officials

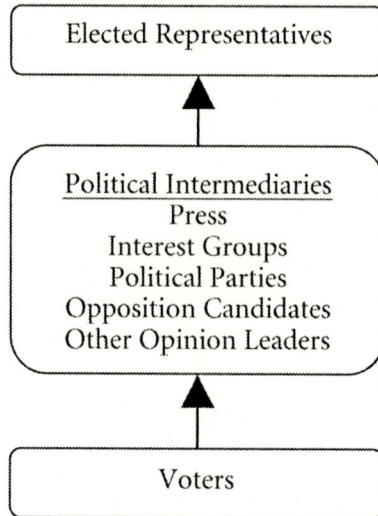

Those who do the delegating are **principals**; those who are delegated to
are **agents**; and the theory that explains the logic of delegation is called

principal-agent theory. When principals expect to gain more than they lose from delegating tasks to an agent, they form an agency relationship.

Agents can be divided into two categories: **object agents** and **information agents.** An information agent provides information about an object agent. The last object agent in a sequence of agents is the **ultimate agent.**

The terms object agent and information agent do not relate to the person but the function of the person. Thus, an elected representative can function as an object agent when passing legislation on behalf of constituents and an information agent when denouncing a political opponent to the same constituents. In a representative democracy, the ultimate object agent is the elected representative.

In an ideal representative democracy, information agents (e.g., mass media and interest groups) function to keep ultimate object agents (elected representatives) accountable to principals (the voters). Of course, this ideal is incompletely achieved in practice. Figure 1-2 illustrates the relationships between the various terms using our new, more universal terminology.

Figure 1-2. Object Agents, Information Agents, and Principals

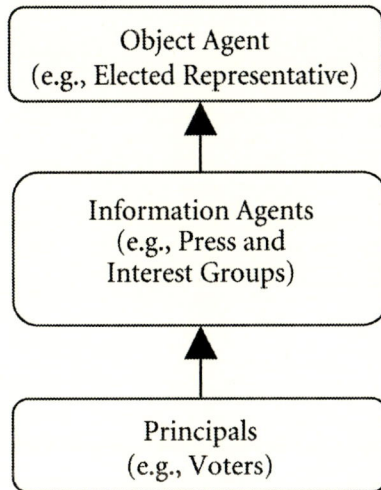

---

[3] John Zaller, *The Nature and Origins of Mass Opinion* (Cambridge [England]; New York, NY, USA: Cambridge University Press, 1992), p. 6.

A **political actor** is any principal or agent who acts in such a way as to influence who gets what from government. Most principal-agent relationships—such as a patient (principal) hiring a doctor (agent)—are not political.

The two central problems of delegation are that 1) principals and agents often have conflicting interests, thus providing a benefit for opportunistic behavior, and 2) it may be prohibitively expensive to eliminate certain asymmetric information between principals and agents.[4] In a democracy, the interests of both intermediaries and elected representatives often diverge from the interests of voters. At the same time, voters may be unable to detect the opportunistic behavior of their intermediaries and elected representatives.

Asymmetric information occurs when one party to a transaction (such as a transaction between a principal and agent) has information not available to the other party and that **private information** has a material impact on the outcome of the transaction. A party to a transaction has an incentive to create asymmetric information only when its interests differ from those of the other party. **Bias** is the act of creating asymmetric information. This is accomplished by selectively changing other political actors' incentive to acquire information. An **information incentive** is the difference between a political actor's benefits and costs of acquiring a particular piece of information. When an information incentive is increased, information is **revealed**. When an information incentive is reduced, it is **hidden**. In this book, I am especially interested in the type of bias involved in hiding information; that is, creating low visibility political environments.

An agent has a **conflict of interest** with its principal when the two actors have different preferences concerning the outcome of a delegated task. For example, an employer seeks to get the most work out of an employee for least cost, and an employee desires the most pay for least effort. We assume **true preferences** (abbreviated as "interests") are fixed. However, as a result of asymmetric information, **perceived preferences** may diverge from true preferences.

---

[4] Lupia and McCubbins, *The Democratic Dilemma*, p. 12. For other qualitative descriptions of principal-agent theory, see: D. Roderick Kiewiet and Mathew D. McCubbins, *The Logic of Delegation: Congressional Parties and the Appropriations Process* (Chicago: University of Chicago Press, 1991), Molho, *The Economics of Information*, chapter 1, John W. Pratt and Richard J. Zeckhauser, "Principals and Agents: An Overview," in *Principals and Agents: An Overview*, ed. John W. Pratt and Richard J. Zeckhauser (Boston: Harvard Business School Press, 1985), pp. 1-36. For an application of principal-agent theory to media, see: Philip M. Napoli, "A Principal-Agent Approach to the Study of Media Organizations: Toward a Theory of the Media Firm," *Political Communication* 14, no. 2 (1997): pp. 207-19.

All other things being equal, as voters' perceived preferences become more aligned with their true preferences, democracy is strengthened.[5]

When the relations between principals and agents are characterized by conflicts of interest and asymmetric information, we expect rational agents to engage in opportunistic behavior (also called "shirking" behavior). For example, unmonitored employees may spend their work time doing personal business rather than working for their employer.

Opportunistic behavior for our purposes is defined as behavior that increases the agent's welfare at the expense of the principal's welfare. The payoff from opportunistic behavior, the **opportunistic payoff**, is the motive for bias. Since bias facilitates opportunistic behavior, it can be viewed as a type of opportunistic behavior. An example of bias would be an employee who pretended to work whenever his boss walked by his cubicle. The opportunistic behavior is the work time devoted to personal business, and the opportunistic payoff the difference in the employee's utility from doing personal business as opposed to work.

The relationship between the various terms is summarized below. A conflict of interest provides a motive for bias. If bias goes undetected, a condition of asymmetric information is created. This asymmetric information, in turn, may provide the means to get away with opportunistic behavior without penalty.

Conflict of Interest ➔ Bias ➔ Asymmetric Information ➔ Opportunistic Behavior ➔ Opportunistic Payoff

If an agent is lucky, asymmetric information may exist without its having to incur the expense of bias. In this case, the cause and effect sequence is much simpler.

Asymmetric Information ➔ Opportunistic Behavior ➔ Opportunistic Payoff

But hoping for this cause and effect sequence is akin to a student not studying the night before an exam in the hope that a blizzard will hit and cause school to be cancelled. Most political actors must rely on bias if they hope to create asymmetric information. The focus of this book is not on how political

---

[5] Robert Alan Dahl, *Democracy and Its Critics* (New Haven: Yale University Press, 1989), pp. 111-12, 81-82, Benjamin I. Page, *Who Deliberates?: Mass Media in Modern Democracy*, *American Politics and Political Economy* (Chicago: University of Chicago Press, 1996), p. 1.

actors exploit asymmetric information—the simple cause and effect sequence—but how they seek to create it.[6]

When people in the real world reason about the probability of opportunistic behavior, they can use conflicts of interest, bias, and asymmetric information as predictors. None of these states of the world proves opportunistic behavior—at least by legal and rigorous academic standards—but each does increase its odds, and it is in the realm of the uncertain that real people live their lives and make decisions. Indeed, in common discourse, people often use the concepts of conflict of interest, bias, and asymmetric information interchangeably with the concept of opportunistic behavior. In other words, evidence of conflict of interest, bias, and asymmetric information are used as **information shortcuts** for evidence of opportunistic behavior.

I call such indirect evidence of bias the **appearance standard** of evidence and contrast it to the **smoking gun standard** of evidence, where the actual opportunistic behavior is observed. This is similar to the legal distinction between circumstantial and conclusive evidence.

Incentives for agent opportunism can be ranked along an accountability scale. The more likely an agent's opportunistic act will be exposed and penalized, the greater the agent's **accountability** for that act. The greater the accountability for an opportunistic act, the less likely it will take place. Behavior under perfect conditions of accountability is **agency** behavior (also called fiduciary, trustee, or ethical behavior).[7]

Professionals and their lobbying organizations commonly assert that agency behavior can be internally generated—that is, it is a matter of ethics, also described as integrity or character. In contrast, the rational choice perspective that dominates this analysis assumes that agency behavior is the result of externally imposed accountability—that is, a cost-benefit calculus.

---

[6] For a classic study on exploiting asymmetric information and reducing it by mobilizing ordinary citizens, see E. E. Schattschneider, *Politics, Pressures and the Tariff; a Study of Free Private Enterprise in Pressure Politics, as Shown in the 1929–1930 Revision of the Tariff* (New York,: Prentice-Hall, inc., 1935).

[7] The non-mathematical language to describe the relations between principals and agents is diverse and often context dependent. For example, working vs. shirking is often used to describe the difference between agency and opportunistic behavior; e.g., see J. Bendor, A. Glazer, and T. Hammond, "Theories of Delegation," *Annual Review of Political Science* 4 (2001). In my opinion, such language works better to describe conventional employee-employer relations than media-audience relations. I have tried to adopt principal-agent language of maximum generality while not completely abandoning the principal-agent-like language used by media scholars.

No rational agent will ever acknowledge to its principal the existence of a conflict of interest because such behavior would be self-destructive: it would suggest to the principal that the agent should be paid less or even fired. To the extent a conflict of interest is obvious, the agent will need to create a **firewall** that eliminates the conflict of interest and inspires the principal with trust. Chapter 9 looks at firewall claims in journalism and Chapter 11 firewall claims in other professions.

In the case of a local TV broadcast station, it is often claimed that a firewall separates the general manager (motivated by profit) from the news director (motivated by news values). In the case of a member of Congress, it is often claimed that a firewall separates a member's policy staff (motivated by good public policy) from its political staff (motivated by the need to raise special interest money for campaigns).

A firewall claim that is false but believed by a principal is an **opportunistic firewall**. When it is real, it is an **agency firewall**. I shall generally call an agency firewall an **ethical firewall** because corporate codes of conduct, such as for broadcast reporters, are typically known as codes of ethics.

Two Different Effects of Asymmetric Information

The existence of asymmetric information can have two very different types of effects:

1) hurt both parties to a transaction,[8] or

2) give the party with the private information a strategic advantage.[9]

The first case prevails when the uninformed party can reasonably anticipate that it will be made into a sucker in a specific transaction and decisions to hire an agent are made one transaction at a time. For example, an employer will not hire a prospective employee without trustworthy information about the job

---

[8] George A. Akerlof, *An Economic Theorist's Book of Tales: Essays That Entertain the Consequences of New Assumptions in Economic Theory* (Cambridge [Cambridgeshire]; New York: Cambridge University Press, 1984), chapter 2.

[9] Avinash K. Dixit and Barry Nalebuff, *Thinking Strategically: The Competitive Edge in Business, Politics, and Everyday Life*, 1st ed. (New York: Norton, 1991), Inâes Macho-Stadler and J. David Pâerez-Castrillo, *An Introduction to the Economics of Information: Incentives and Contracts*, 2nd ed. (Oxford ; New York: Oxford University Press, 2001).

applicant's competence for the job. When broadcasters assert that "good journalism is good business," they are asserting the incentives of this case.

The second case prevails when the uninformed party is uncertain or doubtful about being made into a sucker or values the entire relationship with the agent more than a specific instance of opportunism. No one expects agents to be saints, just the best alternative among competing agents. For example, most employees can get away with an occasional fake sick day as long as the employer has no way to distinguish between a real and fake sick day. If the employer could tell the difference, he'd most likely force the employee to take an unpaid vacation day.

In case #1, an agent's rational strategy is to eliminate the conditions that foster bias (e.g., by creating an agency firewall) because bias is self-defeating. Only in case #2 is bias a rational strategy.

The vast economic literature on signaling focuses on the incentives and methods for eliminating asymmetric information, given the incentives of case #1.[10] A signal is a costly action that reveals trustworthy information; an example would be a prospective employee signaling his intelligence and work habits by acquiring a college degree from a prestigious university.

Another substantial literature focuses on the incentives and methods for generating asymmetric information, given the incentives of case #2. Machiavelli, for example, argued that rulers should deceive others in order to retain and enhance their power.[11] All of us know that deception is common in life, but we rarely know specifically when someone is deceiving us.

Principals, of course, are not helpless in the face of agent attempts to create and exploit asymmetric information. Once principals detect opportunistic behavior, they can penalize agents by withdrawing compensation. And it may

---

[10] E.g., David Austen-Smith and Jeffrey S. Banks, *Positive Political Theory I: Collective Preference, Michigan Studies in Political Analysis* (Ann Arbor: University of Michigan Press, 1999), Jeffrey S. Banks, *Signaling Games in Political Science* (Chur, Switzerland ; New York: Harwood Academic, 1991).

[11] Niccoláo Machiavelli, Luigi Ricci, and Eric Reginald Pearce Vincent, *The Prince* (London,: Oxford university press, 1935). This literature is arguably most explicit as applied to warfare. For recent examples, see Bruce D. Berkowitz, *The New Face of War : How War Will Be Fought in the 21st Century* (New York: Free Press, 2003), Michael Dewar, *The Art of Deception in Warfare, A David & Charles Military Book* (New York: Sterling Publishing, 1989), Roy Godson and James J. Wirtz, *Strategic Denial and Deception: The Twenty-First Century Challenge* (New Brunswick, N.J.: Transaction Publishers, 2002), Jon Latimer, *Deception in War*, 1st ed. (Woodstock, NY: Overlook Press, 2001), John J. Pitney, *The Art of Political Warfare* (Norman, OK: University of Oklahoma Press, 2000).

be surprisingly easy to detect and punish opportunistic behavior. Competing agents have strong incentives to expose opportunistic behavior to win principals' compensation in the form of money, votes, viewership, or anything else that is valued. Principals can use simple cues to assess the probability of opportunistic behavior.[12] And even if a particular principal is bamboozled, it may not matter as long as a sufficient number of other principals with similar interests are not misled.[13] Nevertheless, principal-agent theory suggests that it is difficult to eliminate all incentives for opportunistic behavior. For example, agents may find it more profitable to collude than compete. Opportunistic behavior is likely to occur, even if its extent is debatable.

Local TV Broadcasters

In this book, I attempt to explain the political influence of one information agent, local TV broadcasters. As an information agent, local TV broadcasters share attributes of both press and interest group. These attributes have traditionally been studied separately. For example, political communication scholars study the media-specific operations of TV broadcasters.[14] Similarly, interest group scholars, who are inclined to view broadcasters as just one of thousands of more-or-less conventional interest groups, study the non-media-specific lobbying activity of TV broadcasters.[15]

When an agent has a conflict of interest with a principal, it can solve this dilemma by splitting itself in two and farming out the conflict of interest to a separate entity. For this to be credible, it must not only claim that there is an ethical firewall separating itself from the entity with the conflict of interest; it must also at least partially implement such a firewall. Thus is born the convenient analytical distinction between media as press and media as interest group.

In Figure 1-3, the dual nature of the TV broadcasters is separated by an ethical firewall. On one side of the ethical firewall are journalists; on the other side

---

[12] Samuel L. Popkin, *The Reasoning Voter: Communication and Persuasion in Presidential Campaigns* (Chicago: University of Chicago Press, 1991), Paul M. Sniderman, Richard A. Brody, and Philip Tetlock, *Reasoning and Choice : Explorations in Political Psychology* (Cambridge [England] ; New York: Cambridge University Press, 1991).

[13] Benjamin I. Page and Robert Y. Shapiro, The Rational Public : Fifty Years of Trends in Americans' Policy Preferences (Chicago: University of Chicago Press, 1992).

[14] E.g., Sparrow, *Uncertain Guardians: The News Media as a Political Institution*.

[15] E.g., Schlozman and Tierney, *Organized Interests and American Democracy*, pp. 72, 98, 377.

are all other company employees. According to standard press treatments,[16] an ethical firewall separates news from business and lobbying operations. News operations fit in the category of press; everything else fits in the category of interest group. The news side operates according to journalistic values; the other side is bound by no such constraints. The business side lobbies Congress for favorable legislation; the news side is a public trustee. In theory and practice, news personnel are psychologically, morally, and organizationally distinct from other broadcaster personnel.

To distinguish between the two attributes of local TV broadcasters, I use the phrases "TV broadcasters as press" and "TV broadcasters as interest group." As we shall later see, the line of demarcation between news and non-news can be fuzzy (and this fuzziness, as we shall also see, can be a great political asset to the business side), but that is a complexity we can ignore for now.

Figure 1-3. Two Principal-Agent Models of Local TV Broadcasters

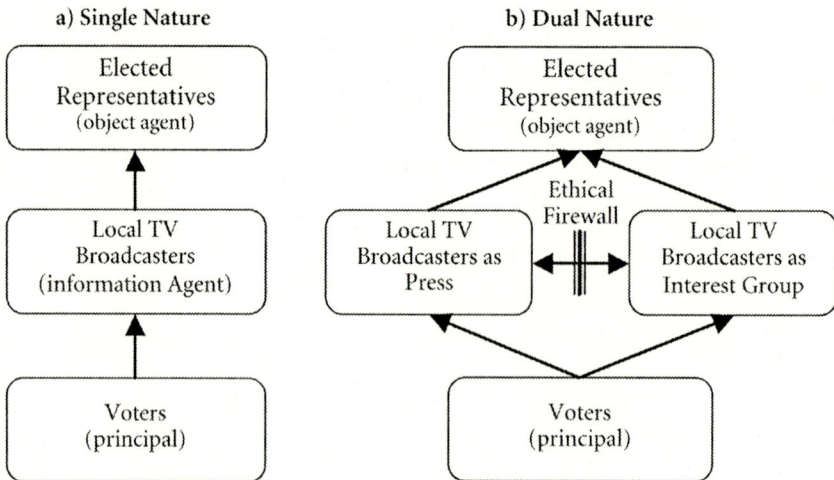

a) Single Nature

```
+--------------------------+
|   Elected                |
|   Representatives         |
|   (object agent)          |
+--------------------------+
             ^
             |
+--------------------------+
|   Local TV               |
|   Broadcasters           |
|   (information Agent)     |
+--------------------------+
             ^
             |
+--------------------------+
|   Voters                 |
|   (principal)            |
+--------------------------+
```

b) Dual Nature

```
            +--------------------------+
            |   Elected                |
            |   Representatives         |
            |   (object agent)          |
            +--------------------------+
               ^              ^
                              Ethical
+------------------+  Firewall  +------------------+
|   Local TV       |  <--||-->  |   Local TV       |
|   Broadcasters as|            |   Broadcasters as|
|   Press          |            |   Interest Group |
+------------------+            +------------------+
               \              /
            +--------------------------+
            |   Voters                 |
            |   (principal)            |
            +--------------------------+
```

---

[16] Ben H. Bagdikian, *The Media Monopoly*, 4th ed. (Boston: Beacon Press, 1992), p. 231, Jay Black et al., *Doing Ethics in Journalism: A Handbook with Case Studies*, 3rd ed. (Boston: Allyn and Bacon, 1999), Bill Kovach and Tom Rosenstiel, *The Elements of Journalism: What Newspeople Should Know and the Public Should Expect*, 1st ed. (New York: Crown Publishers, 2001), chapter 3.

Interest group and political communication scholars have generally accepted the press' self-serving firewall claim without debate or even justification. This is manifested in the fact that the study of interest groups and mass media are considered separate fields of inquiry, each field with its own textbooks, scholars, and journals.

One reason for the analytical separation may be its great convenience. Social scientists are generally rewarded for discovering generalities rather than anomalies. Anomalous cases, unless very significant, are properly ignored. And the reality is that the press is only organized as an interest group on a relatively small set of issues, primarily issues related to information policy, which includes information conduit (telecommunications) and content (media) policy. Since information policy (a tiny fraction of the news) is an anomaly for press scholars, and the press (a tiny fraction of the interest group universe) is an anomaly for interest group scholars, loss of generality by assuming distinct interest group and news activities may appear to be slight.

As I will argue, however, the powers of broadcasters as press and interest group are inextricably intertwined. One cannot understand broadcasters' influence as an interest group without also understanding their influence as press. And vice versa, one cannot understand their influence as press without also understanding their influence as interest group. The resulting need to describe broadcasters in terms of both an interest group and media outlet suggests the need to incorporate their behavior in a more general theory of intermediary behavior; for example, one based on principal-agent reasoning, including the logic of information bias.

In the context of this more general theory of intermediary behavior, we shall see that local broadcasters are similar to other groups in their strategies for creating information bias without detection but are different from other groups in their resources, including legal protections, for doing so. This differs from other accounts of press lobbying,[17] which tend to assume broadcasters' lobbying strategies are different from other groups (e.g., highly constrained by journalistic ethics) while their lobbying resources are similar (e.g., based on campaign contributions).

In this book, I am only interested in studying one type of broadcaster bias—industry policy media bias—because I believe it is common and important, yet rarely studied. Industry policy refers to public policy with a direct

---

[17] E.g., Schlozman and Tierney, Organized Interests and American Democracy. Schlozman and Tierney included the National Association of Broadcasters (NAB) in their study of several hundred interest groups. But they didn't consider that the NAB might have special resources given that its members control local TV and radio news.

bearing on the profitability of the broadcast industry. Media refers to the specific resource used to pursue the bias.

As information industries have converged and the borders of the broadcast industry have expanded to include other telecommunications and media businesses, it becomes increasingly relevant to speak of broadcast industry policy bias as information industry policy bias. For example, the major TV networks are parts of companies that own cable networks, movie studios, daily newspaper chains, record labels, and book publishers. Increasingly, broadcasters also compete with cable TV and telephone companies. And almost every information industry on the face of the earth covets the spectrum (popularly known as the public airwaves) that the FCC has allocated to local broadcasters. This spectrum is the most valuable on earth and is estimated to be worth hundreds of billions dollars if used for non-broadcasting services such as mobile telephone and broadband Internet service.[18]

Although I argue that broadcasters have engaged in opportunistic behavior, I do not thereby want to imply that the broadcast industry is morally different or more culpable than other professions. In my principal-agent theoretical framework, they are merely acting rationally, given their resources. From this standpoint, opportunistic agents, including local TV broadcasters, are no morally different than a hungry lion that instinctively sneaks up on its prey to feed itself. We may dislike the specific behavior, but as scientists we must focus on the underlying universal rationality of the action.

Principal-Agent vs. Objectivity Theory

Journalists have often described their own reporting as "objective" and criticized information that is "biased."[19] Some political communication scholars have also adopted this terminology. Many studies, for example, investigate ideological or partisan bias in the news.[20] Let us call this "objectivity theory." It

---

[18] Snider, *Explanation of the Citizen's Guide to the Airwaves*.

[19] E.g., Robert A. Hackett, "Decline of a Paradigm? Bias and Objectivity in News Media Studies," *Critical Studies in Mass Communication* 1, no. 3 (1984), Michael Schudson, *Discovering the News: A Social History of American Newspapers* (New York: Basic Books, 1978).

[20] W. Lance Bennett, *News, the Politics of Illusion*, 2nd ed. (New York: Longman, 1988). Thomas E. Patterson and Wolfgang Donsbach, "News Decisions: Journalists as Partisan Actors," *Political Communication* 13 (1996). Edward S. Herman and Noam Chomsky, *Manufacturing Consent: The Political Economy of the Mass Media*, 1st ed. (New York: Pantheon Books, 1988).

requires specifying some universal standard of truth, often specifying a method to get at the truth, and then charting any deviations from it.

Many scholars, along with journalists, have come to feel uncomfortable with the language of objectivity theory.[21] It is, after all, notoriously hard to ferret out the truth about what the good society should look like. Reasonable people can and often do disagree. Journalists have tended to retreat to the equally nebulous language of "fairness/unfairness."[22] Scholars have tended to retreat by simply focusing on cataloging the various influences that shape the media.[23] This approach sounds more scientific, but from a normative standpoint is troubling because the relationship between media coverage and democracy, which should be a major focus of political communications research, becomes only implicit and on occasion ignored altogether.

Another way of assessing media content is in terms of the principal-agent framework described above. Unlike objectivity theory, principal-agent theory implies that both the principal and agent engage each other in some type of transaction. In the case of local broadcasters, viewers contribute their attention to watch advertisements that local TV broadcasters can then sell for money. In return, viewers expect to receive editorial information that reflects their own, not broadcasters', interests. Agents have no obligations to people with whom they do not have at least an implicit contract. In the case of local broadcasters, those outside the contract are the people who do not watch their programs and thus bring in no advertising revenues. Similarly, principals have no claims on people they do not hire. In the case of local TV broadcasters, viewers cannot be misled by information they do not watch.

The most important difference between principal-agent theory and objectivity theory is the benchmark used for defining "bias." In objectivity theory, the benchmark of bias is truth—or at least a journalistic method that is supposed to lead to truth. In principal-agent theory, the benchmark is the agent's harm to the principal. In the case of the media, the benchmark is derived, not from some universal standard of truth, but from the specific perceptions and interests of the actual media audience. Socially undesirable behavior occurs when the media can engage in opportunistic behavior with no adverse consequences. It

---

[21] Hackett, "Decline of a Paradigm?.", Schudson, *Discovering the News*, Gaye Tuchman, *Making News: A Study in the Construction of Reality* (New York: Free Press, 1978).

[22] Michael Schudson, "In All Fairness: Definitions of Fair Journalism Have Changed over the Last Two Centuries," *Media Studies Journal*, no. Spring/Summer (1998). Black et al., *Doing Ethics in Journalism..*

[23] Pamela J. Shoemaker and Stephen D. Reese, *Mediating the Message: Theories of Influences on Mass Media Content*, 2nd ed. (White Plains, N.Y.: Longman, 1996).

occurs when a media entity knows something that it does not disclose to its audience and that something would materially affect the audience's assessment of the media's credibility. If the people who actually read or see the story are not misled to act against their own interests, there is no harm.

Obviously, the two theories substantially overlap. If the media misrepresents any material fact to its audience, this is bias under both objectivity and principal-agent theory. For example, if the audience for a TV station has a mixed number of liberals and conservatives, but the news surreptitiously favors conservative interests (e.g., highlights the positive but not the negative consequences of less government), then such behavior could equally well be described as bias under both theories.

But in other cases, the terms might not overlap. For example, if the media outlet is a trade press and its audience a specific industry, the terms might conflict. If the information systematically favored the industry over the general public, the information would be called biased under objectivity theory but not under principal-agent theory. Similarly, if a newspaper's sports page roots for the home team, this would be called bias under objectivity theory but not under principal-agent theory. Alternatively, if a publication is openly partisan (as many United States newspapers were in the 19th century),[24] the information would be called biased under objectivity theory but not under principal-agent theory.

Another difference between objectivity and principal-agent theory occurs when an agent serves a group of principals. In such a case, it is possible for the agent to be acting according to the highest standards of agency behavior with respect to the group interest while simultaneously acting with bias with respect to the vast majority of the individual interests that constitute the group. A news outlet seeking to attract a large audience, for example, will conventionally define agency behavior with respect to the median interest of its audience. But that means that any audience member who doesn't share the median audience interest may observe that the news outlet has an incentive to be biased. This explains how journalists can validly point to the fact that half their audience thinks they're too conservative and half too liberal as evidence that they are neither, while any individual audience member without a middle-of-the-road ideology can validly point to the fact that a media outlet is biased. From the perspective of principal-agent theory, both the journalist and audience member are using the term bias correctly even though they come to diametrically opposed views about who is biased.

---

[24] Thomas C. Leonard, *The Power of the Press: The Birth of American Political Reporting* (New York: Oxford University Press, 1986).

In popular and scholarly literatures, the term "bias" has taken on many different meanings. It might therefore be desirable to replace the term with a more precise phrase such as "create asymmetric information," but the precision would come at the expense of sonority and common usage. Hence, I will continue to use the term bias, but define it as "creating asymmetric information between a principal and agent."

The different meanings of bias suggest a different research agenda for studying bias. For example, questions concerning bias should be addressed to a publication's audience, not the general public. The bias of a local TV station in Baton Rouge, Louisiana does not depend on the preferences of New York City residents but on the preferences of the station's viewers in Baton Rouge. The bias of Rush Limbaugh's conservative network radio show does not depend on how conservative he is but on whether he distorts facts and misleads his audience in such a way that the audience is harmed. The debate over whether Fox News, a 24 hours cable and satellite news network, has a Republican bias hinges not on whether it favors Republican candidates and positions but on whether its audience is predominantly Republican and aware that its programming favors the Republican cause. In short, the focus is not on external facts but on the relation of those facts to particular audience preferences.

To demonstrate bias, it is not necessary to know the truth; it is only necessary to demonstrate that a material fact affecting the publication's credibility is withheld from the viewing audience. Suppose the general manager of a TV station assigns his sales manager to be the head of fundraising for the political campaign of a local member of Congress and also regularly lobbies that member on information policy issues. The general manager claims this information need not be publicly disclosed because it is immaterial: a strict firewall prevents his lobbying interests from influencing his news employees. Let's suppose an academic researcher has no reason not to believe the manager. If the researcher subscribes to objectivity theory, this conflict of interest will be irrelevant. However, under principal-agent theory, the researcher will shift his focus to audience preferences. If the audience considers the activities of a TV station's business side a material fact when evaluating the credibility of a station's news coverage, then a station harms its audience—and commits an act of bias—when it does not disclose this fact to its audience.

Universal vs. Narrow Media Theory

A major advantage of principal-agent theory over objectivity theory is its generalizability. The relationship between viewer and news outlet is considered just one instance of a larger class of relationships that share essential features. It encourages us to look for new kinds of evidence. And if the media then turn out to be unique—to violate generally accepted principles of human behavior by following codes of ethics at the expense of their own economic self-interest—this discovery takes on added meaning. Principal-agent theory predisposes us to reject claims of media exceptionalism—or any other interest group's claims of exceptionalism—unless there is strong evidence to the contrary. It shifts the burden of proof.

A closely related advantage of principal-agent theory is that it may better reflect the reasoning style of politicians. Objectivity theory assumes that politicians assess the power of the press without respect to the lessons they have learned from their general political experience. However, in a world where information about agent behavior is costly or simply unavailable, that assumption should be questioned. In such a world, principals and agents evaluate each other by the use of simple principal-agent rules of thumb gained from their general experience in life. These information shortcuts—also called "proxies," "heuristics," "cognitive shortcuts," "schemas," or "cues"—then become a foundation for a study of the power and methods of bias.

Methodological Considerations

The fundamental insight necessary to pick a method to study bias is what I call the "paradox of bias," of which the "paradox of news bias" is a special case. The paradox of bias is a logical implication of principal-agent theory. According to principal-agent theory, agents have a strong incentive to hide opportunistic behavior, including bias, because no rational principal would pay someone to harm himself.

One implication is that if bias is discovered, it is no longer useful. The very act of discovery eliminates the motivation for the discovered phenomenon. Since humans can anticipate the act of discovery, they will not practice bias in a way that can easily be discovered or cannot plausibly be denied. And if, by chance, an agent's act of bias has been exposed, the agent will find a new method of bias, if one exists, that has not been exposed and remains unlikely to be exposed. The implication, then, is that if broadcasters are shrewd political actors, we should not be able to find easily observable and verifiable measures of bias even if bias exists.

This has implications for both scholars and politicians. For scholars, it implies that merely looking at public data sources for direct and verifiable evidence of media bias is likely to be a flawed research method. In the context of news bias, an example of a public data source would be a readily accessible news database such as Nexis or Factiva.

Scholars should also not expect a random broadcaster who engages in opportunistic behavior—or people who depend on broadcasters' goodwill—to go on the record with claims of broadcaster bias. It defies common sense to assume that more than a tiny fraction of people will incriminate themselves or others on whose goodwill they depend.[25] And even if a broadcaster did do so—as some have in fact done[26]—it would be easy to discount the evidence as an isolated event.

For politicians, the paradox of bias has a similar methodological consequence: politicians should not expect definitive evidence of media bias to be readily available. As a practical matter, however, this is less of a problem for politicians than it is for academics. For politicians, like voters and other real-world decision makers, must make frequent decisions based on imperfect and non-verifiable information. They also have inside information not available to academics.

It is this distinction between the methodological standards of the politician and the methodological standards of the academic that turns out to be the key to understanding the power of broadcasters. The academic seeks the smoking gun; the politician, whom the broadcaster seeks to influence, will settle for reasonable probability. In this book, we study the power of broadcasters indirectly through the experience and perspective of the politician.

Another methodological implication of the paradox of bias is that ultimate agents, such as elected representatives, will always say that information agent bias does not influence their behavior, even when they know otherwise. The

---

[25.]A remarkable illustration of this principle was the revelation that the 1951 Brooklyn Giants baseball team used a hidden telescope to steal other teams' signals during the playoffs and the month preceding the playoffs. The entire team knew of the deceit but no one found it in their interest to expose it for close to five decades. See Joshua Harris Prager, "Was the '51 Giants Comeback a Miracle, or Did They Simply Steal the Pennant," *Wall Street Journal*, 31 January 2001, p. A1.

[26] E.g., Bernard Goldberg, *Bias: A CBS Insider Exposes How the Media Distorts the News* (New York: Perennial, 2002). Jon Lieberman, "Why I Stood up to Sinclair," *Broadcasting & Cable*, 25 October 2004, p. 48.

reason is that elected representatives who want to be re-elected must always publicly claim to represent their constituents. A member of Congress who publicly admitted that his behavior was influenced by interest group or broadcaster bias would in effect be publicly acknowledging that he should be thrown out of office for not representing his constituents. Consequently, it is not useful for a researcher to ask members of Congress or their staffs if they personally fear broadcaster bias because, regardless of whether they do or don't, the rational course of action is for them to say no.[27]

It's true that if a member of Congress could confidently answer the question anonymously, this logic wouldn't apply. But it is exceedingly difficult to build up such trust between a researcher and more than a few members of Congress when the researcher cannot be punished for violating the trust and the consequence of that violation for the elected official could be electoral injury.

A third implication of the paradox of bias is that principals will give isolated evidence of opportunistic behavior disproportionate weight. This is captured in the Latin aphorism: "Falsus in uno, falsus in omnibus." (English Translation: "Untrue in one thing, untrue in everything.")[28] Or, as President Abraham Lincoln observed: "If you once forfeit the confidence of your fellow citizens, you can never regain their respect and esteem."[29] Meanwhile, evidence of agency behavior will be discounted. This double standard of evidence is reflected in the folk wisdom that "credibility takes a long time to build, but can be quickly lost" and the lobbyist's dictum that "you get credibility in teaspoonsful and lose it in gallons."[30]

It may seem unfair and lacking methodological rigor to apply one standard for proving agency behavior and another for opportunistic behavior. But principals recognize that it is much harder to get evidence of opportunistic

---

[27] In contrast, the paradox of bias does not preclude a frank answer to the question: "do you think that other members of Congress fear or hope for broadcaster bias?" But that's like conducting a presidential opinion poll by asking members of the public what they think other citizens think of the president: the result is likely to be less accurate than asking the public what they themselves think of the president.

[28] Note that this principle has legal standing in a court of law; e.g., John R. Wilke, "For Antitrust Judge, Trust, or Lack of It, Really Was the Issue," *Wall Street Journal*, 8 June 2000, p. A1.

[29] Abraham Lincoln and Don Edward Fehrenbacher, *Speeches and Writings*, *The Library of America* (New York, N.Y.: Viking Press, 1989).

[30] Alan Rosenthal, *The Third House: Lobbyists and Lobbying in the States* (Washington, D.C.: CQ Press, 1993), p. 121.

behavior, so they disproportionately weigh any evidence of such behavior in judging an agent. That includes members of Congress evaluating their local broadcasters' agency claims. And it should also apply to academics evaluating local broadcasters' agency claims. To weigh evidence of opportunistic and agency behavior equally is to make no adjustment for the ability and incentive of local broadcasters to make one type of evidence readily available but not the other.

CHAPTER 2:

A Typology of Broadcaster Bias

"Only the cuckoo fouls its own nest."

—Harold P. See, Vice President, Chronicle Broadcasting[1]

Since conflicts of interest generate bias, we can categorize biases by the type of conflict of interest that generates it. In this book, I focus on only one type of broadcaster bias: bias involving the common policy interests of the local TV broadcast industry and employing the industry's media as a resource for bias. I label this "industry policy bias."

In this chapter, I locate industry policy bias in a larger universe of potential broadcaster biases. Figure 2-1 categorizes biases and shows the small niche occupied by industry policy bias. I make no claim that what is true of broadcasters' industry policy bias is true of their other types of bias, so it is useful to draw boundaries around my subject of study. However, I also don't make the claim that different types of broadcaster bias are unrelated. All types of bias are interrelated in that, under conditions of incomplete information, evidence of one type of bias, especially a closely related type of bias, can be used to infer the likelihood of another type of bias. This reasoning will be central to the argument developed in Chapter 11, the Argument by Analogy.

---

[1] Chronicle Broadcasting Co., 40 F.C.C.2d, Docket 18500, 3 May 1973, p. 875. See Chapter 13 for a detailed discussion of the Chronicle Broadcasting case from the 1970s.

Figure 2-1. A Typology of Broadcaster Bias

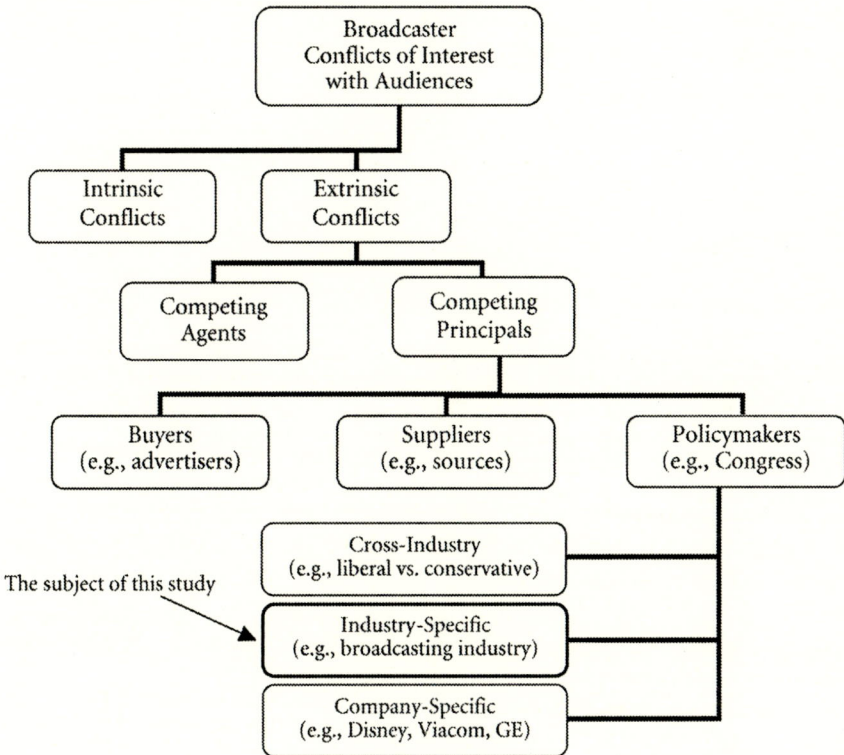

Figure 2-1. A Typology of Broadcaster Bias

Conflict of Interest Defined

To specify a conflict of interest, we must first identify the agent and principal to which the conflict of interest applies. In the case of broadcaster bias, we will take the agent as the owner of an FCC-licensed local broadcast TV station, and the principal as the collective interests of the broadcaster's local TV audience. Therefore, a conflict of interest would be any local TV broadcast owner's incentive to act against the interests of his local TV audience.

Local Broadcast TV Owner Interests

Let us assume that local broadcast TV owners ("media owners") are driven by the profit incentive. Obviously, human beings, including media owners, are motivated by more than profit. Nevertheless, our typology will be based on the assumption of the profit motive. This assumption is reasonable for several reasons.

Owners are stockholders, and stockholders generally invest in companies to maximize their financial returns. It is true that some investors seek to invest in "socially conscious" mutual funds and stocks, but these represent a negligible fraction of the investing public. And even for this small fraction of investors, media companies are generally not viewed as fitting in this universe of socially conscious companies.

The consequence of marketplace competition among companies, including media companies, is that companies that don't seek to maximize profits tend not to grow and buy other local broadcast TV outlets. They also become good targets for hostile takeover; an entrepreneur can acquire them and make a fast buck. As taught in introductory economics, profit-driven owners are not only most likely to survive but also to either acquire their less profitable competitors or drive them into bankruptcy.

As a result, successful companies tend to hire and reward employees who, whether or not they acknowledge it or are even aware of it, act in such a way as to maximize profits. It is true that most companies and employees publicly profess to be motivated by their clients' good—journalists who claim to be motivated by "journalistic values" would be a prime example of this—but nothing is more banal in human affairs than the protestation of altruistic behavior in situations where the appearance of selfish behavior might exact penalties.

Broadcast companies also have legal reasons to pursue profit. Today, most local broadcast TV stations are owned by public companies. As public companies, these companies have a legally enforceable fiduciary obligation to pursue profits for their shareholders.

It is true, of course, that the interests of media owners and the interests of society do not always conflict. This was the idea behind Adam Smith's invisible hand: competition forces companies to attend to customer needs even when the company's motive is purely profit-driven. According to this reasoning, since catering to consumer needs maximizes consumer welfare, the profit motive enhances, not detracts from, social welfare. This is also the theory behind such famous phrases as "what's good for GM is good for America" and media companies' frequent assertion that "good journalism is good business."[2]

But Adam Smith makes a number of assumptions that are open to dispute. One of the most implausible is that parties to a transaction, such as audiences consuming news programming, are perfectly informed. In the real world, asymmetric information between parties to a transaction is common. Accordingly, opportunistic behavior at the margin often has a higher rate of return than fiduciary behavior. The fact that American government spends more than $2 trillion a year is testament to the fact that the public and politicians, for a variety of reasons, do not believe the marketplace left to its own devices invariably maximizes consumer welfare.

Audience Interests

We shall assume that audiences are interested in information that suggests whether or not local TV broadcasters are acting in their interests. Specifically, audiences want information about a local TV broadcast station that might make a *material* difference in their evaluation of that station's broadcast information. To assume otherwise would be to claim that principals like to be hurt by agents, a violation of principal-agent theory.

Audience interests can be divided into those that are informed and uninformed. Audience interests are uninformed when they lack the information necessary to know their own true preferences. When speaking of a conflict of interest, the reference point in this book will always be to an audience's true preferences, not their perceived preferences.[3]

In reality, audiences are made up of individuals, each with different interests. As I use the term, however, the "audience's interest" refers to a unitary actor, analogous to the "median voter" or "public interest," that somehow aggregates and represents the interests of all its members.

A further distinction is between an audience's individual and collective interests. Individuals may have strong incentives to free ride on the efforts of

---

[2] E.g., Valerie Basheda, "She's So Fine: Wall Street's Media Analysts Have an Impact on the Way Newspaper Companies Operate," *American Journalism Review*, July/August 2001. Felicity Barringer, "Los Angeles Times Issues Unsparing Report on Itself," *New York Times*, 21 December 1999, p. C2.

[3] This is admittedly a controversial distinction, but nevertheless a vital one. The controversy lies in the fact that it is hard to measure a preference—a "true" preference—that someone hasn't yet formed and may never form. Given the difficulty in measuring true preferences, all sides to an argument will tend to claim that they have true preferences on their side. Not to accept the distinction between true and perceived preferences is to deny the value of democratic deliberation.

others; to act in ways that are individually rational but collectively harmful.[4] For example, rational individuals may prefer to watch entertainment programming as opposed to the hard news programming that enhances democratic accountability and collective well-being. In this chapter, when I refer to a conflict of interest between media owners and audiences, I will be referring to an audience's collective interests unless explicitly stated otherwise.

One reason for using collective audience interests as the principal is that when media organizations seek special privileges and subsidies from government, they claim to act on behalf of these interests. They may deny, perhaps even ridicule, the idea that a meaningful distinction can be made between individual and collective interests. But they do not openly claim that collective interests should be sacrificed for individual interests.

Conflicts of Interest

A conflict of interest represents a financial incentive for a local broadcast TV organization not to act in the best interests of its audience. These conflicts of interest can be divided into intrinsic and extrinsic.

Intrinsic Conflicts

Conflicts of interest are intrinsic to any principal-agent relationship in that a rational agent will seek to do the minimum work necessary to please a principal. The emphasis here is on shear laziness or cheapness rather than an external conflict of interest. Consider a media owner's incentive to provide quality news when viewers lack the incentive to discriminate among news providers based on quality. If the quality of the news is a function of the amount spent on it, then a conflict of interest arises if reduced news costs leads to a material decrease in news quality that individual viewers lack the incentive to detect. In such a "lemons market" situation of asymmetric information, low-cost/low quality news organizations will drive high-cost/high-quality news organizations out of the market. The surviving media organizations, the "lemons," will be those that abuse their viewers' trust. Examples of intrinsic bias might include viewers who

---

[4] E.g., Mancur Olson, *The Logic of Collective Action: Public Goods and the Theory of Groups, Harvard Economic Studies, V. 124* (Cambridge: Harvard University Press, 1965), Elinor Ostrom, *Governing the Commons: The Evolution of Institutions for Collective Action, The Political Economy of Institutions and Decisions* (New York: Cambridge University Press, 1990).

cannot distinguish between a news organization with twenty news bureaus and another with five, a news organization that generates 80% of its news from press releases and another that gathers its own news, and a news organization that carefully fact checks its stories and another that does not.

Extrinsic Conflicts

Conflicts of interest may also be extrinsic to the defined principal-agent relationship. This occurs when an agent competes with other agents or serves other principals in addition to the principal used to define the principal-agent relationship.

Competing Agents. Successful competitors—including cable TV, satellite TV, newspapers, and fellow broadcasters—may diminish a broadcaster's profitability. Therefore, broadcasters have an incentive not to distribute information that helps competitors, even if this information would be useful to audiences. Examples include crediting a competitor's scoops, reporting on a competitor's contributions to the community, carrying a competitor's product ads, and carrying a competitor's issue ads.

Competing Principals. To maximize profit, media owners may have to satisfy a number of different constituencies with competing interests. These competing constituencies include:

1. suppliers (e.g., news sources and subjects)

2. buyers (e.g., advertisers)

3. policymakers (e.g., legislators)

Each of these three constituencies may be viewed as a source of a distinct conflict of interest. Profit can only be maximized to the extent that opportunistic behavior with respect to these constituencies can go undetected. Accordingly, media owners have strong incentives to mislead audiences about the influence of competing principals in shaping media content.

1) **Suppliers.**[5] Some news suppliers are paid with cash. Many, however, are paid with favorable coverage. If undisclosed, the exchange of news for favorable

---

[5] In the case of ad supported media, audiences are a type of supplier. *See Bruce M. Owen and Steven S. Wildman, Video Economics (Cambridge, Mass.: Harvard University Press, 1992).* Audiences supply media companies with attention that they can then sell to advertisers. In return for their attention to ads, media companies compensate audiences with free entertainment and credible information.

coverage may conflict with an audience's interest, which often centers on finding out the truth. Sometimes broadcasters can raise false expectations among news suppliers, thus avoiding a conflict of interest with viewers. For example, in the common technique of "charm and betray,"[6] reporters may act friendly, flirty, or empathetic to create an unstated expectation of positive coverage. The final news product, however, may reveal that this was merely salesmanship to get sources to open up. This type of deceit, like the hidden cameras used in many investigative reports,[7] benefits audiences and therefore may be consistent with the highest standards of fiduciary behavior on behalf of audiences. Successful deceit on behalf of media audiences is most likely when news suppliers are relatively unsophisticated and unlikely to be important, long-term news sources. But with high level politicians such as mayors, members of Congress, and governors, this type of fiduciary behavior is unlikely to be effective. These press savvy individuals are careful to keep their guard up. Hometown reporters who burn bridges with these key sources may soon lose the privileged access needed to generate exclusive stories and hold on to their jobs. National reporters are less vulnerable to this type of pressure because if they alienate one member of Congress, 534 others are still available as sources.

2) **Buyers.** Advertisers provide the major source of revenue for local TV broadcasters. Advertisers want consumers to feel good about their products so they will buy them. They have little incentive to place ads with news media that give them unfavorable coverage. News media may therefore have strong incentives to avoid programming that would alienate major advertisers, even if the public would find such programming useful and interesting.[8] Examples include cigarette companies (whose ads are now banned from TV) that may not want reports on the ill-effects of smoking; local car dealers that may not want reports on shady sales practices; and pharmaceutical companies that may not want reports on generic substitutes for their high priced proprietary products.

Advertisers also may want favorable news exposure. This may be as innocuous as using an advertiser as a source when most any source would do. Or it may involve something more controversial such as running an advertiser's

---

[6] Evan Wright, winner of a 2004 National Magazine Award, calls this the "reporter's motto." See Sharon Waxman, "Sparing No One, a Journalist's Account of War," *New York Times*, 10 June 2004, p. B1.

[7] Michael Cieplay, "Television's Tiniest Stars," *New York Times*, 20 November 2002, p. B1.

[8] Bagdikian, *The Media Monopoly*, chapter 9, Erik Barnouw, *The Sponsor: Notes on a Modern Potentate* (New York: Oxford University Press, 1978).

video press release as news when the press release is neither newsworthy nor balanced.

3) **Policymakers.** Government policy can have a major impact on media profitability. A change in public policy, such as taking away a broadcaster's license or granting new spectrum rights to an incumbent broadcaster, can have a greater impact on the long-term market value of a media organization than running its existing business or entering new businesses via conventional market mechanisms. But the public policies advocated by broadcasters are not necessarily in an audience's interest. For example, as we shall see in the next chapter, during the 1990s broadcasters lobbied for changes in tax, copyright, telecommunications, and other laws that may have more than doubled the long-term market value of their government granted spectrum licenses. Leading authorities considered some of these policies, such as warehousing vast amounts of extremely valuable spectrum, to be irresponsible and against the public interest. The type of bias of primary concern to us in this book, industry policy bias, is a variant of this type of bias.

Three Levels of Policymaker Conflicts

Based on the extent of collective action problems, we can hierarchically organize three types of conflict of interest—and hence bias—between policymakers and media organizations: 1) company-specific, 2) industry-specific, and 3) cross-industry. In company-specific policymaker bias (henceforth, "company bias"), all the benefits from the bias go to the company that creates the bias. For example, if General Electric, the parent company of NBC's TV network, lobbied for a military contract that would solely benefit itself, this could result in company bias.

In cross-industry policymaker bias (henceforth, "cross-industry bias"), the benefits of the bias go to a large fraction of the United States population. For example, if the NBC TV network had a liberal bias, the tens of millions of other liberals in the United States might benefit from that bias as well as NBC.

Industry-specific policymaker bias (henceforth, "industry bias") falls in a middle ground. The benefits of the bias primarily go to the members of a particular industry; for example, if NBC-owned local stations exert pressure on candidates that take certain stands regarding broadcaster spectrum rights,[9] the several dozen other broadcasting companies that control most industry revenue would also benefit. For any given industry, the strength of the incentive to

---

[9] NBC, "The Case against Broadcast Spectrum Auctions," (New York: NBC, March 1996).

engage in industry bias tends to be directly proportional to the number of industry members.[10]

Company and cross-industry bias have both been the subject of intensive scholarly investigation. Company bias is often studied in the context of growing media conglomerates and concentration. For example, a classic question might be: "how does Disney, one of the twenty most valuable conglomerates in the world, report on itself now that it owns the ABC TV network?" Or: "How does General Electric, the most valuable company on the face of the earth, report on itself given that it owns the NBC TV network?" Many books and articles on the evils of media concentration focus on the dangers of company bias.[11]

Cross-industry bias has been the favorite type of bias studied by political communication scholars. Specifically, political communication scholars have been intensely interested in whether the media have a liberal or conservative bent.[12] Similarly, interest group scholars have been intensely interested in whether the interest group system has a pro-business bias or represents all segments of the population equally.[13] Surely, most political scientists would agree that a finding that the media system has a liberal bias is more significant than a finding that Disney does not report on allegations of pedophilia within its theme parks. Similarly, a finding that the interest group system has a pro-business bias is more significant than a finding that one type of telecommunications lobby has a distinct advantage over another type.

Policymaker bias, including industry bias, can be divided into two types, depending on whether the broadcaster is the principal with the politician the

---

[10] See Olson, *The Logic of Collective Action*.

[11] Dean Alger, *The Media and Politics*, 2nd [rev.] ed. (Belmont: Wadsworth Pub. Co., 1996), Bagdikian, *The Media Monopoly*, Neil Hickey, "So Big: The Telecommunications Act at Year One," *Columbia Journalism Review*, January/February 1997, George Seldes, *Lords of the Press* (New York,: J. Messner, 1938).

[12] S. Robert Lichter, Stanley Rothman, and Linda S. Lichter, The Media Elite, 1st ed. (Bethesda, Md.: Adler & Adler, 1986), Michael Parenti, Inventing Reality : The Politics of the Mass Media (New York: St. Martin's Press, 1986), Thomas E. Patterson, "The News Media: An Effective Political Actor?," Political Communication 14, no. 4 (1997), David H. Weaver and G. Cleveland Wilhoit, The American Journalist : A Portrait of U.S. News People and Their Work (Bloomington: Indiana University Press, 1986).

[13] Theodore J. Lowi, *The End of Liberalism: The Second Republic of the United States*, 2d ed. (New York: Norton, 1979), E. E. Schattschneider, *The Semisovereign People: A Realist's View of Democracy in America* (New York: Holt, Rinehart and Winston, 1960), Schlozman and Tierney, *Organized Interests and American Democracy*.

agent, or the politician is the principal with the broadcaster the agent. The first type can be called the "good politician/bad broadcaster" type because the broadcasters are the principal and thus have the upper hand. The second type can be called the "bad politician/good broadcaster" type because the politicians are the principal and thus have the upper hand.

The bad politician/good broadcaster type is implicit in the First Amendment. It has been reported on in detail in dozens of books and endless TV news programs.[14] It is a favorite subject of memoirs by print and broadcast journalists,[15] and decades old examples are still the subject of front page news.[16] It is routinely used by broadcast lobbyists when they want enhanced monopoly power or more public subsidies with fewer obligations.[17] Sometimes, week after week of *Broadcasting & Cable* go by with little respite from editorials with moral exhortations that broadcasters need to bravely withstand government intimidation.[18]

All this, even if overdone in the trade press, deserves study. Politicians, as history amply demonstrates, have incentives to muzzle potential critics and otherwise control political information. When media interests are dependent on politicians' goodwill, this natural tendency is undoubtedly exacerbated. The

[14] E.g., Marvin Barrett, *Moments of Truth?* (New York: Crowell, 1975), Carl Bernstein and Bob Woodward, *All the President's Men* (New York,: Simon and Schuster, 1974), Corydon B. Dunham, *Fighting for the First Amendment: Stanton of CBS Vs. Congress and the Nixon White House* (Westport, Conn.: Praeger, 1997), Bruce W. Sanford, *Don't Shoot the Messenger: How Our Growing Hatred of the Media Threatens Free Speech for All of Us* (New York: Free Press, 1999).

[15] Benjamin C. Bradlee, *A Good Life: Newspapering and Other Adventures* (New York: Simon & Schuster, 1995), Walter Cronkite, *A Reporter's Life*, 1st ed. (New York: A.A. Knopf, 1996), Daniel Schorr, *Clearing the Air* (Boston: Houghton Mifflin, 1977).

[16] Walter Pincus and George Lardner, Jr., "Nixon Hoped Antitrust Threat Would Sway Network Coverage," *Washington Post*, 1 December 1997, p. 1.

[17] E.g., John Eggerton, "Armey Takes Aim at Belo," *Broadcasting & Cable*, 14 October 2002, p. 22.

[18] E.g., "Asking the Tough Questions," *Broadcasting & Cable*, 29 March 2004, p. 30, "Morrow's Unhappy Anniversary," *Broadcasting & Cable*, 15 March 2004, "Separation Anxiety," *Broadcasting & Cable*, 19 May 2003, p. 48, Watergate is also a favorite theme; for example., "The 'Screw' Tapes and Letters," *Broadcasting & Cable*, 8 December 1997, p. 130, Chris McConnell, "Nixon vs. the Nets," *Broadcasting & Cable*, 8 December 1997, Bruce Fein, "It's About Time To Kill the Caps," *Broadcasting & Cable*, 27 January 2003, p. 28, "What's in the 'Public Interest'?" *Broadcasting & Cable*, 11 March 2002, p. 53, Bill McConnell, "Representing Media; Lawyer Blake is in the Middle of Sweeping Changes in Broadcasting," *Broadcasting & Cable*, 11 March 2002, p. 53.

classic example is Watergate, where the Nixon Administration threatened the *Washington Post* with reprisal, including loss of broadcast licenses, for unfavorable news coverage. Nixon himself was caught on tape vowing: "I will kill them," with "them" referring to the *Washington Post*.[19]

But the good politician/bad broadcaster type of industry bias, where broadcasters can intimidate politicians into giving them valuable, industry-specific property rights, also deserves study, yet has rarely been studied, especially in the scholarly literature.[20] This type of broadcast industry bias is the subject of investigation here.

The Likely Effectiveness of Industry Bias

In picking a type of bias to study, it is necessary to recognize that the effectiveness of bias is likely to vary by type of bias. Accordingly, when political scientists choose a type of bias to study, a major consideration should be the likelihood that a particular attempted bias will be effective, where effectiveness is a function of the difference between the anticipated benefits and costs of the bias. The type of bias with the greatest effectiveness may not win the political science bias sweepstakes—such an award would presumably be reserved for a discovery of cross-industry bias—but the result could still be important.

There are a number of reasons to believe that industry bias might be unusually common, especially in comparison to cross-industry bias. First, the selective incentives for industry bias are much stronger than for cross-industry bias. For example, a $100 billion dollar tax break for corporations in general must be shared with literally millions of companies, generating a relatively paltry return on lobbying efforts. But a $100 billion subsidy for the 25 companies

---

[19] Joseph Finder, "Abuse of Power," *New York Times*, 16 November 1997, p. 13.

[20] As we shall see in Chapter 10, allegations and stray anecdotes about such bias are bountiful. But that is different from sustained analysis. Those who have attempted rigorous content analysis have generally assumed direct and unsophisticated mechanisms of bias. See Roya Akhavan-Majid and Gary Wolf, "America Mass Media and the Myth of Libertarianism: Toward an 'Elite Power Group' Theory," *Critical Studies in Mass Communication* 8 (1991): pp. 146-49, Gilens and Hertzman, "Corporate Ownership and News Bias.", Alf Pratte and Gordon Whiting, "What Newspaper Editorials Have Said About Deregulation of Broadcasting," *Journalism Quarterly* 61 (1986), J.H. Snider and Benjamin I. Page, "Does Media Ownership Affect Media Stands? The Case of the Telecommunications Act of 1996" (paper presented at the Annual Meeting of the Midwest Political Science Association, Palmer House Hilton, Chicago, Illinois, 10-12 April 1997).

that dominate local TV broadcasting would come to $4 billion on average per company.

Second, collective action problems are greater for cross-industry bias because the number of beneficiaries is larger.[21] Continuing with the example above, the general corporate tax cut benefits millions of companies whereas just 25 companies divvy up the lion's share of the spectrum granted to local TV broadcasters. Given the relatively small number of industry beneficiaries, the beneficiaries have less incentive to free ride on the lobbying efforts of others.

Third, voters' incentive to detect cross-industry bias is generally greater. On the benefit side, a politician's systematic liberal or conservative bias is likely to have a much greater effect on a given citizen than a handout to a single relatively small industry. When a voter learns the candidate's party label, he acquires a vast store of useful information. When he learns the candidate's stand on issues only benefiting one industry, the electoral benefit is negligible.

On the cost side, since cross-industry bias tends to cut across many more issues, it is relatively easy to detect. For example, a liberal or conservative slant necessarily cuts across many issues, so a voter, candidate, or competing information agent has many opportunities to ferret out an ideological orientation.

Voters also get a huge amount of information assistance from others. Both the political process and the media that report on it are highly structured around partisan ways of presenting information. Guides to liberal and conservative positions are readily available for anyone who pays even modest attention to politics and the news. Even toddlers know the labels Democrat and Republican. Any time a media outlet shows a partisan bias, an army of partisans, including the surrogates of political candidates, is likely to point this out.

The government also helps. In a primary election, voters choose ballots based on party labels; and in a general election, candidates get party labels next to their names in order to help voters choose.

The relative incentive to engage in company versus industry bias is more problematical. On the one hand, the selective incentives for engaging in company bias are greater. On the other hand, the risk of exposure is also probably greater. All companies with broadcast properties have a common interest in hiding industry wide opportunistic action. But this is not true of company bias. For example, NBC may have an incentive not to disclose that its parent company has been convicted of price fixing, but ABC and CBS and other media outlets have no such incentive.

Of course, the effectiveness of industry bias is ultimately an empirical, not a theoretical question. But reasoning along these lines suggests it might be an

---

[21]See Olson, *The Logic of Collective Action*, chapter 2.

unusually fruitful place to look for media bias. In particular, the transfer of property rights worth tens of billions of dollars from the public to the broadcast industry during the 1990s would seem to be a good testing ground for evidence of industry bias. If industry bias doesn't exist when the stakes are so high, it probably doesn't exist at all.

The Significance of Broadcast Industry Policy Bias

Is broadcast industry policy bias significant? The answer to this question is obviously subjective. But what cannot be disputed is that broadcast industry policy bias, small as it is in the total world of potential biases, is growing in significance. One reason is that the broadcast industry is converging with the overall information industry. Telecommunications conduit industries (such as broadcast TV, landline telephone, mobile telephone, satellite TV, and cable TV), consumer appliance industries (such as TV, computer, and telephone), and content industries (such as broadcasting, newspaper publishing, and magazine publishing) are all converging toward a common, digital, Internet-based language to produce, transmit and receive information. A consequence of this convergence is that the scope of broadcaster interests has expanded to include the much larger information industry.

At the same time, the information industry continues to grow in importance, both as a percentage of GDP and as driver of economic, cultural, and political change. By 1996, the information sector constituted 7% of all value added services in the U.S. economy.[22]

In particular, broadcasters have exclusive or primary rights to a large portion of the most valuable spectrum. Spectrum, which uniquely facilitates mobile communications, is often said to be to the information age what land was to the agricultural age and energy to the industrial age: the most valuable natural resource contributing to wealth creation and civilization.[23] Efficient use of this spectrum may largely determine the cost of information transactions within the United States. To the extent that broadcasters succeed in influencing information policy, the impact on society could be large.

---

[22] Department of Commerce, "The Emerging Digital Economy II," (Washington, DC: U.S. Department of Commerce, Office of Policy Development, June 1999), p. 16.

[23] See Snider, *Explanation of the Citizen's Guide to the Airwaves.*

Conclusion

Potential broadcaster biases can be categorized based on the type of principal-agent conflict of interest that gives rise to the bias. One category of conflict of interest—those involving public policy—can be categorized hierarchically according to the incentive for acting upon the conflict of interest. A conflict of interest is most likely to be acted upon if the benefit of the resulting bias only accrues to the few and the risk of both detecting and penalizing the bias is slight. According to this calculus, partisan bias appears to be a bad investment compared to information policy bias.

CHAPTER 3:

Broadcast Industry Policy Interests

"[T]he media system is the result of explicit public policies and not natural law."

—Robert W. McChesney, The Problem of the Media[1]

"One cannot say that there is a coherent and logical public policy toward the news media. Instead,…such policies and practices emerged in incremental, particularistic, and inchoate manners,…far from philosophical questions of what kind of information is required for and in a democracy."

—Timothy Cook, Governing with the News[2]

In the late 1980s and early 1990s, many analysts expected the terrestrial, over-the-air broadcast TV industry to become a dinosaur thanks to new competition from cable TV, satellite TV, and optical fiber delivered TV-on-demand.[3] In some respects, the analysts were correct. Today, more than 80% of Americans get their primary TV signal via either cable TV or satellite TV.[4]

---

[1] Robert Waterman McChesney, *The Problem of the Media: U.S. Communication Politics in the Twenty-First Century* (New York: Monthly Review Press, 2004), p. 7, Snider, *Explanation of the Citizen's Guide to the Airwaves*, p. 1.

[2] Timothy E. Cook, *Governing with the News: The News Media as a Political Institution, Studies in Communication, Media, and Public Opinion* (Chicago: University of Chicago Press, 1998), p. 39.

[3] George F. Gilder, *Life after Television* (Knoxville, Tenn.: Whittle Direct Books, 1990). Brand, *The Media Lab.* "Broadcast Television in a Multichannel Marketplace," (Washington, DC: FCC's Office of Plans and Policy, 1991). Margaret E. Kriz, "The Fight for Access," *National Journal*, 8 July 1989, p. 1732. Florence Setzer and Jonathan Levy, "Broadcast Television in a Multichannel Marketplace," (Washington, DC: FCC Office of Plans and Policies, June 1991).

[4] Thomas W. Hazlett, "The U.S. Digital TV Transition: Time to Toss the Negroponte Switch," (Washington, DC: AEI-Brookings Joint Center for Regulatory Studies, 2001).

These TV delivery platforms for the most part carry local broadcast TV channels, but these channels now constitute less than 10% of the total number of channels available to the typical viewer.[5] In addition, close to 30% of households receive broadband Internet service, which can provide low quality TV-on-demand. From close to 100% of TV audiences in 1980, less than 50% now watch broadcast TV on a typical evening.[6]

Nevertheless, local TV broadcasting remains highly profitable. Operating margins in large U.S. markets are typically in the range of 40% to 60%. In 1997, ABC owned stations earned $460 million on $975 million of revenue; CBS owned stations earned $325 million on $836 million of revenue; NBC earned $550 million on $1,000 million of revenue; and Fox earned $500 on $1,050 million of revenue, for an average operating profit of 48%. Only CBS earned less than 50%.[7] These numbers are remarkable. In the words of *Washington Post* editor Leonard Downie: "There is no legal way to make this much money in the U.S. except in local television."[8] In addition, local TV broadcasters now have a majority ownership share in 40% of the top 90 TV networks carried by cable and satellite TV, and a minority ownership share in a large fraction of the balance.[9]

The explanation for the continued prosperity of broadcasting has at least partly to do with government policy. Over the years, the government has enacted a large number of policies to enhance the profitability and market value of local broadcast TV stations. These government subsidies to broadcasters can be divided into those given directly via taxpayers and those given indirectly via regulations imposed upon buyers, suppliers, and competitors.

---

[5] FCC, "Annual Assessment of the Status of Competition in the Market for the Delivery of Video Programming: Tenth Annual Report," in *CS Docket 01-129* (Washington, DC: FCC, 28 January 2004). Note that if those who illegally receive cable and satellite TV are included, the figure may be over 90%.

[6] Jonathan Levy, Marcelino Ford-Livene, and Anne Levine, "Broadcast Television: Survivor in a Sea of Competition," (Washington, DC: FCC Office of Plans and Policies, September 2002), p. 22.

[7] See Steve McClellan, "Nets are Big 4's Weakest Link," *Broadcasting & Cable*, 2 March 1998, p. 4.

[8] Leonard Downie speech at Woman's National Democratic Club, Washington, D.C., 15 May 2002.

[9] Michael E. Clements and Amy D. Abramowitz, "Ownership Affiliation and the Programming Decisions of Cable Operators" (paper presented at the Telecommunications Policy Research Conference, Arlington, Virginia, 2 October 2004), p. 5.

Appendix A lists the Congressional bills and federal agencies the National Association of Broadcasters (NAB) lobbied during 1996. Most activity centered on Congress (105 bills or resolutions) and the FCC (23 dockets). The information, derived from broadcasters' legally mandated lobbyist disclosure, provides a sense of the scope of broadcaster lobbying. But it provides no information about the specific issues lobbied or the intensity of the lobbying. For example, the "Seven-Year Balanced Budget Reconciliation Act of 1997" is a huge document but broadcasters focused their lobbying on a tiny section pertaining to the requirement that they give back their "loaned" digital spectrum at a fixed time. Of the 105 bills, probably the "Telecommunications Act of 1996" required more time and money than all the other bills combined. Much of this type of information can only be ferreted out by relying on non-government documents, including interviews with broadcasters, government officials, and lobbyists. The analytical description of broadcaster interests that follows offers what I believe to be a more helpful description of what broadcasters want and get from government.

The inner box in Figure 3-1 models the private market forces influencing broadcast industry profitability and asset values. This model is derived from Harvard Business School Professor Michael Porter's model of industry market structure.[10] Government policy affects all these components of market structure, so it is depicted as a force outside the inner box.

Figure 3-1. Government's Impact on Broadcast Industry Market Structure

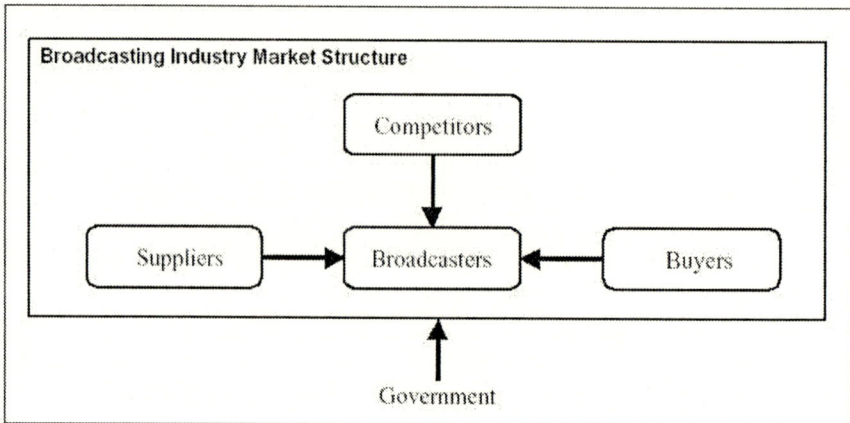

---

[10] Michael E. Porter, *Competitive Advantage: Creating and Sustaining Superior Performance* (New York: Free Press, 1985).

The same entity may simultaneously be a supplier, buyer, and competitor. For example, a viewer is a "supplier" while watching ads and a "buyer" when paying a fee for the programming; and a cable TV company is a "supplier" while carrying a local TV broadcast program and a "competitor" when it also carries its own programming.

A commercial broadcaster is defined as an entity with an FCC license to 1) use the spectrum associated with one of channels 2 through 69 on the TV dial (excluding channel 37, which is unused), 2) broadcast at least one high power TV signal with the right to provide more than 30 seconds per hour of original programming,[11] and 3) do so as a for-profit company. Consistent with this definition, we can divide the broadcast industry into two component businesses: content ("programming") and conduit ("telecommunications"). The two are closely linked in that content is transmitted over conduit and the profitability of each business depends on the other. An example of content is a TV news program; an example of conduit is spectrum.

A buyer is an individual or entity that purchases the broadcasters' end-product. Advertisers are the best known buyers in the local TV broadcasting business. But increasingly broadcasters sell their content to other distributors such as cable TV, satellite TV, and even DVD; and also sell rights to use their spectrum to short-term data subscribers and long-term lessees.

A supplier is a company that provides inputs to the broadcast industry. Suppliers can be divided into those that provide downstream and upstream products to broadcasters.

An upstream product is an input to production; a downstream product is an input to product distribution. An example of an upstream supplier is Hollywood. An example of a downstream supplier is cable TV.

Competitors are any potential entrants or substitutes for broadcaster products. Direct competitors provide an identical product; indirect competitors provide close substitute products.

The broadcast industry's value creation chain runs from upstream suppliers, to broadcasters, to downstream suppliers (distributors), and buyers (see Figure 3-2). For example, broadcasters buy programming from Hollywood (the downstream supplier), distribute it through cable TV (the distributor), and sell the audiences thus captured to advertisers (the buyers). Each player in the value creation chain, including broadcasters, adds value to the finished product. It is in the broadcasters' interest to concentrate the profits from this value creation chain in its own node of the chain.

---

[11] This provision excludes low power TV stations and TV translator stations, which can also operate in the TV broadcast band.

Figure 3-2. Broadcast Industry Value Creation Chain

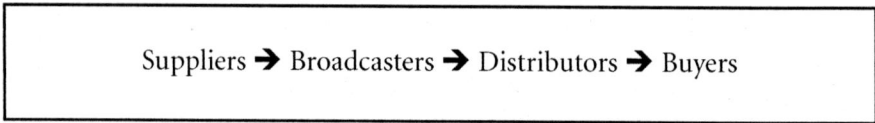

Suppliers ➜ Broadcasters ➜ Distributors ➜ Buyers

Entry and exit barriers determine the profitability of both competitors and broadcasters (Figure 3-3). The higher the barriers for competitors to enter the broadcasting business, and the lower the barriers for broadcasters to exit the broadcasting business and enter other businesses, the higher the profits of broadcasters and the lower the profits of competitors.

Figure 3-3. Profitability of Broadcast Industry Value Creation Chain

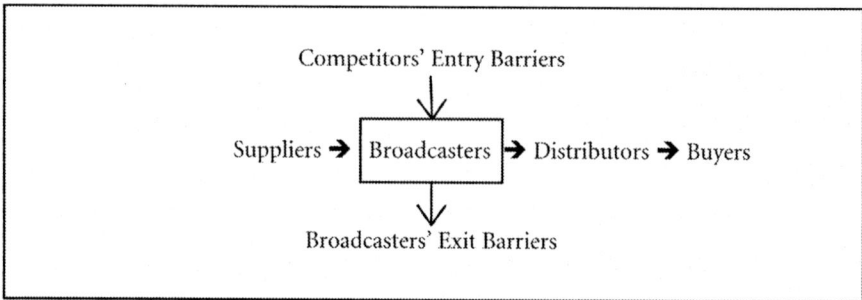

Competitors' Entry Barriers
↓
Suppliers ➜ | Broadcasters | ➜ Distributors ➜ Buyers
↓
Broadcasters' Exit Barriers

Broadcasters lobby the government to enact public policies ensuring that the interaction of these forces serves to maximize their own long-term profitability and wealth. Legg Mason Precursor founder Scott Cleland, a prominent telecommunications analyst, has gone so far as to observe that the broadcast industry now pursues a "Congressional business model," seeking profits through government subsidies, not market competition.[12]

Direct Subsidies to Broadcasters

Spectrum. Broadcasters have lobbied to build a telecommunications network at public expense. Unlike wireline telecommunications providers, which seek preferential access to public roads and rights-of-way, broadcasters have sought preferential access to spectrum, colloquially called the "public airwaves."

---

[12] Comments to broadcasters at their annual convention: "Yahoo's Yang Warns NAB Not to Slow Convergence in Washington," *Communications Daily*, 13 April 2000, p. 5.

Spectrum rights licensed to local TV broadcasters are typically worth far more than their physical assets. For example, in the very largest TV markets, the physical assets of a station may be worth less than $10 million while the spectrum assets are worth hundreds of millions of dollars.[13]

Broadcasters' spectrum can be divided into two major categories: retail and industrial.[14] Industrial spectrum is used as an input to production. A major use of industrial spectrum is for electronic news gathering—sending information from the field back to the station. For example, a reporter at a crime scene will send raw footage back to the station for editing. Retail spectrum is what broadcasters use to transmit signals to the home. Americans are very familiar with this spectrum because it is labeled channels 2 through 69 on their TV sets.

Broadcasters are currently allocated 402 MHz for retail uses and approximately 3,700 MHz for industrial use. However, even though broadcasters have more industrial than retail spectrum, the retail spectrum is worth far more because it is located in the highly desirable lower frequencies—the "beachfront property" of the airwaves. The market value of spectrum allocated to the broadcast industry for retail and industrial purposes is in the vicinity of $500 billion.[15] Broadcasters pay no monetary compensation to the government for use of this asset.[16]

---

[13] John M. Higgins, "As Broadcasters Giveth, They Taketh in Billions," *Broadcasting & Cable*, 6 April 1998, p. 80. See also the 10-Ks filed with the Securities and Exchange Commission by major broadcasters such as Hearst, Gannett, Paxson, and Sinclair. In the early 2000s, FASB changed its general accounting rules for intangible assets. As a result, for the first time in history broadcasters must list their FCC licenses as a separate line item in their annual reports. However, the valuation need not be market value; only the contribution of the FCC license to a broadcaster's ongoing business.

[14] Snider, *Explanation of the Citizen's Guide to the Airwaves*, p. 40.

[15] Wall Street media analyst Thomas Wolzien places the value of the broadcasters' retail spectrum alone at $367 billion. See Tom Wolzien, "Whose Bandwidth Is It Anyway" (paper presented at the National Association of Broadcasters Futures Summit, Monterrey, California, 25 March 2001). See Chapter 12 for a discussion of this valuation.

[16] Broadcasters currently claim to provide $9.8 billion a year in non-monetary compensation for both TV and radio spectrum (they don't break down the $9.8 billion between radio and TV industries). See NAB, "A National Report on Local Broadcasters' Community Service," (Washington, DC: NAB, June 2004). These numbers, however, are not verifiable and have had to be taken purely on trust because broadcasters refuse to provide the data necessary to verify them. Meanwhile, broadcasters have powerful economic incentives to inflate the numbers. See Comments to FCC of Echostar in the matter of *Broadcast Localism*, MB Docket 04-233, 1 November 2004.

Broadcasters seek to increase the value of their spectrum by a number of different strategies. These include:[17]

- **Increase the geographical range of their licenses by various means,**[18] including lobbying for higher power levels for their transmitters; mandated manufacture of receivers with improved sensitivity to weak, distant signals; redefined TV market definitions; must-carry rights on cable and satellite TV systems reached by homes with weak or no over-the-air broadcast signals; exclusive rights to translator stations in nearby rural areas; and rights to build higher towers that cover greater distances. Letters to members of Congress reveal numerous requests for increased power levels on a case-by-case basis. In the aftermath of the Telecom Act of 1996, the FCC's new table of allotments allowed numerous UHF stations to increase their power levels.[19]

- **Appropriate the "guard bands" between stations.** With the transition to digital technology, both the radio and TV bands have a lot of newly usable spectrum that incumbent broadcasters have sought to acquire for themselves. The typical lobbying pattern has been for broadcasters to veto any non-incumbent use of the guard bands. The result is that the only politically realistic way to bring the guard band spectrum into productive use is to give it to incumbent broadcasters. Through such a strategy, individual AM and FM broadcasters were able to double the frequency bandwidth of their spectrum holdings.[20] In the TV band, much the same result has been achieved by giving UHF stations greater geographic coverage, thus eating into the guard bands in adjacent markets.

---

[17] See Appendix C for a detailed chronological account of these efforts as part of the broadcasters' transition to "advanced TV."

[18] See Appendix D for a valuation of the opportunity cost of this spectrum in the context of the broadcasters' transition to "advanced TV."

[19] Chris McConnell, "More Channels, More Power for DTV," *Broadcasting & Cable*, 23 February 1998, p. 6, NAB, "A National Report on Local Broadcasters' Community Service." See also MSTV's brochure to recruit local broadcast TV members: "Promoting the Technical Quality and Future of Free and Universal Local Broadcast Service," (Washington, DC: MSTV, 2000). Chris McConnell, "FCC Urged to Strike Blow Against UHF Handicap," *Current*, 25 November 1996. "Fox UHF Affiliates Object to Digital Plan," *Broadcasting & Cable*, 22 September 1997, p. 22.

[20] FCC First Report and Order in the matter *of Digital Audio Broadcasting Systems and Their Impact on the Terrestrial Radio Broadcast Service*, Docket 02-286, 17 FCC Rcd 19990, released 11 October 2002.

- **Win spectrum flexibility for their licenses.** Licenses have traditionally been awarded to provide a particular service at a particular location with a particular technology. Eliminating these restrictions can be highly valuable. Consider 6 MHz allocated across the United States for a particular TV channel. Restricted to a traditional broadcast programming stream,[21] it may be worth $390 million.[22] But if sold to provide the highest valued service demanded by the market, worth $7.2 billion.[23] In practice, winning spectrum flexibility may involve many "minor modifications." Although each modification appears minor in itself, over time they add up to complete flexibility—with no additional public compensation.

- **Trade low value spectrum (such as a UHF station) for high value spectrum (such as a VHF station).** As part of the broadcast DTV transition, UHF stations on channels 52-69 get to migrate to the more valuable lower channels, 2-51. All stations have been loaned a second channel and the option to retain the one they consider most valuable to themselves.

- **Prevent the government from authorizing the use of unused portions of the broadcast band that competitors or broadcasters might want to use at a later date.** An example of an unused portion is an "unlicensed underlay," which allows a low powered unlicensed device, such as garage door opener, to coexist on the same frequency as a high power broadcast channel.[24]

---

[21] That is, a single, one-way, high-powered, ad-supported, standard definition TV programming stream.

[22] Coleman Bazelon, Michael Rothkopf, and Troy Kravitz, "The Value of the Airwaves," in *Explanation of the Citizen's Guide to the Airwaves*, ed. J.H. Snider (Washington, DC: New America Foundation, 2003), p. 19.

[23] Ibid. Today the market places the highest valuation on 3G mobile telephone/Internet service, including a return path (for interactive information), low-power transmission (which allows spectrum reuse in small cells), non-restricted bits (bits of any type, not just TV bits), and flexible payment (allowing for direct consumer payment as well as indirect payment via ads).

[24] See Snider and Holmes, "The Cartoon Guide to Federal Spectrum Policy." See also Comments to FCC of the National Association of Broadcasters in the matter of *Unlicensed Operation in the Broadcast Band*, MB Docket 04-186, 30 November 2004. An unlicensed underlay is to a TV broadcast what a whisper is to a loud band at a rock concert. While the rock concert (the high-powered broadcast) is playing, it is still possible for two concert goers to whisper to each other without disturbing anybody outside of the immediate vicinity of the whisper.

The gradual transfer of spectrum rights to broadcasters over many decades is akin to a hot dog stand licensee in New York's Central Park gradually appropriating the exclusive spaces ("guard bands") between hot dog stands, winning rights to operate in perpetuity, and evolving from a hot dog stand to a sit down restaurant to a giant office building with a mall including a tiny hot dog stand on the lower floors—all with no increase in the original hot dog stand license fee.

Land. Broadcasters lobby for free or discounted rights to build broadcast towers on public property.[25] Broadcasters transmit their signals from towers. To maximize coverage, broadcasters seek to place transmitters several thousand feet above ground level. To achieve such heights, they can build a tower from ground level or place a short tower on a tall object such as a skyscraper or mountain. Broadcasters estimate a typical ground level tower costs in the vicinity of $2 million.[26]

In the West especially, but also throughout the United States, the government owns many mountains ideal for broadcast towers. Broadcasters seek to receive the use of this land at below market rates. Once they get exclusive access to this land and build a tower, they can resell unused tower space to other wireless providers. In certain urban areas, broadcasters may be able to place their antennas on top of tall public buildings. In New York City, nine TV stations transmitted from the top of the World Trade Center, a publicly owned building.[27] In California, an acre of a national forest was sold to a local broadcaster so it could continue to broadcast without violating U.S. Forest Service rules.[28]

Zoning. Broadcasters lobby to build broadcast towers in communities that don't generally allow 2,000-foot-high structures. This requires federally mandated zoning exemptions for broadcasters. Sometimes there is fierce

---

[25] Petition of the National Association of Broadcasters Regarding Rental Schedule for Communication Uses, before the Office of the Secretary, U.S. Department of Interior, 13 December 1995. See also Statement of the National Association of Broadcasters, Submitted to the House Subcommittee on National Parks, Forests, and Public Lands, and The House Subcommittee on Environment Energy and Natural Resources on the Issue of Oversight of Federal Communication Sites, 12 July 1994; "Forest Service/Bureau of Land Management" in NAB Legislative Issue Papers, 102nd Congress, August 1992, pp. 15-17; and "Forest Service Fees," NAB Legislative Issue Papers, 104th Congress, October 1995, p. 10.

[26] Broadcasters' estimate for members of Congress. See NAB, "Spectrum Auction Action Tool Kit," (Washington, DC: National Association of Broadcasters, 1996).

[27] It was leased to a private company in July 2001.

[28] Cyril T. Zeneski, "Committee Would Sell National Forest Service Property to Radio Station," National Journal News Service, 20 September 2000. The Senate Energy and Natural Resources Committee passed the legislation in a markup without a recorded vote.

opposition to such exemptions. Many residents believe that a 2,000-foot high tower near their homes reduces property values, endangers their safety, and creates an eyesore.[29] In addition, the tall, lighted towers apparently kill millions of neotropical birds a year.[30]

The resulting broadcast towers can be extremely profitable. A broadcaster can lease space on a tower to dozens of different wireless services, including multiple mobile telephone operators. A well-situated tower near a major urban area can bring in revenue of more than $1 million a year and operating profits of more than 80 percent of revenue.[31] Reports one broadcast accountant: "I have heard of a station that made more money from renting its tower than it did from selling advertising."[32]

Broadcasters also lobby to make it illegal for local zoning authorities and community association covenants to ban rooftop or other external antennas, which many consider to be unsightly and a cause of reduced property values.[33]

Government Information. Along with other press entities, broadcasters lobby to gain subsidized and preferential access to government information and

---

[29] E.g., Karen Anderson, "Fighting the Towers-To-Be: Community opposition, local zoning, FAA conflicts make for rocky road to DTV," *Broadcasting & Cable*, 5 April 1999, p. 46. On the safety issue, the only hazardous consequence to humans I have been able to identify occurred on 9/11, when the broadcast towers on the World Trade Center made it impossible for helicopters to evacuate people from the upper floors. The result was that hundreds of people died who might otherwise have been saved. See Scot J. Paltroy and Queena Sook Kim, "No Escape: Could Helicopters Have Saved People From Trade Center?—Police Choppers Hovered, But Roof Was Locked," *Wall Street Journal*, 23 October 2001, p. A1.

[30] On the birds, see http://www.abcbirds.org/policy/towerkill.htm and Gavin G. Shire et al, "Communications Towers: A Deadly Hazard to Birds" (Washington, DC: American Bird Conservancy, June 2000). The FAA mandates the lights for all towers over 199 feet high. Unfortunately, neotropical birds get confused by the lights at night and crash into the towers.

[31] "Broadcast Towers: Managing Your Vertical Real Estate," panel discussion at NAB 1998, Las Vegas, Nevada, 6 April 1998. At this panel broadcasters were advised: "You have two key assets: a tower and a license," and "If you're going to build a tower, why not build it big enough to be a profit center." A number of towers in recent years have been so overloaded with revenue producing transmitters that they have collapsed. One presenter promised that a very popular tower can bring in revenues of a "couple million dollars a year."

[32] Erick Steinberg, "Assessing the Cost of Tower Maintenance or Purchase," *Financial Manager*, August/September 2002.

[33] Comments to FCC of the National Association of Broadcasters in the matter of *Restrictions on Over-the-Air Reception Devices: Television Broadcast and Multichannel Multipoinnt Distribution Service*, CS Docket No. 96-83, 1996.

facilities.[34] Advantageous access may be codified in law or simply institutional-
ized as a matter of practice. Consider Congress.[35] Broadcaster privileges include
free office space and staff support within the U.S. Capitol;[36] special tables and
documents in committee rooms; special tables in House and Senate restaurants;
entry through separate doors to Congressional buildings; immunity from certain security precautions, which speeds entry to and from the Capitol; free
access to telecommunications conduits throughout the Capitol for audio/video
connections; exclusive rights to video coverage of Congressional proceedings;
press aides in every Congressional office to educate reporters about government
affairs and write at least the first draft of many stories; television studios in the
Capitol that provide reporters with prepackaged video clips and story lines
delivered free to their local TV stations; preferred service from the Library of
Congress; privileged and extensive access to government officials, agendas, and
documents; and, on occasion, subsidized transportation, including parking
spaces at the Capitol and Reagan National Airport.

International, weather, and crime news are also heavily subsidized by the
government. The federal government spends hundreds of millions of dollars
on a foreign broadcast service whose board is dominated by domestic broadcasters.[37] Unlike the BBC, which has both a domestic and international version, the Smith-Mundt Act (22 USC 1461) makes it illegal for the U.S.
government broadcast service to distribute its information domestically.[38] But
it is perfectly legal for commercial broadcasters to benefit from the fruits of

---

[34] For another look at such subsidies, see "The Subsidized News Media," in Cook,
Governing with the News: The News Media as a Political Institution, chapter 3.

[35] For a list of select privileges, see "Daily Press Galleries Information Guide," (Washington,
DC: U.S. Congress, 1999), Radio-TV Gallery, "Rules for Electronic Media Coverage of
Congress," (Washington, DC: Radio-TV Gallery, 1999), *[Rules of the House of
Representatives for the Year 1997–1998]*, House; No. 1001 (Boston, MA: House of
Representatives, 1997).

[36] Although the staff is paid for by U.S. taxpayers, Capitol Hill press organizations control
the hiring and firing of staff. See "NPC to Daschle Re: Senate Press Club Gallery," *Record*,
Washington, DC: National Press Club, 1 August 2002, p. 1.

[37] Vanessa O'Connell, "Radio Mogul Heads U.S. Arabic TV Network," *Wall Street Journal*,
26 March 2003, p. B4. Broadcasting Board of Governors 2003 Annual Report, available at
http://www.bbg.gov/reports/03anrprt.pdf.

[38] The key relevant section is that information "shall not be disseminated within the United
States, its territories, or possessions, but, on request, shall be available in the English language at the Agency, at all reasonable times following its release as information abroad, for
examination only by representatives of United States press associations, newspapers, magazines, radio systems, and stations, and by research students and scholars, and on request,
shall be made available for examination only to Members of Congress."

this government subsidized international broadcasting system. Explains the Taxpayer Assets Project: "U.S. commercial television and radio interests have lobbied to retain the Smith-Mundt Act restrictions on U.S. citizen access to the information, in order to limit 'competition' from this U.S. government information service."[39] One of the great ironies of the Smith-Mundt Act is that it exempts the federal government's so-called video news releases that are fed to local TV stations and broadcast by local TV stations as bona fide news with no mention of their source. The Bush Administration spent $254 million during its first four years on outside contracts to PR agencies that developed such spots for at least 20 federal agencies and that were run as hard news on hundreds of local TV stations.[40]

The National Weather Service provides, free of charge, most of the up-to-the-minute weather data used by broadcasters.

Local police often provide media with free transportation ("ride-alongs") when they conduct potentially high profile raids and searches on private property.[41] Media also get privileged access to police radio communications and access to police stations, including the crime blotter.

Broadcasters also lobby to prevent the release of any information that might put themselves at a strategic disadvantage. For example, broadcasters have vigorously resisted efforts to disclose information about their profitability because that would undermine their lobbying efforts seeking government subsidies. They have also vigorously resisted efforts to create publicly accessible archives of their programming.[42] During the past decade, one type of programming claim has become especially noteworthy. When lobbying Congress and the FCC, broadcasters claim to provide billions of dollars a year in public service announcements.[43] Broadcasters use these claims to justify their public subidies, but they strenuously resist efforts to allow third parties to verify the claims, despite the fact that the claims are widely viewed as controversial.[44]

---

[39] James Love, "The U.S. Information Agency On the Internet Not For American Citizens?" (Washington, DC: Taxpayer Assets Project, 26 April 1995). Many commercial broadcasters, including Margita White, long-time president of MSTV, have served on the boards of the various international broadcasting boards.

[40] David Barstow and Robin Stein, "Under Bush, a New Age of Prepackaged News," *New York Times*, 13 March 2005, p. A1.

[41] Kathleen Kirby, "Look Over Your Shoulder," *Communicator*, December 1998, p. 48

[42] See the numerous broadcast industry comments in FCC Notice of Proposed Rulemaking in the matter of *Retention by Broadcasters of Program Recordings*, MB Docket 04-232, 2004.

[43] NAB, "A National Report on Local Broadcasters' Community Service."

[44] E.g., see comments of Echostar Satellite in FCC Notice of Inquiry in the matter of *Broadcast Localism*, MB Docket 04-233, 1 November 2004.

Legal Immunity. Along with other press entities, broadcasters lobby for legal and institutional privileges not accorded to other professions.[45] These privileges relate to the gathering and distribution of information, and include immunity from subpoenas, libel, fraud, lobbyist disclosure, copyright, trespassing, and in-kind campaign finance limits. Many are justified as a logical elaboration of the First Amendment of the United States Constitution. Some legal immunities are embedded in law; others result from public officials' de facto fear of coming into conflict with an institution with great power to influence public opinion. Most media privileges in Congress, for example, are not embedded in law but grew out of the mutual convenience of lawmakers and the press.

Broadcasters share a number of immunities not available to print publishers. For example, they are exempt from the requirement to deposit a free copy of their work in the Library of Congress, and they are largely exempt from the "fair use" exemptions in copyright law. For example, it is illegal for a library to store a broadcast news program for more than one year or a public affairs program at all. It is also illegal, as a result of recently passed "broadcast flag" legislation, to retransmit over the Internet for personal or educational use an excerpt from any broadcast program, including a news or public affairs program. For example, it is illegal to send grandma via the Internet a highlight from Johnny's championship Little League game, an excerpt of which was broadcast on the local TV evening news. Broadcasters also have some unique copyright exemptions on the use of information property published by non-broadcast entities (see indirect subsidies from suppliers and distributors below).

Taxes. Broadcasters have lobbied for exemption from a variety of taxes including the sales tax, property tax, capital gains tax, corporate income tax, and miscellaneous fees. Broadcasters are exempt from sales tax on their advertising revenues, from which they derive the lion's share of their revenue, because advertising is untaxed in all 50 states, thanks in part to vigorous and frequent broadcaster lobbying.[46] In some states, broadcasters are exempt from

---

[45] For example, media lawyer John P. Burger argues that broadcasters shouldn't be penalized for using hidden cameras and that trespass laws shouldn't be used to punish journalists gathering news. In Bill Kirtz, "Tips from the Trenches," *Quill*, March/April 1999, p. 33.

[46] E.g., "Florida Ad Tax is Repealed After Massive Broadcaster Lobbying," *TV Today*, 14 December 1987, p. 2.

sales tax on select major expenditures.[47] At least 13 states grant broadcasters an exemption from sales tax on digital TV equipment.[48] California broadcasters have sought tax exemptions for TV production. Most TV shows are produced in California.

In New York City, ABC, CBS, and NBC have sales-tax exemptions, property-tax abatements, and discounted electricity rates. Some broadcasters may have their local telephone taxes waived.[49]

Broadcasters have lobbied over the years to reduce income taxes by lobbying for depreciation of spectrum licenses,[50] even though spectrum is not a depletable asset.[51] Depreciation reduces income taxes as the values of assets are gradually expensed.[52]

Despite the fact that broadcasters use a natural resource owned by the public—the public airwaves—broadcasters have fought paying user fees based on the value of the resource as opposed to the much lower fee based on the FCC's cost of simply administering its broadcast license program. Usually, the amount of a fee for use of a publicly owned natural resource is related to the value of the resource.[53]

---

[47] Joli Goldberg et al., "Plan Strategically to Reduce Tax Costs and Increase Cash Flow," *The Financial Manager*, April/May 2002. Memo from Art Brooks, President of the Arizona Broadcasters Association, to Arizona TV General Managers, 23 May 1998. In many states, newspapers are also exempt from taxes on any equipment or supplies used to produce a newspaper; e.g., Robert Sandler, "Missouri House Votes to Raise Newspaper Tax," Associated Press, 15 April 2004.

[48] Robynn Tysver, "TV Station Tax Break Considered," *World-Herald Bureau*, 9 March 2000, p. 13.

[49] Ralph Nader, "Socialism for the Rich," The *New York Times*, 15 May 1999, p. A22.

[50] "New IRS Regulations and Their Impact on Broadcast Acquisition," *TV Today*, 5 May 1986, "NAB Asks Regulatory Agencies For Alternative To HLT Definition," *TV Today*, 30 September 1991, "House Tax Plan Benefits Broadcasters," *TV Today*, 17 May 1993.

[51] Alan Murray and Jackie Calmes, "Tax Report," *Wall Street Journal*, 4 September 1991, p. A1.

[52] E.g. "Depreciation of Intangibles," *Review and Summary of NAB Congressional Activities During the 100th Congress* (Washington, DC: NAB, December 1988), p. 2.

[53] Bill Heniff Jr., "User Fees: Applicable Budget Enforcement Procedures," (Washington, DC: Congressional Research Service, 2000). Doug Halonen, "Are Broadcasters Getting Off Cheap?" *Electronic Media*, 8 February 1999, p. 58. Note that mobile telephone operators (which use spectrum) and cable TV operators (which use public roads) pay fees for their public rights of way. Mobile telephone operators both paid for their spectrum at auction AND pay substantial taxes. But most spectrum licensees follow the broadcasting precedent and only pay for the cost of FCC administration.

Broadcasting is extremely well suited for barter transactions and income tax management. Broadcast stations are often at the center of barter systems because advertising time on mass media is widely sought by local businesses and thus forms a type of universal currency. Broadcasters also purchase programming from outside vendors not for cash but for advertising time, which can then be sold like cash. Barter offers great flexibility to control the recognition of profits and losses and to assign monetary values to transactions.[54]

For many years, broadcasters could indefinitely defer capital gains tax by selling to an organization purportedly controlled by minorities.[55] This exemption was closed in 1995 in the wake of revelations that it was providing large media companies, hiding behind minority front groups, with tax breaks worth hundreds of millions of dollars. Since then, there have been numerous attempts to reinstate some type of capital gains tax break for sale of broadcasting properties to minorities. A reduction of the capital gains tax from 28% in the mid-1990s to 15% today has lessened pressure to reinstate this tax break.

Broadcasters can also defer capital gains tax via like-kind exchanges. All businesses can avoid capital gains tax via like-kind exchanges. But the intangible nature of an FCC TV license combined with the huge potential capital gains tax associated with their rapid increase in market value over the last few decades, may lead to perverse incentives.[56]

---

[54] Wayne C. Frankenfield, "Broadcast Accounting: Are We Sitting on a Powder Keg?," *The Financial Manager* October/November 2000. For a general description of how barter can be misused, see Susan Pullian and Rebecca Blumenstein, "SEC Broadens Investigations into Revenue-Boosting Tricks," *Wall Street Journal*, 16 May 2002, p. A1. Edward Wyatt, "A Whole Other Type of E-Trade," *New York Times*, 20 October 1999, p. C1. After the Enron accounting fiasco, FASBE tightened up some of the accounting flexibility associated with asset swaps: "FASB Expert Predicts Higher Hurdles for Reporting Gains on Asset Swaps," *Managing the General Ledger*, July 2003, p. 5.

[55] Jonathan Rauch, "Color TV: Diversity Mongering at the FCC," *New Republic*, 10 December 1994.

Erwin G. Krasnow, "A Case for Minority Tax Certificates," *Broadcasting & Cable*, 15 December

1997, p. 80. Lindsey Kelly, 'Minority Media Owners Protest Axing Tax Certificate Incentive," *Electronic Media*, 30 January 1995, p. 2.

[56] David R. Marcus, "Defer Taxes on FCC Licenses with Like-Kind Exchanges," *Financial Manager* June/July 2002. Christian McBurney, "IRS Like Kind, Tax-Free Ruling," *Financial Manager*, December/January 2001. Christian McBurney, "IRS Like Kind, Tax-Free Ruling—Part II," *Financial Manager*, February/March 2003.

Indirect Subsidies

Broadcasters seek to buy inputs at the lowest possible cost. This applies both upstream and downstream the value creation chain. The distinction between upstream and downstream is useful when trying to make sense of broadcasters' apparently inconsistent lobbying arguments.[57] Depending on whether an industry is upstream or downstream the value creation chain, a broadcaster must often make entirely opposite economic and First Amendment arguments to justify a particular subsidy. For example, a broadcaster wants upstream suppliers to have no intellectual property rights (so the broadcaster can appropriate their content for free), but wants the opposite intellectual property relationship with downstream distributors or buyers.

Suppliers. Perhaps the most important upstream supplier for a broadcaster is its audience. Although it is non-intuitive to think of advertising audiences as suppliers, this is how TV economists view them.[58] Broadcasters buy audience attention ("eyeballs"), which they then sell to advertisers. It is in the broadcaster's interest to ensure that these eyeballs watch the maximum endurable amount of advertising per hour and cannot filter out ads. For example, broadcasters sued SonicReplay when it made it too easy to record and skip over broadcast ads.[59]

Program suppliers are also another upstream supplier. Local TV broadcasters get national network programming for "free." What they give the networks in return for their programming is some of the advertising time inserted in the networks' programs. Networks are so pleased to get local broadcasters' over the air, satellite, and cable TV distribution for their ads, that they see no reason to charge directly for their programming.

One way broadcasters get programming at the lowest possible cost is to hinder upstream suppliers from selling to competitors such as cable TV, satellite TV, and Internet TV. This gives broadcasters extra bargaining power. Even

---

[57] FCC Chair Kennard alluded to this inconsistency when he observed: "The broadcasters play a blame game. They argue against government intervention in their industry. But then they demand that we come as intrusive as possible in other industries." Stephen Labataon, "FCC's Rift With Industry is Widening," *New York Times*, 16 October 2000, p. C2.

[58] Roger G. Noll, Merton J. Peck, and John J. McGowan, *Economic Aspects of Television Regulation, Studies in the Regulation of Economic Activity* (Washington,: Brookings Institution, 1973).

[59] Jefferson Graham, "PVRs Change the Broadcast Picture; Networks Sue Over Ad Skipping," *U.S.A. Today*, 14 August 2002, p. 1D.

though they have been weakened since the 1970s, the sports, movie, syndicated, and network exclusivity rules continue to serve this function.[60]

Copyright law also helps keep broadcasters' costs low. For example, unlike music providers via restaurants, record stores, cable, satellite, and the Internet, terrestrial radio broadcasters do not have to pay for performance rights—a fee to musicians and singers who record songs.[61] Radio broadcasters have argued that since they provide free promotion to record companies for their recordings, they shouldn't have to pay for them. Radio broadcasters do have to pay royalties to composers, but these are a token amount of revenues—approximately 3.5%.

In contrast, those that broadcast over the Internet ("webcasters") must pay .07 cents per song per listener in performance fees, even when the music programmed over the Internet and over an FCC licensed radio station are identical.[62] This is exactly the type of asymmetric regulation based on arbitrary technological differences that the Telecommunications Act of 1996 and most subsequent telecom policymaking was supposed to eliminate.

When a broadcaster acquires a program, it also automatically acquires so-called moral rights. These moral rights allow broadcasters to edit, crop, and otherwise change purchased programming without permission from the author of the programming. In Europe, authors retain these moral rights when their work is purchased.[63]

---

[60] E.g., Kenneth Creech, *Electronic Media Law and Regulation*, 3rd ed. (Boston: Focal Press, 2000), chapter 8, Christopher H. Sterling and John M. Kittross, *Stay Tuned: A History of American Broadcasting*, 3rd ed., *Lea's Communication Series* (Mahwah, N.J.: Lawrence Erlbaum Associates, 2002). In 1999, the exclusivity rules were extended to satellite TV. See David Hatch, "Decisive Win for Landmark Satellite Bill," *Electronic Media*, 3 May 1999, p. 1.
[61] Laura Asplund, "Jack Zwaska, Spirited Combat," *The Financial Manager*, February/March 2001, Andrew Gordon, *Understanding Broadcast & Cable Finance: A Handbook for the Non-Financial Manager* (Des Plaines: BCFM Press, 1994), chapter 12. Interview with Frances Preston, President of Broadcast Music, Inc., *Broadcasting & Cable*, 25 October 1999, p. 43.
[62] Drew Clark, "Lobbying: A Battle Royal Over Internet Royalties," *National Journal*, 14 December 2002. Anna Wilde Mathews, "U.S. Sets Compromise Rate for Webcast-Music Royalties: Initital fee is .07 U.S. cents a song per listener, Wall Street Journal Europe, 24 June 2002.
[63] NAB, "Moral Rights," in *Legislative Issue Papers, 102nd Congress* (Washington, DC: NAB, August 1992), Register of Copyrights, "Droit De Suite: The Artist's Resale Royalty," (Washington, DC: United States Copyright Office, December 1992).

Distributors. Broadcasters seek to get distribution of their programming at the lowest possible cost. With cable TV must-carry rules, they are guaranteed free distribution on local cable TV, even if the area of the cable TV system is larger than the area of the over-the-air broadcast signal. Broadcasters are also guaranteed minimum technical quality of carriage, so even if an over-the-air UHF channel has a snowy image or is impossible to receive behind a dense object such as a tall building, the cable TV version of the channel must be as good as the UHF signal at the transmitter. In the late 1990s, must-carry rights for a TV channel without a major network affiliation were worth as much as $13.88 per subscriber.[64] Broadcasters also have control of the channel number at which the cable TV company offers its programming. Broadcasters have a similar set of must-carry rights with satellite TV providers. The big difference is that must-carry rights are negotiated on a cartel basis. If a satellite provider wants to carry one local broadcast channel from a local market, it must either carry all the local broadcast TV channels from that market or carry none at all. This is known in the broadcast industry as "carry one, carry all."

Broadcasters have also lobbied for more than $1 billion in government backed loans for rural TV service. The idea is to subsidize the delivery of local broadcast programming to rural areas that wouldn't otherwise receive such programming in an easily accessible way.[65] In 1999, the federal government awarded $3.32 million in grants to improve broadcast digital receivers and antennas.[66]

Broadcasters have lobbied to prevent distributors from having control over the broadcast content they carry. Thus, they oppose allowing cable TV companies to modify broadcast programming in any way, including providing localized emergency information when broadcasters are unable to provide this information because of the large geographic area of their signals.

In general, broadcasters seek copyright laws that make Internet distribution of their programming illegal or legal depending on whether they have exclusive

---

[64] John Higgins, "Paxson Renders Unto TCI," *Broadcasting & Cable*, 4 May 1998, p. 6. See also Aaron Barnhart, "Cable, Cable Everywhere But Not a Thing to Watch: Niche Programming Struggles for Air Time," *New York Times*, 23 December 1996, p. D7. One public broadcaster leased only its must-carry rights to a commercial broadcaster for $4.25 million over an 8-year term. Wayne Walley, "Public Broadcaster Sells Must-Carry Rights," *Multichannel News*, 14 October 1996, p. 95.

[65] Adriel Bettelheim, "Senators Unveil Satellite TV Subsidy Bill," *CQ Weekly*, 26 February 2000, p. 418. David Hatch, "Rural Loan Bill Hits Senate," *Electronic Media*, 28 February 2000, p. 4. David Hatch, "NAB's Fritts: Now New Net Protection," *Electronic Media*, 19 June 2000, p. 8.

[66] See "Taking Antennas to New Heights," *Broadcasting & Cable*, 15 November 1999, p. 17.

rights to that programming. Thus, radio broadcasters, which have automatic rights under copyright law to rebroadcast music recordings without compensation for performers, believe they have an inherent right to redistribute music over the Internet. But TV broadcasters, which have exclusive contracts with national TV networks, call this "theft" and have vigorously fought it.[67]

As of this writing, broadcasters are seeking multicasting must-carry rights, which provide all the above rights for any data broadcasters can send on their 19.4 mbps digital channel. Currently, broadcasters only have must-carry rights for a single free (ad-supported) TV programming stream and must negotiate for carriage of any additional bits of information that can be carried within their 6 MHz channels. With digital TV, broadcasters can provide more than ten standard definition TV programs in the spectrum previously used to transmit just one standard definition TV program.[68]

Buyers. Broadcasters have an ever expanding array of revenue generating business models to complement and eventually even replace their traditional model based on advertising. We'll divide buyers into traditional (advertisers) and non-traditional (other).

1) Traditional (advertisers). Broadcasters have lobbied to prevent any bans or restrictions on advertising, including gambling, liquor, auto, political, and pharmaceutical advertising.[69] For example, broadcasters oppose mandatory disclosures of harmful pharmaceutical side effects because this would discourage pharmaceutical advertising, which brings in $1.7 billion per year in TV advertising.[70] Advertising for state lotteries, which often distorts the odds of winning and ill effects of losing, is a half billion dollar annual market.[71]

---

[67] Kevin Maney, "Ruling Stops iCraveTV Transmissions to USA," *USA Today*, 9 February 2000, p. B1.

[68] J.H. Snider, "Is Multicasting Must-Carry a Must-Giveaway?," (Washington, DC: New America Foundation, 2003), J.H. Snider, "Should DTV Must-Carry Be Expanded, Sunset, or Preserved as-Is?," (Washington, DC: New America Foundation, March 2005).

[69] E.g., NAB, "Advertising Restrictions," in *Legislative Issue Papers, 101st Congress* (Washington, DC: NAB, February 1989), NAB, "Alcohol Ad Warnings," in *Legislative Issue Papers, 104th Congress* (Washington, DC: NAB, September 1995).

[70] Doug Halonen, "A Bitter Ad Pill to Swallow: Legislation threatening drug spots galvanizes industry," *Electronic Media*, 12 May 2002, p. 1. Lisa Belkin, "Freed from Federal Restrictions, Pharmaceutical Companies are Flooding Television with Ads," *Mother Jones*, March/April 2001, p. 31.

[71] Nicholas Thompson, "Snake Eyes: Even Education Programs Can't Redeem State Lotteries," *Nicholas Thompson*, December 1999, p. 17. See also: Timothy L. O'Brien, *Bad Bet: The inside Story of America's Gambling Industry*, 1st ed. (New York: Times Business, 1998).

Broadcasters have lobbied against campaign finance proposals to require them to give political candidates free or discounted air time.[72] In a presidential election year, political ads bring in 5% to 7% of total local broadcast TV advertising revenues.[73]

Broadcasters have lobbied to prevent any changes that might reduce the tax advantages of advertising, which is still their dominant source of revenue.[74] They oppose sales taxes on advertising or changing the formula for the corporate income tax deductibility of advertising. For example, efforts to amortize advertising expenditures over a number of years rather than in the year they are incurred are opposed.[75] Even when the advertising is for products such as cigarettes, gambling, and alcohol widely deemed to have negative externalities (i.e., socially harmful effects), broadcasters have lobbied to give advertisers a tax break. The result is a tax system that subsidizes advertiser financed information (e.g., "free" TV, including advertorials and home shopping stations) at the expense of information consumers pay for directly (e.g., subscription TV and the type of information published by *Consumer Reports*).[76]

2) Non-Traditional.[77] In the early days of broadcasting, there was no economical way to charge for broadcasting because there was no affordable way to exclude individuals from receiving a TV signal who hadn't paid for one. With the advent of cable TV, it became easy to exclude non-payers simply by disconnecting the wire that connected them to the network. With digital technology and new encryption technology, it has become increasingly cost-effective to exclude non-payers. Generally, as new technology allows broadcasters to charge for their programming, they have tried to restrict the realm of free/ad-supported TV. Since most subsidies to broadcasters have been given in the

---

[72] E.g., NAB, "Campaign Finance Reform," in *Legislative Issue Papers, 106th Congress* (Washington, DC: NAB, August 1999).

[73] Doug Halonen, "Cry Raised Against Cheap Political Spots," *Electronic Media*, 9 April 2001, p. 3.

[74] E.g., Paige Albiniak, "Ad Deductions Threatened: McCain bill would amortize deductions," *Broadcasting & Cable*, 24 January 2000, p. 26, NAB, "Ad Tax Deductions," in *Legislative Issue Papers, 103rd Congress* (Washington, DC: NAB, February 1994).

[75] The theory here is that the benefit of advertising lasts more than a year and should thus be accounted for like other investments. The higher short-term advertising expense on the accounting statement reduces income and thus income taxes.

[76] For an argument that the priorities should be reversed, see Snider and Ziporyn, *Future Shop*.

[77] For a discussion of the history of free TV, see J.H. Snider, "The Myth of Free TV," (Washington, DC: New America Foundation, June 2002).

name of preserving free TV, it has been a bit awkward for broadcasters to lobby to add pay TV revenue revenues to their advertising revenue streams. Broadcasters have for the most part accomplished this remarkable feat by arguing that pay TV revenues subsidize its free TV users and programming. In other words, by killing free TV, they are able to save it.

In urban areas with tall buildings (such as New York City) or rural areas with mountains (such as parts of Vermont), broadcasters have had trouble providing usable over-the-air TV service. The problem is that the terrestrial airwaves cannot get through tall buildings or mountains. Viewers thus have the choice of getting their local broadcast TV signals via a pay service (usually cable or satellite TV) or doing without.

As described earlier, more than 80 percent of Americans now receive their local broadcast TV programming via a pay TV service such as cable or satellite. Although the law mandates that broadcasters get free carriage of their programming on these distribution outlets, it doesn't mandate that audiences get analogous free viewing rights. Specifically, broadcasters can use either their must-carry rights (zero cost mandatory carriage) or their retransmission consent rights (a negotiated fee for carriage) depending on their bargaining strength. A home shopping channel that a cable or satellite TV provider doesn't want opts for must-carry. A local network-affiliated TV station with high ratings opts for retransmission consent. In the case of satellite TV, viewers may pay an average of about $6 per month for a package of local broadcast TV channels. A substantial part of this revenue goes to pay the retransmission consent fee negotiated with local broadcasters.

As part of their retransmission consent negotiations, broadcasters are allowed to negotiate cable or satellite carriage of additional channels. As a result, broadcast station groups all own cable and satellite networks, and over 90 percent of all cable TV networks are now either owned by cable TV operators or by local broadcast owners. Independent entrepreneurs have practically no chance of securing cable carriage for themselves. The cost for viewers of this is not higher prices but reduced innovation and diversity in TV programming.[78]

As content has migrated to the Internet, broadcasters have also sought to charge for content. CBS, for example, charges for access to news on its website.

---

[78] Doug Halonen, "Looking Back at Retransmission," *Electronic Media*, 4 March 2002, p. 1; see also Testimony of Neal Schnog before the Committee on Energy and Commerce, U.S. House of Representatives, Hearing on The Status of Competition in the Multi-Channel Video Distribution Marketplace, 4 December 2001.

Most local TV is provided by the large TV networks. The networks retain the copyright to the programming and retain rights for all redistribution at a later time. The transcripts of some of the public affairs programs are made available on services such as Nexis or Factiva—but only for a fee.

Broadcasters have won a requirement that all consumer equipment that can record a broadcast TV or other data signal include the ability to read a "broadcast flag," which restricts viewer copying and reuse of programming copied off-the-air. Traditionally, broadcasters lacked the technology to charge viewers for their programming, so a consumer was able to copy programs off-the-air and watch or share them later without paying an additional fee. Broadcasters have sought increasingly restrictive laws to prevent such viewing and sharing.[79]

Broadcasters have lobbied to have the government both force consumers to purchase TV sets with built-in broadcast digital tuners and force TV set manufacturers to label TV sets in a way that would make any set without a broadcast DTV tuner sound defective. To the exent a broadcast DTV tuner becomes a sunk cost for a consumer but a cable or satellite DTV tuner becomes a marginal cost, broadcasters have a comparative advantage.[80]

Finally, in the Telecom Act of '96, broadcasters received the right to charge audiences directly for more than 90% of their spectrum's information carrying capacity. As long as broadcasters provide one standard definition TV program stream on an ad-supported basis, they can charge however much they want for the remainder.

Barriers to Entry

Broadcasters have sought to increase barriers to entry into broadcasting for potential competitors because high barriers to entry increase broadcasters'

---

[79] FCC Report and Order in the matter of *Digital Output Protection Technology and Recording Method Certifications*, Docket 04-193, released 12 August 2004, FCC Report and Order and Further Notice of Proposed Rulemaking in the matter of *Digital Broadcast Content Protection*, MB Docket 02-230, FCC 03-273, released 4 November 2003. These rulemaking gave broadcasters a "digital broadcast flag." Current broadcaster lobbying efforts focus on closing the "analog hole."

[80] The FCC has mandated that in a phased implementation plan all new TV sets sold must include a broadcast DTV tuner but not a cable or satellite DTV tuner. The FCC has also mandated that TV sets labeled "cable ready" include a broadcast DTV tuner, even though the term cable ready historically only meant that a TV set could pick up programming without a separate settop box. See Appendix C for details.

monopoly power and profits. The most obvious barrier to entry in the broadcasting business is a Federal Communications Commission license. To broadcast over the airwaves, it is necessary to have an FCC license. From a broadcasters' perspective, there are three types of FCC licenses, ranked in order of competitive threat:

First, a license to broadcast TV programming over channels 2-69. These channels have been grossly underutilized. The average TV market in the U.S. receives only 7 channels, about 10% of the channels on the TV dial. On a population weighted basis (large markets such as New York City, Chicago, and Los Angeles have more channels), the average American has slightly more than 13 channels, about 20% of the channels on the TV dial.[81] Broadcasters have opposed allowing the FCC to license the unused channels unless they were the recipients. In 1997, the FCC obliged by "loaning" incumbent broadcasters a second channel to migrate to digital TV.[82] Similarly, in 1999 Congress barred new low power FM licensees from getting access to unused FM channels while virtually doubling incumbent licensees' bandwidth to migrate to digital radio—this time without any promise that the additional spectrum would ever be returned to the public.[83]

Attached to the possession of an FCC license to use channels 2-69 are a host of secondary rights, which have been described above. These rights give broadcasters a cost advantage over competitors.

Second, a license that allows broadcasting but not on channels 2-69. From the 1950s through the 1970s, the FCC was notorious for discouraging the development of cable TV as a competitor to over-the-air broadcasting.[84] More recently, satellite has been held back to minimize competition with the local

---

[81] Thomas W. Hazlett, "The Wireless Craze: An Essay on Airwave Allocation Policy," *Harvard Journal of Law and Technology* (Spring 2001).

[82] Joel Brinkley, *Defining Vision: The Battle for the Future of Television*, 1st U.S. ed. (New York: Harcourt Brace, 1997). A much more efficient transition system would have involved only one channel, thus requiring no second channel loan/giveaway. See Chapter 12 for a discussion of this.

[83] FCC First Report and Order in the matter of *Digital Audio Broadcasting Systems and Their Impact on the Terrestrial Radio Broadcast Service*, MM Docket 99-325, released 10 October 2002. Bill McConnell, "First Step for Digital Radio," *Broadcasting & Cable*, 8 November 1999, p. 20.

[84] E.g., see Thomas P. Southwick, *Distant Signals: How Cable TV Changed the World of Telecommunications* (Overland Park, KS: Primedia Intertec, 1999).

broadcast industry.[85] The U.S. was years behind Europe in awarding licenses for satellite radio and TV in part because of opposition from U.S. broadcasters. Broadcasters have lobbied to make it illegal for satellite radio to provide local information such as local news, weather, and sports.[86] In the Satellite Home Viewer Improvement Act of 1999, they also successfully lobbied for satellite TV "carry one, carry all" rights, which requires that a satellite operator either carry none or all local broadcast TV channels in a market. These rights tie up large amounts of satellite spectrum, which reduces satellite capacity for competitors.

Third, a license that allows use of the airwaves but not for broadcasting. Spectrum has often been allocated in such a way to make it illegal to provide broadcasting type services. Even so-called flexible use spectrum for mobile telephone service bars broadcasting service.[87] On the other hand, given today's spectrum technology and economics, it's hard to imagine why any spectrum licensee, given a choice, would want to provide traditional broadcast service over large swaths of low frequency airwaves, which can generate higher revenue when used for interactive mobile services. This explains why broadcasters have been devoting an increasing fraction of their lobbying energies to winning the right to abandon their traditional broadcasting business.

Barriers To Exit

At the same time that broadcasters have lobbied to erect barriers to entry for others seeking to compete with broadcasters, they have lobbied to lower barriers

---

[85] Clayton Kuntz, "DARS Wars: The Government Strikes Back," *Via Satellite*, April 1997. Radley Balko, "All Politics Is Local: How Broadcasters Want to Silence Satellite Radio, Issue #71," *Cato TechKnowledge*, 20 January 2004, Thomas Hazlett, "Why the FCC Should Scrap Its Absurd Rules for Satellite Radio," *Slate*, 16 March 2004.

[86] E.g., NAB petition for declaratory ruling to FCC in the matter of *Establishment of Rules and Policies For the Digital Audio Radio Satellite service in the 231-2360 MHz Frequency Band, Radio Service Terrestrial Repeaters Network*, IB Docket 95-91, GEN Docket 90-357, 14 April 2004.

[87] E.g. "...allowing cellular frequencies to be used for the transmission of news, sports, weather, etc., would, in essence, turn the service into a broadcasting service, and therefore run counter to the primary purpose for which the service was created—to improve the nation's mobile radiotelephone service." Comments to FCC of the National Association of Broadcasters In the matter of *Amendment of the Commission's Rules to Authorize Cellular Carriers to Offer Auxiliary and Non-Common Carrier Services*, RM-7823, 26 November 1991, p. 6

to entry for broadcasters seeking to enter others businesses or simply to exit the broadcasting business. Broadcasters, for example, have lobbied aggressively to win as much flexibility as possible to use their spectrum to enter new businesses. The have lobbied to exit the free TV business (exclusive reliance on ad-supported content) and enter the pay TV business; lobbied to allow themselves to sell their licenses to the highest bidder, regardless of the use the bidder intends to make of the spectrum; lobbied to allow portions of their spectrum to be leased to others who have non-broadcasting business models; lobbied to prevent any transfer taxes when they sell their licenses; lobbied to use retransmission consent to negotiate not only cash but also cable carriage, which gives them a strategic advantage over other entrepreneurs seeking to start cable and satellite TV networks; and lobbied to revoke media consolidation laws, which prevent them from entering any media market they choose.[88]

Ultimately, broadcasters may seek to abandon their traditional business altogether.[89] They know that their spectrum is far more valuable when used for non-broadcasting services such as mobile telephone or Internet service. In more than 30 U.S. TV markets, including New York City, more than 90% of Americans now receive TV via cable or satellite TV. One study found that the value of local broadcaster's spectrum used for analog TV is only about 5% of its value if auctioned for its highest valued use.[90]

---

[88] An important exception is the ownership limit for large TV networks. Local TV stations are fearful that if the large TV groups acquire too many local TV stations, the local TV stations will lose their bargaining power in negotiating with the networks for programming. In 2003, Congress and the FCC eliminated many ownership restrictions but substantially kept the local TV station ownership cap in place.

[89] E.g., Thomas Hazlett, Senior Fellow at the Manhattan Institute, Testimony on the Digital Television Transition before the United States Senate Commerce Committee, 9 June 2004. Steve McClellan, "The Bandwidth Battle," *Broadcasting & Cable*, 25 September 2000. Michael Feazel, "FCC Rejects Sinclair Bid to Allow New DTV Standard," *Communications Daily*, 7 February 2000, p. 1. Greg Schmidt, of LIN Broadcasting and former MSTV President, Presentation at Forum on Spectrum Management Policy Reform sponsored by the National Telecommunications and Information Administration, National Academies of Science, Washington, DC, 12-13 February 2004.

[90] Bazelon, Rothkopf, and Kravitz, "The Value of the Airwaves.".

Conclusion

The broadcast industry lobbies over a wide range of issues and agencies. Issues specifically affecting the broadcast industry include copyright, tax, land use, and spectrum policy. Government agencies and offices include the FCC, NTIA, Copyright Office, Bureaus of Land Management, FTC, and Financial Accounting Standards Board. In terms of economic importance to the broadcast industry, spectrum policy is the most important issue and the FCC the most important agency.

CHAPTER 4:

The Ultimate Object of Broadcaster Bias—Candidate Decisions

"Clearly, the more information a citizen has, the more influence over government policy he is likely to exercise.... Conversely, the less a citizen knows about policy alternatives, the fewer specific preferences he can have, and the more likely it is that government will ignore him in making decisions."

—Anthony Downs, An Economic Theory of Democracy[1]

This chapter and the next three develop a general model of information agent bias. No distinction is made between the logic of bias for local broadcasters and other information agents. Nor is a distinction made in the logic of bias when media and non-media assets are used.

This chapter focuses on the relations between voter incentives to acquire information and the decisions of candidates. The next three chapters look at strategies and resources for changing those incentives.

Power and Incentive Structure

Let us assume that power is the ability to change the incentive structure of other actor(s) to bring about a desired outcome. An actor's incentive structure is the full set of costs and benefits of behaving one way rather than another.

> [A]ctors have power over others to the extent that they can manipulate others' incentive structure. Taking away options from a choice set, or making the costs of an action higher or lower, or making the

---

[1] Anthony Downs, *An Economic Theory of Democracy* (New York,: Harper, 1957), p. 249.

benefits higher or lower..., will encourage some actions and discourage others.[2]

This approach to understanding power is consistent with the rational choice literature. Behavior is predicted based on the benefits and costs of different courses of action.[3]

The final stages of the democratic process involve voters electing their representatives, and then those representatives doing their job of representation. But voters and elected leaders can only exercise that power based on the information they possess. Political power can thus be exercised by changing the incentives of voters and their representatives to acquire information. Accordingly, we shall conceptualize the power of the broadcasters (or any political actor) in terms of their resources to change others' incentives to acquire political information. This formalizes the common aphorism that "information is power."

The view that political power stems from control of information is not necessarily inconsistent with the view that it stems from control of money. Money, after all, is used in politics to gather, process, and distribute information, including information in the form of organizational expertise, political consultants, TV ads, news coverage, direct mail, and face-to-face meetings. Transportation, telecommunications, and campaign organizations can also be seen as information expenditures because they are the infrastructure necessary to support an information campaign. Money, therefore, may be viewed as a proxy for the power to change information incentives. Unlike information, money has the advantage of being quantifiable. This makes it especially appealing to quantification oriented academics and journalists. But many information incentives, such as those created by the structure of our democratic institutions, cannot easily be controlled by money. Thus, a focus on information resources as opposed to monetary resources may lead to a more comprehensive and nuanced view of the influence process.

---

[2] Keith M. Dowding, *Power, Concepts in Social Thought* (Minneapolis: University of Minnesota Press, 1996), p. 5.

[3] E.g., Ibid, Prajit K. Dutta, *Strategies and Games: Theory and Practice* (Cambridge, Mass.: MIT Press, 1999), Alvin I. Goldenson, "Toward a Theory of Social Power," in *Power: Readings in Social and Political Theory*, ed. Steven Lukes (New York: New York University Press, 1986), John C. Harsanyi, "Measurement of Social Power, Opportunity Costs, and the Theory of Two-Person Bargaining Games," *Behaviorial Science* 7 (1962), James D. Morrow, *Game Theory for Political Scientists* (Princeton, N.J.: Princeton University Press, 1994).

The primacy of information over money as a means to power may be the fundamental difference between market and democratic systems of power. Control of information incentives is the lingua franca of democracy, whereas control of monetary incentives is the lingua franca of markets.

The view that political power ultimately stems from control of information incentives is surely incomplete. What good is information if you cannot vote or don't have choices for which to vote?

Consider electoral systems. They have important information properties, such as the transparency of ballots, the time to campaign between primary and general elections, and political opponents' access to accurate legislative records. But their impact is more fundamental than just changing information incentives. For example, if an electoral system is designed so that blacks or women or low income individuals are discouraged or prevented from taking the physical act of voting, this affects the distribution of power regardless of the information voters possess.

Nevertheless, if we assume a democracy in which the vast majority of adults have the right to vote, laws are equally applied to opponents and supporters, and killing off or otherwise systematically intimidating opponents is not tolerated, then information power comes to the fore. I believe that this is the case in advanced Western democracies such as that in the United States.

Exercising Power

In a representative democracy, political actors seek to influence how elected candidates vote on public policies and manage the government. They achieve this influence largely by changing how elected officials perceive their self-interest. Assuming elected officials are motivated by the desire to seek re-election, this involves changing how voters perceive their self-interest.

An intermediary (or information agent) is a political actor who directly changes voters' information incentives. Local TV broadcasters are one of the most powerful intermediaries in our contemporary democracy.

Assuming local TV broadcasters are rational, we would expect them, on average, to increase other political actors' incentives to acquire information favorable to their interests and reduce their incentives to acquire information unfavorable to their interests. The qualifier "on average" is used because presenting some information harmful to one's own interest is often essential to creating credibility and confusing others about one's own interests. For example, salespeople often strive for credibility with sophisticated customers by acknowledging widely known product flaws before the customer has a chance to raise them. According to this logic, maximizing bias, constrained by the risk of discovery and penalty, is the essence of a rational political actor's political strategy. This logic is the same whether the political actor is a broadcaster or any other type of information agent, and whether the broadcaster is playing the role of interest group or media outlet.

Bias, then, is the essence of "rational lobbying." To assert that a political actor is unbiased is to assert that they are irrational. Note that this definition of bias focuses on the intentions, not the results, of political actors seeking to change information incentives. It is possible that the invisible hand of competition among political actors will lead to public enlightenment, even if each actor's motives had exactly the opposite goal.

The Democratic Decision Sequence

A generic model of intermediary influence on public policy outcomes can be conceived of as a series of interlinked decisions. The sum total of these decisions is the four step democratic decision sequence.

1. Intermediaries Choose Voter Incentives to Acquire Information

2. Voters Acquire Information

3. Candidates Acquire Information and Choose Attributes

4. Voters Choose Candidates

Our primary interest is in stage #1—how and why intermediaries change actual voter information incentives or at least candidates' perception of them. But to understand the logic of stage #1, it is helpful to first understand the logic of the later three stages. In game-theoretic fashion, we will reason backwards, starting with stage #4 and then moving stage-by-stage down to #1. This chapter will cover stages #2 through #4; the next two chapters will cover stage #1, which, in turn, will be divided into substages.

Advantages of This Model

The primary purpose of this model is to explain the mechanisms by which control of voter information incentives leads to political power. The specific approach taken to do this—a universal, multistage model of the democratic process—has some advantages. By universal is meant all types of intermediaries rather than one type. By multistage is meant the sequence of decisions from intermediary information investment to voter choice at the polls.

Most models of the democratic process are particularistic: they focus on a narrow range of political actors (e.g., political parties, candidates, or interest groups) and a single step in the democratic decision making process. Examples include legislators making committee decisions,[4] the media setting the agenda,[5] candidates selecting their positions,[6] and interest groups contributing to campaigns.[7]

An advantage of particularistic models is scholarly rigor. Data sets are smaller and theories can be richly textured to fit the nuances of a particular situation.

But scholars who develop particularistic models can sometimes wear strategic blinders and overlook broad patterns and goldmines of relevant data. The underlying logic of a situation may be clearer if there are many more cases that can be used as points of reference. For example, if political communication scholars recognized that ethical "firewall" claims regarding conflicts of interest are pervasive in personal and professional life, then unsubstantiated journalistic firewall claims might be viewed merely as "cheap talk." Instead of asking reporters about their ethical behavior (which may be akin to asking "are you cruel and amoral?"), attention might shift to the specific conditions that make ethical claims credible. The burden of proof concerning the nature of firewalls might shift from those seeking to prove opportunistic firewalls to those seeking to prove ethical firewalls. Uncomfortable questions would have to be raised about why general managers are so secretive about both their lobbying activities and interactions with news personnel, notably news directors.

Similarly, a focus on a single stage of the democratic process may lead to confusion because effective political actors may make strategic decisions with

---

[4] Keith Krehbiel, Information and Legislative Organization, Michigan Studies in Political Analysis (Ann Arbor: University of Michigan Press, 1991).

[5] Shanto Iyengar and Donald R. Kinder, *News That Matters : Television and American Opinion, American Politics and Political Economy* (Chicago: University of Chicago Press, 1987), Maxwell E. McCombs, Donald Lewis Shaw, and David H. Weaver, *Communication and Democracy: Exploring the Intellectual Frontiers in Agenda-Setting Theory* (Mahwah, NJ: Lawrence Erlbaum Associates, 1997).

[6] Downs, *An Economic Theory of Democracy,* James M. Enelow and Melvin J. Hinich, *Advances in the Spatial Theory of Voting* (Cambridge [England] ; New York: Cambridge University Press, 1990), Kenneth A. Shepsle and Mark S. Bonchek, *Analyzing Politics : Rationality, Behavior, and Institutions,* 1st ed. (New York: W.W. Norton, 1997).

[7] West and Loomis, *The Sound of Money: How Political Interests Get What They Want.*

all stages of the democratic process in mind. For example, many political communication scholars study how the mass media affect public opinion about public policy.[8] But if scholars do not clearly keep in mind that the purpose of changing public opinion is to change the behavior of public officials, they can make serious blunders. They may assume, for example, that the way to study telecommunications bias in the media is to study the way the media present telecommunications issues.[9] But if the ultimate goal of the media is to pressure public officials to enact favorable telecommunications policies, the media may find an indirect approach more effective. Instead of biasing telecommunications coverage, for example, media owners may influence telecommunications policy by controlling the amount of "free media" received by their politician friends and enemies. The end result—influencing legislators on telecommunications policy—is the same, but the means are very different.

Stage #4: Voters Choose Candidates

Voters support changes from the status quo that increase their utility and oppose changes that do otherwise. Utility is a measure of a voter's satisfaction with one state-of-the-world as opposed to another. Figure 4-1 describes relative voter utility for an incumbent and challenger candidate. The status quo utility of zero is the level of satisfaction with the current incumbent. In this case, about half the voters prefer the challenger over the incumbent.

---

[8] E.g., Iyengar and Kinder, *News That Matters : Television and American Opinion*, McCombs, Shaw, and Weaver, *Communication and Democracy: Exploring the Intellectual Frontiers in Agenda-Setting Theory*, David Protess and Maxwell E. McCombs, *Agenda Setting : Readings on Media, Public Opinion, and Policymaking, Communication Textbook Series. Journalism* (Hillsdale, N.J.: Erlbaum, 1991).

[9] Gilens and Hertzman, "Corporate Ownership and News Bias.", Snider and Page, "Does Media Ownership Affect Media Stands?"

Figure 4-1. Distribution of Voter Preferences Across Candidates

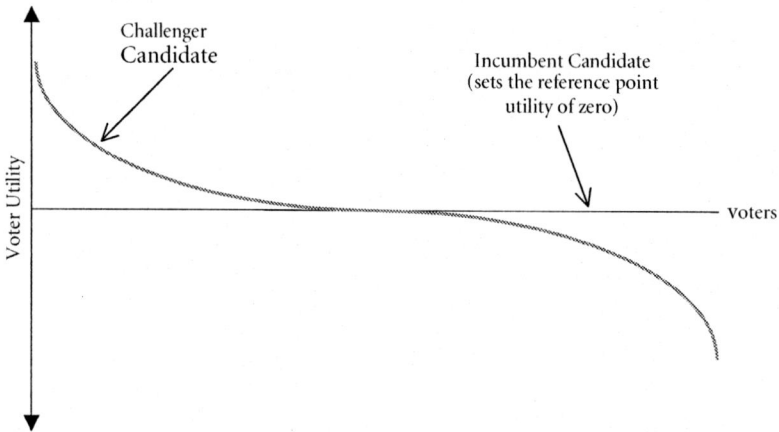

In choosing between multiple candidates (or policies), a voter compares the net changes from the status quo and picks the candidate (or policy) with the highest utility. Figure 4-2 describes this choice for a single voter with multiple candidate options. In this case, since candidate B offers more utility than candidates A, C, and D, this voter would choose candidate B. Candidate A, the incumbent, is used as the reference point and thus has a utility of zero.

Figure 4-2. A Single Voter's Choice Among Candidates

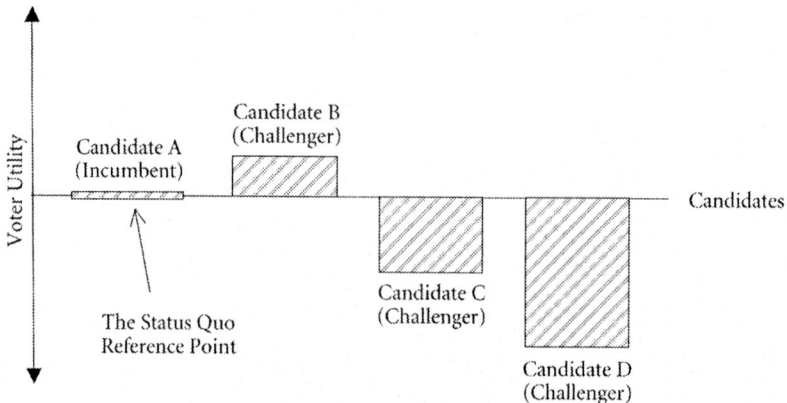

We can distinguish between two types of utility: perceived utility ("perceived preferences") and true utility ("true preferences"). This corresponds to the common distinction between "preferences" and "interests." The true utility curve represents what the voter's utility curve would look like if information costs were zero. Of course, information costs are not zero in the real world, so the true utility curve is a purely hypothetical construct. Thus, when voters actually make decisions, they use their perceived utility curve, not their true utility curve.

There is no necessary relationship between the perceived utility curve and the true utility curve. In an ideal democracy, the perceived and true utility curves for a given candidate would be identical. In a second best democracy, the perceived utility curve would always closely shadow the true utility curve.[10] In Figure 4-3 we see a second best situation where the perceived utility curve closely shadows the true utility curve. The perceived utility curve represents the difference in perceived utility between candidates A and B. The true utility curve represents the difference in true utility between candidates A and B.

Figure 4-3. Perceived vs. True Utility Curves in a Successful Democracy

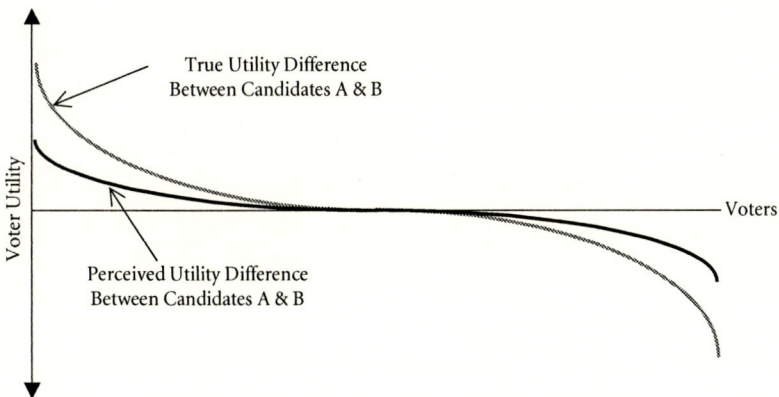

---

[10] Under conditions of scarce voter and societal resources, the second best ideal has the advantage of practicality. Even if it were theoretically possible for society to subsidize voter information costs to the extent that they were brought to zero, it would be undesirable to do so because of the prohibitive cost.

In the real world, the difference between true and perceived utility will often vary across voters because information costs and benefits tend to be distributed highly unevenly across voters.[11] In Figure 4-4, we see a significant discrepancy between the perceived and true utility curves. If voters know their true utility curve, candidate B wins a majority of votes. But if they only know their perceived utility curve, then candidate A wins a majority of votes. In other words, the outcome of the election is changed because voters are confused about the candidates.

Figure 4-4. Perceived vs. True Utility Curves in a Failed Democracy

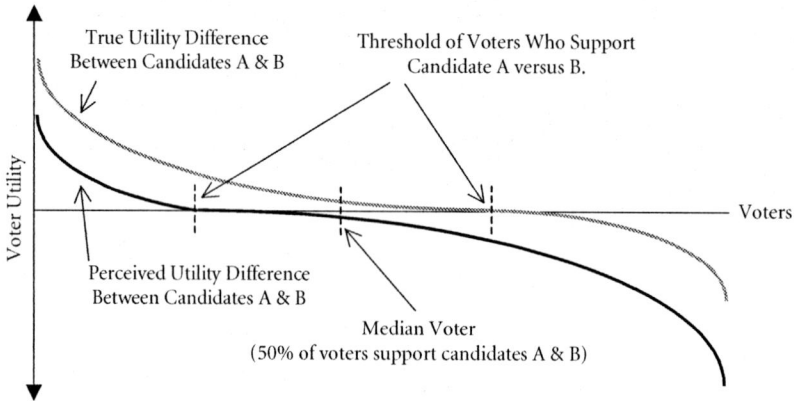

Objects vs. Attributes

In the previous discussion, the voter's object of decision is a candidate. But the same logic applies whether the voter's object of choice is a candidate or a candidate's attributes. When an individual voter assesses the utility associated with a particular candidate, the voter does so based on an aggregate evaluation of all a candidate's attributes. The candidate utility curve, therefore, may be viewed as an aggregation of many attribute utility curves. Figure 4-5 illustrates the relationship between candidates and candidate attributes. Each node may be

---

[11] Michael X. Delli Carpini and Scott Keeter, *What Americans Know About Politics and Why It Matters* (New Haven [Conn.]: Yale University Press, 1996), Downs, *An Economic Theory of Democracy,* Popkin, *The Reasoning Voter.*

viewed as an object of decision, and each subordinate object as an attribute of the object above it.

Figure 4-5. A Sample Relationship Between an Object and Its Attributes

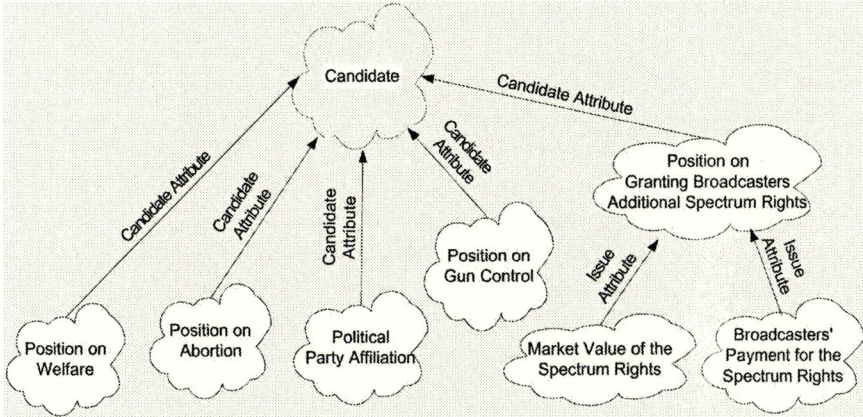

Stage #3: Candidates Choose Attributes

Let us assume that successful political candidates seek election; they have no intrinsic policy preferences. This assumption is controversial[12] but commonly employed in models of legislative voting behavior.[13] We can therefore deduce that legislators who want to stay in office choose actions based on constituent preferences.

A corollary is that candidates are not interested in voters' true preferences, only voters' perceived preferences (i.e., what people actually believe, not what they might hypothetically believe in an ideal democracy). If a candidate attribute is not salient to voters, it does not affect their voting calculus and therefore legislators' re-election prospects. If an attribute does not affect legislators' re-election prospects, it does not affect their political behavior and is therefore

---

[12] E.g., Richard F. Fenno, Home Style : House Members in Their Districts (Boston: Little, Brown, 1978).

[13] E.g., R. Douglas Arnold, *The Logic of Congressional Action* (New Haven: Yale University Press, 1990), Downs, *An Economic Theory of Democracy,* David R. Mayhew, *Congress: The Electoral Connection, Yale Studies in Political Science ; 26* (New Haven: Yale University Press, 1974).

politically irrelevant. In other words, candidates classify voters into two basic groups with respect to every attribute: those who are politically relevant, and those who are politically irrelevant. Only those who are politically relevant help shape the perceived preference curve. When all attributes of an issue for a voter are non-considerations, then the voter is politically irrelevant to a candidate on that issue. This mindset is reflected in the common political aphorism that "the squeaky wheel gets the grease." Rob Owen, NAB Director of U.S. Senate Government Relations, put it this way: "If a Congressman doesn't hear from folks on a specific issue, members assume people are okay with it."[14] Another variant is former Senate Russell Long's oft quoted observation about the politics of tax reform: "Don't tax you. Don't tax me. Tax that fellow behind the tree."

Not surprisingly, those who study candidate and voter decision making rarely distinguish between perceived and true utility curves. As long as information is costly, a true utility curve will never exist in the real world. It is simply a hypothetical construct useful for certain types of theoretical analyses—such as the type of theoretical analysis that seeks to explain why intermediaries attempt to change voter information incentives.

Figure 4-6 depicts "the candidate's decision." Candidates are only concerned with perceived utility, so the graph only includes the perceived utility curve. Graphically, the area under the utility curve depicts the quantity of constituent support for a particular change versus the status quo. The dividing point between voters who support and oppose the change from the status quo is V_x. In choosing between the status quo and a change, candidates compare the areas under supporter and opponent curves and, all other things being equal, pick the side with the largest area (i.e., greatest perceived utility). This is commonly described as picking the side with the greatest political or popular support[15]. On this issue, the largest area belongs to supporters of a change from

---

[14] Presentation at legislative issues briefing, 2001 State Leadership Conference of the National Association of Broadcasters, J.W. Marriott Hotel, Washington, DC., 12 March 2001.

[15] The term popular in this context tends to suffer from ambiguity. In a democracy, what ultimately count are votes, not intensity of voter preferences. But voters only vote on the aggregate results of thousands of day-to-day decisions made by legislators. This makes it rational for legislators to make day-to-day decisions based on the intensity of voter preferences. Legislators add the voter preference curves for countless attributes to arrive at a final tally of anticipated support and opposition. In the final cumulative tally, legislators focus on voters rather than voter preference intensities. To the extent that voters choose candidates based on only a few considerations, the assumption that candidates care about voter intensity, not votes, needs to be qualified.

the status quo, so a rational, re-election seeking politician would seek to position himself aligned with those voters.

Figure 4-6. The Candidate's Decision Based on Voter Preferences

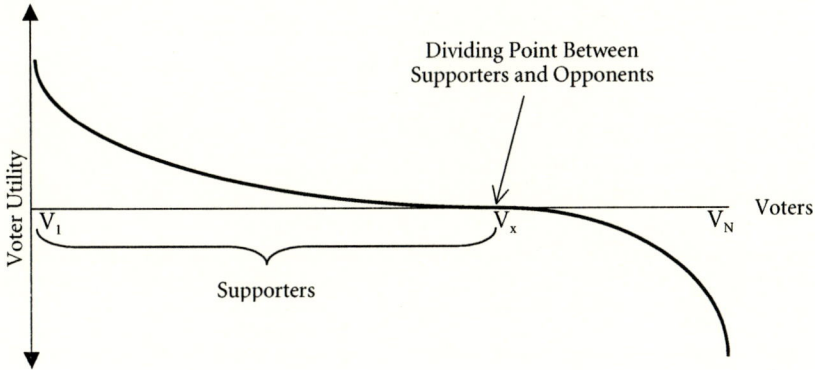

Candidates Acquire Information

The goal of changing voters' information incentives is to change the voters' perceived utility curve. But it is not necessary to actually change voters' perceptions; it is merely necessary to change how candidates currently or might come to perceive those perceptions. Interest groups, for example, often exert great effort to exaggerate grassroots support for positions they favor. One variation of this phenomenon is so common that it is given a name: astroturf. The idea is that grass is real but astroturf is fake grass, so astroturf is fake grassroots support. The fact that candidates have highly imperfect knowledge of voter preferences, especially on relatively obscure issues, suggests that there is ample room for intermediaries to foster false candidate perceptions of voter perceptions. However, whether intermediaries change real voter perceptions or merely candidates' perceptions of those perceptions, does not significantly affect the logic of bias for purposes of this book. Our discussion will focus on how voters acquire information.

Stage #2: Voters Acquire Information

Voters deciding whether to acquire a piece of information ask themselves whether the benefit of the information outweighs its cost.[16] The voter's **information benefit** is the difference in utility from possessing and not possessing a piece of information. The voter's **information cost** is all expenditures in time, money, and other resources—measured in foregone utility—to acquire a piece of information. The voter's **information incentive** is the difference between the benefit and cost of possessing a piece of information. Only if the information incentive is positive is the information acquired. Once information is acquired, it becomes **salient**. A salient piece of information used in a specific decision context is a **consideration**.

Benefits

Information benefits can be divided into a number of categories. One distinction is between collective benefits (benefits to society) and individual benefits (benefits to the individual voter). As Olson[17] argued, problems associated with collective action may lead social benefits to exceed individual benefits. A primary criterion of good democratic institutions is that they transform collective benefits into individual benefits. But for our purposes, we can ignore collective benefits as irrelevant to the individual voter's decision-making process.

Individual benefits can be divided into consumption and investment benefits. Consumption benefits are consumed in the process of acquisition rather than useful as a means to make a later decision. An example of a consumption benefit would be watching entertainment programming. An example of an investment benefit would be watching a candidate debate that will later make it possible to cast an informed vote.

Individual investment benefits can be divided between consumer and citizen benefits. Consumer investment benefits relate to the selection of products

---

[16] Cost-benefit analysis is uniquely difficult to apply to information acquisition because of the seeming paradox that an individual cannot know how much information is worth until he has the information. Nevertheless, it is common to ignore this dilemma in models of information search; e.g., George Joseph Stigler, "The Economics of Information," in *The Essence of Stigler*, ed. Kurt R. Leube and Thomas Gale Moore (Stanford, Calif.: Hoover Institution Press, Stanford University, 1986). Most people make frequent investments in information (e.g., in comparison shopping for a car) despite not knowing the exact value of that information.

[17] Olson, *The Logic of Collective Action*.

and services such as vacations, cars, and doctors. Citizen investment benefits relate to decisions such as learning about political issues and candidates for public office.

Individual citizen investment benefits can be divided between direct and indirect benefits. Direct benefits relate to information relevant to a particular electoral choice. Indirect benefits relate to information relevant in making all other political decisions. An example of an indirect benefit would be learning a decision rule such as how political parties differ. This decision rule may have relevance to hundreds of future decisions. An example of a direct benefit would be learning a candidate's party affiliation.

Usually, a decision to acquire political information is done without reference to a particular electoral contest. Indeed, most public policy information is learned between elections when citizens do not even know who is running for office. This general type of information nevertheless has electoral value because it helps voters learn such information as their party affiliation, their ideology, their positions on various issues, and the individuals and organizations (i.e., agents) to whom they can later delegate information costs. Of course, there are important exceptions to this rule; for example, when the public watches a candidate debate. But we can generally assume that citizens rarely acquire information for its benefit in a particular electoral contest.

A single piece of information may have multiple types of benefits. For example, a local TV broadcaster may learn about the value of spectrum in part to plan his business (a consumer investment benefit), guide his long-term strategy for dealing with the FCC (an indirect citizen investment benefit), and evaluate the Congressional candidates in his media market (a direct citizen investment benefit).

When deciding whether to acquire a specific piece of information, individuals care about the total benefit, not the component benefits. Accordingly, they may acquire information that has a major impact on the outcome of an electoral contest for reasons having little or nothing to do with that contest.

Some individuals acquire information for purely entertainment reasons that are nevertheless useful in their political decision-making. For example, many people watch *Saturday Night Live* and *David Letterman* for purely entertainment reasons. Nevertheless, those shows frequently provide news and commentary on current events and politicians. Similarly, most people watch prime time TV during election season for the entertainment programming, not the political ads between the programming.

Given the important role of entertainment in the acquisition of political information, the consumption benefit is likely to be large relative to other benefits. Given the minimal incentive most citizens have to acquire political information,[18] the combined total of direct and indirect citizen investment benefits is likely to be small. Given the difficulty in knowing what specific information will later be useful in a particular election, direct citizen investment benefits are likely to be negligible.

Figure 4-7 depicts the different types of benefits for acquiring a particular piece of political information across a sample of voters. The specific benefit levels will vary by issue and voter.

Figure 4-7. Different Types of Information Benefits Across Voters

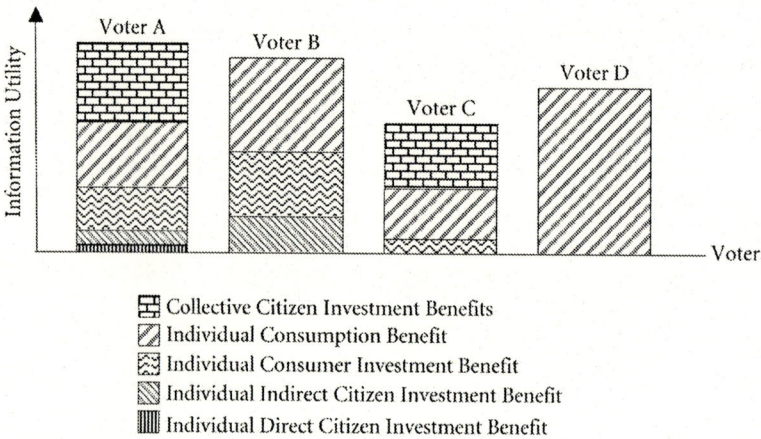

The relative size of different types of benefits is also likely to vary by type of election. For example, Americans tend to invest a lot more time into direct political information for presidents than for members of Congress.[19]

Costs

Costs can be divided into those that are already expended (sunk costs) and those that are incremental (marginal costs). Since sunk costs are already

---

[18] Downs, *An Economic Theory of Democracy,* John A. Ferejohn and James H. Kuklinski, *Information and Democratic Processes* (Urbana: University of Illinois Press, 1990), Bernard Grofman, *Information, Participation, and Choice: An Economic Theory of Democracy in Perspective* (Ann Arbor: University of Michigan Press, 1993), Popkin, *The Reasoning Voter.*
[19]Delli Carpini and Keeter, *What Americans Know About Politics and Why It Matters,* pp. 74-75.

expended, they do not factor into a voter's calculus of the marginal net benefit of acquiring a new piece of information. Sunk costs can be thought of as the facts and theories that constitute a voter's pre-existing store of knowledge. Consider a voter's marginal cost of acquiring information about broadcasters' digital spectrum. If the voter already understands what spectrum is and why certain low frequencies are becoming increasingly valuable, then the marginal cost of learning about the broadcasters' particular spectrum is reduced. Similarly, if a voter has formulated a position on the use of public assets by private companies, then the marginal cost of evaluating an elected official's stand on this particular public asset is reduced. Another example is voters' identification with a political party (a sunk cost) as opposed to their discovery shortly before an election of a new candidate's party label.

Marginal costs vary systematically based on the life experiences of voting groups. For example, broadcasters will have much lower costs than average voters for evaluating a given spectrum policy issue because broadcasters acquire the necessary background information as part of their jobs.

Marginal costs also vary systematically based on the nature of available intermediaries. For example, if spectrum policy is a non-partisan issue, then average voters cannot delegate the costs of acquiring information about spectrum to the political parties.

Putting Costs and Benefits Together

This analysis of costs and benefits suggests that the reasons people acquire information and the reasons they support a candidate are distinct and may be largely independent of each other. In other words, the critical information voters' use in making voting decisions may not be acquired specifically to make those voting decisions. This is consistent with the common scholarly formulation that "free" (i.e., zero marginal cost) information is vital to the workings of the democratic process.[20] The disconnect between the political impact of information and the reasons voters acquire it may give intermediaries great leverage in exercising influence.

The individual costs and benefits of acquiring a particular unit of information across all voters are depicted in Figure 4-8 ("The Decision to Acquire Information About an Attribute"). The area under the information benefit curve includes all four types of individual benefits but excludes collective benefits as irrelevant to the voter's decision.

---

[20] E.g., Downs, *An Economic Theory of Democracy*, p. 222, Popkin, *The Reasoning Voter*, chapter 2.

Figure 4-8. The Decision to Acquire Information About an Attribute

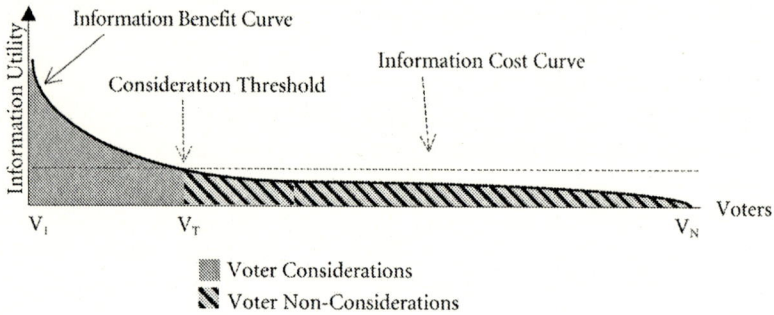

Benefit (B) is the total benefit of the information to the individual. The magnitude of the benefit is the difference between the voter's expected utility with and without the information. Cost (C) is the individual's resource expenditure to acquire the information. The salience threshold point (T) is the point at which the benefit of a piece of information equals its cost.[21] Only if $B > C$ may a piece of information become incorporated into a voter's perceived preferences with respect to a particular decision. The number of Voters (N) is the number of voters who will vote in a particular candidate election. The nth voter

---

[21] The salience threshold point (T) relates to just one type of information threshold—the decision whether to acquire a particular piece of information. After a piece of information is acquired, there are three other information thresholds that must be met before the information becomes electorally salient. These are short-term memory, long-term memory, and processing. If a piece of information turns out, after acquisition, to have no short-term use, it will not be stored in short-term memory or used to adjust an issue or candidate tally. Even after information is kept in short term memory, it will usually not be retained until the next election unless it is periodically refreshed by new information. Finally, the human mind can only simultaneously process a limited number of considerations. Psychologists often set the number of considerations at seven plus or minus two. For a discussion of various information processing models, see Terry Connolly, Hal R. Arkes, and Kenneth R. Hammond, *Judgment and Decision Making: An Interdisciplinary Reader*, 2nd ed., *Cambridge Series on Judgment and Decision Making* (Cambridge, U.K. ; New York: Cambridge University Press, 2000). However, the information-gathering threshold is especially important to intermediaries because it is the most direct one they can control through manipulation of information costs. All other thresholds only come into play after the information has entered the human brain. Thus, they are harder to manipulate.

is V_N; the first voter is V_1; and the voter at the salience threshold point is V_T. In this distribution of voters, only those to the left of V_T will acquire the relevant piece of information. For these voters, the information becomes a *considera-tion*. For voters to the right of V_T, the information is a *non-consideration*. The cost curve is depicted as constant not because it is in real life but because it makes it easier to see the various relationships highlighted in Figures 4-8 and 4-9.

The difference between the information benefit and cost curves can be summarized in a single information incentive curve. Intermediaries seek to change costs and benefits only as a means to change information incentives, which represent the "bottom line." Figure 4-9 summarizes the data in Figure 4-8 as an information incentive summary curve. Since the cost curve was arbi-trarily depicted as a constant, the shapes of the benefit and incentive curve are identical. To clarify the underlying logic of changing information incentives, it is helpful to distinguish between information costs and benefits, so in future graphs both will be shown.

Figure 4-9. An Incentive View of the Decision to Acquire Information

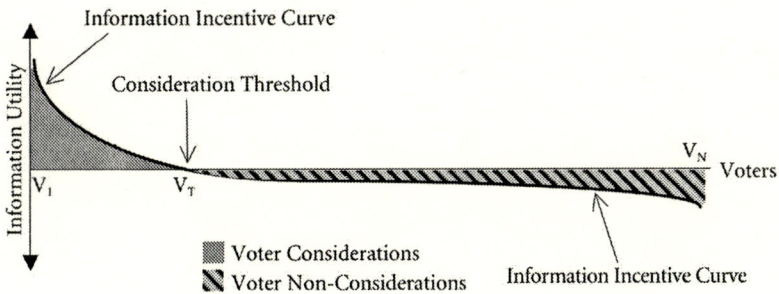

Good vs. Bad Changes from the Status Quo

This model of information salience does not distinguish between information that makes a voter feel good or bad about a proposed change from the status quo. For example, let us assume that a particular piece of information sug-gests that the value of a public asset (such as spectrum) is worth $100 billion. This is a positive piece of information for those who might be given the asset from the government at no charge. But this same piece of information might be a negative for the taxpayers who have to pay for the gift. Figure 4-10 captures this idea by distinguishing between information that builds support or opposition to a change from the status quo.

Figure 4-10. Distinguishing Between Supporters and Opponents

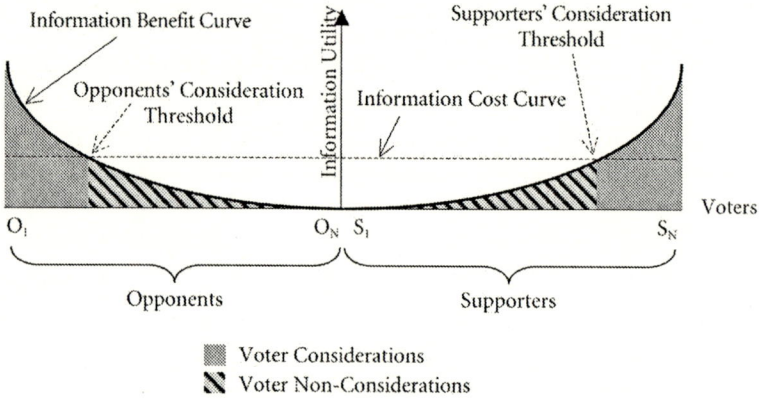

The Information Decision and the Perceived Utility Curve

After a new piece of information is acquired, it triggers the creation of a consideration, which either in the present or future may be attached as a positive or negative attribute to an object, such as a political candidate.

The reason the information acquisition decision is important is that it affects the voters' perceived utility curve. Figure 4-11 captures this idea by distinguishing between an information acquisition curve and a perceived attribute utility curve. The attribute utility curve represents the change in utility revealed by the acquisition of information about an attribute. Voters who attach a positive (above the x-axis) utility to a given piece of information are supporters. Those who attach a negative (below the x-axis) utility are opponents.

Figure 4-11. Change in Perceived Utility from Acquiring Information

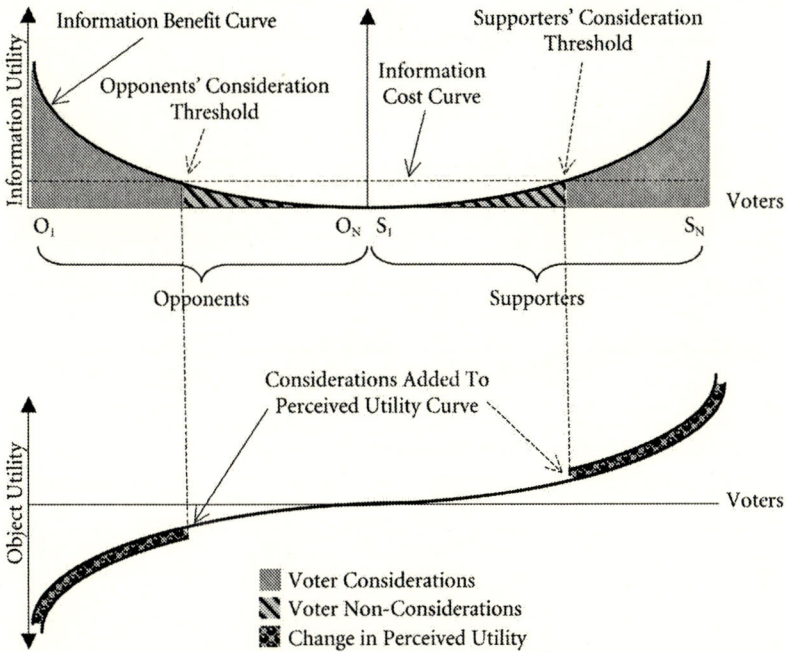

The specific way information acquisition changes preferences is a source of great debate among those who study political psychology.[22] For example, political psychologists debate the extent to which individuals 1) keep all considerations in their heads and aggregrate them when needed, or 2) keep a running tally of considerations in their heads, usually in the form of a summary affect toward an object. What is not controversial is the basic principle that new information can change voters' choices in predictable ways. If this wasn't the case, candidates, lobbyists, and others seeking to persuade voters would give up doing so.

Aggregate Change

Each utility change associated with acquiring information about an object attribute can be serially added to form an aggregate utility curve with respect

---

[22] Ibid, Ferejohn and Kuklinski, Information and Democratic Processes.

to that object. The result of countless such additions is an aggregate perceived utility curve. Figure 4-12 illustrates a perceived utility curve as an aggregation of many small considerations. Adding many small considerations across many voters is assumed to lead to a smooth distribution.

Figure 4-12. Perceived Utility as an Aggregation of Considerations

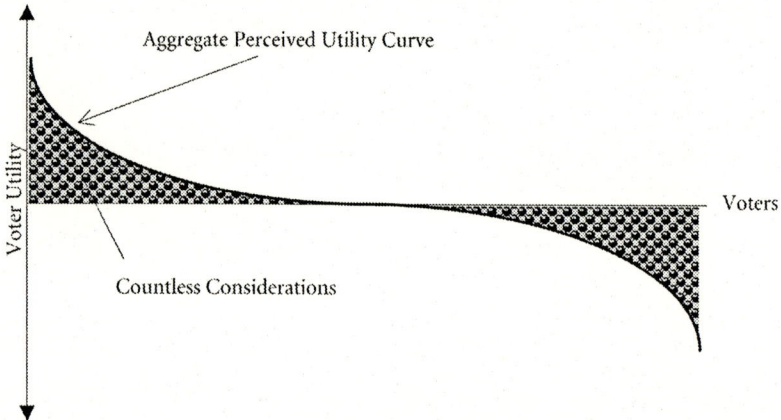

Note that in this model the basic building blocks of an individual voter's decision-making, considerations, are discrete units. But the aggregation of those units generates a continuous curve. Thus, this model of voter information processing has both discrete and continuous properties. At a micro level, changing information incentives across voters, attributes, and time has lumpy effects. But at a macro level, these lumps are smoothed out. An analogy to this lumpy model of political power is contemporary physics, where the deepest levels of nature are ruled by discreet units such as atoms and quarks, but their visible manifestations appear continuous.

Conclusion

The ultimate goal of policy bias is to change the behavior of policymakers. In a democracy, policymakers are assumed to respond to voter preferences, which, in turn, are influenced by the information available to voters. Therefore, controlling voter information incentives, the subject of the next chapter, lies at the heart of the effective exercise of political power.

CHAPTER 5:

Strategies of Broadcaster Bias to Maximize Impact

"In the lobbying business, information is power."
—Kathy Ramsey, Senior Vice President, NAB Government Relations

In the previous chapter's descriptions of stages 2 through 4 of the democratic decision sequence, we assumed that a voter's incentive to acquire information is fixed. This is a common assumption among models of legislative decision-making. Now we turn to stage 1, an intermediary's ability to change a voter's incentive to acquire information.

Intermediaries increase the incentive to acquire positive information and decrease the incentive to acquire negative information. **Positive information** is defined as any information about an attribute that will increase support for an intermediary's preferred policy. **Negative information** is the opposite. This suggests that the power of intermediaries comes not from outright lying but from the ability to selectively change information incentives at the margin. The general effect of this strategy, if successful, is that in their electoral calculations politicians will be disproportionately responsive to interest groups who are willing and able to make the biggest investments in voter information incentives.

Figure 5-1 summarizes the overall strategy of changing information incentives so that the perceived preferences of the median voter move closer to the true preferences of the intermediary. Politicians seeking to win elections choose policies on particular issues that correspond to the perceived preferences of the median voter. Therefore, intermediaries seek to shift the median voter's perceived preferences closer to their own.

Figure 5-1. Effect of an Intermediary's Information Campaign

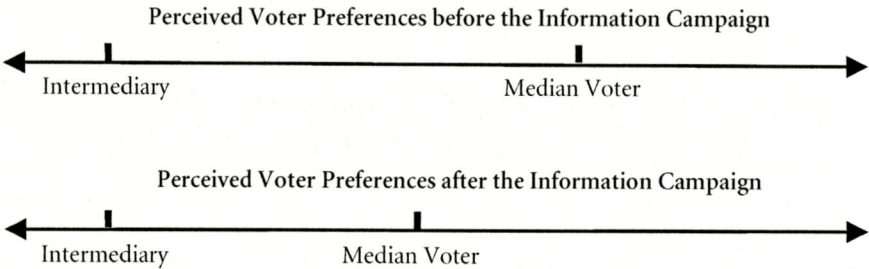

Perceived Voter Preferences before the Information Campaign

Intermediary   Median Voter

Perceived Voter Preferences after the Information Campaign

Intermediary   Median Voter

The ability to selectively change information incentives is ultimately the ability to control which information voters will take into consideration when evaluating issues and candidates. The concept of selectively changing information incentives is loosely equivalent to common concepts in the political science literature such as "changing the scope of conflict," "mobilization," "activation," "bias," "priming," "agenda setting," and "framing." These terms are often employed in a narrower sense than employed here. For example, both framing and agenda setting often refer to changing information incentives, but framing suggests changing information incentives at a micro level (the attributes of an issue) whereas agenda setting suggests changing information incentives at a macro level (the issue itself).

Popular culture has many sayings that take as obvious the strategic utility of one person controlling information at another's expense. Examples include "don't leave a paper trail behind," "don't tip your hand," "sweep it under the rug," "pull the wool over their eyes," "hide your tracks," "pursue a hidden agenda," "wear a poker face," "make a back door attempt," "seek an information edge," "provide window dressing," and "pay lip service."

Military strategists involved in information warfare efforts—variously called "intelligence," "propaganda," and "psychological operations"—have their own terminology. One major recent book called the different components of information warfare "denial" and "deception."[1] Denial refers to the security systems in place to preserve military secrets. Deception refers to framing information in such a way as to mislead the public and potential opponents.

There is a certain refreshing candor in the way military historians and strategists speak of denial and deception. Indeed, a whole bookshelf could easily be filled with military books proudly describing famous deceptions that

---

[1] Godson and Wirtz, *Strategic Denial and Deception.*

fooled the enemy.[2] Who, for example, could possibly be opposed to camouflage that saves the lives of hometown soldiers? In contrast, I could not find a single lobbying book that made such self-congratulatory claims. Certainly, one major difference between lobbying and military strategy is that fooling the enemy is something to brag about while fooling the American public isn't. Why write a book if the result is to be publicly vilified rather than praised? The same goes with sports. Feints in sports are publicly applauded. Saying that someone "faked everybody out" is a compliment. No quarterback has ever been shamed for leading his opponents to think he was going to pass the ball in one direction when his real intent was to pass it in another direction.

Rather than use morally charged terms such as "deception" or "propaganda" to describe lobbying, I have chosen to emphasize the more epistemologically neutral language of "information incentives." This continues in the tradition of other epistemologically neutral terms in the political communication literature such as framing, priming, and agenda setting. Even when I use the more loaded language of bias, I try to do so in a way that emphasizes bias as a universal human motive such as lust and aggression rather than anything uniquely associated with a particular group or individual.

Intermediaries change voter information incentives by changing the differential between benefits and costs. The basic strategic logic of changing information incentives does not change whether we vary both benefits and costs or hold one constant and vary the other. To simplify our graphical analysis, therefore, we will hold benefits constant and vary costs. We could just as easily have

---

[2] Leigh Armistead, Joint Forces Staff College (U.S.), and United States. National Security Agency/Central Security Service., *Information Operations: Warfare and the Hard Reality of Soft Power*, 1st ed., *Issues in Twenty-First Century Warfare* (Dulles, Va.: Brassey's, 2004), Berkowitz, *The New Face of War : How War Will Be Fought in the 21st Century*, Robert J. Bunker and Institute of Land Warfare (Association of the United States Army), *Information Operations and the Conduct of Land Warfare*, *Land Warfare Papers ; No. 31* (Arlington, VA: Institute of Land Warfare, Association of the United States Army, 1998), Dorothy Elizabeth Robling Denning, *Information Warfare and Security* (New York: Addison-Wesley, 1999), Richard Forno and Ronald Baklarz, *The Art of Information Warfare: Insight into the Knowledge Warrior Philosophy*, 2nd pbk. ed. (Boca Raton, Florida: Universal Publishers, 1999), Robert E. Neilson, *Sun Tzu and Information Warfare: A Collection of Winning Papers from the Sun Tzu Art of War in Information Warfare Competition* (Washington, DC: National Defense University Press, 1997), Thom Shanker and Eric Schmitt, "Firing Leaflets and Electrons, U.S. Wages Information War," *New York Times*, 24 February 2003, Edward Waltz, *Information Warfare: Principles and Operations* (Boston: Artech House, 1998), Gary F. Wheatley and Richard E. Hayes, *Information Warfare and Deterrence* (Washington, DC: Institute for National Strategic Studies, National Defense University, 1996).

held costs constant and varied benefits. Of course, in the real world, both information costs and benefits vary.

Political actors have incentives to change the information incentives of three different types of political actors: 1) voters (principals), 2) other intermediaries (information agents), and 3) elected representatives (object agents). For our purpose in this chapter, these distinctions will be ignored because they don't change the logic of changing information incentives.

Intermediaries Choose Voter Information Incentives

Intermediaries choose two types of information incentives about candidates: candidate attributes and source attributes. When intermediaries choose incentives for voters to acquire information *about candidates*, they are changing *perceived candidate attributes*. When intermediaries choose incentives for voters to acquire information *about the credibility of sources of information about candidates*, they are changing *perceived source attributes*. In this chapter, we will focus on incentives to acquire information about candidate attributes, and then end with a discussion of incentives to acquire information about source attributes.

The distribution of voter information incentives facing a candidate is characterized by four variables: voter information utility, voters, candidate attributes, and time. This roughly corresponds to Lasswell's[3] famous description of the study of political persuasion: "Who says what to whom with what effect?" In this case, the "who" is the intermediary, the "what" is the attribute, the "whom" is the voter, and "what effect" is the change in incentive to acquire information. All that we have added is the time dimension—a much neglected variable in the study of political persuasion. Accordingly, we will investigate intermediary incentives to:

1. Change Information Incentives Across Voters

2. Change Information Incentives Across Attributes

3. Change Information Incentives Across Time

For each variable, we will start with a general theoretical discussion, and then provide examples. Many of the examples are drawn from the broadcast industry. The examples suggest that in a variety of different circumstances,

---

[3] H.D. Lasswell, "The Structure and Function of Communication in Society," in The Communication of Ideas, ed. Lyman Bryson (New York: Harper & Row, 1948).

broadcasters are like other intermediaries in that they act rationally when investing in voter information incentives. In this context, "rationally" means "seeking to bias voter decision-making."

Information Incentives Across Voters

"The most powerful special interests want private settlement [of conflict] because they are able to dictate the outcome as long as the conflict remains private.... It is the weak who want to socialize conflict, i.e., to involve more and more people in the conflict until the balance of forces is changed."

—E.E. Schattschneider, The Semisovereign People[4]

Intermediaries may selectively change information incentives for some voters but not others. When an intermediary increases information incentives, its intent is to **reveal** information. When it does the opposite, its intent is to **hide** information.

The vast majority of the literature on intermediaries focuses on strategies intermediaries use for increasing voter information incentives to acquire favorable information.[5] The model presented in this chapter suggests that decreasing voter information incentives to acquire unfavorable information may be just as effective. Since we live in a society obsessed by government, corporate, and personal secrecy, this omission is striking and may largely be explained by scholars' over reliance on published and other easily available and verifiable information.

As a rule, when an intermediary hides information from a principal, it receives the greatest payoff when the act of hiding remains hidden. Otherwise, the intermediary's credibility will be damaged. That is because a reasonable principal will infer from the act of hiding that something unfavorable would

---

[4] Schattschneider, *The Semisovereign People: A Realist's View of Democracy in America*, p. xxiii.

[5] E.g., Alger, *The Media and Politics*, Jeffrey M. Berry, *The Interest Group Society*, 3rd ed. (New York: Longman, 1997), Timothy E. Cook, *Making Laws and Making News: Media Strategies in the U.S. House of Representatives* (Washington, D.C.: Brookings Institution, 1989), Doris A. Graber, *Mass Media and American Politics*, 4th ed. (Washington, D.C.: CQ Press, 1992), Schlozman and Tierney, *Organized Interests and American Democracy*, John R. Wright, *Interest Groups and Congress : Lobbying, Contributions, and Influence, New Topics in Politics* (Boston: Allyn and Bacon, 1996).

otherwise be revealed. Not surprisingly, we live in a world where intermediaries tout their openness to their principals and claim that the cost of hiding information from them is prohibitive, so they never do it.

Figure 5-2 depicts the impact of selectively changing information costs across voters for a single attribute at a particular point in time. In the status quo, both the information benefit and cost curves are perfectly symmetrical across both supporters and opponents. The result of all this symmetry is that the perceived utility of both supporters and opponents is also identical. Now suppose a political actor is able to lower information costs for supporters and raise them for opponents. The perceived utility of supporters now outweighs the utility of opponents, so the political actor has shifted the balance of power with respect to this attribute in favor of supporters.

Figure 5-2. Selective Changes in Information Costs

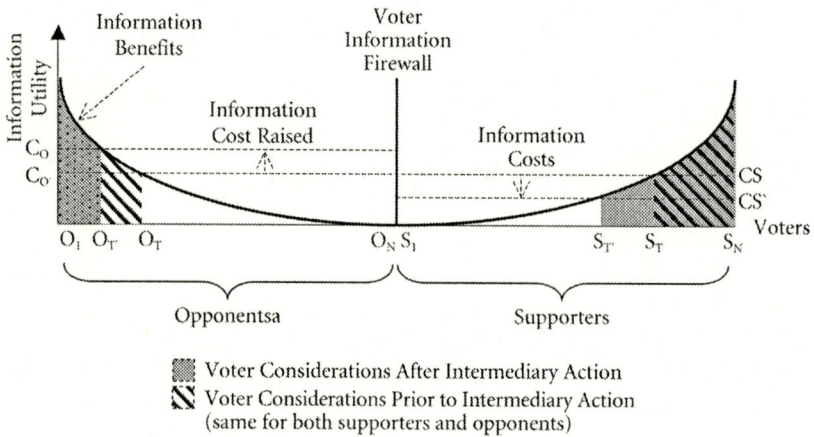

Voter Considerations After Intermediary Action

Voter Considerations Prior to Intermediary Action
(same for both supporters and opponents)

Voter Firewall

Any strategic asymmetry in information incentives across voters, such as that depicted in Figure 3, is a "voter information firewall." A voter firewall separates friends and foes, supporters and opponents. On one side of the firewall information costs are high; on the other side information costs are low. Other types of firewalls, discussed later, create strategic information incentive asymmetries across time and candidate attributes.

The firewall between supporters and opponents suggests the great importance of secrecy in effective political persuasion. A political actor's political power may be greatly diluted if it cannot selectively change information incentives across supporters and opponents.

Intermediaries can use a large variety of tools to increase supporters' incentives, including communications media such as mail, e-mail, faxes, telephone calls, newsletters, and face-to-face communication. Opponents may be excluded from these communications through standard trade association and corporate lobbying security measures such as computer firewalls, guarded entry and exit, document shredder machines, technical language or code words (only understood by insiders), exclusive invitations to events, reliance on unverifiable face-to-face communication, and confidentiality clauses in employee contracts. Group membership criteria, combined with social and economic incentives for maintaining group norms of secrecy, are also likely to be employed.

A vivid example of the potential strength of secrecy norms—when buttressed by self-interest—is the behavior of the 1951 Brooklyn Giants, one of the most famous teams in baseball history.[6] For close to 50 years the entire team—including players, coaches, and support staff—was able to keep a secret that if disclosed would have damaged their collective reputation. During the 1951 baseball season, the team engineered a miraculous come-from-behind end-of-season record by violating baseball norms of fair play. The team used a secret telescope hidden in the centerfield scoreboard to read the opposing catcher's signals at home plate and convey that information through an elaborate communication scheme to batters at the plate. Knowing the type of incoming pitch dramatically increased the Giants' batting percentages and runs scored.

The National Association of Broadcasters has a provision in its bylaws banning any board member from releasing confidential information: "While directors may take positions that differ from the position of the Association, they shall not in so doing utilize non-public information or data that they obtained through their service on the board."[7] By a simple majority vote, the

---

[6] Prager, Joshua Harris, "Was the '51 Giants Comeback a Miracle, Or Did They Simply Steal the Pennant," *Wall Street Journal*, 31 January 2001, p. A1.

[7] Harry Jessell, "Plumbing Problem: NAB's crackdown on leaks threatens sunshine tradition," *Broadcasting & Cable*, 9 January 2001, p. 18. Note that the author praises the NAB's tradition of openness to the trade press without recognizing that the trade press to which he refers is a sympathetic audience that usually takes on the role of broadcast industry advocate. Other legitimate researchers and reporters have been given no such access. See also Doug Halonen, "NAB aims to stop leaks by its directors," *Electronic Media*, 1 January 2001, p. 2.

NAB board may kick out any director it determines has violated the secrecy rule.

According to Tom Sweatt, head of security at NAB, no one can enter the NAB building without first making an appointment. Upon entering, everyone is televised, then registers, receives a pass, and must be escorted within the building at all times. Many internal doors have alarms and some internal doors can only be opened with special passes.[8] These security precautions were in place prior to 9/11.

Most firewalls, however, are created by far more subtle means. Decker Anstrom, the former executive director of the National Cable & Telecommunications Association, describes the way these work: "In Washington, the language is oblique. There are certain codes and secret signals, and people rarely are very direct about things."[9] This gives insiders who can accurately interpret the signals a huge advantage. Far more typical of the way voter firewalls are created is the broadcasters' FCC filings, which are on the public record, but are typically written in a way that requires not only a Ph.D. in engineering to merely comprehend at face value, but also a lot of contextual knowledge to understand their economic and policy implications.[10] Similarly, broadcaster favored clauses in legislation may be public but their purposes invisible to the press and public.[11]

Motive vs. Result

Often when an intermediary that supports a position invests in supporting information, an intermediary that opposes that position will invest in opposing

---

[8] Telephone interview with New America Foundation research assistant Irene Hahn, 14 March 2001. Ironically, when the FCC attempted to put in place similar security precautions, broadcast lobbyists objected. See Chris McConnell, "Lawyers hope to preserve drop-in lobbying: New security, building, commissioners could cut down on informal visits to FCC," *Broadcasting & Cable*, 27 October 1997, p. 22.

[9] Lee Hall, "Give Anstrom the Business," *Electronic Media*, 23 August 1999, p. 2.

[10] FCC Report and Order in the matter of *Amendment of Parts 73 and 74 of the Commission's Rules to Establish Rules for Digital Low Power Television, Television Translator, and Television Booster Stations and to Amend Rules for Digital Class A Television Stations*, MB Docket 03-185, released 30 September 2004.

[11] A reasonable person, for example, might have concluded that in the Telecommunications Act of 1996 broadcasters were legally mandated to provide ad-supported ("free") TV with the bulk of their spectrum. In fact, however, that was not the case. See discussion on Free TV in Chapter 13.

information. Both intermediaries may then engage in an information arms race, with each making additional information investments to expose the other's weaknesses. A general increase in voters' incentive to acquire information may characterize the resulting equilibrium. Consequently, more voters become politically relevant with respect to that attribute, and the perceived utility curve comes to more closely resemble the true utility curve. One political science term for such a result is "expanding the scope of conflict."[12] Like the invisible hand of the marketplace, each party changes voter information incentives for purely selfish reasons, but the resulting competition over voter information incentives leads to enhanced democracy as voters become better informed about their options.

An important implication of this analysis is that we must distinguish between the motive for and result of bias. The motive for bias is the purely selfish goal of increasing voters' incentive to acquire positive information and decrease their incentive to acquire negative information. But in a competitive environment, the result may be an overall lessening of asymmetric information. According to this analysis, the greatest danger to a democracy occurs when those who have disproportionate control over information dissemination—whether they are incumbent office holders, the media, or other mobilized interest groups—have a common interest adverse to the public. This is the classic case against media consolidation.[13]

In Figure 5-3, the information cost level starts at C_S for supporters and C_O for opponents. Intermediary A lowers information costs to C_{S1}. Intermediary B responds by lowering information costs to C_{O1}. Intermediaries A and B keep responding in this fashion until in equilibrium information costs are C_{S*} for supporters and C_{O*} for opponents. The result is that the attribute in question becomes politically relevant for many more voters.

---

[12] Schattschneider, *The Semisovereign People: A Realist's View of Democracy in America*. For the argument that increasing the visibility of a policy area reduces the ability of interest groups to exercise power at the expense of the general public, see Michael T. Hayes, *Lobbyists and Legislators: A Theory of Political Markets* (New Brunswick, N.J.: Rutgers University Press, 1981), Theodore J. Lowi, *The End of Liberalism: Ideology, Policy, and the Crisis of Public Authority*, [1st ed. (New York,: Norton, 1969).

[13] Mark N. Cooper, *Media Ownership and Democracy in the Digital Information Age: Promoting Diversity with First Amendment Principles and Market Structure Analysis* (Stanford, Calif.: Center for Internet & Society, Stanford Law School, 2003), McChesney, *The Problem of the Media: U.S. Communication Politics in the Twenty-First Century*.

Figure 5-3. Changes in Information Costs with Intermediary Competition

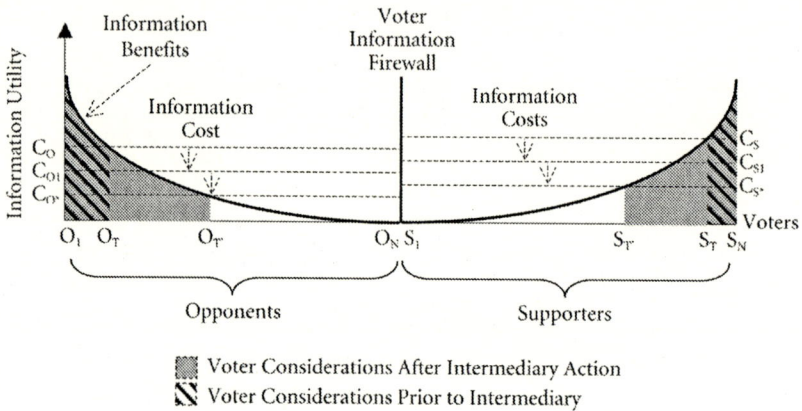

Voter Considerations After Intermediary Action
Voter Considerations Prior to Intermediary

Changes in Information Incentives and the Perceived Utility Curve

Figure 5-4 links changes in information incentives to changes in the perceived utility curve. Specifically, it illustrates the cumulative impact of changing information acquisition incentives across many voters. In this example, the impact of the cost shifts is that supporters' perceived utility comes to outweigh opponents' perceived utility, so power shifts in favor of supporters. The point V_x0 marks the crossover of supporters and opponents on the true utility curve. The point V_x1 marks the crossover of supporters and opponents on the perceived utility curve. The point V_m marks the median voter.

Figure 5-4. Shift in the Perceived Utility Curve

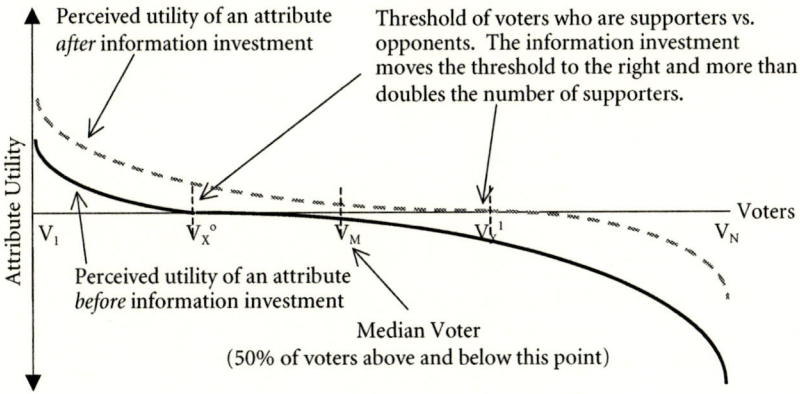

Figure 5-4. Shift in the Perceived Utility Curve

Voter Trustworthiness

An intermediary's expected supporters can be divided by their level of trust-worthiness. In practice, intermediaries are unsure who their supporters are and even more unsure who they can trust to maintain a firewall. If confidential information is publicly released, the information firewall and all the strategic advantages that come from it are eliminated. Therefore, all other things being equal, intermediaries will carefully guard unfavorable information and only distribute it to trustworthy individuals.

For example, The U.S. military does not reveal to the U.S. public informa-tion that it does not want enemies to see because it cannot prevent enemies from seeing information generally available to U.S. citizens. All other things being equal, as the number of individuals targeted for a message increases, the ability to keep the message secret decreases.

Often, trustworthiness can be thought of in hierarchical and organizational terms. Those at the top of the organization are the most trusted and those out-side the organization are the least trusted. The NAB, for example, carefully tar-gets different messages to its executive board of directors, its TV and radio boards of directors (who elect the executive board), its state leaders (state asso-ciation presidents, executive directors, and board members), state legislative liaison captains (two for each member of Congress), its rank-and-file mem-bers, its associate members, and the general public.

The safest assumption for an organization is that no one should be entrusted with sensitive information who doesn't need it to do a particular job.

This strategy, called "information compartmentalization," is a fundamental method United States national security agencies use to prevent sensitive information from getting into enemy hands. For example, this explains the seeming miracle that tens of thousands of people work in national security—mostly in the U.S. military—but relatively few secrets are released publicly. Similarly, Washington DC trade associations that pursue unpopular or controversial agendas rely heavily on information compartmentalization.

Some of this information targeting has to do with pure efficiency: it's inefficient to provide people with information they don't want or cannot use. But the NAB's many steps to ensure secretiveness and their top grassroots and Washington lobbyists' belief that if they release sensitive information they will be viewed as traitors, suggests that a lot more than mere efficiency is involved.

The NAB may be especially prone to information compartmentalization because of the nature of the business its members are in. Broadcasters are extremely adept at getting messages out to the public. So a dissenting member is well positioned to do extensive damage. The result is that the NAB may be forced into a position of unusually high mistrust of its own members.

Voter Trustfulness

An intermediary's supporters often recognize the problem that not everyone is trustworthy and that it is very hard to maintain secrecy. Thus, as long as they trust their representatives to act on their own behalf, they may acquiesce when their leaders withhold information or even lie about their actions. The lies, although harmful to opponents, are viewed as "white lies" by supporters. This is a form of **strategic self-ignorance**, and it is equally effective whether it is real or for the sake of appearance.

We see this type of behavior in many spheres of life. The American public does not complain when the military does not reveal its strategic plans or other confidential information. Nor does it mind when the military uses strategic miscommunication so the enemy is put off guard. The public understands that such actions are taken on its own behalf. Similarly, athletics often involves sending misleading signals to the opposing team. No fans complain when the quarterback keeps his game plan confidential or intentionally deceives the opposition (and his fans) about the person to whom he will give possession of the ball. This type of behavior is also endemic among members of Washington, DC interest groups, especially when they know their group is pursuing an unpopular course of action.

Some groups have more trusting members than others. The more trusting the members, the less the information they require, so the greater the ease in keeping confidential information. For a variety of reasons, the current NAB may be especially blessed in this regard.

The NAB has an excellent track record of representing its members' interests, so its members trust it. In 1982, Edward Fritts was elected president of the NAB. During the early years of his tenure, many NAB members doubted his abilities. Accordingly, he sent substantial information to rank-and-file members describing his accomplishments. In 1987, for example, he sent a detailed memo to members describing the legislative and regulatory accomplishments of the NAB during the first five years under his leadership. A 1987 article in *National Journal* noted that one of NAB's major weaknesses was that its members wouldn't grant its lobbyists autonomy.[14] As Fritts developed a successful track record, however, he was able to restrict the flow of information to these members. Annual reports to rank-and-file members were dropped and compendiums of legislative and regulatory achievements were restricted to only the most trusted member leaders. Today, NAB members are only given minimal documented information about the inner workings of their association. To the extent possible, potentially damaging information is restricted to their elected representatives on the NAB executive board of directors. Nevertheless, I found no evidence that NAB members were dissatisfied with this state of affairs.

NAB members are also politically sophisticated. They know their interests without being banged on the head, and they also know their organization often lobbies for laws—such as spectrum giveaways—that would be unpopular if subject to popular scrutiny. Such a combination of forces begs for secrecy, and the NAB is happy to provide it on behalf of its members. NAB members also don't seem to mind when the NAB actively misrepresents key information not only to the public but also to its own membership. In 1996–1997, for example, touting the high cost of the digital TV (DTV) transition was central to the NAB's lobbying campaign to get free spectrum for digital TV. I had lunch with one general manager at NAB's annual convention in 1997 who readily determined that NAB's numbers were unrealistically high, but it didn't bother him. He knew that it was NAB's job to "push a line," and he could readily get accurate information simply by talking to vendors at the show.

Similarly, NAB's science and technology department wrote a confidential report to TV members about the costs of transitioning to DTV. In the version of the report sent out before the FCC awarded the DTV licenses to incumbents, NAB conspicuously left blank a very sensitive piece of information—the

---

[14] Burt Solomon, "Measuring Clout," *National Journal*, 4 July 1987, p. 1706.

lower bound cost of the DTV transition. It was as if an NAB lobbyist looked at the final report and decided it would be crazy to include this controversial information, so crossed it out. That in itself was a clear signal to TV members. Only subsequently, when the licenses were in the broadcasters' hands, was this blank filled in.[15]

The type of factors described above may be common to many trade associations. But there is one factor that may make NAB members especially prone to cherish their ignorance—or at least the *appearance* of ignorance. Broadcasters are in the business of journalism, and it is universally understood that conventional lobbying creates the appearance of a conflict of interest and thus lowers a media outlet's reputation for journalistic integrity. If broadcasters are ignorant of the NAB's conventional lobbying activities, they cannot fairly be blamed for having a conflict of interest. However, it is also true that broadcasters only need to plausibly claim ignorance, not actually be ignorant. By merely pretending to be ignorant of the conventional lobbying done on their behalf, they can have their cake and eat it, too. This distinction between real ignorance and merely apparent ignorance is central to the distinction between opportunistic (selfish) and ethical (altruistic) information firewalls. As we will see in later chapters, broadcaster claims of an ethical information firewall, which includes self-imposed ignorance, may disguise an opportunistic firewall designed to hide information from the public.

Teasing out the exact nature of the broadcasters' strategic self-ignorance is not easy. Think of the typical American who doesn't want to know the details of how their dinner was slaughtered and dismembered. Are those people really ignorant? Or do they simply not want to think about the implications of their actions? My sense is that both factors are at play. Similarly, broadcasters may act in a way that terrifies members of Congress and yet be oblivious of the implications of their own actions. One caveat is that some broadcasters are perfectly aware of how at least some members of Congress perceive the power of their local broadcaster. But they don't care as long as the politician's perception is born out of what they believe to be unjustified paranoia. This type of broadcaster believes he would never allow his economic self-interest to conflict with his journalistic integrity. If politicians believe otherwise, that is not his fault.

---

[15] The initial report was dated 29 January 1997; the amended report with the blank filled in was dated 11 July 1997. NAB, "Digital Television Broadcasting: A Status Report from NAB Science & Technology," (Washington, DC: NAB, 29 January 1997), Appendix A, p. 5.

Information Incentives Across Attributes

"The definition of the alternatives is the supreme instrument of power."

—Schattschneider, The Semisovereign people[16]

"No one ever lies. People often do what they have to do to make their story sound right."

—William H. Ginsburg, lawyer for Monica Lewinsky[17]

The model so far has assumed that intermediaries can change information incentives in relation to only one candidate attribute. But obviously, intermediaries can change information incentives across many candidate attributes. To capture this dimension of choice, we can add a third dimension: candidate attributes. Candidate attributes can be thought of as occupying an infinite space—as varied as all the considerations that could conceivably influence one's opinion of a candidate. Each of these attributes may be characterized by a variety of parameters, including a voter benefit and cost to acquire information about it

From the perspective of an individual intermediary's interests, candidate attributes can be sorted on a scale from favorable to unfavorable. A rational intermediary can be expected to increase incentives to acquire information about favorable attributes and decrease incentives to acquire information about unfavorable attributes. In the political communication literature, similar terms for this strategy would be "framing," "priming," and "agenda setting." More cynical terms, widely used by Washington political consultants to describe opponents' actions, but also sometimes their own, are "creating a smokescreen," "making noise," "generating political cover," and "diverting attention."[18]

---

[16] Schattschneider, *The Semisovereign People: A Realist's View of Democracy in America*, p. 66.

[17] Francis X. Clines, "Lewinsky Dismisses Her Lawyer and Hires Washington Veterans," New York Times, 3 June 1998, p. A1.

[18] For an example of telecom lobbyists explaining their message strategies as a way "to keep up the noise level," see transcripts of interviews with top Baby Bell government affairs representatives compiled by Elizabeth Books, Vice President for Communications, United States Telephone Association, and sent along with a summary memo to them on 1 November 1996. The interviews were done in preparation for a planned "repositioning" PR campaign costing tens of millions of dollars to influence the FCC's implementation of the Telecommunications Act.

Attribute Firewalls

In Figure 5-5, the x-axis now refers to attributes rather than voters. Attributes, like voters were before, are divided into two categories: favorable and unfavorable. An intermediary lowers the cost of information about favorable attributes and raises the cost of information about unfavorable attributes. The result is an "attribute firewall," with high incentives to acquire attribute information on one side of the wall and low incentives on the other side. The selective subsidization of attributes is the essence of framing. For reasons unknown to this author, attribute firewalls have received far more attention in the political science literature than either voter or time firewalls.

Figure 5-5. Information Incentives Across Attributes

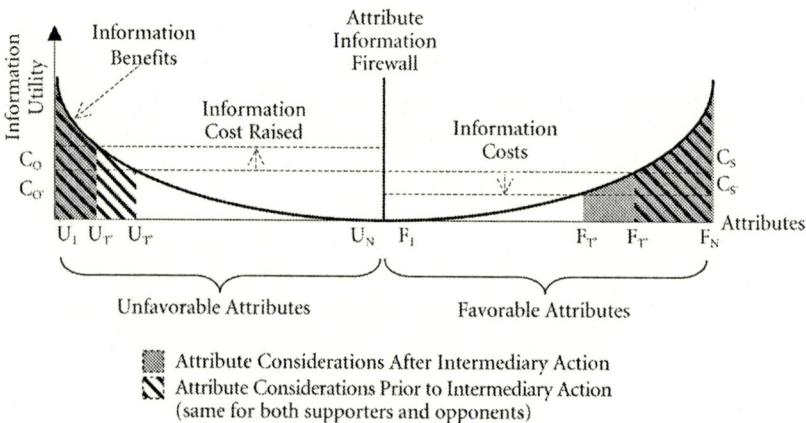

Attribute Considerations After Intermediary Action
Attribute Considerations Prior to Intermediary Action
(same for both supporters and opponents)

Pure vs. Mixed Attribute Strategies

It may not be in an intermediary's interest to engage in a **pure strategy** of raising information incentives on favorable attributes and lowering them on unfavorable attributes. The alternative is to engage in a **mixed strategy** where on average information incentives on favorable attributes are increased but in any specific case they may be reduced. The key point of a mixed strategy is that the unit of analysis shifts to the net favorability of a set of information investments rather than the favorability of just a single information investment.

This is a much more sophisticated and effective strategy for engaging in bias, which can only succeed if it is undetected. For many practical information campaigns, a pure strategy of bias is just too obvious to be effective. Spies often have to help their enemy in order to build trust to gather the information necessary to hurt their enemy on some more fundamental mission. Salespeople may need to offer information about competitors and other harmful information if they are to win their customers' trust. Similarly, broadcasters often find it in their interest to come across as objective and even-handed in how they present their case, whether lobbying one-on-one or broadcasting over the airwaves. Every broadcaster has a story of a time when he acted against his own interests. And he tells this story again and again. In the spring of 1996, for example, CBS ran a story about the spectrum giveaway to broadcasters. Everybody who criticized the media's coverage of the giveaway was reminded of this fact.

Independent vs. Dependent Attributes

Attributes may be dependent on each other with the result that if you know one attribute, you may be able to predict another attribute. An attribute that allows you to predict a cluster of other attributes is an information shortcut. Often there will be many different information shortcuts that allow you to make the same conclusion. For example, you may be able to infer that a neighbor is a Republican by multiple means, including the political signs they put up in their yard, the elephant pin they wear on their lapel, the club they belong to, and their views on gun control and abortion.

Candidate-Linked vs. Candidate-Stranded Attributes

Attributes that might appear to hurt or help a candidate may not in fact do so unless these attributes can be specifically linked to the candidate. For example, the editorial pages of the *Wall Street Journal* and *New York Times* denounced the "spectrum giveaway" to the TV broadcasters contained in the Telecom Act of 1996. But unless readers were also given information to attach the names of individual legislators to this outcome, the negative coverage of the giveaway lacked significant political consequence in terms of affecting legislators' re-election prospects. A consequence of such complex causal linkages is that attributes near the top of the attribute hierarchy tend to have far greater political weight than attributes at lower rungs because even a single broken link near the top can nullify investments in attributes lower down.

The creation of stranded attributes (also known as "plausible deniability") goes to the heart of legislative strategy when an interest group pursues a potentially unpopular strategy. For example, most of the most controversial policies affecting broadcasters are given politically virgin births. They are delegated to the FCC, done in an unrecorded markup session, tagged on a huge appropriations bill with a voice vote, or done in conference committee—all places that avoid recorded votes and the leaving of publicly verifiable fingerprints.[19] As we shall see, the relationship between broadcast general manager and broadcast news director is also like this. A curtain of darkness covers it, so linkages between news and general management decisions are as mysterious as the linkage between the spectrum giveaway and individual members of Congress.

The Scope of Attributes

The scope of attributes that can be used to exert political pressure on candidates is vast. Accordingly, a common error when looking for bias is to conceptualize the domain of attributes too narrowly. Closely related to this problem is the prohibitive cost of checking for bias across all possible dimensions. To the extent that the scope of attributes is large, key events are likely to pass under a researcher's radar screen.

Direct vs. Indirect Attributes. A direct attribute is a public policy that an intermediary hopes to influence. In the case of local TV broadcasters, this would include a candidate's position on government policies with a direct bearing on the broadcasters' bottom line.

An indirect attribute is anything else that may reflect well or poorly on a candidate. This might include a candidate's track record of racism, policy flip flops, reckless drinking, special interest deal making, and sexual misconduct.

Usually, candidates care relatively little how local broadcasters portray their stands on the relatively small universe of direct, industry-specific issues such as whether broadcasters should or shouldn't provide monetary compensation for use of spectrum worth tens of billions of dollars. Americans neither know nor care about such issues. When I ran for office as the Democratic nominee in Maryland's District 33a (population 76,000), I knocked on about 7,000 doors and attended about 25 debates. Many issues were raised during these voter contacts, including gun control, abortion, education, criminal justice, healthcare, the state deficit, and the Governor's marital infidelity. But not once was an issue of information policy raised, despite the fact that broadcasters, cable

---

[19] As a rule of thumb, this type of strategy will only work when an issue is non-partisan because it relies on the tacit support of fellow legislators.

operators, and telephone companies actively lobby the state legislature. To my knowledge, no candidate in American history has ever lost an election on such an issue.

In some respects, the importance of indirect attributes seems so obvious that it is hardly worth mentioning. We all know in our day to day lives that when people seek retribution, the focus is on harming the enemy at his weak point, not directly countering the enemy's arguments. In politics, this is often called "payback" and everyone who watches politics closely knows the behavior is pervasive. As Representative Billy Tauzin warned: if they opposed his House-passed broadband Internet bill favoring the Baby Bells, "[Senator Hollings] and other senators would be attending a lot of funerals [for their own bills] on the House side."[20]

Broadcasters also frequently have this payback mindset in relation to the FCC. Reports *Electronic Media* of Representative Tauzin's charge of such payback:

> According to the lawmaker, broadcasters and other licensees are so afraid of FCC retaliation that they won't go public with stories about their alleged mishandling at the agency.... Tauzin also alleged that the retaliation...comes in the form of delays or even denials of licensing opportunities.[21]

The article then goes on to report an anonymous industry source: "The last thing anyone in this town who is regulated by the FCC is going to do is attack the agency. It's a given."[22]

The most vivid confession of a payback threat that I've ever heard from a journalist came from fearless muckraking syndicated columnist Jack Anderson. When the Nixon Administration, through FBI Director L. Patrick Gray, went after Anderson and subpoenaed his telephone records, Anderson used his leverage over Senator Majority Whip Robert Byrd to block the subpoena. In his autobiography, Anderson describes his payback threat to Byrd this way: "'Bobby, I've got more newspapers in West Virginia than Pat Gray

---

[20] Cited in Yochi J. Dreazon, "Hollings, at 80, Is Hitting Some High Notes," *Wall Street Journal*, 21 March 2002, p. A24.

[21] Doug Halonen, "Intimidation Charges: Rep. Tauzin claims retaliation fears have slowed reform efforts," *Electronic Media*, 1 November 1999, p. 44.

[22] Ibid.

has,' I said. My message was clear: If I ever found any dirt on him, I had an audience in his home state that would love to read about it."[23]

Strangely, the political communication literature has had little to say about the use of indirect bias to exert political influence. This is presumably because direct attributes are easy to identify and lend themselves to more affordable data collection. On issues with a vast number of direct attributes, such as partisan bias, this distinction is not material. But as the number of direct attributes drops, as in industry and company bias, the distinction grows in importance. As we will see in Chapter 10, it may also be the type of bias most feared by legislators.

Fixed vs. Flexible Attributes. An important restriction on the use of direct and indirect attributes is whether they are fixed or flexible. Only fixed indirect and flexible direct attributes are usable for exercising influence.

A flexible attribute relates to the future and is therefore within a candidate's ability to change. An example is a position on a proposed telecommunications bill that a fellow legislator has introduced for committee consideration.

A fixed attribute relates to the past and is therefore irrevocable. An example is a candidate's past action such as a divorce, extramarital affair, or illegal activity.

Intermediaries seek to influence information incentives only on flexible direct attributes and fixed indirect attributes. If a direct attribute were already fixed, it would be pointless to lobby over it because, by definition, the lobbying would be fruitless. If an indirect attribute were flexible, the effect of lobbying would be to change a candidate's position on the flexible attribute. But since indirect attributes have no intrinsic interest to an intermediary other than to change a friend or foe's re-election prospects, this would be a waste of resources.

In the case of local broadcasters, we would not expect them to lobby on proposed transportation, environmental, or military issues that have no significant impact on their bottom line (these are indirect flexible issues). But if a candidate has already taken a position on any of these issues (indirect fixed issues), broadcasters may use that position as ammunition to reward political friends and punish enemies. Similarly, there is no strategic advantage in a broadcaster lobbying a candidate on a specific information policy issue that

---

[23] Jack Anderson and Daryl Gibson, *Peace, War, and Politics: An Eyewitness Account*, 1st ed. (New York: Forge, 1999). Cited in Mark Feldstein, "Getting the Scoop," *Washington Monthly*, January/February 2000, p. 50. Anderson also reports that "Congress and the White House were afraid to take on [FBI Director J. Edgar] Hoover because of his dossiers crammed with dirt on these politicians." Cited in Ibid.

has already been settled (a direct fixed issue). But if it hasn't been settled (a direct flexible issue), the logic is reversed.

Process vs. Substantive Attributes. The process by which an agent makes a decision is often as important to principals as the decision itself. That is because principals can use information about the decision making process to infer information about the quality of the resulting decision and the motives of the agent making the decision. A central prerequisite of procedural trust is openness. Principals will often infer that if an information agent is secretive, the agent has something to hide. And if the agent hides something with respect to an audience, it's probable he is acting against the interests of that audience. Therefore, smart information agents go to great lengths to convey an aura of openness. They hate being in the public position of hiding information.

Often, it is very easy to hide information from the public because of the simple principle that the public doesn't know what it doesn't know. Someone usually has to convey to the public that material information is available and being withheld before the public will take note. This may be a very steep hurdle.

On many occasions I spent an hour or more with a high powered lobbyist and got absolutely no useful information. The question I kept thinking about is "why is this person talking to me when he clearly doesn't want to provide me with the information I'm looking for?" In reflecting over this seeming paradox, I came to the conclusion that the lobbyist, like any good politician, wanted to convey that he and his cause had nothing to hide. By demonstrating to me that he was accessible and seemingly answering my questions, he was engaging in PR on behalf of himself and his client. An alternative explanation was that the lobbyist was interested in learning about me and my research questions, even though the ostensible purpose of the interview was to learn from the lobbyist. But since I rarely did much talking and did not reveal my research hypotheses, the lobbyist probably was not spending his time efficiently if that was his goal.

Similarly, when a news director gives a general manager a heads up on a potentially harmful story to a member of Congress or anyone else, this decision making process is not reported on the news or anywhere else because it would raise a doubt in the viewer's mind about the ethical firewall claim made by TV stations.

Claimed vs. Actual Attributes. Attributes do not have to exist in reality; they merely have to be claimed or otherwise exist in people's minds. Nor do claimed attributes need to be explicitly stated; they can be conveyed via symbols. The test for a claim is not the explicit stated message but the message inferred by an audience. Many important claims are not explicitly stated. A 30 second political TV ad, for example, typically makes many of its most important claims via symbolism. Similarly, local TV news anchors, chosen in part for their appearance of trustworthiness, often act as if they were involved in producing and writing the story they are telling, when in fact they are merely reading a script from a teleprompter.[24] When a story later proves fraudulent, the producer, not the anchor "script reader," may get fired by the TV station, even though the anchor is presented as the story's chief correspondent.[25] The story may not even have been created by a local station reporter. Instead, it may have been purchased from a national news service or derived from a press release.[26]

Consistent vs. Inconsistent Attributes. Attributes do not have to be consistent with each other. Generally, when it is in a political actor's self-interest to hold two inconsistent views, he will do so. One reason this is so easy to get away with is because voters often need a large amount of background information to know that two seemingly unrelated issues are actually related and perhaps even inconsistent. On telecommunications issues, this background information rarely exists, thus inviting huge amounts of self-serving inconsistencies. For example, when competitors seek to use government to restrict broadcasters' programming, broadcasters call this "violating the First Amendment" and may make references to Watergate or some other government press abuse. But when broadcasters seek to use the government to restrict competitors' speech, such as to make it illegal for satellite radio broadcasters to carry local programming, they will discount First Amendment considerations or interpret the First Amendment in a different way.

Source vs. Merit Attributes. Merit information relates to the merits of an attribute. Source information relates to the credibility of the source of information about an attribute. Political actors typically spend large amounts of time cultivating credible third parties who will act as their spokespeople in making arguments about the merits of the issues. The NAB, for example, subsidizes and houses the Broadcast Educators Association, the leading association of academics

---

[24] E.g., Steve McClellan and Dan Trigoboff, "Role Confusion in TV News: 'Newstand' Fiasco Highlights Unclear Lines Between Reporters and Producers," *Broadcasting & Cable*, 13 July 1998, p. 14. In England, journalists often candidly refer to anchors as "news readers," Calvin Trillin, "Class Acting," *Brill's Content*, p. 62. Saturday Night Live has done a skit, Wake Up and Smile!, based on the premise of what might happen if an anchor's teleprompter was cut; see Terry Gross, "Adam McKay talks about his career and his new movie starring Will Ferrell, 'Anchorman,'" in *Fresh Air, National Public Radio*, 8 July 2004.

[25] Steve McClellan, "CNN Takes a Fall," *Broadcasting & Cable*, 6 July 1998, p. 10.

[26] U.S. Senate members collectively send out to their local TV stations as many as 60 video press releases a week. Advertising agencies send out countless more. For an example, see Melody Peterson, "A Respected Face, but Is It News or an Ad?" *New York Times*, 7 May 2003.

who study broadcasting. Credible academics pursuing research favorable to NAB interests are identified. These voices are then amplified in the policymaking community.

Source attributes may be viewed as a form of shortcut or summary attribute. If a fact is presented by a credible source, the audience can attach a lot of weight to the fact without additional research. Without such a source, the audience must do its own research regarding the merits of the fact.

Correlated vs. Causally Related Attributes. In evaluating candidates or any objects, voters are not restricted to causally related attributes. They may also rely on correlated attributes, also called cues, shortcuts, symbols, proxies, and signs. Samuel Popkin relates the story of how Gerald Ford lost the Hispanic vote because he didn't know how to eat a tamale. Hispanics could infer that if he didn't know how to eat a tamale he probably also didn't know much about Hispanic culture and needs, despite what his handlers told him to say. His ignorance of tamales probably also reflected the fact that he didn't share Hispanic interests. It might have been more to the point to look at Ford's track record on Hispanic issues and query him about current issues of concern to Hispanics. But the fact that President Ford didn't know how to eat a tamale may have given them all the information they needed with much less expenditure of effort.[27] Nevertheless, politicians can still attempt to misuse correlations to mislead the public. Another politician could know how to properly eat a tamale yet be less supportive of Hispanic interests.

Like other political actors geared to managing public perceptions, broadcasters make a lot of use of misleading correlations. For example, broadcast general managers who control their stations' local news are careful not to show themselves or their news employees publicly supporting a political candidate. Public interactions are likely to be aloof and even antagonistic. But in many cases it would be a mistake to infer that these general managers aren't privately friends, campaign supporters, or otherwise politically involved with the people their stations' cover.

Unit of Attributes

Individual vs. Grouped Attributes. Attributes can be grouped together. In many cases, it's advantageous for an interest group to link separate attributes with other attributes that then become the practical object of decision. If the individual attribute is unpopular but the overall package of attributes is popular, then linking the unpopular and popular attributes may win support for the

---

[27] Popkin, *The Reasoning Voter*.

unpopular attribute. Often the linked issues can be totally unrelated to the individual issue the intermediary seeks to influence. For example, when an interest group gets a member of Congress to attach a rider to a must-pass omnibus bill that cannot be amended on the floor of the House, it fundamentally changes legislators' political calculus. Now the unit of decision is the omnibus bill, not the individual rider. And the legislator can fairly claim that he had no responsible choice but to vote for the rider. As long as the amendment doesn't kill the omnibus, it can catch a ride to passage—hence the term "rider." The NAB used this strategy when it wanted to kill the FCC's proposal to allow Low Power FM (LPFM) radio in the unused FM radio guard bands, which it wanted to acquire for its members as part of its transition to digital radio. LPFM was very popular among a number of important Congressional constituencies, including local church groups. Members of Congress didn't want to appear to be voting against it, yet couldn't delegate that unpleasant task to the FCC because its Chair, William Kennard, strongly supported LPFM and refused to back down. By using a rider to prevent LPFM, the broadcasters could use Congress to block the FCC without forcing Congress to take responsibility for its actions.[28]

Competitive vs. Cartelized Attributes. The unit of a subsidized attribute is not fixed but subject to bargaining among political actors. When political actors negotiate a grouped attribute among themselves, it becomes an information logroll. When the information logroll is not only for mutual benefit but also avoids public competition over the merits of the component sub-attributes, it becomes an information cartel.

---

[28] Senator McCain describes the low visibility strategy behind LPFM in a speech on the Floor of the U.S. Senate: "[T]he special interest forces opposed to low power FM—most notably the National Association of Broadcasters and National Public Radio—have mounted a vigorous behind-the-scenes campaign against this service....[T]here is no way they could have carried that vote on the floor of this senate. There is no way they could have deprived all of these small business people, all of these religious organizations, all of these minority groups—but they stuck it into an appropriations bill, a piece of legislation that never had a single bit of debate and would never have passed through the Commerce Committee, of which I am the chairman, if it had been put to a vote.... I apologize. I apologize to you for this action—behind closed doors...." See "Low Power FM Radio Service," 106th Congress., 2nd Session, *Congressional Record*, 26 October 2000, p. S11100. In the House, with NAB loyalist Billy Tauzin at the helm of the House Commerce Committee, the politics of LPFM were different. Tauzin passed the measure in a markup hearing on a voice vote; that is, with no recorded votes. See Molly M. Peterson, "House Committee Moves to Stop Low-Power FM Radio Licensing," National Journal News Service, 29 March 2000.

In the battle over the Telecom Act of 1996, broadcasters logrolled with many of their ostensible competitors. The cable industry promised not to go after the broadcast industry's spectrum giveaway if the broadcasters promised not to go against the cable industry's rate deregulation, a provision that broadcasters had fiercely lobbied for four years previously. Similarly, the wireless telephone industry was primarily concerned with winning the right to build cellular phone towers without local interference. They opposed the broadcasters getting free spectrum when they had to pay tens of billions of dollars several years before to buy a small patch of inferior spectrum. But as long as the broadcasters promised not to compete directly against them in the PCS business and didn't oppose their interests in the Telecom Act of 1996, they avoided vigorous public opposition.

Telcos, cable companies, and broadcasters also had a joint interest in ensuring that no incumbent spectrum licensees would ever have to pay for renewing their licenses or seeking additional information carrying rights within their licensed frequency bands. The NAB frequently pointed out to these competitors this common interest in not paying market rates for use of the public airwaves.[29] If the competitors went after the NAB's spectrum, the NAB would go after theirs. Admittedly, the broadcasters' spectrum was far more valuable than the spectrum assigned to its competitors. But the amount of spectrum, an estimated 1.5 GHz for cable companies and 10 GHz for telcos, was not trivial.

Effects of Varying Attributes and Voters Jointly

So far we have looked at the impact of changing attributes and voters individually. But they can also be varied jointly as part of a coherent strategy. As long as different audiences have different incentives to acquire attribute information, political actors will send them different messages, even when the ultimate lobbying goal is the same.[30] For example, when the NAB lobbies the FCC, Congress, the press, and the public directly (via public service ads) it uses different individuals with different expertise that emphasize different things. NAB engineers will talk engineering to FCC engineers; NAB former Congressional staffers will talk

---

[29] "Spectrum Allocation: The Best Kept Secret in Washington—Broadcasters' competitors are intense users of 'free' spectrum," unpublished report of the National Association of Broadcasters. Various versions were handed out to competitors from summer 1995 through spring 1996.

[30] This strategy of sending different messages to different audiences can be depicted with a 3 dimensional version of the 2 dimensional graphs I have used thoughout this chapter. I leave this visualization to the reader's imagination.

·legislation with current Congressional staff; NAB former reporters will talk about an interesting news angle with the press; and an NAB ad agency/grassroots consultant will provide emotion- and symbol-driven ads directed to the general public.

Information Incentives Across Time

"In politics, timing is everything."

—anonymous political maxim

"Citizens do not instruct legislators on how to vote, nor do they necessarily have well-defined policy preferences in advance of Congressional action. Legislators nevertheless have strong incentives to consider citizens' potential preferences when they are deciding how to vote for fear that making the wrong choice might trigger an unfavorable audit. The fear is…that challengers will investigate fully a legislator's voting record and then share with citizens their interpretations of how he or she has gone wrong."

—R. Douglas Arnold, The Logic of Congressional Action[31]

The three preceding dimensions—utility, voters, and attributes—can vary over time. This requires extending our model to a fourth dimension and incorporating time. Let us assume that a given voter and attribute remain fixed over time; only information incentives vary. This assumption allows us to focus on the strategic impact of changing information incentives over time.

At what point in time do politicians care about a voter's perceived utility curve? Is it at the present time (U_p) or at a time some point in the future (U_{el})? Let us assume that legislators seek re-election. Then they should ultimately only care about the voters' perceived utility on Election Day because that is what determines Election Day results. A corollary is that intermediaries should only ultimately care about anticipated perceived utility on Election Day, not present perceived utility

But the present is also important. Politicians will use voters' present perceived utility as an indicator of future perceived utility because there may be a lot of inertia to perceptions, making them very expensive to change at a later date. Similarly, a political actor can exercise power not only by credibly threatening or

---

[31] Arnold, *The Logic of Congressional Action*, pp. 272-3.

promising to change information incentives in the future, but also by signaling future information incentives via changes in present information incentives.

In reality, a campaign for election is made up of many mini-deadlines, not just an Election Day deadline. Deadlines for filing campaign contributions, for example, are often important news events. Political actors often cannot afford to let these deadlines slip by without taking proactive measures.

Time Firewall

Figure 5-6 illustrates one way a voter's incentive to acquire information can vary over time. In this case, an attribute that is not currently politically relevant to a voter becomes politically relevant before the next election. The individual voter's benefit from acquiring information does not change over time, but at some point before the next election an intermediary invests in lowering the voter's information costs, thus making it worthwhile (since $B > C$) for the voter to acquire information about the attribute. The time at which this investment is made is the "time information firewall." Time firewalls become most interesting when they are potential firewalls rather than real firewalls; that is, when an intermediary can change present behavior by credibly threatening or promising to create a time firewall at some future time.

Figure 5-6 Information Incentives Across Time

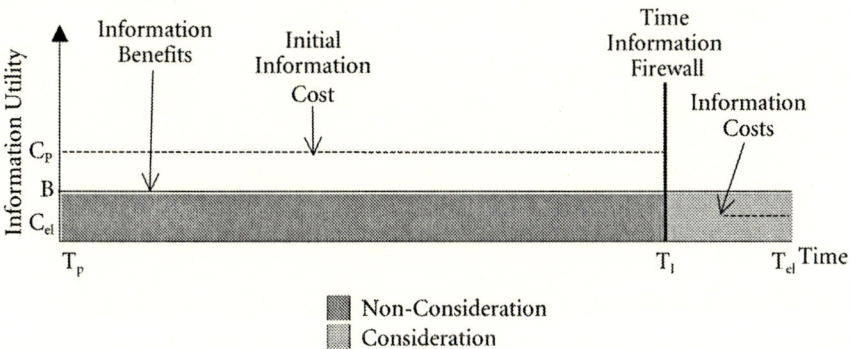

Non-Consideration
Consideration

Political actors can not only provide information about a pre-existing attribute (a prior "event"); they can also create the event that becomes the attribute. Even when a political actor is fundamentally interested in providing information about a pre-existing act, the act of providing information creates a new event. That is, every political act is in itself a new event.

When a political actor creates a new event, he may also be able to control the accessibility and verifiability of this event for those who weren't present to observe it. An inaccessible and unverifiable event creates a time firewall for all voters not present at the event. Figure 5-7 illustrates the cost and benefit of acquiring information about an event that takes place at time T_1. In the first case, a verifiable record of the event wasn't created, so the information cost is high and the voter not present at the event cannot acquire trustworthy information about it. In the second case, an accessible, verifiable record was created, so the voter not present can easily acquire trustworthy information about it.

Figure 5-7. Information Costs with and without a Verifiable Record

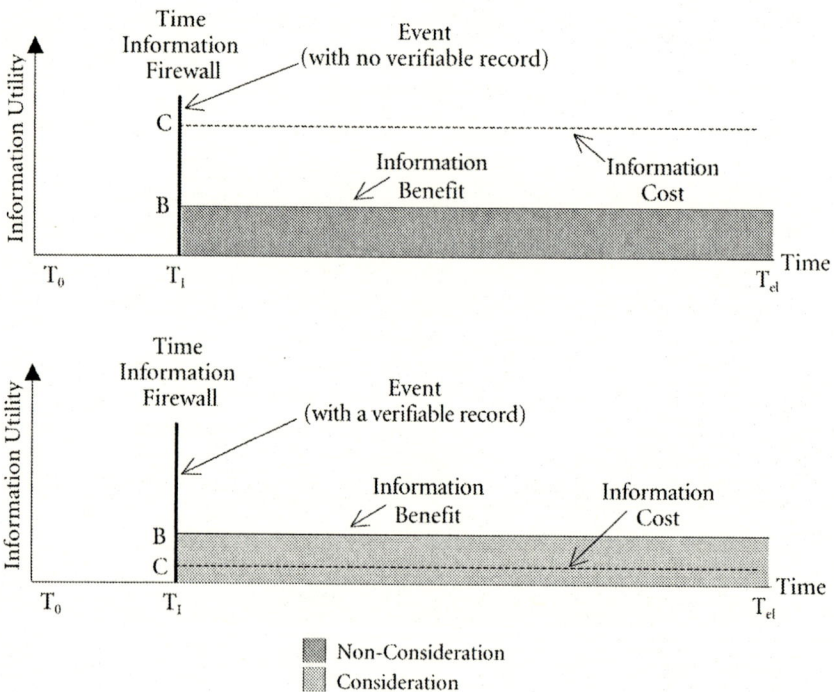

The difference between a verifiable and non-verifiable record depends on the context of a situation. Standards of verifiability, for example, differ among courts, mass media, and public opinion. Sometimes the standards appear quite clear. An unrecorded face-to-face meeting between two individuals is widely considered to be an unverifiable communication. A signed letter, in contrast, is widely considered to be a verifiable communication. But what of a

subtle pattern of broadcast TV program news behavior in Baton Rouge, Louisiana that requires collecting thousands of hours of TV coverage to identify and document? Neither commercial databases nor non-profit libraries archive local broadcast TV programming.[32] In theory, a consumer in the Baton Rouge media market could watch and record such programming for his own use. But the cost of creating such a verifiable record—let alone doing anything effective with it—for some speculative future use is prohibitively expensive. Alternatively, the viewer could request a copy of the programming from his local TV station. But even if the station complies—and it is under no legal obligation to do so—at more than $100/hour for program videotapes, a viewer's budget is not likely to take him very far. Thus, it may be said that in theory the TV news programs in Baton Rouge could have a verifiable record but that in practice creating such a record would be prohibitively expensive.

When local broadcasters lobby their member of Congress, they typically do so face-to-face, over the telephone, in private letters, or in other ways that don't leave a public, verifiable record.[33] Unflattering information may also be expunged from the public record. For example, when FCC Chair William Kennard made some unflattering remarks about the NAB's lobbying at the 1999 NAB Show, this was expunged from the video of the speech posted on the NAB's website.[34] When Brad Dick, Editor of *Broadcast Engineering Magazine*, made colorful remarks about the purported costs of the broadcasters' digital TV transition at the 1998 NAB show, these were missing from the official NAB printed proceedings.[35] All audio tapes of NAB shows, made by private vendors such as Sound Images, Inc., must be turned over to the NAB within two years.

The political cost of not paying adequate attention to issues of verifiability is vividly illustrated by the case of Miriam Santos, the Chicago City Treasurer who ran for Illinois Attorney General and got caught on tape approaching a broker and requesting a campaign contribution in return for doing continued business with the City. The result was that a jury convicted Santos of defrauding the City. The general consensus among knowledgeable political observers was that a) the type of quid pro quo involved in the Santos solicitation is

---

[32] A major reason libraries have not recorded local broadcast TV programs is because doing so under the Copyright Act of 1976 would be an illegal copyright infringement. Libraries may record local broadcast TV programming free of charge. But they are limited to archiving it for less than one year.

[33] The NAB keeps remarkably detailed written records of such contacts but these are not publicly available. See Chapter 14 for a description of how this system works.

[34] "Please Stand By," *Broadcasting & Cable*, 26 April 1999, p. 15.

[35] "Using Market Forces to Implement DTV," Presentation by Brad Dick at the 52nd Annual Broadcast Engineering Conference, at the NAB Show, Las Vegas, Nevada, 9 April 1998.

common in Illinois politics, and b) that Santos was stupid because she allowed herself to be made accountable for actions that should have been easy to plausibly deny. As *Chicago Tribune* reporters Bob Secter and Rick Pearson summed up what most politicians learn in their cradle: "Always delegate the money-collectinng work to a flunky," and "Glare, seethe, or stare daggers if you must, but never utter a syllable that could be construed as a threat and captured by a hidden recording device." The authors add: "What seemed amazing to many political veterans was how easy it might have been for Santos to stay out of harm's way and accomplish the same goal."[36]

The Watergate tapes, which cost Richard Nixon his presidency, are also a vivid reminder of the cost of keeping a verifiable record. Nixon thought he could keep the existence of the tapes secret and, in any case, not have to publicly disclose them until long after he left office, if then.

Distance Between Perceived and True Utility Over Time

In comparing the distance between perceived and true utility on Election Day and the present, the distance may be closer, farther away, or equal. Usually, Election Day perceived utility is closer to true utility than present day perceived utility. The reason is that voters' incentive to acquire information is usually greatest shortly before an election.[37] In the days and weeks leading up to an election, intermediaries, including the press and candidates, invest heavily to reduce voters' incentive to acquire information. Accordingly, voters who acquire information earlier in the election must invest a premium to acquire the same information. Voters are also likely to forget what they have learned by Election Day or ignore information without immediate utility, so early investments may waste money. Therefore, rational voters who anticipate lower search costs at election time often wait until the end of the election campaign before acquiring information. Figure 5-8 illustrates the aggregate change in information incentives over time. In reality, of course, the curves may not change smoothly. For a low visibility political contest for the state legislature, for example, we might expect the cost curve to suddenly drop a notch on the day when the local daily newspaper runs a profile and endorsement of the competing candidates.

---

[36] Bob Sector and Rick Pearson, "Santos Bungled Art of Fundraising, Experts Say," *Chicago Tribune*, 5 May 1999, section 2, p. 1. See also Matt O'Connor and Gary Washburn, "Santos Done in by Tape," *Chicago Tribune*, 4 May 1999, section 1, p. 1.

[37] Thomas E. Patterson, *The Vanishing Voter: Public Involvement in an Age of Uncertainty*, 1st ed. (New York: Alfred A. Knopf : Distributed by Random House, 2002).

Figure 5-8. Aggregate Information Incentives Across Time

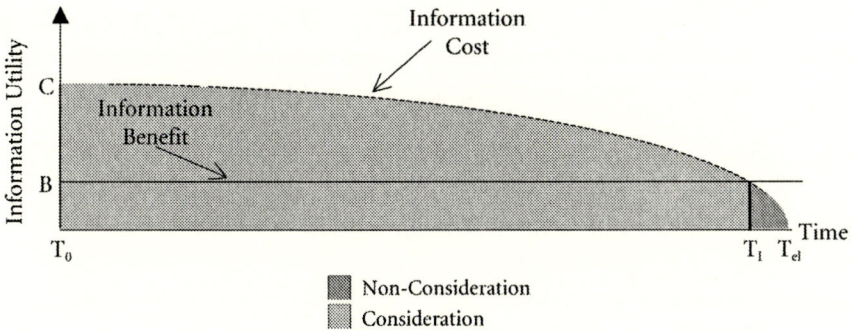

Aggregate vs. Individual Information Incentives

Although aggregate voter information incentives tend to increase as elections approach, incentives for particular attributes and voters may change in many different patterns. Investing early in an election cycle, for example, may establish lasting first impressions when competing information is scarce. Investing in the middle of the cycle may be a good place to "hide" news that would be likely to come out anyway. And investing late in the election cycle may preclude opponents from having a chance to attack back. This helps explain the common political observations that "time is our friend" or "time is our enemy."

Actual vs. Anticipated Information Incentives

> "To win one hundred victories in one hundred battles is not the acme of skill. To subdue the enemy without fighting is the acme of skill."
>
> —Sun Tzu, the Art of War[38]

The emphasis on the future means that a political actor does not have to actually change information incentives in order to exert power. The political actor must merely be able to credibly signal that he can change information incentives. What counts is that a political actor has both the resources and incentive to change voter information incentives, not that it actually does so. It is not

---

[38] Cited in Pitney, *The Art of Political Warfare*, p. 40.

necessary that information incentives are actually increased on Election Day, only that if certain actions were taken they would increase.

This deterrence theory of information incentives is like nuclear deterrence. A nuclear war is deterred because leaders can anticipate the costs of such warfare would outweigh the benefits. Similarly, broadcasters can deter legislator behavior without having to actually exercise bias. They just have to signal to legislators that they have the resources and incentive to do so. A critical caveat is that the signals sent to legislators need not be verifiable by third parties. The only requirement is that they be credible to legislators.

Game theory sets up problems like this. An actor looks at his set of available actions and the likely response to each of those actions by other players. He then takes the action that maximizes his payoff. According to this logic, broadcaster bias would never actually have to occur to overwhelmingly influence legislators' actions. Thus, the entire enterprise of doing media or any other type of content analysis to search for bias should be fruitless. The only valid method must rely on examining incentives and resources.

Anticipating the future and avoiding actions that will lead to unpleasant consequences is the essence of human intelligence. Human don't walk into the cages of lions because they know they would be eaten alive. Similarly, members of Congress may not poke sticks into the eyes of their local TV broadcasters out of fear that they, too, would be eaten alive.

Rates of Investment

Sometimes it's better to invest quickly and at other times slowly. If you have to release unfavorable information that will inevitably be noticed, it's usually better to release it all at once so the story washes over quickly. Similarly, if you have favorable information to release, sometimes it's better to release it all at once so that it will attain critical mass and lead to some desired action.

Sometimes a go slow strategy is more effective. Unfavorable information released in small isolated bits may not reach a threshold of public attention. Alternatively, favorable information whose components will be individually noticed may best be released gradually.

All this depends less on the information per se to be released than on the information incentive thresholds in the environment in which it is released. Table 1 summarizes the four basic investment rate decisions based on whether the information to be released is favorable or not and whether the individual components of the information to be released would be salient to the public or not.

Table 5-1. Factors Affecting Rates of Investment

	Are the individual information components salient?	
	Yes	No
Favorable Information	Slow	Quick
Unfavorable Information	Quick	Slow

Local TV broadcasters (as well as many other spectrum licensees) have made heavy use of the go slow lobbying strategy in their acquisition from the federal government of property rights to spectrum. By accumulating hundreds of billions of dollars worth of spectrum and other rights gradually, they have been able to keep each individual acquisition—and thus the total acquisition—below the public's radar screen.

Originally, broadcasters were given a narrowly circumscribed short-term license to use the public airwaves. In return, they promised public service obligations. Gradually, broadcasters got their license terms extended from 3 to 5 to 8 years. Gradually, they eliminated the risk that a competitor could win their license at the end of their license term. Gradually, they eliminated quantifiable and verifiable public service obligations. Today, both the government and the private sectors treat broadcaster licenses as private property, which largely reflects the fact that broadcast licenses are essentially irrevocable.[39]

If these changes had been implemented all at once, broadcasters would have had to face significant mobilized opposition because the giveaway of billions of dollars of natural resources would have been too obvious. Spread over decades, however, many changes were almost invisible—often not even meriting back page newspaper coverage.

Another example of a go slow strategy is the tactic of asking for case-by-case waivers of FCC regulations rather than a blanket waiver. A blank waiver triggers due process and lots of visibility. Nobody except direct competitors have an interest in following a case-by-case waiver. *Broadcasting & Cable* described the proposed use of this strategy when the broadcasters wanted to slow down the DTV transition: "In June [2001], Tauzin encouraged NAB and its TV-station members to ask the FCC individually for deadline extensions, rather than asking for a blanket waiver. Tauzin thought making such a request would seem like the industry was trying to avoid the transition."[40]

---

[39] J.H. Snider, "The Decline of Broadcasters' Public Interest Obligations," (Washington, DC: New America Foundation, 2004).

[40] Paige Albiniak, "Stations 'Waiver' on DTV," *Broadcasting & Cable*, 20 August 2001, p. 6.

A go fast strategy can be especially effective when combined with a last minute strategy. In their use of last minute riders on omnibus bills, such as budget reconciliation bills[41] and appropriations bills,[42] broadcasters combined a go fast strategy with a last minute strategy (so-called "midnight amendments," the goal of which is to anonymously ride through passage in pitch dark). These bills are massive documents, accumulated over many months of work, and with tremendous inertia leading up to a statutory deadline. If a political actor can insert a rider in a huge, must-pass bill just before a vote, opponents may have no time to discover and scrutinize the rider, let alone mobilize opposition to it.

The Time Frame of the Decision

An election is actually made of many deadlines, not just the final election. For example, there may be deadlines for registering as a candidate, receiving interest group endorsements, and voting in the primary election. Each one of these deadlines may be characterized by a time firewall.

Whether one's time horizon is just the next election or extends beyond may impact strategy. If the time horizon is just the next election, then a political actor can say or do almost anything just days before the election without worrying about long-term reputation effects. One way candidates and broadcasters address this problem is not to avoid reputation harming activities but merely to hide them by having surrogates engage in those activities. They can then plausibly deny at a later time that they were in any way involved.

Effects of Varying Time and Attributes Jointly

Subsidizing linked attributes over time can lead to impressions of causality. Two types of misleading causal impressions may be especially valuable in exerting political power

---

[41] E.g., the Budget Reconciliation Bill of 1997.National Association of Broadcasters, "Legislative Issue Papers, 105th Congress, 1st Session," (Washington, DC: National Association of Broadcasters, 1997), p. 7.

[42] E.g., see "Radio Broadcasting Preservation Act of 2000" (House bill H.R. 3439 and Senate bill S. 3020), enacted on 31 December 2000 as part of the Commerce-Justice-State Appropriations bill. The House Commerce Committee passed this on a voice vote. See Molly M. Peterson, "House Committee Moves to Stop Low-Power FM Radio Licensing," *National Journal News Service*, 29 March 2000.

Partial Causality. Many events are the result of a long and complex chain of causality, where causality is empirically observed as a change of attributes over time. Hiding part of that causal sequence from the public can be of great strategic advantage. It's been found, for example, that a videotape that just shows police beating a suspect has a very different impact on juries than one that shows the prior behavior of the suspect leading to his beating. Similarly, the public's perception of a videotaped confession is very different if only the victim's confession is taped rather than the full interaction between the interrogator and victim.

Broadcasters made heavy use of partial causality in their fierce lobbying campaign for additional spectrum to provide digital TV services. The spectrum, if sold on the open market, was estimated to be worth as much as $70 billion.[43] To secure this spectrum, broadcasters made certain compromises. Both FCC regulations and Congressional statute mandated that broadcasters couldn't receive a large windfall from the government,[44] so broadcasters reduced the perception of a windfall by promising to give the spectrum back by a date certain and spend huge sums on HDTV without any new revenues to offset them. This gave members of Congress the political cover they needed to give the broadcasters the spectrum.

However, as soon as the legislation was passed giving broadcasters the spectrum, the broadcasters began ridiculing the limitations imposed on their use of the spectrum. They started calling the digital transition an "unfunded government mandate," as though the transition was forced upon the broadcasters rather than something the broadcasters strong armed the government into doing. They frequently observed that the government was forcing them to spend large amounts of money on an uneconomical service (HDTV) while turning off a service, analog TV, which many Americans clearly wanted. From this they concluded that they should be loaned the spectrum indefinitely without government restrictions on its use. In the words of a spokesperson for Sinclair Broadcast Group, one of the largest broadcast groups in the United States:

> We have government-mandated standards and rollout dates, and now an imposed consumer-adoption deadline. Meanwhile, China and Russia have adopted a free-market model. How truly bizarre. What's next in our Soviet-style approach to DTV?[45]

---

[43] This number is discussed at length in Chapter 12.

[44] Communications Act of 1934 (47 U.S. C. §151), *Ashbacker Radio Corp. v. FCC* (1945).

[45] Doug Halonen, "Proposal Would Vacate UHF by '07," *Electronic Media*, 18 March 2002, p. 1.

The Texas Association of broadcasters conducted a poll of 800 randomly selected adults across Texas in January 2001 and found that over a third of Texans "are aware that their local television stations are spending millions of dollars converting from analog to digital transmission systems to comply with a *federal mandate* [italics added]."[46] Greg Kelly, general manager of Channel 3 (KCRA-TV) in Sacramento, California, nicely summed up the broadcasters' general line: "Congress shoved this down everyone's throats."[47] The government mandate line was also used to win a sales tax exemption on DTV equipment from 13 states.[48]

Clearly, when the public is only given information on the broadcasters' government mandated obligation and not the huge gift of public assets that led to the creation of those mandates—it is not being given crucial policy information.

False Causality. Making scientific causal inferences is prohibitively difficult in day-to-day life. No citizen has the time to find exhaustive evidence for every causal inference they make. This offers intermediaries an opportunity to create the impression of false but plausible causal inferences. A student who doesn't do his homework and blames his dog for eating it is banking on his ability to convince his teacher of a false but plausible causal claim.

Effect of Varying Time and Voters Jointly

Voters use the support of other voters as a cue to determine their own preferences. Political actors can exploit this cue to create momentum effects.[49] Getting a few key opinion leaders as supporters, for example, can quickly generate a much larger group of supporters.

Another strategy is to target highly motivated individuals early (such as party activists) and less motivated ones later on (such as the general public), even if there is little logical relation between the support of the early and later supporters. This phased audience strategy, where early and late adopters are distinguished, identified, and provided with different messages, is also widely used in corporate marketing campaigns.

---

[46] "Texas Broadcasters Enjoy 80% Approval Rating," press release of the Texas Association of Broadcasters, 6 March 2001. Baseline & Associates conducted the survey for the Texas Association of Broadcasters.

[47] Stephanie McKinnon McDade, "Ready or Not: High definition TV will one day beam its way to Sacramento," *Sacramento Bee*, 3 November 1998.

[48] E.g., Tysver, "TV Station Tax Break Considered."

[49] Larry M. Bartels, *Presidential Primaries and the Dynamics of Public Choice* (Princeton, N.J.: Princeton University Press, 1988).

Information Incentives About Information Sources

In addition to changing voter incentives to acquire information about *candidate attributes*, intermediaries seek to change voter incentives to acquire information *about the credibility of sources of information about candidates*. These investments apply across voters, attributes, and time just like investments about the merits of candidates. Credibility is an attribute of sources, and can be divided into two components: interests and expert ability. Voters want sources that have similar interests to their own and that have expert ability to act on those interests.[50]

Intermediaries divide sources into allies and enemies. With allies, they invest in information that suggests the sources have expert ability and similar interests to voters. Conversely, with enemies, they invest in information that suggests the source has conflicts of interest and bad judgment.

In 1995, for example, the Campaign for Broadcast Competition was put together to oppose the spectrum giveaway to broadcasters that was later contained in the Telecom Act of 1996. The Alliance put together a coalition of liberal and conservative citizen groups. The NAB discovered that the Coalition received $20,000 in funding from the Cellular Telecommunications Industry Association. The NAB then used this information to attack the credibility of the Campaign and all the consumer groups associated with it.

Similarly, the NAB hires certified experts to attack the research results of other researchers. In 2000, during a Congressional hearing, an NAB-hired consultant accused a much more credentialed opponent of engaging in "junk science."[51] The debate centered on whether low power FM stations could be

---

[50] Lupia and McCubbins, *The Democratic Dilemma*.

[51] Spoken testimony of Dr. Charles Jackson on behalf of NAB before the House Commerce Committee Telecommunications & Finance Subcommittee on "Spectrum Integrity and HR 3439, the 'Radio Broadcasting Preservation Act of 1999,'" 17 February 2000. The opponent, engineering Professor Theodore Rapapport, was the author of one of the leading textbooks in the field of wireless communications and is currently director of the Wireless Networking and Communications Group at the University of Texas, Austin. Responding to testimony on an unrelated technical issue, a judge in Florida later found that Mr. Jackson, "while qualified in this field, lacked credibility." See CBS Broad., Inc. v. Echostar Communications Corp., No. 98-2651, 2003 U.S. Dist. LEXIS 9707, (S.D. Fla. June 10, 2003). In this case, the FM broadcasters wanted to prevent the current guard bands between stations from being used to increase competition, and they also wanted the guard band spectrum for their own future digital radio service, which would eventually allow them to broadcast over a larger terrain and provide multiple FM programming streams

inserted into the FM band without creating unacceptable interference to the programming of incumbent FM broadcasters.

There are numerous ways to discredit opposing information sources. These include critiquing their source of financing, their non-mainstream ideology, poor judgments from the past, hidden agendas, and laziness. If one has a heads up on a likely opponent, one can even set up a situation that can be used for a later attack. For example, one can arrange for a grievous attack on that individual. And when that person attacks back, call it sour grapes. An employee identified as a potential whistleblower, for example, can be charged with some type of incompetence or immoral behavior, and then fired. If the person then attacks the company, the attack can then be derided as coming from a person with an axe to grind. Perhaps the most common way an individual's credibility is attacked in politics is simply to accuse that person of playing politics. This, in effect, says that an individual will say anything to win public support, so his utterances cannot be assumed credible.

Among the ways to build the credibility of friendly information sources include enhancing their democratic legitimacy (so that they "represent" the public's interest), touting their credentials (e.g., degrees, work experience, and institutional affiliations), hiding their financial compensation (e.g., many expert reports by academics and others are paid for by industry interests), and generating symbols that imply both their affinity with the common citizen and expert knowledge (e.g., birth in a wholesome town, unpretentious clothes, and professional demeanor).

---

and other data as a minor modification of their FM license. A million dollar FCC funded study later confirmed that the NAB study was wrong. See FCC, "Report to the Congress on the Low Power Fm Interference Testing Program Pub. L. No. 106-553," (Washington, DC: FCC, 19 February 2004), Mitre, "Experimental Measurements of the Third-Adjacent Channel Impacts of Low-Power Fm Stations," (McClean, VA: Mitre, May 2003). Reed Hundt, the former FCC Chairman, characterized the NAB/Jackson incident as "fraudulent tape recordings of fake interference." Quoted in Kim McAvoy, "Hundt: Nothing but Net," *Broadcasting & Cable*, 10 April 2000, p. 68.

Source Information About Oneself

"People judge communication by its source so when you deny people full knowledge of that source of information they are losing something important about evaluating the message."

—Kathleen Hall Jamison, Dean, Annenberg School for Communication[52]

A special category of source information is information about oneself. A political actor with a low level of credibility will seek to bias perceptions of its own incentives and secretiveness, and that of its paid fronts.

Bias Perceptions of One's Own Incentives

It is hard to overestimate the importance that interest groups with "special" interests place on hiding their own incentives. Hiding one's own incentives is, of course, a staple of bargaining theory.[53] Each party in a negotiation wants to hide its "reservation" price so as to maximize its negotiating leverage. A party's reservation price is the minimal acceptable outcome that will make the transaction worthwhile for it. Each negotiation involves a range of acceptable outcomes for the participants. By narrowing the range of perceived acceptable ranges, one gains negotiating leverage. What is true of marketplace negotiations is also true of lobbying. Lobbying is often successful to the extent one is successful distorting perceptions of one's own incentives. Sometimes this results in apparent inconsistencies. For example, broadcasters often say one thing to members of Congress and another thing to Wall Street. To members of Congress, they plead poverty so as to win bigger subsidies and more favorable regulation; to Wall Street, they promise bigger profits so as to boost their stock price. To reconcile the apparent inconsistency, they banish the press from attending sales presentations to Wall Street analysts.[54] Other venues that might

---

[52] Cited in Jeffrey H. Birnbaum, "Advocacy Groups Blur Media Lines: Some Push Agendas by Producing Movies, Owning Newspapers," *Washington Post*, 6 December 2004, p. A1. See also Kathleen Hall Jamieson, *Dirty Politics: Deception, Distraction, and Democracy* (New York: Oxford University Press, 1992).

[53] Howard Raiffa, *The Art and Science of Negotiation* (Cambridge, Mass.: Belknap Press of Harvard University Press, 1982).

[54] Randall Smith, "Dow Jones Quits DLJ Conference Over Media Ban," *Wall Street Journal*, 7 December 1999, pp. C1, C17.

reveal embarrassing inconsistencies, such as the NAB Futures Summit, which explores future broadcast industry profit opportunities, ban the public and unfriendly press.

Bias Perceptions of One's Own Secretiveness

Principals are very suspicious of any evidence of agent secretiveness because they rightly infer that the reason for secretiveness is often to withhold information that would reveal opportunistic behavior; in other words, agents aren't secretive unless they have something to hide. Thus, it is never in an agent's interest to appear secretive in its agency relationship with a principal.

John Dean, Counsel to President Nixon during Watergate, expressed the mindset vividly: "The White House will take a public posture of full cooperation but privately will attempt to restrain the investigation and make it as difficult as possible to get information and witnesses."[55] This type of secrecy, combined with a PR laden campaign to signal the opposite, is pervasive in politics.

The best way for an agent to avert suspicions of secrecy is to convey the impression that its interests are identical to those it serves. This helps explain why so many politicians have the "common touch." People trust those who are like themselves.

But conveying an impression of openness also helps. For example, the public can freely wander within Congressional buildings and enter the open door to their representative; when constituents enter the door of a well run Congressional office, they are greeted with expressions of great friendliness, including an effusive desire to help the constituent and provide any desired information. Yet, as anyone knows who is familiar with the inner workings of Congress, there is a second culture in the back offices closed to constituents. There, a huge premium is placed on staffers who can be trusted to keep secrets. And those secrets often involve hiding information that, if known to constituents, would signal a conflict between constituent interests and the representative's actions.

Similarly, journalistic codes of ethics place a huge premium on disclosing conflicts of interest with the public. And, in a variety of subtle ways, this aura of openness is constantly promoted to the public. Yet, as we will see in

---

[55] Testimony of John Dean before the United States Senate Watergate Committee, 25 June 1997.

Chapters 14 and 15, local TV stations have many highly significant financial and political conflicts of interest that are rarely, if ever, disclosed to the public.

Bias Perceptions of a Front Group's Incentives

> "[P]rinces should let the carrying out of unpopular duties devolve on others, and bestow favors themselves."
>
> —Machiavelli, *The Prince*, Chapter 19

Whenever a political actor is widely known to have a conflict of interest with the public, the political actor has an incentive to hide his presence by exerting influence through one or more intermediaries. Such influence laundering is one of the main activities of Washington, DC lobbyists, and is a staple of Washington, DC political reporting.[56]

The influence laundering mindset is partially captured in the lobbyist's maxim that "the better you are, the quieter you should be about it,"[57] a variation on President Theodore Roosevelt's famous "speak softly and carry a big stick." Being recognized as a "hidden hand interest group" and "wily in being underestimated" are among the most valued traits in an accomplished DC trade association lobbyist. Explains broadcast and cable industry trade press writer Alicia Mundy: "[I]n Washington, even if you've won the battle, you don't crow about it. That annoys politicians, who don't want to read they've caved in or been bought off."[58] Billionaire Jerry Perenchio, Chairman of Univision, the Hispanic network that is now one of the largest TV groups in America, described his own management philosophy this way: "Stay clear of the press. No interviews, no panels, no speeches, no comments. Stay out of the spotlight—it fades your suit."[59]

Figure 5-9 depicts influence laundering as involving two steps: A secondary (unpublicized) principal hires an intermediary, and the intermediary seeks to influence the primary principal (the publicly touted principal).

---

[56] E.g., John Mintz, "Utilities Secretly Lobbied Congress," *Washington Post*, 11 May 2000, p. A1; Nicholas Confessore, "Meet the Press: How James Glassman Reinvented Journalism—As Lobbying," *Washington Monthly*, December 2003.

[57] "The Powers of Persuasion," *Broadcasting & Cable*, 22 December 1997, p. 50.

[58] Alicia Mundy, "What Spectrum Issue?," *Mediaweek*, 15 April 1996.

[59] Rick Wartzman and Lisa Bannon, "A Media Mogul Who Steers Clear of Media? Publicity-Shy Univision Chief Captures a Huge Market in Spanish Language TV," *Wall Street Journal*, 13 August 1999, p. A1.

Figure 5-9. Hiding Conflicts of Interest via Intermediaries

Secondary Principal (Media) ➔ Intermediary ➔ Primary Principal (Voters)

If a secondary principal believes its interests are congruent with the primary principal's and that primary principal sees the influence relationship the same way, then the secondary principal will not create a firewall hiding its lobbying activity. Most consumers groups, for example, are quite open in their lobbying. Similarly, political parties are comparatively transparent compared to most trade associations.

However, if the interests of the primary and secondary principals would be perceived to conflict, if known, then an opportunistic firewall will be established between the primary and secondary principals. That firewall can be established in a number of different places. In case A, "the good intermediary," the firewall is established between the secondary principal and intermediary. In case B, "the bad intermediary," the firewall is established between the intermediary and the primary principal. In case C, there is a sequence of intermediaries, and the bad intermediaries are separated from the good ones by a firewall. Figure 5-10 shows these three cases. The arrow marks the flow of influence. The vertical line marks the point at which the flow of influence is hidden. The difference between a "good" and "bad" intermediary hinges on whether the intermediary's identity, if known, would help or harm the secondary principal's cause.

Figure 5-10. Influence firewalls and Intermediaries

Case A: The Good Intermediary
Secondary Principal ➔ | Good Intermediary ➔ Primary Principal

Case B: The Bad Intermediary
Secondary Principal ➔ Bad Intermediary ➔ | Primary Principal

Case C: The Sequence of Bad, then Good, Intermediary
Secondary Principal ➔ Bad Intermediary ➔ | Good Intermediary ➔ Primary Principal

In case A, the secondary principal tries to hide the nature of his connection with the good intermediary. The reason is that if the primary principals knew who was behind the "good" intermediary, they would use this information to discount the information provided by the intermediary and perhaps also damage the reputation of the secondary principal. For example, many special interest groups hire "front" groups with do-good sounding names to serve as their public representatives. These front groups rarely highlight their sponsors. To some extent, these types of relationships are pervasive in politics. Interest groups devote huge energy to cultivating third parties to make their case. Often this may involve hidden conflicts of interest. For example, the National Consumers League (NCL) lent its name in support of NAB positions during both the fight over the Cable Act of 1992 and the Telecom Act of 1996. NCL's executive director came out of the public relations field, and NCL is often dependent on broadcasters for publicity. A reasonable person might infer that NCL's dependence on broadcasters' goodwill represents a conflict of interest. But this dependence is not publicly disclosed. RTNDA has also occasionally played this role for broadcast owners. In an article describing the history of RTNDA, former RTNDA Paul Davis describes the origin of RTNDA as financed by the TV networks and serving as a sort of front group for them lobbying on government openness and First Amendment issues: "[T]he networks had a common agenda on most FOI [Freedom of Information] issues and felt RTNDA's motives would be seen as less driven by profits than the networks or an ownership group such as NAB."[60]

In case B, the "bad" intermediary tries to hide both its actions and its secondary principal's from the primary principal's. This is useful when the intermediary provides a valuable political service to the primary principal but engages in an action harmful to the primary principal. For example, special interest groups, like politicians, often try to hide the identities of individuals and firms that engage in controversial activities such as opposition research, polling, focus groups, and grassroots mobilization. These are activities that, when done very professionally, are associated with propaganda and giving a group an unfair advantage over the rest of the public. The use of surrogates to engage in unpopular but useful activities is pervasive not only in politics but

---

[60] Paul Davis, "Moving to Washington: Rtnda Is a Major Player in Washington in First Amendment and Foi Battles Because of the Vision and Bullheaded Persistence of Its Early Leaders," *Communicator*, September 1995, p. 113. Given NAB's extensive use of secrecy in lobbying the government, farming off the fight for government openness to RTNDA helps NAB avoid the charge of hypocrisy. To the best of my knowledge, RTNDA has never sought openness in a way that would harm the NAB.

also business. In business it is often called the good guy/bad guy routine. The car salesman, for example, is the customer's best friend who wants to give the customer the requested discount or feature. But the salesman then goes to the manager who, acting the part of the bad guy, says no. The good guy acts as if the bad guy is independent of his control, so he is not to be blamed for the bad guy's actions. In fact, however, they are working as a team. Similarly, local broadcasters hire the NAB to be their bad guy. When the NAB acts rationally in the pursuit of broadcaster interests, the local broadcaster can profess total ignorance and even disagreement.

In case C, there is a division of labor between intermediaries. The intermediary that makes the final pitch to the primary principal is the "good" intermediary. But a "bad" intermediary comes before. This type of complex sequence is much closer to the reality of interest group politics. Just as organized crime syndicates try to launder their money through a sequence of hard-to-follow links, interest groups often seek to do the same. Broadcasters, for example, will hire the Media Institute, which will then hire academics. On the surface, the Media Institute is a perfectly credible foundation seeking greater First Amendment liberties for American media.[61] But it turns out upon closer inspection that when broadcasters' lobbying agenda conflicts with the First Amendment rights of other media, such as cable operators, the Media Institute keeps mum.[62] The Media Institute was formed as a joint endeavor of three media policy PR firms: Timmons & Company, the Sawyer/Miller Group, and Griffin Johnson.[63]

Of course, in the real world, things are more complex. There are no neatly separated "good" and "bad" intermediaries. It is merely a matter of degree. But the basic logic described here is equally valid. At the margin, intermediaries will hide unfavorable information about themselves and reveal favorable information. And the intermediaries that are most visible will also appear to be the most trustworthy.

---

[61] This credibility may be important to help ensure that contributions to the Media Institute are tax deductible. The National Association of Broadcasters Education Foundation (NABEF), for example, is a non-profit, tax deductible foundation set up by the NAB to fund research by "impartial third parties," including the Media Institute.

[62] It is also mum about funding sources. See Ken Silverstein, "His Biggest Takeover Ever: How Murdoch Bought Washington," *Nation*, 8 June 1998. Over the years, this author has repeatedly tried to attend Media Institute luncheons and been refused. The Media Institute is known as one of the few think tanks in Washington covering communications policy that will only allow industry allies to attend its events.

[63] Alicia Mundy, "Jack Valenti's Last Stand," *Business Dateline*, January 1991, p. 28.

Lobbyist, gift, and campaign disclosure laws, as well as tax considerations, must also factor into any discussion of the influence laundering systems. For example, by filtering money through think tanks, donor contributions are tax deductible and both policymakers and lobbyists don't have to disclose them.[64] Similarly, by using outside groups as surrogates while leaving no traceable evidence of coordination, politicians and interest groups can escape campaign finance restrictions.[65]

Two Mechanisms for Plausible Deniability

There are two ways a secondary principal can get an intermediary to do an unpopular deed without specifying the deed and thus preserving plausible deniability for causing the deed. One is to provide the intermediary with a goal but not specify the means. If the means come to light, the secondary principal can rightfully deny it authorized those means, although they might be implied by the goal. For example, in a candidate's political campaign, allies (also called "surrogates") might do the necessary but unpopular dirty work of attacking opponents not because the candidate told them to do so but because they knew it was helpful in getting their candidate elected, especially if the candidate could distance himself from the attack. Similarly, a TV station might hire a private detective to gather certain information for a news story without specifying the means of gathering it. The investigator may then use deceptive means that would embarrass the TV station but are necessary to get the information. If the investigator is then caught lying, the station can then claim it neither knew about nor sanctioned such behavior.

Another way to preserve plausible deniability is to specify the means but not the real goal. Often no goal needs to be given to get a subordinate to pursue a certain goal. For example, few legislative aides if told to do something will press for reasons why if they sense their member of Congress doesn't want to be bothered with explanations. However, even if pressed to give a goal to justify the means, generally dozens of plausible goals can be given for any means. For example, it is a simple matter for an elected official to tell his policy staff to pursue a specific policy for high-sounding reasons even if he pursued the policy as a payoff to a campaign contributor. Similarly, if pressed, a local television manager can come up with a million plausible and high minded journalistic

---

[64] Richard Morin and Claudia Deane, "Lobbyists Seen Lurking Behind Tank Funding," *Washington Post*, 19 November 2002, p. A23. Benjamin Wallace-Wells, "In the Tank: The Intellectual Decline of AEI," *Washington Monthly*, December 2003, pp. 24-26.
[65] See the Federal Election Campaign Act, 2 U.S.C. §441b(a)

reasons not to give a particular politician airtime or to avoid running a damaging story about him.

Neither the goal nor the means need even be explicitly stated. For example, a legislative aide who wants to remain employed may only need to use common sense to infer his boss's goals and the best means to achieve them. Asking for either explicit goals or means, by revealing the aide's incompetence, may be grounds for dismissal.[66]

Conclusion

Let's assume the information investment model presented in this chapter accurately reflects how a rational legislator would reason about the likelihood of information agent bias when 1) an agent has a serious conflict of interest with his constituents, and 2) he and his constituents have incomplete information about the agent's behavior. Under such circumstances, a rational legislator should place the burden of proof not on those seeking to prove agent bias but on those seeking to prove agent ethical behavior. This conclusion would apply regardless of whether or not the agent happened to be a broadcaster.

To change the burden of proof, agents and their advocates must change the circumstances. They must be able to provide overwhelming evidence that verifiable evidence of a particular bias could be detected and punished with a high probability.

When unverifiable agent claims conflict with agent incentives, the benefit of the doubt should be given to incentives. And when the incentives for bias are huge and the legislator's career could be at stake for making an incorrect estimate of the likelihood of bias, then the burden of proof on agents and their advocates should be correspondingly greater.

---

[66] Shakespeare articulated this strategy of plausible deniability in Antony and Cleopatra. Menas tells his boss Pompey that he could easily cut the throats of Pompey's rivals for the throne of Rome. Pompey responds that Menas should just have done it "and not have spoke on't! In me 'tis villany; in thee't had been good service." Cited in Joseph E. Persico, "Deception is Part of the Art of War, But Shhhhhh!" *Wall Street Journal*, 28 February 2002, p. A1.

CHAPTER 6:

Strategies Of Broadcaster Bias to Minimize Costs

The process of maximizing political power with limited information resources can be broken down into two stages. In the last two chapters, we looked at strategies for maximizing outputs—political power. In this chapter, we look at strategies for minimizing the cost to generate that output.

Political Efficiency

Let's assume that intermediaries are economically rational. They will continue to invest in changing information incentives as long as the return on their information investment is larger than their opportunity cost of capital. Consider a choice of investing a dollar in lobbying public officials or producing the news. If the marginal return of a dollar spent on lobbying for government subsidies is greater than the marginal return of a dollar spent on improving the news, the dollar will go to the lobbying.

When choosing among inputs to change voter information incentives, these rational intermediaries choose inputs that will generate the greatest amount of output (political power) at the least cost. The ratio of the output to the input is the **political productivity** of an input.

Political productivity is maximized by investing in lobbying inputs with the lowest marginal cost per unit of change in net political support. **Net political support** is the difference between the areas under the perceived utility curves of positive and negative issue attributes across all voters at a particular point in time.[1] The purpose of an intermediary's information investment is to change

---

[1] In a democracy, preference aggregation is lumpy because each person is given one vote regardless of their preference intensity. Each voter aggregates candidate attributes by intensity. But among voters, each voter gets the same weight regardless of his or her preference intensity. For purposes of this discussion, we can ignore this lumpiness of voter preference aggregation because it does not change the basic strategic logic of information investments.

net political support. Figure 6-1 defines net political support for a voter as the difference between areas B and A.

Figure 6-1. Net Political Support

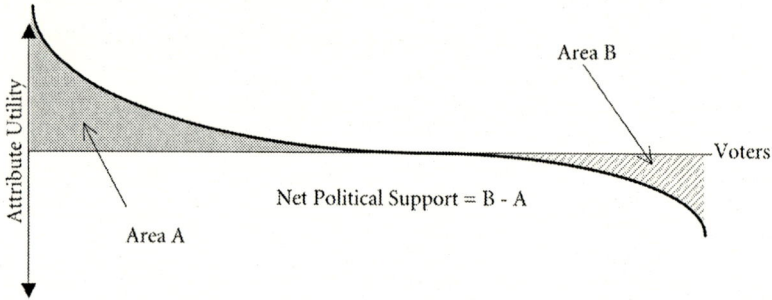

Figure 6-2 depicts a ranking of inputs based on their marginal political productivity. The marginal political output (or productivity) is defined as the change in net political support resulting from a political actor's investing one utility in a particular input. A change in one utility for a given political actor may be measured in money, time, or any other valued resource that must be given up to change a voter's perceived utility curve. The equilibrium is the choice of input (I) that maximizes output (O) per utility of investment.

Figure 6-2. Political Efficiency of Different Inputs

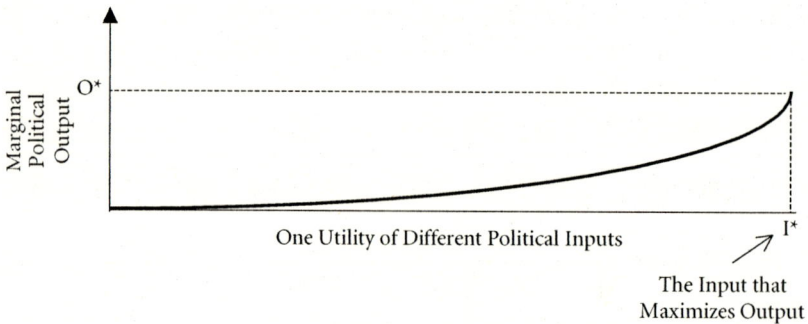

Short-term vs. Long-term Information Incentive Investments

Intermediary information investment decisions can be grouped into three time-based categories: 1) how best to employ *existing* laws, regulations, norms, technology, and voter knowledge—**the short term**, 2) when to create *new* laws, regulations, norms, technical innovations, and voter knowledge—the **long term**, and 3) attempts to create fundamentally new laws (e.g., changes in the U.S. Constitution), technologies (e.g., the invention of the Internet), and institutions (e.g., the United Nations' Telecommunications Union)—the **very long term.**

The **short term** is a time period when some lobbying inputs can be varied. A **fixed input** (or "factor") is one that cannot be changed in the short term. For example, an intermediary cannot change the FCC's lobbying disclosure laws and regulations in the short term. A **variable input** is one that can be changed in the short term. For example, an intermediary can increase or decrease the amount of political advertising in the short term.

For all practical purposes, we can think of the **very long-term** as equivalent to the state-of-nature. It would be quixotic for an intermediary to hope to change these inputs to the lobbying process. Therefore, they do not enter into lobbying strategy.

The short-term and long-term do not correspond to specific time periods. They may be thought of as occupying a continuum. But it is important to keep these distinctions in mind, if only because the academic literature and the popular press are so heavily focused on investments in short-term inputs into the lobbying process.

Intermediaries who have invested in long-term assets are more politically efficient than those lacking such assets. An intermediary with a stable of long-term, trusting relationships with members of Congress, for example, has an advantage over one lacking such relationships, even if they both have the same short-term lobbying budget. As we shall see in the next chapter, what make the broadcasters remarkable are not their political strategies or their morals but their long-term political assets, which make their political productivity extraordinarily high.

The relationship between short- and long-term costs in the economic marketplace has parallels to the relationship between short- and long-term costs in the political marketplace. Just as owning an expensive state-of-the art factory may boost a firm's economic productivity, an industry may make an investment in a regulation, such as a loophole in a lobbyist disclosure law, to increase

its political productivity. But political and economic assets have one fundamental difference. Economic assets maximize monetary return; political assets
maximize political power.

Figure 6-3 depicts the inputs that can be varied over the short- and long-
term. The short-term equilibrium is the choice of input (I_{ST}) that generates
maximum output (O_{ST}) per utility of investment. The long-term equilibrium
has the same maximizing relationship between input (I_{LT}) and output (O_{LT}).

Figure 6-3. The Productivity of Inputs in the Short- and Long-Term

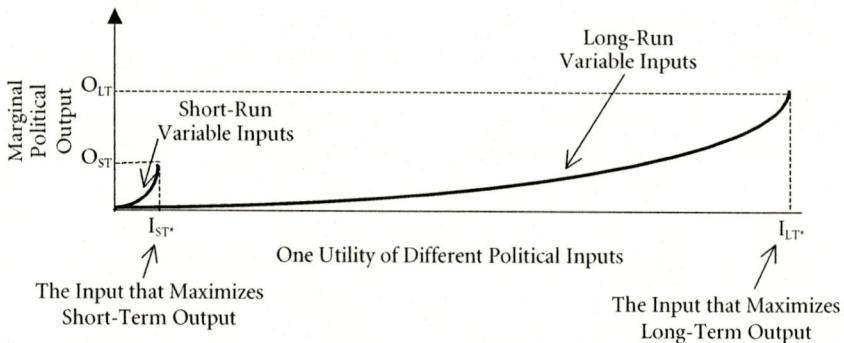

The long-term curve spans a greater number of inputs because more inputs
can be changed in the long-term. For example, it may be possible to build a
political relationship in the long-term that is not possible to build in the short-
term.

Some long-term inputs are highly politically efficient while others may be
even less efficient than short-term inputs. A rational political actor will never
use an input with a low political efficiency.

The maximum of the long-term curve is never below the maximum of the
short-term curve. This is because the long-term curve is a superset of the
short-term curve and because with more time more efficient investments can
be made. For example, contrast the return from making spectrum grants to
broadcasters an off-budget allocation versus hiring a lobbyist every year to
keep the spectrum grant in the budget. If the U.S. government budget had an
annual line item for the annual lease value of the broadcasters' spectrum and
accompanying rights, the additional visibility would create great pressure during every Congressional budget cycle to either cut the line item or ensure the
public was getting its money's worth. By incurring a long-term investment to

keep spectrum out of the annual Congressional budget, the broadcasters prevent a series of much more costly short-term battles.[2]

Similarly, the NAB may want to win a particular battle in a Congressional committee (a short-term perspective) but it is also worth resources to ensure that the most favorable Congressional committee possible gets jurisdiction over the contested issue (a long-term perspective). This helps explain why the NAB has fought to keep spectrum auctions out of the Congressional budget committees and in the Congressional telecommunications committees. When the issue comes up in the budget committees, the opportunity cost of the spectrum becomes vividly apparent; no spectrum auctions explicitly means less money for other, popular programs. This helps mobilize opposition. But when the issue comes up in the telecommunications committee, the issue may be framed in such a way that there is no explicit acknowledgment of the opportunity cost of giving spectrum rights worth billions of dollars to some of the largest corporations in America.

Long-term investments may be made in both government and private institutions. Examples of private investments include trade associations, other interest groups, and the press. Examples of public investments include FCC, Judicial, and Congressional norms and laws.

Inputs into lobbying may be divided into three categories: human, media, and institutional.

Human Inputs

The political actors we have used in our model of strategic behavior are candidates (as ultimate agents), voters (as principals), and intermediaries (elite information agents), including broadcasters. Intermediaries create voter information incentives, which in turn determine candidate incentives. As described in Chapter 4, the flow of influence is as follows:

Intermediaries ➔ Voters ➔ Candidates

We can thus identify three broad classes of human inputs—candidates, voters, and intermediaries—each of which shows variation in efficiency with regard to a particular lobbying goal.

---

[2] Bill Heniff Jr., "Off-Budget Status of Federal Entities: Background and Current Proposals," (Washington, DC: Congressional Research Service, 1999).

Candidate Efficiencies

The efficiency of contributions to candidates is a function of both candidate electability and policy stands. Political actors don't want to waste resources on candidates with a small chance of being elected, even if their policy stands are perfectly aligned with their own. Even a candidate with policy stands strongly opposed to a given political actor on most issues may be supported by that political actor if the candidate is viewed as unbeatable and persuadable on at least some issues.

It turns out that the electability of different candidates varies greatly. Incumbent members of the U.S. House of Representatives, for example, had more than a 95% chance of winning re-election during the late 1990s. Since political actors don't like to invest in losers, the lion's share of campaign contributions and other resources go to incumbents. NAB PAC money, for example, is overwhelmingly focused on incumbents.

Since the Congressional election system is rigged to favor incumbents, the power of any interest group, even the most powerful, is severely constrained. Let's assume, for example, that broadcasters can sway 1% of the electorate. Compared to the number of people employed in the broadcast industry, that is a huge number. But compared to the percentage by which most incumbents win re-election, it's a small fraction. Thus, even the most powerful interest groups have limited power over a determined Congressional opponent who, as the democratically elected champion of the people, has carefully chosen to take on no more than a handful of special interests.

Figure 6-4 illustrates the importance of electability. Assume that for a given political actor the policy stands of Candidate A are far preferable to those for Candidate B. Yet in the status quo distribution of voter preferences, Candidate A gets 10% of the vote whereas Candidate B gets 90%. Thus, even if the political actor had the resources to double Candidate A's support to 20%, it still wouldn't be enough to ensure victory, so it would be a bad investment.

Figure 6-4. Electability of Candidate A vs. Candidate B

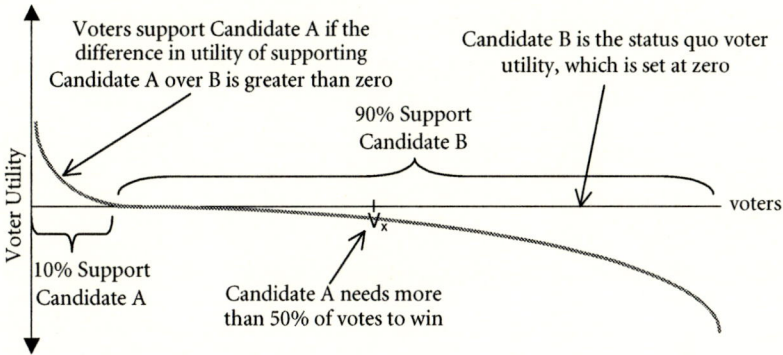

Voters support Candidate A if the difference in utility of supporting Candidate A over B is greater than zero

Candidate B is the status quo voter utility, which is set at zero

90% Support Candidate B

voters

Voter Utility

10% Support Candidate A

Candidate A needs more than 50% of votes to win

Voter Efficiencies

The relative cost and benefit curves facing specific voters with regard to specific issues at specific moments in time is a variable affecting the efficiency of different information investments. Political actors want to minimize the cost of achieving a particular change in support or opposition. In the last chapter, all voters, attributes, and moments were classified into favorable or unfavorable sets. There were no targeted investments within members of these sets. But, all other things being equal, a rational political actor will invest resources in particular attributes for particular voters at particular points in time with the least expensive ("easy") to change information incentives.[3] The property of easiness or hardness is a function of the cost to make salient a particular attribute for a particular voter at a particular time. A rational political actor will invest in easy voters on easy issues at easy moments while avoiding hard voters on hard attributes at hard moments, for only in this way can political productivity be maximized.

As I learned when running for the Maryland House of Delegates in the 2000 primary and general elections, most advice for candidates from political consultants and how-to campaign books centers on identifying easy voters, easy

[3] E.g., E. G. Carmines and J. A. Stimson, "The 2 Faces of Issue Voting," *American Political Science Review* 74, no. 1 (1980), Downs, *An Economic Theory of Democracy,* Marion R. Just, W. Russell Neuman, and Ann Crigler, "An Economic Theory of Learning from News," (Cambridge: Joan Shorenstein Barone Center, 1992).

attributes, and easy points of time, and focusing scarce campaign resources on them.

Figure 6-5 illustrates that the property of easiness is a function of the shape of the incentive curve. When the difference between the status quo benefit and cost of information is negative in sign and large in magnitude, changing the salience of a piece of information is hard. When the status quo benefit of information is only slightly larger than the cost, changing the salience of a piece of information is easy. When a voter has already acquired a piece of information, the salience of a piece of information is unchangeable.

Figure 6-5. Difficulty (cost) to change the salience of a piece of information

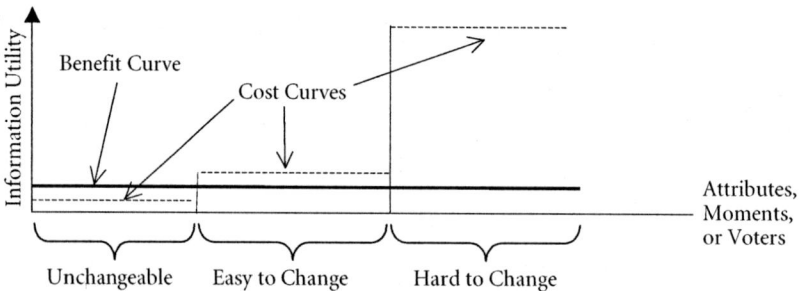

Easy voters are uncommitted to a candidate, yet likely to vote and already motivated to acquire the information that will give the candidate making the information investment an advantage. Easy attributes tend to involve information acquired in the course of everyday life. And easy moments tend to be located at a point in time, such as near Election Day or after a crisis, when voters' demand for political information is greatest and their cost of information most heavily subsidized by other intermediaries. Related terms for easy attributes, easy voters, and easy moments, are "wedge issues," "swing voters," and "teachable moments."

The NAB invests large sums of money in lobbying research to identify persuadable voters and the most effective ways to frame issues.[4] KRC Research & Consulting, a division of the Bozell-Sawyer-Miller Group (BSMG),[5] now part of Interpublic Group, one of the world's three largest diversified lobbying firms,[6] did the research for the broadcasters' 1996 media campaign to win the

---

[4] This research is briefly mentioned in Mundy, "What Spectrum Issue?."

[5] Then known as Robinson, Lerer, Sawyer, and Miller.

[6] Louis Jacobson, "Gobbled Up," *National Journal*, 7 April 2001, p. 1014.

public's support for the broadcasters' spectrum agenda.[7] BSMG also did the lobbying research for the National Cable and Telecommunications Association's $18 million media campaign in 1993–1994 and the United States Telephone Association's $20 million media campaign in 1996–1997. The quality of the research is comparable to what a Fortune 500 consumer products manufacturer such as Proctor & Gamble would use before launching a major new consumer product. The purpose of the research is not to identify the public interest but to persuade a susceptible subset of the public that an industry's private interest is identical to the public interest.[8] Heavy reliance on such sophisticated research to frame issues has given telecommunications policy language a remarkably Orwellian flavor, where competition is monopoly, free is pay, and fairness is corporate welfare.[9]

A private contractor for KRC Research & Consulting, Shugoll Research, got the NAB in trouble when, using a common consumer product focus group incentive, it offered to pay nine Congressional staff $150 to participate in a February 28, 1996 focus group on spectrum allocation issues. Senator McCain publicly complained, and the NAB had KRC Research immediately fire the subcontractor.[10]

---

[7] Results were embedded in the NAB's 1996 Spectrum Auction Action Toolkit (described in Chapter 15) and presented at a session called "Spectrum Auctions and the Industry Campaign" by Edward Reilly, KRC Research & Consulting, at the NAB's State Leadership Conference, Park Hyatt Hotel, Washington, DC, 4 March 1996.

[8] For a description of this type of survey research, see Carl M. Cannon, "Hooked on Polls," *National Journal*, 17 October 1998, Lawrence R. Jacobs and Robert Y. Shapiro, *Politicians Don't Pander: Political Manipulation and the Loss of Democratic Responsiveness, Studies in Communication, Media, and Public Opinion* (Chicago, IL.: University of Chicago Press, 2000), Alex Williams, "The Alchemy of a Political Slogan: In Focus Groups, Pollsters Test the Words That Shape the Issues," *New York Times*, 22 August 2004, section 9, p. 1.

[9] BSMG has also provided promotional advice to TV stations. For example, it advocated the following advertising line for CBS station KYW-TV in Philadelphia: "Eyewitness News. We're there for you." Randall Rothenberg, "The Boom in Political Consulting," *New York Times*, 24 May 1987, section 3, p. 1.

[10] Jeannine Aversa, "McCain: Research Firm 'Way Over the Line' with Hill Payment Plan, *Associated Press*, 6 March 1996; Mary Jacoby, "McCain Zaps Survey Firm That Offers to Pay Senate Staffers for Focus Groups," *Roll Call*, 29 February 1996; Sarah Pekkanen, "How Lobbyists are Changing the Lobbying Game," *The Hill*, 12 February 1997; Dennis Wharton, "Hundt ties station licenses to kidvid," *Variety*, 11-17 March 1996, p. 30.

Agent Efficiencies

Principals delegate a lobbying task to an intermediary (the "information agent") to enhance their political productivity. Principals choose a particular agent because of that agent's competence and incentives to change audience information incentives with respect to particular attributes at a particular point in time. Principals want agents who have interests congruent with their own and greater competence to pursue those interests,

Incentives. Ideal agents should not have any conflicts of interests with a principal. Since all agents have some conflicts of interest, the issue of incentive compatibility is always a measure of degree rather than kind. When the agent is an "expert," it is often enough to merely demonstrate that the agent is "independent"—that is, does not have any obvious conflicts of interest. The presumption is that, absent conflicting evidence, an expert will adhere to the scientific method or some other impartial method of formulating judgments. For example, an academic's peer reviewed article on an information policy issue is likely to be considered more credible than a story placed on the same topic written by a known PR specialist working for a trade association with a known axe to grind. Most big budget national lobbying campaigns involve identifying and, if necessary, recruiting independent third parties with no obvious financial or personal gain from a proposed policy. The NAB, for example, has traditionally invested in a variety of independent institutions such as the Media Institute, Broadcast Educators Association, and Roper (the polling firm),[11] who themselves either generate or solicit information under their own name. Again and again in its political marketing campaigns, the NAB reminds its state lobbying leaders that "the power of having credible third parties articulating our message is immense."[12]

Insofar as some agents, for the same amount of money, appear more impartial than others, the efficiency of agents will vary. All other things being equal, for example, a plug for a medical treatment within a TV news program is worth more than one within an ad, and democratic legitimacy for a point of view is greater when it stems from a name brand polling firm often cited in the media (such as Roper) than one with an unrecognized name.

---

[11] E.g., "Turned On, Tuned In To TV," The *Public Pulse*, May 1991, p. 1.

[12] National Association of Broadcasters, "A Model State Marketing Plan: The Marketing of Broadcaster's Public Service Record," (Washington, DC: National Association of Broadcasters, 1998), p. 11.

Competence. An agent should have a cost advantage over oneself with respect to investing in information incentives. This cost advantage involves the gathering, processing, and distribution of information, with distribution including both a cost advantage in publicizing favorable information and hiding unfavorable information. This plays itself out in hiring a welter of individuals, each with a different lobbying expertise. For example, a trade association will often employ different individuals with expertise in lobbying the executive branch, Congress, the press, the courts, and their own members. The employees will either be in-house staff or independent contractors. Larger trade associations, such as the NAB, will employ or subcontract with individuals with even more specialized expertise—for example, expertise in lobbying House Democrats vs. House Republicans on a particular House committee. Sometimes an individual will be hired because of her efficiency in communicating with a single especially important individual such as a committee chair or a narrow class of individuals such as Congressional press secretaries. Many individuals are hired not because of their audience expertise but because of their issue attribute expertise. For example, the NAB has substantial in house engineering and research departments and contracts out for specialized information with think tanks, professional consultants, and academics. Lastly, timing expertise, while inextricably tide to audience and issue attribute expertise, is a vital expertise for influencing the legislative process. Timing expertise involves knowing the best moment or rate at which to do any form of lobbying, which includes slipping in a particular clause in a piece of legislation, looking for a particular piece of information, or issuing a press release.

The most widely studied act of delegation in the interest group literature may be the campaign contribution. In the classic make or buy decision that all organizations must face, many organized interests have come to the conclusion that candidates are more efficient than themselves in changing voter information incentives. Candidates usually have superior knowledge about their own and their opponents' strengths and, weaknesses as well as their constituents' preferences, knowledge, and points of persuasion.

Political actors may also vary in the penalty they face for being caught in an act of opportunistic behavior. Thus, there may be gains to be had from delegating the risk of being caught in opportunistic behavior to other political actors. This assumes that the political actor who engages in the opportunistic behavior will take at least some of the blame if this behavior is exposed.

It turns out there are many political actors willing to take on this blame for a fee. Consider this description of Hilary Rosen, Chair of the Record Industry Association of America, who represented the U.S. recording industry [including companies with significant broadcast interests] in fighting Napster and other free uses of music.

> Reviled by college kids, music fans, and more than a few recording artists for the RIAA's role in forcing the shutdown of Napster, Rosen is seen as the embodiment of a venal corporate culture.... As industry figures urged her on from the sidelines, Rosen withstood a level of vitriol that stunned friends.... The presumption in these attacks was that Rosen was calling the plays for the music business and not the other way around. She seems to prefer it that way; she gets paid $1 million a year to shelter the executives from criticism. But, in fact, according to those closest to her, she's not the hard-liner in the crusade against file-sharing. Yes, she's the frontwoman. But there are five CEOs backing her up—and they sometimes make her look like Mary Poppins.[13]

Similarly, a broadcast TV news magazine may hire an outside private detective to gather information for a story at least in part because the private detective won't be embarrassed if caught engaging in certain activities that would embarrass a news outlet. As long as the news outlet didn't verifiably ask for a controversial data collection method when it hired the private detective, it can plausibly deny any knowledge of the private detective's actions.[14] This is easy to do because written contracts typically specify desired results, not the means by which they are achieved.

Media Inputs

Different media are more or less efficient in changing voter information incentives. These efficiencies can be divided into three categories: voter, attribute, and time.

Voter. Different media have different costs to reach a given audience size with a given quality of information. One important cost variable is one-to-one vs. one-to-many media. Examples of the former are the telephone and face-to-face communication. Examples of the latter are broadcast TV and mass circulation daily newspapers. In terms of cost per audience member, one-to-one

---

[13] Matt Bal, "Hating Hilary," *Wired*, February 2003, pp. 98-9.

[14] Douglas Frantz, "Law Confronts a Peddler in Private Data," *New York Times*, 1 July 1999, p. A1. In this case, media outlets hired out a company called Press Pass Media, which in turn hired out private detective companies.

communication tends to be more expensive than one-to-many communication.

One important quality variable is high vs. low fidelity communications, with high-fidelity defined in terms of the ability to replicate face-to-face communication. Video is a high fidelity form of communication and text a low fidelity form. Another important quality variable is live vs. recorded. The immediacy of a live event may generate a more engaged audience.

The NAB uses a wide variety of media depending on the audience they want to reach. Communications with members of Congress, top-ranked Washington lobbyists, and senior grassroots operatives rely heavily on one-to-one media such as the telephone and face-to-face meetings. Communication with station general managers and other local grassroots operators has relied more heavily on one-to-many communications such as *Congressional Contact*, a monthly newsletter, and *Telejournal*, a monthly satellite broadcast. Access to *Congressional Contact* and *Telejournal* are very tightly controlled. To reach the general public, the NAB heavily relies on the mass media, including print and video ads, and print and video news media. News media is cultivated through an extensive network of colleagues in the news business.

Attribute. The form of media has a large impact on the number and type of attributes that can be considered. Some media allow for presenting much more detailed considerations than others. Roughly in order of decreasing detail are scholarly publications, think tank reports, print mass media, and electronic mass media. Highly motivated audiences, such as academics and other opinion elites, tend to want much more detailed information than the general public.

To appeal to opinion leaders, the NAB will often commission detailed expert studies, often by academics. Sometimes these will not actually be distributed but only held in reserve in case opposition develops and they are needed for countervailing firepower. In contrast, the print and video press releases sent to the mass media are likely to be short and written at an elementary school reading level.

Time. Media have large differences in their verifiability by third parties at a future time. As a general rule, intermediaries want verifiable records regarding information favorable to their interests and unverifiable records regarding information unfavorable to their interests.

Information whose future positive or negative valence remains uncertain represents a special category. In this case, a verifiable record is desirable—but only if the intermediary controls the record. When broadcasters videotape members of Congress at the exclusive annual Congressional breakfast at the annual NAB show in Las Vegas, at the annual NAB State Leadership Conference in Washington, DC, at the monthly Washington representatives' breakfast at NAB headquarters, or even at Congressional committee hearings on Capitol Hill,[15] it may be said to be creating such a controlled record.

Institutional Inputs

Institutions are made up of individuals, which have different incentives and expertise. Thus, efficiency considerations that relate to individuals also apply to the institutions in which they belong.

But institutions are more than the sum of the individuals that make them up. They also have distinctive legitimacy and powers. In order to be effective in pursuing their government interests, an interest group may work through a vast array of different organizations. Figure 6-6 lists some of the organizations local TV broadcasters work with as part of their lobbying efforts.

---

[15] The case of the Capitol Hill hearing may confuse readers. After all, aren't Congressional hearings public? And aren't they often broadcast over C-SPAN? The answer is that it is generally illegal for non-news media to videotape Congressional hearings, and C-SPAN doesn't allow its footage to be used for political purposes. The only regular exception to this rule that I know of is the NAB, which appears to leverage its media connections to get a verifiable video record for its own political purposes.

Figure 6-6. Institutions through which local TV broadcasters exert influence

FEDERAL GOVERNMENT

Executive Branch
- White House
- Federal Communications Commission (FCC)
- Federal Trade Commission (FTC)
- Department of Interior

Legislative Branch
- Members of Congress and their staff
- various Congressional committees (notably the House and Senate Commerce Committees)
- Congressional Budget Office
- Library of Congress (including the Congressional Research Service and Copyright Office)
- General Accounting Office
- Press galleries
- Press secretary associations

Judicial Branch
- Supreme Court
- Lower Courts

STATE GOVERNMENT
- Executive Branch
- Legislative Branch
- Judicial Branch

NON-GOVERNMENT

Broadcast Industry Trade Associations
- Maximum Service Telecasters (MSTV)
- Motion Picture Association of America (MPAA)
- National Association of Broadcasters (NAB)
- Radio-Television News Directors Association (RTNDA)
- State broadcasting associations

PR and Research Firms
- Bozell Sawyer Miller Group (BSMG) Worldwide (sold to Weber Shandwick Worldwide, now part of Interpublic Group)
- Chlopak, Leonard, Schechter and Associates (owned by Omnicom Group, Inc.)
- Edelman Associates
- KRC Research (a division of BSMG Worldwide)
- Mellman Group

Pollsters
- Roper
- Wirthlin Worldwide

Local Non-Profits
- Rotary clubs
- Chambers of commerce
- Red Cross
- State press clubs

National Non-Profits
- Ad Council
- Congressional Club (for Congressional spouses)
- National Consumers League
- U.S. Senate Press Secretaries Association

Academics/Thinktanks
- National Association of Broadcasters Education Foundation (NABEF)
- Broadcast Educators Association
- Media Institute
- Quello Center

Issue Specific Trade Association Allies
- American Association of Advertising Agencies (advertising restrictions and taxes)
- American Gaming Institute (gambling advertising)
- Beer Institute (alcohol advertising)
- National Rifle Association, Christian Coalition, National Right to Life Committee (political advertising)

Washington, DC Lobbyists & Law Firms
- APCO Associates
- Black, Kelly, Scruggs and Healey
- Capitoline/MS&L (Manning, Selvage, & Lee)
- Davidson Colling Group, Inc.
- Dewey Ballantine
- Dow, Lohnes and Albertson
- Higgins, McGovern et al.
- Jenner & Block
- Johnson, Smith et al.
- Moir & Hardman
- Podesta.com
- Shaw Pittman
- Skadden, Arps et al.
- Wiley, Rein, & Fielding

One important difference among institutions is their visibility to the press and general public. Some institutions are much better at keeping secrets or promoting ideas. Consider the different lobbying disclosure laws in Congress versus the FCC. When a broadcaster lobbies a proceeding at the FCC, he must file an ex parte stating who he met and what he said. That information then gets published in the FCC's public record, where it becomes available for all competitors to see. In contrast, a broadcaster can lobby a member of Congress to his heart's content, and no one needs to know anything about it. Clearly, a broadcaster concerned about visibility is better off working through Congress. But that's only part of the story.

Since senior members of Congress can influence the FCC without leaving a paper trail, an interest group like the broadcasters that can effectively work through Congress can lobby the FCC without a verifiable public trace.[16] Similarly, the White House is exempt from disclosure laws that pertain to federal agencies. Thus an interest group that can lobby the White House directly may have a comparative advantage.

Even within Congress, some institutions are lower visibility than others. For example, it's usually easier to hide controversial measures in appropriation committee bills than commerce committee bills. Since appropriations bills tend to be large and passed at the last minute, public scrutiny of their contents is more difficult. Conference committees, which include representatives from both the House and Senate, are also a good place to hide controversial measures, because they aren't subject to open meeting requirements or roll call votes.

Just as some institutions are better for keeping secrets, others are better for getting a message to the public. The president of the United States, for example, has unparalleled access to the media to get out his message.[17] Similarly, if broadcasters can get a senior senator to make a statement, it's likely to get more coverage than if an FCC bureau chief made the same statement. Rarely, however, do broadcasters seek the limelight; the shadows are where they prefer to do their lobbying.

---

[16] Members of Congress are also exempt from the "sunshine period" restrictions on lobbying the FCC. This restriction bans contact with the FCC from a week before a decision (that is, when an item is put on the following week's agenda for an FCC commissioner vote) until the day the vote actually takes place. See Christopher Stern, "Getting Their Message Across to the FCC," *Washington Post*, 27 March 2003, p. E01.

[17] Samuel Kernell, *Going Public : New Strategies of Presidential Leadership*, 2nd ed. ([Washington, DC]: CQ Press, 1993). Jeffrey Tulis, *The Rhetorical Presidency* (Princeton, N.J.: Princeton University Press, 1987).

Consider this interchange at a panel on Low Power FM political strategy at the 1999 NAB State Leadership Conference. The moderator was John David, NAB's Executive Vice President of Radio, and the panelists Jack Goodman, NAB's General Counsel, and Lynn Claudy, NAB's Senior Vice President of Science & Technology. A local broadcaster asks the panel about using a Congressional appropriations committee to kill the FCCs low power radio proposal.

> **Local Broadcaster:** I have a question for you Jack. There's been some discussion about trying to make an end run around the FCC by trying to get our Congressional delegation to attach an amendment to allocate zero dollars to the Commission to pursue this effort. Is that a realistic opportunity for us?"
>
> **Jack Goodman:** I think that that is always possible, but those are the sorts of things that have to be attached at the last minute. If you put them in the beginning, they tend to fall apart and fall away. It's something to consider, and I know that Mike and Jim [presumably Mike Waring and Jim May in NAB's government relations department] are looking for opportunities to do that [put in a rider]. But typically that kind of rider is best done in the dark of night at the last minute.
>
> **John David (interjecting):** That's why you pay your NAB dues, for those dark at night moves.[18]

There are also huge differences in the disclosure requirements of different interest groups. Federal security law, for example, requires brokerage firms to retain electronic mail relating to the brokerage firm's business for three years, so the government has the evidence it needs to enforce its security laws.[19] In contrast, broadcasters, who in theory have even greater public interest obligations in return for their government subsidies, face no such disclosure requirement.[20]

There is also the question of simple institutional smarts. For example, during the late 1990s, Microsoft faced great government scrutiny partly because it kept careful records of its e-mails and thus could have those e-mails subpoenaed and

---

[18] Comments at the NAB State Leadership Conference, 3:15pm-4pm panel on Low Power FM, Washington Monarch Hotel, Washington, DC, 9 March 1999.

[19] Gretchen Morgenson, "Wall St. Firms Said to Break E-Mail Rule," *New York Times*, 7 May 2003, p. C1.

[20] Snider, "The Decline of Broadcasters' Public Interest Obligations."

used as incriminating evidence.[21] In contrast, smart DC trade associations, such as CTIA and NCTA, routinely destroy their correspondence and reports so that they cannot be put in such a compromising position. Similarly, smart FCC commissioners and other public officials clean out their e-mail correspondence so that members of Congress cannot request to see them.[22] If something needs to be put in writing, it can be done without a date, author, and other identifying information. A remarkable number of lobbying documents are handed to members of Congress without document dates, which reduces their utility to researchers and reporters who later come upon them and want to place them in historical context. I have also seen Congressional staffers send each other undated notes signed with a name in an indecipherable scribble.[23] TV reporters are also routinely told to keep the threat of subpoenas in mind and destroy or keep journalistic information depending on whether it would help or harm their corporate interests. Examples of corporate interests would be winning a TV station's FCC license renewal and winning a libel case brought against the station.[24]

It is important to recognize that the most efficient way to influence a particular branch of government may be indirectly via another branch. For example, the courts are often deferential to Congressional intent, especially on complex, technical issues such as telecommunications regulation. As a result, broadcasters are able to take their very strong base of support in Congress and leverage it into support in the judicial branch. In the Supreme Court's 5-4 Turner decision, for example, the majority opinion chose to defer to Congressional judgment, despite doubts about the wisdom of pursuing TV programming diversity via complex regulatory mandates to carry TV programs on cable systems.[25] The alternative would have been to seek to break the broadcast-cable duopoly by encouraging new forms of competition and speech, including

---

[21] E.g., Joel Brinkley, "Microsoft Undercut in Effort to Depict Rival as Thriving: E-Mails Suggest a Selective Search for Data," *New York Times*, 5 June 1999, p. B4.

[22] Interview with former FCC Commissioner Susan Ness, 22 May 2004.

[23] An example is the correspondence between Congressional aides leading to the breaking of the Republican leadership's pledge to then Senate Majority Leader Bob Dole not to "loan" broadcasters a second channel and give them spectrum flexibility until Congress introduced spectrum reform legislation. See Chapter 15 for a discussion of this incident.

[24] Kathleen Kirby, "Should You Save Story Files?" *Communicator*, February 1999.

[25] "Judgments about how competing economic interests are to be reconciled in the complex and fast-changing field of television are for Congress to make," wrote Justice Kennedy for the majority. "If Congress sought to address anti-competitive behavior by cable system operators, it passed the wrong law," wrote Justice O'Connor for the minority. See *Turner Broadcasting System, Inc. v. FCC*, 520 U. S. 180 (1997).

satellite TV, broadband Internet service, and non-discriminatory broadband network access for all information providers, not just FCC licensed TV broadcasters.

Similarly, through its control of the reappointment of FCC Commissioners and the annual FCC appropriation, Congress has tremendous power over the FCC's agenda and rulemakings even when it passes no legislation and leaves no public trace. In the words of former FCC Commissioner James Quello:

> [T]he FCC is an 'arm of Congress,' created by Congress to implement Congressional legislation and intent. It was not created to implement the non-legislated policies policies or directives of the executive branch whether Democratic or Republican. The commissioners may owe their confirmation to the president, but they owe their confirmation and financial appropriations to Congress.[26]

Congress can also play a big part in seemingly private industry deals. House Commerce Committee Chairman Billy Tauzin, for example, hosted a regular broadcast digital TV roundtable, where he invited industry leaders to negotiate a voluntary deal with each or face government regulation. Said his spokesman Ken Johnson: "Everyone recognizes that Congress is insistent on this transition [from analog to digital TV] taking place. Either the affected industries work collaboratively or Congress and the FCC will do it for them, either through regulation or legislation."[27] FCC Chair Michael Powell, picking up on Tauzin's cue, threatened regulations unless the industry could come up with voluntary agreements to his liking.[28]

Conclusion

Political actors are rational in that they not only seek to maximize bias but also seek the most efficient means to do so. They will invest in voters, attributes, and points in time that are "easy" and they will invest in agents, media, and institutions that also generate maximum impact at least cost. Options available to minimize cost heavily depend on the decision making timeframe. In the long-run, the range of cost effective inputs increases. If an intermediary acts

---

[26] E.g., See James Quello, "If I were chairman (again)," *Broadcasting & Cable*, 4 October 1998, p. 19.

[27] Neil Munro, "Jousting for Television's Holy Grail," *National Journal*, 8 June 2002, p. 1723.

[28] Ibid.

rationally to minimize its costs of exercising bias, then its claims of acting as a public trustee are undermined.

CHAPTER 7:

Information Assets for Broadcaster Bias

"Broadcasters control the most powerful promotional engine on the planet. Why do we not use it to make the public aware [or not aware] of our case and promote and preserve our businesses?"[1]

—Nat Ostroff, Vice President, Sinclair Broadcast Group

"[A broadcaster] is no different than any other constituent. What can a broadcaster do to a congressman? Nothing. And he won't try to do anything either."

—Eugene Cowan, ABC Representative on NAB Board[2]

In previous chapters, we looked at ways strategies of bias are independent of a political actor's assets. For example, the principle that a political actor increases incentives to acquire favorable information and decreases incentives to acquire unfavorable information does not depend on whether the resource used to change incentives is money, airwaves, or face-to-face communication. Similarly, the principle that a political actor picks the least expensive resource to achieve a particular result is independent of the assets available to that political actor.

Assets are important because they determine both the likely success of a bias strategy and the particular way it is likely to be implemented. The idea that political actors differ most fundamentally in their assets but not their strategies typically conflicts with the self-descriptions of political actors. Political actors

---

[1] Nat Ostroff, "Cable Should Pay for DTV Signal," *Broadcasting & Cable*, 19 January 2004, p. 49.

[2] "The Broadcast Lobby: Resistant to Change," in *The Washington Lobby* (Washington, DC: Congressional Quarterly, 1979), p. 206. Cowan served on NAB's board from 1972 to 1990. The claim may be viewed as ironic because Cowan takes credit for pushing to hire Fritts and inaugurate the era of much more aggressive grassroots broadcast lobbying. Author's interview with Eugene Cowan on December 23, 1998.

with similar assets typically claim that they, but not their opponents, are motivated to act in the public welfare and would therefore never engage in the type of purposeful bias described in the previous chapter. Never mind that just about every agent on the face of the earth makes the same claim.

The claim may either be based on altruistic motives (I act in the public interest because it is the moral thing to do) or selfish motives (I act in the public interest because it is in my self-interest to do so). But the bottom line in both cases is a promise that the agent won't act opportunistically.

Types of Assets

Political assets can be divided into two basic categories: voter preference assets and information assets. Voter preference assets refer to the status quo preference distribution of voters, and information assets refer to the ability of principals and their agents to change that status quo preference distribution.

Voter Assets

An interest group pursuing a popular cause among well-informed voters can be said to have more voter assets than one pursuing a popular cause among ill-informed voters. Conversely, an interest group pursuing an unpopular cause among ill-informed voters can be said to have more voter assets that one pursuing an unpopular cause among well-informed voters. In Figure 7-1, political actors favoring supporters of a particular candidate attribute have greater voter assets than opponents because the number of informed supporters is larger than informed opponents.

Figure 7-1. Preference Curve of Informed Supporters and Opponents

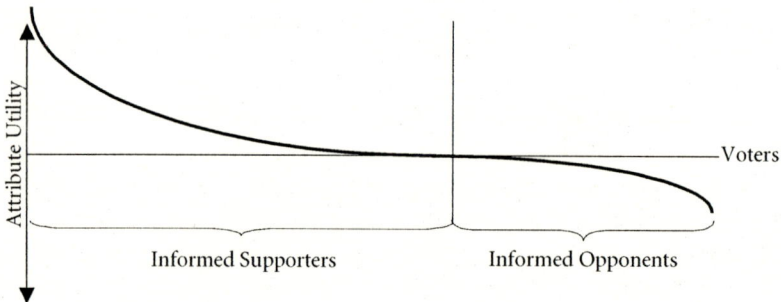

Figure 7-1 doesn't tell us about the relative costs to inform opponents and supporters. Figure 7-2 provides this missing information. In this example, political actors favoring the supporters have greater voter assets because, although both supporters and opponents have equal numbers of voters, the cost to make supporters aware of their own preferences is less.

Figure 7-2. Considerations of Supporters vs. Opponents

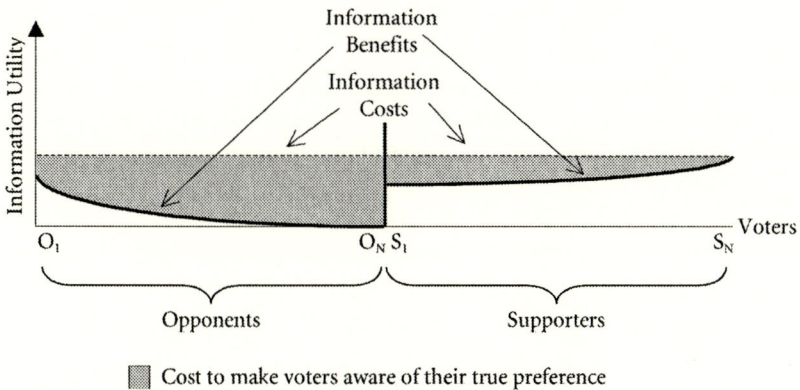

Cost to make voters aware of their true preference

Some interest groups are blessed with favorable voter preferences assets. Either they are pursuing a popular cause or they are pursuing an unpopular cause but the issue is so obscure that it is only salient to their members. Broadcasters have pursued both types of causes, but the spectrum rights give-away was decidedly in the second category. The spectrum rights were of immense concern to broadcast owners. But most members of the public could have cared less, if only because they didn't know about it.

In this chapter, our primary concern is with how information assets vary among political actors and how broadcasters may be blessed with a remarkable array of long-term information assets, largely stemming from the nature of the business they are in.

Information Assets

An information asset lowers the cost of changing voter information incentives. A monetary asset is a type of information asset because money can be used to buy media and expertise, which can in turn be used to change other political actors' information incentives. However, monetary assets are only a subset of information assets.

Some assets, such as laws and institutional norms, generate political influence over a relatively long period of time, whereas other assets, such as money used to purchase a lobbyist, generate political influence over the short-term.

The key feature of information assets that interests us is that long-term information assets vary across political actors. As we saw in the last chapter, different inputs have different efficiencies in changing voter information incentives. But now we observe that the level of efficiency doesn't merely depend on the input. It may also depend on who is using the input. Depending on their other assets, political actors may need to spend different amounts to achieve the same result. For example, the marginal expenditure needed to influence a local TV news director's political coverage is incomparably smaller for the news director's boss than for just about any other political actor. This may also help explain why history is rife with aspiring politicians who purchased media outlets and then used them as a springboard to a political career,[3] and businessmen who purchased media outlet as a lobbying and PR vehicle for their non-media businesses.[4] Today, in contrast, media owners appear more inclined to view the media business as a profitable and glamorous end-it-itself rather than a stepping stone to something else.[5]

Figure 7-3 shows the political efficiency curves for two different political actors. For actor A, one dollar has three times the political efficiency as one dollar for actor B. In other words, the political efficiency multiplier for a marginal dollar of political expenditures is three times as high for actor A as for actor B.

---

[3] Most of the examples are from prior to the 20th century, when partisan politics and the press were tightly linked. For early linkages of political and journalistic careers, see Denis Brian, *Pulitzer: A Life* (New York: J. Wiley, 2001), David Nasaw, *The Chief: The Life of William Randolph Hearst* (Boston: Houghton Mifflin, 2000).

[4] E.g., Grace Glueck, "Walter Annenberg, 94, Dies; Philanthropist and Publisher," *New York Times*, 2 October 2002, p. A1, Alicia C. Shepard, "Big Sky's Big Player," *American Journalism Review*, October 1999, p. 33, Jean Strouse, *Morgan: American Financier*, New York: Random House, 1999.

[5] An apparent exception might be my home town's local publisher, Philip Merrill, who currently has a position in the Bush Administration. See "Bush Picks Media Chairman for Bank," *Associated Press*, 30 September 2002. Noi Mahoney, "Merrill Confirmed to Ex-Im Bank," *Capital* (Annapolis, MD), 16 November 2002, p. A1. Still, this publisher's greatest loyalty appears to be to his highly profitable publication, not his political career.

Figure 7-3. Political Efficiency of Different Political Actors

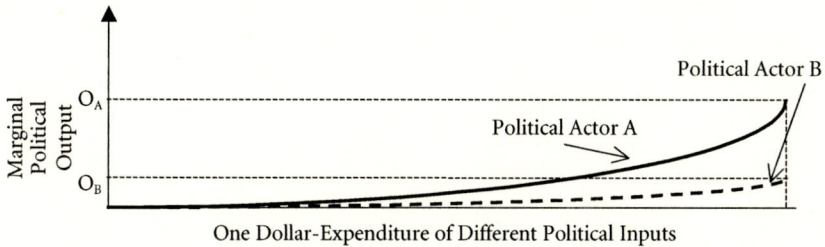

One Dollar-Expenditure of Different Political Inputs

The most widely studied short-term asset is money. Almost any political actor can use money to hire top flight Washington lobbyists, purchase prime-time media ads, and make campaign contributions.

Examples of long-term assets are relationships with celebrities, journalists, and politicians. Political actors in the TV and entertainment business may have easier access to these assets as a consequence of the business they are in.

A great advantage of monetary assets is that they allow for easy, quantitative comparison across groups. For example, the amount spent on Washington lobbying or campaign contributions is widely perceived as a meaningful measure of relative political power among different interest groups. In contrast, long-term political assets do not allow for easy, quantitative comparisons across groups. The situation differs in business, where there are well established markets and widely accepted accounting measures for long-term assets such as intangibles, property, plant, and equipment.

A major difference between practicing politicians and quantitatively oriented political scientists is that the former are concerned with a political actor's total assets, whereas the latter tend to analyze only easily measurable monetary assets.

Actor-specific information assets can be divided into company-specific and industry-specific. Industry-specific assets are shared by all members of an industry. Company-specific assets are only shared by a single company. In this chapter, we focus on the industry-specific information assets of local TV broadcasters. Local TV broadcasters are an interesting case because of the extraordinary scope and magnitude of their industry-specific assets. A look at fungible information assets—for example, their total lobbying expenditures—thus provides a highly misleading assessment of their assets for pursuing bias.

The most widely cited industry-specific information asset in the interest group literature involves the collective action problem.[6] Industries made up of many companies have a greater collective action problem than industries composed of few companies. More generally, the more members in a group, the less incentive each has to contribute to the group's welfare.

The collective action problem has especially intrigued political scientists because it conflicts with democratic theory. According to democratic theory, all other things being equal, the more supporters one has, the stronger one should be. From an Olsonian information asset perspective, however, it turns out that more supporters can be a liability.

Broadcasters' Short-Term Monetary Assets

Local broadcasters spend a large amount of money to pursue their legislative agenda. One reason exact numbers are hard to pin down is because expenditures are reported by company, not industry, and some companies are in multiple industries. The four major broadcasting networks, ABC, CBS, NBC, and FOX, each of which owns many local broadcasting stations, are each part of large conglomerates that compete in many different industries. NBC, for example, is owned by General Electric, the largest company in the world. And ABC is owned by Disney, one of the twenty largest companies in the world.

Another reason numbers are hard to pin down is that many lobbying groups divide their assets between national, state, and local lobbying. Cable TV companies, for example, invest their greatest assets lobbying at a local and state level because of the critical importance of local franchise agreements, often regulated by the state, in determining the profitability of their businesses. In contrast, the broadcast industry is predominantly regulated at the national level.

Another reason is that the accounting for campaign contributions and expenditures is riddled with loopholes. Many types of expenditures, such as grassroots lobbying and PR, do not have to be reported. And many others can be given indirectly—e.g., through relatives and independent groups—so that they are not readily traceable.

Finally, numbers are hard to pin down because government enforcement of campaign finance laws and especially lobbying laws is lax. There are so many legal loopholes to the laws that it's hard to imagine why anyone would bother with illegal activities. Given the discretion in categorizing whether or not an

---

[6] Olson, *The Logic of Collective Action.*

activity is lobbying, it's amazing how few government enforcement actions there have been.

Consider the National Association of Broadcasters. It reports lobbying expenditures of only about 10% of its total expenditures. Given that lobbying is the prime function of the NAB, the low expenditure rate is surprising. Are the NAB's in-house engineers and other researchers lobbyists? They and the government may not think of themselves that way. But their actual work primarily supports the NAB's lobbying efforts, so it is at least debatable whether their compensation could be viewed as a lobbying expenditure.

Table 7-1 shows local radio and TV broadcaster campaign contributions for every Congressional cycle from 1990 through 2002. For comparison purposes, I have included a number of other industries in the information business. The general pattern of increased expenditures for broadcasters is roughly matched by increased expenditures for the other industries.

Table 7-1. Campaign Contributions from 1990 through 2002

	TV & Radio Stations	Movie Production	Cable TV	Telephone Utilities	Computer Industry
2002	$5,446,737	$10,516,326	$6,191,300	$16,723,545	$26,642,563
2000	$7,024,024	$11,137,091	$8,542,549	$19,101,445	$39,584,423
1998	$2,426,091	$4,544,942	$3,479,248	$15,300,816	$9,498,923
1996	$2,334,832	$5,964,382	$4,085,530	$15,509,726	$9,418,538
1994	$1,393,613	$3,214,099	$2,849,491	$8,258,190	$4,331,975
1992	$1,530,450	$5,220,906	$3,327,250	$8,881,216	$5,340,862
1990	$745,482	$1,727,851	$1,647,800	$6,013,990	$1,563,519
Total	$20,901,229	$42,325,597	$30,123,168	$89,788,928	$96,380,803

Source: Center for Responsive Politics.

Even if local broadcasters' total monetary expenditure on influencing public policy could be precisely parsed from their total parent company expenditures, the number would be a highly imprecise guide to their information assets. This is because of the nature of the broadcasting business, which provides broadcasters with highly efficient political resources. A broadcaster's dollar spent on lobbying is likely to go much further than another political actor's dollar.

At the state level, the discrepancy between broadcasting and other telecom industries appears to be much greater. Consider Illinois. According to the Illinois Campaign for Political Reform, during the 1995–1996 election cycle, Ameritech (the local telephone company; later acquired by SBC) was the 9th highest contributor to candidates running for state offices and the Cable Television and Communications Association of Illinois the 11th highest. No broadcast entity showed up in the top 20 contributors. The same database shows that the Cable TV and Communications Association of Illinois gave $2.0 million to candidates running for state offices from January 1, 1993 to June 30, 2004; Ameritech/SBC $2.6 million; and the Illinois Broadcasters Association nothing.[7]

Broadcasters' Long-Term Information Assets

A major reason industries differ in their long-term political assets is because different industries have different political economies of scope. Economies of scope refer to a situation where the marginal cost of Activity A is *less* because a firm or entity already engages in Activity B. Diseconomies of scope refer to a situation when the marginal cost of Activity A is *higher* because a firm or entity already engages in Activity B. The contribution here is to extend this concept to the political sphere and assert it is fundamental to understanding the political power of the broadcast industry.

Other reasons for differing long-term assets include luck and strong leadership. Some industries are blessed with laws and institutions that give them a comparative lobbying advantage. Sometimes these laws and institutions are a matter of luck. Other times they are the creations of far-sighted leadership. Usually there is a combination of luck and leadership.

Economies of Scope—Group Size

As a byproduct of marketplace activities, interest groups differ in their size. A staple of the interest group literature is that members of small groups tend to have significantly greater incentives to lobby than members of large groups.[8] Olson's work on the problem of collective action has inspired much of this

---

[7] http://www.ilcampaign.org.

[8] Frank R. Baumgartner and Beth L. Leech, *Basic Interests: The Importance of Groups in Politics and in Political Science* (Princeton, N.J.: Princeton University Press, 1998), Virginia Gray and David Lowery, *The Population Ecology of Interest Representation : Lobbying Communities in the American States* (Ann Arbor: The University of Michigan Press, 1996), Olson, *The Logic of Collective Action*, Schlozman and Tierney, *Organized Interests and American Democracy*, Jack L. Walker, *Mobilizing Interest Groups in America: Patrons, Professions, and Social Movements* (Ann Arbor: University of Michigan Press, 1991).

literature.[9] According to Olson's theory, there is a significant difference in the incentives of individuals to pursue individual and group interests. Individuals may belong to groups but will only pursue group interests to the extent they correspond to individual interests. The problem is that individuals cannot capture for themselves the full benefits of actions they conduct on behalf of the group. They must share the benefits with the full group. The result is that individuals have strong incentives to free ride on the group benefiting activities of others. Another consequence is that the smaller the group, the less the free riding incentives apply. This explains why producer groups tend to be much more effective in politics than consumer groups: producer groups tend to be much smaller than consumer groups and thus suffer from fewer collective action problems.

The collective action problem captures one important cost difference across interest groups. But there are many other systematic cost differences for which it provides no explanation.

Economies of Scope—Fundraising

Political activity is often viewed as a collective good because individuals have strong incentives to free ride on the efforts of others. The broadcast industry is remarkable in its ability to get third parties to pay for its lobbying activities, thus allowing its members to reap the benefits of lobbying without paying the cost.[10]

Annual Convention. The NAB receives more than half its revenue from its annual convention in Las Vegas. Ranked by *Tradeshow Week* as one of the ten largest trade shows in America,[11] the NAB convention attracts close to 100,000 paying attendees as well as hundreds of high paying exhibiters. Attendees come from all over the world and from corporate, cable, satellite, and other non-broadcaster video producers. Only a small fraction are NAB members. The primary reason broadcasters and others attend the NAB show is for reasons wholly unrelated to lobbying; they come to purchase equipment and programming and learn profit-making skills.

---

[9] Olson, *The Logic of Collective Action.*

[10] Jack Walker observed that the ability of groups to raise non-member money was a major source of variation among groups, but his typology of outside funding sources doesn't include trade shows. See Walker, *Mobilizing Interest Groups in America: Patrons, Professions, and Social Movements.*

[11] "The Ten Largest Trade Shows of 2001," *Tradeshow Week*, 5 August 2002.

In 1999, *Broadcasting & Cable* estimated the NAB convention would cost $10.1 million and bring in $33 million, netting the association $22.9 million, a 69% "profit" margin, to fund other association activities.[12] The $10.1 million figure includes a half dozen parties and events for the bJroadcasters' top grass-roots lobbyists and PAC contributors.

Among major trade associations, NAB receives one of the smallest percentages of total revenue from membership dues and assessments. The average for all trade association is 48.9%.[13] NAB's is 24.6%; The United States Telephone Association's, in contrast, is 83.7%.

The tax advantages of this type of revenue base for the NAB are considerable. Convention expenses, but not lobbying dues, are tax deductible. That is, taxes are based on sources of funds, not uses of funds. Usually there is a high correlation between sources and uses of funds. But the broadcast industry is an exception to this general rule.

One reason for the success of the NAB show compared to other video shows may be the glamour and publicity skills the NAB can bring to the show as a result of its membership. It's a rare industry trade show that can attract a U.S. president, yet the National Association of Broadcasters has done so repeatedly. And it's standard for famous news personnel to attend the NAB show and moderate high level panels.

It is hard to estimate how much of the NAB budget is allocated to lobbying. But it is clearly larger than is brought in by member dues.

One fundraising advantage the NAB received from the federal government is that during the mid-1980s its annual convention was designated an "International Trade Show" by the U.S. Department of Commerce, with the consequence that U.S. embassies promoted them worldwide at U.S. taxpayer expense. By the late 1980s, international attendance had increased 50 percent.[14] Today, the NAB annual convention attracts a worldwide audience. In 2003, an NAB affiliated group called the Advanced Television Systems Committee (ATSC) received $400,000 from the federal government to promote the U.S. digital TV standard to foreign countries.[15]

Non-Commercial Sustaining Announcements (NCSAs). At a local level, broadcast state associations, which play an active role in both national and state lobbying, receive a large fraction of their funds from NCSAs. NCSAs are a

---

[12] "Broadcasters and Bucks," *Broadcasting & Cable*, 11 January 1999.

[13] Society of Association Executives 1997, p. 52.

[14] Special mailing to NAB members, "Highlights of NAB's Service to Broadcasters: 1982–1987," October 1987.

[15] "Broadcast," *Communications Daily*, 3 March 2004. "Broadcast," *Communications Daily*, 2 April 2004.

hybrid of paid ad and public service announcement (PSA) but are generally categorized under the general heading of PSA. Local stations contribute time for NCSAs to their state broadcast association, and the state associations then pocket the revenue from the ads. None of this revenue derived from local stations is deemed a political contribution.

Only government and non-profit organizations can qualify to purchase NCSAs. Purchasers of NCSAs pay a fee to the state broadcasting association. In return, local broadcasters give them preferred airtime (in comparison to non-paying PSAs) and an accounting of when and how frequently their spots ran. In the state of Idaho, for example, the special privileges of an NCSA campaign cost $10,000 (minimum) per quarter. In Illinois, NCSA recipients receive "approximately $7 in value for every dollar in grant money." In Kentucky, NCSA recipients pay one-third the value of the airtime; in Florida, the rate is 25% of the value of the airtime. Broadcasters claim to "pay" for their public spectrum and other special privileges with these PSAs. But they also can be viewed as indirect taxpayer support of local broadcast lobbying organizations.[16] State broadcast associations bundle NCSA receipts to fight initiatives in particular states that might set harmful precedents for broadcasters in other states. In Arizona, approximately 56% ($180,000) of the $319,000 annual budget of the Arizona Broadcasters Association comes from NCSAs.[17] If this were representative across all state broadcasting associations, the total value of NCSAs would be about $10 million, less than .2% of the total value of

---

[16] NAB's spokesperson has denied including NCSAs in NAB's public service calculations submitted to Congress. But the questionnaire and supporting documents given to local stations about their public service activities made no mention that NCSAs were to be excluded, and the NAB provides no data to verify its spokesperson's claim. The term "NCSA" is an old Federal Communications Commission (FCC) logging term indicating that radio and television stations receive no revenue for the announcement. Since only non-profits can receive NCSAs and the receipts go to the state broadcast association, not the local station, it is not clear why a local station would exclude NCSAs from PSA totals unless explicitly told to do so. Moreover, state broadcasting associations highlight that NCSA receipts go to supporting public service type activities such as student scholarships, job fairs, and the emergency alert system.

[17] See memo from Art Brooks, President of the Arizona Broadcasters Association, to members of the Arizona Broadcasters Association, 30 January 2003. See also "B&C's Annual Wrap of Non-Profits," *Broadcasting & Cable*, 16 February 2004, p. 24.

PSAs broadcasters claim to provide for free every year.[18] Compared to the total claimed value for PSAs, $10 million may sound negligible, but there are very few industries with such a massive state lobbying effort.

Alternative Broadcast Inspection Program (ABIP). Another fundraising advantage the broadcasters have is that their state trade association dues are partially federally mandated. By law, the FCC must investigate local TV stations to ensure they are complying with federal laws. But instead of monitoring local TV stations directly, it may contract out the monitoring task to the state broadcasting associations. Specifically, state broadcasting associations run what is called the Alternative Broadcast Inspection Program (ABIP). Instead of paying the FCC for station inspections, stations can pay their local broadcast association. If the state broadcast association conducts the inspection, the local broadcaster receives three years of immunity from surprise FCC inspections. The local broadcaster also receives confidentiality if any problems are found. I have no information about the percentage of state broadcasting association revenues that come from this source of funds.

Taxpayer Subsidies. Along with other trade associations, the NAB receives a large taxpayer subsidy for its lobbying operations. Lobbying expenditures are not tax deductible, but the government has a very narrow definition of what constitutes a lobbying expense. Thus, the NAB only needs to report $4.7 million of its $34.8 million budget as a lobbying expense, although it is common knowledge that lobbying is NAB's primary mission.[19] The result is that NAB's corporate members can take a tax deduction for their various NAB contributions, including dues and convention activities. Any firm that combines both lobbying and non-lobbying activities may also be well-positioned to shield its lobbying activities from taxation.[20] In contrast, if an individual contributes directly to a political cause, none of the contribution is tax deductible.

---

[18] In 2002, state broadcasting association had total revenues of approximately $17 million. See Ibid. Multiplying 56% by $17 million gets approximately $10 million. For 2003, broadcasters claimed to provide $7.3 billion in PSAs. See NAB, "A National Report on Local Broadcasters' Community Service."

[19] I cannot recall reading a single profile of NAB, including in the broadcaster friendly trade press, that didn't describe lobbying as its primary activity. In dozens of conversations with former NAB insiders and others involved in the Washington telecom policy community, I never heard anyone assert otherwise.

[20] W. John Moore, "By the Numbers," *National Journal*, 30 September 2000, p. 3082.

The NAB has a trust fund with tens of millions of dollars in it. Thanks to another loophole for trade associations, this trust fund can earn income tax free, and can then be used to cover lobbying expenses.[21]

In my former hometown of Wilmette, Illinois, when the PTAs, League of Women Voters, Boy Scouts, Girl Scouts, and churches wanted to become active in the selection of school board members, they were told to stop their activities or lose their non-profit status.[22] But the NAB can keep its non-profit status and a tax-deduction on dues while aggressively lobbying members of Congress and influencing their re-election prospects.

Arguably, the trade association taxpayer subsidy,[23] which NAB has vigorously supported,[24] probably dwarfs total private and public federal campaign spending, making the public subsidy for presidential elections a pittance in comparison.[25]

Economies of Scope—Access & Relationships

With enough money, an interest group can purchase just about any access it wants. But it can nevertheless be a great boon if an interest group has a substantial cost advantage in acquiring this access. It is in the nature of the broadcasting business that local TV broadcasters have extraordinary access to movers and shakers in all walks of life. That is largely because it controls a resource that these movers and shakers seek access to on favorable terms.

---

[21] "Administration Proposes Spectrum Fee on Broadcasters," *Television Digest*, 8 February 1999.

[22] Diane Lipkin, "PTAs, League Should Join School Caucus," *Wilmette Life*, 1 April 1999, p. 15.

[23] The American Society of Association Executives has led the lobbying for the trade association tax loopholes; e.g., see "Grassroots Advocacy Emphasized at 2001 Legislative Summit of American Society of Association Executives," *Association Management*, 1 August 2001, p. 8.

[24] In January 1994, under the leadership of the American Society of Association Executives, NAB and a coalition of ten other associations filed a complaint in the U.S. District Court in Washington, D.C. challenging the constitutionality of certain provisions of the 1993 Omnibus Reconciliation Act, including those restricting the tax deductibility of interest group lobbying expenses. See *TV Today*, 10 January 1994.

[25] Ironically, the relatively small public subsidy for presidential campaigns has received much more scholarly and press attention than the much larger public subsidy for large corporate interest groups. One reason for this skewed interest may be that the presidential campaign subsidy involves a check off on every U.S. tax return. Consequently, the subsidy is obvious; all taxpayers, reporters, and scholars are reminded of it when they fill out their annual tax return.

Members of Congress and Other Politicians. Broadcasters and politicians have a symbiotic relationship.[26] Broadcasters need politicians to create appealing news and public affairs programs. Politicians need broadcasters to get on the air and get their message out. In order to get on the news, many members of Congress visit radio and TV stations more than any other type of business in their district. When they come to the station, general managers and other broadcast lobbyists have an opportunity to talk to them and build a relationship. Sometimes non-news personnel sit in on the editorial meetings where members of Congress discuss their issue agendas, including issues of communications policy. To secure such access, most other constituents would expect to be major campaign contributors or employers within the Congressional district.

Members of Congress also like attending parties and events with local broadcasters. Until honoraria were banned in 1989, broadcasters were the second largest source of honoraria for members of Congress.[27] At the annual NAB convention, as many as 40 members of Congress would regularly attend, far more than for the annual trade shows of the other major telecommunications interest groups, including the telephone and cable industries. What distinguished the broadcaster convention from other conventions was not the honoraria, but the chance to hobnob with their local broadcasters and get news coverage for their pet projects.[28] The invitation to the NAB show asks

---

[26] Cook, *Governing with the News: The News Media as a Political Institution,* Cook, *Making Laws and Making News.*

[27] Carol Matlack, "Getting Around the Rules," *National Journal,* 12 May 1990, p. 1138.

[28] In recent years, the number of members of Congress attending the NAB convention has dropped precipitously. In 1998, only four attended at NAB's invitation: Sen. McCain (Chair, Senate Commerce Committee), Sen. Burns (Chair, Senate Communications Subcommittee), Rep. Crapo (House Commerce Committee), and Rep. Bilrikis (House Commerce Committee). A fifth, Sen. Lieberman, also attended, but was not invited to official events such as the Congressional Breakfast. NAB's current philosophy is quality over quantity. According to Steven Stockmeyer, former NAB VP of government affairs, the purpose of having so many members of Congress at the NAB convention was not to lobby them but to impress NAB members. NAB members no longer need to be impressed. Moreover, other forums, including monthly Washington breakfasts, the annual NAB state leadership conference, the annual NAB radio convention, dinner parties at the home of NAB President Edward Fritts, public awards dinners (perhaps the most popular lobbying venue today), and the semi-annual NAB board meetings (held at splendid resorts while Congress is in recess), are more convenient and often less controversial places for members of Congress to hobnob with broadcasters.

members of Congress to fill out a card with the "names of broadcasters you would like to see while in Las Vegas."[29] Detailed briefing information notes: "Where possible, we try to coordinate dinner parties with your local broadcasters."[30] The NAB convention has also attracted every President or Vice President of the United States since Eisenhower.[31]

Top Congressional aides report that the broadcasters' annual grassroots blitz on Capitol Hill is the best received of all the telecom industry groups. During this blitz, more than 250 local broadcasters from every state in the country visit all 535 Congressional offices.

The annual parties state broadcast delegations hold in the U.S. Capital are also well attended. It is reported that Senator William Proxmire never attended receptions, with the exception of the annual Washington D.C. party of the Wisconsin Broadcasters Association.[32] Their purely social party, held a day or two before their blitz on Capitol Hill, regularly attracted a majority of the Wisconsin Congressional delegation. It even attracted former members of Congress who have been retired for many years.[33]

Most members of Congress are on a first-name basis with key local broadcasters. Members of the key judiciary and commerce subcommittees often also have close friendships with local broadcasters. Some of these relationships began early in the politician's career when he was a school board member, city

---

[29] E.g., Invitation from Sharon Goldener, NAB broadcast liaison, to Representative Swift, February 16, 1984.

[30] Memo from NAB Government Relations to all members of Congress participating at the NAB Show, March 1987. The March 1987 NAB Show had 41 members of Congress in attendance.

[31] During the Clinton Administration, only Vice President Gore attended the NAB convention. But President Clinton did speak via satellite before the annual meeting of CBS affiliates, an event that caused a stir in the press when the President predicted the new Dan Rather and Connie Chung CBS News team "will be great together" and Dan Rather replied "If we could be one-hundredth as great as you and Hillary Rodham Clinton have been in the White House, we'd take it right now and walk away winners." That was a remarkable comment coming out of a TV news anchor. See Howard Rosenberg, "The Restoration of Dan Rather," *Broadcasting & Cable*, 4 October 2004, p. 34. Scott Williams, "CBS' Dan Rather Teams with Connie Chung for 'CBS Evening News,'" *Associated Press*, 1 June 1993.

[32] Interview with former representative and chair of the House intellectual property subcommittee, Robert Kastenmeier, on 24 December 1998. One reason may be that the executive director of the Wisconsin Broadcasters Association also orchestrated Congressional debates during campaign season. See Eliza Carney, "Tuning Out Fee TV," *National Journal*, 12 April 1997.

[33] Ibid.

councilor, state representative, mayor, or governor. The relationship was culti-vated as the politician gradually moved up the ranks to Congress. Some of the broadcast lobbyists may even have moved up the ranks with the member of Congress—starting as a political reporter, moving into news management, and then into other management positions.

Rep. Sonny Callahan's (R-Alabama) tribute in the Congressional *Record* to D.H. "Buck" Long nicely captures the special relationship between broadcaster and member of Congress:

> Mr. Speaker, on June 1, 1998, D.H. "Buck" Long will retire from his long-time service as President and General Manager of WKRG-TV, Inc., the CBS affiliate in my hometown of Mobile, Alabama.
>
> For over 30 years, Buck has...set an example for his peers and employees alike by giving much back to his community.... Buck has also believed the public deserves to be kept informed with a top-notch news department and public affairs division that is second to none. Along these lines, I would be remiss if I didn't mention one such program, The Gulf Coast Congressional Report, which has been a mainstay on WKRG for more than 20 years. In fact, with Buck's strong support, several of my colleagues and I, most notably former Congressman Earl Hutto and the Senate Majority Leader, Trent Lott, have been able to appear on WKRG on a regular basis keeping the viewing audience in Northwest Florida, Southwest Alabama and the Mississippi Gulf Coast informed on the latest news coming out of Washington.... Not long ago, the Alabama Broadcasting Association named Buck Alabama Broadcaster of the year....
>
> Mr. Speaker, Buck Long is a good friend but more than that, he is a good citizen.[34]

Another perk that broadcasters use to build relationships with politicians is the public service announcement. For example, every two years spouses and children of members of Congress (disproportionately from rural areas) tape at least one PSA for a cause of their choice, which is then broadcast throughout their Congressional district. In 1997, 104 spouses and children participated. A hallmark of all PSAs is that they are on non-controversial subjects (e.g., "don't drink while driving"). They involve no political cost and always are designed to make the politician or his relative look good.

---

[34] 105th Congress, 2nd session, *Congressional Record—Extensions*, 20 May 1998, 144(65), p. E918.

Broadcasters' ready access to politicians is not limited to members of Congress. It also includes governors, mayor, state legislator, and local legislators. But the underlying logic facilitating relationship building is similar. Of particular note in recent years has been broadcasters' relationship with big city mayors. Mayors control cable TV franchise renewal agreements, so can exercise great leverage over cable companies in broadcasters' negotiations for more favorable retransmission consent and preferred channel positioning.[35]

Opinion Leaders. As part of their normal business operations, broadcasters develop close ties with opinion makers in the communities in which they reside. According to NAB's report on community service, executives at 81% of local TV stations "consult with local community leaders in deciding the issues and causes for community service programming."[36] The report continues: "In fact, most stations have become institutions upon which countless other beneficial organizations literally depend for their livelihoods and their ability to function effectively."[37] The slogan of the broadcasters' theme song at its annual convention, played just before NAB President Edward Fritts' keynote address, is "friends in local places." In the early 1980s, Fritts rose to the position of NAB president on the strength of his pledge to strengthen broadcasters at the grassroots.

One executive director of a state broadcaster association put it this way: "Broadcasters live or die based on their relations with the local community. The most important thing we do is maintain a close liaison with the local community. If there is not a good relation with your community, you won't get any advertising dollars." Accordingly, broadcasters tend to be active participants in local Chambers of Commerce and Rotary Clubs—places where relationships with potential advertisers can be cultivated. The members of these clubs also tend to be community leaders. Politicians often seek invitations to these clubs, partly because they are good places to meet potential contributors.

Broadcast employees are extraordinarily involved in charitable organizations. Among the service clubs NAB cites are Kiwanis, Jaycees, Elks, Lions, Optimists, Big Brothers/Big Sisters, American Legion, Knights of Columbus, Masons, Boys/Girls Clubs, Junior Achievement, and 4H.[38] NAB claims the following example is typical: "One television station in Rochester, Minnesota,

---

[35] E.g., Bill Carter, "Reprieve for Houston TV Station," *New York Times*, 3 March 2000, p. C18.

[36] NAB, "A National Report on Local Broadcasters' Community Service," (Washington, DC: NAB, 1998), p. 8.

[37] Ibid., p. 11.

[38] Ibid., p. 9.

polled its 51 employees and found they had commitments to 138 charitable organizations. General Manager Jerry Watson of KTTC-TV explained: 'It's just the mindset of the broadcaster to serve the community and to be involved.'"[39]

Broadcasters also serve on the boards of many prominent community organizations. One reason may be that part of a broadcaster's job is to get out into the community and learn about it. The broadcaster learns not just about the non-profit organization but develops a relationship with what are likely to be prominent community figures. Another reason for board membership may be that broadcasters are in high demand to serve on boards. They bring prestige to a board, valuable community contacts (including with the press), and expertise in the publicity business. Moreover, broadcasters can usually get on prestigious boards at a significant discount. A board seat at an arts organization like New York's Whitney Museum that might cost a business person $100,000 may well be given for free to someone in the media.[40]

On the other hand, local broadcasters rarely serve on the boards of for-profit companies, perhaps because it might create the appearance of a conflict of interest.

Large urban media markets such as New York City, Los Angeles, and Chicago, each with dozens of members of Congress within its TV station boundaries, are in a different situation. They provide less incentive for each local broadcaster to cultivate relationships with both members of Congress and the community leaders that influence them in those areas. NAB indirectly acknowledges its weakness in large markets when it observes in its community service report: "Particularly in smaller markets, local TV and radio stations serve as indispensable organs of communication and organization."[41]

Press Secretaries. It does not show up in any disclosure form, but one of the most unusual assets broadcast lobbyists have is their special relationship with Congressional press secretaries, one of the most important positions in a Congressional office.[42] Press secretaries are often the public mouthpieces for members of Congress, operating as their spokespeople and writing speeches, floor comments, and op-eds for them.

---

[39] Idid., p. 11.

[40] Lisa Gubernick, "Buying Your Way On To A Board," *Wall Street Journal*, 7 May 1999, p. W4.

[41] James L. Baughman, *Television's Guardians: The FCC and the Politics of Programming, 1958–1967* (Knoxville: University of Tennessee Press, 1985), p. 74, NAB, "A National Report on Local Broadcasters' Community Service," p. 11.

[42] Cook, *Making Laws and Making News.*

Press secretaries are often former local reporters, sometimes from the hometown broadcaster. Some press secretaries will go back to reporting after their Congressional stint.[43] A major part of their job is to get favorable coverage on media.[44] They also write member speeches, floor statements, press releases, and op-eds that may touch on issues of communications policy. When other telecom lobbyists visit a Congressional office, they will usually meet with only the telecom aide and possibly the member of Congress. When grassroots broadcasters lobby, the press aide will often also be present. Sometimes the press aide even handles broadcaster issues.

During the mid-1990s, the NAB had extraordinary access to Congressional press secretaries and was arguably the chief sponsor, albeit very discreetly, of the Senate Press Secretaries Association. Mike Waring, an NAB senior Vice President during the spectrum giveaway to broadcasters, was a former Congressional press secretary and had as one of his chief responsibilities until he left the NAB the cultivation of the press secretaries. As an alumnus of the Senate Press Secretaries Association, he was allowed to attend their monthly social get together. According to several Senate press secretaries, he was a well-beloved member of the association. The premier social event of the press secretaries association was an annual train trip to New York City orchestrated by the NAB. The press secretaries traveled together to New York City and then met top reporters such as Tom Brokaw, Dan Rather, and Peter Jennings to learn how to get on the air.

The NAB also sponsors other how-to and social events for the press secretaries, including a post-election speech by a prominent political commentator. The get-together offers an opportunity for NAB lobbyists to mingle with the press secretaries. Other regular contacts between the press secretaries and the NAB include arranging PSAs for Congressional spouses and children and reviewing Congressional profiles for the broadcasters' grassroots publication, *Congressional Contact*. The press secretary for the chair of the House Judiciary Committee considered Mike Waring to be a close personal friend and talked to

---

[43] Jack Barry's career may be illustrative. He started as a radio show host in 1948, later served as press secretary to Senator Leahy (D-VT), then returned to anchor a local public affairs TV program. In retirement he ran for Vermont state senate and won. Upon his death, both Senators Jefford (R-VT) and Leahy (D-VT) included tributes to him in the *Congressional Record*. See 105th Congress, 2nd Session, *Congressional Record*. 9 May 1997, 143(57, 60), p. S 4269. See also an earlier tribute to him as a public affairs commenter: 99th Congress, 1st Session, *Congressional Record*, 1 August 1985, 131(106), p. S10768.

[44] E.g., see Congressional ads for press secretaries in the help wanted pages of *The Hill* and *Roll Call*.

him frequently. The judiciary committee is responsible for copyright law, a primary area of broadcaster lobbying. According to one former NAB official, the value of press secretaries is not that they can help the broadcasters much, but they can do a lot of harm. Having a relationship with a press secretary makes that person think twice about saying something negative about a position advocated by broadcasters. Some Congressional press secretaries will give their bosses statements that are virtually identical to NAB lobbying talking points. NAB loves the type of credibility this can bring its cause.

Broadcast reporters. Needless to say, the broadcast managers who control the news have daily access to their news directors, high profile news staff, and any other reporter they might choose. Moreover, those news staff are dependent on managers for their income, news assignments, quality of work life, and job recommendations. No other lobbyists have the same quality and quantity of access to broadcast reporters as do the local broadcast managers who orchestrate the grassroots lobbying on behalf of the broadcast industry.

Non-Broadcast Mass Media. Broadcasters tend to develop relationships with other local media, most notably local newspaper personnel, at press clubs, elite community organizations (e.g., Rotary), journalism schools, news events, and joint task forces (e.g., a permanent "Open Government Task Force" on open meeting and public record legislation). Sometimes there is a symbiotic relationship between the local newspaper and the local broadcaster, even when they are owned by different companies. In many communities, TV stations invite local newspaper reporters to serve as commentators on public affairs and news shows, sometimes on a regular basis. Of the top 15 daily newspapers in the United States, 12 are owned by companies that also own local TV stations. Of the top 100 daily newspapers in the United States, 51 are owned by companies that also own local TV stations.[45] When the TV and newspaper staffs are both located in the same city, as in top ten markets Chicago, San Francisco, and Dallas, there is likely to be "synergy" between the two staffs. They will co-produce websites, share building space, perhaps even share floor space in the newsroom. For example, in Chicago, the *Chicago Tribune* newspaper has a TV studio for its 24 hour TV news channel in the *center* of its newsroom. These relationships might make it easier for a broadcaster to get favorable news, such as an op-ed, placed in a local newspaper. During the early

---

[45] See Appendix B. List of top 100 newspapers and TV ownership interests derived from the 2003 edition of *Editor & Publisher Yearbook*. TV ownership interests supplemented with data from SEC filings. Some daily newspapers managed as part of holding companies may be excluded from this list because owners have no legal obligation to disclose ownership links between separate corporations.

1996 fight over new spectrum rights for broadcasters, at least a dozen general managers wrote op-eds in local newspapers favoring the broadcasters' position. The op-eds were then clipped and used in the lobbying campaign on Capitol Hill.

Broadcast Academics. Broadcasting is one of the most glamorous and sought after professions in America. Partly as a result, it occupies a disproportionate space in the local university. Only a minority of American industries have closely affiliated academic departments. There are probably more shoe sales people in America than local TV broadcasters. Yet universities don't have departments devoted to shoe salesmanship—or even retail sales in general.

Of course, there are many trade oriented academic fields such as law, medicine, and business that retain close relationships with the subjects of their study. Still, the relationship between the NAB and the Broadcast Educators Association (BEA) is noteworthy. The BEA is the primary professional association of broadcast scholars and also publishes the leading academic journal in the field. The BEA has its headquarters in the NAB headquarters building, receives free office space, and receives an approximately $30,000/year subsidy for the salary of its executive director. The BEA holds its annual trade association meeting at the same location as the NAB, provides academic research awards funded by the NAB, and strives to place the best students of its members in NAB-affiliated companies. NAB representatives, given a position of great honor at BEA, also attend other broadcast related academic conferences where they can scout for supportive voices and do other useful broadcast industry reconnaissance. On top of a research award, an NAB funded BEA scholar can receive free lodging and transportation to the annual BEA conference in Las Vegas. If the NAB finds the paper useful, it may even distribute it to decision makers at the FCC and on Capitol Hill. Most of the papers, however, are held in reserve in case a situation arises where one of them might be politically useful.

Vendors. In Washington, DC, vendors often lobby on behalf of the industries they supply. But in TV production, there is a special relationship between broadcasters and their vendors. One reason is that commercial TV broadcasting is on the most glamorous side of the video production business—far more glamorous than advertising or other corporate video work. It's so prestigious that the largest and wealthiest broadcast companies like ABC, CBS, NBC, and Fox often get a special manufacturers' discount in part because they are prized clients that can be touted to other video purchasers.

One powerful lever the NAB has to control vendors is the annual NAB Show, the major annual trade show of the worldwide video production community. As a point of contrast, Comdex, until recently the major computer industry trade show, was owned by a private company unaffiliated with a trade association.

The NAB Show is so dominant that many vendors wait until the show to introduce their products. What may be most remarkable is that only a small fraction of the approximately 100,000 attendees are NAB members, so the NAB's leverage extends far beyond the relatively narrow buying power of its own members. Although exhibit space is presumably sold on a first-come, first-served basis, the conference speaking slots are controlled by NAB. The NAB determines who speaks and gets dubbed as an industry leader providing cutting edge and high quality products. Like free news coverage on TV, vendors view these slots as extremely valuable publicity opportunities. Not surprisingly, they are not inclined to bite the hand that feeds them. And some, like Harris Corporation (the leading producer of broadcast digital TV transmitters), produce "third party" surveys and other materials that the NAB can use in its lobbying. A rational vendor would presumably think twice about providing any testimony to the FCC, Congress, or the press that would contradict NAB's official lobbying line and technical statements.

Fungible Relationships. Relationships developed with opinion leaders and other high status individuals as a routine part of operating a broadcast business can then become a universal currency that can be employed to cultivate other relationships and exercise political influence. For example, broadcasters can use their relationships with state press clubs, charities, and business groups to arrange desired speaking engagements for members of Congress. And they can use their relationships with governors, mayors, business leaders, and other prominent individuals to facilitate face-to-face meetings and fundraising opportunities for members of Congress.

Economies of Scope—In-House Lobbying Talent

Broadcast lobbyists are also unusually skilled and interested in politics. In a metropolitan area there may be far more McDonalds franchisee operators than broadcast general managers, but the broadcaster is likely to be the far more accomplished lobbyist. One reason for this skill discrepancy may be that many people drawn to broadcasting are interested in politics. Many stations have at least one employee who enjoys being around politicians and being a political player. Another reason for the skill discrepancy may be that interacting with politicians and studying politics is part of the business of a local broadcaster. Some station groups include grassroots political activity as part of the job evaluation of the general manager. A testament to the affinity between broadcasters and politicians is that, on a proportionate basis since 1980, more former local broadcasters may have become members of Congress than any other profession, including lawyer.[46] For example, when the Telecom Act of 96 was passed, there were three members of the U.S. Senate that claimed to be former local broadcasters: Senators Conrad Burns (R-MT), Kay Bailey Hutchison (R-TX), and Rod Grams (R-MN).[47] In addition, the wife of Senator Russell Feinstein (D-WI) was the former executive vice president of the Wisconsin Broadcasters Association. The Stennis Center for Public Service starts off its biography of Representative Al Swift, who started his career as a local broadcast producer and news director before moving on to a 16 year career in Congress: "Al Swift has divided his career almost equally between broadcasting and Congress—finding in the two jobs more similarities than differences." It then goes on to quote Swift that working as a member of Congress as opposed to a broadcaster "you need exactly the same qualities, except that you have to know how to produce solutions instead of programs."[48]

Economies of Scope—Glamour

Broadcasters control fame and thus are surrounded by famous people. This makes broadcasters glamorous themselves and gives them a set of celebrity connections that may be useful in lobbying. Nobody exploits such celebrity

---

[46] Obviously, there are many more lawyers in Congress. But the pool of potential lawyers is also much larger. One president, Ronald Reagan, "The Great Communicator," also started out as a local broadcaster. He worked as an announcer at WOC-AM and WHO-AM before starting his better known career in movies and TV. Vice President Gore also started out as a reporter—but for the *Nashville Tennessean*, a newspaper. Italy's Prime Minister, Silvio Berlusconi, owns Mediaset, the country's main broadcasting group, with reportedly about half of Italy's TV audience. See Paschal Mooney, "Monopolisation of the *Electronic Media* and Possible Abuse of Power in Italy," *Council of Europe*, 3 June 2004.

[47] In addition, in the period leading up to passage of the Telecom Act there were at least seven members of the House of Representative who were former broadcast journalists: Kweisa Mfume (MD, 1987–1996), Susan Molinari (NY, 1990–1997), Willie Hefner (NC, 1979–1995), Robert Dornan (CA, 1977–1983 and 1985–1997), Al Swift (WA, 1979–1995), Scott Klug (R-WI, 1991–1999), Ron Klink (D-PA, 1993–2001). In addition, Jay Johnson (D-WI), a TV anchorman, was elected in 1996. At least two former TV anchorman, Mike Schneider (D-NJ) and Mark Baker (R-IL), ran for Congress in 1996 and made it to the general election as major party candidates. TV anchor Mike James (D-WA) ran for U.S. Senate in 1994, and then, after being defeated, returned as news anchor to KIRO-TV.

[48] See biography of Al Swift at http://www.stennis.gov/Congressional%20Bios/alswift.htm,

connections better than the Motion Pictures Association of America (MPAA)), which represents Hollywood. A majority of MPAA's members, including all four of the major TV networks, also own local TV stations. The MPAA has a movie studio in Washington DC that shows premiers of movies and often has top Hollywood celebrities on hand. Once a month about 15–20 Congressional aides from the judiciary and commerce committees go to a primarily dinner/social event at the MPAA that includes a first-run movie. Perhaps the premier annual social get together for members of the judiciary and commerce committees is also held at the MPAA. This is how *Forbes* describes the value of MPAA's glamour power.

> Say you're running for Senator. Whom do you want standing next to you in the TV shot? A colorless captain of industry or Clint Eastwood? Therein lies much of the power of Jack Valenti, the veteran president of the Motion Pictures Association of America (MPAA). Get one of his celebrities to your money-raiser and you're guaranteed a turnout.
>
> Valenti has a $60 million budget, but his almost limitless supply of celebrity power for photo ops and endorsements is priceless.[49]

The NAB, like many other wealthy trade associations, reserves box seats at Jack Kent Cooke Stadium and the MCI Center for major sports events.[50] Unlike other associations, however, the broadcasters have special relationships with team owners and sports celebrities. Broadcasters, who buy TV and radio rights, are often a team's largest customer. Indeed, the relationship between sports and broadcasting is so close that many local professional teams are owned by companies that own local broadcast stations. A vivid example of the use of such contacts occurred at the 1996 Democratic National Convention. The Tribune Company owns newspapers and local TV stations as well as the Chicago White Sox. It invited all delegates to the convention to an on-field batting practice with team members. Tribune's lobbyists also invite top politicians like House Commerce Committee Chair Billy Tauzin to sit in the announcer's

---

[49] Dyan Machan, "Mr. Valenti Goes To Washington," *Forbes*, 1 December 1997, p. 66.

[50] There is no public record of these tickets because of a ruling of the Congressional ethics committees that box seats can be valued at $48, even though the actual ticket prices are much higher. The lobbyist disclosure law requires gifts above $50 to be disclosed. See Dayn Perry, "Insider Baseball," *Washington Monthly*, December 2001, p. 10. John Solomon, "Whose Game Is It, Anyway," *Washington Monthly*, December 1999, p. 31.

box—and chat off-air with famous announcers like Harry Caray—during Cubs games.[51]

Washington parties sponsored by the TV networks are among the most popular with lawmakers and offer an opportunity for lawmakers and broadcaster lobbyists to mingle. The televised CBS Kennedy Center Honors, held every December, is one of the most popular. The program honors a half dozen leading performers in the arts. The President, Vice-President, and dozens of members of Congress are usually in attendance. Before the event is a cocktail party and afterward is a big dinner where stars from the television show mingle with the guests. The broadcasters' top lobbyists, some of them former members of Congress or senior aides, mingle in the crowd. Anyone who buys a ticket, including cable and telephone companies, can also attend the show and associated events. One senior commerce committee aide described the event this way: "This is a great ticket. It's a great event. The President is there and the vice president. The commerce committee is all invited and the FCC commissioners. Everybody shows up in a tux and it's really great. CBS has the keys—the tickets—that they distribute to various folks."

NBC has a similar Christmas in Washington show. Before the show it hosts a reception where politicians and broadcast lobbyists mingle. NBC's annual affiliates meeting, where it plots out political strategy for the coming year, is held in *Saturday Night Live's* studio.[52]

The networks may also host a televised inaugural gala. The 1996 CBS Inaugural gala was not unique, but the fact that it was televised may give it a special cachet.[53] At the 1992 Republican National Convention, Hearst Corporation (owner of a large TV broadcasting group and the local newspaper, the Houston Chronicle), Capital Cities/ABC, Inc. (owner of local TV station KTRK-TV), and NAB hosted parties. The NAB party, called "The Best Little Party in Texas," was hosted by Representative Bob Michel. All three parties were by invitation only and could be expected to exploit media connections to draw the politicians and provide "quality time" for the media lobbyists to mingle with the politicians they sought to influence.[54]

---

[51] Chris McConnell and Paige Albiniak, "Take me out to the ballgame," *Broadcasting & Cable*, 24 August 1998, p. 20.

[52] Michele Greppi, "NBC, Affiliates Focus on Digital Must-Carry Rules," *TelevisionWeek*, 21 April 2003, p. 3.

[53] For background on the political utility of inaugural events, see Leslie Wayne, "Companies Raise $35 Million for Inauguration," *New York Times*, 18 January 2001, p. A1.

[54] "Party Time, Texas Style," *Roll Call*, 17 August 1992.

Washington broadcaster lobbyists also invite select FCC commissioners and members of Congress to the Emmys. Anyone can attend the Emmys who can afford a ticket, but presumably it is something special to attend under the auspices of the event sponsors. As one Congressional aide described the event: "You're utilizing your access to many different things. Your access to TV, movie stars. It's an opportunity to mingle with the stars. As a lobbying device, it's quite extraordinary."

The invitation only White House Correspondents Dinner—featuring the U.S. President, Hollywood stars, and the Congressional leadership—is not exclusively controlled by broadcasters. But it is another place where senior politicians, journalists, and broadcast lobbyists mingle. The journalists draw the politicians. And the politicians draw the broadcast lobbyists. More than 90% of those in attendance are invited guests of reporters and their parent companies.[55] In 1998, for example, News Corporation reserved a table with Rupert Murdoch (News Corporation CEO), Peggy Binzel (New Corporation chief Washington lobbyist), Billy Tauzin (House Commerce Committee Chair), Billy Tauzin's wife (Cecile), and News Corporation White House correspondents (from Fox News).[56]

At the Radio and TV Correspondents Dinner in 1996, the President, First Lady, and Speaker of the House were all in attendance, as well as famous TV journalists such as Dan Rather, Barbara Walters, and Walter Cronkite. Surrounded by broadcast journalists, NAB chief lobbyist Jim May and Senator McCain, soon-to-be-chair of the Senate Commerce Committee, bantered about spectrum policy.[57]

Another popular event for politicians, broadcast reporters, and broadcast lobbyists to mingle is NAB's annual Service to America symposium. In 2004, NBC News White House correspondent David Gregory gave the keynote

---

[55] "Keeping Dinner Down: The White House Correspondents' Association tries to thake Its bad image," *Brill's Content*, May 1999, p. 28.

[56] Silverstein, "His Biggest Takeover Ever." See also Kim Masters, "Murdoch to Launch Magazine for Conservatives," *Washington Post*, 1 May 1995, p. D1.

[57] Mundy, "What Spectrum Issue?." The 2002 guest list, reported in *National Journal's* Daybook on 21 March 2002, includes a who's who of Washington DC's movers and shakers from the President and his wife down to the complete House and Senate leadership and down from there to the chairs of the committees with jurisdiction over broadcast issues. Only lobbyists invited by the news media—presumably excluding non-media lobbyists—can be invited to this event. For a description of the difficulty getting tickets to this and other reporter-politician-lobbyist parties, see Alicia C. Shepard, 'Schmoozing with the Stars," *American Journalism Review*, July/August, 1996.

luncheon address, and Deborah Norville of MSNBC was master of ceremonies for the awards dinner in the evening. Last year, when First Lady Laura Bush was given the humanitarian award, Bob Schieffer of CBS News was the emcee. The year before that, when New York Mayor Rudolph Guiliani was given the humanitarian award, Cokie Roberts of ABC News was the emcee.[58]

Glamour may also play on FCC staffers. Attending a broadcast TV event is not only likely to be more glamorous than attending a satellite TV event; it might also help to open a more glamorous post-FCC future career. The young FCC staffers who do the technical analyses and write the FCC rules rarely see the FCC as more than a stepping stone to a future career. All other things being equal, given a choice between alienating a non-glamorous potential employer and a glamorous one, the temptation will be to sacrifice the less glamorous one.

Broadcasters themselves have become part of the celebrity culture, so much so that when politicians host dinners for other politicians they now feature both famous news reporters and their bosses. For example, when President Clinton feted British Prime Minister Tony Blair, more than a dozen top TV news anchors and their bosses were invited, including Peter Jennings, ABC news anchor, and Jack Welch, CEO of GE (parent of NBC).[59] CBS TV President Leslie Moonves was a repeat golf partner of President Clinton.[60]

Economies of Scope—Opposition Research

TV stations are bombarded with damaging information about candidates, especially as the end of a campaign nears. As the *New York Times* notes, "Every campaign has people who work behind the scenes, feeding unflattering facts about opponents to the news media."[61] I noticed this myself when I ran for the House of Delegates in Maryland. The candidates were all sweetness and light in public—no one wanted to be perceived as running a negative campaign— but behind the scenes there was a great effort to badmouth opponents to reporters. And with rare exception, the comments were made off-the-record, often by surrogates.

---

[58] Layton, "Lobbying Juggernaut." This article describes how state broadcasting associations also hold awards events where members of Congress are given awards, journalists emcee the events, and broadcast station executives mingle with the politicians.

[59] "Prime Ticket," *Broadcasting & Cable*, 9 February 1998, p. 16.

[60] Kyle Pope, "CBS Shelves Fall Mob Series As Too Violent," *Wall Street Journal*, 20 May 1999, p. B1.

[61] Sheryl Gay Stolberg, "All's Fair? Clark Rivals Irked by an Aide's Tactics," *New York Times*, 16 January 2004, p. A1.

This information can be very valuable. Often candidates have spent tens of thousands of dollars or countless hours collecting the information. And they give it to the local media, usually on an exclusive basis (because they don't want to be identified as the source of the information), for completely free.

In my experience with local reporters, the biggest problem is shear laziness. They are overwhelmed with candidates—often hundreds even in small media markets. And their editors give them very little space to run articles, thus diminishing their incentive to do work. The result is they are heavily influenced by campaigns who cleverly give them easily digestible "free" information, either off-the-record or by surrogates. This "private campaign" can sometimes be more important than the "public campaign."

Local TV stations are also in an excellent position to pass on opposition research to favored candidates. In Fall 2000, U.S. Representative Frank Pallone faced a challenger with independent backing from an entity called Americans for Job Security (AJS) that was beginning to take out a lot of TV ads. As an independent entity, none of the funding for AJS needed to be disclosed. In an article in *Campaigns & Elections*, Timothy Yehl, a Pallone campaign aide, describes the opposition research problem the campaign faced:

> You didn't know how much money they had on hand, you didn't know how much they had raised, you didn't know what they had spent it on. It was difficult to trace their media buys, to trace where they were going, because they're not regulated. That's the heart of the problem, there's not disclosure.[62]

Brad Lawrence, the Pallone campaign's media consultant, then describes how to address this type of opposition research problem: "You try to find out from the station who is contacting them, what agencies, under what entity...."[63]

Indicative of the potential political power of the media, private detectives hired to do opposition research not only frequently pretend to be reporters but actually are former reporters and use their media contacts to get their dirt aired. Reports the *New York Times*:

> Feeding an almost insatiable demand for negative information in today's world of bruising politics, private investigators are playing a larger—though mostly hidden—role in the public arena.... Today's

---

[62] Philip D. Duncan, "Incumbent in the Crosshairs," Campaigns & Elections, December/January 2000, p. 31.
[63] Ibid.

breed of investigators includes...ex-journalists who can tap old news contacts to get negative information published. Operating with little regulation or accountability, the detectives spy on opponents by posing as reporters...."[64]

The article then goes on:

No incident better demonstrates the power of private investigators than the runoff for Houston mayor in 1991 between Bob Lanier, a millionaire businessman, and Sylvester Turner, a Harvard-educated lawyer and State Representative.

Six days before the vote, Houston's ABC affiliate broadcast a report questioning whether Mr. Turner had a role in an insurance scam in which a former law client had faked drowning....

Mr. Turner blamed the report on Mr. Lanier, an accusation that the campaign and the TV station denied. Mr. Turner never recovered and lost by an eight-point margin.

Mr. Turner later sued the station and its investigative reporter for libel, and in trail in 1996 the link between the Lanier campaign and the broadcast was finally discovered.... The jury found that the broadcast was false and that the station had shown a reckless disregard for the truth...."

The key point is that if a local station does want to favor one candidate over another, it will often have plenty of inexpensively gathered exclusive information, combined with equally inexpensive surrogates—to make its case without substantial economic cost or risk to itself.

Economies of Scope—Public Non-Involvement

For a variety of reasons involving the nature of broadcast issues, it has been remarkably easy for the broadcast industry to render the public politically irrelevant on its key pocketbook issues involving rights to spectrum and intellectural property.

Technical Issues. A cost advantage the broadcasters have is that many of their telecommunications and copyright issues are technical and difficult for

---

[64] Douglas Frantz, "Plenty of Dirty Jobs in Politics And a New Breed of Diggers," *New York Times*, 6 July 1999, p. A1.

the public and reporters to understand. Nor do members of the public and reporters see great benefit to themselves in mastering the vital technical details of these issues. The result is that broadcasters have been able to easily mask an issue of great public policy importance (e.g., the future of wireless communication in the information age) as an obscure technical debate (e.g., about the validity of a complex mathematical equation used to gauge the interference created if a new service uses the "white space" in the broadcast band).

MSTV, an organization ostensibly devoted to providing technical information on broadcasting issues, is a master at such subterfuge. Many of its FCC filings involve issues of great economic and public policy consequence. But since they are often framed in engineering terms, the public is effectively disenfranchised from the debate and may have little or no idea what is at stake.

Non-Partisan Issues. Unlike issues such as abortion and gun control, broadcasters' major pocketbook issues remain non-partisan. This is a problem because the party system has long been seen as a way to inform the public and give them a meaningful role in the political system. As we have previously seen, in conditions of low visibility lobbying, special interest groups have an advantage.

Democratic and Republican leaders sometimes see no advantage in turning an issue into a partisan issue. An example is the Savings & Loan Scandal that cost Americans hundreds of billions of dollars.[65] Both parties were involed in passing the legislation that helped to bring the Scandal about. The result was that bringing it to public attention via the party system would have hurt incumbents of both parties.

Similarly, the cozy relationship between local broadcasters and incumbent members of Congress gives members of Congress no incentive to call the public's attention to broadcast industry pocketbook issues via the party system.

The major exceptions to this rule, such as children's programming requirements, the Fairness Doctrine, and violence on TV, tend to be of relatively minor financial consequence to the broadcast industry and of either great public salience (violence and children's programming on TV) or great political salience (the Fairness Doctrine).[66]

Economies of Scope—Legal

Among the professions, the media may be unique in having a Constitutional amendment addressed to their industry. The First Amendment includes the

---

[65] E. E. Schattschneider, *Party Government* (Westport, Conn.: Greenwood Press, 1977).

[66] Many Democrats took the Fairness Doctrine extremely seriously. They were worried that its abolition might give the Republicans a political advantage.

text: "Congress shall make no law...abridging the freedom of speech, or of the press...." What this means in practice is that the media—unlike doctors, lawyers, accountants, stock brokers, real estate agents, and hundreds of other occupations that deal in information—are immune from conventional legal obligations to make them accountable for their actions. Their accountability must come through the marketplace.

Of course, First Amendment immunity is shared not only by broadcasters but also all media. But insofar as broadcasters control the most powerful medium for local public affairs information—especially in the eyes of members of Congress—they may be able to use their press immunity to greater effect.

The broadcast industry's legal advantages may be attributed to a variety of factors, including luck, smart lobbying, and the political resources that come from being in the broadcasting business. Regardless of the source of the laws, it's clear that the laws put at least some of the broadcasters' lobbying competitors at a disadvantage. The number of laws and government institutional norms that treat members of the media more favorably than other members of the public is quite remarkable. Here are some examples.

First Amendment. The public, politicians, and the courts are extremely wary of any proposal that in any way might restrict the free speech of the press, including broadcasters. It is now common to write laws forcing politicians to make decisions in public, keep good public records, abstain from voting on issues where they have a conflict-of-interest, and disclose their personal financial interests and activities. Similarly, disclosure and conflict of interest laws apply to the more than 800 licensed occupations in the United States, including accountants, lawyers, and investment advisors. Yet attempts to write similar ethics, conflicts-of-interest, and disclosure laws for broadcasters would invite howls of protests on First Amendment grounds.

Campaign Finance. There is an adage in politics that a dollar given to a candidate in secret is worth a lot more than if given in public.[67] This is because no candidate wants to be accused of taking money from a special interest if and

---

[67] This was a guiding inspiration of Larry Makinson, former Executive Director of the Center of Responsive politics, who devoted his career to reducing the advantage that comes from secret lobbying. See http://www.opensecrets.org. Many articles describe the value campaign contributors place on secrecy and the numerous ways campaign contributions can be given in a way to obscure the identity of their source. Examples include: Don Van Natta Jr. and John M. Broder, "The Few, the Rich, the Rewarded Donate the Bulk of G.O.P. Gifts," *New York Times*, 2 August 2 2000, p. A1. Gregg Hitt, "Battle for the House Has Big Bucks Fueling Grass-Roots Tactics: Secretive GOP Group Hides Donors Inside Loophole," *Wall Street Journal*, 22 March 2000, p. A1.

when he takes an action on behalf of that interest group. One of the major exemptions in campaign finance law is for news organizations.[68] If an interest group purchases an ad on behalf of a candidate (or gives the candidate money to spend on his own PR), that's a campaign contribution that must be reported to the Federal Election Commission. But if a broadcaster provides face time or favorable coverage to an ally, this need not be reported. Nor, of course, is it necessary to report when a broadcaster provides no coverage or unfavorable coverage of a foe. There are also no limits on contributions, which is why one recent article on the news media exemption had the title: "Latest Path Around Soft-Money Ban: Buy a TV Station."[69]

TV Archives. The lack of an FEC contribution database would be less significant if there were an independent record of media content. But since the beginning of local TV broadcasting, no such record has existed.[70] One reason is that copyright law has discouraged its creation. Libraries may keep old newspapers. But it is illegal for them to keep old TV broadcasts without the permission of the broadcaster. The Library of Congress collects daily newspapers from hundreds of newspapers across the United States. But it collects no local TV broadcasts. Even those who want to study live broadcasts face legal obstacles. FCC regulations, for example, make it illegal to send live local TV

---

[68] See the Federal Election Campaign Act, 2 U.S.C. §431(9)(B)(i). "The term 'expenditure' does not include any news story, commentary, or editorial distributed through the facilities of any broadcasting station, newspaper, magazine, or other periodical publication, unless such facilities are owned or controlled by any political party, political committee, or candidate." Senator Mitch MicConnell has repeatedly and loudly complained about this loophole. See Mitch McConnell, "'Reform' Hurts Freedoms," *USA Today*, 23 March 2001, p. 16A.

[69] Randy Dotinga, "Latest Path around Soft-Money Ban: Buy a TV Station," *Christian Science Monitor*, 17 December 2003, p. 02. The article was written in response to a National Rifle Association plan to circumvent soft-money limitations by buying a radio or TV station to gets its message across. See also Richard L. Hasen, "Double Standard: Media Corporations Have the Power to Endorse Candidates, but Other Companies Don't," *Brill's Content*, February 1999, p. 109.

[70] James H. Snider, "Local TV News Archives as a Public Good," *The Harvard International Journal of Press/Politics* 5, no. 2 (2000). Local broadcasters have even resisted creating the most basic programming logs for public use and accountability. See Theodore M Hagelin and Kurt A. Wimmer, "Broadcast Deregulation and the Administrative Responsibility to Monitor Policy Change: an Empirical Study of the Elimination of Logging Requirements," *Federal Communications Law Journal* 38(2), pp. 201-282. More recently see Comments to FCC of the New America Foundation In the matter of *Retention by Broadcasters of Program Recordings*, MB Docket 04-232, released 27 August 2004.

broadcasts outside the local geographic boundaries determined by FCC licenses. And the FCC has recently mandated "broadcast flag" technology to ensure that the Internet is not used to bypass this usage restriction.[71]

Moreover, a TV station has no legal obligation to provide TV footage, at any price, to someone who requests it. That's true even if reasonable grounds exist to believe a station provided false information.[72]

Lobbyist Disclosure. Lobbyist disclosure laws require that professional lobbyists who lobby on specific legislation or rulemakings disclose their compensation for such activities. This exempts other important types of lobbying, including grassroots lobbying, public relations, educational events, and lobbying at the national political conventions. These exemptions are very important to broadcasters because, for reasons discussed in Chapter 9 on broadcasters' ethics claims, local TV broadcasters hate to leave a verifiable paper trail of their lobbying activities. Of course, these lobbying exemptions benefit other groups as well. But it is rare to pursue an effective "qualitative" grassroots lobbying strategy without backup from traceable campaign contributions. A grassroots lobbying consultant for the broadcast industry explained to me the distinction. A **qualitative** grassroots operation is based on a few key contacts per Congressional district rather than an outpouring of grassroots support. A grassroots campaign based on a couple of local TV station managers seeing a member of Congress is a qualitative grassroots campaign. A grassroots campaign based on thousands of anti-abortion constituents contacting their member of Congress is a **quantitative** campaign.

Another major distinction between a quantitative and qualitative campaign involves the nature of the grassroots. The norm in quantitative campaigns is for the grassroots to be composed of constituents. In contrast, a qualitative grassroots lobbyist is more likely to be a campaign contributor, celebrity, or friend. In the case of local TV station lobbyists, the grassroots often aren't constituents— just employed by stations that broadcast into areas with constituents.

The Official U.S. Budget: The largest subsidy the broadcast industry has received from the federal government is free use of the public airwaves. Since the government does not estimate the value of this resource and put it on its balance sheet, there is no impact on its balance sheet when it gives away rights to use such a resource. In other words, spectrum giveaways can be exempt from the annual budgetary process and made all-but-invisible. In contrast, it

---

[71] FCC Report and Order and Further Notice of Proposed Rulemaking in the matter of *Digital Broadcast Content Protection*, MB Docket 02-230, FCC 03-273, released 4 November 2003.

[72] E.g, Greg Farrell, "Lurching Into Reverse," *Brill's Content*, July/August 1998.

would be illegal for Congress to sell the furniture in its Congressional offices at below market rates and without accounting for the transaction in its budget. Of course, if Congress wanted to, it could go to the Congressional Budget Office and get an estimate of the value of rights to use the public airwaves. But it is under no obligation to do so and has generally chosen not to do so when the broadcasters have requested new rights to spectrum.

Inside Access to Information. A host of laws exist to further reporters' access to government information. Reporters, for example, get privileged access to the U.S. Capitol and Library of Congress, free office space and staff support in the Capitol building, unrestricted use of TV footage from Congressional proceedings, and exemption from subpoenas (so-called "shield laws") involving their sources of information.[73] The result of these formal laws, as well as countless norms that give journalists access to information undreamed of by ordinary citizens, gives reporters a privileged position to find dirt and other information that might be useful to a lobbyist.

One oddball perk the NAB receives is the right to videotape Congressional hearings. Most hearings are videotaped by bona fide news organizations or not videotaped at all. Lobbyists are rarely given rights to videotape hearings. The NAB is an exception, however. It often receives rights to tape the hearings, and then includes hearing highlights in its monthly telecasts to station general managers and grassroots lobbyists.[74] For a variety of poorly understood reasons, the NAB may in fact be the only registered lobbying organization in the U.S. that can use Capitol video footage for political purposes. C-SPAN owns the copyright to its footage and explicitly forbids any use of its footage for political purposes, and the only other outside group with access to Congressional video footage is bona fide news organizations, who also own the copyright to their footage and don't allow it to be used for political purposes.[75]

Another perk that NAB members sometimes receive is the privilege, like bona fide news staff, of not having to wait in line to get into hearing rooms. In

---

[73] E.g., Dan Trigoboff, "Press Shield Law Upheld," *Broadcasting & Cable*, 8 November 1999, p. 37. Thirty states and the District of Columbia have reporters' shield laws. See Kathleen Kirby, "Look Over Your Shoulder," *Communicator*, December 1998, p. 47.

[74] Taping rights are granted by committee chairs. Examples of NAB privileged tapings are the Senate Banking, Housing, and Urban Affairs Committee hearing on Loan Guarantees and Rural Television Service on 1 February 2000, and the House Energy and Commerce Committee hearing on Advancing the DTV Transition on 2 June 2004.

[75] J.H. Snider, "Should the Public Meeting Enter the Information Age?," *National Civic Review* 92, no. 3 (Fall 2003), James H. Snider, "Senate Hypocrisy over "Hot" Testimony," *Chicago Tribune*, 27 January 1999.

Washington, DC, hearing rooms are limited in size. Only press, staff of committee members, and witnesses, can generally get into hearing rooms without waiting outside in a line. Getting into some hearings is so precious that lobbyists hire line standers to hold a place for them in line, sometimes beginning many hours before a hearing begins.[76] But committee members like to do favors for their local broadcasters. So when they come to town to attend a hearing, the red carpet is laid out. One local broadcaster told me that when he wanted to attend the Monica Lewinsky hearing, one of the most publicized hearings in the history of Congress, he simply let his senator know he wanted to attend, and he was then bumped to the front of the line. Less privileged citizens waited in line more than 24 hours just in the attempt to attend the hearing.

Broadcast Financial Data. Many regulated and subsidized industries, including broadcasters, make frequent pleadings about their high costs and low revenue. This helps them secure laws to enhance their profitability. But not all of these claims are equally verifiable, in part because the government collects cost and revenue information about some regulated and subsidized industries but not others. For example, the FCC has detailed information about the costs of telephone companies, but it collects virtually no information about the costs of the broadcast industry. This strengthens the bargaining position of the broadcasters. If the local telephone industry asks for a rate increase on the access charges of long-distance telephone companies, the long-distance industry and the government are in a relatively good bargaining position. Broadcasters, however, provide no more financial information to either the government or public than most unregulated and unsubsidized industries. Broadcasters consider detailed information about their cash flow, net profits, public service, and assets, to be highly confidential. A major reason is that disclosure of such information would hinder their lobbying efforts, which are frequently premised on the assumptions that the broadcast industry provides a "free" (i.e., ad-supported) service and thus cannot survive without special government protection and subsidies. For example, in seeking new spectrum for advanced television services in the Telecom Act of 1996, broadcasters claimed that digital TV conversion costs were so high that they couldn't afford both to purchase the spectrum and convert their stations to digital. The government didn't verify these claims.

---

[76] E.g., Doug Halonen, "Waiting is the Hardest Part," *Electronic Media*, 29 May 1995, p. 24. This article describes telecom firms willing to spend $1,500 to get into an important House Commerce Committee vote, with a representative from the association of independent TV broadcasters getting in for free.

Ex Parte. The Ex Parte laws are designed to prevent one interest group from getting an unfair advantage over another. They require that an interest group that lobbies the FCC about a particular proceeding must publicly disclose the time, participants, and substance of the meeting. Interest groups carefully watch these ex parte filings and use them to ferret out false claims and counter their opponents.

But the Ex Parte laws have loopholes. When an interest group lobbies Congress about a specific proposed law, it needn't file anything analogous to an ex parte. And although in theory Congress must file an ex parte when it lobbies the FCC, in practice Congress exempts itself from ex parte disclosure. For example, members of Congress can clearly reveal their preferences to FCC staff, but merely by labeling their communications a status request on a particular proceeding, eliminate the disclosure requirement. And, of course, Congress has huge power over the FCC. Through the appropriations process, it controls what the FCC can and cannot do. An FCC staffer who acts against the wishes of Congress can have his pet projects zeroed out. Similarly, it has oversight and appointment powers. Reappointment as an FCC Commissioner requires U.S. Senate approval. And an FCC official who acts against the wishes of a Congressional authorization committee may be hounded with requests for stacks of documents.

Since the broadcasters' base of support is in Congress, this gives them an advantage over other groups in FCC battles. The typical pattern is for Congress to delegate its dirty work on behalf of special interests to the FCC. Thanks in part to the de facto Congressional exemption from ex parte filings, it can do so without leaving an incriminating public record.

Widely attended events, such as those put on by the largest and wealthiest trade associations, have also been exempt since 1997. A small group of public interest activists must file an *ex parte* when they meet with FCC officials. But a large group of broadcasters that meet with FCC officials at an exclusive event at the annual NAB Show are exempt. Broadcasters got a special ruling that they could benefit from the new exemption before others.[77]

---

[77] "Waiver of Ex Parte Sunshine Prohibition in DTV Proceeding," FCC Public Notice #97-122," Washington, DC: FCC, 4 April 1997. The waiver included the following text: "The Commission believes that participation by Commission personnel in the scheduled panels and presentations associated with the NAB convention, which may involve discussions of the Commission's DTV Reports and Orders, will serve the public interest.... In light of the foregoing, the Commission is waiving the Sunshine Period prohibition contained in its currently effective *ex parte* rules, 47 C.F.R. Section 1.1203...."

National Party Conventions. The national party conventions are taxpayer funded extravaganzas that are largely exempt from lobbyist and gift disclosure laws.[78] In recent decades, their electoral and democratic importance has declined. But they thrive as backroom vehicles for special interest influence. Broadcasters get to participate in this influence game on bargain basement terms. This is largely because of the important role broadcasters play at the conventions.

The major TV networks have premium suites at the conventions. These suites, equipped with bars and other amenities, are a luxurious way to watch the conventions. The suites are open to network reporters, preferred members of Congress, and network lobbyists. For example, at the ABC suite, a member of Congress may stop by to watch the convention and chat with well-known columnist George Will who is sitting at the bar watching the convention. Next to George Will may be ABC's chief lobbyist, a former senior Congressional aide himself.

At both the Democratic and Republican conventions, the NAB tries to provide some type of service which helps solidify its relations with the national party leaders. During conventions in the 1990s, the NAB provided 200 television monitors for VIP suites and delegate lounges. The NAB also hosts a number of low-key events at the conventions. For example, in 1988 the NAB hosted a small dinner party with Vice Presidential nominee Dan Quayle and NAB President Eddie Fritts. It also hosted tennis activities with NAB Government Affairs VP Jim May, Vice President Dan Quayle, Representative Tom Bliley, and Senators John Warner and Ted Stevens. At various other social occasions, NAB President Eddie Fritts met with Senators Alan Simpson and Thad Cochran, and Representatives Carlos Moorehead and Norm Lent. The contacts focused on key Congressmen with power over broadcast issues.[79]

Internal Documents. Some regulated or subsidized industries are required to keep internal documents for a period of years so the government can subpoena documents and perform an audit.[80] Lobbying organizations are exempt from such disclosure, presumably because it would appear to chill political

---

[78] E.g., Damon Chappie, "Ethics Evens Field for GOP: Change opens door to freebies at conventions," *Roll Call*, 3 August 2000. For a view of how this loophole benefits media companies, see "Laurel to ABC's World News Tonight," *Columbia Journalism Review*, November/December 1996, p. 32. This is also a rare case of a news outlet reporting on its parent company's lobbying.

[79] *TV Today*, 22 August 1988.

[80] E.g., Randall Smith, "Wall Street Has E-Mail Problems," *Wall Street Journal*, 2 August 2002, p. C1.

speech, the most protected form of speech in our system of government. But there are consequences to such reticence. It makes the lobbying disclosure laws—and many other laws, for that matter—all but impossible to enforce. The consequence is that many DC trade associations have a policy of destroying or at least not keeping on premises any document that isn't essential and might be subject to a subpoena. As the Director for Regulatory Policy at the Cellular Telecommunications & Industry Association explained to me while we were waiting for a Senate hearing to begin: "If you keep that stuff around, sooner or later you'll get a document request. A lot of it is harmless, but some of it might not be."[81] Kathleen Kirby, a regular columnist in *Communicator* and a lawyer for Wiley, Rein & Fielding with TV station clients, provides the following advice to TV and radio news directors: "The most critical question to answer when you are deciding whether to retain or destroy journalistic material is how your organization would react should that material be subpoenaed." Her document retention advice contains not a word about the public's interest, journalistic standards of accountability, or upholding the law.[82]

Economies of Scope—Media

> To a politician, television is a drug. So, broadcasters find themselves the dealers, the pushers.
>
> —Barry Diller, Owner, USA Networks[83]

> What if a $70 billion robbery took place and it didn't make the 6 o'clock news? Most of us would assume it never happened. That's the power of TV.
>
> —David Morris, Columnist, Saint Paul Pioneer Press[84]

Let's suppose that broadcasters have no risk of being both caught and penalized for using their media assets to lobby. Of course, this is a ridiculous assumption. But it is nevertheless a useful reference point for thinking about

---

[81] Conversation with Christopher E. Guttman-McCabe in the U.S. Senate Commerce Committee Room, 31 July 2001.

[82] Kathleen Kirby, "Should You Save Story Files?" Communicator, February 1999.

[83] Barry Diller, Speech to the Schroder Wertheim "Big Picture" Media Conference, NBC Professional Transcripts, 2 April 1997.

[84] David Morris, "Broadcasters Keep Public in Dark About $70 Billion Public Gift to Them," *Saint Paul Pioneer Press*, 29 July 1997, p. 7A.

the fears a member of Congress might have about the power of his local broadcasters.

Candidate Ads. Members of Congress spend a large fraction of their time raising money to purchase TV ads for their next political campaign.[85] According to Competitive Media Reporting, federal candidates in recent two-year election cycles have spent upwards of $400 million on political ads on local broadcast TV stations.[86] As journalism professor and political writer Mark Danner put it, "politicians have become forced to become a species of bagmen who collect money from the wealthy and deliver it to television in order to sell themselves to voters."[87] Placement, cost, and disclosure of these ads are heavily regulated by the FCC but there is a perceived margin of discretion left to the broadcaster.

Political ads generally come in different categories with sharply varying price tags, including: fixed (guaranteed to run on a particular date at a particular time), non-preemptible (guaranteed to run only during a particular day-part or program), preemptible with notice (guaranteed to run only if notice is not given by a set time before the ad is to be aired), or run-of-schedule (a preemptible spot that may be scheduled at any time at the discretion of the station and without prior notice). Does the broadcaster give the candidate timely information about an opponent's advertising plans? Does the politician get the absolutely best deal for his money? Does he buy a run-of-schedule ad but in fact get the privileges of a fixed ad? Does he buy a preemptible ad with one day notice but in fact get two day notice or one week notice? Does the Member of Congress get the best time or worst time within a non-preemptible time segment (e.g., 3pm vs. 5:30pm in a 3pm-7pm drive time daypart)?

Members of Congress care tremendously about such issues, which explains why FCC regulations governing political advertising are so voluminous. There is also tremendous suspicion that local broadcasters "gouge" members of Congress, as reflected in the 2001 Congressional floor debates on proposed campaign finance legislation.[88] Reports one of the broadcast trade magazines:

---

[85] E.g., Alliance for Better Campaigns, "Profiteering on Democracy: How the Television Industry Gouged Candidates in Campaign '02," (Washington, DC: Alliance for Better Campaigns, 2002).

[86] Steve McClellan, "'98 Political Spending Tops $530 million," *Broadcasting & Cable*, 11 January 1999, p. 15.

[87] Mark Danner, "The Shame of Political TV," *New York Review of Books*, 21 September 2000, p. 101.

[88] David Rogers, "Senators Move to Restrict the Amount TV Stations Can Charge for Political Ads," *Wall Street Journal*, 22 March 2001, p. A24.

"Senator after senator came up [during the floor debate] and told their war stories about how much they're paying."[89]

Most general managers rise through the ranks of the advertising sales department. And sales personnel are likely to also take on the role of station lobbyist. Indeed, in some communities a station ad executive is not only a major rainmaker and bundler for Congressional candidates, but also the chief of fundraising. In rural America, a broadcast ad manager is an excellent person for this role because of his active participation in the local business clubs such as Rotary and the Chamber of Commerce, and his contacts with many of the major businesses and sources of sizable contributions in his community.

In such an environment, a member of Congress might reasonably reflect on the facts that the ad manager is a passionately involved political player rather than a neutral observer, knows the member's political stands and friends and enemies, receives as much as 40% of his campaign expenditures (which go to purchase TV ads), has inside information about his own and his opponent's last-minute advertising attack campaign, can pull ads deemed false or in poor taste, and has discretion over vital details about when a political or issue ad runs.

One of the most interesting areas of station discretion is whether it will prosecute a candidate who has taken one of its video or audio segments—or a transcript of a segment—and used it in a campaign ad. The stations generally claim that they have a copyright to all their programming but there is a fair use exemption that candidates can claim makes their use legal. The stations have a number of options in this situation: take legal action, threaten the candidate with legal action but take no action, complain about the activity in a news segment, use the media outlet to take some other retribution, or do nothing.[90] A close variant on this situation is when the request for copyright permission to use a video segment comes from an independent entity such as a filmmaker or candidate supporter. For example, when documentary filmmaker Robert Greenwald wanted to use a one minute segment of an interview on *Meet the Press* between NBC's Tim Russert and President Bush, NBC refused, explaining that the segment is "not very flattering to the president."[91]

Another area of station discretion concerns the degree to which it extends credit to political candidates. The FCC makes it illegal for a station to require an advance payment when a candidate has an "established credit history." The

---

[89] Doug Halonen, "Cry Raised Against Cheap Political Spots," *Electronic Media*, 9 April 2001, p. 3.

[90] Dan Bischof, "Politicians sometimes cross the line in using news copy to advance their campaigns," *The News Media & the Law*, Winter 2001, p. 10.

[91] Lawrence Lessig, "Copyrighting the President," *Wired*, August 2003, p. 94.

point is that stations should not treat credit requests by politicians any differently than it does credit requests by commercial entities. Otherwise, there is impermissible discrimination. The FCC adds, "so long as a station's policies are not designed as subterfuge to favor particular candidates and are applied even-handedly to all, impermissible discrimination does not occur."[92] Szabo Associates notes the difficulty of enforcing such even-handedness: "Among the practical implications of forcing broadcasters to evaluate candidates' creditworthiness is that it invites the very discrimination that it seeks to prohibit. The practice particularly favors incumbents, who are more likely to have an advertising history with the station as well as larger campaign coffers than challengers."[93]

An important caveat is that the voluminous federal government rules restricting station discretion on running and charging for candidate ads only apply to Federal candidates. Ads for state and local candidates, like the issue ads discussed below, are exempt from such rules.

Issue Ads. Issue ads run by groups not directly linked to a candidate are a very important part of the political process, and here local TV broadcasters have almost complete discretion. NAB's advice to its members describes this discretion as a way to pursue truth: "[L]icensees are responsible for everything they air. If a product ad is false, misleading or deceptive, the station may have to answer to the FTC or FCC. While there is no 'truth in political advertising' law, why not ask ourselves whether a political ad would appear on our stations if subjected to the same standards applied to product ads."[94] This discretion is often used—and complained about by politicians and interest groups.

For example, when Senator McCain (R-Arizona) ran for President, he complained to local broadcasters about ads that supporters of Governor Bush (R-Texas) ran against him. Letters from the McCain campaign to local broadcasters complained that the ads were "demonstrably false" and "we believe you have an obligation not to run an advertisement that has been shown to be untrue." The local TV stations did not pull the ads.[95]

---

[92]Szabo Associates Inc., "Should Broadcasters Extend Credit to Political Candidates? Governmental Regulations Cause Confusion and Concern," *The Financial Manager,* August/September 1996. *Financial Manager* is published by the Broadcasting & Cable Financial Managers Association.

[93] Ibid.

[94] "The Role of Broadcasters in the Political Process," (Washington, DC: National Association of Broadcasters, 1986).

[95] "FCC, FEC Investigating McCain Campaign Ad Complaints," *Communications Daily,* 8 March 2000, p. 4. "Bush Supporter Says He's Behind $2 Million Attack Ad," *Associated Press,* 4 March 2000.

When the AFL-CIO ran "issue education" ads critical of Republican candidates in 11 Congressional districts, 14 local TV stations pulled the ads. The National Republican Congressional Committee requested that the ads be pulled. Said the NRCC spokesman:

> We're not going to violate anyone's right of free speech. But when they are as deceptive as the labor unions have been, we will strongly encourage our Members' campaigns to contact the stations. And in many instances, the stations have been very open and responsive.[96]

When Republican ads attacked incumbent Representative Moore (D-Missouri) on social security, a local TV station refused to carry them, and this was reported on the front page of the *Wall Street Journal*.[97]

The *New York Times* ran an article describing the ubiquity of these claims and counter claims by political operatives seeking to control what issue ads are run by local TV stations. The article begins: "Television station managers in small communities across the nation are being forced this fall to adjudicate a barrage of demands from Democrats and Republican Party lawyers pressuring them to pull political advertisements in closely fought Congressional races—or face the risk of a defamation suit." The article concludes that "the actions by the political committees have transformed station managers and their lawyers into some of the most powerful political players on the scene today." [98]

The *Washington Post* wrote a very similar story: "In a fast and furious guerilla war involving high-powered lawyers and high-pressure threats, both Democratic and Republican operatives are finding ways to silence the other sides' ads. And local stations keep caving in."[99] The analysis was confirmed with a quote from Brown University Professor Darrell West: "Politicians have

---

[96] Benjamin Sheffner, "Please Stand By...TV Stations Nix Some Union Ads," *Communications Daily*, 20 June 1996. The Republican National Committee wrote a letter to more than 250 local TV stations in 2004 asking them not to run anti-Bush ads from MoveOn.org. See "Broadcast," *Communications Daily*, 9 March 2004.

[97] *Wall Street Journal*, 22 October 1999, p. A1. A similar incident occurred some years later in Virginia, with four local TV stations pulling the ads. See "Richard E. Cohen, "The GOP's Social Security Blanket," *National Journal*, 5 October 2002, p. 2894.

[98] Adam Nagourney and Adam Clymer, "Local Television Stations Become the New Arbiters of Political Fair Play," *New York Times*, 2 October 2002, p. A23.

[99] Howard Kurtz, "Hearing 'Foul,' Stations Pull Political Ads: Broadcasters Yield When Candidates Call Opposing Party Spots Misleading," *Washington Post*, 20 September 2002, p. 14.

realized they're not helpless. The can appeal to the goodwill of local broadcasters."[100]

The *Wall Street Journal*'s version of this story started with the general observation that "candidates on both sides of the aisle are using their familiarity with local reporters, editorial writers, and TV-station managers to paint [attack] groups as unwelcome interlopers—well before the attackers air their first commercial." It then cites Senate Minority Leader Daschle's campaign as an example. The campaign early on sought "to 'educate' local TV stations about the law regarding third-party ads—including the part that says they don't have to run them and can require editing of them."[101]Perhaps the most interesting aspect of this discretionary power is that local station executives so often disagree about whether a particular ad should be pulled, and, if not, how to run the ad. A station may run an ad, for example, but add the disclaimer "this ad does not reflect the views of this station." In its magazine for members, the Radio-TV News Directors Association has acknowledged that such decisions are a matter of discretion and may be handled differently by different news directors within the same broadcast market.[102]

Public Service Media. Broadcasters claim to be the largest providers of public service in the United States. This is how they claim to "pay for" the spectrum and other subsidies granted to them by members of Congress.[103] In 1998 broadcasters claimed to provide $6.8 billion in public service a year. [104] NAB's president argued that this is a conservative number and that the real number might be three times as large, or $19.6 billion.[105] This is a huge number. In

---

[100] Ibid.

[101] Jeannine Cummings, "Candidates Learn to Defuse Outside Groups' Attack Ads," *Wall Street Journal*, 20 July 1998, p. A20.

[102] "Tough Calls: Your station's management has refused to air a controversial political ad, making your station the only one in the market not running the ad. Do you report this?" *Communicator*, November 2000, p. 56.

[103] E.g. NAB, "A Model State Marketing Plan: The Marketing of Broadcaster's Public Service Record," (Washington, DC: NAB, 1998), NAB, "Spectrum Auctions," in *Legislative Issue Papers, 104th Congress* (Washington, DC: NAB, October 1995), p. 16.

[104] During 1998, these numbers were delivered to every member of Congress, every U.S. governor, and many state representatives. Numerous comments in the public record by members of Congress and governors can be found praising them. The numbers were the linchpin of the broadcasters' efforts to avoid paying for their new digital spectrum rights with new public interest obligations.

[105] Chris McConnell and Paige Albiniak, "Putting a Price on Community Service," *Broadcasting & Cable*, 6 April 1998, p. 71.

contrast, total PAC expenditures for all Congressional candidates in the 1995–6 election cycle were only $201 million.[106] Total non-religious charitable expenditures in the entire United States during 1997 were only $68.49 billion and total corporate contributions to charity were only $8.20 billion.[107]

The breakdown of the $6.8 billion was $4.8 billion for public service announcements, $2.1 billion raising money for charities and other causes, and $148 million for free airtime for candidate debates, candidate forums and national party convention coverage. The largest component of these contributions is public service announcements (PSAs). The recipients of these ads are a who's who of local non-profit organizations and community leaders. They have a lot to lose by getting on the wrong side of their local broadcasters.

PSAs build a reservoir of IOUs that broadcasters can draw on in time of political need.[108] Recipients can also be expected to think twice before publicly opposing a group that has given them something valuable. In times of need, broadcasters routinely call on PSA recipients to write letters to Congress and provide members of Congress with political cover for positions that might otherwise appear to be the product of special interest politics. During the lobbying battle leading up to passage of the Cable Act of 1992, members of Congress received 22,000 letters from non-profits in support of broadcasters.

PSAs Used Directly for Broadcast industry Lobbying. Some PSAs directly complement the broadcast industry's lobbying efforts. For example, local broadcasters have lobbied for more than a decade to make sure that direct broadcast satellite (DBS) operators cannot undermine their advertising base by carrying network TV signals or cherry picking local channels for coverage. In the late 1990s rural broadcasters ran many PSAs warning DBS subscribers that it was illegal to receive broadcast signals through a satellite dish if they couldn't be received through an over-the-air signal. The PSAs were not explicitly advocacy because they simply reminded viewers of the law. Similarly, in

---

[106] Anthony Corrado, *Campaign Finance Reform: A Sourcebook* (Washington, D.C.: Brookings Institution, 1997), 141.

[107] AAFRC Trust for Philanthropy, "Giving USA 1998," (Sewickley, Pennsylvania: AAFRC Trust for Philanthropy, 1998).

[108] See Chapter 14 for details on how public service media is leveraged for political support.

[109] In 1997 the value of TV and radio stations was $141.7 billion and their cash flow was $9.4 billion. See John Higgins, "As Broadcasters Giveth, They Taketh in Billions," *Broadcasting & Cable*, 6 April 1998, pp. 80, 82. Stations are customarily valued based on cash flow. Using a conventional cash flow multiple of 15 (e.g., $141.7 billion divided by $9.4 billion equals 15), the resale value of a $6.8 billion cash flow is $102 billion.

1996 broadcasters ran what one article estimated were $9.5 million of PSAs in favor of "free TV."[110] The ads were designed to apply pressure on select members of Congress who might be tempted to ask broadcasters to pay for new spectrum rights valued at tens of billions of dollars. The ads made no mention of the new spectrum rights the broadcasters sought.

To outsiders, these PSAs may look like political or marketing ads on behalf of broadcasters, but that is not how the NAB characterizes them to its members or how local stations tally them in their biannual tally of public service to the nation.[111]

News. According to dozens of sources, local TV news is the most watched and trusted of the major mass media.[112] Positive "earned media" (the opposite of advertising or "paid media") is highly sought after by members of Congress.[113] Compared to paid media, it both saves them money and maximizes the credibility of their messages. Therefore, controlling a local TV station's news content could be a useful political resource.

Most grassroots lobbying by local television broadcasters is done via local television station general managers. Sometimes one or more subordinates outside the news department will take over day-to-day lobbying responsibilities, but the general manager will likely be aware of major lobbying goals and strategies.

The chief grassroots broadcast lobbyist (a.k.a. "the general manager") will have extraordinary access to and influence over the news director as part of his management responsibilities.[114] If the local television station provides local news (and more than 75% do), the news department may generate a large fraction of the station's profits and include 50% or more of total employees. The news director will report directly to the broadcast lobbyist.

---

[110] Arthur E. Rowse, "A Lobby the Media Won't Touch," *Washington Monthly*, May 1998, p. 9. See Chapter 15 for details.

[111] See Chapters 14 and 15 for details. Other media industries also use their airwaves for political purposes. For example, Charlie Ergen, CEO of satellite TV operator Echostar, has run a program called *Charlie Chat* to lobby his viewers on satellite legislation. See Paige Albiniak, "Echostar Ruffles Feathers," *Broadcasting & Cable*, 13 August 2001, p. 26. One noteworthy difference is that I'm not aware that Echostar includes the value of these ads in a tally of public service that it claims to Congress and the FCC is how it pays for its spectrum.

[112] E.g., Frank Newport and Lydia Saad, "A Matter of Trust," *American Journalism Review*, July/August 1998, pp. 30-33.

[113] Cook, *Making Laws and Making News,* Stephen Hess, *The Ultimate Insiders : U.S. Senators in the National Media* (Washington, D.C.: Brookings Institution, 1986).

[114] For a detailed discussion of this argument, see Chapter 13.

The broadcast lobbyist will hire and fire the news director and set the terms of the news director's contract. At his own discretion, he may be actively involved in determining major line items in the news budget. He may be actively involved in the hiring and firing process of news anchors and other key news personnel. If he is in a top 30 news market, he will have overnight ratings every day informing him how the evening news did against the competition.[115] Depending on his interests and background (e.g., many general managers are promoted from the position of news director), he may make frequent suggestions for news coverage. If the station temporarily lacks a news director, he may take over the news director's role. As a rule, he will communicate with the news director on a daily basis.

Control over news could be used to reward friends and punish enemies. For example, a broadcast lobbyist could use his contacts and control of the news agenda to kill negative stories and give the green light to positive stories. Positive news might simply consist of giving more face time to an incumbent. In a world where political opponents bombard TV stations at the last minute with negative stories about their opponents, the station manager who makes the call whether to run these stories is potentially in a very powerful position.

Control over debates is a major source of potential news bias. TV stations only air a small fraction of debates that candidates seek. For example, the Committee for the Study of the American Electorate found that during the 1992 election cycle local TV stations only aired debates for 8 of 17 U.S. Senate races and 36 of 107 U.S. House of Representatives races.[116] In addition to deciding which candidates to debate, local TV stations often get to decide how many debates to cover, when in the Election cycle to cover them, what time of day and week to host the debate, what format they will take, and who will ask

---

[115] The existence of local competition and overnight ratings helps explain the high turnover of news directors. Every TV market has a last place TV news program and in a large market up to four or five also-rans. Overnight ratings remind a general manager of this fact on a daily basis. In contrast, most local newspaper markets have no direct competition and therefore no last place editor. Neither the newspaper publisher nor editor typically study circulation figures on a daily basis. In addition, newspaper circulation figures provide less detail than TV ratings. A TV rating is broken down program by program or even minute by minute. Audience switching costs are low and there is high audience variation based on content. In contrast, a newspaper is purchased as a package, readership of individual articles is hard to track, and reader disinterest in a particular article is unlikely to lead to lost revenue because reader switching costs are high.

[116] Cited in Pat Nason, "Analysis: Politics as Profit Center," *United Press International*, 18 August 2004.

the questions. Opportunity for abuse is rampant. In general, candidates who are ahead in the polls (usually incumbents) don't want debate whereas those that are behind (usually challengers) do. As American Enterprise Institute Fellow Norman Ornstein has argued, TV stations have means at their disposal to force those who are ahead into televised debates, and they do exercise that power at their own discretion.[117]

Ad watches are another area where local TV broadcasters have huge potential clout. Many ads are potentially misleading. As Professor Kathleen Hall Jamieson observed, 52% of all the ads broadcast by Republican and Democratic presidential candidates during the fall 2002 election season contained misleading information.[118] Through "adwatching," dissecting the content of political ads, local TV stations can decide which misleading information to highlight and which to ignore.

Lastly, public affairs TV programs, although lightly watched, represent another news vehicle where favors can be granted and withdrawn. Michelle Malkin, a syndicated columnist, reported in the *Seattle Times* that politicians got to pick their interviewers on KONG-TV's public affairs shows.[119] Seattle's KONG-TV is owned by Belo Corporation, one of the nation's largest media companies with a diversified group of TV, newspaper, and cable properties.

Entertainment Programming. A lot of entertainment programming on broadcast television covers politics. This includes the *Late Show with David Letterman, Late Night with Conan O'Brien, Tonight with Jay Leno, Entertainment Tonight, Access Hollywood, Politically Incorrect* with Bill Maher, and *Saturday Night Live.* Politicians sometimes appear on these shows and have even announced their candidacies on them.[120] The *New York Times* has periodically kept a runny tally called "campaign laugh track," ranking the most joked about politicians on late night TV monologues.[121] *Hotline*, which summarizes mass

---

[117] Norman Ornstein, "Broadcasters Need to Do More to Give Candidates Air Time," *Roll Call*, 23 June 2004.

[118] Kathleen Hall Jamieson, "Scholarship and the Discourse of Election Campaigns," *Chronicle of Higher Education*, 22 November 1996, p. 28.

[119] Michelle Malkin, "What's Really Wrong with Seattle TV Media," *Seattle Times*, 9 February 1999.

[120] E.g., during the summer of 2003, Arnold Schwarzenegger announced his candidacy for governor of California on the Jay Leno show, with an audience of 6.2 million nightly viewers. See "Schwarzenegger Uses Savvy to Handle Media: Image-Conscious Schwarzenegger Works to Keep Media Under Control As California Governor," *Associated Press*, 25 April 2004.

[121] "Campaign Laugh Track," *New York Times*, 5 March 2000, p. 5.

media coverage for Washington's insiders, every day reprints the political jokes told over the previous 24 hours. Says *Hotline* Editor-in-Chief Craig Crawford: "I'm personally of the view that a good joke goes further in the public arena than the most finely crafted speech.... If the first lady is getting trashed..., I think that the first lady's staff and Democrats and Republicans in Washington...need to know."[122] According to the *Chicago Tribune*, "40 percent of people under 30 years of age get their information about presidential politics from late-night comedy."[123]

Few dispute that corporate interests influence entertainment programming. It's no surprise, for example, that on New Year's Eve, ABC, owned by Disney, features events at Disney theme parks. Advertisers also routinely pay to have their products inserted in story lines.[124] By extension, it's possible that entertainment programmers could pursue a political agenda.[125] For example, when *Saturday Night Live* pulled an animated satire of its corporate parent's use of media in lobbying, a reasonable person might wonder if corporate interests were involved regardless of whether or not *Saturday Night Live*'s executive producer, Lorne Michaels, said it was pulled because "I don't think it worked comedically"[126] The satire was called "Media-opoly," specifically mentioned NBC owner General Electric, and included the jingle "They can use [their media outlets] to say whatever they please and put down the opinions of anyone who disagrees."[127]

Broadcaster Diseconomies of Scope

Clearly, broadcasters also have significant diseconomies of scope in lobbying. In at least some respects, broadcasting is an extraordinarily visible industry, if

---

[122] Robert Schmidt, "Hotline's Heat," *Brill's Content*, November 1999, p. 112.

[123] Roger Simon, "The Media Presidency," *Chicago Tribune*, 25 January 1998, p. A1.

[124] E.g., Suzanne Vranica and Brian Steinberg, "The Robot Wore Converses: Chaos reigns as marketers, media scramble to negotiate product-placement deals," *Wall Street Journal*, 2 September 2004, p. B1.

[125] Many entertainment programs are subject to the FCC's equal time rule, so station discretion is limited. See Craig Kilborn, "My Couch Is Too Small for 135 Candidates," *New York Times*, 30 August 2003, p. A25.

[126] Frazier Moore, "Free Speech Is Fine, but Bill Moyers Wonders: Can You Afford It?," *Associated Press*, 7 June 1999.

[127] Ibid. In 2004 Saturday Night Live ran a similar cartoon satire poking fun at FCC Chairman Powell's recent indecency fines of TV network programming. This was deemed funny. See "Broadcast," *Communications Daily*, 9 March 2004.

only because more than 99% of Americans have TV sets and watch local TV broadcast programming. This visibility breeds scrutiny and criticism.

Broadcasters are also uniquely crippled in their ability to use employees for lobbying. For example, when the CEO of BellSouth, one of the major local telephone companies, wanted to apply grassroots pressure on Congress during the lobbying leading up to passage of the Telecom Act of 1996, he wrote a letter to all his employees and asked them to contact their member of Congress. A local TV broadcaster would never dare to do this with close to half his employees—his news staff—because such an action is almost impossible to hide and would undermine the credibility of the news staff when it became public.[128]

Similarly, most broadcasters discourage or even penalize news employees from contributing to candidates for public office. ABC spokesman Jeffrey Schneider, for example, says that all political contributions are barred "to maintain our professional reputation for fairness and impartiality."[129] Sometimes senior executives and non-political reporters are allowed to contribute.[130] But I was not able to find a single instance where political reporters were allowed, let alone encouraged, to contribute to candidates.

Broadcasters and their allies tend to dwell on these diseconomies of scope in lobbying. They claim that it is not in their self-interest to use their control of the airwaves for lobbying purposes because the public would discover and penalize such use. We will evaluate these diseconomies of scope claims in Chapters 13.

Conclusion

In Plato's Republic, Book II, there is the famous story of the Ring of Gyges, who discovers a ring that allows him to exercise power invisibly:[131] The story is told to Socrates by one of his students, Glaucon.

> According to the tradition, Gyges was a shepherd in the service of the king of Lydia; there was a great storm, and an earthquake made an

---

[128] See Cheryl Bolen, "From Hours of Discussions to Non-Negotiable Demands: The History of the Failed 1994 Telecommunications Bill," *Bureau of National Affairs*, No. 226, 28 November 1994, p. C6.

[129] Howard Kurtz, "Journalists Not Loath to Donate to Politicians: Media Companies' Policies Vary Widely," *Washington Post*, 18 January 2004, p. A1.

[130] Ibid.

[131] Plato, *The Republic*, trans. Benjamin Jowett (Vintage Books, 1991).

opening in the earth at the place where he was feeding his flock. Amazed at the sight, he descended into the opening, where, among other marvels, he beheld a hollow brazen horse, having doors, at which he stooping and looking in saw a dead body of stature, as appeared to him, more than human, and having nothing on but a gold ring; this he took from the finger of the dead and reascended.

Now the shepherds met together, according to custom, that they might send their monthly report about the flocks to the king; into their assembly he came having the ring on his finger, and as he was sitting among them he chanced to turn the collet of the ring inside his hand, when instantly he became invisible to the rest of the company and they began to speak of him as if he were no longer present. He was astonished at this, and again touching the ring he turned the collet outwards and reappeared; he made several trials of the ring, and always with the same result—when he turned the collet inwards he became invisible, when outwards he reappeared. Whereupon he contrived to be chosen one of the messengers who were sent to the court; where as soon as he arrived he seduced the queen, and with her help conspired against the king and slew him, and took the kingdom.

Suppose now that there were two such magic rings, and the just put on one of them and the unjust the other. No man can be imagined to be of such an iron nature that he would stand fast in justice. No man would keep his hands off what was not his own when he could safely take what he liked....

If you could imagine any one obtaining this power of becoming invisible, and never doing any wrong or touching what was another's, he would be thought by the lookers-on to be a most wretched idiot, although they would praise him to one another's faces....

Would broadcasters be able to resist using such power if they had it? Socrates contends, in his reply to Glaucon, that Gyges is the exception, not the norm. But even if Socrates' optimistic assessment of human nature is correct,[132] would a politician want to take the risk on an issue such as spectrum that matters a huge amount to broadcasters but isn't even on the radar screen of the average American? To that question, we now turn.

---

[132] One economist designed an elegant study to show that a large fraction of people would act like Gyges, if given the proper incentives. See Stephen J. Dubner and Steven D. Levitt, "What the Bagel Man Saw," *New York Times Magazine*, 6 June 2004.

Part II:

Case Study: The Great Spectrum Giveaway

CHAPTER 8:

Was it Reasonable for Legislators to Anticipate Broadcaster Bias?

"Do media organizations pursue policy objectives through their publications or broadcasts? On this fundamental question there is a curious disjuncture between the communications literature and common sense. Most sophisticated observers of the media, at least nonacademic observers, would say, 'of course.'…But communications scholars tend to dismiss such possibilities out of hand…. How could such a thing be managed? Journalists take pride in their independence and in professional norms of objectivity. Surely media *owners* do not influence what journalists say or print!"

—Benjamin I. Page, The Mass Media as Political Actors[1]

"[T]he literature is asymmetrical, with many more journalist's-eye views of the process than perspectives from the politicians' side."

—Timothy Cook, Governing with the News[2]

In the Telecommunications Act of 1996, Congress awarded broadcasters rights to use spectrum that if sold at auction would have been worth tens of billions of dollars. The broadcasters called the spectrum a "loan" because they were technically required to give back an equal amount of spectrum at some future date. But it was an interest free loan with an indefinite duration and an ambiguously defined amount of principal subject to diminishment. Moreover, the bundle of spectrum rights they would have at the end of the loan period was far more valuable than the bundle of rights they started with.

---

[1] Benjamin I. Page, "The Mass Media as Political Actors," *PS: Political Science and Politics* 29, no. 1 (1996): p. 21.

[2] Cook, *Governing with the News: The News Media as a Political Institution*, p. 12.

Reed Hundt, then chair of the Federal Communications Commission, said that granting digital channels to broadcasters was "the biggest single gift of public property to any industry in this century."[3] The National Cable Television Association, which often lobbies against broadcasters, said in a nationally syndicated AP story that the grant "makes the sale of Manhattan for a few beads look like a hard bargain."[4] William Safire, a nationally syndicated *New York Times* columnist, described the grant as a "ripoff" worthy of "yesteryear's robber barons."[5] Common Cause called the broadcasters' free spectrum the "Godzilla of Corporate Welfare."[6] Adam Thierer, Director of Telecommunications Studies at the Cato Institute, called it "one of the most unjustified giveaways and biggest boondoggles in American history. You have to count it as the greatest victory the NAB ever had."[7] Senator Lieberman said giving the spectrum away is "a little like the Indians selling Manhattan Island for $24."[8] Senator McCain called it "one of the great scams in American history"[9] and explained that "No other commodity owned by the American people—not our national forests, not our public lands, not anything, would be given away as this incredibly valuable commodity was to broadcasters."[10] Lawrence Grossman, former president of NBC News, called it "the greatest giveaway of publicly owned resources in history...."[11]

What explains the broadcasters' legislative triumph? The argument put forth in Part II of this book is that at least part of the explanation may have to do with legislators' expectations of broadcaster media bias. Would it have been reasonable for a legislator who opposed the spectrum provisions in the Telecom Act of 1996 to fear broadcaster media bias? Was it reasonable for a legislator to believe that broadcasters would act rationally when faced with a huge

---

[3] "FCC Begins Digital TV Channel Allocations," *Television Digest*, 29 July 1996, p. 2.

[4] Jeannine Aversa, "FCC Oks Pricey Digital TV," *Associated Press*, 4 April 1997.

[5] William Safire, "Stop the Giveaway," *New York Times*, 4 January 1996, p. A21.

[6] Letter to solicit new members, June 1999; see also Jeannine Aversa, "Airwave Allocation Called Big Giveaway: Sale of TV Spectrum Could Raise Billions," *The San Diego Union-Tribune*, 8 April 1997, p. C1.

[7] Neil Hickey, "TV's Big Stick: What the Broadcast Industry Gets What It Wants in Washington," *Columbia Journalism Review*, September/October 2002, p. 51.

[8] Elizabet Corcoran and Paul Farhi, "4 Senators Propose U.S. Auctions of Airwaves for New TV Channels," *Washington Post*, 23 May 1995, p. C1.

[9] James O. Goldsborough, "A Meaningful Campaign Finance Proposal," *San Diego Union-Tribune*, 20 March 1997, p. B9

[10] David Hatch, "McCain hits DTV giveback," *Electronic Media*, 13 July 1998, p. 1.

[11] Lawrence Grossman, "Corporate Culture," *The Nation*, 3 June 1996, p. 23.

financial incentive to use their media as a lobbying resource? I argue that it was reasonable and label this the "Allegation," with a capital "A." Note that I am not making the claim that the broadcasters did in fact exert such bias, just that it would have been reasonable for legislators who opposed broadcaster interests to fear such bias, or for those who supported broadcaster interests to hope for such bias. To the extent legislators' fears or hopes were reasonable, it would conflict with media's public trustee claims.

A Principal-Agent Definition of the Allegation

News media typically claim that their first loyalty is to the interests of their audiences, not their shareholders and business managers hired to represent those shareholder interests. Figure 8-1a depicts these trustee claims. The arrow points from a principal to an agent. The person who delegates a task to another is the principal. The person who accepts that trust and promises to act on behalf of the principal is the agent. Figure 8-1b depicts the media's trustee claim in the more abstract and generalized terminology of principal-agent theory. A dash across a line of potential influence represents a claim that those interests do not in fact influence the agent and that the agent therefore has no conflict of interest.

Figure 8-1. Media's Ethical Claims in Principal-Agent Terms

1a) Media Terminology

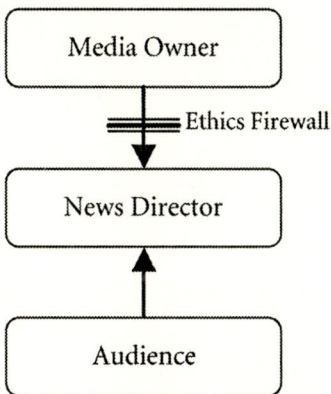

Media Owner
↓ Ethics Firewall
News Director
↑
Audience

1b) Principal-Agent Terminology

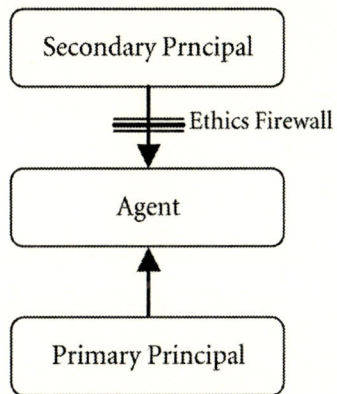

Secondary Prncipal
↓ Ethics Firewall
Agent
↑
Primary Principal

The person the agent claims to serve when there is a conflict of interest between two principals is the primary principal. The person the agent claims not to serve in such a conflict is the secondary principal. It's quite possible that the claim will vary depending upon which audience it is made to. Politicians, for example, are notorious for claiming to act on behalf of any audience they happen to be speaking to. Similarly, a news director may privately profess to his general manager and employer that he is the primary principal while at the same time publicly professing to audiences that they are the primary principal. When I use the term primary principal, I will always mean the claim made to media audiences, not media owners.

Every dashed line pointing from a secondary principal to an agent is termed an ethics firewall. Media will typically claim the existence of many such ethics firewalls because, as outlined in Chapter 2, potential conflicts of interest are numerous. In the literature on journalistic ethics, what is here labeled the ethics firewall is commonly called "the separation of church and state."[12]

The Allegation of Bias asserts that the agent is influenced by the interests of a secondary principal, even when those interests conflict with the interests of the claimed primary principal. Figures 8-2a and 8-2b depict this situation simply by removing the dash/ethics firewall that signifies non-influence. Now the agent is a dual agent because he no longer has undivided loyalty to his primary principal.

Figure 8-2. The Allegation of Bias in Principal-Agent Terms

1a) Media Terminology

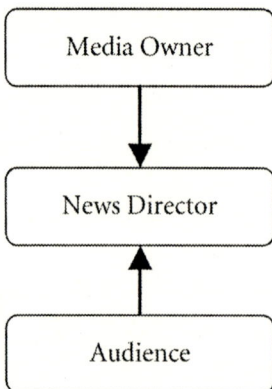

```
┌─────────────────────┐
│     Media Owner     │
└─────────────────────┘
           │
           ▼
┌─────────────────────┐
│    News Director    │
└─────────────────────┘
           ▲
           │
┌─────────────────────┐
│      Audience       │
└─────────────────────┘
```

1b) Principal-Agent Terminology

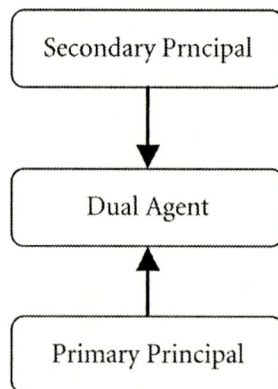

```
┌─────────────────────┐
│  Secondary Prncipal │
└─────────────────────┘
           │
           ▼
┌─────────────────────┐
│     Dual Agent      │
└─────────────────────┘
           ▲
           │
┌─────────────────────┐
│  Primary Principal  │
└─────────────────────┘
```

[12] E.g., Bagdikian, *The Media Monopoly*, p. 231, Kovach and Rosenstiel, *The Elements of Journalism*, p. 62.

In the case of the Media, the Allegation asserts that legislators are skeptical of reporter (agent) claims to always represent the interests of their audiences (primary principal) when they have much to gain by acting in the interests of their media owners (secondary principals) unless there is an exceptionally credible separation of Church & State (ethics firewall).

Structure of the Argument

In Chapter 9, we look at media's ethical claims. Then in the succeeding chapters we look at four types of arguments—from authority, analogy, cause, and example—addressing the Allegation that legislators have reasonable grounds to doubt those claims. These types of arguments are taken from Northwestern University Professor David Zarefsky's classic textbook on rhetoric.[13]

1) The argument from authority looks to statements by respected individuals. In this case, we look at allegations that members of Congress were indeed fearful of broadcaster media bias.

2) The argument from analogy looks at evidence from situations with a similar incentive structure outside the realm of broadcast policy. If broadcasters and other political actors claim to be public trustees but act opportunistically in one situation, it is reasonable to infer that in other situations with similar incentive structures they might do the same.

3) The argument from cause looks at broadcaster incentives to lobby for spectrum with media resources. If a broadcaster's cost-benefit analysis points to the desirability of broadcast policy media bias, then it is reasonable to believe that some broadcasters might act on their self interest.

4) The argument from example looks at lobbying case studies involving broadcast policy media bias. In this case, we look at broadcasters' use of their own media during lobbying for the Cable Act of 1992 and Telecommunications Act of 1996.

The arguments are meant to be complementary, and are ordered roughly in ascending methodological rigor and declining availability of readily accessible public information.

According to the paradox of bias (see Chapter 1), evidence of bias, including media bias, should be hard to come by. But not all such evidence should be

---

[13] David Zarefsky, *Argumentation: The Study of Effective Reasoning* (Chantilly, VA: Teaching Company, 2001), sound recording, David Zarefsky, *Public Speaking : Strategies for Success*, 3rd ed. (Boston: Allyn and Bacon, 2002).

equally hard to come by. The hardest type of evidence should be actual behavior, a "smoking gun" (the argument by example). General life experience of similar situations (the argument from analogy) may be easier to come by because it draws upon a much larger pool of potential evidence. Similarly, collecting detailed cost-benefit data (the argument from cause) may be easier than collecting data about actual behavior (the argument from example) because it is usually harder to hide information about incentives for bias than actual behavior of bias.

In terms of methodological rigor, the arguments from authority and analogy cannot do much more than establish doubt that media trustee claims, per se, may not be credible in the eyes of a reasonable person. They help shift the burden of proof onto those claiming media trustee behavior. The extent to which they shift this burden of proof is heavily dependent on the ability and incentives of media agents to hide direct evidence of bias.

The arguments from cause and example provide higher quality evidence than the argument from analogy because both arguments may be viewed as a special case of the argument from analogy, with a greater number of potentially confounding variables controlled for.

The overall argument strategy relies heavily on circumstantial evidence. However, the piling on of circumstantial evidence raises doubt. And it is such doubts, in my opinion, that make it reasonable for politicians to anticipate broadcast policy media bias if they act against broadcaster interests. Politicians live in a world where circumstantial evidence dominates their decision making process. Given the paradox of bias, a rational politician should have little expectation that definitive evidence of widespread broadcaster policy media bias will ever be produced.

In many transactions between a principal and agent, the paradox of bias is not a problem. Many products can be evaluated before being acquired ("search goods"). Many others can be evaluated after being acquired ("experience goods"). Still others cannot be evaluated even after purchase ("credibility goods').[14] Government often responds to the existence of credibility goods by passing disclosure, conflict of interest, and quality of service regulations. This explains, for example, why there are more than 800 licensed occupations in the United States, including many, such as financial advisors, which provide nonpolitical information services.[15] But First Amendment considerations have

---

[14] F. M. Scherer and David Ross, *Industrial Market Structure and Economic Performance*, 3rd ed. (Boston: Houghton Mifflin, 1990).

[15] Benjamin Shimberg, *Occupational Licensing: A Public Perspective* (Princeton, N.J.: Center for Occupational and Professional Assessment, Educational Testing Service, 1982).

traditionally precluded the government from regulating public affairs media—even when such media, as argued in Chapter 2, create information products whose credibility audiences have great difficulty evaluating. Journalistic codes of ethics are the way media deal with this marketplace failure. But it is a solution that may inspire less than 100% confidence in reasonable politicians.

On the one hand, therefore, we have a system of media regulation (or its absence) that invites abuse. On the other hand, the remedy would appear to be far worse than the problem. Nobody wants elected officials regulating the very media that in a democracy functions to hold them accountable to voters. But, as the body of this book argues, this may come at a price.

In this book's concluding chapter, we will see that this type of dilemma is not limited to media—it's endemic to all democratic reform. And it's solution should also not be specifically directed at media but that much larger problem.

CHAPTER 9:

Media Trustee Claims

"Some have questioned whether newspapers and other media organizations can lobby legislators one moment and cover them the next. Can the 'Daily Press' report fairly about 'Sen. Jones' if the senator voted for (or against) a bill that the newspaper's parent company lobbied for (or against)?

After 23 years of representing media interests in Washington, I believe the answer is unequivocally yes. Further, it's an insult to the professionalism of the newsroom to think otherwise.

The well-known wall that separates news and business operations at newspapers is no myth."

—John Sturm, NAA President and Former NAB Board Member[1]

"[I]t is not essential…that a prince should have all the good qualities that I have enumerated…but it is most essential that he should seem to have them."

—Machiavelli, *The Prince*, Chapter 18

All successful agents claim to act on behalf of their principals. This is because no rational principal would "hire" an agent whose intent was to harm the principal. Similarly, when soliciting audiences, the media claim to act on behalf of those audiences. Media make this claim in a number of different ways, some explicit and some implicit. Journalistic codes of ethics are among the clearest and most explicit ways media trustee claims are made.[2]

---

[1] The NAA is the Newspaper Association of America and is to the newspaper industry what the NAB is to the broadcast industry. John F. Sturm, "Lobbying for More Than Just Assets: The lobbyists protect the business interests, which promote the vitality of the news media," *Media Studies Journal*, Fall 2000, p. 99.

[2] For an excellent recent overview of media ethical claims, see Kovach and Rosenstiel, *The Elements of Journalism*.

The **Radio-Television News Directors Association** (RTNDA) is the premier association that represents news directors on local radio and television broadcast stations. It is located in Washington, DC less than a mile from both the White House and the National Association of Broadcasters (NAB). Every RTNDA member must sign RTNDA's ethics code before joining.[3] Many successful news directors who move up to management positions later join the NAB. RTNDA's ethics code includes the following major headings:

> PREAMBLE: Professional electronic journalists should operate as trustees of the public, seek the truth, report it fairly and with integrity and independence, and stand accountable for their actions.
>
> PUBLIC TRUST: Professional electronic journalists should recognize that their first obligation is to the public....
>
> FAIRNESS: Professional electronic journalists should present the news fairly and impartially, placing primary value on significance and relevance....
>
> INTEGRITY: Professional electronic journalists should present the news with integrity and decency, avoiding real or perceived conflicts of interest....
>
> INDEPENDENCE: Professional electronic journalists should defend the independence of all journalists from those seeking influence or control over news content.

The "Independence" clause specifically claims an ethics firewall:

> **Professional electronic journalists should:**
>
> Gather and report news without fear or favor, and vigorously resist undue influence from any outside forces, including advertisers, sources, story subjects, powerful individuals, and special interest groups.
>
> Resist those who would seek to buy or politically influence news content or who would seek to intimidate those who gather and disseminate the news.
>
> Determine news content solely through editorial judgment and not as the result of outside influence.

---

[3] Barbara Cochran, "Holding the Banner High," *Communicator*, September 1997, p. 38.

Resist any self-interest or peer pressure that might erode journalistic duty and service to the public.

Recognize that sponsorship of the news will not be used in any way to determine, restrict, or manipulate content.

Refuse to allow the interests of ownership or management to influence news judgment and content inappropriately.

The **American Society of Newspaper Editors** (ASNE) represents newspaper editors, a position analogous in seniority to TV news director. Its ethics code begins:

The primary purpose of gathering and distributing news and opinion is to serve the general welfare by informing the people and enabling them to make judgments on the issues of the time. Newspapermen and women who abuse the power of their professional role for selfish motives or unworthy purposes are faithless to that public trust.

The **Society of Professional Journalists** (SPJ) represents rank-and-file reporters from both print (including newspapers and magazines) and electronic media (including both radio and TV). Like the RTNDA ethics code, the SPJ ethics code is often posted in the newsrooms of local broadcast stations. Its ethics code includes the following text:

PREAMBLE: Members of the Society of Professional Journalists believe that public enlightenment is the forerunner of justice and the foundation of democracy. The duty of the journalist is to further those ends by seeking truth and providing a fair and comprehensive account of events and issues....

Seek Truth and Report It

Journalists should be honest, fair and courageous in gathering, reporting and interpreting information....

Act Independently

Journalists should be free of obligation to any interest other than the public's right to know....

Be Accountable

Journalists are accountable to their readers, listeners, viewers, and each other.

The "Act Independently" clause contains the following ethical firewall claims:

Journalists should:

Avoid conflicts of interest, real or perceived.

Remain free of associations and activities that may compromise integrity or damage credibility.

Refuse gifts, favors, fees, free travel and special treatment, and shun secondary employment, political involvement, public office and service in community organizations if they compromise journalistic integrity.

Disclose unavoidable conflicts.

Be vigilant and courageous about holding those with power accountable.

Deny favored treatment to advertisers and special interests and resist their pressure to influence news coverage.

Be wary of sources offering information for favors or money; avoid bidding for news.[4]

The **National Press Club,** located near the White House and Capitol Hill, is the premier news club for the nation's elite media. Prominent politicians and other influential leaders speak there on a daily basis, and the walls are covered with photographs of famous politicians and reporters who have spoken there. TV outlets and daily newspapers from throughout the country pay for their Washington, DC reporters to belong to the National Press Club. Many state level press clubs also have reciprocal rights to use the National Press Club. The foyer leading into the Press Club displays "The Journalist's Creed" adjacent to the elevator at eye level, so it's hard for any National Press Club member or visitor to miss it. The Creed is also prominently displayed on the National Press Club's website and in its annual directory sent to members. It reads:

I believe in the profession of journalism.

I believe that the public journal is a public trust; that all connected with it are, to the full measure of their responsibility, trustees for the public; that acceptance of a lesser service than the public service is a betrayal of this trust.

---

[4] Black et al., *Doing Ethics in Journalism*, pp. 6-8.

I believe that clear thinking and clear statement, accuracy, and fairness, are fundamental to good journalism.

I believe that a journalist should write only what he holds in his heart to be true.

I believe that suppression of the news, for any consideration other than the welfare of society, is indefensible.

I believe that no one should write as a journalist what he would not say as a gentleman; that bribery by one's own pocketbook is as much to be avoided as bribery by the pocketbook of another; that individual responsibility may not be escaped by pleading another's instructions or another's dividends.

I believe that advertising, news, and editorial columns should alike serve the best interests of readers; that a single standard of helpful truth and cleanness should prevail for all; that the supreme test of good journalism is the measure of its public service....

The **Newseum,** based in the Washington, D.C. metro area, is the most visited and influential museum of the print and electronic news industry. When visitors enter the Newseum, they see the following journalistic codes of ethics in slogan form plastered all over the wall across from an inscription of the First Amendment:[5]

- All the news that's fit to print.
- An independent newspaper.
- Balanced news, fearless views.
- Dedicated to the people's right to know.
- Friend of the people it serves.
- Give light and the people will find their own way.

---

[5] Note that many of the above slogans are no longer on print publication mastheads. They are historical slogans. But this fact is nowhere acknowledged at the Newseum. The simplest explanation for this riddle is that these are indeed the standards the media like to claim for itself not only when they want audience trust but also when they want government perks, including a media friendly interpretation of the First Amendment. On the other hand, media lawyers don't like explicit claims that might come back to haunt media outlets in a court of law. Thus, by farming out self-serving ethical claims to third parties such as the Newseum, the media are able to claim the benefits of such claims without the legal liability that might otherwise attach to them.

- I have never regarded the paper as merely a piece of private property to be conducted for mercenary ends; but rather as an institution to be managed for the public good.
- If you don't want it printed, don't let it happen.
- It is a newspaper's duty to print the news and raise hell. It will be the people's paper, run strictly in their interests, guarding jealously their rights and maintaining boldly their cause.
- Light for all.
- Little good is accomplished without controversy, and no civic evil is ever defeated without publicity.
- Service is the rent we pay for the space we occupy in this world.
- The conscience of the nation.
- The Leader guards the reader.
- The newspaper that says what others won't.
- The old reliable.
- The paper that gives it to you straight.
- The stinging truth.
- The truth and nothing but the truth.
- The tyrant's foe—The People's Friend.
- To give the news impartially, without fear or favor.
- Truth in preference to fiction.
- We don't make the news; we report it.
- What the people don't know WILL hurt them.
- Without or with offense to friends or foes, we sketch your world exactly as it goes.

The **Public Broadcasting Service** (PBS) provides programming to hundreds of non-profit local TV stations. Its ethics code starts:

Editorial integrity in public broadcasting programming means the responsible application by professional practitioners of a free and independent decision-making process which is ultimately account-able to the needs and interests of all citizens. Programming based on principles of editorial integrity will guarantee journalistic objectivity, as well as fair and balanced presentation of issues.

Public Radio New Directors Incorporated (PRNDI) represents news directors at hundreds of public radio stations. Its ethics code includes:

> Whereas PRNDI members serve many communities and interests that deserve news programs of the highest standards of honesty, fairness, integrity, balance, compassion, and technical quality;
>
> Now, therefore PRNDI does advance and call upon members to follow this code of ethical conduct...
>
> Strive to eliminate personal, station, or community bias....
>
> Responsibly evaluate the newsworthiness of all broadcast items and guard against undue pressure from non-news personnel...."[6]

A brief submitted to the U.S. Supreme Court on behalf of major media outlets, including broadcasters ABC, CBS, Gannett, Hearst, NBC, New York Times, E.W. Scripps, Tribune, and Washington Post, included the following opening:

> From the time individuals first consider becoming journalists, two principles are drilled into them....
>
> The first is that telling the truth about matters of public interest is what journalism, at its best, is all about. Journalists who consult codes of ethics written about their chosen field read the repeated exhortation that their role is to "seek truth and repeat it" and that "truth is their guiding principle"....
>
> So is the journalistic norm that in the course of gathering news, journalists should affirmatively seek the truth from those who have it.... This applies to the gathering of news both about the government and the private sector....
>
> For journalists, then, the notion that liability may be imposed upon them for doing nothing more or less than reporting truthfully about newsworthy events is deeply disturbing.[7]

---

[6] Cited in John Dinges et al., editors, "Independence and Integrity: A Guidebook for Public Radio Journalism," Washington, DC: *National Public Radio*, 1995

[7] Bartnicki et al. v. Vopper, No. 99-1687, Supreme Court of the United States, Brief Amici Curia of Media Entitites and Organizations in Support of Respondents, 25 October 2000, pp. 2-5.

The **National Association of Broadcasters,** the leading trade association representing local broadcast TV management, has no formal journalistic ethics code. But affirmative ethical statements are nevertheless occasionally made. For example, in lobbying against the Fairness Doctrine, it repeatedly claimed that "broadcasters do provide coverage of both sides of controversial issues."[8] In arguing against spectrum auctions, the NAB asserted "Broadcasters follow a higher standard for serving the public interest than the government requires. The fact that very few licenses have ever been revoked is testament to the responsible manner in which broadcasters have used the airwaves and served the public."[9]

Some individual publications and media chains also have their own journalistic codes of ethics.[10] Here are two elite newspapers, both owned by companies with modest broadcast holdings:

> *New York Times:* "The goal of The *New York Times* is to cover the news as impartially as possible—"without fear or favor," in the words of Adolph Ochs, our patriarch.... Conflicts of interest, real or apparent, may come up in many areas. They may involve the relationships of staff members with readers, news sources, advocacy groups, advertisers, or competitors; with one another, or with the newspaper or its parent company.... In keeping with its solemn responsibilities under the First Amendment, The Times strives to maintain the highest standards of journalistic ethics.... [N]o one may do anything that damages The Times' reputation for strict neutrality in reporting on politics and government.... Our fundamental purpose is to protect the impartiality and neutrality of the Times and the integrity of its report.... Journalists have no place on the playing field of politics.... In particular, they may not campaign for, demonstrate for, or endorse candidates, ballot causes or efforts to enact legislation.... Staff members may not themselves give money to, or raise money for, any political candidate or election cause."[11]

---

[8] Fairness Doctrine," Legislative Issue Papers, October 1995, p. 9.

[9] NAB, "Talking Points," in *Spectrum Auction Action Tool Kit* (Washington, DC: NAB, January 1996), p. 26.

[10] For a good list of journalistic codes of ethics, see the website of the American Association of Newspaper Editors. http://www.asne.org/index.cfm?id=387. It is noteworthy that I was able to find nothing comparable for local broadcast TV outlets.

[11] *New York Times,* "Ethical Journalism: Codes of Conduct for the News and Editorial Departments," January 2003 edition, available at http://www.poynterextra.org/extra/ethics.pdf.

Washington Post: "The newspaper's duty is to its readers and to the public at large, and not to the private interests of the owner. In the pursuit of truth, the newspaper shall be prepared to make sacrifices of its material fortunes, if such course be necessary for the public good. The newspaper shall not be the ally of any special interest, but shall be fair and free and wholesome in its outlook on public affairs and public men."[12]

Here are two smaller market newspapers:

Spokane Spokesman-Review: "Business, advertising and political interest of management personnel must not be allowed to influence news content.… the editorial department must retain its special status as watchdog for the readers, inherent in which is the responsibility to report stories regardless of the economic or political ramifications. The newspaper should report matters regarding itself or its personnel with the same vigor and candor as it would other comparable institutions or individuals."[13]

Columbus Ledger-Enquirer: "Our newspapers report the news without regard for our own interest. We do not give favored news treatment to advertisers or special-interest groups. We report matters regarding ourselves and our staff and families with the same standards we apply to other institutions and individuals."[14]

Individual broadcasters are much more likely than newspapers either not to have a detailed ethics code or to keep the one that they have a secret. But this doesn't mean that they don't have widely touted news slogans that make agency claims, albeit ones that amount to little more than legally sanctioned branding puffery. In Washington, DC, the news slogans of the three major network affiliated TV stations are: Working 4 You (NBC's WRC-TV, Channel 4); Seven On Your Side (ABC's WJLA-TV, Channel 7), and Whatever It Takes (CBS' WUSA-TV, Channel 9). Other similar slogans are Fair and Balanced (Fox's News Channel), Watching Out for You (ABC's KEZI-TV; Eugene, Oregon), News You Can Count On (Fox's KTBC-TV; Austin, Texas), Your Eye on Austin (CBS' KEYE-TV; Austin, Texas); The Eye of Texas (CBS' KTVT-TV;

---

[12] *Washinngton Post*, "Standards and Ethics", 16 February 1999 edition, available at http://www.asne.org/ideas/codes/washingtonpost.htm.
[13] Black et al., *Doing Ethics in Journalism*, p. 108.
[14] Ibid, p. 110.

Dallas, Texas), and Station of the People (CBS' KCBS-TV; Los Angeles, California).

Implicit Claims

Many local media outlets lack their own formal journalistic codes of ethics. And of those that do, only a small fraction publicize them. Despite scouring dozens of local TV news websites, I could not find a single one that posted an ethics code. And although all the major TV networks have codes of ethics, they consider them confidential documents. The only way I got the ethics statement for NBC news was to promise the national reporter who gave it to me that I would not reveal her name. I also needed to assure her that my use was scholarly. The primary reason for this secrecy is that media lawyers believe that making a formal ethics claim creates a legal liability on the part of the corporation.[15]

The basic legal and public relations strategy is to let the networks have their cake and eat it, too. By making individual reporters sign the confidential ethics documents, the legal and public relations burden of violation gets shifted from the corporation onto individual reporters. The company can assert that it has an ethics policy and that all violations are the fault of individual reporters, not the company.

The most common type of public ethics claims are made implicitly. One reason may be that implicit ethics claims may be the most believable. Given a choice between believing the salesman who says he would never lie and the salesman who has a trustworthy manner, most people would choose the one with the trustworthy manner. Accordingly, a rational media outlet will try to demonstrate by its behavior that it follows a strict journalistic ethics code.

One type of implicit claim is the absence of any public claims contrary to the codes of ethics. Most media organizations have employees that belong to media associations that promulgate codes of ethics and expect members to abide by them. Yet, I have never heard of a media organization telling its employees that they cannot belong to such associations because the journalistic codes of ethics they are expected to abide by as members in good standing conflict with their employer's interest.

A similar piece of evidence by omission is the deafening public silence among media spokespeople, including journalists and media owners, that opportunistic action in relation to the public is acceptable. Over the years, I have been a regular reader of many magazines devoted to press criticism. But I

---

[15] Jeffrey Marks, "Raising Ethical Issues," *Communicator*, February 1995, p. 19.

have yet to read an article where a spokesperson for a reputable media organization touts ethical violations or asserts that the interests of his organization's owners should take precedence over the interests of his organization's media audience. Often, the interests of media owners and viewers will be described as identical. Questions that suggest the possibility of a conflict of interest will be dismissed, perhaps as not reflecting an adequate understanding of the logic of Adam Smith's invisible hand, where self-interest is transformed through competition into the public interest. In other words, the possibility of a conflict between media owners' profit goals and the interests of their media audience will not be acknowledged.

Another type of implicit ethics claim is by commission. The act of commission is to hide any evidence of behavior contrary to the claims of an ethics code. For example, reporters are expected to act aloof to politicians when in front of a public audience. Their off-camera behavior may be totally different, but as long as the audience is unaware, their actual behavior doesn't matter.

Perhaps the most telling fact is that when a media organization is accused of violating a core journalistic ethics standard, it doesn't try to argue that the standard should not apply to itself, only that the evidence doesn't warrant the claim of a violation or that it was an aberration not representing corporate policy.

If all the public hears are denials of breaches of ethical conduct, and if it never hears any claims that a company sanctions such breaches, it can easily put one and one together and infer that a media organization claims to act as the public's trustee, even if the organization doesn't explicitly make that claim.

In lobbying for the spectrum giveaway contained in the Telecom Act of 1996, broadcasters had numerous opportunities to deny media ownership bias.

The *Wall Street Journal* reported on Senator McCain's allegation of broadcaster media bias, then ran a denial by one of his local TV broadcasters. The story ran just before the FCC gave broadcasters their new digital TV licenses:

> Jon Ruby, who runs the NBC television station in Tucson, Ariz., says he's known and admired Sen. John McCain for 10 years. But lately the Arizona Republican has been making some tough demands on Mr. Ruby's friendship.
>
> Mr. McCain wants broadcasters to pay billions of dollars for licenses to offer advanced, digital television…. Mr. McCain says the broadcast lobby is the most powerful lobby he has confronted in his 14 years in Congress…. Mr. McCain says: "They have never threatened me, but it's clear when they come in, they're the people who carry my message."…Broadcasters reject that notion. "Nobody that had any conscience about running a good news operation would ever

embargo a senator or a congressman," Mr. Ruby, the Tucson station manager, says.[16]

The Associated Press, in a nationally distributed newswire, reported on Common Cause's allegation of broadcaster media bias, then ran a denial by NAB spokesperson Dennis Wharton. The story ran the day the FCC gave broadcasters their new digital TV licenses:

> [A Common Cause Report] said broadcasters are particularly effective lobbyists because they have the 'power to report and shape the news' and 'control how and if members of Congress appear on television. That makes legislators extremely reluctant to take them on.'.... NAB spokesman Dennis Wharton called Common Cause's assertions 'baseless.'[17]

Broadcasting & Cable, the leading trade magazine of the broadcast industry, ran this denial of broadcaster media bias by a local broadcaster and NAB board member:

> Broadcasters deny that they would use their control of the airwaves to strong-arm politicians. 'It's getting legislators to understand what our business is about and getting them to understand the contributions that we make to our communities,' says Anderson, who is also vice president of the NAB radio board."[18]

The *Boston Globe* reported McCain's allegation of broadcaster media bias and then ran a denial by a local Boston TV station general manager, who also happened to be an NAB spokesperson[19] and his station's on-air commentator:[20]

---

[16] Bryan Gruley, "Senator McCain Puts Spotlight on Broadcasters With Demands for TV License Fees, Free Air Time," *Wall Street Journal*, 17 March 1997, p. A20.

[17] "Watchdog says broadcasters' donations buy influence," *Associated Press*, 4 April 1997.

[18] Paige Albiniak, "King of the Hill," *Broadcasting & Cable*, 22 December 1997, p. 18.

[19] Paul La Camera served as a broadcast industry representative on the President's Advisory Commission on the Public Interest Responsibilities of the Broadcasters, popularly known as the Gore Commission. The NAB strongly opposed the agenda of the Gore Commission and La Camera represented their position. E.g., Bill McConnell, "Loud Public Interest Earful," *Broadcasting & Cable*, 23 October 2000, p. 27.

[20] Karissa S. Wang, "Editorials Help Stations Stand Out," *Electronic Media*, 26 March 2001, p. 23.

McCain said members of Congress are cowed facing an industry that can make or break their careers.... 'The broadcasters carry the message of the politician,' McCain said, explaining why so many members of Congress side with the industry. 'I have never been threatened by a broadcaster and I never will be. But it is an unstated, unspoken message always in the room.'

Paul La Camera, the president and general manager of Boston's WCVB-TV...said McCain's comment is nonsense. Though La Camera said the station's news director reports to him, he said he would never suggest that news coverage be altered according to whether a member of Congress supports or opposes the industry. 'It's outrageous,' La Camera said. 'If I tried to do that, it would be immediately exposed.'"[21]

Conclusion

Ethics claims made by broadcasters and other media outlets to act on behalf of their audiences are not unusual. They are made by all agents in relationship to their principals. Legislators, like people in all walks of life, are constantly bombarded by people making such claims. The task is to determine when and to what extent it is reasonable to believe such claims. That is the subject of the next five chapters.

---

[21]Michael Kranish, "Campaign Finance Bill Shows TV's Clout: Networks Help Scuttle Free Ads," *Boston Globe*, 25 December 1997, p. A1. McCain may be unusually well positioned to make such an allegation because his own early political career was given a huge behind-the-scenes boost by the publisher of Arizona's largest newspaper. See Douglas Frantz, "A Beer Baron and a Powerful Publisher Put McCain on a Political Path," *New York Times*, 21 February 2000, p. A14.

CHAPTER 10:

The Argument from Authority

One type of evidence for the Allegation is the argument from authority. The argument from authority comes in direct and indirect varieties. The direct variety claims that the source of the broadcasters' power specifically stems from their control of the airwaves. The indirect variety makes a claim that might lead a reasonable person to make that inference himself. When a claim is made by many respected and diverse sources, it has more credibility.

The Direct Allegation

In the year preceding passage of the Telecom Act of 1996 and in the several years following its passage when the Act was interpreted and implemented, the Allegation of politically motivated media bias was levied in a wide variety of respected print media.[1] Sometimes news articles and editorials would attribute the Allegation to a named source. But usually it would be attributed to an anonymous source or stated as a simple matter of fact. Sometimes it would be countered with an opposing view but usually it was not. Even when an opposing view was stated, the Allegation represented a serious challenge because it raised a doubt in the reader's mind, especially when the reader was given little or no evidence concerning the Allegation's merit.

America's most respected and influential daily newspapers repeatedly made the Allegation.

> *Wall Street Journal*: Broadcasters control the one thing politicians care about more than money: television time. It is hard to find a member of Congress who doesn't fear that crossing the owner of his or her local broadcast station will translate into an immediate

---

[1] Snider was able to find only one such charge in TV broadcast media, although it is possible that others exist. See Chapter 15 for details.

reduction in air time. So when broadcasters come knocking, members of Congress answer.[2]

New York Times: The broadcast industry has power in Washington for two reasons: It spends millions in campaign donations and on high-powered lobbyists that work Congress and the F.C.C.... More important, however, the industry has the power of television: Its stations nationwide determine how politicians are portrayed to their voters back home.[3]

Washington Post: Traditionally, politicians have been wary about taking on broadcasters during election years, when exposure on local and national TV news is crucial.... 'If I were a candidate for president, I surely would not want to...alienate broadcasters at this stage of my campaign,' one lobbyist said.[4]

The *Wall Street Journal* printed the Allegation four times between December 27, 1995 and September 29, 1997. It made the Allegation a fifth time on March 17, 1997, but along with a broadcaster denial.[5] The *New York Times* printed the Allegation four times between February 25, 1996 and July 23, 1997.[6] No *New York Times* Allegation was accompanied by a broadcaster denial.[7] The

---

[2] Alan Murray, "Broadcasters Get a Pass on Campaign Reform," 29 September 1997, p. 1.

[3] Leslie Wayne, "Broadcast Lobby's Formula: Airtime + Money = Influence," *New York Times*, 5 May 1997, p. C1

[4] Mike Miles and Paul Farhi, "Dole Statement Snags Phone, Cable TV Bill," *Washington Post*, 11 January 1996, D8.

[5] The four additional *Wall Street Journal* Allegations: "I-Way Detours," 27 December 1995, p. A10, "Asides," 26b April 1996, A20, "Off the Dole," 24 January 1996, p. A14, Alan Murray, "Digital TV Giveaway Foils Campaign Reform," 17 March 1997, p. A1.

[6] The three additional *New York Times* Allegations: Max Frankel, "Digital Castles in the Sky," 25 February 1996, p.38; "Another Broadcast Giveaway," 25 June 1997, p. A26, William Safire, "Broadcast Lobby Triumphs," 23 July 1997, Leslie Wayne, "Broadcast Lobby's Formula: Airtime + Money = Influence," *New York Times*, 5 May 1997, p. C1.

[7] The *New York Times* ran letters from senior broadcasters disputing the assertions in its editorials. However, none of these writers, including the NAB's president, chose to dispute the Allegation. In his role as panel discussant at the 1998 Telecommunications Policy Research Conference, the head of NAB's research department, Rick Ducey, read a paper presented by this author providing evidence of broadcaster news bias. At no point during his very brief critique of the paper did he question the author's findings.

Washington Post printed the Allegation six times between January 11, 1996 and July 20, 1997, including twice in Herb Block cartoons.[8]

The Associated Press, which distributes its stories to more than a thousand local newspapers, carried the Allegation twice within a week, each time with a broadcaster rebuttal. The first of the two articles ran immediately after the FCC implemented the portion of the Telecom Act allocating new spectrum rights to broadcasters.

> Critics call it the biggest corporate giveaway of the century: broad-casters getting television channels worth billions of dollars.... Over the last decade, major broadcast interests have given more than $9.5 million in political contributions, Common Cause reports. Broadcasters are effective lobbyists and have the power to shape the news and control how and if politicians get on the air.... Broadcasters rebut those charges.[9]

Nationally syndicated *New York Times* columnist, William Safire, made the Allegation: "Because TV stations dictate local coverage, the broadcast lobby strikes bipartisan terror in officeholders' hearts."[10]

Nationally syndicated *Washington Post* political cartoonist, Herb Block, made the Allegation (see Figures 10-1 and 10-2).[11]

---

[8] The other major daily newspaper in Washington, DC, the *Washington Times*, also made the Allegation: "[B]ecause politicians are generally afraid of offending the broadcasters who shape their own media coverage, the NAB might just get what it wants." See "The Specter of Spectrum," *Washington Times*, 28 March 1997, p. A18.

[9] Jeannine Aversa, "Airwave Allocation Called Big Giveaway: Sale of TV Spectrum Could Raise Billions," *San Diego Union-Tribune*, 8 April 1997, p. C1. See also "Watchdog says broadcasters' donations buy influence," *Associated Press*, 4 April 1997.

[10] William Safire, "Broadcast Lobby Triumphs," *New York Times*, 23 July 1997, p. A21.

[11] Herb Block, "We Know You Politicians Want To Look Good on Television—And Before You Go, Here's a Little Release for You to Sign," *Washington Post*, 27 July 1997.

Figure 10-1. Herb Block Cartoon—"We know you politicians…."

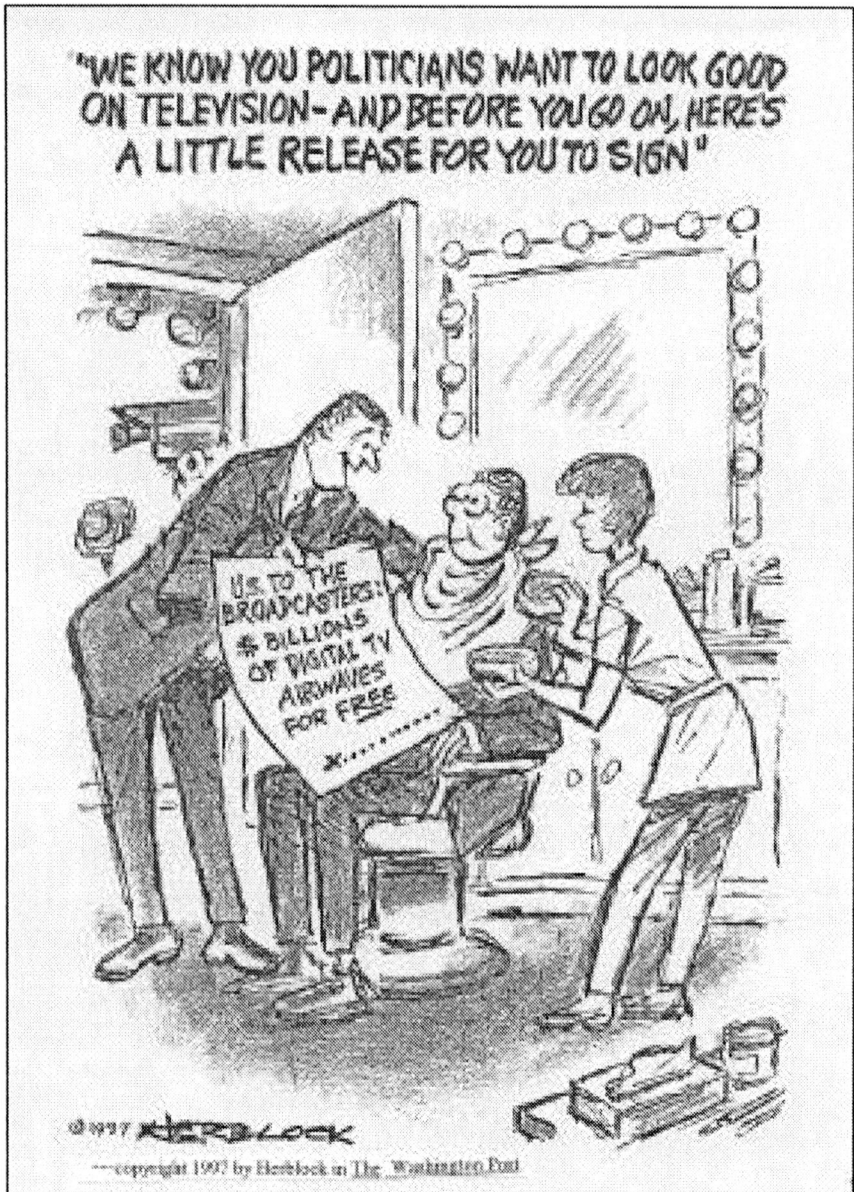

Figure 10-2. Herb Block Cartoon—"In some countries...."

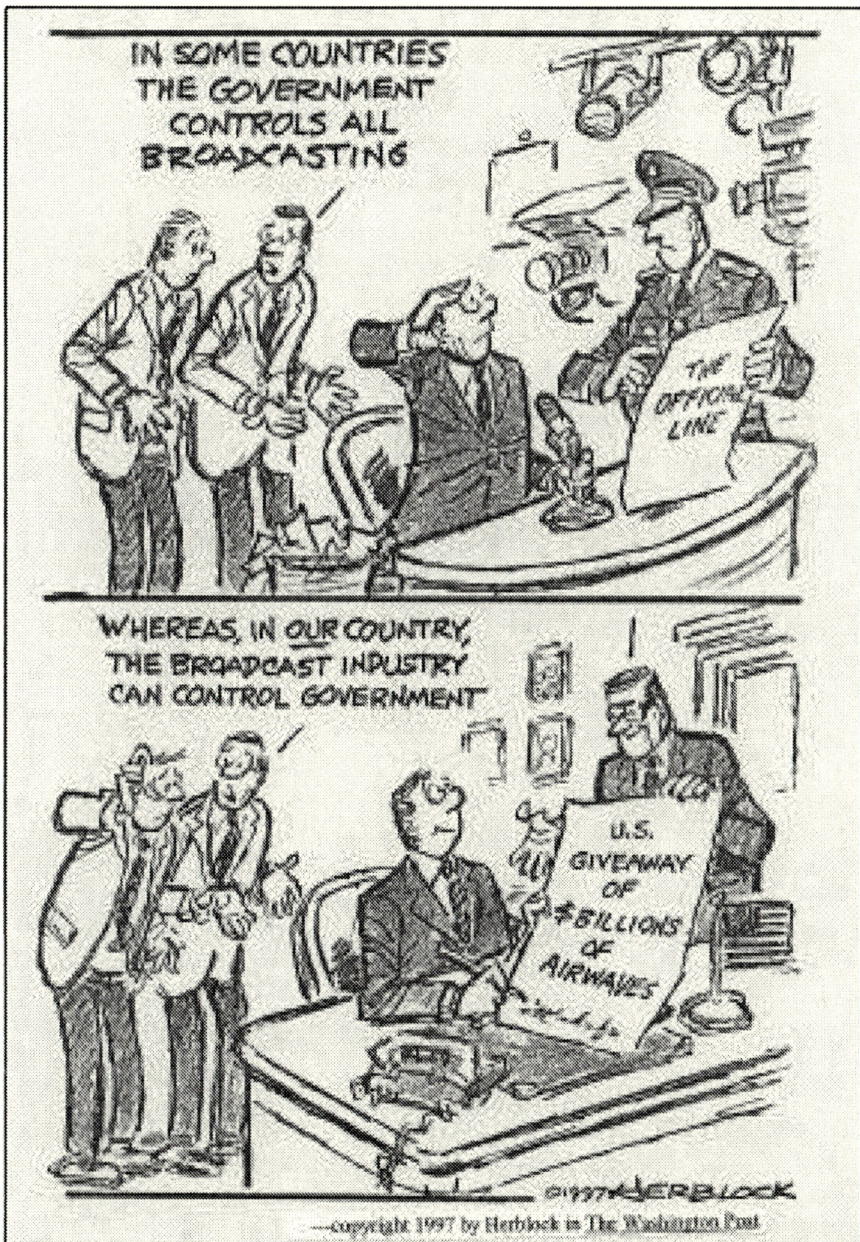

Influential Washington-based media that specialize in covering Congress made the Allegation:

> **National Journal:** The NAB gave more than $660,000 in political action committee (PAC) contributions in the recent election.... Even more important than such contributions may be lawmakers' fear of challenging TV stations, on which they depend heavily for news coverage and ad discounts.[12]

> **The Hill:** The most important ally for the industry may not be their high-priced talent in Washington, but the unwitting news directors of local TV stations, said...Paul Taylor, a former *Washington Post* reporter.... 'There is a rather vulgar connection made in the minds of members, who are reluctant to take on broadcasters,' Taylor said. 'They worry they may not get on the 6 o'clock news.'[13]

The oldest and arguably most prestigious of the journalism reviews ran the Allegation three times between July 1995 and September 1998:[14]

> *Columbia Journalism Review:* In election years, politicians develop a special attentiveness to the needs of local TV entrepreneurs, whose goodwill, airtime, and contributions they need to get re-elected.[15]

---

[12] Eliza Newlin Carney, "Campaign Finance: Tuning Out Free TV," *National Journal*, 12 April 1997. On the NAB's 1992 effort to win cable reregulation, Kirk Victor writes: "The NAB, the big winner so far, has discovered how to fully flex its political muscle. Particularly in a year when politicians are in a state of high anxiety, the folks in charge of soundbites have a lot of clout." See Kirk Victor, "The Clash of the Titans on Cable Regulation," *National Journal*, 16 May 1992, p. 1177.

[13] Earnon Javers, "Lobbyists Oppose Free Air Time For Candidates," *The Hill*, 26 March 1997, p. 8.

[14] Neil Hickey, "Revolution in Cyberia," *Columbia Journalism Review*, July/August 1995, p. 45, Neil Hickey, "What's at Stake in the Spectrum War? Only Billions of Dollars and the Future of Television," *Columbia Journalism Review*, July/August 1996, p. 42, Sheila Kaplan, "Payments to the Powerful," *Columbia Journalism Review*, September 1998, p. 54. The Review ran it a fourth time in September 2000. See Charles Lewis, "Media Money," *Columbia Journalism Review*, September/October 2000, p. 24.

[15] Hickey, "What's at Stake in the Spectrum War?," p. 42.

Influential public affairs magazines made the Allegation:[16]

Washington Monthly: The media's role as information provider to the public puts them in a class apart. One aspect of that power is the media lobby's ability to act in its own interest virtually without fear that it will face much, if any public scrutiny.... This role as information provider also gives the media the ability to make or break any public servant with the use—or non-use—of news and commentary.[17]

The New Republic: [B]roadcasters back home...are the figures, far from Capitol Hill, who hold the ticket to every congressman's heart—access to the six o'clock news....This is not the sort of currency that's openly exchanged. On the contrary, broadcasters insist in private and in public that they never barter journalistic coverage for bottom-line favors. And they may mean it. But not many politicians believe them. They're as jaundiced about the media's ethics as the media are about theirs. They live in a world where image is a fragile commodity, where paranoia is a survival tool and where it's taken as a given that if the station manager, the news director and the anchorman think you're a helluva guy, that's a very good thing.[18]

The Nation: Media companies are especially powerful in Washington because they have more than money to hand out. 'TV and newspapers are the gatekeepers of public perception and can make a politician popular or unpopular,' says Reed Hundt. 'Politicians know that in their bones; the only ones who don't are the ones who didn't get elected.'[19]

---

[16] Note that the *Weekly Standard*, financed by Rupert Murdoch, did not cover the story.

[17] Arthur E. Rowse, "A Lobby the Media Won't Touch," *Washington Monthly*, May 1998, p. 10. The *Washington Monthly* made the Allegation three times between June 1995 and November 1999. See Warren Cohen, "Halting the Air Raid: Auctioning the Air Waves," *Washington Monthly*, June 1995, p. 30, Charles Peters, "Tilting at Windmills," Washington Monthly, November 1999, p. 4, Sheila Kaplan, "One Special Interest the Press Doesn't Cover: Itself," *Washington Monthly*, December 1988, pp. 36-46.

[18] Paul Taylor, "Superhighway Robbery: America's Broadcasters V. The Public Good," *New Republic*, 5 May 1997, p. 20.

[19] Silverstein, "His Biggest Takeover Ever," p 18. In the same issue of *The Nation*, another article concludes: "The N.A.B. is a master at using its member stations to pressure Congress." See Bill Meisler, "Field Guide to Lobbyists," *Nation*, 8 June 1998, p. 27.

The American Prospect: The Old Washington truism is that every member of Congress quivers to think what the TV station back home might do in the way of negative coverage. Have they good reason to tremble? Would television stations really succeed in manipulating their reporters to serve the industry's purposes? Or could it be that the NAB is a convenient bogeyman for Congress?

"I think that's right," Taylor [a former *Washington Post* reporter and advocate of free airtime for candidates] says. "But listen: I've always been impressed by the extent that politicians live in fear of real and imagined enemies."[20]

Regulation: When Congress applies more serious pressure for the return of the old licenses, the broadcasters will threaten dirty public-information and lobbying campaigns and less-than-favorable political advertising treatment.[21]

The two most influential journals dedicated to covering the emerging information economy made the Allegation:[22]

Wired: So long as broadcasting is protected from the free market by legislators who depend on TV to get themselves reelected, Congress will continue to give broadcasters special treatment and favors, and consumers will suffer.[23]

Industry Standard: Congress...donated an extra channel of spectrum space to every TV station to allow for a stately analog-to-digital conversion. (All this despite Bob Dole's warning of a "$72 [*sic*] billion giveaway" to the broadcasters, before he remembered from whom he had to buy his commercial time, and promptly clammed up.)[24]

---

[20]Dave Denison, "Don't Mess with Television," *American Prospect*, 5 June 2000, p. 37.

[21] Adam Thierer, "The Great Taxpayer Rip-Off of 1995," *Regulation*, no. 4 (1995): p. 22.

[22] The *Industry Standard*, which in the late 1990s took over *Wired*'s role as the leading magazine of the digerati, also made the Allegation. See Harry Shearer, "Bad Reception," *Industry Standard*, 26 February 2001, p. 27.

[23] Charles Platt, "The Great HDTV Swindle," *Wired*, February 1997, p. 191. See also Common Cause, "Your Master's Voice," *Wired*, August 1997, Mark Lewyn, "The Great Airwave Robbery," *Wired*, March 1996, p. 115.

[24] Harry Shearer, "Bad Reception," *Industry Standard*, 26 February 2001, p. 27.

Widely read trade journals that cover the media industry, including *Broadcasting & Cable*, *Electronic Media*, *Hollywood Reporter*, *Daily Variety*, and *Communications Daily* contained the Allegation. Unlike articles in the mass media, these articles usually contained a brief broadcaster rebuttal:

> **Broadcasting & Cable:** Critics say broadcasting's grass-roots clout comes not from the power of the arguments but from its control of the airwaves that politicians need to get elected or re-elected….
>
> Broadcasters deny that they would use their control of the airwaves to strong-arm politicians. "It's getting legislators to understand what our business is about and getting them to understand the contributions that we make to our communities, says Anderson,…vice president of the NAB radio board."[25]

Many of the Allegations fit in a common place within an article. At some point an author would seek to explain the broadcasters' success on Capitol Hill. The first and most discussed explanation would be the Broadcasters' campaign contributions. After 1996, when select lobbying expenditures became available, these might also be reported. Numbers and sometimes even an impressive-looking table might accompany this explanation.[26] Then, almost as an afterthought, the Allegation would be made.

---

[25] Albiniak, "King of the Hill," p. 18. See also Matt Pottinger, "A Digital License 'Giveaway'?" *Hollywood Reporter*, 4 April 1997, p. 3, "Telecom Act is Only Partly Successful, Tauzin Tells NATPE," *Communications Daily*, 27 January 2000, p. 3; "Watchdog says broadcasters' donations buy influence," *Daily Variety*, 4 April 1997; Doug Halonen, "NAB now rides a wave of Capitol clout," *Electronic Media*, 14 December 1998, p. 1. Sometimes even the broadcasting trade press did not bother with a rebuttal, reporting the allegation as fact; e.g., "Paige Albiniak, "Looming Specter of Spectrum Fees," *Broadcasting & Cable*, 19 January 1998, p. 11.

[26] A classic illustration of this point is Common Cause's report: "Channeling Influence: The Broadcast Lobby and the $70 Billion Free Ride," (Washington, DC: Common Cause, 2 April 1997). The lion's share of the report focuses on campaign contributions and lobbying expenditures.

Surprisingly, those who rely on campaign contributions often misuse them because they don't understand broadcaster politics. Following the practice of the Center for Responsive Politics and Common Cause, many define broadcaster expenditures as including Hollywood and the TV networks. This masks the fact that local TV stations are relatively small contributors, especially in comparison to their major competitors such as the telephone and cable industries.

Although the overwhelming majority of the published Allegations were contained in print publications, I found several on TV. CNN, a cable TV network not affiliated with broadcast TV, had an especially hard hitting program on its show called "Reliable Sources." In a segment focused on the spectrum giveaway, *Washington Post* Media reporter Howard Kurtz, Martin Schram of the Scripps Howard Institute, *Los Angeles Times* media reporter Jane Hall, and Meredith McGehee from Common Cause all express their opinion that the broadcasters didn't cover the spectrum giveaway for obvious self-interested reasons. This is balanced with an NAB assertion that this allegation "is ludicrous." And then John Podhoretz of *The Weekly Standard*, says:

> It is very hard to see, in the history of giveaways, a giveaway larger than this giveaway…and I think the secret here is…that it is understood that congressmen, and if you talk to their press secretaries, they will tell you, you don't want to have fights with networks because if you have fights, they're afraid if they have fights with networks that if they become real critics of the networks that they will be hostilely covered.[27]

I also found one allegation in a major broadcast TV news program from ABC's Nightline.[28] The ABC reporter who made the Allegation, Jeff Greenfield, had regularly attended NAB conventions. The NAB paid him as much as $12,000 for speaking at these conventions and moderating a panel of industry leaders.[29]

> JEFF GREENFIELD: There is also a major public policy question to be answered here….

---

[27] CNN Reliable Sources, 6 April 1997, Federal Document Clearing House Transcript # 97040600V50.

[28] I also found one program on C-SPAN where Paul Taylor made the Allegation without rebuttal: "Congress is the one place in Washington that is most sensitive and intimidated by the broadcast industry….Congress is intimidated by the broadcasters, I think, more than by their money and their lobbying clout, by the fact that they perceive broadcasters as the ticket onto or off the 6 o'clock news back home and that's obviously a very important place to be." See C-SPAN's National Journal Roundtable—Paul Taylor: Free TV Update, 28 October 1997. C-SPAN, unlike ABC, owns no local television stations. Its board is entirely made up of cable industry executives, some of whom nevertheless have significant local broadcast TV holdings.

[29] Alicia C. Shepard, "Take the Money and Talk," *American Journalism Review*, June 1995, p. 18.

FOREST SAWYER: Is this going to be a political brouhaha, Jeff?

JEFF GREENFIELD: I don't think it's going to be a major one, primarily because broadcasters have so much political clout—you know, politicians kind of like to be on television....[30]

An important qualification is that many media outlets did not run the Allegation with equal prominence or timeliness. For example, the *New York Times* and *Wall Street Journal* ran the Allegation before and after the broadcasters received their free spectrum. They also ran it on their editorial pages. In contrast, both the *Chicago Tribune* and *Washington Post*, each with significant broadcast properties, only ran the Allegation after the broadcasters had triumphed. And neither ran the Allegation as an editorial or as a front-page story. The ABC Allegation above was run long after the broadcasters had secured the spectrum and was made as an incidental comment in a story primarily about the wonders of HDTV. After the comment was made, the moderator, Forest Sawyer, immediately changed the subject and did not even attempt to present an opposing view.

Non-profit groups on the left and right made the Allegation:

Heritage Foundation: Adam Thierer, an economic policy fellow at the conservative Heritage foundation...says, that NAB lobbyists carry with them an "implied threat" whenever they go to Capitol Hill—the threat that a lawmaker won't get his face on the 6 o'clock news unless he goes along with the NAB's agenda....[31]

Center for Media Education: Jeff Chester, executive director of the watchdog Center for Media Education, also said members of Congress feel if they "cross NAB, they will simply disappear from local news coverage."[32]

Media Access Project: "Broadcasters are renowned for being cheapskates," says Andrew Schwartzman of the Media Access Project. "But

---

[30] Digital TV—Coming Soon to a TV Near You," *ABC Nightline*, 22 April 1997. C-SPAN's National Journal roundtable discussion with Paul Taylor had a brief discussion of the Allegation on October 28, 1997.

[31] Paul Farhi, "Their Reception's Great," *Washington Post*, 16 February 1997, p. H1 ; see also Thierer, "The Great Taxpayer Rip-Off of 1995," p. 22.

[32] Cited in Doug Halonen, "NAB now rides a wave of Capitol clout," *Electronic Media*, 14 December 1998, p. 1. The Center for Media Education is now called The Center for Digital Democracy.

their power comes from controlling the content of what goes into every voting home."[33]

Common Cause: How has the broadcast industry been able to get so much support for its grab of $70-billion worth of corporate welfare?.... They have the power to report and shape the news, including the power to control how issues affecting their own operations—such as the spectrum giveaway—are covered. They also control how, and if, Members of Congress appear on television. That makes legislators extremely reluctant to take them on.[34]

Center for Public Integrity: [T]he media industry is widely regarded as perhaps the most powerful special interest in Washington.... [N]o other sector of the economy has the perceived power to shape coverage in the news, a factor that greatly increases the media companies' lobbying weight."[35]

Fairness & Accuracy in Reporting (FAIR). The truth is, TV producers and correspondents know that probing the political donations of one's boss is not the surest path to job security or advancement. A surer path is self-censorship.

So certain questions don't get asked....For those of you who get your news from television, here's what you missed: Last month, the Federal Communications Commission carried out the will of Congress by awarding valuable new digital frequencies to the current TV license-holders—and doing so free of charge....

So how to explain what Congress did? In a word, Congress got "nabbed" by the National Association of Broadcasters. One of Washington's most powerful and feared lobbies, NAB has...members in every Congressional district with unique power to shape the image of politicians for better or worse.[36]

Consumers Union. Broadcasters are the "dominant mechanism that the public uses to get news," says Gene Kimmelman, co-director of

---

[33] Warren Cohen, "Halting the Air Raid (Auctioning the Air Waves)," *Washington Monthly*, June 1995, p. 30.

[34] "Channeling Influence," p. 17.

[35] Lewis, "Media Money," pp. 20-21. See also: "Off the Record: What Media Corporations Don't Tell You About Their Legislative Agendas," (Washington, DC: Center for Public Integrity, 2000), p. 7.

[36] Jeff Cohen, "TV Industry Wields Power in DC," *Baltimore Sun*, 4 May 1997, p. 6F.

the Consumers Union's Washington office. "They control the imagery of what people learn about public officials. They can show a candidate picking his nose, his hair blowing the wrong way, making a funny face or a silly comment. They can make you look like a fool or a brilliant politician."[37]

Prominent public officials in charge of information policy made the Allegation:

Ken Johnson, spokesman for Representative Billy Tauzin, Chair, House Commerce Committee: To a large extent, members of Congress owe their elections to being able to tell their message on TV. In the back of their minds, no one wants to alienate their local broadcaster.[38]

Senator McCain, Chair, Senate Commerce Committee: McCain said members of Congress are cowed facing an industry that can make or break their careers.... "The broadcasters carry the message of the politician," McCain said, explaining why so many members of Congress side with the industry. "I have never been threatened by a broadcaster and I never will be. But it is an unstated, unspoken message always in the room."[39]

Representative Barney Frank, Ranking Minority Member, House Intellectual Property Subcommittee: We know [broadcasters] have enormous discretion over what goes on the air each night and what doesn't.... It's not that members of Congress fear out-and-out retribution. It's more subtle. They worry that the station might decide to just ignore the shit out of them. Now I happen to be at the stage of my career where if they never say another word about me, a blessing on their head. But, for a lot of members, it can have a chilling effect.[40]

Reed Hundt, Chair, Federal Communications Commission: Only the broadcast lobby uses the public property of the airwaves to threaten representatives in Congress with significant alterations of

[37] Hickey, "TV's Big Stick."

[38] Doug Halonen, "NAB Now Rides a Wave of Capitol Clout," *Electronic Media,* 14 December 1998, p. 1. See also Albiniak, "King of the Hill," p. 18.

[39] Kranish, "Campaign Finance Bill Shows TV's Clout," p. A1.

[40] Taylor, "Superhighway Robbery," p. 21.

the public's perceptions in order to retain their private benefits. They have a tool that no one else has, and they use it.[41]

Senator Ernest Hollings, Ranking Minority Member, Senate Commerce Committee: Our broadcaster friends are the most powerful I know of…. They can change votes right and left, and that is quite understandable. We live and breathe by TV, and that is our reelection. If the local broadcaster calls you, you are going to do him a favor.[42]

On the other hand, Barney Frank later retracted his Allegation:

It's not fear that they will keep you off the air. It is that they are very powerful economic interests within your district. Everybody represents stations…. And they are influential people, and they have a lot of people who work for them, and they come and lobby you just like any other group.[43]

And at least one other member of Congress, Representative Maurice Hinchey, disputed its veracity:

I don't think the broadcasting industry would do that. I mean, if there was any indication of that, I would raise hell. I'd find ways to raise hell about it.[44]

Personal Interviews

In part to better assess the validity of the Allegation—the alleged link between broadcaster control of news and broadcaster political power regarding telecommunications policy—I interviewed more than 50 Washington insiders. These included prominent officials responsible for telecommunications policy

---

[41] Albiniak, "King of the Hill.". See also: Silverstein, "His Biggest Takeover Ever."

[42] Sheila Kaplan, "The Powers That Be—Lobbying," *Washington Monthly*, December 1988, p. 44. Hollings made this comment after his defeat on the Fairness Doctrine in the late 1980s. In 1977 he made a similar statement shortly after he became chair of the Senate Communications Subcommittee (The Washington Lobby, 3rd Ed., Washington, DC: *Congressional* Quarterly, October 1979).

[43] Cited in Dave Denison, "Don't Mess With Television," *American Prospect*, 5 June 2000, p. 37.

[44] Ibid.

at government agencies (the Federal Communications Commission and the National Telecommunications Information Administration), Congress (members, personal staff, and committee staff), and lobbyists (e.g., the National Association of Broadcasters, National Cable Television Association, and United States Telephone Association). I asked these individuals a variety of questions, but the two questions I asked most consistently were: 1) who were the major interest group players lobbying the Telecom Act of 1996 (I occasionally asked the same questions about the Cable Act of 1992), and 2) why were they politically effective. Notably, I rarely mentioned my focused interest on the local TV broadcasters. I concluded from these interviews that the elite print publication reporters who made the Allegation were accurately reflecting common perceptions by political insiders who were speaking off-the-record. Liberals and conservatives, Democrats and Republicans, supporters and opponents of the broadcasters' policy agenda—they all made the Allegation.

In many cases, individuals made these comments on a not for attribution basis. Often, when individuals made these comments, they would lower their voices, tell me this wasn't for attribution, and ask me to turn off my recorder. For the rest, I am not providing attributions because the individuals involved may have had no idea that this is what I would pull out of our conversations to use. Sometimes more than an hour would go by before the issue of the broadcasters would even arise, for they represented only one of numerous groups involved in the Telecom act. Once the broadcasters came up, I might launch into a discussion of the broadcasters' PAC contributions and their Washington lobbying. Perhaps only then would somebody smile at me, the smile of an insider looking at a naïve academic, and in a good natured way remind me of one important fact: the broadcasters control the legislators' access to their constituents.

> "No politician wants a broadcaster against them."
>
> "They're extremely powerful because they control the debate."
>
> "They're the gatekeepers into the voters' home.... You don't have to be a rocket scientist to understand their power. Part of getting elected is understanding the power of local TV."
>
> "If the broadcasters decide you don't exist, you don't exist."
>
> "Broadcasters don't need to pay for access; they're the ones getting your message out."
>
> "They control the networks, the media; that's people's worst fear."

"A staff person thinking about a vote situation would never put himself in a position of alienating (TV broadcasters) near the election."

"You never pick a fight with someone who buys ink by the barrel."

"The most dangerous place to stand is between a politician and a television camera." "I would never devalue the power of the broadcaster community in this country."

"They have something more important than money. They have something money cannot buy. They have access. They are your access to people back home."

"You live and die through the media. You'll do anything you have to do to get on the media….you spend a lot of time thinking about how you can ingratiate yourself with these folks. Say you're in a heated campaign getting down to the end. You say one thing. Your opponent says another. Neither side has conclusive evidence. Who does the media give the benefit of the doubt? You or the opponent? A politician's future depends so much on the media that you tread very carefully."

"Politicians can you give you legions of information about how the media has slanted the news. It's inherent in their business to be a bit paranoid about this type of thing. To disinterested observers it may sound paranoid. It's so nuanced, God knows."

"We're at their mercy. If we schedule 10 press conferences, only one will get covered. They can pick and choose."

"The networks have power. Sure they do. Damn right they do. They have a lot of power given the nature of our democratic system these days. The networks are the place the average American gets information about how the government operates. No legislator would want to get crosswise with a broadcaster. There is always the issue of whether the industry might bias the presentation because they control the airwaves. To sit here and tell you they're not important would be naive on my part."

"Fish gotta swim and politicians gotta get on the evening news." "Broadcasters talk about themselves in a very different way than other interest groups. They talk about all the wonderful local service they do. They cloak themselves in localism. This is a codeword for: 'I have access to the local media market; if you want to be re-elected, you want me to cover you positively.' If I am a politician, I say: 'That's right, I need them to reach the voter. I need them to be friendly to me even if they in fact never editorialize. They don't have to be negative. All they have to do is keep me off the news. If I become invisible, I'm dead.'"

Books by respected telecommunications industry reporters made the Allegation. Joel Brinkley, a *New York Times* Pulitzer prize winning telecom reporter (and son of ABC news anchor David Brinkley), wrote in his book on the history of HDTV:

[B]roadcasters had often found that one good way to sway the FCC was to get congressmen on their side. Usually that wasn't especially difficult. When these people went home to visit their districts, they *loved* [sic] to be on TV.... [M]embers of Congress were loath to take on the broadcasters; they needed to be on TV to get reelected.[45]

Thomas Southwick, a prominent writer in cable trade publications, wrote in his history of the cable industry:

Broadcasters understood far better than cable operators how to influence the political process. They made sure each member of Congress knew the station managers in his district. And members of Congress understood that these managers could transmit the images of politicians to millions of voters.... Broadcasters...were able to make their local news shows sources of both profit and political clout.[46]

Broadcasters have also made this Allegation against each other. In 1998, the American Federation of Television and Radio Artists (AFTRA) lobbied aggressively for a Massachusetts law banning non-compete clauses. TV reporters dislike non-compete clauses because they restrict their ability to move from one station to another in the same market, even when they are fired. The Massachusetts Broadcasters Association (MBA) lobbied against AFTRA's position and lost. *Broadcasting & Cable* reported the reaction of MBA's chief lobbyist:

The initial reaction from a disappointed Massachusetts Broadcasters Association: The new law "sucks." The association also complains

---

[45] Brinkley, *Defining Vision*, pp. 23, 376.
[46] Southwick, *Distant Signals*, p. 356.

that big-time TV reporters exploited their celebrity before a bunch of relatively gutless politicians, using a veiled threat to keep publicity-hungry candidates off the air. But association executive director Al Sprague commented later that "I have to respect what my opponent did."[47]

In striking contrast to the MBA executive director's use of the Allegation, one of MBA's most prominent members, local TV General Manager and NAB activist Paul La Camera, denounced the Allegation as "outrageous" when made in the context of the spectrum giveaway.[48]

Bill Daniels, described by *Broadcasting & Cable* as "the father of cable"[49], has encouraged his colleagues to build up their local news coverage for political leverage. He holds up the local broadcasters as his example:

> Our battles with adversaries will be never-ending. So, one of the things we have to accomplish is to mobilize our satisfied customers…. [A] way to galvanize our customers is to expand our local news programming. Local news has given broadcasters a lot of clout in their markets, particularly with politicians. We should become a highly visible news source as well….[50]

---

[47] Dan Trigoboff, "The Noncompetitive World of TV News," 21 September 1998, p. 38.

[48] Kranish, "Campaign Finance Bill Shows TV's Clout," p. A1.

[49]"Breaking the Mold," *Broadcasting & Cable*, 13 March 2000, p. 118; see also. Southwick, *Distant Signals.*

[50] Bill Daniels, "A Defining Moment," *Broadcasting & Cable*, 16 November 1998. Just a few months earlier the Federal Election Commission granted Daniels' request to give candidates free airtime ("media commentary") without treating it as a political contribution. See Paige Albiniak, "Daniels Gets Free Airtime Green Light," Broadcastinng & Cable, 7 September 1998, p. 14. In an interview with me on 11 September 2000, NCTA President Robert Sachs strongly denied that seeking political power was a reason local cable TV companies were bolstering their local news programs. The denial seemed to conflict with the spirit of NCTA's own grassroots manual (see following footnote), which suggests using local public affairs programming as a political resource.

Incidentally, the cable industry appears to have taken Bill Daniels' sage advice to heart.[51]

I interviewed more than a dozen former NAB executives and grassroots lobbyists. Although none of them explicitly said that NAB encourages media bias, I was repeatedly told that it is well understood in NAB government affairs

---

[51] NCTA's Washington Handbook for the 105th Congress (1997–1998), includes the following advice for grassroots strategies: "The importance of cable system operator involvement in grassroots lobbying cannot be over-emphasized…. There are many strategies for strengthening your relationships with your Member of Congress. The following courses of action are meant to provide you with ideas that you may adapt to fit your circumstances with your representatives and senators…. **Political Cablecasting:** Our elected officials are constantly seeking new avenues to reach constituents. If your system has local origination cablecasting and ad insertion facilities, ask your representative or senator to participate in call-in programs or electronic town hall meetings. In addition, you can provide air time for Members of Congress who produce 30- or 60-second PSAs on issues of importance to them. **Participation in Campaigns:** Your participation in your Member's campaign provides an excellent way to get to know the candidate, his/her close associates and other members of the community who support the candidate." See also Rosenthal, *The Third House*, p. 117.

When I ran for the Maryland House of Delegates in 2002 as a major party candidate, the head of government affairs for my local cable system offered me and all other candidates a five minute "interview," which the cable company ran 21 times (3 times a day, 7 days a week) on CNN's Headline News channel. They gave all the candidates questions upfront, asked no follow-up questions, allowed candidates to retape the interviews until they were happy, and assured me that no record would be kept that a future opponent could access. The coverage was admittedly a great public service in a political district that had no local broadcast TV coverage. But the coverage also served to cultivate a relationship with future delegates to the state legislature. More recently, my County's cable company, Comcast, withheld ads highly critical of the County Executive, the County's chief elected official. The County Executive is the person responsible for negotiating the cable TV franchise agreement. See Eric Collins, "Police Union Ads Attack Owens," *Maryland Gazette*, 6 August 2003, p. A2.

During the Government Relations session at Forum 2000, the annual meeting of the Cable Television Public Affairs Association, held 12 March 2002 at the Ritz-Carlton in Washington, DC, Janice Caluda, Vice President of the Florida Cable Telecommunications Association, told attendees that Florida's cable association provides new legislators with training on how to act on TV, starting with a "dear in the headlights interview" and finishing with "10 Rules for Effective Behavior on TV." The advantage to cable companies, she says, is that "there is nothing more powerful than the media we possess. With one exception: developing a relationship with people through the medium we possess."

that members of Congress are uniquely fearful of their local broadcaster and that this helps NAB.[52] NAB takes no responsibility for such fears and believes they are due to Congressional paranoia. According to NAB reasoning, if Congressmen want to indulge themselves in such paranoia, it is not the NAB's responsibility to dissuade them from it.

Although the Allegation appears to have increased in frequency during the 1990s, it goes back many years.

Two highly respected books by former broadcasting insiders made the charge. Corydon Dunham, the former Executive Vice President and General Counsel of NBC, slipped into a book that otherwise provided an extremely flattering account of the broadcasters' heroic struggle for the public benefit against evil politicians who want to control the news for their own benefit: "The affiliates had political clout. Representatives and Senators back home who wanted favorable coverage for reelection listened to them."[53]

Erwin Krasnow, the former NAB General Counsel, co-authored with an academic perhaps the most widely cited book on broadcaster politics. He made the Allegation several times in his book but did not elaborate upon it or support it with any evidence.

> Since media exposure over the airwaves is practically essential for election to Congress, usually the only politicians who criticize the media with relative impunity are national leaders, who are too prominent for the media to ignore them or elected officials who come from one-party or 'safe' districts. By contrast, a congressman may be reluctant to criticize local broadcasters if his reelection depends in great measure on the amount and tone of the exposure obtained from them.[54]

During an hour long interview with Erwin Krasnow, now a broadcast lobbyist and multi-billion dollar dealmaker with Verner, Liipfert, Bernhard, McPherson, and Hand, I asked him if he could remember any evidence that led him to include this Allegation in his book. He could recall nothing.

---

[52] E.g., interviews with NAB's Senior VP, TV Department, Dick Hollands, on 12 March 1998 and former NAB Senior VP, Public Affairs & Communications, Walt Wurfel, on 29 September 1997.

[53] Dunham, *Fighting for the First Amendment*, p. 75.

[54] Erwin G. Krasnow and Lawrence D. Longley, *The Politics of Broadcast Regulation* (New York,: St. Martin's Press, 1973), p. 72.

A 1979 book by *Congressional Quarterly* staff titled *The Washington Lobby* contained profiles of major Washington lobbies. It started its profile of the broadcast lobby with the following assertion:

> The broadcast industry lobby has been called one of the most powerful in Washington. To the casual observer it operates like most other Washington lobbies, but in one very important respect it differs. The broadcasters have a unique relationship with elected public officials: Members of Congress rely on broadcast news coverage to remain in the public eye and thus promote their re-election.
>
> A politician's need for broadcast exposure in his home district is seldom discussed, but widely recognized by broadcaster and politician alike. Broadcast lobbyists, especially, are aware that it can be a potent lobbying tool even if never brought up.[55]

Unlike other books with this Allegation, this book does provide a concrete anecdote, one of the best known among old telecom lobbyists. In the mid-1970s there was a major effort in the Ford Administration to deregulate certain industries, including cable. At the time, the FCC heavily regulated the cable industry so as not to pose a competitive threat to broadcasters. The Ford Administration went ahead with its other deregulatory initiatives but dropped its cable initiative after vehement broadcaster lobbying.[56] One anonymous network executive was accused of threatening the Ford Administration with bad TV coverage during the upcoming presidential election if he continued his deregulatory initiative. However, the supposed recipient of this threat, Administration official William Seidman, a former TV broadcaster himself, denied having received any such threat.[57]

Widely cited and respected broadcast industry scholars have made the Allegation: Robert W. McChesney, a professor at the University of Illinois, wrote:

---

[55] John Leo Moore, Robert Healy, and Margaret Thompson, *The Washington Lobby*, 3d ed. (Washington: Congressional Quarterly, 1979), p. 205.

[56] In the late 1970s, the Supreme Court ruled that some of the key cable TV restraints were unconstitutional. This helped inaugurate a decade of annual double digit growth within the cable industry.

[57] More than twenty years after the event, I called William Seidman to ask him about it. He continued to deny the threat was ever made. Telephone conversation with L. William Seidman, 4 June 1998.

The NAB and the other corporate media lobbies are so strong not merely because they are rich and give lots of money to politicians' campaigns, though they are and they do. Far more importantly, the corporate media control news and access to the media—something politicians respect even more than money."[58]

Thomas W. Hazlett, a professor at the University of California, Davis, and former FCC Chief Economist, wrote:

[B]roadcasters are able to compensate policy makers for rents in all the traditional forms, plus they are able to make in-kind donations at wholesale cost. Perhaps even more important are negative in-kind contributions: declining to broadcast news favorable to a candidate or coalition, electing to broadcast negative information or allegations, or choosing to give airtime to a challenger, are all editorial decisions.[59]

James Baughman, a professor at the University of Wisconsin, wrote:[60]

In the absence of much organized constituent involvement, congressmen were more likely to accept the entreaties of local station managers who had been helpful in reelection campaigns....[61]

Within individual districts, radio and television stations offered an efficient source of exposure, a reminder to voters of a representative's name and positions.... A South Carolina congressman confessed: "Any person in politics benefits, ordinarily, by any radio or television interview. The honest politician will tell you that he knows the value of being placed before the public in the off season, when there is no political contest involved. It is an advertisement at its best insofar as his ambitions are concerned."[62]

---

[58] McChesney, *Rich Media, Poor Democracy*, p. 65.

[59] Thomas Hazlett, "Assigning Property Rights to Radio Spectrum Users: Why Did FCC License Auctions Take 67 Years?," *Journal of Law & Economics* 41, no. 2 (1998): p. 546. Hazlett is currently a senior fellow at the Manhattan Institute for Policy Research.

[60] Braughman also identified what may be the earliest high profile allegation of news bias by TV broadcasters. In November 1959, *New York Times* columnist James Reston predicted that "Congress in an election year is not going to want to punish the TV industry too hard." See Baughman, *Television's Guardians: The FCC and the Politics of Programming, 1958–1967*, p. 49.

[61] Ibid., p. 74.

[62] Ibid., p. 130.

The Indirect Claim

In literally hundreds of articles the broadcast industry is described as "mighty" or "powerful" or a "lobbying juggernaut,"[63] with little or no explanation as to why the broadcast industry deserves such a description. The language can be quite varied: from Alan Murray of the *Wall Street Journal* describing broadcasters as having "legendary lobbying muscle"[64] to nationally syndicated *New York Times* columnist William Safire hyperbolically writing: "Media plutocrats intimidating politicians to get a lucrative spot on the spectrum for nothing are villains."[65] NAB President Eddie Fritts, in a much quoted phrase from a

---

[63] A 14 August 2004 Nexis search with the search string "National Association of Broadcasters and powerful w/5 broadcasters" netted 350 cites, including false positives but also missing many with the same intent but using different locutions. Examples include: "Must-See TV?" *Christian Science Monitor*, 18 March 1997, p. 20; Stephen Labaton, "Business Awaits Its Regulator-In-Chief," *New York Times*, 8 October 2000, p. C11. William Safire, "Stop the Giveaway," *New York Times*, 4 January 1996, p. A21. Tim Jones, "Panel on TV Standards Shuns New Regulations," *Chicago Tribune*, 6 November 1998, p. 1. Robert A. Rankin, "FCC to Unveil Proposal for Free Political TV ads," *New Orleans Times-Picayune*, 31 March 1997, p. E15.

[64] Alan Murray, "FCC May Try to Fix Campaign Financing," *Wall Street Journal*, 4 August 1997, p. A1.

[65] William Safire, "Will Dole Fight?" *New York Times*, 8 August 1996, p. A27. In another Op-ed, William Safire writes that the broadcast lobby "has long been able to put the arm on Congress" but does not clarify why they have been able to do this. See William Safire, "Good Guys Win 2," *New York Times*, 29 January 1996, p. A17. Molly Ivins, another nationally syndicated columnist, writes in one Op-ed: "Although the digital broadcast section of the bill is "in abeyance" for now, if you look at the vote in Congress (414-16 in the House and 91-5 in the Senate), you can see how much appetite our politicians have for taking on the broadcasters." See Molly Ivins, "Big Biz Got Gold Mine; We Got The Shaft," *South Bend Tribune*, 13 February 1996, p. A7. In another Op-ed, which also describes the broadcasters' spectrum "ripoff", Ivins explains why the reduction in ownership caps contained in the Telecom bill is dangerous: "Murdoch, in case you haven't heard, is notorious for interfering with the news and editorial content of his media properties…. Come on, team, think about this. How many politicians and journalists are going to be willing to stand up and criticize Rupert Murdoch…when he has a lock on one-third of all the media in this country?" See Molly Ivins, "Can You Spell R-I-P-O-F-F?" *Sacramento Bee*, 6 August 1995, p. F2. Murdoch owns Fox, one of the four major TV networks in the United States. Although Ivins, like Safire, wrote many Op-eds attacking the "spectrum giveaway," she attributed broadcasters' power on this issue to their campaign contributions. This is striking because in her many

September 1995 speech given to his members, said: "No one has more sway with members of Congress than the local broadcaster."[66]

In some cases, it may be reasonable to infer that the missing explanation is the broadcasters' control over the airwaves, as when then Speaker of the U.S. House of Representatives, Newt Gingrich, asserted in an interview in *Broadcasting & Cable* magazine that "[t]he practical fact is, nobody's going to take on the broadcasters."[67] This Gingrich quote was widely reported in a variety of publications as an explanation for why the broadcasters got the spectrum flexibility clause in the Telecom Act. Given Gingrich's personal beliefs[68] and his claimed aversion to government regulation and handouts, his support of the spectrum clause in the Telecom Act might be otherwise hard to explain. As the *Wall Street Journal* editorialized:

> ...Republicans have buckled under to broadcasters' pressure this year.... The only way we can explain it is to quote Newt Gingrich's comment earlier this year: 'Nobody in Congress wants to 'take on' the broadcasters.' Presumably, the Speaker and his colleagues fear that if they don't let broadcasting keep its handout, the network news divisions will pummel them nightly until their approval ratings sink to record lows.[69]

Given that during this period Gingrich was being disloyal to his wife and sleeping with an aide 23 years his junior, he might have had especially good

---

Op-eds about the evils of media concentration she either implicitly or explicitly (see above) makes the Allegation. A *Wall Street Journal* editorial describes Congress as "paralyzed by its thralldom to local TV broadcasters." See "You Ain't Seen Nothing Yet," *Wall Street Journal*, 15 March 1999, p. A18. Nationally syndicated columnist Susan Estrich, former National Campaign Manager for Dukakis for President, asks simply and rhetorically as though the answer were self-evident: "what politician wants to alienate the local television stations?" See Susan Estrich, "What $70 Billion Won't Buy on TV News," *Houston Chronicle*, 16 June 2000, p. A42.

[66] "Tough Challenges Ahead," *Communications Daily*, 12 September 1995, p. 1.

[67] Kim McAvoy and Don West, "Newt Gingrich: The Great Liberator for Cybercom," *Broadcasting & Cable*, 20 March 1995, p. 6.

[68] The staff of the Progress & Freedom Foundation, Gingrich's personal think tank, were strongly opposed to giving the broadcasters free spectrum. In their views—and in the public views of the Republican leadership—the Telecom Act was to encourage competition, not to enact major barriers to entry and innovation.

[69] "I-Way Detours," *Wall Street Journal*, 27 December 1995, p. A10. See also Paul Taylor, "Air Time in the Bank," *Washington Post*, 2 April 1997, p. A17.

reason to be fearful of the broadcasters. As the saying goes, people who live in glass houses shouldn't throw stones.[70]

Another indirect form of the Allegation may be the explanation of broadcasters' power with the assertion that "television broadcasters...own stations in every Congressional district."[71] This is also the political explanation of their own power that broadcasters use most often. Says NAB President Eddie Fritts: "The strength of NAB is that we have local stations in virtually every district in America."[72]

Critical to interpreting this statement is recognizing that the definition of owning a station in every Congressional district is left ambiguous. Normally, when used in a political context, having a presence in every district implies having an office with employees who live and vote in that district. But that is not necessarily the case in the local TV broadcast industry. In 1996, there were 210 TV markets but 435 Congressional districts. Within a given TV market, TV stations are usually clustered together near the population center. That means that if TV markets were evenly distributed across Congressional districts, there would be approximately one TV market for every two Congressional districts. But Congressional districts are not evenly distributed. For example, the New York City TV market, the most densely populated TV market in the United States, encompasses 35 Congressional Districts.[73] In contrast, Alaska has six TV markets for just one Congressional District. This lumpy distribution of broadcaster stations means that there are many Congressional districts with either only a handful of local TV broadcaster employees or none at all. The number of Congressional districts with politically significant numbers of non-news employees (the only type allowed to lobby) is smaller still.

What broadcasters, therefore, seem to mean by "own stations in every Congressional district" is that a local TV news station COVERS every

---

[70] David D. Kirkpatrick, "Marianne Gingrich Wants to Sell A Book About Her Ex-Husband," *New York Times*, 18 July 2000, p. C7, Jane Manners, "A Wandering Eye On Newt: Why the press did—or didn't—cover the former House speaker's private life," *Brill's Content*, November 1999, p. 36.

[71] Edmund L. Andrews, "Dole Steps Up Criticism of Telecommunications Bill," *New York Times*, 11 January 1996, p. D2. See also Paige Albiniak, "A House Divided," *Broadcasting & Cable*, 28 June 1999, p. 11, Paige Albiniak, "Reform Takes Form," *Broadcasting & Cable*, 2 April 2001, p. 15, Doug Halonen, "Cry Raised Against Cheap Political Spots," *Electronic Media*, 9 April 2001, p. 26.

[72] Paige Albiniak, "A House Divided," *Broadcasting & Cable*, 28 June 1999, p. 18, *Communications Daily*, 8 March 2000, p. 10.

[73] Arnold, *Congress, the Press, and Political Accountability*, p. 3.

Congressional district. Indeed, when the NAB holds its annual state leadership conference in Washington DC and then blitzes every Congressional office with local broadcasters, it defines a local broadcaster as one who covers a Congressional district, not one who lives in that Congressional district.

But why should this confer power on local broadcasters? There are thousands of other consumer products that are also sold and used in every Congressional district. Yet members of Congress rarely accord special consideration to manufacturers of products just because those products happen to be used by constituents in their districts. A shoe manufacturer seeking a tariff on foreign shoes, for example, would be expected to use its grassroots organization to lobby only those members of Congress with factory workers in their districts. Similarly, when I call my member of Congress as a regular citizen, the member wants to know my address to determine that I am indeed a constituent within his district. All other things being equal, non-constituents are treated as second class citizens.

There are also countless other professions, including dry cleaner, dentist, accountant, electrician, carpenter, and so on, that have both far more constituents and geographic dispersion than local TV broadcasters, yet are not known for being especially powerful. The assertion that television broadcasters own stations in every Congressional district therefore begs the question. It cannot be interpreted literally as an explanation of broadcaster power but as a code for saying the exact opposite of what it seems to imply. Instead of implying that broadcasters are like other groups with members in every Congressional District, it implies that broadcasters own a political resource that has remarkable properties. And what may be most remarkable is that broadcasters' control what constituents learn about political candidates and others seeking favorable publicity in every political district in the United States. To be fair, if radio broadcasters are included in the analysis, then NAB does have members in virtually every Congressional district in America. But radio broadcasters do not typically lobby passionately on behalf of TV broadcasters, which explains why the NAB has separate radio and TV boards: the two different groups don't trust each other. Mimicking this organizational separation, the NAB provides different newsletters and lobbying game plans for the two different groups of broadcasters, and assigns a separate radio and TV broadcast liaison for all 535 members of Congress.

Yet another indirect form of the Allegation is that some authors accuse broadcasters of self-serving news bias but don't take the extra step of asserting that this leads to their power on Capitol Hill. For example, nationally syndicated columnist Molly Ivins denounced the "rip-off" of giving free spectrum to broadcasters, and then asserted "The reason you don't know jack about this bill [The Telecom Act of 1996] is because the people who own the media are the ones who are going to make all the money from it."[74] It is a reasonable inference to go from the observation that local TV news doesn't cover an issue to the claim that this could have an impact on legislators. But Ivins and other who accuse the media of not covering certain issues don't explicitly make that claim, perhaps because they consider it self-evident.

PBS President Pat Mitchell made the same type of indirect Allegation when she testified before the British parliament on the U.S. system of public TV:

> With just one month left before the vote [on media consolidation], there had been just one mention of it on a national network news-cast; not because it wasn't news, but because it wasn't news that the dominant news organizations necessarily wanted to tell. They had, to use an old expression, 'a dog in the fight.'
>
> …I'm pleased to report to you that PBS was an exception to the news 'blackout' on the proposed FCC ruling just as we had been in 1996 when the Telecommunications Bill was voted into law, a law that resulted in the great spectrum giveaway. As we did then, PBS did report the story, did attempt to connect the issues to the democratic values potentially threatened.[75]

Sometimes the Allegation is not so much indirect as simply ambiguous or even muddled. *Communications Week* ran an article that argued that a Senate bill advocating reform of spectrum policy had little chance of success in part because of "vigorous lobbying from the very corporations that regularly grill politicians on the nightly news."[76] But the reader was left guessing the connection between news coverage of politicians and the inability to pass spectrum management reform.

Finally, there are the ubiquitous statements that today's media are driven by profits. Nowadays it is practically a cliché for leading journalists to complain, as did Walter Cronkite at the annual Radio-Television News Directors Association (RTNDA) meeting in 1997, about the "greed" of corporate owners and their "mad scramble for ratings and…profits" in the broadcasting business.[77] As long as no names are mentioned, this type of speech can be

---

[74] Molly Ivins, "The Politics of Airwaves," *Arizona Republic*, 7 February 1996, p. B5.

[75] Testimony of Pat Mitchell before the House of Lords, London, England, 26 June 2003, p. 8.

[76] Bill Freeza, "Parrying Pressler's Press for Reform," *Communications Week*, 8 July 1996.

[77] Steve McClellan, "Journalists Look Inward: Ethics and Credibility Much on the Minds of RTNDA," *Broadcasting & Cable*, 22 September 1997, p. 7.

quite popular among journalists. Cronkite got a standing ovation from his audience of radio and television directors. He also went out of his way to flatter his audience by tapping into their mindset of being a victim rather than perpetrator of media ethics violations: "[G]et the monkey off your back and put it on the money men…. Let the battle cry be 'editors, not auditors!'" he himself cried.[78] Even *Broadcasting & Cable*, the boosterish trade magazine for the broadcast industry that's never seen a broadcast industry subsidy it didn't like, praised Cronkite's pious sentiments:

> Walter Cronkite seemed to be just the right person at the right place at the right time last week as he gave his news heirs a good talking-to about what they ought to be doing…. Cronkite laid much of the blame for broadcast journalism's credibility gap on corporate parents' mad scramble for ratings and profits, which in turn, he said, adversely affects journalistic quality and credibility…. TV news's rallying cry, he said, should be "editors, not auditors." We like the sound of that.[79]

In the most respected academic and industry forums, Cronkite is joined by a chorus of leading journalists. Writing to his fellow broadcast journalists, Don Hewitt, executive producer of *60 Minutes*, laments: "today broadcast journalism is every bit as market-driven as the 'anything-for-a-vote' congressman and the 'anything-for-a-buck' businessman we hold up to ridicule."[80] Lowell Bergman, former executive producer at *60 Minutes*, writes: "There once was a firewall between the commercial-entertainment side and the public service 'news' side of broadcasting. That fire wall has been breached. It is the specter haunting the broadcast 'news' business today.[81] The prominent journalist

---

[78] Ibid.

[79] "And that's the way it is," *Broadcasting & Cable*, 22 September 1997, p. 90.

[80] Don Hewitt, "Blame Me," *Communicator*, February 1995, p. 38.

[81] Lowell Bergman, "Network Television News: With Fear and Favor," *Columbia Journalism Review*, May/June 2000, p. 51. Contrary to the implications of the Hewitt and Bergman statements, CBS issued a press release with the following statement: "Unlike the *New York Times*' own ethical problems, there is no question about the accuracy or integrity of CBS News' reporting. CBS News does not pay for interviews, and it maintains a well-established separation from other parts of Viacom." The statement was made in response to a *New York Times* story that CBS had offered to pay Jessica Lynch, including a book and made-for-TV movie from other Viacom subsidiaries, in return for her telling her Iraqi war story on CBS. P.J. Bednarski, "How To Get Bad Press: CBS News Created Its Own Media Mess," *Broadcasting & Cable*, 23 June 2003, p. 37.

Harold Evans puts the media's dilemma this way: "The challenge of the media is not to stay in business, but to stay in journalism."[82] Former *New York Times* editorial writer Geneva Overholser writes in the *Columbia Journalism Review:* "We report scantily on ourselves as a business. And more than a few of us pull punches when it comes to reporting something our owners or our advertisers might not like."[83] Pulitzer-prize winning journalist David Halberstam eloquently describes the hypocrisy of media ethics statements:

> The older generation, whatever its flaws—and they were considerable—felt a sense of obligation and responsibility—not just to the people who worked in their newsrooms but also…to the people who bought their newspapers and listened to and watched their networks and their news programs. And that sense of personal responsibility for what they put out is, I think, largely gone. That proprietarial generation has been replaced by a managerial generation for whom the only index which matters is the price of the stock and a belief, never openly expressed of course, that the real customers are not the people who buy the paper or who listen at night, but the people who buy the stock.[84]

Long-time NAB board member William O'Shaughnessy, owner of two radio stations, describes his competitors in much the same way:

> Most radio stations have fallen to absentee owners and speculators who use radio stations as chattel. [These owners] are just asset managers. They're not broadcasters.[85]

William F. Baker, President of New York City's non-profit TV station WNET-TV and former President of commercial broadcasting group Westinghouse Television, has explained the "failure" of his commercial colleagues as resulting from "the entry of a generation of managers with little or

---

[82] Paul Klite, "Tabloid Fever," *Television Quarterly* 27, no. 4 (1996): p. 29.

[83] Geneva Overholser, "Front-page Ads and Other Supposed Threats to Credibility," *Columbia Journalism Review*, September/October 2000, p. 72.

[84] Speech excerpt cited in "The Annenberg School Celebrates 40 Years of Research and Teaching," *Newslink* 10(1), Philadelphia, Annenberg School for Communication, Spring 2000, p. 18.

[85] "William O'Shaughnessy," *Broadcasting & Cable*, 18 September 2000, p. 70.

no commitment to the product and absolute devotion to the ever-increasing profitability of their television properties."[86]

The legion of insider statements—consistent with academic studies[87]—that media organizations are driven by profits, not journalistic values, doesn't necessarily imply that the media would use media to further their lobbying objectives. But it is certainly an obvious implication of such statements when self-interest would seem to point in that direction; for example, when billions of dollars are at stake, as was the case with the broadcasters' digital spectrum.

The Problem of Missing Evidence

A remarkable feature of the direct Allegation made by scholars, journalists, and other credible sources is their lack of concrete and verifiable supporting evidence. None cite or make a definitive study to support their claims. Some provide anecdotes, usually undocumented, but none that couldn't be readily refuted by broadcasters or dismissed as an isolated case.

One brief article in *U.S. News & World Report* had perhaps the most concrete evidence to support the Allegation. However, the legislator who was the object of the influence denied it had any impact on his behavior.

> McCain argues that legislators are reluctant to oppose the NAB because it represents TV stations that also present news about Congress. In most cases, that pressure is subliminal, McCain says.

---

[86] William F. Baker and George Dessart, "Down the Tube: An Inside Account of the Failure of American Television, New York: BasicBooks, 1998. See also William F. Baker, "The Lost Promise of American Television: Eyeballs for Sale," *Vital Speeches of the Day*, 1 September 1998.

[87] The argument that media do not generally show a liberal or academic policy bias is not necessarily inconsistent with the argument that media are profit driven. News objectivity is now widely held as the most profitable form of journalism; E.g., David T. Z. Mindich, *Just the Facts : How "Objectivity" Came to Define American Journalism* (New York: New York University Press, 1998), Schudson, *Discovering the News*. This literature can therefore coexist with the literature asserting media are generally driven by the profit motive; e.g., Thomas Kunkel and Gene Roberts, "The Age of Corporate Newspapering: Leaving Readers Behind," *American Journalism Review*, May 2001, John H. McManus, *Market-Driven Journalism: Let the Citizen Beware?* (Thousand Oaks, Calif.: Sage Publications, 1994), Howard Tumber, *Media Power, Professionals, and Policies* (London ; New York: Routledge, 2000), Doug Underwood, *When MBAs Rule the Newsroom: How the Marketers and Managers Are Reshaping Today's Media* (New York: Columbia University Press, 1993).

But there are times it's nakedly overt. For example, when Rep. Zach Wamp, a Tennessee Republican, went to one of his hometown TV stations in Chattanooga in January, he found members of the news department at one end of a conference table and the station's business managers at the other. First, reporters asked him about his political views. Then, he said, station executives grilled him on their legislative agenda. Wamp had already said he opposed plans like McCain's, which he calls a "broadcasters' subsidy" for politicians. But he acknowledged that being lobbied in the presence of reporters—and by the reporters' bosses—"makes the bells go off in your head."[88]

The lack of concrete and verifiable evidence to back up the Allegation was also one of the most noteworthy features of my interview feedback. During my interviews regarding the Telecom Act of 1996, when I would hear somebody make the Allegation, I would ask: "do you have any hard evidence?" In response, the interviewee would often look at me as though I were an idiot (some even expressed open contempt) because the question had revealed to them that I understood nothing about politics or human life. They felt that the threat of broadcaster news bias was obvious but that no broadcaster would be stupid enough to provide me with a verifiable case study. When I pressed for hard evidence, the type of answer I generally got referred to what the interviewees thought of as similar situations, even though it wasn't what I had asked for. Some examples came from the newspaper and cable industries, not the broadcast industry. Former Representative Dan Glickman's pummeling by the cable industry was well-known within the commerce and judiciary committees.[89] The cable industry in Kansas ran numerous ads attacking him for a position he took (he nevertheless won the election). So also was the newspaper industry's 1989 campaign against Representative Tauke, Representative Swift, and Senator Burns for supporting telephone company provision of online

---

[88] Kent Jenkins, Jr., "Learning to Love those Expensive Campaigns," *U.S. News & World Report*, 10 March 1997, p. 29.

[89] Glickman served on the House Judiciary Committee, including the Copyright Subcommittee. Only the Telecommunications Subcommittee of the House Commerce Committee is of greater political importance to the broadcast industry. In 2004, Glickman was appointed president of the Motion Pictures Association of America, which represents Hollywood and is dominated by the four largest companies with broadcast TV networks (News Corporation, Viacom, Disney, and General Electric). Glickman's son is president of Spyglass Entertainment, a producer of broadcast TV shows and Hollywood movies.

classified ads (called "electronic Yellow Pages").[90] Classified ads account for about 40% of total newspaper revenue and are generally considered to constitute the bulk of industry profits.

The few broadcaster anecdotes I heard about were ancient and came from the FCC. FCC Chief of Staff Blair Levin told me that when President Ford proposed a plan in the 1970s to deregulate the cable industry, the broadcasters threatened to show footage every night of him stumbling off Air Force One.[91] But he didn't know if the story was apocryphal or real. Another senior FCC official told me that he had heard rumors that Senator Pastore, chair of the Senate Commerce Committee, had been blacked out in the early 1970s for crossing his local broadcasters. But this FCC official didn't know the origin of the rumors. I was not able to verify either rumor.

Unfortunately, I did not realize until late in the interviewing process that my search for hard evidence, while meeting conventional standards of proof used by political communication scholars, was not the type of evidence that politicians needed to make important political decisions. I had assumed that politicians employed rigorous standards of scientific reasoning to draw their conclusions, when gut reasoning was sufficient for their purposes. It eventually became apparent to me that broadcasters could send signals to politicians about the extent of their propensity to use the airwaves to reward friends and punish foes without this propensity being verifiable by third parties, such as political communication scholars, using research methods such as content analysis.

The Skepticism of Political Communications Scholars

Political communication scholars are generally skeptical of claims and evidence that media owners use the media to pursue their public policy interests.

---

[90] All three members of Congress were also noted allies of the local broadcast industry. Both Conrad Burns and Al Swift were former local broadcasters, with Swift rising to the rank of news director. Tom Tauke, now head of government relations for Verizon, coached the broadcasters during the 1980s on how to be more effective political players and was one of only three members of the U.S. House of Representatives ever to win one of the NAB's annual Grover Cobb Memorial Award for broadcasting and Government Relations. Tauke won in 1987. The two other House recipients were Billy Tauzin (1986) and Sam Ervin (1976, the year the award was inaugurated).

[91] Interview with Blair Levin, 11 August 1997.

This is manifested in the paucity of contemporary studies on this type of bias.[92] Presumably, there would be more studies on this type of bias if political communication scholars thought they might find a positive result. It is hard to get work published when the result is a null hypothesis. As Doris Graber sums up the literature, perhaps with slightly excessive conclusiveness: "A number of content analyses of [political] events definitely refute the charges of political bias, if bias is defined as deliberately lopsided coverage or intentional slanting of news."[93] Usually, the question of industry policy media bias is simply ignored.[94]

How can we reconcile the research results of political communication scholars with the apparent views of insiders? I suggest that those making the Allegation are drawing inferences by using a different method than that used by scholars. Which method is better may not have a simple answer but may depend on the context of a situation and the type of evidence likely to be available. In this regard, it is noteworthy that scholars have made their assessment of media industry policy bias despite the fact that there has never been a major study of such bias. If they had studied such bias, they might have concluded that the conventional tools used to study bias were inadequate.

---

[92] Recent exceptions include Gilens and Hertzman, "Corporate Ownership and News Bias.", McChesney, *The Problem of the Media: U.S. Communication Politics in the Twenty-First Century,* Sparrow, *Uncertain Guardians: The News Media as a Political Institution.*

[93] Doris A. Graber, *Mass Media and American Politics,* 2nd ed. (Washington, D.C.: CQ Press, 1984), p. 97. See also Page, "The Mass Media as Political Actors," p. 21.

[94] E.g., Arnold, *Congress, the Press, and Political Accountability.*

CHAPTER 11:

The Argument From Analogy

"Falsus in uno, falsus in omnibus."

> —Latin for "Untrue in one thing, untrue in everything."

"If you see one cockroach going across the floor, there's a pretty good chance there are others behind the baseboard."

> —The Cockroach Theory[1]

In day to day life, people often reason by analogy. They seek to understand a less familiar situation by recourse to another more familiar situation. When both situations exhibit similarities in the essential characteristic being compared, the analogy is apt. In this chapter, the analogies that interest us involve situations with similar underlying incentive structures; specifically, a principal-agent incentive structure with a dual agent. Strictly speaking, apt analogies can prove little more than that talk is often cheap and that even the most heartfelt protestations of agency/ethical intent (such as those that broadcasters often make) should be treated with at least a grain of skepticism.

However, lay people are not so rigorous in the inferences they make. They intuitively grasp that certain clusters of behavior often go together; that if an agent has a political resource and is revealed to have a conflict of interest with a claimed principal, there is a better than zero chance that the resource will be used adversely to the interests of the claimed principal. They further understand that agents have no incentive to reveal evidence of opportunistic behavior, so they will give far more weight to evidence of opportunistic behavior than agency behavior. When the incentive and ability to hide opportunistic behavior is very great, even shoddy, indirect evidence of opportunistic behavior may trump copious direct evidence of agency behavior.

---

[1] An 18 December 2004 search on Nexis found 330 references to the "The Cockroach Theory" from 12 August 1987 to 10 December 2004. The cockroach theory is generally applied to financial markets but is applied here in the context of opportunistic behavior.

Recognizing the low standard of evidence required by lay people, broadcasters ban reporters and even broadcast management from engaging in any type of public display of political behavior.

Like argument by authority, argument by analogy is a highly efficient mode of reasoning because it requires minimal knowledge of the particulars of a situation. External knowledge dominates the analysis.

Principal-Agent Theory as the Basis for Analogies

By defining broadcaster bias in principal-agent terms, we specify the underlying incentive structure of the analogy. Once this underlying incentive structure is clear, we have a powerful tool for drawing inferences. Figure 11-1 describes the underlying incentive structure of interest to us here: an agent with a potential conflict of interest. The conflict of interest is generated when the publicly proclaimed principal, the primary principal, must compete with another principal, the secondary principal. An agent with a conflict of interest is a dual agent.

Figure 11-1. The Underlying Incentive Structure of the Analogy

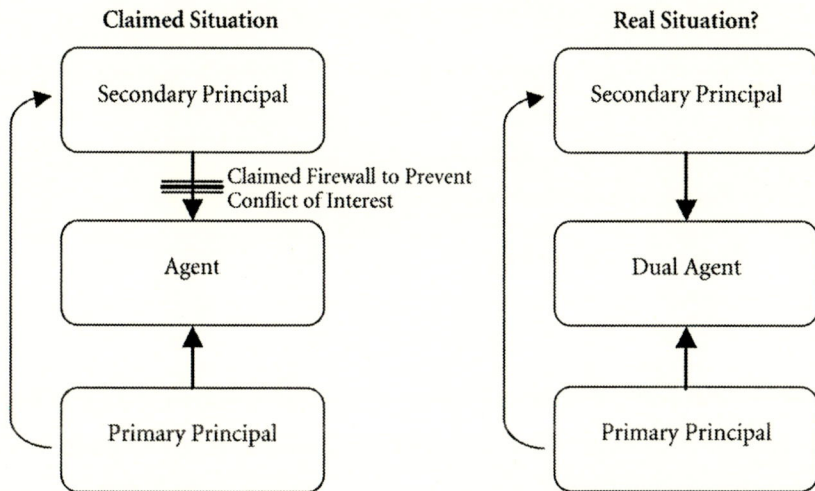

Each arrow points from a principal to an agent. An extra arrow is added between the primary and secondary principals because when both secondary principals publicly lobby, they claim to be acting as an agent on behalf of the primary principal.

The analogy works by drawing an inference from a reference case to a test case, where both cases involve the behavior of a dual agent. Figure 11-2 shows our test case. In this case, the media owner and his business oriented employees is the secondary principal; the news director and the reporters who work for him is the agent; and the audience is the primary principal. The publicly claimed ethics firewall assures the audience that those responsible for the media content of the broadcast outlet have undivided loyalty to their interests. The question is whether the news director has mixed loyalties. If so, the expected result would be bias to the extent it could go undetected and unpenalized.

Figure 11-2. The Test Case

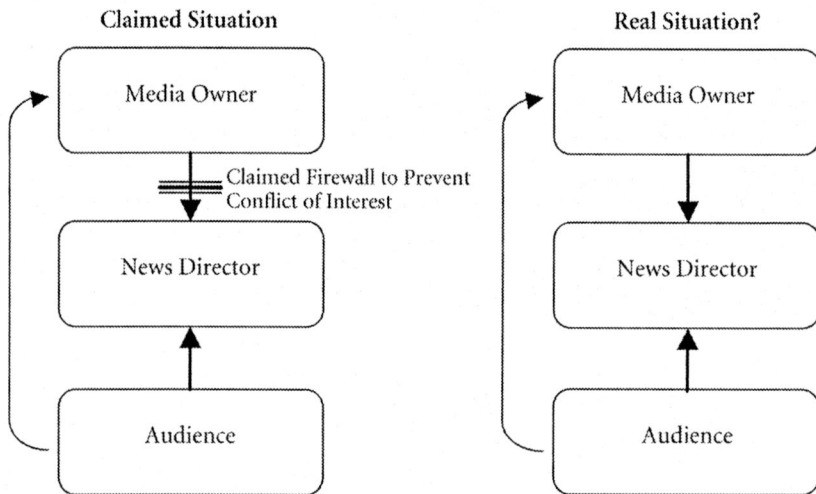

When the underlying structure of a class of analogies is clearly specified, the class of analogies becomes a theory. Thus, dual agent analogies become transformed into dual agent theory, and the Allegation becomes a mere instance of the law of dual agent behavior.

Theories are useful because they help us identify relevant and irrelevant data and make accurate inferences from data. Dual agent theory, for example, leads us to expect that all dual agents and secondary principals will implicitly or explicitly publicly claim some type of agency/ethics firewall. But it also leads us to ignore such claims unless it can be proved those claims are costly and that the expected cost of bias outweighs its benefit. A costly legal claim would be one enforceable in a court of law at a reasonable expense. A costly marketplace claim would be one that would lead to a loss of profit independent of any government action.

Dual agent theory allows us to test the firewall claims of broadcast media against the claims of other dual agents in similar situations. The result may be that the public claims of TV general managers and TV news directors to act in the interest of their audience may be given no more prima facie credence than a politician's claim not to be influenced by special interest campaign contributions or a lobbyist's protestations to be motivated only by the public interest.

Humans as Principal-Agent Theorists

If an individual determines he is faced with a principal-agent relationship, he can use his entire experience with other principal-agent relationships as a basis for predicting what will happen in this particular relationship, given his incomplete information.

To describe someone as a "principal-agent theorist" may suggest that that person has some esoteric knowledge. But the knowledge in fact only refers to commonsense perceptions about how people interact in day-to-day situations and decide whom to trust. Every adult has personally experienced or observed thousands of principal-agent relationships in his or her life. As suggested earlier, the daily act of one person (the "principal") delegating a task to another (the "agent") is what makes modern civilization possible. Therefore, most people are pretty sophisticated principal-agent theorists, even if only in the narrow sphere in which they live. Members of Congress, in particular, tend to be outstanding principal-agent theorists because rising to their powerful positions requires an exceptional ability to read and make sound inferences from other people's salient interests. And since almost all agents to some extent have mixed loyalties, any competent principal-agent theorist will also be familiar with dual agent situations.

Reference Cases From Other Industries

Many trade associations and corporations make ethics claims. These claims are typically very similar in structure to the ethics claims made by journalists. A claim is made that the agent does indeed act on behalf of the principal he claims to act on behalf of while somehow avoiding conflicts of interest that might impel him to act otherwise.

Most ethics claims are not codified in formal codes of ethics. However, it turns out that many trade associations and corporations do have formal codes of ethics. For example, the Ethics Officers Association says it has 975 members, including more than 50% of Fortune 100 companies.[2] A review of codes of ethics reveals that the professional narcissism associated with journalistic codes of ethics—the idea that a particular agent has a higher moral calling than agents in other professions—is common. Written codes often exist in professions, like broadcasting, where consumers have limited ability to judge the quality of the product they receive, and so must depend on the good faith of those providing the product. Hundreds, if not thousands, of organizations publish codes of ethics that assert that their members act in the interests of their customers and the general public. Some codes of ethics, such as those issued by associations representing lawyers (the American Bar Association) and doctors (the American Medical Association), are long and detailed. Others, such as those put out by associations representing journalists, are relatively short and simple. Regardless of variations in length and detail, the basic types of ethical claims contained in these codes of ethics, including journalistic codes of ethics, are largely interchangeable.

Consider the following sample of ethics claims by a diverse group of industries.

Realtors' Codes of Ethics

The National Association of Realtors, which describes itself as the world's largest professional association with 750,000 members, is also the premier association representing real estate brokers.

> Under all is the land. Upon its wise utilization and widely allocated ownership depend the survival and growth of free institutions and of our civilization…. Such interests impose obligations beyond those of ordinary commerce. They impose grave social responsibility and a patriotic duty…. The term REALTOR® has come to connote competency, fairness, and high integrity resulting from adherence to a lofty ideal of moral conduct in business relations. No inducement of profit and no instruction from clients ever can justify departure from this ideal.[3]

---

[2] From www.eoa.org/AboutEO, 31 December 2003.

[3] "Code of Ethics and Standards of Practice," National Association of Realtors, effective 1 January 2001.

Lawyers' Codes of Ethics

The American Bar Association is the premier association representing lawyers.

> A lawyer shall not represent a client if the representation of that client will be directly adverse to another client....

> The lawyer's own interests should not be permitted to have an adverse effect on representation of a client. For example, a lawyer's need for income should not lead the lawyer to undertake matters that cannot be handled competently and at a reasonable fee.... A lawyer may not allow related business interests to affect representation, for example, by referring clients to an enterprise in which the lawyer has an undisclosed interest.[4]

Doctors' Codes of Ethics

The American Medical Association is the premier association representing doctors.

> Under no circumstances may physicians place their own financial interests above the welfare of their patients. The primary objective of the medical profession is to render service to humanity; reward or financial gain is a subordinate consideration. For a physician unnecessarily to hospitalize a patient, prescribe a drug, or conduct diagnostic tests for the physician's financial benefit is unethical. If a conflict develops between the physician's financial interest and the physician's responsibilities to the patient, the conflict must be resolved to the patient's benefit.[5]

Lobbyists' Codes of Ethics

The American League of Lobbyists is the premier association serving Washington DC lobbyists, including employees and outside contractors of the NAB. Its ethics code includes the following text:

---

[4] "Model Rules of Professional Conduct, 2001 Edition," (Chicago, IL: American Bar Association, 2000).

[5] "E-8.03—Conflict of Interest: Guidelines" (Chicago, Illinois: American Medical Association, 2000).

The professional lobbyist will always deal in accurate, current and factual information, whether it is being reported to the employer or client, government officials, the media or professional colleagues, and will not engage in misrepresentation of any nature.

The professional lobbyist will acquire enough knowledge of public policy issues to be able to fairly present all points of view.

The professional lobbyist will avoid conflicts of interest...and where conflict is unavoidable will communicate the facts fully and freely to those affected.[6]

What can one learn from the widespread existence of such agency claims? The most obvious lesson is that agency claims per se may not be worth much more than the paper they are written on. Consider the cases of two companies, Enron and Arthur Anderson.

Enron

On July 1, 2000, shortly before filing for bankruptcy in one of the most famous cases of corporate fraud, Enron Corporation CEO Kenneth Lay signed his name to the following *Enron Code of Ethics* and distributed it to his employees, asking them to read it and then return a signed "certificate of compliance".[7] The Enron Code opens with this letter from Kenneth Lay: "...We want to be proud of Enron and to know that it enjoys a reputation for fairness and honesty and that it is respected..." Then under the section "Business Ethics" it includes the following text:

Employees of Enron Corp., its subsidiaries, and its affiliated companies (collectively the "Company") are charged with conducting their business affairs in accordance with the highest ethical standards.... Moral as well as legal obligations will be fulfilled openly, promptly, and in a manner which will reflect pride on the Company's name.

---

[6] "Guidelines for Professional Conduct," (Washington, DC: American League of Lobbyists, 1987). The American Society of Association of Executives, the premier trade association for trade associations, has adopted almost identical language as the ALL for its lobbyist guidelines. See ASAE, "Guidelines for Association Lobbyists," (Washington, DC: American Society of Association Executives, 1997).

[7] Caroline E. Mayer and Amy Joyce, "Blowing the Whistle," *Washington Post*, 10 February 2002, p. H1.

Products and services of the Company will be of the highest quality and as represented. Advertising and promotion will be truthful, not exaggerated or misleading....

Illegal behavior on the part of any employee in the performance of Company duties will neither be condoned nor tolerated.

Arthur Anderson

Arthur Anderson, Enron's prestigious Big 5 accounting firm, was also convicted of participating in and covering up Enron's fraud and abuse. Anderson was a member of the American Institute of Certified Public Accountants and instrumental in writing its ethics code.[8] The code reads, in part:[9]

Members should accept the obligation to act in a way that will serve the public interest, honor the public trust, and demonstrate commitment to professionalism.

A distinguishing mark of a profession is acceptance of its responsibility to the public. The accounting profession's public consists of clients, credit grantors, governments, employers, investors, the business and financial community, and others who rely on the objectivity and integrity of certified public accountants to maintain the orderly functioning of commerce. This reliance imposes a public interest responsibility on certified public accountants. The public interest is defined as the collective well-being of the community of people and institutions the profession serves.

In discharging their professional responsibilities, members may encounter conflicting pressures from among each of those groups. In resolving those conflicts, members should act with integrity, guided by the precept that when members fulfill their responsibility to the public, clients' and employers' interests are best served.

Those who rely on certified public accountants expect them to discharge their responsibilities with integrity, objectivity, due professional care, and a genuine interest in serving the public....

---

[8] In 1986. Arthur Anderson President George Anderson chaired the committee that wrote AICPA's Report of the Special Committee on Standards of Professional Conduct for Certified Public Accountants, which revised the accounting profession's Code of Professional Conduct. The report was widely known as the "Anderson Report."

[9] See http://www.aicpa.org/about/code.

All who accept membership in the American Institute of Certified Public Accountants commit themselves to honor the public trust.

To the extent that ethics claims are universal but ethical behavior is not, there will be a tendency to discount ethics claims. A claim in-and-of-itself, therefore, contains little valuable information. Seminal works in the literature on media objectivity have relied on such testimony.[10] But asking journalists whether they act in the public interest should hold no more intrinsic credibility than asking a real estate broker, candidate for public office, or lobbyist.

A Famous Dual Agent Structure in Politics

As the basis for a detailed discussion of the dual agent analogy, let's take the case of a legislator who receives special interest campaign contributions. For our purposes, the strategic position of the legislator and reporter is identical. The legislator and reporter both have a conflict of interest. Legislators need campaign contributions to win re-election; reporters need to please their bosses to keep their jobs. Both have strong incentives to claim an "ethics firewall" exists that prevents this conflict of interest from hurting the general public, their primary principal. Both also have strong incentives to both hide and deny any evidence to the contrary.

In figure 11-3, we see the two sets of principal-agent relationships. Each set is named after the potential "dual agent," the agent that may serve two competing principals. Accordingly, the first set is named the "reporter case;" the second the "legislator case."

---

[10] E.g., Herbert J. Gans, *Deciding What's News: A Study of CBS Evening News, NBC Nightly News, Newsweek, and Time*, 1st Vintage Books ed. (New York: Vintage Books, 1980).

Figure 11-3. The Common Incentive Structure of Two Dual Agents.

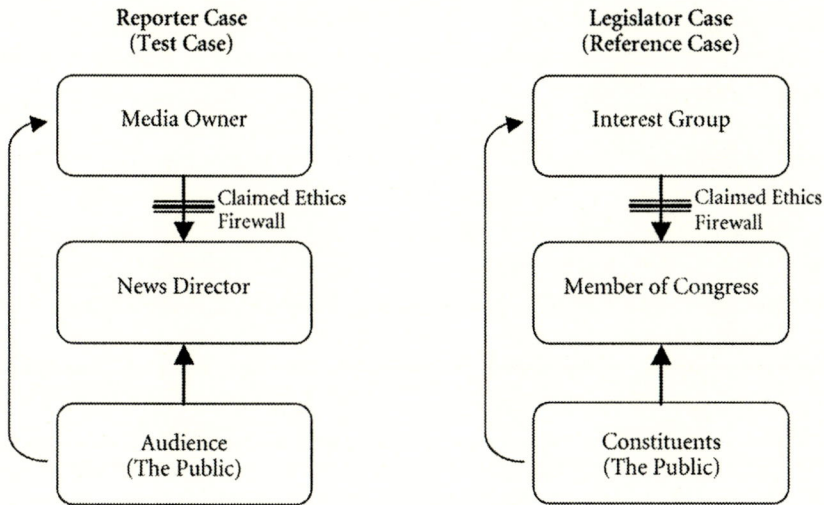

Reporter Case (Test Case)	Legislator Case (Reference Case)
Media Owner	Interest Group
—— Claimed Ethics Firewall	—— Claimed Ethics Firewall
News Director	Member of Congress
Audience (The Public)	Constituents (The Public)

The legislator case is the "reference case" because it is used to make inferences about the reporter case, the "test case."

Each case has the two elements in common that constitute a dual agency situation: 1) An agent that serves two principals with competing interests, one of which is a primary principal and the other a secondary principal, and 2) a claimed "ethics firewall" that prevents the dual agent from acting opportunistically on this conflict of interest.

In the reporter case, the primary principal is the reporter's viewing audience; in the legislator case, it is the legislator's voting constituents. In the reporter case, the secondary principal is the local TV news director's superiors and corporate owners; in the legislator case, it is the special interest groups who provide disproportionate resources to a Member of Congress' re-election campaign. In the reporter case, the ethics firewall is the claimed separation of the business and news sides of their corporate employer. In the legislator case, it is the claimed separation of the political and public policy sides of their offices.

In both the reporter and legislator cases, it should be extremely difficult for third parties to find verifiable evidence of a breach in a claimed firewall, even when such a breach exists. As argued earlier, this lack of evidence may arise because agents (e.g., reporters and legislators) have strong incentives to hide opportunistic behavior from principals (e.g., the public). Consistent with this theory, political scientists have generally had as much difficulty "proving" special interest bias (stemming from campaign contributions) as media ownership bias (stemming from control of media).[11]

The argument here is that a member of Congress can use inside information about the legislator case, which they have direct and intimate knowledge of, to make inferences about the reporter case. For example, let's assume that the two sets of principal-agent relationships described above are strategically identical. If legislators don't believe the claims of interest groups and their colleagues that campaign contributions don't influence policy stands, then it should be easier for them to infer, all other things being equal, that the public trustee claims of broadcast owners and chief reporters may not be credible.[12] In the words of Senator John McCain, co-author of the most significant campaign finance legislation to pass Congress in the last two decades, the campaign finance system is "nothing less than an elaborate influence peddling scheme in which both parties conspire to stay in office by selling the country to the highest bidder."[13] Senator Simon, who spent 42 years in elected office, including 24 in Congress, put it this way: "Anyone in a major elected public office who tells you that he or she is not influenced by campaign contributions is either living in a dream world or is lying."[14]

As we have seen, the legislator case is hardly the only reference case that can be used to draw inferences regarding the reporter case. However, the legislator case is especially useful because it is well known to the public, political scientists, and members of Congress.

---

[11] E.g., S. Ansolabehere, J. M. de Figueiredo, and J. M. Snyder, "Why Is There So Little Money in U.S. Politics?," *Journal of Economic Perspectives* 17, no. 1 (2003), Rosenthal, *The Third House*. Note that Rosenthal concedes that interest groups are likely to have more influence on "minor technical issues" than "big issues." Here the definition of minor technical issue becomes crucial. Is spectrum policy such an issue? Presumably, in Rosenthal's eyes, yes. But this author would beg to disagree.

[12] Elizabeth Drew, *The Corruption of American Politics: What Went Wrong and Why* (Secaucus, N.J.: Carol Pub. Group, 1999), William Greider, *Who Will Tell the People: The Betrayal of American Democracy* (New York: Simon & Schuster, 1992), R. L. Hall and F. W. Wayman, "Buying Time—Moneyed Interests and the Mobilization of Bias in Congressional Committees," *American Political Science Review* 84, no. 3 (1990), Brooks Jackson, *Honest Graft : Big Money and the American Political Process*, Rev. ed. (Washington, D.C.: Farragut Pub. Co., 1990), West and Loomis, *The Sound of Money: How Political Interests Get What They Want*.

[13] Cited in Joan Claybrook, "McCain's Campaign Finance Candor," *Public Citizen News*, September/October 1999, p. 2.

[14] Cited in Roger Simon, "Honest Paul," *Washington Monthly*, April 1999, p. 51. See Paul Simon, *P.S.: The Autobiography of Paul Simon*, 1st ed. (Chicago, Ill.: Bonus Books, 1999).

The public. The possibly corrupting influence of special interests on members of Congress is a staple of popular literature and mass media, and polls show that most Americans believe that special interest influence is a corrupting force in politics.[15] Candidates for Congress, including incumbents, routinely campaign by claiming that their opponents have been bought off by special interests, and Congress passes campaign finance reform with a promise to curb such influence. Meanwhile, the public know that politicians routinely deny being themselves influenced by campaign contributions. Special interests, in turn, routinely deny giving money with the purpose of changing a legislator's behavior.

Political scientists. Political scientists have had great difficulty proving the existence of such special interest group bias, yet they keep trying in recognition of the widespread popular perception—and their own intuition—that such bias would be a manifestation of rational behavior. Douglas Arnold has devoted the better part of a book to explaining this paradox of interest group bias: interest groups give money and legislators accept it only when the public cannot trace the flow of influence.[16]

Congress. Legislators see their colleagues routinely deny being influenced by campaign contributions when they know the truth to be otherwise;[17] they see special interests routinely seeking to influence themselves while publicly denying doing so;[18] and from their own experience they know how easy it is to

---

[15] Both the popular and academic literature is full of anecdotal allegations of policy favors in return for money. E.g., see Harwood Group, "Citizens and Politics: A View from Main Street America," (Dayton, Ohio: Kettering Foundation, 1991), Peter D. Hart, "People Versus Politics: Citizens Discuss Politicians, Campaigns, and Political Reform," (Washington, DC: Peter D. Hart Research Associates, 1991), John R. Hibbing and Elizabeth Theiss-Morse, *Congress as Public Enemy : Public Attitudes toward American Political Institutions, Cambridge Studies in Political Psychology and Public Opinion* (Cambridge ; New York: Cambridge University Press, 1995).

[16] Arnold, *The Logic of Congressional Action*.

[17] In my experience on Capitol Hill, I have routinely heard private cynical comments that a particular legislator was loyal to a particular group because it was a contributor.

[18] In response to the charge that NAB contributions bought off Representative Billy Tauzin, Tauzin's spokesperson Ken Johnson replied "there was no link between contributions and favors from the lawmaker....'Frankly, the only thing anyone can expect for a campaign contribution is a free autographed photograph." Cited in Doug Halonen, "Fishing to be Heard in DC," *Electronic Media*, 7 October 2002, p. 22. Other denials by Johnson on behalf of Tauzin are in David Hatch, "Baby Bell Broadband Brouhaha," *Electronic Media*, 7 May 2001, p. 31. John Bresnahan and Damon Chappie, "Members Quit Weller Tech Group," *Roll Call*, 3 December 2001, p. 1.

avoid creating any traceable and verifiable evidence of special interest influence.[19] The Republican Party's directive to interest groups, "Stop donating so much to the Democrats…or be denied access to Republicans in Congress,"[20] is indicative of the cynicism on this issue by both Democratic and Republican legislators.

Legislator Ethics Claims

Looking at legislators' written codes of ethics, we see that they mirror the structure of media codes of ethics. That, of course, is what makes them codes of ethics.

The U.S. Senate is one of two bodies that constitute the U.S. Congress. Although each body has different codes of ethics, the basic principles contained in them are the same. The U.S. *Senate Ethics Manual* clearly identifies a Senator's primary principal as the public. According to Senate Resolution 266, "[a] public office is a public trust" and each Senator "has been entrusted with public power by the people; that the officer holds this power in trust to be used only for their benefit and never for the benefit or himself or a few."[21] The *Senate Ethics Manual* is 562 pages long and elaborates on this simple principle at length. One section of the Manual describes establishing a firewall of ignorance as a solution to conflicts of interest created by financial contributions from special interests.

> [A] number of Senators have instituted practices to strictly separate fund raising from substantive legislative or constituent casework activities.… If the Senator or staff member does not know if an individual is a contributor, he or she is not required or encouraged to find out. Most Senate staff members are not provided with information regarding contributions and are unaware of whether an individual seeking assistance is a contributor.[22]

---

[19] United States. Congress. Senate. Select Committee on Ethics., *Senate Ethics Manual*, S. Prt. ; 104-60 (Washington, DC: For sale by the U.S. G.P.O., Supt. of Docs., Congressional Sales Office, 1996), pp. 232-3.

[20] Helene Cooper, "GOP to Rebuke Companies for Bipartisan Donations," Wall Street Journal, 9 January 1997, p. A12.

[21] United States. Congress. Senate. Select Committee on Ethics., *Senate Ethics Manual*, p. 234.

[22] Ibid.

The ethics code of the U.S. House of Representatives is similar.[23]

A classic use of this type of firewall occurred when Senator McCain was accused of writing letters to federal regulators on behalf of 15 campaign contributors. McCain aides explained to reporters: "Commerce Committee staff members who draft the letters—most of which aren't even read by McCain—have no knowledge of his campaign fund-raising."[24]

In many years of following Congress in major media, I do not recall a single instance of a member of Congress arguing that he acted against the public interest or allowed special interest campaign contributions or other similar political considerations to affect his legislative behavior. When individual members of Congress are accused of such behavior, they invariably either ignore the allegation or deny it. For example, after describing the campaign contributions of the cable, broadcast, and movie industries leading up to the Cable Act of 1992, *Communications Daily*, the leading newsletter covering communications and broadcast policy, noted: "Lawmakers routinely deny close ties between their votes and PAC financing...."[25] As we have now seen, to do otherwise would be to violate Congressional ethics and risk Congressional censure or even expulsion from Congress.

A Simple Control for Confounding Variables

One subcase of the legislator case is especially useful as a reference case because it controls for confounding variables. That subcase substitutes one particular interest group, broadcast owners, for interest groups in general, as the secondary principal. The reference case is now a closer approximation of the test case, and we can therefore make a more valid inference from the reference case to the test case. That is, the use of broadcast owners rather than interest groups in the reference case by no means guarantees a flawless inference, but it does increase the odds of a correct inference. In both cases now, the secondary principal is the same, the broadcast owner. The new reference case is depicted in Figure 11-4.

---

[23] United States. Congress. House. Committee on Standards of Official Conduct., *Ethics Manual for Members, Officers, and Employees of the U.S. House of Representatives* (Washington: U.S. G.P.O., 1992), pp. 250-1.

[24] John Mintz and Susan B. Glasser, "McCain Interviewed With U.S. for 15 Campaign Contributors," *Washington Post*, 9 January 2000, p. A1.

[25] "Pressure Building for Bush to Sign Cable Bill," *Communications Daily*, September 24, 1992.

Figure 11-4. Reference Case Controlled for the Secondary Principal

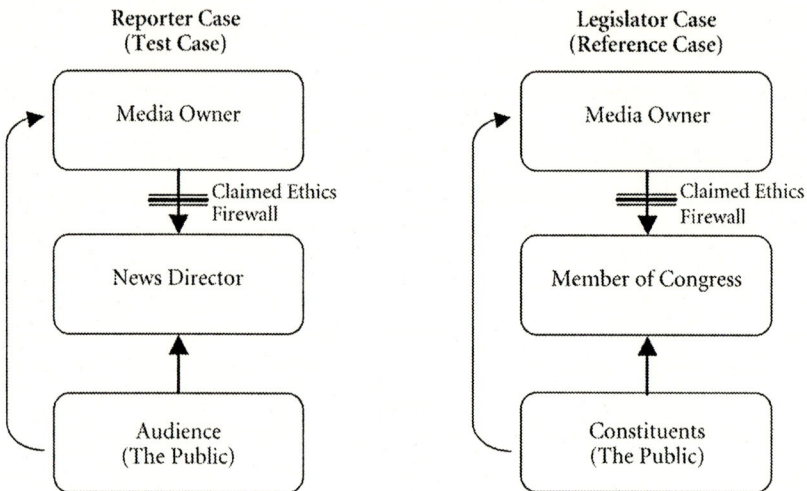

Reporter Case
(Test Case)

Legislator Case
(Reference Case)

Media Owner

Claimed Ethics
Firewall

News Director

Audience
(The Public)

Media Owner

Claimed Ethics
Firewall

Member of Congress

Constituents
(The Public)

Broadcaster lobbyists have not come together as a group and composed their own formal, written ethics code. However, their ethics code can easily be inferred from how they react when accused of not pursuing the public interest.

To the best of my knowledge, a broadcaster owner-lobbyist has never publicly asserted that he lies, provides inaccurate information, or in any other way acts against the public interest. This is equally true regardless of whether the lobbying resource is media or non-media.

The National Association of Broadcasters states the position clearly: "Broadcasters speak up when they feel their cause is just. They exercise their Constitutional prerogative to petition the government for relief of grievances. When broadcasters seek change in public policy, it is change that is in the best interests of broadcast television, the viewing public and the nation."[26]

In 1997, a broadcast TV station general manager responded to criticism of the NAB's lobbying tactics with the following defense: "The NAB is doing a great job. In the last two or three years they have very fairly presented the broadcasters' picture to the Congress."[27] This period of time, 1995–1997, covered the broadcasters' peak lobbying for free spectrum rights.

---

[26] NAB, "Talking Points," p. 28.

[27] Comments of Michael McDougald, president and general manager of McDougald Broadcasting Corporation, cited in Paige Albiniak, "King of the Hill," *Broadcasting & Cable*, 22 December 1997, p. 18.

In 1996, after Congress gave the broadcasters what they had lobbied so hard for, "NAB spokeswoman Patti McNeill said charges that the digital license distribution was the result of influence-buying are 'ridiculous.'"[28]

However, when the NAB sends out solicitations to raise money for its PAC, called TARPAC (for Television and Radio Political Action Committee), its message is different.[29] An April 1998 solicitation to potential TARPAC contributors says: "The stronger we are as a PAC, the stronger our ability to the job we need to do in Washington."[30] An April 1997 solicitation says: "TARPAC ensures that when the chips are down, Congress will hear our voice on key bottom-line issues."[31] A 1990 how-to guide for TARPAC State chairman and members of the TARPAC board of directors says: "Your role in building TARPAC has a very practical importance: The more successful you—and others on the TARPAC Team—are, the better chance we have to shape the decisions of Congress on issues that affect us."[32]

Perhaps the most interesting feature of the more precise reference case is that broadcasters can manipulate it to send signals to legislators. Broadcasters know that legislators will use their own direct experience to make inferences about what they cannot experience. Therefore, if broadcasters simply act like every other interest group in both their private contacts with legislators and in their public claims, this can be enormously informative for legislators trying to make inferences about broadcasters' behavior in a media setting. In other words, if broadcasters act opportunistically in one context (conventional lobbying) while making great efforts to hide this behavior from the public, then

---

[28] Matt Pottinger, "A digital license 'giveaway'?" *Hollywood Reporter*, 3 April 1997, p. 3.

[29] A remarkable feature of the broadcast industry is the degree to which PAC contributions come from the NAB. According to an Open Secrets report of the top 20 campaign contributors from the local radio and television industry for the 1995–1996 election cycle, only the NAB contributed PAC money. All the other stations relied on either soft money or individual contributions. In contrast, for local telephone companies for the same period, 14 of the top 20 contributors contributed PAC money to candidates. For local cable companies, the figure was 8 of 20. One explanation is that local broadcast stations with news departments don't like to publicly indicate direct support for a particular candidate. Individual and soft money donations create a buffer between the station and the contribution to the candidate. See http://www.opensecrets.org/industries.

[30] "Time to Renew Your Pledge," *Leaders of the PAC*, Washington, DC: NAB, 5(2):1. *Leaders of the PAC*, launched in 1993, is a monthly NAB publication for TARPAC contributors.

[31] TARPAC brochure handed out to NAB members at the April 1997 NAB Show.

[32] "TARPAC Fundraising Manual," (Washington, DC: NAB, 1990).

legislators can infer that when incentives are very similar in another context (use of media for lobbying), broadcasters will act similarly.

This signaling system is effective largely because legislators have much better knowledge than the general public of the broadcasters' conventional lobbying behavior. Broadcasters must engage in conventional lobbying behavior, if only to inform legislators of their needs. But the broadcasters are careful to ensure that their passionate special pleading is done face-to-face or in other ways that are unverifiable and thus subject to plausible deniability. Based on this private, unverifiable, information, legislators draw their inferences about the likelihood of broadcaster bias.

A More Rigorous Control for Confounding Variables

A more rigorous inference can be drawn when both the agent and secondary principal are controlled. Now the secondary principal acts as an agent in relation to another principal, which differs in the reference and test cases. In Figure 11-5, we substitute the TV news director for the legislator. Variation now occurs at the level of the type of ownership interest at stake, with the test case industry-specific policymaker bias and the reference case advertiser bias. Both policymakers and advertisers control resources that media owners want and thus serve as secondary principals to news directors, filtered through the interests of media owners. In this discussion, the reference case is advertiser bias, but it could also be any of the other common forms of media bias outlined in Chapter 2. The inference is of the following nature: If a news director is willing to engage in media bias in relation to one secondary principal, an advertiser, he is likely to be willing to engage in bias in relation to another secondary principal, a policymaker.

Figure 11-5. Reference Case Controlled for the Agent & Primary Principal

Policymaking Case
(Test Case)

Advertising Case
(Reference Case)

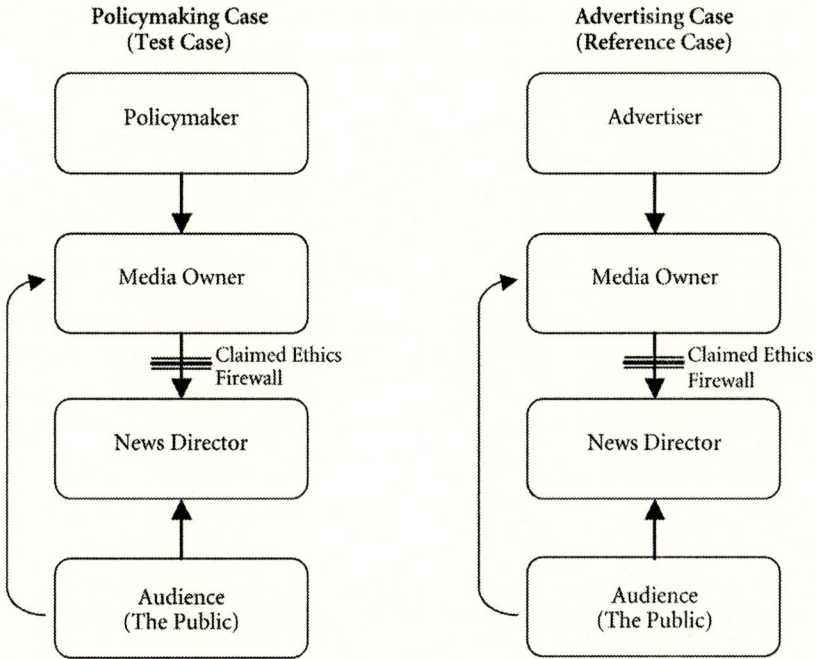

Media routinely claim that advertiser interests don't affect editorial content. Yet the literature on media criticism is full of reports that advertisers influence content.[33] The trade and popular press also carry abundant reports on advertiser bias, such as car dealers influencing negative news coverage of their business,[34] advertisers vetoing programs with violent or other socially

---

[33] Blake Fleetwood, "The Broken Wall: How Newspapers Are Selling Their Credibility to Advertisers," *Washington Monthly*, September 1999, Marion Just and Rosalind Levine, "News for Sale: Half of Stations Report Sponsor Pressure on News Decisions," *Columbia Journalism Review*, November/December 2001.

[34] E.g., "In The Driver's Seat," *Broadcasting & Cable*, 29 May 2000, p. 58. "Karissa S. Wang, "KCBS News to Expose Car Dealers," *Electronic Media*, 15 May 2000, p. 1A.

controversial content,[35] advertisers with health messages seeking placement of those messages in entertainment program scripts, [36] and advertisers getting their logos inserted in news programming.[37]

In an ethics debates on advertisers bias in *Communicator*, the magazine for radio and television news directors, one news director concedes that advertisers get privileged news exposure: "Management always encourages the news department to consider sponsors when doing stories and our reporters follow that as a rule, making exceptions when we know the best source is not a sponsor."[38] Another story in *Communicator* praises a reporter in Los Angeles, one of the top five TV markets in the U.S., who resisted the pressure of advertisers and station management:

> Joel Grover was expecting trouble. The head of the special investigations unit at KCBS-TV in Los Angeles had pitched the same story countless times at various stations—a series exposing how some car dealers can rob customers easily without being detected.
>
> But over the years, Grover learned it isn't an easy sell, as the auto industry shovels big advertising bucks into radio stations, TV stations and newspapers....
>
> "I've been a reporter for 19 years, and I can't tell you how unusual it is, what just happened at KCBS," he says. "Doing investigative stories about car dealers is taboo in local television. The majority of stations won't touch this story, no matter how important, no matter how

---

[35] E.g., Chuck Ross, "USA [owner of ten local TV broadcast stations] Cozies Up To Advertisers," *Electronic Media*, 18 December 2000, p. 1. At Cato event on television violence televised by C-SPAN on 27 May 1997, NBC Counsel Rick Cotton explained that the market, rather than government, was a sufficient filter for violence because advertisers previewed all major programs to ensure they don't have unacceptable levels of violence.

[36] E.g., Spencer S. Hsu, "TV Stations Say Ads on Abstinence Had Strings," *Washington Post*, 4 June 1998, p. D1. The sources for this article were all stations that refused the deal proposed by the health advertiser, but they also were quoted as saying that other unnamed stations competing with their stations accepted the deal.

[37] Howard Kurtz, "CBS Reporter Creates Internal Furor Over Nike," *Washington Post*, 11 February 1998, p. D1.

[38] Colleen Reynolds, "Tough Calls: The sales department has sold advertising time to a brokerage and is asking for a weekly segment in your newscast on personal finances featuring someone from the brokerage. What do you do?" *Communicator*, May 2000, p. 48.

legitimate. I've worked at six stations in my career, and this is the first station, the first management that would ever allow me to do this."[39]

The article is framed not to disparage the journalistic ethics of other stations but to praise the ethics of KCBS-TV, the only station mentioned by name in the article. An editorial in *Broadcasting & Cable*, read by TV station general managers and staff on the Congressional telecom subcommittees, articulates the same view about the KCBS-TV incident:

> In local TV, car dealers are the backbone (or perhaps that should be drive train) of many ad budgets. So TV reporters may be reluctant to investigate allegations of unethical behavior by dealers. But that is just what KCBS-TV Los Angeles did. And when faced with some angry dealers threatening to drive their six-figure ad accounts off the lot, the station's general manager told them to go ahead.[40]

Another article in *Communicator* provides a profile of a muckraking reporter whose station general manager shielded the reporter from "business and advertising pressure."[41] Although there is no mention at all that other stations might not uphold such high journalistic standards, a logical but unstated implication for the reader is that the article is newsworthy precisely because such behavior is out of the ordinary.

Advertising bias can also work in reverse, with stations insisting that entities take out ads if they want program coverage. This includes stations insisting that musicians buy advertising or play at station-sponsored concerts as a condition of playing their songs,[42] TV networks requiring fees in return for brand and product placement within a show,[43] and editing out billboard ads at bona fide news events whose TV exposure hasn't been paid for.

---

[39] "The Story Behind KCBS-TV's Series on Car Dealers," *Communicator*, July 2000, p. 12.

[40] "In The Driver's Seat," *Broadcasting & Cable*, 29 May 2000, p. 58. See also "Karissa S. Wang, "KCBS News to Expose Car Dealers," *Electronic Media*, 15 May 2000, p. 1A, and Just and Levine, "News for Sale," p. 3.

[41] Al Tompkins, "Total Recall," *Communicator*, October 2000, pp. 23-25.

[42] Laura M. Holson, "With By-the-Numbers Radio, Requests Are a Dying Breed," *New York Times*, 11 July 2002, pp. C1, C4.

[43] Steve McClellan, "Grading Product Placement," *Broadcasting & Cable*, 15 December 2003, p. 1. Stuart Elliott, "Hiding a Television Commercial in Plain View," *New York Times*, 24 May 2002, p. C1. Michael McCarthy, "Digital Ads Show Up In Unexpected Places," *USA Today*, 23 March 2001.

According to a survey of news directors conducted by the Project for Excellence in Journalism, a third of news directors say they've been pressured to kill negative stories—or do positive ones—about sponsors. The same survey found that two-thirds of stations now run "sponsored" news segments.[44]

Another type of bias involves companies in which media companies have equity interests, including sports teams,[45] hotels,[46] Internet startups,[47] and theme parks.[48] There is source bias, where reporters and stations get subsidies from the sources they cover, including sports teams, entertainment shows,[49] and travel destinations.[50] And there is cross-promotion bias within a TV station, where hard news shows promote other type of station programming.[51] This is *Broadcasting & Cable*'s editorial on the commercial corruption of news.

> Once journalists endeavored—at significant economic sacrifice—to avoid even the appearance of conflict of interest. But much of today's corporate-controlled TV journalism seems to be defined not by

[44] Cited in Howard Kurtz, "ABC Fires Radio Host Matt Drudge," *Washington Post*, 17 November 2000, p. C1.

[45] Bob Edwards, "Integrity of Sports Journalism," *National Public Radio*, 3 November 1999, transcript available via Nexis, Kelly Heyboer, "Fair Game? Things can get quite tricky when a commpany that owns a news organization invests in a sports franchise in the same town," *American Journalism Review*, October 1999, p. 50, Jane Manners, "Smells like Team Spirit: *Dallas Morning News* reporters wonder about their owner's sports deal," *Brill's Content*, October 1999, p. 42, David Shaw, "Crossing the Line," *Los Angeles Times*, 20 December 1999, p. V3.

[46] E.g., "Sinclair Stations Fed Pro-Advertiser Story," *Electronic Media*, 1 May 2000, p. 1. Steve McClellan, "Hey, Big Spender!" Broadcasting & Cable, 19 April 1999, p. 60.

[47] Leslie Kaufman, "The Sock Puppet That Roared: Internet Synergy or Conflict of Interest," *New York Times*, 27 March 2000, p. A4.

[48] ABC News routinely promotes Disney during news coverage of major holidays such as New Year's Eve and Thanksgiving. See also Howard Kurtz, "ABC Kills Story Critical of Owner Disney," *Washington Post*, 14 October 1998, p. C1. Carol Guensburg, "When the Story Is About the Owner," *American Journalism Review*, 1 December 1998.

[49] Sharon Waxman, "Spoon-Fed News: When the nation's television critics make the pilgrimage to Pasadena twice a year, the networks lavish them with heavy doses of propaganda along with free meals, glitzy parties and trinkets," *American Journalism Review*, October 1998, pp. 36-9.

[50] Cerra Whittelsey, "Press Credentials, $298," *Columbia Journalism Review*, March/April 1999, p. 13.

[51] Eric Effron, "And This Just In?" Brill's Content, July/August 2000, p. 44-5. Barbara Mattusow, "You Call This News?" *The Washingtonian*, April 1996, p. 39.

avoiding cross-industry interests but promoting them. And many who should be on the front lines in the battle to preserve journalistic integrity not only fail to voice loud protests but defend this "synergy" as they elevate corporate interests to news events. And we've been told that, in some organizations, if news executives want to advance into the business side of television, they'd better be willing to do things a news purist might not be comfortable with.... [I]nstead of the fabled wall separating the "church and state" of editorial and marketing, there is a door marked "Enter" and increasing financial pressure to do so.

We were struck on our visit to the Promax convention last month with how often the marketers there were encouraged to enlist the news department to cross-promote a new syndicated show. We shouldn't have been, of course. For years, sweeps periods have been filled with "news" stories about the casts or subjects of shows or movies leading into those newscasts....

Local news as a promoter of prime time is everywhere.... and the viewers can never be sure whether the decision to run a story is based on news value or shareholder value.[52]

Another type of bias involves competitors, including stations refusing to carry ads by existing or even would-be competitors,[53] replacing promotional banners of competing TV stations,[54] refusing to run a movie ad for a movie starring a disliked former employee,[55] deleting a reference to a competitor in a U.S. President's speech,[56] and refusing to carry the promotional ads of competing cable TV networks.[57] Their competitors, the cable TV companies, do the same.[58] In *Communicator*, a news director responded to a question concerning whether she'd cover a competing station's banner at a news event:

---

[52] "Plug at 11," *Broadcasting & Cable*, 17 July 2000.

[53] Lee Romney, "Univision Begins Internet Venture," *Los Angeles Times*, 28 June 2000.

[54] Bill Carter, "CBS Is Divided Over the Use of False Images in Broadcasts," *New York Times*, 13 January 2000.

[55] "Wright Does the 'Dirty Work,'" *Broadcasting & Cable*, 15 June 1998, p. 49.

[56] "Radio Station 'Blew It' By Censoring Bush," *Seattle Times*, 19 June 2004.

[57] "Notebook," *Television Digest*, 20 February 1995.

[58] Seth Schiesel, "Cable Giants Refuse to Sell Ads to Internet Competitors," *New York Times*, 8 June 2001.

The ultimate question you have to ask is whether the event is newsworthy. If the answer is yes, then you cover it. Do you make a conscious attempt to avoid shooting your competition's banners? Probably. Do you shoot and include the emcee from your competition? Probably not.[59]

TV stations also refuse to run ads critical of valued advertisers[60] or advertising in general.[61]

Another completely different category of deceptions involve those that don't hurt viewers but others such as advertisers and competitors. Examples include charging advertisers for a fixed length ad and then secretly squeezing those ads so extra ads can be inserted;[62] inflating circulation statistics and thus advertising rates of subsidiaries with newspaper properties;[63] and plagiarizing content from local daily newspapers without crediting or paying them.[64]

Of course, journalistic ethics are not uniform across all media outlets. But they also don't vary merely randomly or in accordance with the journalistic integrity of particular reporters and their bosses. Presumably, as the chance of exposure and penalty for unethical conduct increases, the likelihood of that conduct decreases. For example, media ethics may vary as a function of the

---

[59] Tamara McGregor, "Tough Calls: A competing station has attempted to turn a public event into an event of its own by setting up banners with the station's logo and convincing organizers to let one of the station's anchors act as emcee. How do you handle this?" *Communicator*, February 2001, p. 40.

[60] Kelly Greene and Laurie McGinley, "AARP to Alter TV Ad That Touts More Scrutiny of Drug Purchases," *Wall Street Journal*, 14 May 2002, p. B6.

[61] Robert Berner, "A Holiday Greeting Network's Won't Air: Shoppers Are 'Pigs,' *Wall Street Journal*, 19 November 1997, p. A1.

[62] Michele Greppi, "Time Squeeze Probe Widens," *Electronic Media*, 17 December 2001, p. 1. Michele Greppi, "Squeezed Shows Upset Agencies," *Electronic Media*, 19 November 2001. p. 1. Michele Greppi, "CBS Time Squeeze Scandal Widens," *Electronic Media*, 12 November 2001, p. 1. Michele Greppi, "KDKA Cheating on Spots," Electronic Media, 5 November 2001, p. 1. One CBS executive anonymously explained why so many CBS stations were caught using a Time Machine: "There's so much pressure from Mel [Mel Karmazin, Viacom's chief operating officer, including responsibility for CBS] to do whatever you've got to do." Ibid, p. 28.

[63] Jacques Steinberg, "After Circulation Scandal, a Move to Build Trust," *New York Times*, 17 August 2004. Two of the three companies involved in the scandal, Belo and Tribune, were among the largest and most respected TV broadcasters in the United States.

[64] Lori Robertson, "Toledo's Blade Strikes Back," *American Journalism Review*, January/February 2000, p. 10.

national visibility of the media outlet. In my hometown suburb of Severna Park, Maryland (population 30,000), the local newspaper, a monthly publication, has minimal journalistic standards. It will routinely publish press releases as news items. It will give candidates who purchase large ads front page coverage for major candidate announcements. And the publisher will call up writers asking for contributions to favored political candidates covered in its news pages. Editorial standards tend to improve with the size, competitiveness, and national visibility of the media market, with the *New York Times*, *Wall Street Journal*, and *Washington Post* widely perceived to be at the top of the heap.[65]

Ironically, the media with the highest journalistic standards may be those that receive the most criticism. In the history of the *Severna Park Voice*, there has probably never been a serious article critiquing its journalistic standards. In contrast, there have been dozens of books, countless scholarly articles, and probably tens of thousands of competing newspaper articles that have at one time or another critiqued the journalistic standards of the *New York Times*. This doesn't mean that the publisher of the *Severna Park Voice* wouldn't take great offense at any public suggestion that his journalistic standards weren't up there with those of *The New York Times*. The point is that media critics have a perverse incentive to critique the publications with the highest journalistic standards rather than the worst, and that the quality of journalism tends to be in direct proportion to its susceptibility to public criticism.

Similarly, with broadcast TV, the vast majority of expert media criticism focuses on the national programming of the four major TV networks. Local TV broadcast programming, most notably news and public affairs programming, are all but invisible, especially in smaller markets.

A reasonable inference can be made that if media outlets will engage in advertiser and other forms of bias when it suits their interest, there is a high probability they will also engage in policymaker bias when, assuming the risk of exposure and penalty are no greater, they have an ever greater interest at stake. This is extremely efficient reasoning because it means a politician or anyone else with only a little knowledge of a broadcasters' self-interest can make valid, if less than perfect, inferences.

As more and more variables are controlled, argument by analogy converges with argument by example. In argument by example, the generic principals, agents, and issues of the reference and test case are the same.

---

[65] E.g., A study by the Project for Excellence in Journalism found that twice as many small market TV stations felt sponsorship pressure on news than their large market counterparts. Black et al., *Doing Ethics in Journalism*, 141.

Evidence of the Power of Broadcaster Analogies

One of the best pieces of evidence of the power of analogies is the broadcasters' own fear of them; in particular, their fear that the public will infer media bias from non-media bias. A vivid illustration of this occurred in 1986 when NBC's President Robert Wright proposed establishing an NBC political action committee (PAC) financed by employee contributions. Traditionally, newspaper and broadcasting companies had avoided setting up their own PACs because of the appearance of news bias it would create for their news divisions. Wright's proposal caused a furor within the press, including his own company, and he was forced to give it up, if only for a time. Brandon Tartikoff, president of NBC Entertainment, explained why not only news but also entertainment employees couldn't be allowed to contribute: "I wouldn't want...somebody in Iowa or Montana or Michigan or someplace else to think that the programming arm of a network had any sort of political debt." He continued that the entertainment division should remain "apolitical" and "not be seen as taking sides on issues."[66] A CBS spokesman explained why the CBS Corporation, one of the two other TV networks at the time, lacked a PAC: "We feel that having a PAC would be inconsistent with being a major and significant news organization.... We want to keep the political process separate from our job of informing the public."[67] A *New York Times* editorial against NBC's proposed PAC summed up the conventional press view: "The appearances for the network are bad enough. It is a business, but it is also a primary instrument of information and opinion that depends on public trust. Mr. Wright exempts NBC News from his contribution program, but try making that distinction to ordinary citizens."[68] Nevertheless, it is important to note that although NBC gave up its proposal for an impossible-to-hide PAC, its conventional, outside-the-public-eye lobbying never abated and arguably became more intense than ever in the years leading up to passage of the Telecom Act.[69]

---

[66] Cited in "NBC's Tartikoff: No to PAC," *Broadcasting*, 12 January 1987, p. 128.

[67] Cited in "Wright Ponders PAC for NBC," *Broadcasting*, 15 December 1986, p. 58.

[68] "Speaker Wright, Meet Mr. Wright," *New York Times*, 10 December 1986, p. A30.

[69] According to interviews with telecom lobbyists, the breakdown of the rank-and-file broadcaster's inhibition against conventional lobbying is widely considered one of the NAB's greatest triumphs since Eddie Fritts took over the organization in the early 1980s (see Chapter 14). The new mindset doesn't condone any form of lobbying, only lobbying that doesn't leave a public, verifiable record. It's a mindset where appearance counts for everything and reality for nothing; where if you're caught you're dumb and bad, and if you're not, you're smart and good. NBC's Robert Wright learned that lesson in the 1980s and has practiced it successfully ever since.

Disney Chairman Michael Eisner expressed a similar mindset when *Broadcasting & Cable* reported that he "is not personally raising money for any candidates because he wants to keep ABC's news division, which Disney owns, removed from political efforts."[70] But such claimed scruples do not prevent Eisner (and his army of paid lobbyists, including TV general managers from ABC's own stations) from frequently and personally lobbying politicians on broadcast issues.[71]

Another example of broadcasters' fear of this type of reasoning and the corresponding effort to hide evidence of conventional lobbying occurred when network TV executives collectively refused an invitation to stand next to President Clinton during the February 8, 1996 signing of the Telecom Act of 1996. This was no ordinary bill signing. The Library of Congress reported its significance this way:

> The event was historic in two ways: The Telecommunications Act of 1996 was the first bill to be signed into law at the Library of Congress and the first to be signed in cyberspace. After the president signed the bill on paper, he also "signed" it electronically....
>
> President Clinton began his remarks by thanking the Library for hosting the signing. "My understanding is this may be the first time in three decades when a bill has been signed on Capitol Hill."
>
> The event was fraught with symbolism, from the setting—the high-domed Main Reading Room...to the pen used for the signing: the same one President Eisenhower used when he signed the Interstate Highway Act of 1957, "which met the challenge of change...and literally brought Americans closer together," the President said. "That same spirit of connection and communication is the driving force behind the Telecommunications Act of 1996."[72]

The bill signing, featuring a telecommunications skit by famous comedian Lily Tomlin, was designed to attract TV coverage. Very few bill signings feature a soundbite skit by a famous comedian.

---

[70] Paige Albiniak, "McCain Builds War Chest," *Broadcasting & Cable*, 22 March 1998, p. 22.

[71] E.g., "Eisner Pitches to Gore," *Broadcasting & Cable*, 22 March 1999, p. 18.

[72] Guy Lamolinara, "Wired for the Future: President Clinton Signs Telecommunications Act of 1996," *Library of Congress Information Bulletin* 55, no. 3 (1996): p. 43-45. See also: Mike Mills, "Ushering In a New Age in Communications; Clinton Signs 'Revolutionary' Billl Into Law at a Ceremony Packed With Symbolism," *Washington, Post*, 9 February 1996, p. C1.

Ending the bill signing, the Librarian of Congress pointed to the statue in the dome nearly 160 above his head: "There is a lovely lady looking down on us today.... She is lifting back the veil of ignorance...."[73]

But, in fact, there was a deep deceit associated with the event. Some 400 people were in attendance, including telecom CEOs with important interests at stake. These included Ray Smith of Bell Atlantic, Ted Turner of CNN, Brian Roberts of Comcast, Gerald R. Levin of Time Warner, Glenn Jones of Jones Intercable, Bert Roberts of MCI, Jean Monty of Northern Telecom, and John Hendricks of the Discovery Channel. But none of the major broadcast executives who had so passionately lobbied the President and Congressional leaders on the bill (see Chapter 15) were in attendance.[74] A reasonable explanation of their behavior is that it was in their strategic interest to lobby the President in private while providing no public demonstration of their political interests and influence. In other words, instead of "lifting back the veil of ignorance" at this event "fraught with symbolism," they were sending a message to viewers and journalists that their news outlets were objective and disinterested observers of the event rather than active and passionate participants in shaping its outcome.

A major journalist ethics textbook explains the rationale for the appearance standard of ethics, with the assumption that non-broadcasters will reason by analogy:

> How can a news organization legitimately cover [a story] if that news organization is a player rather than an observer? Yes, journalists and their organizations can keep saying, 'We remain objective. We have not been compromised by our involvement." But it is impossible to prove that point. You cannot prove that you haven't bent too far one way or the other. You cannot defend your decisions for what you did cover and what you didn't cover.[75]

The FCC acknowledges broadcasters' need to appear impartial with a striking exemption from its reasonable access rules. The reasonable access rules entitle Federal candidates to reasonable access to purchase airtime from

---

[73] Ibid.: p. 45.

[74] Like other top Washington telecom lobbyists, Eddie Fritts and Jim May did attend. But the network CEOs who had traveled to Washington, DC only weeks before to personally lobby the politicians attending the signing were conspicuously absent. See Brooks Boliek, "Clinton Pen Puts Future at Our Doorstep," *Hollywood Reporter*, 9 February 1996.

[75] Black et al., *Doing Ethics in Journalism*, 141.

commercial radio and television stations. But the broadcasters are granted a news exemption so they can keep up the appearance of an ethical firewall: "In order to maintain journalistic integrity of the news programming, stations may deny a federal candidate the right to buy advertising time during news programming."[76]

Survey Evidence

Substantial survey evidence indicates that many journalists, citizens, and members of Congress, draw general ethical inferences from their experiences with the media, and that these inferences lead them to be skeptical of media ethics claims. The point of this evidence is not that the media deserve this level of mistrust, only that such mistrust of the media is widespread and thus should not be viewed as extraordinary or paranoid among members of Congress in the case of high stakes broadcast spectrum policy.

Journalists

A 2004 survey of journalists by the Pew Research Center in association with The Project for Excellence in Journalism and The Committee of Concerned Journalists found 66% of national reporters and 57% of local reporters believed that bottom-line pressure hurt news coverage.[77] The same survey quotes a local TV station manager as saying: "Journalism is becoming more and more a business operation. What news stories will make our station/newspaper most profitable? This has always been part of the 'business' but now it has become the major factor."[78]

In a commentary accompanying the survey results, leading media ethicists and former journalists Bill Kovach, Tom Rosenstiel, and Amy Mitchell, summarize the findings.

> [Journalists] think business pressures are making the news they produce thinner and shallower. And they report more cases of advertisers and owners breaching the independence of the newsroom.... Five years ago we found that financial pressures in the

[76] Campaign Legal Center, "The Campaign Media Guide," (Washington, DC: Campaign Legal Center, 2004), p. 6.

[77] Pew Research Center, "Bottom-Line Pressures Now Hurting Coverage, Say Journalists," (Washington, DC: Pew Research Center for The People & The Press, 2004), pp. 1, 48.

[78]Ibid., p. 2.

newsroom 'was not a matter of executives or advertisers pressuring journalists about what to write or broadcast.' It was more subtle than that.

Unfortunately, that is less true today. Now a third of local journalists say they have felt such pressure, most notably from either advertisers or corporate owners. In other words, one of the most dearly held principles of journalism—the independence of the newsroom about editorial decision-making—increasingly is being breached."[79]

Other findings from the study include:

- 28% of national reporters and 23% of local reporters say lack of credibility/public trust is the most serious problem facing journalism today.

- 61% of local broadcast journalists say that the distinction between reporting and commentary has been seriously eroded.

- Only 13% of local broadcast journalists are very confident that a news organization that is owned by a corporate parent can do a good job covering news about the parent company.

National and local reporters in general and local broadcast reporters in particular consistently grade the quality of local television news below other major media outlets. See Table 11-1.

Table 11-1. Journalists' Grading of News Quality by Type of Media Outlet

Type of Media Outlet	National Reporters (all)	Local Reporters (all)	Local Broadcast Reporters
Major National Newspapers	B+	B	B
Typical Daily Newspaper	B-	B	B-
Network TV News	C+	B-	B-
Cable TV News	C+	C+	C+
Local TV News	C-	C	C+

---

[79] Ibid., pp. 27-28.

A 2000 survey by the Pew Research Center, done in association with *Columbia Journalism Review*, asked local journalists and local news executives a variety of questions about self-censorship. Executives included superiors on the business side of a local broadcaster or daily newspaper. One question asked: "In your opinion, to what extent do corporate owners influence news organizations' decisions about which stories to cover or emphasize?" In response, 16% of journalists said "a great deal" and 31% "A fair amount," giving a majority (51%) saying either "a great deal" or "A fair amount." The executives perceived much less censorship but still enough to send chills down the spine of a politician: 3% of executives said "a great deal" and 24% said "a fair amount."[80]

Another question asked: "In your experience, do journalists sometimes purposely avoid covering certain stories that they believe are truly newsworthy?" More than a third (42%) of local journalists replied "yes." The reasons given included bosses/editors/management wouldn't support (16%), advertising concerns (16%), corporate concerns (10%), and bosses/managers would retaliate (6%).[81]

Probing further, the survey asked: "How often, if ever, do you think the journalists you know avoid a newsworthy story because the story would be embarrassing or damaging to the financial interests of a news organization's owners or parent company?" In response, 44% of local journalists said "commonplace" (11%) or "sometimes" (33%).[82] When the question was slightly modified to ask whether the journalist personally avoided such issues, the response dropped almost in half, with 24% saying often (3%) or sometimes (21%).[83]

The Roper Center and Freedom Forum surveyed 323 Washington-based bureau chiefs and Congressional correspondents and got 139 responses. A large majority (80%) believed that journalists' personal or professional opinion of a member of Congress often or occasionally affected the tone of their coverage.[84]

---

[80] Andrew Kohut, "Self-Censorship: Counting the Ways," *Columbia Journalism Review*, May/June 2000, p. 43. See also: Pew Research Center, "Self Censorship: How Often and Why," (Washington, DC: Pew Research Center, 2000), p. 9.

[81] Pew Research Center, "Self Censorship: How Often and Why," p. 10.

[82] Ibid., p. 13.

[83] Ibid., p. 18.

[84] Povich Elaine S., *Partners & Adversaries: The Contentious Connection between Congress & the Media* (Arlington, Va.: Freedom Forum, 1996), p. 172.

A 2003 study published by the Radio and Television News Directors Foundation asked television news directors "How much of the time, if any, do you think news reporting on local television is improperly influenced by...."[85] Table 11-2 shows the percentage who replied "often" or "sometimes."

Table 11-2. TV News Directors Views of Improper Influences on Local TV News

Source of improper influence	"often" or "sometimes" (%)
Elected Officials	34.1
Advertisers	43.6
TV Station Owners	37.0

In 1999, the Public Agenda Foundation, with the *Columbia Journalism Review*, polled 125 senior journalists across the U.S. Its findings about handling mistakes included the following:

> Fully 70 percent of the respondents feel that most news organizations do a "poor" or "fair" job of informing the public about errors in their reporting....

> Almost four in ten feel sure that many factual errors are never corrected because reporters and editors are eager to hide their mistakes....

> Broadcast news is the "most susceptible" medium for letting inaccuracies creep into reporting.[86]

In 2001, the Project for Excellence in Journalism with the *Columbia Journalism Review* surveyed 118 news directors about advertiser influence on news content. More than half (53%) report advertiser pressure to kill negative stories or do positive ones. The survey reports that "The pressure to do puff pieces about sponsors occurs 'constantly,' 'all the time,' 'everyday,' 'routinely,' and 'every time a sales person opened his/her mouth.'"[87] A large percentage of

---

[85] Cited in Bob Papper, "2003 Local Television News Study of News Directors and the American Public," (Washington, DC: Radio Television News Directors Foundation, 2003), pp. 29-30.

[86] Neil Hickey, "Handling Corrections," *Columbia Journalism Review*, July/August 1999, p. 42.

[87] Just and Levine, "News for Sale," p. 2.

stations also succumb to the pressure in various ways: mention by announcer (68%), sponsored segment (64%), logo in newscast (48%), sponsor story or interview (8%), and mention by newscaster (6%).[88] One local TV affiliate promised local businesses three favorable local news segments (one each for the morning, midday, and evening newscasts) for $15,000.[89]

Even broadcast executives appear to be quite skeptical of the ethical claims made by their peers. Ted Turner started his media career as an owner of local TV stations, founded CNN and sold it to Time-Warner (one of the world's largest media conglomerates and owner of the WB broadcast TV network), graduated to Vice Chair and 10% owner of Time-Warner, and now, in forced retirement, has expressed many colorful comments about the news bias of his colleagues. Here's a quote from an article he authored himself:

> [on media consolidation] you saw little news from ABC, CBS, NBC, MSNBC, Fox, or CNN on the FCC's actions.... One never knows for sure, but it must have been clear to news directors that the more they covered this issue, the harder it would be for their corporate bosses to get the policy result they wanted. [90]

He elaborates:

> The ability to control the news is especially worrisome when a large media organization is itself the subject of a news story. Disney's boss, after buying ABC in 1995, was quoted in LA Weekly as saying, "I would prefer ABC not cover Disney." A few days later, ABC killed a "20/20" story critical of the parent company. [91]

He then goes on to describe a similar anecdote concerning NBC. The Disney quote is especially ironic because of ABC's propensity to give vastly disproportionate coverage of Disney. Turner then concludes with this zinger, which gets right to the heart of the matter.

> Naturally, corporations say they would never suppress speech. But it's not their intentions that matter; it's their capabilities.[92]

---

[88] Ibid.

[89] Lou Prato, "Punishing the Ethically Challenged," *American Journalism Review*, September 1999, p. 86.

[90] Ted Turner, "My Beef with Big Media," *Washington Monthly*, July/August 2004, pp. 35-6.

[91] Ibid., p. 36.

[92] Ibid.

Turner's greatest ire is directed against Rupert Murdoch, CEO of News Corporation, which owns dozens of local TV stations and the Fox News Channel, CNN's chief rival. The *Wall Street Journal* cites Turner as complaining that "Mr. Murdoch uses his media properties as business weapons to attack rivals."[93] In *Broadcasting & Cable*, Turner's views are portrayed as paranoid.

> Turner calls Murdoch…"a frightening person" who dreams of world domination. "He literally has control of Britain," Turner says. "I talked to Tony Blair many years ago. I said, 'Tony, why don't you crack down on Rupert a little? He's got too much control of Britain.' He said, 'Ted, I wouldn't have been elected. I wouldn't be in my job without Rupert. I can't go after him.' What about that?"[94]

But a chorus of other broadcast executives appears to agree with Turner. In an *Atlantic Monthly* piece that contrasts the media ethics of CBS with Fox, a broadcaster (presumably from CBS) anonymously alleges that "Murdoch has been shameless about using his journalism for the advancement of his business interests."[95] In another article, News Corporation General Counsel Arthur Siskind all but admits that ownership interests influence news content by arguing that the practice is widespread:

> "Every publication is used to further its own interests from time to time. He says Mr. Murdoch does it "no more than anyone else."[96]

Comments to the FCC are also full of cynical comments made by one broadcaster about another. In the fight between local TV affiliates and the networks with which they are affiliated, local affiliates claimed their programming choices better reflected the public interest. One affiliate called the TV networks "pirates."[97] The NAB and Network Affiliated Stations Alliance (NASA) claimed that stations owned by the Big 4 TV networks "must

---

[93] Eben Shapiro, "Media: Turner, Murdoch Play Latest Drama on Bigger Stage," *Wall Street Journal*, 30 September 1996, p. B1.

[94] "Turning Point," *Broadcasting & Cable*, 2 August 2004, p. 7.

[95] James Fallows, "The Age of Murdoch," *Atlantic Monthly*, September 2003, p. 90. See also Robert Greenwald, "Outfoxed: Rupert Murdoch's War on Journalism," (Carolina Productions, 2004).

[96] Elizabeth Jensen and Eben Shapiro, "It's a Thin Line…." *Wall Street Journal*, 28 October 1996, p. A6.

[97] Joe Flint, "How the top Networks Are Turning the Tables on Their Affiliates," *Wall Street Journal*, 15 June 2000, p. A8.

inevitably pursue economic objectives" inconsistent with their public interest responsibilities.[98] Disney, owner of the ABC network and more than a dozen local TV stations, countered in its FCC filing: "A local station's clearance decision often has little to do with the abstract notions of the public interest and everything to do with money."[99]

Public TV broadcasters have frequently charged commercial TV broadcasters with putting self-interest above audience interests. Says Ellen Hume, Executive Director of PBS's Democracy Project to facilitate an informed and active citizenry: "Our mission is to serve the public. We're not a profit-making commercial enterprise."[100]

Broadcasting & Cable Editor-In-Chief Harry A. Jessell summarizes the truthfulness of hundreds of broadcasting licensing promises over the decades. The promises, which turned out to be worthless, concerned integrating station management and ownership; that is, keeping station ownership local.

> Of course, just about everybody lied. They all promised integration. But, as soon as the FCC wasn't looking, the winning applicant would leave town, sell to the highest bidder, or pay off any local who fronted for the applicant and head for the bank.[101]

Jessell offers no explanation why *Broadcasting & Cable* did not report on those lies when it might have made a difference.

---

[98] Cited in "35% Cap Necessary to Preserve Localism—NASA, NAB Tell FCC," *Communications Daily*, 12 February 2003, p. 5.

[99] Doug Halonen, "Networks Say Affiliates Abuse Pre-Emptions," *Electronic Media*, 30 July 2001, p. 2.

[100] Cited in "Where's the Fire," *Broadcasting & Cable*, 2 February 1998, p. 106. Note that the editors of *Broadcasting & Cable* shot back: "commercial broadcasters are able to do both."

[101] Harry A. Jessell, "The Joy of Broadcasting," *Broadcasting & Cable*, 16 December 2002, p. 47. Note that *Broadcasting & Cable* failed to condemn these lies when they occurred and something could be done about them. Moreover, even now, no names are proffered. Although the article purports to praise one of the last, dying breed of local broadcasters, its hidden morality tale is that both the government and trade press reward liars, with the truth left for suckers and failures.

Public

A 2004 Pew Internet and American Life Project poll asked Americans if they agreed with the statement: "I often don't trust what news organizations are saying." A majority (53%) agreed with the statement.[102]

A 2003 Pew Internet and American Life Project poll asked: "In general, do you think news organizations are pretty independent, or are they often influenced by powerful people and organizations?" A large majority (70%) responded that the media are often influenced by powerful people and organizations.[103]

A 2002 Pew Research Center and American Life Project poll found the following results.[104]

- 58% of Americans believe the news media gets in the way of society solving its problems.

- 56% of Americans think news organization reports are often inaccurate.

- 55% of Americans think that news organizations don't care about the people they report on.

- 67% of Americans think that news organizations try to cover up their mistakes.

- 36% of Americans think that news organizations are immoral.

- 59% of Americans think that news organizations are politically biased in their reporting.

A 2004 First Amendment Center survey done in collaboration with the *American Journalism Review* stated: "Overall, the news media tries to report the news without bias." In response, 39% strongly disagreed and only 15% strongly agreed. The survey also stated: "The falsifying or making up of stories in the American news media is a widespread problem." In response, 37% strongly agreed and only 12% strongly disagreed.[105]

---

[102] Pew Research Center for the People & the Press, "News Audiences Increasingly Politicized," Washington, DC: The Pew Research Center, 8 June 2004, p. 33.

[103] A Pew Internet and American Life national survey conducted 19 June to 2 July 2003. See http://nationaljournal.com/members/polltrack/2003/national/03media.htm.

[104] Pew Research Center national survey conducted 8-16 July 2002. See http://nationaljournal.com/members/polltrack/2002/national/02media.htm.

[105] "State of the First Amendment 2004," (Arlington, Virginia: First Amendment Center, 2004). The survey is excerpted in "A Skeptical Public," *American Journalism Review*, August/September 2004.

A 2002 Harris poll asked "Would you generally trust each of the following types of people to tell the truth or not?" Table 11-3 shows the percent who were mistrustful.[106]

Table 11-3. Public Mistrust of Various Occupations

Occupation Group	Not trust to tell the truth (%)
Stockbrokers	66
Lawyers	65
Trade union leaders	56
Journalists	53
Members of Congress	52
TV newscasters	46
Pollsters	43
Bankers	41
Accountants	35
The president	30
Civil servants	27
Judges	27
Military officers	26
Clergmen or priests	26
Ordinary man or woman	23
Police officers	21
Scientists	21
Doctors	17
Professors	16
Teachers	12

A 2003 CNN/Gallup/USA Today poll asked: "Please tell me how you would rate the honesty and ethical standards of people in these different fields—very high, high, average, low or very low?"[107] Table 11-4 shows the percent who said very high or high.

---

[106] Harris national survey conducted 14-18 November 2002.
See http://nationaljournal.com/members/polltrack/2002/national/02media.htm.
[107] CNN/Gallup/USA Today national survey conducted 14-16 November 2003. See http://nationaljournal.com/members/polltrack/2003/national/03media.htm.

Table 11-4. Public View of Ethical Standards of Various Occupations

Occupation Group	Ethical standards high or very high (%)
Nurses	83
Medical doctors	68
Veterinarians	68
Druggists/Pharmacists	67
Dentists	61
Policemen	59
College teachers	59
Engineers	59
Clergy	56
Phsychiatrists	38
Bankers	35
Chiropractors	31
State governors	26
Journalists	25
Senators	20
Business executives	18
Congressmen	17
Lawyers	16
Stockbrokers	15
Advertising practitioners	12
Insurance salesmen	12
HMO managers	11
Car salesmen	7

A 2002 CNN/Gallup/USA Today poll asked a random sample of the public the following question: "For each of the following groups, please tell me whether most of the people in them can be trusted or that you can't be too careful in dealing with them? Table 11-5 shows the percentage who said "can't be too careful."[108]

---

[108] CNN/Gallup/USA Today national survey conducted 22-24 November 2002. See http://nationaljournal.com/members/polltrack/2002/national/02media.htm.

Table 11-5. Public Mistrust of Various Occupations

Occupation Group	"Can't be too careful" (%)
Teachers	15
Middle class people	21
Military officers	24
Police officers	26
Protestant ministers	26
Poor people	28
Coaches of youth sports	28
Doctors	31
Rich people	41
Professional athletes	45
Catholic priests	48
Accountants	57
Journalists	58
Stockbrokers	58
Government officials	69
Lawyers	70
CEOs of large corporations	73
Car dealers	81

The same 2003 study published by the Radio and Television News Directors Foundation that asked television news directors "How much of the time, if any, do you think news reporting on local television is improperly influenced by…." (Table 11-2) also asked the public the same question.[109] Table 11-6 shows the percentage of the public who replied "often" or "sometimes."

Table 11-6. Public Views of Improper Influences on Local Television News

Source of improper influence	"often" or "sometimes" (%)
Elected Officials	68.2
Advertisers	73.9
TV Station Owners	75.0

[109] Povich Elaine S., *Partners & Adversaries*, p. 157.

New York Times columnist Frank Rich summarizes the public's view of the U.S. press:

> Pity, though not too deeply, the American press. Once the wisecrack-ing truth seekers of "The Front Page" and the brave gumshoes of "All the President's Men,"...Hollywood no longer depicts reporters in ruthless pursuit of criminals, high and low. Now they are the crimi-nals.[110]

A *Brill's Content* focus group conducted by pollster Frank Luntz summa-rized viewer attitudes with this comment by a postal worker.

> [T]hey're out there for the money. They're out there to get ratings. They're out there to sell commercial slots. And that's it. That's the bottom line.[111]

Politicians

The Roper Center and Freedom Forum surveyed all 535 members of Congress and got 155 responses.[112] To the question, "Have you ever been 'burned' by a reporter who either wrote or broadcast a bad or false story?" 89% replied "yes."[113] To the question, "In general, how would you rate the job that televi-sion broadcasters in your state or district do in serving their viewers/listeners'

---

[110] Frank Rich, "So Much for 'The Front Page,'" *New York Times*, 2 November 2003, section 2, p. 1.

[111] Frank Luntz, "Reality Talks: Twenty citizens who gathered to talk about the media sound off on its bias and sensationalism—and why they keep coming back for more," *Brill's Content*, September 2000, p. 70.

[112] Cited in Povich Elaine S., *Partners & Adversaries*, p. 159. The survey could have been more useful if it clearly distinguished between the news and business sides of media organ-izations. For example, it asks: "Have you ever complained to a reporter's supervisor about a bad or false story?" but it leaves it ambiguous whether the supervisor might be a general manager rather than a news director. The general context of the survey implies the supervi-sor is on the news side of the news outlet. But since members of Congress typically have far closer relationships with general managers than news supervisors, that should be the most likely person for members of Congress to complain to if they want to go over the head of the local reporter.

[113] Ibid., 158.

overall information needs, political and otherwise?" 78% replied "fair" or "poor." Only 1% replied "Excellent."[114]

A striking finding in a report by the American Society of Newspaper Editors is that "members of the public who have had actual experience with the news process are the most critical of media credibility." In other words, "adults that have been close to the news process are more likely to believe that the news media are biased."[115] The survey includes in its definition of close "those who have been subject of news stories (or been interviewed),"[116] which would be a fitting description of the relationship between members of Congress and the press.

In 1998 the Pew Research Center had personal interviews with 81 members of Congress. Pew asked members of Congress for their overall opinions about news media coverage of the federal government. Only 1% gave the news media the top score of "excellent" while 26% gave it the bottom score of "poor" and another 50% gave it the second-to-bottom score of "only fair." Asked their overall opinion of the news media, only 4% of members of Congress said "very favorable."[117]

Strong evidence that legislators fear media bias was legislators' creation and long-time support of the FCC's Fairness Doctrine as it related to programming on "controversial issues of public importance." The Fairness Doctrine was put in place to ensure that the broadcast media didn't abuse their power. The public was indifferent to the Fairness Doctrine while the broadcasters strongly opposed it. Yet despite these political dynamics, a majority of members of Congress sought to preserve the Fairness Doctrine. The FCC revoked the main features of the Fairness Doctrine in 1987. In response, Congress passed legislation to reinstate it, only failing because of a presidential veto. In 1987, despite strong broadcaster opposition, the Senate vote for the Fairness Doctrine was 59-31 and the House 259-157. Explained *Broadcasting* (later *Broadcasting & Cable*): "members of Congress...make no secret of their lack of faith in broadcasters' fairness."[118] One interpretation of these results, then, is that at least 66% of voting senators and 62% of voting representatives feared a substantial risk of broadcaster bias. This interpretation is bolstered by the fact

---

[114] Christine D. Urban, "Why Newspaper Credibility Has Been Dropping," (Reston, Virginia: American Society of Newspaper Editors, 1998), p. 21.

[115] Ibid.

[116] Campaign Legal Center, "The Campaign Media Guide," pp. 6-13.

[117] Pew Research Center, "Washington Leaders Wary of Public Opinion," (Washington, DC: Pew Research Center, 17 April 1998).

[118] "Reagan Vetoes Fairness Doctrine Bill," *Broadcasting*, 29 June 1987, p. 27.

that the FCC has never dared to revoke the Fairness Doctrine as it relates to election-related programming involving candidates. Broadcasters continue to be required to provide candidates with "equal opportunities" (also referred to as "equal time") and "reasonable access" to broadcast coverage.[119] When I asked Senator Paul Simon (D-Illinois) why he was such a strong supporter of the Fairness Doctrine, he answered it was because "I never met a broadcast owner who wasn't a Republican." Senator Simon started his career as a newspaper reporter and eventually acquired a chain of 13 newspapers before switching over to a career in politics.[120] *Campaigns & Elections*, the premier magazine for political candidates, polled 362 recent state legislative candidates through a grant from the Pew Charitable Trusts. It found that "most [candidates] do not think the press was fair to them in their last race." It went on: "Less than half of the respondents (45 percent) think that the media didn't favor either candidate and was fair to all of them. But most of the remainder thought there was some bias and, by a lopsided 45-7 percent margin, said the bias favored their rivals."[121]

In Montana, home of broadcaster cum U.S. Senate Communications Subcommittee Chair Conrad Burns, local press critic Nathaniel Blumberg, former journalism dean at the University of Montana, delivered a speech in the Montana House of Representatives. In the speech, he criticized Montana's news corporations because they "regard their newsroom employees as little more than cogs in a money machine." After Blumberg's speech, legislators from both parties gave him a standing ovation.[122]

---

[119] Campaign Legal Center, "The Campaign Media Guide," pp. 6-13.

[120] Interview with Senator Paul Simon, 6 February 1998, Evanston, Illinois.

[121] Ron Faucheux and Paul S. Herrnson, "See How They Run: State Legislative Candidates," *Campaigns & Elections*, August 1999, p. 24. The poll was conducted under the auspices of Paul S. Herrnson, professor of political science at the University of Maryland.

[122] Charles Layton and Mary Walton, "The State of the American Newspaper," *American Journalism Review*, July/August 1998, p. 51. In Montana, more than 95% of daily newspaper circulation is controlled by out-of-state media conglomerates. At the time of Blumberg's speech, two conglomerates with substantial broadcasting interests, Gannett and Lee Enterprises, controlled more than 80% of Montana's daily newspaper circulation. As if confirming Blumberg's argument, the Associated Press filed a story with Blumberg's colorful quotes, but the Gannett owned newspaper in the state, the *Great Falls Tribune*, edited them out. Ibid, p. 42. See also Alicia C. Shepard, "Big Sky's Big Player," *American Journalism Review*, October 1999, p. 30, and "Montana," *Editor & Publisher International Yearbook 1994* (New York City: Editor & Publisher, 1994).

One trade association writer, reviewing *New York Times* reporter Joel Brinkley's book on the DTV transition, observed that most members of Congress "trust broadcasters as much as Taiwan does Mainland China."[123]

Anecdotes about politicians' mistrust of the press are legion. One bumper sticker in the 1992 presidential election was "Annoy the media. Re-elect Bush." A reporter who spent 14 years covering politics for the *New York Times* explains:

> You'd go into any Bush rally and somebody would get up and tell the story of Bush's beautiful little granddaughter who was visiting the White House, and there was a terrible thunderstorm, and she was petrified and went running into the President. He said, "Don't worry, dear. When someone tells a terrible lie, God thunders in heaven." She feels better and goes back to sleep. At 2:30 in the morning, the worst thunder she'd ever heard goes on and on, and this time she's really scared. She goes to see the President and he says, "It's OK. The Washington Post just started rolling off the press."[124]

Senator Slade Gorton (R-Washington), a member of the Senate Commerce Committee, refused to seek an endorsement from the *Seattle Post-Intelligencer*, owned by the Hearst media conglomerate, explaining that the newspaper was "Just another special interest group." [125] *The Seattle Post-Intelligencer* endorsed Senator Gorton's Democratic opponent.[126]

In retirement, Senator Simpson (R-Wyoming) wrote a book called "Right in the Old Gazoo: A Lifetime of Scrapping with the Press." In it he includes the observation: "It doesn't take any sensible politician ten minutes in the presence of a modern journalist to know pretty well which side he or she is on."[127]

Speaker of the House Newt Gingrich on multiple occasions publicly stated that "bias in the media" is "overwhelming,"[128] albeit in the context of partisan bias; for example, "the liberal slant of the news media is responsible for the current "Republican period of being in a funk…. The bias in the media is so

---

[123] Alicia Mundy, "Brinkley: The Next Generation," *MediaWeek*, 14 April 1997, p. 36.

[124] E.J. Dionne, "Fourth Annual Philip M. Foisie Memorial Lecture," Chicago Athletic Club, Chicago, Illinois, 12 May 1999.

[125] John H. Fund, "The Power of Talk," *Forbes MediaCritic*, Spring 1995, p. 55.

[126] E.g., "Angry Voters Turn To The GOP," *Seattle Post Intelligencer*, 10 November 1994.

[127] Alan K. Simpson, *Right in the Old Gazoo: A Lifetime of Scrapping with the Press*, 1st ed. (New York: W. Morrow, 1997), p. 15.

[128] "Discussion on Newt Gingrich and the Elite Media," *CNN Reliable Sources*, 6 April 1997.

overwhelming that all the voters hear is the [anti-Republican] background noise."[129]

After the 2000 presidential election, House Commerce Committee Chair Billy Tauzin (R-Louisiana) held a hearing to determine whether the major TV networks may have been involved in a conspiracy to help the Democrats on election night.[130]

In 1996, Senate Majority Leader and Republican presidential nominee Bob Dole (R-Kansas) accused broadcasters of "bullying Congress and running a multi-million-dollar scare campaign to mislead the public."[131]

In 2004, 26 Democratic members of Congress wrote to the President of CBS Television accusing it of exercising programming and ad bias in favor of Republicans at the expense of Democrats.[132]

In 1998, a chief argument the Republican leadership used against the McCain-Feingold campaign finance legislation is that it would prevent Republicans from raising money necessary to circumvent a news media biased against them.[133]

Conclusion

Inferences by analogy may not be rigorous but they are efficient and therefore widespread. To the extent that direct evidence of agent bias is hard to come by, principals may compensate by relying on imperfect analogies.

A more accurate but difficult to do type of inference anticipates the future costs and benefits of a particular act of bias. In the next chapter, we will look at broadcasters' anticipated costs and benefits of engaging in media bias with respect to a particular agenda: winning free spectrum rights from the government.

---

[129] John Yang, "Gingrich Tells Activists to Outgun 'Elite Media,'" *Washington Post*, 23 April 1996, p. A6.

[130] "Billy Tauzin's Magical Media Tour," *Electronic Media*, 19 February 2001, p. 8.

[131] Christopher Stern, "Dole: Broadcasters 'bullying Congress,'" *Broadcasting & Cable*, 22 April 1996, p. 6.

[132] Letter to Leslie Moonves, 23 January 2004.

[133] Alison Mitchell, "The Senate Votes to Keep Alive Bill on Campaign Gifts," *New York Times*, 25 January 1998, p. A1.

CHAPTER 12:

The Argument from Cause: Benefits

"The name of the game is spectrum, spectrum, spectrum."

—Bud Paxson, Chairman of Paxson Communications[1]

"Nothing was more certain to rouse the broadcasters. Above all else, [broadcasters] held sacred the eleventh commandment: Thou Shalt Not Give Up Spectrum."

—Joel Brinkley, Defining Vision[2]

One way for a legislator to anticipate a broadcaster's behavior is to look at their incentives. What benefits might broadcasters receive from winning new public airwaves? What costs might broadcasters incur if they used their existing control of the airwaves to help them secure this benefit? In this chapter, we will look at the benefits. In the next chapter, we will look at the costs.

A key assumption of this argument is that politicians believe people act in their own self-interest. If a politician hurts a person's interests, that person will seek to punish the politician and use all effective means to do so. This is politics 101, and central to the operating assumptions of any Congressional office. As *Campaigns & Elections* cautions candidates, "The most effective interest groups in American politics did not get that way by being gracious losers. When you cross them in the policymaking arena, you can be sure they will return the favor...."[3] As applied to broadcasters, this political principle means that if a rational broadcaster had a powerful motive for wanting the spectrum and the expected penalty for using media as a political weapon were slight, he would use that weapon.

---

[1] Kathleen Gallagher, "Paxson's TV Channels Make Stock Look Good to Analyst," Milwaukee Journal Sentinel, 6 May 2001, p. 4D.

[2] Brinkley, *Defining Vision*, p. 10.

[3] Charles Mahtesian, "Payback is Hell," *Campaigns & Elections*," February 2000, p. 22.

Legislators can use two types of reasoning and corresponding sets of facts to determine the economic benefit broadcasters expected from winning new spectrum rights. Using high-information reasoning, legislators directly calculate the economic benefits broadcasters would attain. Using low-information reasoning, legislators observe broadcasters' behavior to make the same calculation.

Of course, broadcasters are well aware that legislators and viewers look at their incentives to assess the probability of news bias. That is why broadcasters are so fearful of publicly revealing their true political preferences. As we have seen, a primary reason broadcasters don't want the public to know which members of Congress they lobby and what they lobby them about is that this would reveal their incentives to the public. By providing a motive for bias, doubt is cast on their news reporting.

High-Information Reasoning

Calculating the value of the airwaves is one way to assess broadcasters' incentives. Today, there is a general consensus that the airwaves are one of the most valuable natural resources of the information economy and that the broadcast band between channels 2 and 69 occupies the beachfront spectrum because of its desirable propagation characteristics, including its ability to pass through objects such as trees and walls.[4]

What was the opportunity cost of the digital TV spectrum the broadcasters received? The broadcasters argued that the spectrum they would receive had minimal value. But by February 1996, there was ample widely available evidence, notably the billions of dollars raised from PCS airwaves auctions during the prior 14 months, that the airwaves the broadcasters wanted were worth a king's ransom.

The receipts from auctions begun in late 1994 and completed in early 1996—more than $20 billion for the U.S. Treasury—were widely reported on the front pages of business sections in major daily newspapers such as the *Washington Post* and *New York Times*.[5] The *New York Times* called it the

---

[4] Snider, *Explanation of the Citizen's Guide to the Airwaves.*

[5] E.g., Edmund L. Andrews, "Winners of Wireless Auction to Pay $7 Billion," *New York Times*, 14 March 1995, p. D1. Edmund L. Andrews, "$6 Billion Bid So Far in Latest F.C.C. Auction for Airwaves," *New York Times*, 14 February 1996, p. D1; Edmund L. Andrews, "In Auctions of Airwaves, The Sky Seems To Be the Limit," *New York Times*, 26 February 1996, p. D1. A caveat is that one of the major auction purchasers, Nextwave, later went bankrupt and did not pay for its licenses. See Simon Romero, "Nextwave Victory May Not Prove Too Lucrative," *New York Times*, 28 January 2003.

"biggest auction in history"[6] and the *Guinness Book of World Records* recorded it as such in its next edition. At the FCC, any reporter, CEO, lawmaker or FCC employee who visited FCC Chair Reed Hundt's office beginning in 1995 would have seen a giant, wall-mounted $7.7 billion check, which is the sum the U.S. government received from its first ever spectrum auction started in late 1994 and completed on March 13, 1995. In case anyone missed the giant check, the Chairman proudly claimed to the press that spectrum auctions were one of his major achievements.[7]

Members of Congress clearly got the message, as evidenced by the dozens of Congressional bills and presidential budgets in the coming years that would use proposed spectrum auction receipts to fund pet programs under the Congressional pay-go budget rules, which required new programs to be funded either with new revenue or program cuts.[8] Reported *Broadcasting & Cable*: "it's clear that the $9 billion raised by the FCC from PCS auctions during the past 10 months has captured Congress's attention." It then quoted House Telecommunications Subcommittee Chair Jack Fields: "A lot of us are asking questions that have never been asked before. Is it really fair for [broadcasters] to use [a second channel] for a commercial service when [the spectrum] was never subject to the auction process?"[9]

On March 16, 1995, an op-ed by nationally syndicated *New York Times* columnist William Safire, estimated the value of all spectrum could soon reach $500 billion and that the value of the broadcasters' portion might be $120 billion. He concluded: "Even if accompanied by payment of rent to the government, the exclusive arrangement sought by broadcasters would be an

---

[6] Ibid., p. D1.

[7] "105th Congress May Tighten Control of Spectrum Management," *Land Mobile Radio News*, 8 November 1996.

[8] Interview with G. William Hoagland, Staff Director, Senate Budget Committee, 18 September 1996. See also the weekly bulletin of the Senate Budget Committee majority staff. For the week of 9 September 1996, it includes the following information: "Spectrum auctions round out the new offsets the President has proposed. In addition to the $31 billion in auction receipts he expects in the 1997 budget, the President has subsequently proposed $7.6 billion more from spectrum to offset new spending and an increasingly long list of "social engineering" tax incentives." See also Christopher Stern, "White House Says Auctions Will Raise $32 Billion: Budget for FY '97 targets $17 billion from returned spectrum," *Broadcasting & Cable*, 25 March 1996, p. 19.

[9] Kim McAvoy, "Congress Sees Gold in Them Thar Second Channels," *Broadcasting & Cable*, 10 April 1995, p. 23.

outrageous taxpayer ripoff…. [W]e want top dollar for our public property."[10]

In response to Safire's column, four U.S. Senators wrote a letter to FCC Chair Reed Hundt requesting that the FCC value the spectrum Congress intended to give incumbent TV broadcasters for digital TV.[11] During the infighting over the proposed Telecom Act, Safire's column would also be widely distributed on Capitol Hill.

On May 5, 1995 the FCC estimated the value of the broadcasters' digital spectrum, if sold by auction, at between $11 and $70 billion dollars.[12] The $70 billion figure was extrapolated from the value of recent spectrum sales for PCS, a new wireless telephone service. The $11 billion figure was extrapolated from the projected sale price of a recent analog TV license with no tangible assets attached to it. The actual sale of the analog TV license was for far more than initially projected, thus leading to a revised estimate on September 5, 1995, using the same extrapolation method, of $37 billion.[13]

Over the coming months, the $70 billion figure was the one most widely used in the print press when referring to the potential magnitude of the spectrum "giveaway." The $70 billion figure was also the one used by Senate Majority Leader Bob Dole when he held up passage of the Telecom Act because of this "giveaway." FCC Chair Reed Hundt and his successor William Kennard repeatedly used it.[14] All major newspapers and trade association publications repeatedly cited the $70 billion number.

---

[10] William Safire, "The Greatest Auction Ever," *New York Times*, 16 March 1995, p. A25.

[11] Letter from Senators Lieberman, Kerrey, Conrad, and Leahy to FCC Chair Reed Hundt, 7 April 1995. The letter includes the following text: "We understand that the Commission will soon consider proposals to grant each existing television station an additional 6 MHz channel…. Estimates, noted by Mr. Safire, have been made that suggest this spectrum could have a market value of $120 billion, based on the results of the recent auctions conducted by the FCC…. Please provide an estimate of the range of value of licenses to be issued for the spectrum if it were to be auctioned."

[12] Letter from Robert M. Pepper, Chief of the FCC's Office of Plans and Policy, to Senator Joseph I. Lieberman, 5 May 1995

[13] Letter from Robert M. Pepper, Chief of the FCC's Office of Plans and Policy, to Senator Joseph I. Lieberman, 6 September 1995.

[14] E.g., "What Does $70 Billion Buy You Anyway?" Remarks of FCC Chairman William E. Kennard, New York City, Museum of Television and Radio, 10 October 2000, Bill McConnell and Paige Albiniak, "The Chairman Steps Out," *Broadcasting & Cable*, 16 October 2000, p. 14.

In response to these claims of highly valuable spectrum, the NAB commissioned a report by Charles J. Jackson and John Haring of Strategic Policy Research.[15] On August 16, 1995 the report was distributed to House and Senate Commerce Committee staffers with a cover letter from Jim May, NAB VP of Government Relations. The letter summarized what it said was the report's key conclusion: "Under the best circumstances, auctions of reversion channels could raise between $2-3 billion dollars by 2002."[16] Reversion channels meant channels that would "become available following the complete transition to digital by broadcasters."[17]

One key assumption of the report was that the reversion channels would flood the market with 200 MHz of spectrum.[18] The other key assumption was that mobile telephone companies already had enough spectrum for any conceivable mobile telephone demand (the report estimated existing mobile phone capacity of approximately 2 mobile phones for every U.S. resident).[19] With little or no new forecast demand for spectrum combined with a significant increase in spectrum supply, the price of spectrum would plummet.

---

[15] Some months later the broadcasters hired another economist, MIT Professor Jerry Hausman, who testified before the Senate Budget Committee on 14 March 1996 that even the CBO numbers were too high because the correct valuation benchmark was the sale of UHF TV stations over the prior six years (1990–1995, with half those years prior to passage of the Cable Act of 1992). The analysis assumed that a purchaser of a UHF station could reasonably have assumed that at some point in the not too distant future he would win digital flexibility on his analog channel, so purchasing an analog UHF channel was a good proxy for purchasing a digital channel. For a very different view, see Charles J. Jackson and John Haring, "Pitfalls in the Economic Valuation of the Electromagnetic Spectrum," (Bethesda, Maryland: Strategic Policy Research, 1995).

[16] The actual report suggested a valuation of between $2 and $10 billion, with a strong emphasis on the low end of that scale. Presumably, most staffers would only read the cover letter summary. In any case, the 12 page report contained no calculations, just a verbal account of considerations that went into the analysis.

[17] Jackson and Haring, "Pitfalls in the Economic Valuation of the Electromagnetic Spectrum," p. 9.

[18] Ibid., p. 10.

[19] Specifically, it estimated that current allocations of spectrum for the mobile telephone industry would already support 1 million mobile phones in the District of Columbia, with a population a bit larger than a half million. It then extrapolated from that market to the rest of the country. Ken Belson, "Verizon Moves to Head Off Nextel in a Spectrum Swap," *New York Times*, 9 April 2004.

After distributing the report to a handful of policymakers, the NAB withdrew it from circulation, and the broadcast trade press never reported on its existence. Any number of plausible reasons may explain why the NAB chose not to publicize the report. Most obviously, the low NAB valuation seemed less credible than ever.

On September 6, 1995, approximately two weeks after the report was distributed to allies on Capitol Hill, the FCC submitted a revised letter to the four senators who had previously submitted a valuation request. This letter, as noted above, changed the $11 billion estimate to $37 billion, based on new information. In late fall 1995, the second major auction of PCS licenses began, and this time it generated revenues for comparable spectrum even higher than the first PCS auction. When the months-long auction was completed in spring 1996, receipts would total over $10 billion. That spectrum was not as high quality as the broadcasters' spectrum, and it was for only a small fraction of the 200 MHz of spectrum used as the basis for the calculations in the Jackson-Haring study.

Another problem was that one of the Jackson-Haring assumptions, the return of 200 MHz at the end of the transition to HDTV, conflicted with other NAB priorities. The 200 MHz figure was useful for the argument that the returned spectrum would flood the market and thus reduce the value of spectrum. But the NAB was also aggressively lobbying to reduce the amount of spectrum that would have to be returned at the end of the HDTV transition. The success of the latter lobbying campaign is evident in the shrinkage of spectrum that the broadcasters would be forced to return at the end of their HDTV transition. In its letters to the four senators in May 1995, the FCC estimated that "over 150 MHz of contiguous spectrum could be recaptured."[20] In its December 1995 and March 1996 estimates, the CBO would also use 150 MHz of returned spectrum in its calculations. Gradually, under intense broadcaster lobbying, even the 150 MHz would be whittled down, until by the time the FCC rules were finalized in April 1997, the amount to be returned at the end of the DTV transition was reduced to 108 MHz. Regardless of the NAB's reasons for not publicizing this particular report, the report marked the last time the NAB would not only publicly distribute a figure valuing the market value of its members' spectrum, but also provide an alternative that could be disputed by others.

Behind the scenes, however, the NAB worked to critique the FCC's number by getting the Congressional Budget Office (CBO) to come up with a lower number, which is the number the Congressional budget committees would have to use when considering using auctions to balance the budget or fund other programs. The NAB was terrified that a high CBO number would play a

---

[20] Letter from Robert M. Pepper to Senator Joseph I. Lieberman, 5 May 1995.

key role in solving the budget crisis. During fall 1995, Democratic and Republican lawmakers were bitterly feuding over how to balance a large CBO forecast budget deficit, and some key lawmakers hoped to use spectrum receipts to eliminate the deficit. Eventually, in late December 1995 and early January 1996, this feud would shut down the entire federal government. In the midst of this shutdown and debate over broadcast spectrum valuations, the front page of the *New York Times* would show a picture of Congressional leaders negotiating with President Clinton, with Senate Majority Whip Trent Lott holding an NAB briefing document, presumably including a discussion of the disputed spectrum valuations.[21]

A large CBO spectrum valuation might allow Congress to solve the budget crisis by auctioning the channels the broadcasters wanted free. Given a choice between auctioning spectrum and cutting Medicare, Aid to Dependent Children, and other high profile services, broadcasters were worried that it was their spectrum interests that might be sacrificed.

Accordingly, over the summer of 1995, NAB independent contractor Charles Jackson, co-author of the report described above and former senior Congressional staffer covering telecom policy, lobbied the CBO to come up with a lower figure than the FCC's. He gave his report to senior CBO spectrum analyst and colleague David Moore, including the calculations missing from the printed version described above. Jackson specifically asked that the report not be publicized. And his request was honored. When the CBO report came out, it closely followed Jackson's valuation method but did not explicitly cite that it had received or in any way used Jackson's report.[22]

In December 1995, the Congressional Budget Office (CBO) valued the spectrum at $6 billion. On March 14, 1996, the CBO revised its estimate to $11 billion and $12.5 billion, based on two different scenarios.[23] The CBO used a fundamentally different valuation method than the FCC. It downplayed the results of actual PCS auctions (the FCC's method), instead relying on forecasted supply and demand (the NAB's method).

Also of note, the Office of Management and Budget (OMB) broadcast spectrum valuations were consistently two to three times the size of CBO spectrum

---

[21] Jerry Gray, "Battle Over the Budget," *New York Times*, 8 January 1996, p. A1.

[22] Like Congress but unlike the FCC, the CBO can be lobbied without leaving a public record. Anyone lobbying the FCC on an ongoing proceeding must file an ex parte, which must include any submitted written matter.

[23] Statement of David H. Moore, senior analyst in the Natural Resources and Commerce Division of the Congressional Research Service, before the Senate Committee on the Budget, 14 March 1996.

valuations. This difference between the White House and Congress was especially striking because on non-broadcast spectrum valuations the CBO and OMB came up with almost identical numbers.[24]

Although the NAB stopped providing its own formal spectrum valuations for public consumption, it did seek to ridicule the FCC valuations. In its recommended "talking points" for local broadcasters when lobbying members of Congress, the NAB wrote: "Estimates of $70 billion or $40 billion from the auction of digital TV spectrum are nothing more than "pie in the sky" numbers. There is nothing to suggest that auctions of the digital channels TV broadcasters are slated to use temporarily will raise anything near those numbers. Indeed, the numbers could be less than $6 billion."[25]

In subsequent years, spectrum in different bands would be auctioned for widely varying amounts. But what is clear is that the NAB's spectrum valuation was wildly inaccurate. Indeed, the FCC's $70 billion figure may have been too conservative. In the years following the Telecom Act, there was a rapid increase in the value of low frequency spectrum such as the broadcasters possessed.

During the late 1990s, close to $100 billion of spectrum was auctioned in Europe at rates substantially higher than that used as the basis for the $70 billion valuation.[26] In January 2001, some of the most sophisticated U.S. telecommunication companies, including Verizon and Sprint, purchased spectrum for close to $16 billion that had been previously auctioned in 1996 for $4.7 billion. The rate per megahertz (MHz) per person in the 2001 auction was significantly higher than the rates used to derive the FCC's $70 billion spectrum valuation in 1995.[27] One FCC Commissioner argued the $16 billion figure was artificially

---

[24] "A Comparison of CBO and OMB Estimates of Receipts from Auctions of the Electromagnetic Spectrum," 5 March 1997, unpublished document prepared by CBO staff. "Administration Offer of December 7, 1995—7 Year Plan, Spectrum Auctions," 9 December 1995, unpublished document prepared by Senate Commerce Committee staff.

[25] "A Call to Arms for Television Broadcasters," a lobbying toolkit sent to local broadcasters in late January 1996 by NAB Government Relations, p. 8.

[26] An auction in 2000 for 140 MHz in Britain raised $35.5 billion; an auction in 2000 for 145 MHz in Germany raised $45.5 billion; and a later auction in Italy raised $11.6 billion.

[27] In September 2002, the bidders had to return the spectrum. That spectrum was originally purchased by Nextwave in the 1996 PCS auction for $4.7 billion. When Nextwave subsequently defaulted on its payments to the FCC and sought bankruptcy protection, the FCC repossessed Nextwave's licenses and re-auctioned them in January 2001. Nextwave sued, arguing that the licenses couldn't be repossessed by the FCC. In September 2002, the U.S. Supreme Court sided with Nextwave, thus forcing the bidders to return the licenses to Nextwave.

low because of substantial "legal risk" stemming from the dubious ownership of the spectrum.[28]

On March 25, 2001, Thomas Wolzien, Senior Media Analyst at Sanford C. Bernstein & Company, told broadcast industry leaders at the exclusive broadcaster only NAB Futures Summit that the total value of spectrum allocated for channels 2-69, based on auctions of spectrum for mobile telephone service, was worth $367 billion.[29] Another analyst at the Futures Summit, Bishop Cheen from First Union Securities, valued the spectrum at over $400 billion.[30] Verizon, the largest mobile telephone company in the U.S., is legally obligated to file an annual report to the FCC called a "10K." In its 2003 10K, Verizon includes a valuation of $42 billion for its spectrum licenses. That spectrum has a bandwidth less than 10% of the bandwidth occupied by TV channels 2-69, and also may occupy slightly less valuable, higher frequency spectrum.

Spectrum values have declined a bit from their peak in the late 1990s and early 2000s but in 2004 there was broad consensus that low frequency unencumbered spectrum was worth in the vicinity of $500 million/MHz—more than the average valuation in the 1996 PCS auctions.[31]

By 2001, the broadcasters' trade publication, *Broadcasting & Cable*, no friend of broadcast spectrum auctions, could take the $70 billion dollar figure and the notion of a giveaway as a given: "Maybe Congress should have auctioned the

---

[28] Harold Furchgott-Roth, "The Price of FCC Integrity: $15 Billion," *Wall Street Journal*, 8 August 2001, p. A12. The Commissioner's legal analysis proved correct. After losing interest on their bid deposits for 18 months, the U.S. Supreme Court forced the winning bidders to return their licenses to Nextwave.

[29] Tom Wolzien, "Whose Bandwidth Is It Anyway," Paper delivered at the National Association of Broadcasters Futures Summit, Monterrey, California, 25 March 2001. See also "Broadband Could Hurt Broadcasters' Keeping Spectrum, NAB is Told," *Communications Daily*, 27 March 2001.

[30] Bishop Cheen, "Digital Spectrum: Television's Deeply Hidden Value," Paper delivered at the National Association of Broadcasters Futures Summit, Monterrey, California, 25 March 2001. See also an earlier report by Cheen: "Monetizing the Hidden Value in TV Spectrum," (Charlotte, North Carolina: First Union Securities, 3 July 2000).

[31] In April 2004, Verizon Wireless offered $5 billion as an opening bid on 10 MHz that the FCC was deciding whether to auction or give to Nextel as part of a spectrum swap. The FCC later used this benchmark in its own valuation of the spectrum. See Linda Moore, "Public Safety Spectrum," (Washington, DC: Congressional Research Service, July 2004), J.H. Snider and Michael Calabrese, "Speeding the DTV Transition: A Consumer Tax Credit Can Unplug Analog TV, Reduce the Deficit and Redeploy Low-Frequency Spectrum for Wireless Broadband," (Washington, DC: New America Foundation, 2004).

spectrum to broadcasters and given them full First-Amendment rights in the bargain, but they didn't and have been complaining about the lost $70 billion ever since."[32]

In an ironic twist, the Association of Public Television Stations (APTS) in early 2004 used the $70 billion figure in a series of FCC filings, Congressional documents, and press releases. APTS represents public television stations, and it was lobbying to receive the revenue from its members' returned channels to fund public television.[33] More generally, as broadcasters begin to think of themselves as spectrum sellers rather than buyers, the less politically oriented among them have begun to publicly cite much higher valuations of spectrum to gain negotiating leverage and boost stock prices.[34]

At a U.S. House Energy and Commerce Committee hearing on "Advancing the DTV Transition" held on June 2, 2004, Telecommunications Subcommittee Chair Fred Upton asked FCC Media Bureau Chair Kenneth Ferree for a ballpark estimate of the value of the 108 MHz of spectrum to be returned. Ferree replied "tens of billions," whereupon Upton asked the other panelists, including NAB President Eddie Fritts, if any disagreed. No one did.

The Broadcasters' Framing of the Valuation Argument

"Like *L.A. Confidential,* you can never tell from surface appearances what is really going on in the DTV saga."

—Reed Hundt, Former FCC Chair[35]

---

[32] "Lead and Get Out of the Way," *Broadcasting & Cable,* 5 March 2001, p. 54.

[33] "PTV's Analog Switch-Off Draws Mixed Response From Wireless Industry," *Communications Daily,* 15 April 2004.

[34] E.g., in 2000, Bud Paxson, one of the largest broadcast station group owners, valued channels 60-69 at $30 billion for selling purposes. On a per MHz basis, that comes out to less than the $70 billion FCC estimate, but channels 60-69 are at the highest frequency of the broadcast band and thus are least valuable. See Bill McConnell, "FCC Delays 60-69 Auction," *Broadcasting & Cable,* 7 August 2000, p. 20.

[35] Hundt and Levin, "The Digital TV Shuffle: Now You See It, Now You Don't." Reed Hundt was FCC chair from 1993–1997 and Blair Levin was his chief of staff.

"The sad thing is all the members of Congress who were lied to....
For some reason, it doesn't seem to bother them. I don't know.
Maybe they want to make sure they can get on TV."

—Al Franken, Author and Former Saturday Live Actor[36]

The NAB argued against the idea that the market value of spectrum was the right way to value it. Instead, they responded with a complicated, confusing, and sometimes contradictory set of arguments that all added up to the proposition that accepting additional spectrum rights from the government was an unprofitable, altruistic act by the broadcasters on behalf of the public. This argument can be broken into eight components. There were other arguments brought into the mix, especially before 1995 and after 1997, but a review of the lobbying and public record from 1995–1997 reveals that these were the key arguments.[37]

1. **The Free TV Argument.** The purpose of the transition to HDTV was to preserve free, over-the-air TV.

2. **The Auction Argument.** Preserving free, over-the-air TV and conducting an auction were incompatible goals.

3. **The Status Quo Rights Argument.** Broadcasters already had rights to 6 MHz of spectrum.

4. **The Physics Argument.** Physics dictated that HDTV could only be created by giving each broadcaster a second 6 MHz channel.

5. **The Fairness Argument.** Auctioning spectrum for HDTV would not be fair to broadcasters.

6. **The Loan Argument.** The second 6 MHz channel for broadcasters was a loan, not a giveaway.

7. **The Revenue Argument.** HDTV would not increase broadcasters' revenues.

---

[36] Al Franken, "Take This Media...Please!" *Nation*, 7/14 January 2002, p. 23. Franken's comment was about the 1995 fight over syn-fin but is equally applicable to the spectrum giveaway, which happened at almost the same time.

[37] Over the last few decades, the arguments for broadcaster TV transition subsidies have been like a hydra. As soon as one argument is cut down, another sprouts up to take its place. Lawyers, lobbyists, and other spinmeisters earning upwards of $500/hour are paid for their skill at coming up with plausible sounding arguments to rationalize any policy they want.

8. **The Cost Argument.** HDTV would drastically increase broadcasters' costs.

Free TV Argument[38]

In the early days of broadcasting, the broadcasting community discovered that it was uneconomical to charge viewers directly for their programming. The cable TV industry could cost effectively charge for its programming because it was relatively easy to disconnect cable connections to households that hadn't paid for cable. Broadcast TV, in contrast, had no easy way to exclude non-paying subscribers. Thus, it had to be 100% supported via advertising.

When cable TV came along, broadcasters took their technological handicap and converted it into a political virtue. Broadcasters came to claim that they provided a "free" service while their competitors provided a "pay" service. As a consequence, broadcasters argued that they deserved an array of government subsidies (e.g., free spectrum) and regulatory privileges (e.g., free cable and satellite carriage of broadcast programming) because of this free service to the public. Looking back at 15 years of NAB's legislative issue papers (talking points to use with legislators), I couldn't find a single one that somewhere didn't mention "free TV" as a worthy goal for Congress to pursue. In broadcasters' Congressional testimony and FCC comments, the term "free TV" is endlessly repeated.

Not surprisingly, members of Congress in hearings, bills, and in the press, routinely equate "free TV" with local TV broadcasting. FCC commissioners also make frequent approving references to "free TV." I believe it is fair to say that any member of Congress or FCC commissioner who didn't publicly equate "free TV" with local TV broadcasting would immediately be looked at with suspicion by the broadcasting community. It's become a litmus test that broadcasters use to distinguish friends from enemies.[39]

---

[38] For a detailed discussion of the history and merits of the free TV argument, see J.H. Snider, "The Myth of 'Free' TV," Spectrum Series Working Paper #5, Washington, DC: New America Foundation, June 2002.

[39] In private, the level of cynicism about free TV is quite the opposite. For example, when I asked then Representative Lincoln why no one complained about the broadcasters' free TV campaign, her response was "everyone knows nothing is free." In other words, it was so patently ridiculous, it wasn't worth responding to. Interview with Rep. Blanche Lambert Lincoln, 3 January 1997. Peter Pitsch, former head of the FCC's Office of Plans and Policies, says that when people would talk about free TV, the people in his office would say: "O, you mean commercial TV?" Interview with Peter Pitsch on 9 August 2000.

So it was natural, when broadcasters' sought additional spectrum rights, that this would be sold as a way to preserve and strengthen America's system of free TV. Here's how the leaders of the broadcast industry, featuring the CEO's of the three major TV networks, put it in a letter to President Clinton, which they then distributed on Capitol Hill:

> Without digital capability, our country's free over-the-air system will be permanently relegated to a form of technical and competitive inferiority that would undermine greatly the vitality and viability of free television. At a time when we as a country are legitimately concerned about creating information have's and have not's, it makes no sense to deprive the public of the opportunity to receive for free the high quality picture and sound that would otherwise be available only on a subscription basis."[40]

In fact, however, the new spectrum rights granted to broadcasters did not stipulate that they be used to provide ad-supported/free TV. Instead, they only mandated that broadcasters provide one conventional standard definition program stream within their total 19.4 mbps channel data stream. The rest could be used for whatever they wanted. With 2004 technology, such as Microsoft's Windows Media Player, allowing a standard definition TV channel to fit in a 1 mbps program stream, broadcasters, in effect, are only required to provide free TV on less than 10% of their total data stream capacity.[41]

Congress, the FCC, and broadcasters also took a number of other steps inconsistent with the goal of preserving and strengthening free TV. Broadcasters were allowed to charge cable or satellite companies to carry ad-supported TV channels. Local TV Broadcasters were also allowed to pick a TV transmission standard (8-VSB) that, compared to the European standard (COFDM), maximized the number of bits that broadcasters could transmit in

---

[40] Letter from Tomas Murphy (CEO of ABC, Inc.), Peter Lund (CEO of CBS, Inc.), Robert Wright(CEO of NBC, Inc.), Andrew Fisher (Chair of ABC Television Network Affiliates Association), Ralph Gabbard (Chair of CBS Television Network Affiliates Association), Ken Elkins (Chair of NBC Television Network Affiliates Association), and Eddie Fritts (CEO of NAB) to President Clinton dated January 10, 1996. The three page letter opposed Senator Dole's proposed changes to the spectrum provisions in the Telecom Act. NBC later widely distributed this letter on Capitol Hill in its Congressional briefing book: NBC, "The Case Against Broadcast Spectrum Auctions."

[41] Ken Kerschbaumer, "DVD-Quality Video at 1 Mb/s," *Broadcasting & Cable*, 29 May 2000, p. 38.

6 MHz but provided inferior over-the-air reception. Note that 8-VSB is a subset of the overall U.S. ATSC broadcast DTV standard and COFDM a subset of the overall European DVB broadcast DTV standard.

According to the "bits are bucks" broadcasting DTV theory, sacrificing bit quality for bit rate was a smart economic investment because the vast majority of Americans—and those most valued by advertisers—get their 6 MHz/19.4 mbps local broadcasting signals over cable and satellite. Another economic advantage of 8-VSB was that it had lower energy costs than COFDM. To the extent that an FCC TV license had become a bundle of rights for preferred distribution over cable and satellite TV, energy savings on over-the-air bits went directly to the bottom line.

The government mandated that cable setop boxes be made interoperable with digital broadcasting service, which provided an easy mechanism for broadcasters to exclude non-paying viewers for the first time in the history of broadcasting. And the government mandated that new broadcast TV equipment have the capability to prevent unauthorized retransmission of ad-supported TV programming, which allowed broadcasters to charge for content not viewed in real-time.

Broadcasters argued that pay services were necessary to subsidize the DTV transition for free services. But the experience of Britain proved otherwise. Britain has broadcast DTV TV set penetration rates 11 times those in the U.S.—and the programming is exclusively ad-supported.[42] See Figure 12-1.

---

[42] Snider and Calabrese, "Speeding the DTV Transition." See also Hernan Galperin, *New Television, Old Politics: The Transition to Digital TV in the United States and Britain, Communication, Society, and Politics* (New York: Cambridge, 2004).

Table 12-1. Digital TV Transition Rates in the U.K. vs. U.S.[43]

	Digital Terrestrial (% of all hh)	Digital Cable (% of all hh)	Digital Satellite (% of all hh)	Total Digital[44] (% of all hh)
U.K.[45]	12%	9%	29%	50%
U.S.[46]	1.1%[47]	20.8%[48]	19%[49]	41%

My perception is that most broadcasters privately view the digital transition as a way to quietly kill free TV. Quite simply, if the technology allows them to supplement ad revenue with direct viewer fees, they want the extra revenue. In the words of Jamie Kellner, the CEO of the WB (Warner Brothers) Television Network:

> "I'll tell you what I think. If you get away from a year, two years and three years—and I've not had a drink at lunch—I think we're going to evolve into a paid medium. I think that what we currently call free over-the-air television will no longer be called free."[50]

In another ironic twist, broadcasters argued that HDTV was the way to save free TV. But by the late 1980s it was already clear that while consumers were

---

[43] Data compiled by New America Foundation Program Associate Matt Barranca.

[44] Some digital households may have more than one DTV tuner, thus the total here is an approximation and upper bound.

[45] Based on data from, "Driving Digital Switchover: A Report to the Secretary of State," [report] Ofcom, 5 April 2004.

[46] See FCC, "Annual Assessment of the Status of Competition in the Market for the Delivery of Video Programming: Tenth Annual Report," 28 January 2004.

[47] Based on Consumer Electronics Association estimates for the number of over-the-air DTV tuners shipped between 1998 and the end of 2003. Available at http://www.ce.org.

[48] *See* National Cable and Telecommunications Association data from December 2003, available at http://www.ncta.com.

[49] *See* FCC, "Annual Assessment of the Status of Competition in the Market for the Delivery of Video Programming: Tenth Annual Report," 28 January 2004.

[50] "Beyond 2000: Five top broadcasters talk about the evolution of the TV business in the digital age," *Electronic Media*, 10 January 2000, p. 32.

interested in HDTV, they preferred quality programming, affordable technology, and program choice for the foreseeable future.[51] The British focused on these immediate consumer needs and thus had a successful free DTV transition and a natural progression path to HDTV.[52] The American broadcast DTV transition, in contrast, responded to political, not market imperatives. It pushed for HDTV first and SDTV and mobility second, with the results being low consumer demand, a further weakening of free TV, and ongoing broadcaster requests for additional government handouts to make the broadcasters' DTV transition a success.

The Auction Argument

Broadcasters argued that since they provide a free ("ad-supported") service to the American public, they could not afford to both pay for spectrum at auction and continue to provide their free service to the American public. In the words of NAB's talking points to members of Congress:

> Digital spectrum auctions disrupt the economics of the broadcast industry. They will make it impossible for broadcasters to continue to offer free television to American viewers. The burden would fall heaviest on middle class and lower-income viewers.[53]

In a speech on the Floor of the House, Representative Cliff Stearns, a member of the House Telecommunications Subcommittee, echoed the broadcasters' argument:

> [T]here are many who want broadcasters to give up the old analog spectrum, spend billions of dollars on new equipment to convert to digital TV, and then continue to deliver free TV and pay for the digital spectrum all together. Well, it cannot be done.[54]

---

[51] Neuman, "The Mass Audience Looks at HDTV: An Early Experiment." This authoritative and often cited study was presented at the annual NAB show and then promptly ignored by the broadcasters because it conflicted with their political strategy.

[52] Snider and Calabrese, "Speeding the DTV Transition."

[53] NAB, Spectrum Auction Action Toolkit, p. 21.

[54] Cliff Stearns, "The Spectrum Giveaway is a Misnomer," 105 Congress, 1st Session, 153 Cong Rec H 5830, Vol. 143, No. 108, 28 July 1997.

One weakness in this argument is that so-called "free TV" is actually an extremely profitable business. As noted in Chapter 3, local TV broadcasters routinely earn 40% to 60% gross profits on their "free" service, perhaps the most profitable legal business in America. The profitability of the free TV business is manifested in the fact that in 1996 The Walt Disney Company purchased Capital Cities/ABC, one of the major "free" TV networks, for $19.3 billion.

Another weakness is that the FCC could easily have specified that DTV licenses assigned via auction could only be used to provide ad-supported programming. Joseph Stiglitz, as Chairman of the President's Council of Economic Advisors, the top economist under President Clinton, noted the obvious flaw in the broadcasters' reasoning about the linkage between auctions and the survival of free TV: "[an auction] would not affect the viability of the industry. If it did, the price of the auction would be zero."[55]

The Status Quo Rights Argument

Broadcasters argued that they currently had rights to 6 MHz of spectrum. Thus, after they returned their loaned 2nd channel, they would have the same rights to bandwidth with which they started.

But this wasn't strictly true. What broadcasters had was the right to provide one standard definition TV programming stream. With 1940s technology, that took up 6 MHz. But by 1997, when the FCC awarded broadcasters not only a second 6 MHz channel but vastly expanded rights to the first 6 MHz channel, five to ten standard definition TV programming streams could already fit in that 6 MHz. In other words, the right to provide a certain quality of service—one standard definition TV programming stream—is wholly different from the right to a certain amount of spectrum.

Broadcasters could have been given the right to replicate their service without replicating their spectrum bandwidth.[56] This was the obvious approach advocated by many U.S. telecommunications policy analysts. It was the approach the FCC had frequently taken in the past when moving incumbent

---

[55] "TV Girds for Spectrum Fight," *Television Digest*, 19 February 1996, p. 4. See also Christopher Stern, "ABC's Iger says auction could kill free TV," *Broadcasting & Cable*, 26 February 1996, p. 8, Alan Murray, "TV Giveaway Foils U.S. Campaign Reform," *Wall Street Journal Europe*, 17 March 1997, p. A1.

[56] For a detailed discussion of the ambiguity of the broadcasters' status quo spectrum rights, see J.H. Snider, "Who Owns the Airwaves? Four Theories of Spectrum Property Rights," (Washington, DC: New America Foundation, April 2002).

spectrum users. And it was the approach taken by the successful British broadcast DTV transition.[57] In England, the original approach was to give incumbent broadcasters 30% of each new multiplexed DTV channel. After intense lobbying by British broadcasters, the percentage was increased to 50%.[58] This approach gave existing broadcasters a still substantial spectrum rights windfall, but it also provided an opening for new entrants and increased competition, including a vast expansion of over-the-air radio service.

To counter the service replication argument, broadcasters argued that no system was currently developed that would allow a broadcast DTV signal on 1 MHz and developing one would take many years, thus leaving broadcasters hopelessly behind in the race for DTV.[59] However, the British easily solved this dilemma by separating the right to multiplex from the right to use part of the multiplex. One entity was given rights to broadcast over the entire channel, and then each broadcaster was given must-carry rights to a part of that channel, just the way broadcasters currently have must-carry rights on cable systems.

To counter the service replication argument, broadcasters also argued that neither they nor consumers would have the incentive to switch to digital television without the immediate carrot of HDTV. But, again, the experience of England would prove otherwise. By the end of 2003, as seen in Table 12-1, with only a tiny fraction of the subsidies bestowed on American broadcasters, including no broadcast DTV tuner mandate (starting July 2004 in the U.S.), approximately 11 times the percentage of British viewers (12%) watched broadcast DTV than U.S. viewers (1.1%), and the overall DTV transition, including cable and satellite DTV, was also ahead, with 50% in England vs. 41% in the U.S.[60]

Nor did the British preclude eventually shifting to broadcast HDTV service. A bit-is-a-bit-is-a-bit. If they wanted to allocate more future bits to HDTV service (which by 2004 only required a fraction of a channel), they could. But what the British stressed in their phase I broadcast DTV rollout was offering more TV and radio channels at less cost and with improved reception in mobile environments. The American broadcast DTV standard, driven by the political imperative to give incumbent TV broadcasters as much spectrum as possible while not letting them compete with mobile services, resulted in the

---

[57] For an excellent account of the British broadcast DTV transition, see Galperin, *New Television, Old Politics*, chapters 7-11.

[58] Ibid., p. 232.

[59] NAB, "Spectrum Auction Action Tool Kit," p. 31.

[60] Snider and Calabrese, "Speeding the DTV Transition."

initial launch of a high cost HDTV service with crippled mobile service. TV typically operates in a fixed setting (e.g., a home) whereas radio typically operates in a mobile setting (e.g., a car).

The Physics Argument

The broadcast band consists of two types of channels. Those that are in use and those that serve as guard bands around those that are in use. In the analog era, for any given market, almost 90% of the channels were used as guard bands. As new digital technology allowed those guard bands to be used, the question became who should get access to them. The incumbent broadcasters wanted as much of that guard band spectrum for themselves as they could possibly get. At the very least, they wanted to keep the guard band spectrum out of the hands of potential competitors such as mobile telephone providers.

To capture as much guard band spectrum as possible, broadcasters argued that it would be used for HDTV. HDTV required about five times the amount of spectrum as SDTV. Joel Brinkley does an especially fine job of recounting the history of this political stratagem.

> The FCC's most difficult task was allotting uses for the crowded airwaves. Everyone wanted to transmit on the invisible highway.... The list went on and on, but there were only so many lanes. Of all these users, however, the broadcasters had the choicest space—or spectrum, as it is called.... Now, in the mid-1980s, a new group was clamouring for space—the manufacturers and users of two-way radios.... Nothing was more certain to rouse the broadcasters. Above all else, [broadcasters] held sacred the eleventh commandment: Thou Shalt Not Give Up Spectrum....
>
> Land Mobile repeated its most telling argument: You broadcasters aren't dong anything, and you have no plans for them. Tell us what you'e going to use them for....
>
> Wait a minute, [John Abel, the NAB's strategist] thought...Here's an argument.... The broadcasters could offer the lofty idea that they needed all that extra spectrum so they could *bring HDTV to America* (italics original).[61]

---

[61] Brinkley, *Defining Vision*, pp. 8-10. See also: Thomas W. Hazlett and Matthew L. Spitzer, "Digital Television and the Quid Pro Quo," *Business and Politics* 2, no. 2 (2000).

The other argument used was that fitting an HDTV channel within a broadcaster's existing 6 MHz channel was a violation of physics. Thus, if tens of millions of Americans with analog TV sets were not to lose their free TV, the transition to HDTV would have to take place via a second 6 MHz channel. In its talking points for local broadcasters, NAB repeatedly made this point:

> **The laws of physics prohibit transmitting an analog and a digital signal in the same 6 MHz.** As a result, when television broadcasters go digital, they **must** have an additional 6 MHz of spectrum to accommodate both signals.[62] [the bold highlight is in the original.]

However, it turned out that the laws of physics weren't the problem. There was a short-term technological problem. But it was easy to foresee by 1996 that it might be overcome in the near future if there were motivation to do so.

In 1995, both the NAB and FCC estimated that the vertical blanking intervals and other unused space in an analog TV channel could provide more than 1 mbps (millions of bits per second) of data.[63] By 2003, a company called Dotcast had developed a technology for Disney Corporation that could cram into that space 4.5 mbps,[64] the equivalent of four SDTV program streams using the latest version of Microsoft's Media Player and RealNetworks' Real Player, both available for free and widely available on consumer PCs.

In 1995, too, broadcaster Stanley Hubbard argued a single channel broadcast HDTV transition was possible. And this was reported in *Broadcasting & Cable*.[65]

In 2001, George Nickel, a scientist at Los Alamos Labs, developed a prototype of such a system.[66] The Los Alamos strategy was to start with an HDTV

---

[62] "Spectrum Flexibility," NAB Legislative Issue Papers, May 1995, p. 24. See also NAB Legislative Issue Papers, October 1995, p. 26, and March 1996, p. 26.

[63] Letter from Robert Pepper, Chair, FCC Office of Plans & Policies, to Senator Lieberman, 5 May 1995.

[64] Jon Healey, "Disney Is Thinking Inside the Box; Attempting to bypass the middlemen, the entertainment giant will test a service that beams movies into homes," *Los Angeles Times*, 27 May 2003. Mark Hachman, "Dotcast To Power Disney Set-Top Box," *ExtremeTech*, 18 August 2003.

[65] Christopher Stern, "Hubbard Says Separate Channel is Mistake," *Broadcasting & Cable*, 18 March 1996, p. 12.

[66] Jeff Baumgartner, "Digital Algorithm Developer Seeks Allies Amid Skeptics," *Multichannel News*, 19 March 2001, p. 53. Note that Federal law prohibits Los Alamos scientists from lobbying, which would have been required to make Nickel's DIANA system successful.

image, extract an analog SDTV image, and then add back the extra HDTV detail using the unused data stream.

By 2004, such clever stratagems didn't even appear necessary, as RealNetworks and Microsoft released video compression software that allowed consumer PCs to receive HDTV in a 5 mbps data stream.

Even with technology circa 1995, a single channel HDTV transition could have been easily implemented by using the same type of hybrid, two-stage transition broadcasters were proposing for the FM and AM bands—the so-called IBOC (for in-band, on-channel) digital audio broadcasting transition. With the hybrid approach, consumers would buy dual mode analog-digital sets just like they purchased dual mode mobile phones when phone companies switched from analog to digital service. The extra digital data could be used to provide all sorts of new services and enhancements to the broadcasters' existing analog service. And then at the end of the digital TV transition the analog portion of the channel would be turned off and replaced with a pure digital channel.

The broadcasters' main argument against the hybrid strategy was that the newly usable guard bands at the end of digital TV transition would vary market by market. By repacking the spectrum all at once at the end of the transition, a national band of contiguous spectrum would be created that would enhance auction receipts from sale of the spectrum. But by 1995 such reasoning was already being challenged.[67] For example, inexpensive mobile telephones could roam from market to market, determine which market they were in, and send a signal only on frequencies owned by a particular vendor in that market.

The Fairness Argument

Broadcasters argued that the DTV transition would not only cost them a lot of money in the future but had also cost them a lot of money in the past. Furthermore, they argued that it would be unfair to make them pay for spectrum at auction given all the resources they had invested in advanced TV technology in good faith that they would be given the spectrum as promised. As broadcast station managers and other grassroots lobbyists told members of Congress in early 1996: "The television industry has already invested hundreds of millions of dollars and nine years of research and development in the new digital technology."[68]

---

[67] Letter from Robert Pepper, Chair, FCC Office of Plans & Policies, to Senator Lieberman, 5 May 1995.

[68] NAB, Spectrum Auction Action Toolkit, p. 21. See also "Digital Television," NAB Issue Papers, April 1997, p. 4, which estimates the total spent at $500 million.

There are a number of questionable assumptions in this argument. First, there is a failure to distinguish between the expenditures of the TV broadcasting and consumer electronics industries.[69] The FCC licenses primarily benefited TV broadcasters, not equipment manufacturers. So the most appropriate reference point would have been only the expenditure of TV broadcasters, and these were very modest. It was consumer electronics manufacturers, not broadcasters, who invested the great bulk of the resources in advanced TV. The only significant expenditures of the broadcasters, other than lobbying, were in testing the technologies that the consumer electronics manufacturers came up with. According to the former director of the advanced television testing labs, these expenditures amounted to $26.1 million,[70] and the broadcasters' share $14.5 million.[71]

Second, these expenditures had to be balanced against the prospect of huge gains. A $30 million expenditure in return for the prospect of a $70 billion gain represents a potential return on investment of over 2000:1. It has never been government policy to compensate interest groups for their lobbying expenditures. Given the huge discrepancy between the broadcasters' expenditures and their prospective gains, as well as the lack of a written contract between the government and broadcasters promising broadcasters spectrum flexibility, the expenditures can fairly be viewed as lobbying.

Third, there was a presumption that the broadcasters spent their money to foster a broadcast standard in the public interest. But in retrospect, this has become a highly dubious proposition. A highly paid broadcast lobbyist (and former FCC chairman) was put in charge of picking the broadcast DTV standard. And he was arguably far more interested in securing the TV broadcasters

---

[69] When, on 15 April 1996, Robert Wright gave the keynote address to his fellow broadcasters at the annual NAB convention, he put it this way: "broadcasters have spent ten years and $500 million to develop a unique response to the Congressional mandate to migrate from an analog to a digital signal." At a speech to the National Press Club on 22 June 1995, Wright formulated the source of funds differently: "We estimate that in response to this Congressional and FCC directive, more than $500 million has been spent by U.S. industry in developing digital television." I could find no backup for Wright's $500 million figure, even from the person who calculated it, NBC executive Michael Sherlock. In a 15 January 1998 telephone interview, Sherlock, by then retired, told me he no longer had the documents and apologized that "there aren't documents I can refer you to."

[70] Dupagne and Seel, *High-Definition Television*, pp. 23, 313.

[71] Ibid. See also Robert Pepper letter to Senator Lieberman, 5 May 1995. In an interview this author had with on 15 September 1997, Fannon estimated an additional $12 million in-kind contributions by the broadcasters.

a spectrum windfall than in coming up with the best broadcast DTV standard for America.[72] In a striking setback, by 2004 only 5 countries had adopted the U.S. broadcaster DTV standard (called ATSC) but 36 had adopted the superior European broadcast DTV standard (called DVB). The U.S. broadcasters' top priority was to get the spectrum and then work out the technological kinks, even if it meant making obsolete the broadcast DTV sets of millions of early adopters.

Fourth, by 1996, broadcasters had already received a substantial benefit from their lobbying. The original primary motive for asking for HDTV spectrum was to prevent other industries and potential competitors from getting the unused spectrum.[73] By 1996, broadcasters had successfully warehoused the spectrum for DTV for close to 13 years.[74] That benefit was arguably far greater than the tens of millions of dollars they had spent.

Fifth, the broadcasters expressed no concern about fairness to the American public. The broadcasters were asking for tens of billions of dollars worth of spectrum rights for a measly investment of tens of millions of dollars—clearly, an unfair deal for American taxpayers. The public also lost out on valuable services that could have been provided on those airwaves by competitors. Even after broadcasters received their DTV licenses in 1997, very little productive use was made of their spectrum. By the end of 2003, less than 1% of Americans even had the capacity to use that spectrum for watching TV programs. In contrast, at about the same time that broadcasters got their digital spectrum for free, DBS and mobile telephone operators paid for their spectrum. By the end of 2003, those digital communications providers had tens of millions of customers. Meanwhile, broadcasters were abandoning the uses for which the giveaway of spectrum rights had been justified.

Sixth, there was a question of equity to other companies. Other companies, such as Northpoint, have invested tens of millions of dollars in innovative spectrum concepts and then been forced to bid at auction for an FCC license. Creating a special standard of fairness for broadcasters violated the fundamental principle of jurisprudence that everyone in the same circumstances should be treated equally under the law.

Seventh, the investment the consumer electronics industry made was not specifically on behalf of the broadcasters' DTV standard. The same DTV

---

[72] E.g., Chris McConnell and Don West, "Dick Wiley: Delivering on Digital," *Broadcasting & Cable*, 4 December 1995, p. 32.

[73] Brinkley, *Defining Vision*, pp. 7-10, Hazlett and Spitzer, "Digital Television and the Quid Pro Quo."

[74] MSTV first petitioned the FCC to set aside the spectrum for advanced television in 1983.

technology could be used in TV sets attached to DVD players, cable TV, satellite TV, and even broadband Internet connections. Indeed, it would be those DTV applications, not broadcast DTV, which would drive sales of DTV sets both in the U.S. and the rest of the world. It is also difficult to determine whether key components of the broadcast DTV system, such as signal compression, were a byproduct of research for satellite TV and other digital services or developed specifically for broadcast DTV. To the extent that investment was specific to broadcast DTV, an argument can be made that the purpose was largely to preserve the market power of the consumer electronics industry by placing computer manufacturers at a competitive advantage. For example, one of the most noteworthy features of the planned broadcast DTV system was its use of interlaced rather than progressive scanning to draw TV images on the screen. The computer industry used progressive scanning for its monitors whereas the consumer electronics industry had used interlaced scanning, which meant it controlled the patents and had superior technical expertise in that technology. Ultimately, Microsoft and the rest of the computer industry threatened to derail the giveaway of free spectrum to broadcasters if progressive scanning wasn't made part of the broadcast DTV standard. The compromise worked out by the broadcasting and computer industries—at the expense of the consumer electronics industry—was to allow progressive scanning in return for a written commitment not to lobby for the auctioning of the spectrum assigned to the broadcasters.[75] By 2004, realizing some of the worst fears of the consumer electronics industry, computer manufacturers such as Dell, Gateway, and HP had become major suppliers of flat panel DTV sets.

---

[75] Letter to FCC Commissioner Susan Ness, 26 November 1996. The agreement includes the following passage between the Computer Industry Coalition on Advanced Television Service ("CICATS") and the Broadcasters Caucus. CICATS included Microsoft, Intel, and Hewlett-Packard. "...neither CICATS nor its member companies nor their representatives will directly or indirectly seek to oppose or delay—before the FCC, by judicial review, legislative or otherwise—final adoption of the positions urged by broadcasters and consumer electronics manufacturers in MM Docket 87-268 [the FCC docket on advanced television]....Nor will they support efforts in Congress or elsewhere for auctioning of spectrum allocated or to be allocated for digital television in MM Docket 87-268 or other proceedings related to the launch of digital television. After December 31, 1997, CICATS and its member companies may address other spectrum issues, provided that they do not support efforts for the auctioning of spectrum allocated or to be allocated for digital television in MM Docket 87-268 or other proceedings related to the launch of digital television." See Michael B. Grebb, "Digital Dealings," Wired, 6 December 1996.

The Loan Argument

Broadcasters argued that the extra 6 MHz channel the FCC allocated to them for digital TV was a loan, not a gift, because the broadcasters had to give it back by the end of 2006.[76] Moreover, they argued it was a giveback, not a giveaway, because the spectrum returned at the end of the digital TV transition was "packed" and therefore more valuable than if it had been given away right away without packing.

> The government is not giving the spectrum to broadcasters. It is loaning the spectrum....[A]fter we give back the analog spectrum to the government that we are currently using...[t]he government will then have nationwide blocks of spectrum that will be infinitely more valuable than the spectrum currently mentioned for auction.[77]

But what broadcasters and their Congressional allies meant by a loan was not what most individuals think of as a loan. Indeed, any bank loan officer would have been immediately fired for agreeing to such a "loan" because this loan lacked a payback date, quantifiable and verifiable interest rate, clear description of the item to be returned, and even a payback commensurate with the value of the item loaned. In the words of *Variety*'s Chris Stern, "Only in Washington can you borrow billions of dollars worth of public property, pay no fees and escape without setting a deadline for repayment—and still call it a loan."[78]

Payback Date. When the FCC formally decided to license the additional 6 MHz to the broadcasters in April 1997, it looked more like a real loan because there was an auction date set for 2002 and a fixed return date set for 2006.[79] Doing without interest for ten years, albeit unheard of for a non-government loan, nevertheless seemed a fairly modest subsidy. However, as soon as the broadcasters had the license guarantee, they lobbied to move from a "hard" to a "soft" return date. Knowing how controversial that change might be, they got

---

[76] NAB, "Spectrum Auction Action Tool Kit," p. 29.

[77] Ibid.

[78] Chris Stern, "B'cast 'Loan' Has Xmas Wrapping," *Variety*, 7 August 1997, p. 1.

[79] The 2002 date was set by the Administration and Congress to create a balanced budget. It would have required auctioning the spectrum four years before purchasers could have taken possession of it and would have led to serious discounting of the value of the spectrum because at the end of four years there would have been no credible guarantee that they actually would gain usage rights to the spectrum.

an amendment inserted—at the last minute and with no public debate—in the Budget Act of 1997 (P.L.105-33, Title III).[80] That Act included 3 conditions that would have to be fulfilled before broadcasters would have to return their loan, including that 85% of American households have TV sets that could receive local broadcast DTV signals.

The general consensus was that it would take decades for such penetration to happen. Moreover, senior politicians promised broadcasters that they would never allow the loan to be returned even if the 85% target was reached. In telecom policy circles, this is known as the "granny rule." It asserts that so long as one granny in a Congressional district relies on analog TV, no member of Congress will make that TV obsolete.[81] To the extent the granny rule actually describes the politics of the "loan," the loan will likely be outstanding for decades. In the words of one industry columnist:

> At the current rate, it will take 12,000 years for Americans to replace their 300 million analog TV sets with digital ones, calculated Mark Hyman, Sinclair Broadcast Group vice president of corporate relations. But it will be "only" 4,000 years before there's at least one DTV set in 85 percent of U.S. homes.[82]

Tom Wheeler, the president of CTIA, the trade association for mobile telephone companies, called the three stipulations in the Budget Reconciliation Act "the lobbying loophole of the century." Over the next 7 years, that loophole would give broadcasters huge negotiating leverage and be used to justify many additional broadcaster subsidies to speed reaching the 85% threshold and the return of their "loaned" spectrum.[83] See Appendix C, Period #3.

Later, FCC Commissioner Furchgott-Roth aptly characterized the fantasy of a fixed deadline as "a little white lie to get Congress out of town in 1996."[84] Or, from the convenient perspective of six years later, the Democratic Counsel

---

[80] The broadcasters used the "budget reconciliation process" to accomplish this feat. This process allows Congress to pass legislation, even about non-budgetary matters, without public debate. For a critique of this process, see Senator Byrd's comments on the Floor of the U.S. Senate, "Reconciliation Process Reform," 147 Cong Rec S 1532, Vol. 147, No. 22, 15 February 2001.

[81] Snider and Calabrese, "Speeding the DTV Transition."

[82] Jim McConville, "HDTV Outlook for the next 12 millenia," *Electronic Media*, 12 February 2001, p. 6.

[83] See Snider and Calabrese, 2004.

[84] Bill McConnell, "Delaying Digital TV," *Broadcasting & Cable*, 29 January 2001, p. 55.

to the House Commerce Committee, told broadcasters that "the way Congress determined that deadline was asinine, made no sense and results in a gross mismanagement of spectrum."[85] Bud Paxson, Chair of Paxson Communications, told a convention of broadcasters that in response to an effort to eliminate the fixed deadline "broadcasters will put together a Normandy invasion to Capitol Hill and the FCC."[86]

Interest Rate. Recognizing that an interest free loan with an indefinite duration is not really a loan and creates no incentive for broadcasters to return their spectrum, the Bush and Clinton White Houses repeatedly tried to add a squatting fee to the broadcasters' additional 6 MHz. Each time the broadcasters fought back and argued that "taxing" their spectrum licenses would be unfair and counterproductive.[87] The track record of these proposed fees suggests they may be explained less as an act of political courage than a short-term budgetary gimmick to allow presidents to present a balanced budget to Congress while knowing full well that Congress will not go along with a broadcaster spectrum fee.

Payback Amount. At the end of the digital TV transition, broadcasters would be left with a bundle of rights far greater than what they were giving up. A traditional TV broadcast license gave a broadcaster the right to transmit one standard definition TV program. Using 1940s technology, that required 6 MHz of bandwidth. But with mid-1990s technology, that same service could be provided with 1 MHz; and with 2004 technology, less than .5 MHz. In short, broadcasters were giving up the right to provide one standard definition TV program and getting in return the right to provide more than 12 standard definition TV programs (or 3 high definition programs or any other type of data).

If efficiency was the goal of the digital TV transition, broadcasters could have been required to compress their signals into far less spectrum at the end of the digital TV transition. As noted previously, this was what was done in England. It was also done during the transition period in Germany (to reduce the needed number of transition channels).[88] But in the U.S., broadcasters asked for and received a fundamental redefinition of their license. Instead of possessing rights to provide a particular service, they wanted rights to a certain amount of spectrum to provide any service they wanted. This was a monumental change in

---

[85] Paige Albiniak, "700 MHz Auctions, Take 6," *Broadcasting & Cable*, 29 April 2002, p. 46.

[86] Bill McConnell, "Delaying Digital TV," *Broadcasting & Cable*, 29 January 2001, p. 54.

[87] Many NAB legislative issue briefs from the mid 1990s to the early 2000s contain descriptions of administration proposals to institute spectrum taxes. The broadcasters successfully opposed all of them.

[88] See Snider and Calabrese, "Speeding the DTV Transition."

rights. It meant that when the loan finally terminated, broadcasters would be giving back a bundle of rights worth only a small fraction of the value of the rights they were "loaned."

Broadcasters argued that what the public should focus on was not the spectrum individual broadcast licensees would return at the end of the HDTV transition but what the public would get back as unused TV guard bands were freed up for productive use. Although 68 TV channels are allocated to broadcasters, the average TV market prior to the DTV transition only offered, on a population weighted basis, approximately 13 channels.[89] Most of the rest served as "guard bands" to prevent one channel from interfering with another. Adjacent guard bands were guard bands between stations in the same market (e.g., channel 8 could be a guard band between 7 and 9). Co-channels were guard bands in neighboring markets (e.g., if channel 8 was used in market A, then in neighboring market B it would need to be left as a guard band).

The wonders of digital technology allowed many of these guard bands to be used, which made it possible to stuff the 13 channels into a much smaller fraction of the 68 channels on the TV dial. This would make possible the return of not only the loaned spectrum but also guard band spectrum. In other words, a given broadcast channel that nominally takes up 6 MHz on average really pollutes another 24 MHz or so of nearby spectrum. Digital technology made it possible to clean up a lot of this polluted spectrum.

Unfortunately, Congress and the FCC did not clearly specify what spectrum would be returned at the end of the digital TV transition. This left the door open for the broadcasters to claim a portion of the virgin guard band spectrum as an enhancement to their own licenses.[90] See Appendices C and D. In effect, broadcasters argued that if they cleaned up the polluted guard bands, they should get a cut of them. This sense that they somehow owned the polluted guard bands was how they could speak publicly of the broadcast industry giving up spectrum, rather than gaining spectrum, at the end of the DTV transition.

As we have seen, the FCC allocated 402 MHz of spectrum to broadcasters for use as channels 2-69 (excluding channel 37). Originally, as we have also seen, the NAB claimed broadcasters would return as much as 200 MHz of that

---

[89] Letter from Robert Pepper, Chair, FCC Office of Plans & Policies, to Senator Lieberman, 5 May 1995. Pepper specifically estimates that "the average American home receives 13.3 television channels."

[90] For a discussion of the broadcasters' appropriation of the guard bands, see Appendix C and NAF et al. Economic and Legal Reply Comments to FCC in the matter of *Unlicensed Operation in the Broadcast Bands*, Docket 04-186, 31 January 2005.

after the transition.[91] But as incumbents jockeyed for larger geographic territories and more spectrum, the amount gradually dropped from 200 MHz to 150 MHz to 138 MHz to 114 MHz and then settled at 108 MHz. For example, WLMB-TV was able to increase its coverage from 1.2 million to 2.7 million people as part of the DTV transition. Said the general manager: "We're just giddy! We're so happy we keep kicking ourselves."[92] According to one study, broadcasters won a windfall of $6 billion of this type of guard band spectrum between April 1997 and December 2004—with a lot more yet to come.[93]

The quality of the returned spectrum also was reduced. Generally, the lower frequency VHF channels are much more valuable than the higher frequency UHF channels. They pass through buildings and other obstacles better and thus cover a lot more homes; and they require a lot less energy and thus transmitter size and operating expense to cover a certain distance.[94] Originally, all the VHF channels, 2-13, were to be returned. Then this dropped to 2-6. Finally, it was decided that the only channels to be returned would be the least desirable: channels 52-69. For example, WMFD-TV was able to switch from channel 68 to 12. Reported the *Wall Street Journal*: "Regulators assigned the station to channel 12 for digital broadcasts, a dial position that is far more attractive than its current position at channel 68 in the UHF stratosphere. The lower-number station will require much less transmitting power, which should cut [WMFD's] electric bills."[95]

The great beneficiaries in this process tended to be the UHF channel licensees. They won "spectrum parity" with VHF channels, which meant significantly large geographic areas along with a migration to lower frequency spectrum. Later, the great majority of channels, both UHF and VHF, got an option of two channels from which to keep: their digital or analog. The one with the best frequency or biggest geographic range they could keep.

---

[91] See letter from Jim May, NAB Executive Vice President of Government Relations, to Senate Commerce Committee Counsel, 16 August 1995 and the report that accompanies it: Jackson and Haring, "Pitfalls in the Economic Valuation of the Electromagnetic Spectrum."

[92] David Yonke, "Stations Expects to Double Its Market: WLMB looks to reach 2.7 million in switch to digital TV," *Toledo Blade*, 9 October 2004, p. B3.

[93] See Economic and Legal Reply Comments to FCC of NAF et al. in the matter of *Unlicensed Operation in the Broadcast Bands*, Docket 04-186, 31 January 2005.

[94] According to one broadcaster with 17 TV stations, it pays an average of $360,000/year in energy costs for each UHF transmitter and only $12,000/year for each VHF transmitter. See Steven V. Brull, "Will They Rope 'em With Digital in Dallas? *Business Week*, 26 October 1998, p. 158.

[95] Evan Ramstad, "Digital TV is Set to Transform Industry," *Wall Street Journal*, 22 October 1998, p. B6.

For the most part, the VHF channel owners did not object to the UHF sta-tions' disproportionate gains because they also were getting billions of dollars worth of goodies. This included changing both the parameters and model function that specified a broadcast license's interference protection. The parameters of the model function (F), for example, changed from F(50,50) to F(50,90). That is, in the analog era, the protected coverage area of a broad-caster's license was defined statistically as covering 50% of the locations 50% of the time. In the digital era, that area increased to 50% of the locations 90% of the time. Broadcasters would also later lobby aggressively to modify the pro-tection model itself. For example, in the Satellite Home Viewer Improvement Act, Congress granted broadcasters exclusive rights to a new group of viewers outside their former outermost ("Grade B") protected contour line. And in a variety of FCC proceedings, broadcasters would propose novel theories to expand other rights to viewers beyond their Grade B contour, including the theory that anyone who puts up a tall tower on their property with a direc-tional antenna pointing to a TV transmitter within the Grade B contour should be included in a broadcaster's license area.[96] The right to place trans-mitters in small cells throughout their Grade B contour also would allow broadcasters to reach millions of new viewers.[97] Lastly and perhaps most important, the big television groups that owned the great majority of the VHF channels also owned UHF channels. So, even if they faced more competition at the station level, at a corporate level they were winners.

Another perk that helped the big TV station groups was that the UHF dis-count would not change even though the geographic areas of UHF stations did. According to FCC regulations, no station group could control more than 35% of U.S. homes. This was calculated by adding all the homes in a given metropolitan service areas. But UHF stations were automatically given a 50% discount because of their inferior geographic coverage. In 2003, the small TV

---

[96] See comments to FCC filed in Dockets 04-186, 03-15, and 03-186.

[97] This right was tentatively awarded broadcasters in the FCC's Report and Order in the matter of the *Second Periodic Review of the Commission's Rules and Policies Affecting the Conversion to Digital Television*, Docket 03-15, released 7 September 2004. In the analog era, broadcasters were allowed to retransmit their signals within their Grade B contour with booster stations. But this was qualitatively different from what they could do with the new digital technology. The analog booster technology required that the booster signal be com-pletely hidden from the main signal. For example, it could be placed behind a mountain range that blocked the main signal. With digital technology, in contrast, it could be placed anywhere to create a better signal. Better yet, the new scattered broadcast towers would help lay the foundation for broadcasters to reuse their spectrum like cellular telephone providers.

stations, backed by a public outcry against "media consolidation," strongly opposed raising the cap for TV networks because it would give the networks more bargaining leverage. But in this case they didn't object because both the small and large TV station groups were being given the opportunity to get more spectrum rights (to reach more eyeballs and thus increase advertising revenues) at the expense of the public, not each other.

Broadcasters have also lobbied the FCC to force consumers to purchase TV sets with more sensitive receivers, thus allowing all broadcast stations to be received at greater distances. The alternative approach would be to mandate that receivers have greater sensitivity while broadcasters transmit at lower power levels and only preserve their geographic service areas, thus opening up more spectrum at the end of the DTV transition.

All this was possible because neither Congress nor the FCC nailed down the precise definition of the item being loaned when they gave the loan. The result was endless jockeying to reduce the spectrum rights that would otherwise have to be returned to the public.

The Revenue Argument

Broadcasters wanted additional spectrum rights so they could use their FCC licensees with complete flexibility. This would allow them to generate fundamentally new revenue streams from their FCC license. But they also didn't want to pay for those additional rights.

The flexibility rights request would be like a contractor licensed to graze cattle on federal lands asking for timber, oil, mining, and development rights to the same land without paying an extra penny. Not surprisingly, broadcasters were worried about how this would look in both the court of public opinion and the laws against "windfalls" and "unjust enrichment" that reflect that opinion. The solution they devised to this problem was "HDTV." They would use their new spectrum to provide a single programming stream of HDTV. Moreover, broadcasters could plausibly argue that an HDTV signal would bring in no more advertising revenue than the SDTV signal it replaced[98] while costing a lot more to provide. Adding one and one together, it was thus easy to calculate that HDTV would be a big loss for broadcasters. No windfall there.

---

[98] For example, NAB talking points to grassroots lobbyists proclaimed: "Broadcasters will be reaping no windfalls during the transition. They will have no increase in audience or advertising revenues." ("The Transitioni to Digital Television," NAB Legislative Issue Papers, April 1997, p. 7.) In fact, broadcasters used the DTV transition to both increase their audience sizes and add additional revenue sources.

The legal benefits of this approach were significant. The Communications Act of 1934 (47 U.S. C. §151) and its implementation in the U.S. Supreme Court's *Ashbacker Radio Corp. v. FCC (1945)* decision banned "windfalls" and "unjust enrichment."[99]

The *Ashbacker* decision held that the FCC could make "minor" modifications to licenses without a comparative hearing. But licenses to fundamentally new services had to be granted by comparative hearing.[100]

The FCC appears to have been quite worried about the relevance of *Ashbacker* to the transition to advanced television.[101] As one history of the HDTV transition describes the FCC's strategy:

> Under the Supreme Court's *Ashbacker Radio Corp. v. FCC (1945)* decision, the FCC would have been required to hold comparative hearings if the ATV spectrum assignment had been considered to be a new service. The Commission, as a result, has always taken pains to characterize any national conversion to advanced television as an "improvement" to existing broadcast services.[102]

Accordingly, a central feature of the broadcasters' early argument to get the FCC to allow them to convert from standard definition to high definition TV was that this was a minor (i.e., no big windfall) modification of a license. Broadcasters would transmit the same single programming stream to the same households on both their HDTV and SDTV channels (the "simulcast" requirement). All that would vary was that one of the images would have more detail.

---

[99] In retrospect, the Anti-Deficiency Act and the Miscellaneous Receipts Act may have been better legal grounds than *Ashbacker* to attack this proposed FCC spectrum giveaway. These acts prevent federal agencies from circumventing Congressional spending prerogatives. See Jay Lefkowitz and John O'Quinn, "A Spectrum of Abuse at FCC?" *Washington Times*, 25 July 2004, p. B4.

[100] MSTV, "MSTV White Paper on Broadcaster Flexibility to Provide Additional Service Using New Technologies within Existing Spectrum Allocation," (Washington, DC: Association for Maximum Service Television, 4 April 1994), p. 6. On 5 May 1995, FCC Plans and Policy Chief Robert Pepper wrote Senator Lieberman that the FCC was currently investigating the various arguments concerning the relevance of *Ashbacker* to the DTV transition.

[101] E.g., FCC Second Report and Order/Further Notice of Proposed Rule Making in the matter of *Advanced Television Systems and Their Impact upon the Existing Television Broadcast Service*, MM Docket 87-268, released 8 May 1992, pp. 3342, 3355.

[102] Dupagne and Seel, *High-Definition Television*, p 196. See also Galperin, *New Television, Old Politics*.

Perhaps the main reason the broadcasters went to Congress rather than the FCC to seek spectrum flexibility was to avoid the specific legal risk of violating the *Ashbacker* doctrine and the more general legal risk of violating the clearly expressed Congressional intent contained in the Communications Act to prevent spectrum windfalls.[103]

Solving the legal problem, however, didn't solve the public opinion problem. Thus, broadcasters continued to be adamant that the DTV transition be promoted to the public as the "HDTV" transition until enough HDTV sets were in the market that the spectrum giveaway was politically irreversible. The following letter from senior CBS executives to major TV set manufacturer Panasonic captures this PR and political strategy. The letter was sent six months after the FCC had assigned individual broadcasters their digital FCC licenses but before commercial service had commenced. Meanwhile, Panasonic had started demonstrating less expensive standard definition digital TV sets, the same type of sets used for DVD DTV, which during the late 1990s and early 2000s would drive sales of DTV sets.

> The Panasonic 480 line wide-screen (16 x 9 demo) has been perceived as being "good enough" by some sectors. This could potentially lead to the United States Congress mandating that broadcasters multiplex their signals or combine their signals on a single 6 MHz channel using 480 wide screens rather than "true" HDTV (1080 X 1920). The government would then auction off the other DTV channels to the highest bidder....
>
> [W]e are not operating in a free market decision process. The television channels we have been assigned will not be secure until there are several million HDTV receivers in the hands of the public.... As

---

[103] Two weeks after Representative Billy Tauzin introduced the "spectrum flexibility" amendment into the bill that would become the Telecommunications Act of 1996, MSTV distributed a white paper to broadcaster allies disputing the assertion that Tauzin's amendment, which made no mention of HDTV, was incompatible with Ashbacker: "*Ashbacker v. FCC*, 326 U.S. 327 (1945) does not present an obstacle to the exercise of this authority to authorize broadcasters to respond to consumer demand by using the new technologies to provide services that are *in addition to* [italics in original] their basic main programming services.... In its ATV proceeding, the FCC has determined that it is not creating a wholly new service and that, for convincing public interest reasons, it should restrict initial eligibility for ATV channels to existing broadcasters." See Brinkley, *Defining Vision*, p. 341. Don West and Kim McAvoy, "Staking a Claim on the Future: Interview with Eddie Fritts, President of National Association of Broadcasters," *Broadcasting & Cable*, 19 April 1993.

a result, we are respectfully requesting that you discontinue the multi-format demonstrations until the transition to high definition television is assured.[104]

By 2004, most digital TV monitors sold in the United States were less than true HDTV in resolution. But by then the political imperative to only promote HDTV sets had passed. With millions of DTV sets in the public's hands, the broadcasters' spectrum grab was irreversible.

To the extent that broadcasting leaders acknowledged they could provide multiple streams of SDTV programming instead of HDTV, they talked about "several" or "three to four" programming streams. The possibility that they could fit in a lot more SDTV programming streams or perhaps even multiple HDTV streams was not mentioned publicly.

Now the fact that the enabling legislation proposed by Congress said, at the broadcasters' insistence, not a word about HDTV, made absolutely no difference to the broadcasters' PR campaign. The point was to provide members of Congress with political cover so they could claim with a straight face broadcasters weren't receiving a windfall. But given the discrepancy between the verbal promises and the written laws, there was ample room for confusion. As one well known TV engineer wrote to enlighten his colleagues, who might have been confused from reading mass media accounts:

> There ain't anythin' in Our Beloved Commish's DTV rules sayin' anythin' about HDTV. Zip. Zilch....
>
> Repeat after me: The FCC doesn't require HDTV. The FCC doesn't require HDTV. The FCC doesn't require HDTV.
>
> Got that? Good. Now spread it around.[105]

In fairness, broadcasters didn't get all the flexibility they wanted.[106] In 1993 and 1994, when they first began to aggressively pursue spectrum flexibility,

---

[104] Letter from CBS executives Robert Seidel, Robert Rose, and Joseph Flaherty to Matsushita (parent company of Panasonic) executive Kajitani, 3 October 1997.

[105] Mario Orazio, "Remember the DTV Rules?" *TV Technology*, 29 December 1999, p. 10. Note: Mario Orazio is a pseudonym of a TV engineer who writes an anonymous column for *TV Technology*.

[106] Interview with John Abel, former NAB Executive Vice President, on 18 December 1998. See also Edmund L. Andrews, "HDTV Use for Profit is Pushed," *New York Times*, 2 March 1994, p. D1, S. Merrill Weiss and Rupert L. Stow, "NAB 1993 Guide to HDTV Implementation Costs," (Washington, DC: NAB, 1993).

they hoped to be able to do literally whatever they wanted with their spectrum, include provide two-way, cellular mobile telephone type services. At the time, this was not a particularly controversial statement because it was part of the vision of Vice President Gore's National Information Infrastructure, which was backed by President Clinton. At the annual NAB show in March 1994, NAB President Eddie Fritts demanded a place for broadcasters on the information superhighway:

> Today's system of broadcasting should be tomorrow's superhighway.... With digital technology and flexible use of the spectrum, broadcasters will be well prepared to compete. In tomorrow's race for the gold, Marconi will give Bell a run for this money.[107]

But after the first spectrum auctions in history, which began in late 1994, complete spectrum flexibility for incumbent broadcast licensees became politically untenable because the value of such rights became abundantly clear. It was also clear that the winning bidders, who had just spent $20 billion for their spectrum and included some of the largest corporations in America, would have howled in protest at the unfairness of giving away for free what they had just paid for. Broadcasters would never give up the holy grail of complete spectrum flexibility—but they would have to employ a more subtle strategy and wait for opportune moments to inch that agenda ahead step by step. They had patiently waited more than 40 years to win de facto ownership of their analog FCC licensees. If it took them a few decades to do the same for their digital rights, it would just be a little more water under the bridge.

The Cost Argument

As part of their lobbying campaign to prevent the guard band spectrum from being auctioned and to cultivate the perception that giving incumbent broadcasters digital rights was not a giveaway, the broadcasters emphasized at every opportunity that the transition to HDTV would be hugely costly for themselves to make.

Beginning in early 1995, the broadcasters started publicly claiming that the transition to HDTV would cost each broadcaster $8-$10 million dollars and

---

[107] "NAB—Broadcasting's Place on the Information Highway," *Newsbytes News Network*, 22 March 1994.

the industry as a whole $16 billion.[108] The figures were cited in the mass media, trade press, and endless face-to-face encounters with members of Congress.[109] In early 1996, for example, the NAB sent the following talking points to its grassroots station lobbyists:

> The transition to digital will cost each individual television station between $8-10 million for new equipment—more than some stations' total worth. Stations cannot afford spectrum on top of the costs they must pay for the transition to digital.[110]

In early 1996, the NAB orchestrated a campaign to invite all 535 members of Congress to local stations where they got a detailed explanation of how the $8-10 million figure was derived. Station engineers were duly sent a spreadsheet showing the items that generated the $8-10 million figure. Instructions included the following advice on sending invitations for a television station tour:

> It is important that Members of Congress see firsthand the operation of the station—what equipment and training will be required to make the transition to digital. Broadcasters should extend an invitation in writing to their Member(s) of Congress and Senators to visit the station at their earliest convenience. The letter should be sent to the Member with a copy to the state or district office director with follow-up calls to the director and to the press secretary.... It is important to make similar impressions on local opinion makers, government officials and political leaders, particularly those who may have influence with Members of Congress.[111]

---

[108] See talking points for grassroots lobbyists from NAB Legislative issue papers from May 1995, October 1995, March 1996, August 1996

[109] Examples in the mass media include: Kyle Pope and Mark Robichaux, "Waiting for HDTV? Don't Go Dumping Your Old Set Just Yet," *Wall Street Journal*, 12 Septembere 1997, p. A10, Joel Brinkley, "Getting the Picture," New York Times, 24 November 1997, p. C12, Paul Farhi, "A Defininng Moment for TV? As Digital Broadcast Age Begins, the Outlook is Far From Clear," *Washington Post*, 1 November 1998, p. H1. Gradually, over the coming years, increasingly lower estimates for the cost of the broadcast DTV transition would be used in the press, but I do not recall a single story that would acknowledge how far off the early press reports were.

[110] NAB, Spectrum Auction Action Toolkit, p. 21.

[111] NAB, Spectrum Auction Action Toolkit, p. 33.

This advice was followed by detailed information on what to do during the station tour. The attached spreadsheet, called "Cost Model for Advanced TV Conversion," was three pages in length.

> In taking your Senators or Representatives on a tour of your television station, use the following information that we have provided for you....
>
> See attached spreadsheet.
>
> Use this information, generally a $8 to $10 million total, and plan your station visit from the top to bottom. Make sure that your visiting Senators and Representatives receive a listing of the new digital equipment and a spreadsheet of the costs that will be incurred in the transition to digital.
>
> Be sure that each employee knows how the new digital functions will effect their particular job in a digital station.... It is also important that they realize the cost of their new digital work-station and the overall cost of the new digital station. Members of Congress like to ask questions to employees....
>
> The tour should take no more than an hour. If possible, start off in the control room and follow the functions through the guts of the station—perhaps your chief engineer should conduct the tour.... Try to have a station personality (news, sports, weather anchor, etc.) stop by and say hello. At each stop along the way, show each piece of equipment that will need to be replaced or duplicated with digital technology. These are enormous expenditures that must be spent in order to maintain free, over-the-air television. Your station tour will make it abundantly clear that spectrum auctions must not be dumped on top of the huge costs already incurred by each station.[112]

Based on the HDTV equipment available in 1996, the $8-$10 million estimate seemed reasonable. After all, the market for HDTV equipment was practically non-existent. The industry had had no opportunity to go down a learning curve or benefit from economies of scale.

Yet it was also clear that the assumptions behind this estimate were patently ridiculous. Indeed, many of these assumptions were challenged in NAB's own exhaustive 1993 study of HDTV implementation costs, published before HDTV implementation costs became a central focus of NAB's

---

[112] NAB, Spectrum Auction Action Toolkit, page 56.

lobbying campaign.[113] And in a confidential members only report from January 1997, NAB argued that "the total cost could be $8-10 million" but also provided advice on how to get those numbers down, noting that some stations may be able "to construct a DTV facility for under $1 million, and a few innovative stations may be well under that amount."[114] In early 1997, FCC Chair Reed Hundt called the $8 to $10 million estimates "highly inflated"[115] but was inexplicably ignored in the mainstream press. In the trade press and in product literature, vendors argued "This can be done respectably for a lot less than people think."[116] Comments submitted to the FCC in 1995 and 1996 by highly respected engineers argued that the NAB figures were likely too high by more than an order of magnitude.[117]

---

[113] Weiss and Stow, "NAB 1993 Guide to HDTV Implementation Costs." See also: Joseph Flaherty, "High Definition TV: Transition Scenario for TV Stations," (New York City: CBS, 23 October 1990), James Kutzner and William Zou, "High Defiinition Television: Member/PBS Transition Planning," (Alexandria, Virginia: PBS, March 1991), RMS, "New HDTV Estimates: $12 Million or Less," *Broadcasting*, 29 October 1990, Robert J. Ross, "The Cost of Converting a Broadcast Facility to HDTV: An Update" (paper presented at the 1990 NAB Engineering Conference Proceedings, Philadelphia, Pennsylvania, 1990), William Y. Zou, "ATV Implementation Plan: A Cost Study," (Alexandria, Virginia: PBS, January 1996). See also NAB, "Digital Television Broadcasting," p. 11.

[114] NAB, "Digital Television Broadcasting," p. 11.

[115] Alicia Mundy, "Ness Brokers Digital Deal," *MediaWeek*, 7 April 1997, p. 5. See also Hundt's speech, "A New Paradigm for Digital Television," delivered at Digital Convergence: Reshaping the Media, New York, New York, 30 September 1996. Here Hundt sets the range at $200,000 to $2 million.

[116] Comment of Jim Kutzner, director of engineering for Comark Digital Services, quoted in "DTV Multicast Basics," *Broadcasting & Cable*, 8 September 1997, p. 17.

[117] Letter from Rupert Stow, a CBS engineering consultant, to Saul Shapiro, FCC Director of Technology Policy, 17 January 1996, Reply Comments to FCC of the Digital HDTV Grand Alliance, Docket 87-268, 22 January 1996, pp. 28-9, Reply Comments to FCC of Larcan TTC, Docket 87-268, 12 January 1996. The Rupert Stow comments, which are exceptionally perceptive in analyzing current technology, long-term trends, and offsetting benefits of converting digital technology, were also provided to CBS's chief engineer, Joe Flaherty, on 27 October 1995 and 8 January 1996. In retrospect, even these costs would be an order of magnitude too high. Shortly after the FCC's November 2001 decision allowing stations to retain their licenses with inexpensive, compact, low power transmitters, the trade press reported that "a quick-fix small digital transmitter could keep the FCC from knocking on a station's door and costs less than $10,000." See Jennie L. Phipps, "The Cheap, Fast Approach to Making the DTV Leap," *Electronic Media*, 8 April 2002, p. 7.

Some of the remarkable features of NAB's 1996 estimate were: no forecast reduction in price, no distinction between total and legally mandated costs to hold on to a broadcast DTV license, no distinction between the costs of large and small broadcasters, and no recognition that many of the costs of digital technology were offset by benefits.

No forecast reduction in price. In general, the cost of information technology plummets over time. In one famous formulation known as Moore's law, the performance-price of computer processing power doubles every 18 months. Even between the late 1980s and mid-1990s, the price of HDTV equipment had dramatically decreased—without HDTV even becoming a commercial standard. Broadcasters themselves have frequently submitted filings to the FCC where they assume that the price of technology, such as consumer broadcast DTV tuners, will drop at rates comparable to Moore's Law.[118] Broadcast engineers knew that the price of HDTV equipment would drop after it became commercially available. For example, the editor-in-chief of *Broadcast Engineering* magazine spoke to local TV broadcast engineers at the 1997 NAB convention and essentially said that smart broadcasters would wait at least a few years before buying HDTV equipment, when its price would drop to only a fraction of the price NAB was claiming.[119]

When it suited its interests, NAB was also acutely aware of the tendency for advanced television equipment to decline in price over time. A 1992 NAB report to members noted that in 1990 CBS and PBS estimated the maximum cost per station at $10–12 million, with a much lower cost of $2-$3 million for just passing through a network HDTV feed and insertion of local commercials. It qualified the estimates with the following statement:

> The CBS and PBS cost estimates are viewed by the industry as initial calculations…. [T]hese estimates are certain to be outdated even now. Due to continuing progress in developing the proposed compression, modulation, and processing technologies, it is expected

---

[118] Arthur D. Little, "Assessment of the Impact of DTV on the Cost of Consumer Television Receivers," (Cambridge, MA: Arthur D. Little, 10 September 2001), pp.76-77, 87-88. This report was prepared for NAB and MSTV and submitted by them to the FCC as a written ex parte on 8 November 2001 in the matter of the *Review of the Commission's Rules and Policies Affecting the Conversion to Digital Television*, MM Docket 00-39.

[119] "Using Market Forces to Implement DTV," Presentation by Brad Dick at the 52nd Annual Broadcast Engineering Conference, at the NAB Show, Las Vegas, 9 April 1998. At the same NAB Show, Victor Tawil, a broadcast industry leader, was asked in front of the press what the transition would cost the average broadcaster. He replied: "$8-10 million."

that the range of actual station implementation costs will be significantly less than these early estimates.[120]

Michael Sherlock, NBC's Executive Vice President of Technology, who chaired the broadcasters' caucus on HDTV, insisted at a forum for broadcast executives at the 1992 annual NAB convention that HD equipment need not cost more than today's analog equipment.[121]

One vivid illustration of how far the official NAB figures were off was the cost of HDTV cameras. During the 1996 station tour, the NAB estimated the cost of an HDTV camera as ranging from approximately $350,000 to $400,000. A footnote to the spreadsheet that contained this estimate stated: "Low costs are the lowest estimates for the item.... The estimate for some items has been further reduced to reflect decreasing costs of technology...."[122] In early 2005, Sony introduced a digital HDTV camcorder, the HDR-FX1, for $3,000, less than 1% of the cost of NAB's "low" estimate.[123] By 2004, consumer quality digital SDTV camcorders cost a few hundred dollars and broadcast quality ones were less expensive and vastly more flexible than their analog forbears 8 years previously.[124] Meanwhile, the cost of a 1 hour HDTV videotape dropped to $5, and the cost of a highly rated HDTV editing program, Apple's iMovie HD, cost $80.

Moreover, there was no stipulation in the law that broadcasters even had to transmit, let along create, HDTV programming to keep their digital licenses. All they had to do was broadcast in SDTV. As early as 2001, *Broadcasting &*

---

[120] Marcia L. De Sonne, "Advanced Broadcast/Media Technologies: Market Developments and Impacts in the 90's and Beyond," (Washington, DC: National Association of Broadcasters, 1992), pp. 9-11. See also public comments of NBC's General Counsel, Rick Cotton: Paul Farhi, "Networks Seek More Time For Digital TV's Premiere," *Washington Post*, 4 March 1997, p. C1.

[121] Peter Lambert, "HDTV: A Game of Take and Give," *Broadcasting*, 20 April 1992, p. 6.

[122] NAB, "Spectrum Auction Action Tool Kit."

[123] David Pogue, "Home Video Made to Watch on HDTV," New York Times, 10 February 2005, p. E1.

[124] In 2001, a senior broadcast engineer observed these declining costs to his colleagues: "What I do know is that, back in the era of one-inch HD chip cameras (way, way back in maybe 1996), a high-end, one-camera, one-recorder, one-lens HD package would have set you back a cool million bucks.... Now we've got that $45,000 camcorder. Add a lens—even an HD lens—and you're still at less than a tenth of the cost of the older stuff.... Ayup, we've got HD camcorders that ain't much more expensive than their SD counterparts...." Mario Orazio, "Do You Believe in HDTV? *TV Technology Vendor & Product Directory*, 2001, p. 24. As noted above, the $45,000 HDTV camera of 2001 cost $3,000 in 2005.

Cable could report a broadcaster fulfilling his DTV license obligations "for less than $125,000."[125]

Quite remarkably, despite the price drops, broadcast leaders publicly continued to use the $8-$10 million individual station figure and $16 billion total figure throughout the 1990s.[126] Only in the last few years has the taboo against mentioning lower numbers receded.

Legally mandated vs. other DTV conversion costs. All local TV broadcasters needed to do to keep their new digital license was transmit a DTV signal (the so-called "pass thru" requirement). They did not even have to convert their studios to either HDTV or SDTV digital production; they could continue to produce their own programming in analog and convert to digital at the transmitter.

As it turns out, meeting the "pass thru" requirement costs a small fraction of what it costs to convert an entire station to digital HDTV. The NAB, however, made no such distinction. It assumed that all broadcasters would need to fully convert their operations to digital HDTV at the same time that they started transmitting digital signals. But this was no more necessary than converting transmitters to digital when broadcasters had already begun to convert their studios to computer-based video editing systems. It is easy and inexpensive to convert an analog format signal into a digital format signal.

Quite remarkably, even the pass thru requirement to keep a digital license was largely waived. Specifically, the broadcasters won numerous extensions on their build out requirements. By 2000, less than 10% of commercial broadcasters were broadcasting in digital and of those, a majority were broadcasting at less than a third of their power (equivalent to a ninth of their geographic area of license).[127] Even in 2004, a majority of broadcast stations were broadcasting at a fraction of the power necessary to replicate their analog over-the-air service areas.

The major economic reasons for wanting low power transmitters are simple. The major cost of the transmitter is the portion that generates its power; thus, low power transmitters are much less expensive to purchase than their high power counterparts. Low power transmitters also use proportionately less electricity to operate, thus saving stations $50,000 or more per year. Meanwhile, if the local broadcaster's DTV signal is picked up by cable TV, it can still get its full coverage area.

---

[125] Michael Grotticelli, "Affordable DTV is a Reality," *Broadcasting & Cable*, 23 April 2001, p. 39.

[126] For a list of recent Congressional hearings where broadcasters have had the chutzpah to use these numbers, see Lennard Kruger, "Digital Television: An Overview," Washington, DC: Congressional Research Service, 10 March 2005, p. 7.

[127] "LPDTV," *Broadcasting & Cable*, 13 December 1989, p. 16

Meanwhile, the NAB touted the large number of stations that were broad-casting in digital but steadfastly refused to disclose the power levels at which they were operating.[128] The public impression was that the vast majority of stations were reaching the vast majority of Americans when, in fact, most sta-tions were reaching only a fraction of their audience. The cost of a transmit-ter—and the cost of its electricity bill—is mostly a function of its power level. Lamented one broadcast DTV transmitter company that had dreams of big sales of high-power transmitters: "I tell the [TV stations], 'You're not going to be able to see it unless you're standing next door.' They say, 'I don't care.'"[129]

As long as only a tiny fraction of Americans had DTV sets with broadcast tuners, it was in the interests of broadcasters to postpone their build out as long as possible. By the end of 2003, only about 1 million Americans, less than 1% of households, had purchased DTV sets with broadcast DTV tuners.[130]

Americans could purchase DTV sets to watch DTV on DVDs, satellite TV, and cable TV. Only after a large installed base of DTV sets was out there would it be in broadcasters' interest to finish the build out. Accordingly, most broad-casters warehoused their new digital spectrum as long as they could, petition-ing the FCC again and again to either delay the build out altogether or allow them to transmit signals at low power. The result was that by 2004 most broad-casters were still broadcasting over-the-air to less than half their FCC licensed geographic service area.

No distinction between different costs for different broadcasters. When the NAB and other broadcasters used the $8-$10 million figure, they implied that number was a range among all stations, not an average for all stations. In fact, however, broadcasters faced very different costs to transition to digital TV.[131] Consider the additional cost of adding a digital transmitter to the tower cur-rently carrying their analog transmitter. The NAB assumed that new towers would have to be built to support the additional weight of the new transmit-ters. For a 2,000 foot tower, this could cost several million dollars. But the tower economics of broadcasters varied enormously. Some broadcasters locate their towers on 2,000 foot special towers, but others locate them on top of

---

[128] E.g., Paige Albiniak, "Stations 'Waiver' on DTV: A third of outlets probably won't make 2002 deadline, NAB tells FCC," *Broadcasting & Cable*, 20 August 2001, p. 6.

[129] Jennie L. Phipps, "The Cheap, Fast Approach to Making the DTV Leap," *Electronic Media*, 8 April 2002, p. 7.

[130] Snider and Calabrese, "Speeding the DTV Transition."

[131] Prior to the FCC awarding broadcasters new licenses, the *Washington Post* estimated the range between $700,000 and $10 million. See Paul Farhi, "Networks Seek More Time For Digital TV's Premiere," *Washington Post*, 4 March 1997, p. C1.

mountains or tall buildings. Some broadcasters share a single tower with a half dozen or more other TV broadcasters (as well as mobile telephone operators, AM and FM stations, and other spectrum users). Broadcasters didn't ignore this variation totally. They privately acknowledged a range of costs between 0 and $2 million for upgrading just a tower for DTV. But they came up with an estimated average cost of $1.25 million, which was the basis for the $8-$10 million public estimate.[132]

Offsetting Benefits. Throughout all sectors of American business, companies are replacing analog with digital technology because digital technology saves them money and allows them to compete more effectively. The same economics apply to the media industry broadly and the local TV broadcast industry narrowly. Already by the mid-1990s, cable networks, community access channels, and independent producers were switching to digital technology because it reduced costs and helped generate better products. By 2005, American consumers were buying far more digital cameras and camcorders than analog ones because they were no more expensive and offered superior features. By 2005, too, a $1,000 consumer PC offered more video editing features than a $250,000 professional video editing machine of 1980.

For the same reasons, broadcasters already were transitioning to digital technology long before the so-called DTV transition began. And they would have continued to voluntarily transition their studios to digital technology regardless of whether or not the government granted them additional spectrum rights. PBS President Ervin Duggan captured this idea when he said DTV is "a giant opportunity, occasionally disguised as a problem."[133] Alan Mnuchin, managing director, Lehman Brothers, advised broadcasters that when selling their story to Wall Street (as opposed to Congress and reporters), "You have to make the case that the digital upgrade is investment spending, not just expense."[134]

The offsetting benefits to the DTV transition that broadcasters didn't include in their $8-$10 million net cost estimate include the following:

Broadcasters made no allowance for the fact that lots of equipment, such as broadcast towers, have a natural life cycle, get a tax write off for depreciation, and must periodically be replaced anyway. In 1995, the year before the Telecommunications Act was passed, broadcasters (including radio broadcasters)

---

[132] See "Cost Model for DTV Conversion," in Spectrum Auction Tool Kit, 1996.

[133] "Cable Notes," *Communications Daily*, 8 December 1997, p. 9.

[134] Steve McClellan, "Industry Image is a Problem," *Broadcasting & Cable*, 12 April 2000, p. 46.

spent $445 million on analog transmitters.[135] Observed the CEO of Capitol Broadcasting, "Most stations that I know of replace their equipment over a seven-, eight-, nine-year period.[136] We've got that long to do this." Speaking to fellow broadcasters at the NAB annual convention, the CEO of CBS observed: "We believe that much of the cost...would be normal maintenance replacement."[137]

Broadcasters were able to use the new technology to greatly reduce their labor costs. Through the innovation known as centralcasting, for example, a company owning a group of stations could program them from a single distant station, thus allowing it to automate many jobs and reduce labor costs.[138] Similarly, reporters in the field previously often went out with a camera person and editor. With the new smaller, far more flexible digital cameras, it was much easier for the reporter to take on the job of camera person and editor.[139] For example, during the 2003 Iraqi war and its aftermath, TV reporters often served as camera person and editor. This not only saved TV networks personnel costs but also allowed reporters to get into places they would never before have been allowed with a crew of three and cumbersome, highly visible analog equipment.

Through digital technology, broadcasters have also been able to reduce their building and studio costs.[140] Traditionally, a classy news set had to be built, at great expense, out of bricks and mortar. With digital technology, broadcasters can now create virtual news sets that allow even the smallest broadcasters to look like they have news sets rivaling those of the big four TV networks.

---

[135] "Electronic Market Data Book 1997" (Washington, DC: Electronic Industries Association, 1997), p. 34. The same report, explaining the significance of the FCC's recent DTV mandate, says that "digital equipment generally costs 30 percent more than conventional hardware." Ibid., p. 34. In a brochure handed out at NAB97, Panasonic was even more optimistic: "Media budgets should be eased or unaffected by conversion to digital."

[136] "WRAL's James Goodman: High on HDTV," *Broadcasting & Cable*, 29 September 1997, p. 39.

[137] "Michael Jordan Positions CBS at Top of Media," NAB97 Daily News, 7 April 1997, p. 12.

[138] E.g., Karissa S. Wang, "Ackerley Sees the Future, and It's About Automation," *Electronic Media*, 3 July 2000, p. 8. Steve McClellan, "Union Blues," *Broadcasting & Cable*, 14 December 1998, p. 26.

[139] Mary Coffman, "Going Solo: Why hire a reporter and photographer when you can get both by hiring a video journalist?" *Communicator*, April 2000, p. 33.

[140] E.g., Karen Anderson, "Your New Digital Home: New TV facilities are loaded with computer-based gear that promises to save money and space," *Broadcasting & Cable*, 11 January 1999, p. 72.

Through digital technology, broadcasters could reach more homes within their viewing areas that would otherwise be blocked. In a 1994 memo, CBS Senior Vice President of Technology, Joseph Flaherty, wrote:

> Analyzing the results is a function of distance from the UHF transmitter, up to 10 miles, digital HDTV provided 10 percent more locations with satisfactory reception than NTSC. In the range of 40 to 56 miles from the transmitter, digital HDTV provided 51 percent more locations with satisfactory reception than NTSC.
>
> The impact of these results is clear. Digital transmission provides better coverage and thus more viewers,…and this will ultimately lead to incremental revenue for a commercial television station."[141]

Through digital technology, broadcasters could also turn expensive towers from cost centers into revenue centers. *TV Technology*, reporting on a panel at the annual NAB convention called "Broadcast Towers: Prime Real Estate for the Digital Age," informed its readers: "The conversion to DTV is having a profound effect on the value of broadcast towers—it is turning them into some of the most valued real estate in the United States."[142] At the 1997 NAB convention, one tower vendor soliticited TV broadcasters with the following message: "Let OmniAmerica purchase your tower. You will profit from up front capital and freedom from the hefty financial and management burdens of tower maintenance."[143] A single tower can serve 20 TV and FM stations in a single market plus mobile telephone, public safety, and point-to-point backhaul communications.[144] The extraordinarily tall height of TV towers provides line-of-sight communications to many locations. This makes them premium locations for communication devices using higher frequencies that would otherwise be obstructed by trees and buildings.

For the big TV networks, consumer electronics manufacturers paid for the cost of digital equipment. It was a way for them to showcase their new equipment in a prestigious venue and thus could be written off as a marketing

---

[141] Joseph Flaherty, "ATV How to Do It Whatever It Is" (paper presented at the Bit by Bit into the Future, Hilton Head, South Carolina, 27 September 1994).

[142] Robert Brilliant, "Value of Towers Head Skyward," *TV Technology*, 15 May 2000, p. 12.

[143] Brochure of OmniAmerica, distributed to broadcasters at NAB97, Las Vegas, Nevada, April 1997.

[144] E.g., Glen Dickson, "Dialectric's Tall Deal," *Broadcasting & Cable*, 6 December 1999, p. 78.

expense.[145] It is the same marketing principle that leads Nike to give free sneakers and other perks to professional athletes in the hope that it will bring visibility and credibility to their brand.

The fact that broadcasters didn't take their own costs arguments seriously is reflected in their Form 10-Ks submitted to the Securities and Exchange Commission. For example, in 1997, the Tribune Company, one of the largest broadcasting groups in the U.S., noted in its 10-K:

> Conversion to digital television will require all television broadcast-ers, including those owned by the Company, to invest in digital equipment and facilities. The Company does not believe that the required capital expenditures will have a material effect on its con-solidated financial position or results of operations.[146]

NBC President Robert Wright presents an illustrative case of the way the broadcasters brazenly poor mouthed policymakers on the broadcast DTV transition in order to win subsidies. In 1997, he testified before the President's Advisory Committee on the Public Interest Obligations of Digital Television Broadcasters (known as "The Gore Commission.") The Gore Commission was supposed to make recommendations to Congress for how the broadcasters could compensate the public for their spectrum windfall. At the hearing, he testified that not only were the TV networks in desperate financial straights, but also the high cost of digital TV would not be offset with new advertis-ing.[147] Thus, the TV networks had received no spectrum windfall.

That year NBC made more than $500 million in profit from its owned and operated local TV stations. In a few weeks, it would pay $30 million to broad-cast the Titanic on network TV[148] and $13 million per episode of ER (for a total of $850 million).[149] A year later it would spend a record breaking $823 million to purchase a *single* TV station in San Francisco.[150] At about the same time, other TV networks' spent $18 billion for TV rights to National Football

---

[145] Roger Berger and Greg Spring, "Mitsubishi Deal Has Hidden HD Perks," *Electronic Media*, 17 May 1999, p. 3, "ABC-Panasonic Deal on HDTV," *New York Times*, 27 May 1999.

[146] Tribune Company Form 10-K, Washington, DC: Securities & Exchange Commission, for the fiscal year ended 28 December 1997, p. 13.

[147] Alicia Mundy, "Washington: In Whose Interest?," *Media Week*, 8 December 1997.

[148] Steve McClellan, "Titanic Sails at NBC: Network pays $30 million," *Broadcasting*, 2 January 1998, p. 95.

[149] Bill Carter, "Outbid on Pro Football, NBC Retains 'E.R.' in Record Pact," *New York Times*, 15 January 1998, p. C1.

[150] "TV Stations for $823M," *Broadcasting & Cable*, 22 November 1999, p. 62.

League games,[151] and $6.2 billion for TV rights to NCAA championship games.[152] A one minute ad for the Super Bowl cost $3.2 million.[153]

Purchasing DTV equipment was also an investment to reduce costs. An article in *Electronic Media* reported: "General Electric Chairman and CEO Jeff Immelt says his company will save at least another $1.2 billion in costs this year and as much as $10 billion over the next 10 years from digitization of its subsidiaries, including NBC."[154]

Wright confirmed that "digitizing our operations" was a major part of his business plan to reduce NBC's costs and increase its profits.[155] Another article in *Electronic Media* reported that NBC expected "$150 million in cost savings due to rigorous digitization of its operations."[156] All this became painfully clear to NABET, the broadcast employees' union, where a decimated workforce from DTV automation became the dominant issue.[157]

As evidenced by NBC's continuing stratospheric profits since the broadcasters' DTV transition began, the DTV transition hardly caused the catastrophic fall in profits that Wright implied in his testimony before the Gore Commission.

Argument Summary

The net effect of the broadcasters' claims was to argue that the digital spectrum was not a government giveaway because accepting it would reduce the broadcasters' profitability. The spectrum would bring in no new revenue, raise costs, and have to be returned in ten years. Indeed, according to this argument, accepting the loan of spectrum was an act of economic altruism on the broadcasters' part. When this argument was combined with the argument that the loaned spectrum would be more valuable at the end of the DTV transition

---

[151] Stefan Fatsis and Kyle Pope, "NFL Scores Nearly $18 Billion in TV Rights," *Wall Street Journal*, 14 January 1998, p. B1.

[152] "Basketballs for $6.2B," *Broadcasting & Cable*, 22 November 1999, p. 62.

[153] "Trying to Score Big in 'Ad Bowl,'" *New York Times*, 28 January, 1999, p. C1.

[154] "Digitizing NBC, GE Businesses to Save Billions," *Electronic Media*, 21 January 2002, p. 10.

[155] Diane Mermigas, "Wright, NBC Plan for Uncertainty," Electronic Media, 24 September 2001, p. 22.

[156] Diane Mermigas, "NBC Committed to Net, But Not to NBCi," *Electronic Media*, 16 April 2001, p. 30.

[157] Karissa S. Wang, "NABET's Labor Woes: Union faces changing workplace and priorities," Electronic Media, 15 November 1999, p. 3.

because it would be repacked, NAB President Eddie Fritts could legitimately call the DTV transition a government-mandated broadcaster "giveback."[158]

In subsequent years, the various "giveback" claims would be weakened. The hard loan deadline would be dropped indefinitely. The amount and quality of the spectrum given back at the end of the loan would be reduced; compression technology would allow broadcasters to use their additional 6MHz for a vast array of new services; and the cost of DTV equipment to meet FCC requirements to retain a broadcast license would drop precipitously. Moreover, as described in Chapter 3 and chronicled in Appendix C, broadcasters would seek new subsidies to speed the return of their loaned spectrum. These subsidies included:

- **A Tuner Mandate.** A phased-in requirement that no consumer could purchase a TV set without a broadcast DTV tuner inside it (the mandate begins in July 2004 for high-end TVs and ends in July 2007 for all other TVs).

- **The Broadcast Flag.** A requirement that all digital video devices incorporate a "broadcast flag" to prevent retransmission of an FCC licensed broadcast signal out-of-the-home without payment to the broadcaster.

- **Multicasting Must-Carry.** The right to digital must-carry on cable systems (in addition to analog must-carry).

- **More eyeballs.** Expanded geographic and household coverage for existing broadcast TV licensees.

- **Tax Exemption.** The right to purchase DTV equipment without paying a state sales tax.

- **Lower Energy Costs.** The right to switch from higher frequency spectrum (channels 52-69) to lower frequency spectrum (channels 2-51). This allows broadcasters not only to reach more eyeballs, but also save on energy costs.

- **Distributed Transmission Networks.** The right to divide broadcast license areas into cells. This allows broadcasters to reach viewers otherwise blocked by buildings, hills, and other obstacles; it also positions them to provide mobile service and reuse their spectrum cell-by-cell, helpful for providing broadband Internet service.

- **Underlay Rights.** The right to reuse broadcast spectrum at low power levels. Just as people can whisper to each other in a restaurant playing

---

[158] Associated Press, "Critics Call TV Plan Huge Giveaway," St. Louis Post-Dispatch, April 8, 1997, p. 6a. See also "Broadcasters Say FCC Spectrum Loan Ushers In New Digital TV Age," NAB Press Release, Washington, DC: NAB, 3 April 1997. Dennis Wharton, "No TV Broadcaster Eludes Obligations," Wall Street Journal, 17 October 1997, p. A23.

music in the background, people can reuse spectrum within their own homes and offices that is being used by broadcasters. As more and more low power spectrum devices come to market, these unassigned underlay rights have become increasingly valuable.

Gradually, then, the distinction between the market value and use value of the broadcasters' spectrum is diminishing as the broadcasters seek and win ever-increasing spectrum flexibility. Rank-and-file broadcasters now routinely lament that it is unfair and inefficient that they lack complete spectrum flexibility and cannot use their spectrum to serve needs the market most values, such as broadband Internet service.[159] And in FCC proceedings, broadcasters routinely seek to block uses of their spectrum that don't conflict with their present broadcasting services but might conflict with their future plans to provide new services.[160] They rarely specify what those new services are.[161] But it is reasonable to infer that they are the high-speed interactive services that are widely believed to be the highest valued use of their spectrum.

Perhaps the best evidence of the specious nature of the broadcasters' valuation claims is the markets response to them. According to *Broadcasting & Cable*, the value of a TV station license increased 30% ($19.5 billion) in 1997 (when the FCC finalized the spectrum assignment rules and granted the new licenses) and 29.6% ($15 billion) in 1996 (when the Telecom Act of '96 was passed), for a two year gain of 67% ($34.5 billion).[162]

---

[159] E.g., presentation of Greg Schmidt, LIN Broadcasting, at Forum on Spectrum Management Policy Reform sponsored by the National Telecommunications and Information Administration, National Academies of Science, Washington, DC, 12-13 February 2004.

[160] Comments and Reply Comments to FCC of the National Association of Broadcasters in the matter of *Additional Spectrum for Unlicensed Devices*, ET Docket 02-380, 17 April 2003 and 16 May 2003.

[161] A glimpse is available in the FCC's 2004 Notice of Proposed Rulemaking concerning unlicensed sharing in the broadcast band, which proposes allowing broadcasters to charge others for use of their white space for non-broadcast purposes. *See* FCC Notice of Proposed Rulemaking in the matter of *Unlicensed Operation in the TV Broadcast Bands*, ET Docket 04-186, Released May 25, 2004.

[162] John M. Higgins, "As Broadcasters Giveth, They Taketh in Billions," *Broadcasting & Cable*, 6 April 1998, p. 80. According to the *Wall Street Journal*, the broadcast industry during 1997 was the 2nd best performing of 94 industries studied, "Industry by Industry, Who Leads the Field in Shareholder Returns," *Wall Street Journal*, 26 February 1998, p. R17. For an industry most telecom policy analysts considered a dinosaur, this was a remarkable return on investment.

Low-Information Reasoning

Regardless of broadcasters' objective interests, members of Congress could infer broadcasters' interests through their behavior. This low-information reasoning about interests tends to be much more efficient for decision makers such as legislators because it economizes on the gathering of information. All members of Congress needed to know was that broadcasters passionately wanted new digital spectrum rights in order to infer that opposing the granting of those rights would be at their own political peril.

The Value of the Airwaves

Broadcasters repeatedly stated that winning free spectrum was a life-or-death economic issue for both themselves personally and their industry. More importantly, they signaled through their actions that they would be extremely upset with key legislators who didn't support giving them the spectrum for free.

In a letter to Larry Pressler, Chair of the Senate Commerce Committee and chief architect of the Telecom Act in the U.S. Senate, the President of the NAB wrote:

> Broadcasters want to compete in the world of digital technology, but the imposition of a spectrum auction for the transitional digital channel we need would be tantamount to signing a death warrant on advanced television.[163]

In the trade press, the President of the NAB asserted: "If they try to auction the digital spectrum, they will drive a stake in the heart of free digital TV."[164] The Chair of NAB's Board held a special conference call, telling NAB TV members: "It's time to start beating the drum and let Congress know that [auctions; sic] are wrongheaded."[165] The head of NAB Government Relations criticized

---

[163] Letter from NAB President Edward Fritts to Senate Commerce Committee Chair Larry Pressler, 31 July 1995. In retrospect, Fritts' claim proved absurd. Broadcasters got their spectrum. But it was the satellite, cable, DVD, and broadband Internet markets that led the U.S. transition to digital TV, with broadcast DTV dramatically lagging behind both technologically and in market penetrations.

[164] Doug Halonen, "Telecom Bill Hits Another Snag GOP says no vote until budget accord reached," *Electronic Media*, 8 January 1996, p. 1.

[165] Christopher Stern, "TV Spectrum Under Attack," *Broadcasting & Cable*, 11 September 1995, p. 4.

the menu of options to make broadcasters pay for new spectrum rights this way: "[W]ould you like to be hung or would you like to be shot."[166] The president of the CBS network affiliates board of governors, usually preoccupied moderating fights between CBS and its network affiliates, argued that this issue transcended all their differences: "There's no use worrying about CBS and affiliates if this spectrum thing happens because we've got no business."[167] In one hyperbolic statement, the President of NBC said that forcing broadcasters into an auction would be like "taxing the right to build churches."[168]

In a cover story article, the editor of *Broadcasting & Cable* wrote:

> Broadcasters are at a pivotal moment in their 75-year history: 1995 could be their make-or-break year. It all has to do with the so-callled second channel.... The reality is, if time runs out on the second channel, it runs out on broadcasting as well.[169]

Backing up the rhetoric, the NAB went into war mode during January 1996 after Senate Majority Leader Bob Dole held up passage of key telecom reform legislation because of the spectrum clause pertaining to broadcasters. Accordingly, the NAB put together a world class team of information warfare specialists, including KRC Research and Chlopak & Associates.[170] A special lobbying campaign was launched that would ultimately cost the NAB and its members more than $10 million. As part of that campaign, the NAB sent local TV general managers a "Call to Arms"[171] and then a comprehensive (65 pages

---

[166] Ibid.

[167] Jon Lafayette, "Spectrum Issue Hot Topic at Affiliate Meetings," *Electronic Media*, 22 January 1996, p. 4.

[168] Ralph Kinney Bennett, "The Great Airwaves Giveaway," *Reader's Digest*, June 1996, p. 150. See also: Elizabeth Lesly Stevens, "Mouse-Ke-Fear," *Brill's Content*, December 1998/January 1999, p. 97.

[169] Done West, "The Fateful Battle for the Second Channel: For broadcasters, not a second to lose," *Broadcasting & Cable*, 10 April 1995, p. 22.

[170] Bob Chlopak's background includes: former Executive Director of the Democratic Senatorial Campaign Committee; director of Sawyer Miller's Washington Office; and, currently, Partner, Chlopak, Leonard, Schechter & Associates. Robert Leonard is the former head of the Republican Congressional Campaign Committee. The *Wall Street Journal* has described Chlopak, Leonard, Schechter & Associates as "a bare-knuckles Washington public relations firm." See Ted Bridis, Glenn Simpson, and Mylene Mangalindan, "How Piles of Trash Became Latest Focus In Bitter Software Feud," *Wall Street Journal*, 29 June 2000, p. A1.

[171] Distributed by NAB Government Relations during the last week of January 1996.

in length) "Spectrum Auction Action Tool Kit," which began with the following text:

> We are facing one of the most serious challenges Congress has ever posed for the Broadcasting Industry….Our campaign must, in the immediate future, focus grassroots strength on Members of Congress and their staff. It must prove how digital spectrum auctions are harmful to the future of free local television.
>
> This campaign will require using every tool at our command…. Contact with Members of Congress must reflect the true gravity of the situation.[172]

The 65 page tool kit plus dozens of pages of exhibits included instructions on communicating with members of Congress via writing letters, making calls, arranging visits, attending events, recruiting third parties, giving speeches to local civic and business groups (with politicians in attendance), placing print ads in local papers, and running TV ads. The kit included detailed talking points; rebuttals for opponent arguments; draft newspaper editorials (three options); draft on-air editorials (three options); draft letter to public service announcement and telethon recipients; draft letter to local advertisers; sample letters from numerous organizations (ten samples); draft speech (about 15 minutes in length); print ad slicks (camera ready artwork sent under separate cover); TV ads (sent separately via NAB's monthly *Telejournal* program); and detailed instructions for conducting a station tour.

Local broadcasters writing to members of Congress also used the language of life, death, and outrage. The general manager from a TV station in central Illinois writing to Senator Simon claimed the spectrum auction proposal would "bring about the end of our business."[173] Another local broadcaster writing to Senator Simon called the spectrum auction proposal "a certain death sentence."[174] The general manager from KWHD-TV in Colorada writing to Senator Hank Brown called the auction proposal "outrageous and completely unacceptable."[175]

---

[172] NAB, "Spectrum Auction Action Tool Kit," pp. 1-3.

[173] Letter to Senator Simon on 22 March 1996, with the author's identification information partially blacked out.

[174] Letter from WCIA-TV to Senator Simon with the author's name blacked out, 15 March 1996.

[175] Letter from KWHD-TV General Manager Mark Winslow to Senator Brown, 19 February 1996.

In a more recent debate over auctioning each broadcaster's second TV channel, the FCC Media Bureau Chief, Ken Ferree, vividly described the broadcasters' passion on this issue: "They'd rather eat their children than give up this spectrum. They will hold on to this spectrum to their dying day, if they can."[176] In the words of David Smith, CEO of Sinclair Broadcasting: "The last thing anyone wants to do is concede their spectrum space. It could be too valuable."[177]

Jim Goodmon, CEO of Capitol Broadcasting and star NAB grassroots activist, has characterized his own lobbying style as similar to Plott Hound, North Carolina's state dog: "Having chased a bear into a tree, the hounds have been known to sit at the bottom of the tree until they starve."[178] Goodmon's comment was made publicly in the context of NAB's later and highly popular lobbying battle against the FCC's attempt to raise the network TV media ownership cap. But it also aptly characterizes the passion with which many local TV broadcasters lobbied members of Congress for more spectrum rights in the period surrounding passage of the Telecom Act of 1996.

Clearly, any member of Congress would have had to be very dumb not to recognize that whether or not the broadcasters' new spectrum rights were worth $70 billion or $2 billion, the broadcasters strongly desired to win them.

A Conflict of Interest

To even the most casual observer of the lobbying battle over spectrum rights, it was obvious that broadcasters had a conflict of interest with the public when negotiating with the government. It was in the interest of broadcasters to win additional rights to the public airwaves for as little compensation as possible. And it was in the public's interest to get maximum compensation for those rights. Members of Congress, as the democratic representatives of the public, were supposed to negotiate on behalf of the public.

Perhaps the best evidence that members of Congress were aware of this conflict of interest is that none took credit for the granting of spectrum to broadcasters. Congressional offices send out hundreds of press releases a day touting even tiny programs they have won for their constituents. But no press

---

[176] Ted Hearn, "TV Has 'Death Grip' on Analog Spectrum," *Multichannel News*, 14 April 2004.

[177] Jon Lafayette, "Fox Spooks Affils: Digital spectrum 'grab' reports put affiliates on edge," *Electronic Media*, 1 November 1999, p. 1.

[178] Matthew Rose and Joe Flint, "Behind Media-Ownership Fight, An Old Power Struggle is Raging: A 'Plott Hound' Takes on FCC," *Wall Street Journal*, 15 October 2003, p. A1.

releases were sent out touting the spectrum grant to broadcasters. Nor, if any member of Congress wanted to take credit for the giveaway, would it have been easy to do so. The spectrum giveaway was carefully orchestrated so that members could avoid accountability for their votes. Most of the key provisions dictating the terms of the giveaway were part of large bills that passed with overwhelming majorities. And the actual giveaway was left to the discretion of the FCC. The FCC wasn't explicitly told to give the spectrum to broadcasters. It was simply told that if it wanted to do anything with that spectrum, it could have no other options.

In a similar vein, Congress held no public hearing on the issue prior to passage of the Telecom Act. For a subsidy of this magnitude and with as much controversy associated with it, the absence of a public hearing, if not unprecedented, was at least deafening.

Given that the degree of visibility and accountability Congressional leadership create for a given issue and vote is a carefully weighed political calculation, the lack of visibility and accountability associated with the spectrum grant was a strong indicator that the Congressional leadership thought giving free spectrum to broadcasters was not in the public's interest. Rank-and-file members of Congress would have immediately picked up on this cue from their leadership and acted accordingly.

Conclusion

To the extent that broadcasters had a conflict of interest with the public, broadcasters would have a motive for media bias. This would be tempered by the risk that acting on the motive would be discovered and penalized, the subject of the next chapter.

CHAPTER 13:

The Argument from Cause: Costs

"Hardly a week goes by that I don't get a call from someone in television who's concerned about the business side encroaching on journalism, who wants to know what's appropriate journalistically. There's pressure being brought on news directors from general managers. The news directors tell me 'They keep asking, I keep saying no.' I don't want to be against everything."

—Al Thompkins, Broadcast Journalism Ethicist, Poynter Institute[1]

"The truth shall set you free. Free to look for other employment."

—James Coppersmith, General Manager, WCVB-TV[2]

Let us assume that a broadcaster somehow or other uses his control of a TV station to apply pressure on candidates in pursuit of a public policy agenda narrowly favoring broadcast interests. What is the probability that this behavior would be discovered and cause the broadcaster to suffer a significant penalty?

Broadcasters make two types of claims why they would not use control of the airwaves to pursue a political agenda averse to the public interest: an altruistic claim and a self-interested claim. The altruistic claim is that it would violate journalistic ethics; broadcasters are ethically bound to represent the interests of the public, not their shareholders. The self-interested claim is that it would not be in the broadcasters' self-interest because good journalistic ethics is good business; if journalists didn't act with journalistic integrity, the bottom line would suffer.

---

[1] Cited in Dan Trigoboff, "News Rules," *Broadcasting & Cable*, 11 September 2000, p. 52.
[2] Emily Rooney, "Truth Can Be Trouble," *Communicator*, September 1995, p. 124.

Only the second claim is a cost-benefit claim, and that is all we will focus on in this chapter. But we have earlier discounted the altruistic claim, and we can briefly recap five of those arguments here.

1) *Government laws mandate that the first responsibility of a public corporation's management must be to its shareholders (see Chapter 2),*
   Most state corporation laws mandate that corporations should be run for the economic benefit of their shareholders. For management to do otherwise is to risk legal liability for violating their fiduciary obligations to shareholders.[3]

2) *Marketplace laws dictate that profit-oriented broadcast companies are the most likely to grow and acquire other broadcast companies (see Chapter 2),*
   Basic economic theory predicts that over time profit oriented companies will thrive while unprofitable companies will die. Consequently, when codes of ethics conflict with economic survival, economic survival will take precedence.

3) *Even if altruistic arguments weren't true, it would be in the self-interest of broadcasters to claim they were true (see chapters 1 and 5),*
   This is a consequence of Principal-Agent Theory. Agents will always claim to act on behalf of their principals even when they are acting opportunistically. Machiavelli is a famous early theorist of this type of behavior.

4) *History demonstrates that broadcasters and other professionals who have made such claims in the past have often violated them when it was in their self-interest to do so; this suggests they will do so again in the future (see Chapter 12).*
   This is the argument from analogy. In cases with similar incentive structures, broadcasters and others have made similar altruistic claims while acting opportunistically.

5) *It is extremely difficult to unmask evidence of the type of self-interested behavior known as bias (see Chapter 1).*
   This is the paradox of bias. It should be extremely difficult to unearth bias because there are strong incentives to hide it, and once a particular bias is widely known, it is no longer useful.

---

[3] See "Commission on Public Trust and Private Enterprise: Findings and Recommendations," report of the Conference Board, Inc., 9 January 2003, p. 5.

Having critiqued the altruistic claim, I do not in any way want to imply that many broadcast station employees don't struggle over ethical issues and won't sacrifice their own welfare when there is a conflict between their own welfare and that of the public. But as long as there are reasonable grounds for politicians to worry that not all news managers and reporters are able to rise above their self-interest, politicians will have less than 100% faith in the altruistic claim.

The Self-Interest Claim

Media companies routinely claim that there is no inconsistency between their altruistic and self-interested claims. According to this theory, good journalism is good business because it is in a media company's enlightened self-interest to act in the public interest.[4] In the words of Stanley E. Hubbard, a much cited local TV broadcast owner: "If you serve your community, the profits will take care of themselves."[5] Don Hewitt, Executive Producer of CBS' *60 Minutes*, puts it this way: "you can do good and do well at the same time."[6] ABC News President David Westin offers this rendition: "There's a large moat built around any news organization. If anybody starts messing with it, then...pieces start being written, columns, and work [is] leaked."[7] And Barbara Cochran, President of the Radio-Television News Directors Association (RTNDA), makes the claim as the official keeper of the broadcast TV news ethics code: "The most valuable asset a station or network or news service has is its credibility with the community. Not only does it make journalistic sense to preserve the independence of news, it makes business sense."[8] Note that Cochran doesn't pretend the wall between news and business isn't frequently breached;[9] she is just trying to explain the breaches as poor business judgment. To my knowledge, no broadcaster has ever publicly said otherwise. In many cases, of course, corporate self-interest and the public interest are identical. This is Adam Smith's notion of the "invisible hand." And in the context of local TV, surely the need for viewer trust poses immense constraints on what a TV station can

---

[4] See "Good Journalism, Good Business," a special issue of the *Newspaper Research Journal*, Winter 2004, especially Geneva Overholser, "Good Journalism and Business: An Industry Perspective," *Newspaper Research Journal*, winter 2004, pp. 8-17.

[5] Jim du Bois, "Public Service in the Digital Age," *Format*, January 1998, p. 7.

[6] Neal Gabler, "The 60 Minutes Man," *Brill's Content*, May 2001, p. 110.

[7] Cook, *Making Laws and Making News*.

[8] Barbara Cochran, "Not For Sale at Any Price," Communicator, September 1999, p. 34.

[9] Ibid., p. 32.

do. I am not arguing, for example, that a broadcast station could become a mouthpiece for one of the political parties without this fact being observed by audiences.[10] But I am arguing that there are certain types of bias it may be hard for the public to discover and effectively penalize. In the words of newspaper columnist Molly Ivins, "Bad journalism can be very, very good for business."[11]

This chapter assumes that legislators know a lot about the workings of TV stations. I believe this is a reasonable assumption because members of Congress have both the motivation and experience to understand how the press works.[12] Most members have decades of experience working with the press. They spend large amounts of their time thinking about how to get free press coverage and raise money to purchase campaign ads. They also spend a lot of time in TV stations and other locations talking to both reporters and management. And if, by some chance, a member doesn't know how the TV business works, the probability is high that his press secretary (sometimes a former TV reporter) or campaign manager will.

The Probability of Public Exposure

Let's conceive of media content as shaped by the incentives facing those who create it. What are the incentives of insiders to expose violations of journalistic ethics? Consider the ethics firewall claim:

Business Side ➔ | News Side

We'll now break this claim into its micro components, without clearly marking the place of the ethics firewall.

Owner➔General Manager (GM)➔News Director (ND)➔
Assignment Editor➔Reporter➔TV Audience

---

[10] E.g., just before the 2004 general election, TV broadcasters Sinclair Broadcasting and Pappas Telecasting were forced to back down from attempts to use their airwaves for partisan purposes. See Jim Rutenberg, "Broadcast Group to Pre-empt Programs for Anti-Kerry Film," *New York Times*, 11 October 2004, p. A19. Wyatt Buchanan, "GOP Broadcaster Ordered to Give Dem Equal Time," *San Francisco Chronicle*, 30 October 2004, p. B10.

[11] Molly Ivins, "Some Mauling of the Media," *Fort Worth Star-Telegram*, 31 October 1999, p. 4.

[12] Alliance for Better Campaigns, "Profiteering on Democracy.", Povich Elaine S., *Partners & Adversaries*. Snider, "Local TV News Archives as a Public Good."

Where should the firewall go? Conventionally, it is placed between the general manager and the news director.

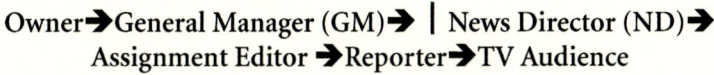

Owner➜General Manager (GM)➜ | News Director (ND)➜
Assignment Editor ➜Reporter➜TV Audience

In reality, however, general managers often act like news directors and news directors as general managers, so the precise placement of the ethics firewall, when defined in terms of persons rather than functions, is ambiguous.

Regardless of where the firewall should ideally be located, the public is unable to see it because all the links between the owner and the TV audience are hidden in a black box.

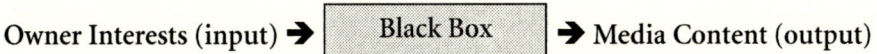

Owner Interests (input) ➜ | Black Box | **➜ Media Content (output)**

The only way for the public to see what's inside the black box is if someone inside it chooses to make it public. But the incentives of players within the black box to reveal ethical breaches may be minimal. We'll specifically look at the incentives of three of those players: general managers, news directors, and reporters.

It also turns out that the information at the inputs and outputs to the black box are not readily available for public, verifiable analysis. Using inputs and outputs to detect media bias, it is necessary for the audience to both have substantial background information about its own self-interest and be able to relate that self-interest to media coverage. But for certain types of bias, that can be very hard to do.

Outputs

One reason is the difficulty in accessing some outputs. The media content archives of local TV news and public affairs programming have not been readily available for scholars, competing journalists, or any other member of the public.[13] For research on national TV news, Vanderbilt University has a video archive. The verbatim transcripts of many national TV programs are also made available on major databases such as Nexis. However, there has never

---

[13] U.S. Congress. Telecommunications, Trade and Consumer Protection Subcommittee, *High Definition Television*, 2nd Session, 25 July 2000. Comments to FCC of the New America Foundation in the matter of *Retention by Broadcasters of Program Recordings*, MB Docket 04-232, 27 August 2004.

been a similar video or verbatim transcript archive for local TV news. A member of the public must either record the programming live or request it from a TV station. Both are impractical endeavors, even for the most highly motivated scholars. Libraries are allowed to record and store local TV programs for a year, then they must be destroyed. Few bother. I know of no large-scale scholarly study of TV bias of any type that relied on requests from local TV stations. And only the most senior scholars with large grants have been able to do large scale tapings of local TV programs.

Another reason is that tapings require that scholars have a hypothesis before a news event so they can record relevant programming as it is aired. But many of the most important questions only become clear a long time after an event has happened. When the Watergate story originally broke, for example, few people had any idea that it would evolve into a major story. It took years before the significance of the story became clear.

Broadcasters, of course, are acutely aware that people who request videotapes of their programs often do so to try to hold them accountable for their programming. This could mean an expensive libel suit or defense of their license against a challenge for not fulfilling their public interest obligations. This mindset is reflected in local broadcasters' aggressive lobbying over the years to limit the contents, duration, and accessibility of their public programming records.[14]

Inputs

On the input side, gathering data may be just as hard because but for somewhat different reasons. By input, I mean evidence of the motivations that might lead broadcasters to have a conflict of interest with the public. This type of accountability involves two elements. First, the public must be able to determine whether its policy interests and the broadcasters' are identical. Second, it must be able to link policy outcomes to the actions of particular legislators or political parties. There are no electoral consequences if every person in the U.S. knows and opposes the spectrum giveaway to broadcasters but cannot assign responsibility for it to particular legislators or parties.

Issues. Let's assume a broadcaster has a conflict of interest with the public with respect to an issue. This may be extremely difficult for the public to ferret out because telecom issues tend to be difficult to understand. They involve new

---

[14] E.g., see the comments to FCC filed by local TV broadcasters in the matter of *Retention by Broadcasters of Program Recordings*, MB Docket 04-232.

and complex technologies catering to wants people may not even know they have. And regardless of the facts, broadcast lobbyists, backed by high powered experts, will always argue that science, economics, and the public interest are on their side. Sorting through competing claims or the claims of just one loud industry voice may be daunting, even for a telecommunications policy expert.

Candidates. Let's assume a broadcaster has a conflict of interest with the public with respect to a candidate. This may be extremely difficult to ferret out because, even if the broadcasters' issue conflict of interest can be ferreted out, the links between broadcasters and their Congressional allies may be carefully hidden. For example, the NAB carefully guards its ratings of individual legislators to protect both its members and individual legislators. Guarding the list protects legislators from being accused of favoring a controversial special interest. It also protects local broadcasters from the appearance of having a conflict of interest when they cover legislators.

Conventional indicators of a potential conflict of interest in covering members of Congress, such as campaign contributions and roll call votes, may be inaccessible. Few local TV broadcasters directly reward their legislative allies with campaign contributions, so a public, verifiable link between broadcaster interest and legislator behavior may be unavailable. Similarly, legislators rarely cast roll call votes on big pocketbook issues involving broadcasters. Most of their influence is exercised behind the scenes, often through the FCC, in such a way that the public would have difficulty knowing whether a particular legislator was a friend or foe of the broadcasters. Aggravating the problem is that legislators' public statements may be highly misleading because they don't correspond to their actual behavior.

The chief sponsors of the Telecom Act of 1996, for example, promised deregulation and competition, yet the spectrum clause pertaining to the broadcast industry was a classic case of corporate welfare and heavy handed industrial policy. House Commerce Committee Chair Billy Tauzin's repeated public condemnation of broadcasters for not fulfilling their promise to provide HDTV programming on their second channel[15] is a classic example of a politician saying one thing and doing something else.[16] Despite his position as chair of the House Commerce Committee, he never actually introduced a bill

---

[15] E.g.,: "One thing is certain. If the broadcasters use any part of the digital spectrum to make money through multicasting, there is going to be a quid pro quo. They are *not*, I repeat not, getting this for free." Quoted in Alicia Mundy, "HDTV or Else," *MediaWeek*, 6 April 1998, p. 24.

[16] E.g., Barbara Matusow, "Heeere's Brian," *Washingtonian*, December 1994.

to enforce an HDTV requirement.[17] And it was Tauzin himself who previously inserted the clause in the Telecom Act of 1996 allowing broadcasters not to provide HDTV programming on their DTV channel. In the cynical words of Tauzin's telecom aid and media spokesperson (spoken in support of Tauzin): "The most overused and least fulfilled phrase on Capitol Hill is 'I promise you.'"[18]

Confusing the analysis of interests even more is that there are large differences on types of issues. Broadcasters grant a lot of leeway to legislators who criticize broadcasters on non-pocketbook or hot air issues such as "violence on television." Legislators get a lot of publicity for holding hearings on such issues, yet rarely pass legislation on them, and when they do, don't materially affect a broadcaster's bottom line. In contrast, sizable pocketbook issues, such as the spectrum giveaway, generate much more intense grassroots broadcaster lobbying while leaving legislators publicly speechless. This discrepancy between words and deeds in the House and Senate Commerce Committees

---

[17] Tauzin was one of the most effective supporters local broadcasters ever had in Congress. The broadcasters were very tolerant of his occasional public outbursts criticizing the DTV transition. They recognize that politicians who want to get re-elected need to project an image of being tough advocates for their constituents. But as long as this persona doesn't correspond to reality, they recognize no material harm is done.

Early in his Congressional career while attending the NAB's 1986 annual convention for its best grassroots lobbyists, Tauzin performed the Billy and Ray Show, coaching local broadcasters on how to lobby members of Congress. In 1994, Tauzin introduced the amendment to the Telecom Act of 1996 that would eventually lead to the warehousing of tens of billions of dollars worth of spectrum rights for the future use of the broadcasters (see Chapter 15). In 1997, he introduced the 85% DTV amendment, "the lobbying loophole of the century," as a rider to the must-pass budget bill.

A measure of NAB's appreciation for Tauzin is that subsequent to passage of the Telecom Act of 1996 they hired his daughter to work with NAB government relations. Tauzin was one of the few members of Congress ever to win the NAB's annual unpublicized Grover Cobb Memorial Award for service to the broadcast industry. Between 1976 and 1996, only two other members of the U.S. House of Representatives and three members of the U.S. Senate (including Ted Stevens, current Senate Commerce Chair) won the award. Usually it goes to a broadcast lobbyist. The award, named after a former senior NAB vice president of government relations, is "awarded to a broadcaster or public official who is involved in government relations important to the broadcast industry and the people it serves. The recipient demonstrates unusual dedication to the improvement of broadcasting's relationship to the federal government."

[18] Doug Halonen, "AOL Ad Plan Irks Broadasters," *Electronic Media*, June 2000, p. 66.

sometimes gives the proceedings an aura of professional wrestling—a sense that the apparent conflict and tough talk is merely for public consumption. Perhaps it should be no surprise that NBC has an equity interest in the World Wrestling Foundation, the primary venue for professional wrestling.[19]

The Black Box

The focus of this chapter is on the incentives guiding the relationships of people within the black box; in particular, the incentives of general managers, news directors, and reporters to expose any breaches in the ethics firewall.

This analysis assumes that the general manager, news director, and reporter are different people. But this assumption doesn't always hold. In Vermont, one individual at a local radio station simultaneously held the role of state broadcast association president, general manager, news director, reporter and public affairs talk show host for members of Congress. More frequently, the general manager at a small station serves as news director but not reporter. When a general manager takes one or more news roles, the ethics firewall is internalized and may be characterized as "integrity."

General Managers. General managers are responsible for the bottom line performance of their stations and clearly occupy the business side of the broadcasting business. This includes both the short-term profitability of the station and the long-term profitability of the parent company and industry. Short-term profitability is purely business oriented and consists of the profit and loss of the station. Long-term profitability is a function of the company's and industry's success in lobbying politicians for favorable public policies.

In group owned stations, lobbying effectiveness is likely to be part of a general manager's periodic job evaluation. A station manager who is incompetent at lobbying may not be fired, but it is nevertheless a mark against him. The NAB is highly effective in identifying general managers with exceptional political skill. This is partly because station managers send Congressional contact

---

[19] Mary Hyman, "Holy Testosterone! The XFL is Comin' At You," *Business Week*, 30 October 2000, p. 130, "Mass Media," *Communications Daily*, 30 March 2000, p. 9. NBC purchased $30 million of World Wrestling Foundation stock and took a 50% ownership stake in World Wrestling Football (WWF). In yet another ironic twist, the NBC executive who helped mastermind the purchase, NBC Sports President Ken Schanzer, was one of NAB's former senior political operatives. Schanzer's pick to run NAB's political action committee, Brian Williams, later rose to be NBC news anchor. "We Love Our Jobs: B&C's Annual Survey Finds a High Degree of Job Satisfaction among News Directors, yet Many Have Eye on Boss' Office," *Broadcasting & Cable*, 11 September 2000, p. 60.

reports to the NAB whenever they meet with a member of Congress. From this information, the NAB is quickly able to determine which general managers can accurately assess a political situation and make the policy sale.

My limited observations lead me to believe that station managers who are also owners or have a significant ownership interest lobby most fiercely. An owner or general manager who does not want to lobby can delegate the day-to-day lobbying tasks to someone at the station who enjoys lobbying and is good at it. Sales managers are often appointed to this role. Many sales managers also later become general managers.

General managers clearly see themselves on the business side of a local TV station. That's why, for example, they don't sign journalistic codes of ethics but, at many stations, force their reporters to. If a firewall exists between the news and business sides of a station, then there is no need for them to sign such an ethics code. Similarly, journalists are strictly banned from lobbying politicians or engaging in any political activity, but general managers are not. General managers or other business side employees of stations not only lobby members of Congress but also become their friends, campaign fund raisers, and grassroots coordinators. A spouse may even work for the local member of Congress. Such activity would usually be cause for firing an individual on the news side of a station.

Broadcast leaders ensure that local managers have all the tools they need to be effective lobbyists. The NAB transmits to the general manager a weekly newsletter (*TV Today*), a monthly videoconference on public policy issues (*Telejournal*), legislative alerts (as many as 4 a week during the heat of a legislative battle), and grassroots lobbying tool kits for issues with significant public opposition (e.g., fights for digital spectrum and against free airtime for federal candidates).[20] State broadcasting associations send the general managers similar types information, although the broadcast industry's political agenda at a state level tends to be much smaller than at a national level. The general manager may, in turn, delegate the task of keeping up with all this information to someone on his staff that isn't on the news side of his business.

The news department is likely to be one of a station's largest and most profitable departments, with up to 65% of station revenue coming from news,[21]

---

[20] In recent years, the NAB has switched to e-mail for its alerts, newsletters, and other time sensitive information. During most of the 1990s, the distribution medium of choice was the fax for both alerts and the weekly newsletter.

[21] Bob Papper and Michael Gerhard, "News Profitability," *Communicator*, November 1998, p. 33.

and gross margins on news average over 50%.[22] Responsible general managers will closely monitor the news side of their business. The general manager will hire the news director, fine tune the news budget, read the overnight Nielsen ratings of news (available in the top 30 markets), and usually meet with the news director on a daily basis, often to make news suggestions. In small markets, especially for local radio stations, the general manager may be the same person. If a news director has been fired or left the station for any reason, the general manager may temporarily take over his or her responsibilities.

The general manager will also be active in the community and generate news ideas. During his contacts with governors, mayors, city councilors, and members of Congress, he will gather data and pass it along to his news staff. The discreet general manager will pass this information along to his news staff as merely suggestions. Reconciling this behavior with the claimed firewall, the general manager will claim that every member of the public also has the right to pass along story ideas to the news department. The general manager, the news director will agree, should have as much of a right to offer story ideas to the news staff as anyone else in the public.

However innocent general managers might view their own lobbying and news behavior, they will jealously guard any information about such activities that might be deemed controversial. It is generally considered very bad form for a station manager to be publicly seen engaged in any political activity or demonstrating friendship with a politician the station covers.

General managers routinely hide information not only from the general public but also their own news departments. For example, NAB lobbying tool kits and *Congressional Contact* (a monthly publication of the NAB to local broadcast station management) are generally kept under lock and key within a TV station. The general manager will justify this based on a concern for preserving the ethical firewall at the station: "I don't want to compromise the news staff by letting them know about my political activities; they might feel compelled to tilt their news in support of those activities." But if the general manager is nevertheless controlling the news agenda, he is merely hiding information from both his reporters and news audiences.

News directors may generously view general managers as just another source of news tips. In the words of one news director: "Everyone in the building should be encouraged to have news ideas: from the GM to janitor. You grab

---

[22] NAB, "1997 NAB/BCFM Television Financial Report" (Washington, DC: National Association of Broadcasters, 1997). Jill Geisler, "Blacked Out," *American Journalism Review*, May 2000, p. 34.

ideas from everyone. A GM's suggestion is just like any other."[23] But for most news directors, the reality is that a news tip from the GM is not like a news tip from the janitor. As one advises his colleagues: "You've got to choose your battles. Save 'going to the mat' for something really important."[24]

Regardless of what news directors and general managers believe, sophisticated politicians clearly believe general managers have substantial control over the news. For example, when a general manager lobbies a politician, the politician often sees this as an opportunity to provide the general manager with news ideas. The politician will devote precious minutes to describing his political agenda. Or the press secretary, who is also in the same room, may describe his agenda for him. For example, Karl Rove, the president's campaign manager, spoke to several hundred top station lobbyists as though he were selling the president's message.[25] The lobbyists came to Washington to lobby the federal government, but Karl Rove was primarily interested in getting out the President's message, pleading for their support on President Bush's tax cut proposal: "You can help provide the reason; a lot of people still need to hear."[26] Newspaper publishers may be no different. At the 2004 annual convention of the Newspaper Association of America, which is to newspaper publishers what NAB is to broadcasters, President Bush, Democratic presidential candidate John Kerry, and Secretary of Defense Donald Rumsfeld all made pilgrimages to pitch their messages.[27]

A reasonable person might clearly see the general manager's behavior as eating his cake and having it too. Station managers know that their stations must convey an impression of journalistic integrity to the public because otherwise the public wouldn't tune in to their stations. On the other hand, in an age when government granted telecom rights and copyrights are worth tens of

---

[23] Telephone interview with former WITI-TV news director Jill Geisler, 29 June 1998.

[24] "Tough Calls: The GM is encouraging you to cover a local food drive since he's involved with the organization that's sponsoring the drive. You don't see much news value in the story, but the GM stands firm, 'asking' you to run it anyway. What do you do?" *Communicator*, October 1998, p. 128. Another news director responded to this tough call strictly as an employee responding to a boss' request: "I would not consider this request at all out of line.... I'd pass the story along.... Tough call? Not at all!"

[25] Speech of Karl Rove, Senior Advisor to the President, at NAB's State Leadership Conference, JW Marriott Hotel, Washington, DC, 11 March 2001.

[26] Ibid.

[27] Annual Convention of the Newspaper Association of America, Omni Shoreham Hotel, Washington, DC, 20-23 April 2004.

billions of dollars, lobbying for government handouts may have more to do with a station's long-term value than running an ongoing business.

When general managers withhold information from their news staff for the staff's own good, this may be viewed as a paternalistic practice that prevents journalists from having the necessary information to fulfill their journalistic responsibilities, including the disclosure of management's conflicts of interests. To the extent journalists don't like making tough ethical decisions, this is indeed a favor to journalists. But even in that case, it is still no favor to the public.

News Directors. If there are a 100 windows in a bank and 99 are securely locked and the 100th is visibly open, in which window will a crook seek to enter? According to the logic in most of the journalism literature, the crook would attempt to go through the locked window and ignore the easy open window. According to the logic here, however, the crook should go through the open window. That open window, in this sequence, is the relationship between the general manager and the news director.

The relationship between general managers and news directors is one of the least studied relationships in the field of political communications. In theory, there is a giant chasm between the two roles in a TV station. But, in practice, the roles are closely related.

News directors are essentially junior managers. Depending on the size of a station, they spend a lot of their time doing things not all that different from general managers, except on a smaller scale.[28] A majority of general managers still come from the business side of a station, but a large fraction come from the news side. And an even larger fraction of news directors aspire one day to become general managers. A survey of news directors conducted by *Broadcasting & Cable* found that more than half (58%) wanted to move up to general manager or some other non-news-group management job.[29] Money is cited as one obvious explanation: "general managers typically earn 40% to 60% more than the news director at the same station."[30] *Communicator*, the magazine for news directors, offers this career advice:

---

[28] Mike Cavendar, "Putting the 'News' Back in News Director," *Communicator*, March 2004, p. 23.

[29] Dan Trigoboff, "Nds Thrive on Gm Track: News Directors Find Doors Open to General Management, with More Making the Jump," *Broadcasting & Cable*, 27 September 1999, p. 51. See also: Kovach and Rosenstiel, *The Elements of Journalism*.

[30] Ibid.

Anyone who aspires to be a general manager needs to really learn all areas of a television station, and learning doesn't mean how mechanical things operate. He or she has to want to help all areas operate, want to solve problems in engineering, want to come up with ideas that will help the sales department sell, want to bring a measure of togetherness to the departments that traditionally dislike each other.[31]

Another *Communicator* article observes: "It's more and more acceptable for news directors to become general managers, and probably 50 have done that in the last three years."[32]

Sometimes RTNDA is surprisingly candid about breaches in the firewall. A bold ad in *Communicator* featured the following training session at RTNDA's annual convention: "At RTNDA99 in Charlotte, news directors can learn more about how to enhance their relationships with general managers by attending 'News and Sales: The New Reality.'"[33]

Many news directors receive stock options in the companies in which they work.[34] And the stock options are specifically designed to align a news directors interests with the interests of the parent company. Some local broadcasters give stock to every news employee, not just news directors. Reports *Broadcasting & Cable*: "Mirroring practices at successful companies such as Starbuck and Wal-Mart, CBS is using its stock as a motivational tool by making every employee a shareholder."[35] The company distributes "stock options representing 10 percent of eligible pay to the retirement plan of every full-time employee."[36]

The career of a news director is also not without risk. In comparison with most professions, turnover among TV news directors is high. The average tenure of a news director is only about two years.[37] Some move on to larger TV

---

[31] Lou Prato, "Moving Up," *Communicator*, October 1996, p. 31.

[32] Bob Papper, Michael Gerhard, and Joe Misiewicz, "Another Growth Year for News and Staff," *Communicator*, June 1997, p. 35.

[33] *Communicator*, September 1999, p. 58.

[34] Joanmarie Kalter, "Burnout," *Columbia Journalism Review*, July/August 1999, p. 32. Bob Papper and Michael Gerhard, "Beyond Salaries," *Communicator*, May 2000, p. 29.

[35] Diane Mermigas, "Wall Street's 'Demigod,'" *Electronic Media*, 17 January 2000, p. 139.

[36] Ibid.

[37] Don Aucoin and Mark Jurkowitz, "Outside Consultants Play a Key Role in Shaping Broadcasts," *Boston Globe*, 30 April 1999, p. A1. Sharon O'Malley, "When the Ax Falls," *Communicator*, September 1998, p. 36. Bob Papper and Michael Gerhard, "Staffing Solutions," *Communicator*, September 1999, p. 61.

markets or into management. Some leave the business for more lucrative positions in public relations, advertising, marketing, and other related businesses. But many are also fired. In any given TV market, there can be only one top-rated news program. Those that aren't in that top spot—especially the news director at the lowest rated station—will often be replaced in the hope of finding another news director who will increase ratings. And it's not just the news director who is under this pressure. If the general manager runs a station that has a poor news rating, his chances of moving on to a larger market are significantly reduced. And he may be fired, too.

News directors will generally give general managers a veto opportunity on any story that the news director believes the general manager may find objectionable.[38] This includes expensive investigative reports, controversial stories that might alienate valued viewing demographics, stories that might result in libel complaints, and stories that might harm the election prospects of a member of Congress. (On the business side, the advertising manager will also give the general manager veto power over controversial political issue ads).

When Nielsen provides the station with audience ratings, the news director will pour over the results with an eye to learning what does and doesn't attract not only large audiences but also audiences that appeal to their target advertising demographic.[39] The news director will then make news decisions largely based on what will net the station the largest advertising dollars. Although the news director may analyze the news component of the Nielsen ratings most closely, he will not be alone in receiving and analyzing them. All senior station management will receive the ratings, and the general manager will be integrally involved in designing news strategies that will boost ratings for desirable

---

[38] This point was made to me in at least a half dozen conversations with news directors and general managers. See also Sharon O'Malley, "GMs Get Candid With News Directors," *Communicator*, September 1999, p. 55. "Tough Calls: While tracking campaign donations for a story on governor candidates, you discover your owner group's CEO is the top contributor for a candidate. How do you handle the story?" *Communicator*, March 2004, p. 44. The American Society of Newspaper Editors provides this advice, based on its survey of best editor-publisher relationships: "Don't Surprise the Boss: Editors take special steps in running their offices to make sure the publisher is never surprised by anything major." "Coping With Your Boss" in *Newsroom Management Handbook*, Washington, DC: American Society of Newspaper Publishers, 1985, p. 4. See also Michael McCarthy et a., "L.A. Times's Groping Articles Spark Outcry," *Wall Street Journal*, 7 October 2003, p. B4.

[39] Carol Guensburg, "Taming the Beast: The Ratings Game," *American Journalism Review*, July 1999, p. S1.

demographics. All these decisions will primarily be based on bottom line considerations.

When a key news hiring decision is made, such as news anchor, the general manager will be intimately involved. A news anchor not to the general manager's liking will not be hired.

One general manager fired a news director for comments made during a regular newsroom meeting. The news director critiqued a proposed report by an African-America reporter that described African Americans' disproportionate propensity to heart disease but didn't mention diet as a possible explanation. The reporter considered the critique racist, and the general manager agreed. It was the fourth news director at that station in four years.[40]

News directors are also not virgins when it comes broadcast policy issues. They will often accompany the general manager to state broadcasting association meetings, where there is invariably a public policy track and lobbying of local politicians.[41] In recent years, RTNDA has hosted its annual convention, advertised as "RTNDA@NAB," at NAB's annual convention.[42] The NAB convention is full of public policy tracks and opportunities to lobby FCC officials and members of Congress. Even if news directors don't attend any of those events, it's reasonable to expect that they would read the program and have some idea of the policy issues that concern their boss.

The president of RTNDA is often treated as a VIP at NAB events, including those featuring public policy and lobbying. To the best of my knowledge, RTNDA has never opposed the NAB on any issue of substance.[43] This is not because of shyness when it comes to expressing public policy preferences. On select free speech and spectrum issues,[44] RTNDA is public and vitriolic and often joins forces with the NAB. Many NAB members are former RTNDA members. A successful TV reporter may start his career with a membership in

---

[40] Dan Trigoboff, "News Director Resigns After Remarks," *Broadcasting & Cable*, 31 August 1988, p. 14.

[41] E.g., see the agenda of the Michigan Association of Broadcasters' *Finding the Key to Broadcast Success: Broadcasting Conference & Expo*, 26-28 February 2001, Lansing Center, Lansing, Michigan.

[42] "Trade Groups to Produce Joint Conferences," *Electronic Media*, 14 January 2002, p. 1.

[43] E.g., Barbara Cochran, "Free Airtime Still a Threat," *Communicator*, February 1998, p. 16. "Guarding the ENG Spectrum," *Communicator*, September 1997, p. 12.

[44] RTNDA doesn't directly lobby on the TV broadcasters' "retail spectrum," channels 2-69, but actively lobbies on its "industrial spectrum," the huge swaths of spectrum the broadcasters have for electronic newsgathering and other backroom operations.

the Society of Professional Journalists, move on to RTNDA, and then graduate to the NAB.

Knowing that senior news staff will be at the NAB convention, public interest groups have occasionally targeted the news directors and well known TV anchors that attend the show. In 2004, for example, a coalition of about a dozen public interest groups including Common Cause, Alliance for Better Campaigns, the Campaign Legal Center, Center for Creative Voices in Media, Center for Digital Democracy, Media Access Project, and Benton Foundation sought to use the NAB conference as a forum for their proposal to get the TV broadcasters to provide more public service obligations in return for the digital must-carry and other rights the broadcasters were lobbying for at the FCC and in Congress.[45] The coalition handed out flyers, held a press conference, and wrote letters to three prominent broadcast journalists in attendance: Ted Koppel (ABC News; recipient of the RTNDA Paul White Award), John Cochran (ABC News; moderator of the NAB panel with FCC commissioners), and Oprah Winfrey (Host of the Oprah Winfrey Show; recipient of NAB Distinguished Service Award).

Reporters. Not all parts of the black box are equally "black." Political communication scholars have devoted much greater resources to studying the relationship between news director and reporter than the relationship between general manager and news director.[46] Most studies of bias focus on outputs; that is, content analysis of the actual output of the news media. Although anecdotal accounts of such behavior abound, I know of no systematic study that looks at the incentives of reporters to slant the news to favor the industry interests of media owners.

A critical insight is that reporters do not need to know the ownership interests of their stations in order to be pawns of those interests. That is because their journalistic discretion is usually highly circumscribed. They can choose how to cover a story. But they cannot choose the type of stories to cover. The news agenda is set by management. Management decides whether a tip provided by an opposition candidate is newsworthy. Management decides whether to invest resources in an investigative story or a public affairs show designed to give a local member of Congress favorable face time. Management decides which reporters to assign to a story.

Reporters are obviously not irrelevant to the news. But for them to exercise journalistic judgment, they need to be informed.

---

[45] Doug Halonen, "Watchdogs Take to the Air at NAB Seek Tougher Public Interest Rules," *TelevisionWeek*, 19 April 2004, p. 12.

[46] Eg., Layton, "Lobbying Juggernaut."

As a rule, low level reporters won't know much about broadcast policy or a general manager's lobbying activities. But this is less true of senior editors and news anchors.

Prominent TV anchors are often called in to moderate public policy and business events for general managers and senior station executives. At the NAB's annual convention, for example, almost every major news anchor at some point in their careers has either given a keynote speech or moderated an industry policy and business panel.[47] Examples include Tom Brokaw (NBC News), Dan Rather (CBS News), Jeff Greenfield (ABC News), Barbara Walters (NBC News and ABC News), Cokie Roberts (ABC News), David Brinkley (ABC News), Bob Schieffer (CBS News), Sam Donaldson (ABC News), Ted Koppel (ABC News), and John Cochran (ABC News).[48] David Brinkley's son wrote an expose of the NAB[49] and the father and son briefly spoke together at the NAB Show. But the father never reported on it during his Sunday morning public affairs talk show.

NBC news anchor Brian Williams not only has moderated NAB policy panels, but also started his career working at the NAB in charge of raising money from station executives for its political action committee, TARPAC.[50] Speaking to NAB members in 1998, Brian Williams began: "I owe nothing but thanks to the NAB, both personally and professionally."[51]

White House correspondence dinners, state press club events, and national party conventions are also places where politicians, station lobbyists, and TV reporters overlap. At the White House correspondents dinner, for example, there will be a smattering of prominent TV lobbyists scattered among the reporters and politicians. And at the national party conventions, the major networks will have some of the best booths overlooking the convention below.

---

[47] Prominent journalists also attend cable trade shows to moderate panels and pitch their parent company's cable networks. For example, for the 1997 Western Cable Show, NBC took a full page ad out in *Broadcasting & Cable* featuring a picture of NBC news anchor Tom Brokaw covering 75% of the page. The ad promises that Brokaw will moderate the opening session of the conference on what the future holds for the cable TV industry. See *Broadcasting & Cable*, December 10, 1997, p. 26.

[48] For a description of ABC News correspondents Sam Donaldson's and John Cochran's advocacy on behalf of the broadcast industry as NAB moderators, see

[49] Brinkley, *Defining Vision*.

[50] Matusow, "Heeere's Brian."

[51] Statement of Brian Williams, as moderator of "A Conversation with Industry Newsmakers," to NAB members at NAB's 1998 annual convention, Las Vegas, Nevada, 6 April 1998.

With great views and food, the booths will be places for senior politicians, network lobbyists, and reporters to hang out together.

Nevertheless, many reporters claim not to know anything about the lobbying activities of their bosses. In 1997, I attended an event at Harvard Shorenstein Center on Press, Politics, and Public Policy featuring ABC News reporter and "20/20" host Barbara Walters as the keynote speaker.[52] During the question and answer period following her speech, I asked why she didn't report on this particular issue. She replied that she knew nothing about it, despite the fact that it was prominently featured in major newspapers such as the *New York Times, Wall Street Journal,* and *Washington Post* as well as all the major broadcasting trade press and trade events. A few weeks later she was the keynote speaker at the annual NAB convention where she thanked ABC network affiliates for carrying her show, acknowledging that they could bump her off at any time if they were displeased with what she said.[53]

Is reporters' claimed ignorance real? Or is it real but purposively created? It is hard to tell. But what is indisputable is that reporters have minimal incentives to do an expose on the political activities and potential biases of their superiors all the way up to news director, general manager, and company CEO. The downside is great, and the upside is negligible. "Don't ask; don't tell" may be the most rational strategy for a reporter because it allows the reporter to claim the ethical high ground without confronting any difficult ethical questions.

For the majority of reporters who lack a trust fund or haven't risen to the top ranks of their profession, the downside of blowing the whistle on a boss' violation of journalistic ethics overwhelms the upside. Observes *America Journalism Review* Editor Rem Reider: "Resigning over principle is rare enough. Going public and explaining precisely why you did so is simply

---

[52] Awards presentation, Harvard Shorenstein Center for Press, Politics, and Public Policy, 19 March 1997.

[53] I later checked the NAB press room for a copy of Barbara Walters' speech. After coming up empty handed, I asked Barbara Walters' assistant for a copy of her speech and was told she didn't have one. The norm at NAB is for the text of keynote addresses to both be available in the press room and available ahead of time for NAB conference organizers. Joel Brinkley, for example, gave NAB the text of his speech before he delivered it. In 2000, the NAB put together a video on the history of the NAB. The video featured an interview with Barbara Walters. See Robert Kapler, "Redstone: Broadcasting Alive and Well." TV Technology. May 15, 2000, p. 10.

unheard of."[54] Bernard Goldberg describes the "sacred code of silence" that leads journalists not to report violations of their code of ethics.[55]

The prime reason for the silence is undoubtedly economic. In an *American Journalism Review* article titled "When the Story is About the Owner," the author sought to explain the difficulty she had getting reporters to speak on the record. One explained: "Nobody's talking because everybody wants [to keep] their jobs."[56]

Another reason is moral: in all businesses, not just journalism, it's looked on as immoral to violate the fundamental trust between an employee and employer.

Another reason is lack of corroborating evidence. For example, it is hard to get colleagues to break their own code of silence; as one reporter observes: "[they] won't risk their own jobs to testify on your behalf."[57]

Broadcast companies have done little or nothing to encourage their TV reporters to engage in such ethics enforcement. Over the years, a small but steady flow of journalists have denounced ethics firewall breeches, but the culprit is rarely the company at which the journalist is employed. Companies do occasionally assign reporters to investigate their ethics firewall breeches,[58] but I know of no instance when that happened before the competition already had the story and the preservation of credibility was at stake.[59] The odds of whistle blowing on a boss being associated with job- or career-termination are much higher than being associated with promotion. To my knowledge, no local TV reporter has ever been praised, let alone promoted within a company, for such

---

[54] Rem Rider, "A Sacred Profession? Not if almighty profits trump public service," American Journalism Review, May 2001, p. 5.

[55] Goldberg, *Bias*, p. 12.

[56] Carol Guensburg, "When the Story Is About the Owner," *American Journalism Review*, December 1998, p. 11.

[57] Emily Rooney, "Truth Can Be Trouble," *Communicator*, September 1995, p. 124

[58] A notable example would be the media reporter of the *Los Angeles Times* reporting on the Staples Center scandal. The LA Times held an ownership interest in the Staples Center but did not reveal that fact when reporting extensively on it. See David Shaw, "Special Report: Crossing the Line," *Los Angeles Times*, 12 December 1999, p. V3.

[59]One news director provided a frank discussion of how competition drives reporting of embarrassing station news: "Is our competition aware of the incident? Is it likely to be reported by other outlets simply because of the connection to my station? If so, I would feel obliged to cover the story, no matter what my personal feelings may be." Lou Kishkunas, "Tough Calls," *Communicator*, December 2000, p. 48.

a move.[60] Yet many have been fired or otherwise furiously attacked for saying anything publicly disparaging about their corporate employers. As CBS News President Andrew Hayward succinctly said when CBS *48 Hours* correspondent Roberta Baskin accused CBS News of going soft on a particular sponsor: "It's amazing, ludicrous and totally baseless."[61] When Sinclair Broadcasting Washington Bureau Chief Jon Lieberman publicly complained on CNN that the company's management was trying to sway the election in favor of President Bush by forcing the news department to air a one-sided documentary against competing candidate John Kerry, the company fired him and issued a formal statement calling him a "disgruntled employee." It also noted that "We are disappointed Jon's political views caused him to violate policy and speak to the press about company business."

As a more general example of this perhaps self-evident logic, I am not aware of a single television news director in the United States who publicly acknowledges that advertisers influence particular TV news content. Yet private surveys indicate that both news directors and reporters believe the practice is widespread.[62] This indicates the strong incentives reporters must have not to whistle blow on bedrock journalistic values.

The current state of journalism awards provides strong evidence that external rewards do not compensate for the lack of internal rewards for whistle blowing. For example, RTNDA, the trade association representing broadcast news directors, promulgates one of the most influential journalistic codes of ethics. It gives out journalism awards in eight categories every year. But it is noteworthy that not one is dedicated to a journalist or news director who upholds that ethics code despite risk to his own career. In contrast, the First Amendment category has three awards, each given for some aspect of working on behalf of press freedom. However admirable such behavior might be, it enhances the privileges, not the accountability, of the press. The mixing of

---

[60] For one of the most famous examples of what happens when a local TV reporter accuses a parent company of news bias on a bottom line issue, see the Chronicle Broadcasting case described below.

[61] Steve McClellan, "Baskin Memo Causes Furor at CBS," *Broadcasting & Cable*, 16 February 1998, p. 10.

[62] E.g., Just and Levine, "News for Sale," p. 2, Pew Research Center, "Self Censorship: How Often and Why," p. 9. Layton, "Lobbying Juggernaut."

broadcast lobbyists, news directors, and legislators at First Amendment award dinners also sends a message to legislators that the firewall has cracks.[63]

To my knowledge, no more than a handful of local TV reporters have ever won an award for exposing the difference between their employer's ethics claims and actual behavior. Since journalism awards are almost always intended to help a reporter's career, an obvious conclusion is that such an award would not be career enhancing. The Associated Press Managing Editors, a prominent journalism association, is remarkably upfront about its standards for giving awards: "[Journalism] awards that reflect unfavorably on the newspaper or the profession should be avoided."[64] When the only way for a journalist to win most of the prestigious awards, such as the Pulitzer or Peabody, is to have their boss nominate them, avoiding whistle blowing awards is not hard.

To be fair, RTNDA and the Associated Press are not representative of all journalistic organizations. Of the many hundreds of journalism awards, there are a few focused on upholding journalistic codes of ethics at the risk of one's own journalism job and career. But these are neither distinguished by their prestige nor prize money. The two I found were the annual Payne Award for Ethics in Journalism and the occasional Ethics in Journalism Award from the Society of Professional Journalists (SPJ). The Society of Professional Journalists also has an annual Research About Journalism award, but this, too, doesn't go to working journalists who risked their jobs. The National Press Club has a press criticism award, but a survey of recent winners suggests it doesn't go to working journalists who risked their job to uphold the ideals represented in NPC's ethics code. The George Foster Peabody Awards, originally established by the NAB to compete with the print oriented Pulitzer prizes, gave a prize to a news anchor in 1997 for upholding ethical values at the expense of her job. But it was given under the catch-all "personal" category. A review of several dozens winners indicated it was an anomaly.

---

[63] The Radio Television News Directors Foundation's Fourteenth Annual Awards Dinner in Celebration of the Fourteenth Amendment, Ritz-Carlton, Washington, DC, 11 March 2004. First Amendment awards were given to U.S. Senators Grassley and Leahy while NBC lobbyist Bob Okun served on the organizing committee and prominent national reporters and local news directors were in the audience. The tax-deductible tickets for this quasi-lobbying event started at $300/ticket. For an analysis of the compromising nature of this event, see Anne Colamosca, "Who's Left Out: Small Markets, Small Paychecks," *Columbia Journalism Review*, July/August 1999, p. 29.

[64] Doing Ethics in Journalism p. 147.

The history of the SPJ's Ethics in Journalism Award may be indicative. By 1998, SPJ had only given this award four times in its 89 year history.[65] That year it gave the award to a husband-and-wife team of journalists who lost their jobs as a result of accusing their bosses of slanting news to favor a powerful advertiser. Their former bosses disputed the award: "'This is not a case of courageous journalists fighting the good fight against evil,' says WTVT-TV news director Phil Metlin, but of 'disgruntled employees doing their best to shine their tarnished reputations.'"[66] One of the disgruntled employees had won 4 Emmy Awards. This particular story had a happy ending for the reporters involved. In 2000, a jury vindicated the two reporters, and in 2001 one of the reporters was hired as the lead investigative reporter for WXYZ-TV.[67]

Broadcast reporters bargaining leverage with management may also be slight. In 1997, starting salaries for radio and TV journalists were $12,000 to $20,000—barely over minimum wage and well below the starting salaries of other occupations with comparable training.[68] Yet stations continue to be flooded with applications for those positions. A reporter with an overdose of ethical sensitivity can easily be replaced.

According to a survey in *Communicator*, 84% of news reporters under contract have a non-compete clause.[69] This means that if they leave their place of employment, they must also pack up and move to another news market if they want to stay in journalism. By making leaving a station so costly, reporters become even more dependent than most employees on their bosses.

Another question concerns how committed most local TV reporters are to journalistic norms of truth-telling. Most schools of journalism train their students in both public relations and journalism. The two sets of skills are viewed as widely overlapping. Many reporters and their spouses move back and forth

---

[65] "'Whistleblowing' Journalist Featured at May 1 Cleveland SPJ Event 'Media Ethics: The Jury is Still Out,'" *PR Newswire*, 20 April 2004.

[66] Dan Trigoboff, "Station Disputes SPJ Award," *Broadcasting & Cable*, 8 November 1998, p. 44.

[67] "Steve Wilson Named Investigative Reporter at WXYZ-TV/Channel 7," *PR Newswire*, 2 September 2001.

[68] Bob Papper and Michael Gerhard, "Radio and Television Salary Survey," *Communicator*, May 2000, p. 32. See also Baughman, *Television's Guardians: The FCC and the Politics of Programming, 1958–1967*, p. 125.

[69] Bob Papper and Michael Gerhard, "Noncompetes: The Norm in TV..." *Communicator*, May 2000, p. 8. The same survey finds that 70% of TV news directors under contract have non-competes, which would similarly influence their incentives to dispute their bosses.

from journalism and public relations. A common career path starts in a low paying reporting job and ends in a high paying public relations job. The top political and marketing PR firms in the U.S. are full of former reporters. Some reporters move back and forth from politics as both politicians and aides of politicians. Many members of Congress employ former local reporters as press secretaries and spokespeople. The political parties at both the state and national level employ many former reporters. Trade associations and corporate government affairs departments in Washington, DC are filled with communications directors who are former reporters. A handful of members of Congress started as local reporters.[70] Others, such as Tim Russert (NBC news anchor), George Stephanopoulos (ABC news anchor), and Brian Williams (NBC news anchor) moved from politics to news. Diane Sawyer (ABC news anchor) moved from TV to politics and back to TV. Some reporters marry politicians, PR flacks, and other people who have been in some way related to their journalistic work.[71]

Many of the finest reporters, with management's consent and encouragement, routinely engage in deception as part of their newsgathering practices. Moreover, as long as these deceptions are in the service of getting the story for the public, they don't violate journalistic norms. *Washington Post* columnist David Broder, one of the most respected journalists in America, wrote this obituary of his colleague Bob Donovan:

> Bob gave the lie to the notion that you have to be hard-nosed to succeed in Washington journalism. He was a sweet-natured gentleman. He was also a great actor. Prematurely white-haired, he would approach an official and, with imploring gestures, say that his paper had just ordered up a story on such and such a subject and he was in desperate need of help.
>
> Thinking "the old fellow" might otherwise be fired, the official would spill his guts—and Donovan, who usually had all but one or two crucial aspects of the story well in hand before he went into his act—would go back to his typewriter and file a story the rest of us

---

[70] Former TV reporters may be the most disproportionately represented profession in Congress; in the state of Wisconsin alone, two of eleven members of the *Congressional* delegation for the 105th Congress were former broadcast reporters. The wife of a third member of the delegation was the former executive vice president of the Wisconsin Broadcasters Association.

[71] Lori Robertson, "Romancing the Source," *Brill's Content*, May 2002, pp. 43-49.

would be scrambling all the next day to duplicate. I never met a better reporter—or a nicer man.[72]

Journalist Janet Malcolm put it more tartly, declaring that "a good journalist was by nature a con artist, drawing people in and gaining their trust, only to betray them for the sake of the story."[73]

Other forms of misrepresentation to get a story may include using hidden cameras,[74] going undercover,[75] lying explicitly,[76] and even breaking the law.[77] There is also the strategy of hiring a private detective to do the misrepresentation so that the reporter can preserve plausible deniability.[78]

Another major category of deception involves deceiving viewers, which is a violation of journalistic ethics. These deceptions are usually minor or even petty in the context of an overall story, but that doesn't make them unreal. One subcategory of these viewer deceptions involves faking events. Examples of event fakery include inserting virtual ads into real life events such as sports events;[79] using a virtual news set that appears to be a real

---

[72] David S. Broder, "Leavitt's Long View," Washington Post, 17 August 2003, p. B7.

[73] Paraphrased in Jonathan Weber, "A Reporter's Reporter," *Industry Standard*, 5 February 2001, p. 7. Her actual quote was: "Every journalist who is not too stupid or too full of himself to notice what is going on knows that what he does is morally indefensible. He is a kind of confidence man, preying on people's vanity, ignorance, or loneliness, gaining their trust and betraying them without remorse." Janet Malcolm, *The Journalist and the Murderer* (New York: Knopf, 1990), p. 1.

[74] Bob Steele, "Hidden Cameras: High-Powered and High-Risk," *Communicator*, September 1997, p. 73. The author observes: "Let's face it. Most hidden camera reporting involves some level of deception, and deception is about causing someone to believe what is not true. Since we are in the business of pursuing truth, there is more than a hint of hypocrisy when we use some form of deceit to pursue the truth. We can only justify that inconsistency and the use of deception when we truly serve a greater principle."

[75] John Seigenthaler and David L. Hudson, "Going Undercover: The public's need to know should be more important," *Quill*, March 1997, p. 17.

[76] Susan Paterno, "The Lying Game," *American Journalism Review*, May 1997, pp. 40-45.

[77] Dean Starkman and Gordon Fairclough, "Report in Business Week Draws Fraud Ruling," *Wall Street Journal*, 28 December 1998, p. A3. Douglas Lee, "Damages Downsized but the Principle Remains: Media must weigh the cost of undercover techniques," First Amendment News, September 1997, p. 8. Lee asks bluntly: "Under what circumstances, if any, may the media break the law in order to gather the news?"

[78] Douglas Frantz, "Journalists, or Detectives? Depends on Who's Asking," *New York Times*, 28 July 1999, p. A14.

[79] "Picture Your Ad Here," *Washington Post*, 14 April 1997, p. A20.

news set;[80] using fake sounds in a real news event; pretending that an old event from earlier in the day is breaking news later in the day;[81] re-enacting events and pretending that the original event is being shown;[82] splicing two separate events together and showing them as if they were one;[83] and pretending that the answer to one question is really the answer to another question.[84] In recent years, one of the most reported on types of fakery in local newscasts is called centralcasting.[85] Here, a reporter that isn't reporting locally pretends to be doing just that.

Pretending to investigate and author a story that one hasn't is an especially common form of viewer deception. A significant fraction of news is actually researched and written by PR firms. As one radio broadcast news anchor observed: "Press releases might not be read on the air verbatim, but they're certainly the basis of stories all the time, and sometimes they are aired almost word for word. The ubiquitous "Health Minute" used by hundreds of TV stations is nothing more than a canned story, with the option of inserting your local voice-over."[86]

Even when a TV station produces its own news, there is often viewer deception about who actually did the work. Viewers largely tune into a station because of the anchor. According to one survey, 58% said the anchor is the "main" or "important" reason they tune into a newscast.[87] When anchors change, viewers shop around.[88] And a major quality that leads viewers to turn

---

[80] Eric A. Taub, "Where Little But the News is Real: Virtual sets give smaller-market broadcasters the look of the big three," *New York Times*, 14 March 2002, p. E1.

[81] Abe Rosenberg, "Let's Stop This—Now!" Communicator, April 19999, p. 51.

[82] Carol Anne Strippel, "Not Necessarily the News," *Communicator*, April 1997, p. 24.

[83] Amy Mitchell and Tom Rosenstiel, "Don't Touch That Quote," Columbia Journalism Review, January/February 2000, p. 34.

[84] Ibid., p. 35.

[85] Anna Wilde Mathews, "A Giant Radio Chain is Perfecting the Art of Seeming Local," *Wall Street Journal*, 25 February 2002, p. A1, Jim Rutenberg, "TV News That Looks Local, Even It It's Not," *New York Times*, 2 June 2003, p. C9.

[86] Cheri Preston, "Tough Calls: You're in the first month of your first job as a reporter for a small station, and the news director hands ou an awareness-raising health story to be read on the day's newscast. Trouble is, the script came from the PR department at a local hospital. How do you handle this situation?" *Communicator*, September 1997, p. 96. For another vivid example, see Barstow and Stein, "Under Bush, a New Age of Prepackaged News," p. A1.

[87] "Viewers Give Local News High Marks," *Electronic Media*, 4 September 1995, p. 29.

[88] David Zurawik, "A Smooth Transition at NBC News," *Baltimore Sun*, 3 December 2004, p. 3F.

to one anchor over another is how much they trust the anchor.[89] This trust can be undermined if viewers learn that the anchor has played no role in researching and writing the story and is merely reading off a teleprompter. Thus, anchors routinely appear to take credit for the words that come out of their mouths and the stories that feature them. Mark Feldstein, a former NBC News reporter, says that "the dirty little secret of television newsmagazines such as '60 Minutes' is that the producer is really the journalist who does all the important editorial work. The on-air correspondents at these primetime newsmagazines are largely front people. They parachute into the story."[90] CNN's famous on-air correspondent, Peter Arnett, blamed his producers and pleaded ignorance when the report he read on-air turned out to be fabricated.[91] *Communicator* reports that the problem is so bad that anchors often don't even take the time to read their scripts before going on the air.[92]

Perhaps the most obvious type of viewer deception is hype. Stations want to keep viewers tuned into a channel, so they hype later programs. Promo spots make excessive use of words like "crisis" and "scandal." The problem of hype in promos is so severe that they are a major cause of libel suits against TV stations, even when the promoted segment is harmless.[93] Says Gary Gibson, head of Minnesota's News Council, "Credibility should be the No. 1 priority. But we're living in a competitive climate where some stations do not value credibility as much as they do promotability. They see the short-term gain; they're trying to prevent the short-term loss."[94]

At other times TV stations don't intend to misrepresent the facts when they put on a program. But after it becomes clear they made a mistake, they still refuse to issue a correction. One survey reported in *American Journalism Review* found that "The perception is almost universal that it's impossible to get a correction on local television news."[95]

---

[89] Jennie L. Phipps, "Building a Better Anchor," *Electronic Media*, 14 February 2000, p. 14.

[90] Cited in John Cook, "'The Dirty Little Secret' of TV newsmagazines," *Chicago Tribune*, 27 September 2004, section 5, p. 1.

[91] Steve McClellan and Dan Trigoboff, "Role Confusion in TV News," *Broadcasting & Cable*, 13 July 1998, p. 14.

[92] Jim Redmond, "Managing the Quality," *Communicator*, April 1997, p. 21.

[93] Sharon O'Malley, "Will Your Promos Land You in Court? Find out at 10!" *Communicator*, June 1998, pp. 24-30.

[94] Ibid., p. 30.

[95] Alicia Shepard, "To Err is Human, To Correct Divine," *American Journalism Review*, June 1998, p. 56.

To be fair, news directors don't necessarily go out of their way to keep reporters in the dark because they may be in the dark themselves. The NAB, for example, carefully guards the names of its Congressional friends and foes, grassroots lobbying subcontractors (who are exempt from the lobbyist disclosure laws), and lobbying kits. But many stations have at least one non-news employee with access to at least some of this information. Reporters could easily ask them for it or walk to their offices and look at it. When meeting with a manager, they could look around, see a large binder on the bookshelf called "NAB: Spectrum Auction Tool Kit," and ask some questions. But they choose not to. Similarly, the NAB library is open to member station employees, including Mike Wallace (CBS' 60 Minutes), Barbara Walters (ABC's 20/20), and Diane Sawyer (ABC's Primetime Live). But my observations of TV news indicate that it has never been used.

In sum, for those who work at local TV stations, from the general manager down to the lowliest reporter, the downside of exposing broadcast policy bias may be considerably greater than the upside.

The Audience for a Disclosure

The penalty from disclosure of an ethics violation is in part a function of the potential viewing public that learns about it. Let's assume, then, that some insider on the news side of a local TV station is willing to go public by spilling the beans on management's violation of journalistic ethics. The odds that a large fraction of local viewers will discover the violation are probably negligible unless management chooses to report it.

Most small media markets have only one daily newspaper and a couple of competing TV stations with news departments. It is simply not part of the professional norms of these media outlets to do investigative journalism of their peers. With the exception of a handful of major newspapers such as the *Washington Post* and *New York Times*, journalism criticism is not done. The media are not unique in their reticence to criticize colleagues and prospective employers; it's been found to be a problem with the enforcement of codes of ethics in hundreds of other professions. But without government enforcement, including licensing boards, legally enforceable disclosure mandates, and legally enforceable conflict of interest prohibitions—all of which have been considered abhorrent for the media on First Amendment grounds—professional self-enforcement takes on added importance.

Another reason that small market media may be less likely to report on each other is that they face minimal competition and can easily enforce mutually self-serving information cartels. A local media outlet that criticized another could make itself vulnerable to a similar expose, which would be to neither company's long-term advantage. This is a major reason why many professions explicitly discourage such criticism by the insiders most qualified to engage in it: it hurts everyone in the profession by damaging the public's esteem for the profession as a whole. A code of silence, except for egregious and obvious ethics violations, is in everyone's interest.

Even those most willing to engage in media criticism—the major popular journals of media criticism such as *the Columbia Journalism Review*, the *American Journalism Review*, and *Brill's Content* (now defunct)—devote the lion's share of their media criticism to large market and prestigious media. Mass market book and magazine publishers, too, are far more likely to publish an expose of the *New York Times* than *The Capital* (covering my hometown county of Anne Arundel, Maryland); and of CBS network news than the news of a local Baton Rouge TV station (in the district of Representative Billy Tauzin, Chair of the House Commerce Committee).

Lastly, a distinctive characteristic of industry media bias is that broadcast media have a common interest in this type of bias. Thus, even broadcast companies in fierce competition with each other would be hurting themselves as much as their competitors by doing an expose on this type of bias.

The same overlapping economic interests may exist for non-broadcast media. More than 50% of local daily newspapers in the top 100 markets are owned by companies with substantial broadcast interests (see Appendix B). Even a newspaper company with no such interests may have a strategic relationship with a local TV broadcaster, such as an agreement to share stories in exchange for publicity. And many broadcast issues, such as the sales tax exemption for advertising, are also newspaper issues (daily newspapers receive about 80% of their revenue from advertising; local broadcasting close to 100%).

All these overlapping economic interests create disincentives for competitors to do exposes of each other—regardless of the number of competitors in a given media market. Consequently, critics of local broadcast TV would be expected to be voices in the wilderness. The audiences that could, in theory, punish local broadcast TV for violating their own ethics claims are unlikely, in fact, ever to be exposed to those criticisms. A revealing if freakish illustration of the lack of transparency within the black box occurred on election night 2000. GE CEO Jack Welch was widely reported to have told his NBC news division to call the election in favor of George Bush. While being grilled during a Congressional hearing, NBC News President Andrew Lack promised to provide the Committee with a videotape of the disputed incident, if such a videotape existed. But, without denying it existed, he later refused to provide the tape.[96] What's remarkable about this incident is that the interaction between the business and news side may have been recorded in a verifiable record. Yet there was no outcry from the National Press Club, RTNDA, Society of Professional Journalists, or other media ethics organization to exploit this unusual situation. They could have requested that NBC voluntarily disclose the record, thus making itself journalistically accountable. Instead, one of them, the Society of Professional Journalists, denounced Rep. Waxman for threatening to subpoena the tapes. *Broadcasting & Cable* called the Waxman threat a "witch hunt" and didn't even acknowledge that the tapes might shed light on a serious breach of an NBC ethical claim.[97]

Penalty for an Exposure

Even if broadcast industry media bias could be discovered and verified by large numbers of potential viewers, it is unlikely that the penalties would be severe. Potential penalties fall into two major categories: government and market-place.

Government Penalties. The two most potent penalties government can impose on broadcasters are libel claims and loss of licensure. Libel is injury to reputation. News that injures a person's reputation may be grounds for a charge of libel. A common defense against libel charges in a court of law is that the news is accurate and fair.[98] But libel law, while exerting a huge influence on the news media, is nevertheless essentially irrelevant to the type of media bias under discussion here because political speech is the highest form of protected speech. Critiquing politicians is what the media is expected to do. And if the media sometimes gets some facts wrong—probably as a result of careless-ness—that is the price to be paid for living in a workable democracy.

A more potent weapon, applicable only to local radio and television broad-cast media, is for government to threaten to revoke a broadcast license. From the passage of the Communications Act of 1934 until today, broadcasters have been awarded licenses to use the public airwaves on condition that they do so in the public interest. Even today, the law still specifies that broadcasters are

---

[96] Doug Halonen, "NBC Fights Potential Subpoenas," *Electronic Media*, 13 August 2001, p. 1. Dough Halonen, "Waxman Pressured to Drop Tape Request: Media groups say ease up on NBC," *Electronic Media*, 10 September 2001, p. 8.

[97] "Don't Give Up The Tape," *Broadcasting & Cable*, 13 August 2001, p. 50.

[98] *The Associated Press Stylebook and Libel Manual*, New York: Addison-Wesley, 1996, p. 282.

public trustees. In the words of one FCC chairman, "[the broadcaster] is not free to maximize profits at the expense of the public interest," and "the essence of the Communications Act's public interest mandate is that broadcasting must be more than a business"[99]

The Supreme Court's *Red Lion Broadcasting Co. v. FCC* (395 U.S. 367) decision in 1969 provides a standard description of the broadcasters' public trustee responsibilities. The Communications Act of 1934 requires broadcasters to act in the public interest. *Red Lion* asserts that the "Fairness Doctrine" inheres in the public interest standard. The fairness doctrine stipulates that "Every licensee who is fortunate in obtaining a license is mandated to operate in the public interest and has assumed the obligation of presenting important public questions fairly and without bias."[100] Consistent with a principal-agent framework, the public interest is defined in terms of the local audience for a broadcast. The licensee is "to conduct himself as a proxy or fiduciary with obligations to present those views and voices which are representative of his community...."[101]

Red Lion acknowledges that the interests of the public and the interests of broadcasters may not be identical. When such a conflict of interest exists, the public interest must come first: "There is no sanctuary in the First Amendment for unlimited private censorship operating in a medium not open to all.... Congress need not stand idly by and permit those with licenses to...exclude from the airways anything but their own views of fundamental questions...."[102]

During the 1960s and 1970s, FCC proceedings reflected the widespread conviction that self-serving ownership influence on news content was not only bad but also should influence who could win, lose, or retain a broadcast license. In the Conglomerate Inquiry, the FCC was worried that if ITT, a large international conglomerate, took over ABC, one of the three major broadcast TV networks, it could adversely affect ABC's programming.

In its comments, ITT assured the FCC that after merging "ABC will operate as a substantially autonomous subsidiary.... [T]he broadcasting operations of ABC will be kept separate from other ITT operations, and the operations of

---

[99] Cited in Nicholas Johnson, *How to Talk Back to Your Television Set*, [1st] ed. (Boston: Little Brown, 1970), chapter 2.

[100] *Red Lion*, p. 7.

[101] Ibid., p. 9.

[102] Ibid., pp. 10-11

ABC as a licensee will be performed unaffected by commercial, communications, or other similar interests of ITT."[103]

In its ruling, the FCC emphasized the importance of these assurances:

> These assurances were reiterated and elaborated with emphasis. It was represented to the Commission...that the news department within ABC is substantially autonomous and is permitted to conduct its journalistic functions free of control or influence by advertisers or the commercial interests of ITT. The assurances and representations on this point were persuasive and we accept them as credible. The autonomy of the news department is also stated to mean that there has been and will be factual and objective reporting of news and discussion of public affairs, neither distorted nor influenced by the personal views of those in ABC outside the news department.... It demands eternal vigilance by all broadcast licenses and will receive our continuing scrutiny for any indication that our reliance upon the assurances and safeguards set out on this record was not warranted.[104]

The FCC then goes on to observe that the separation of programming from commercial influence is rigorously adhered to by broadcasters, not just in their news but in all their programming: "Fully recognizing this as the sine qua non of a reliable and healthy broadcast service, we, nevertheless, find in our experience with numbers of other licensees who encompass, along with broadcast interests, large and diversified non-broadcast activities, no indication of abuse of their public trust through the intrusion of their non-broadcast concerns upon the objectivity of their news reporting or commentary and no demonstrated detriment in any other programming sectors."[105]

Another FCC case concerned an attempt to prevent the renewal of Chronicle Broadcasting Company's San Francisco TV and radio licenses because of alleged ownership bias in reporting the news. The holdings of Chronicle Broadcasting's parent company, Chronicle Publishing Company, included the San Francisco Chronicle (the largest daily newspaper in San

---

[103] ITT letter to FCC on 25 July 1996, cited in FCC Memorandum Opinion and Order in the matter of *Applications By American Broadcasting Companies, Inc. for Assignment of Licenses...*, Docket 16828, 7 F.C.C. 2d 245, 9 Rad. Reg. 2d (P & F) 12 (1966), release number 66-1186, adopted 21 December 1966, p. 253.

[104] Ibid., p. 253. See also Bagdikian, *The Media Monopoly*, pp. 98-101.

[105] Ibid.

Francisco), KRON-TV (a San Francisco TV affiliate), KRON-FM (a San Francisco FM radio affiliate), and numerous cable systems in the San Francisco area. Chronicle Publishing wanted to acquire cable TV franchises in the greater San Francisco area. Mayors and other elected officials were typically instrumental in awarding these exclusive local cable TV monopolies. Two reporters of the Chronicle Broadcasting Company accused senior management of encouraging them to provide favorable TV coverage of elected officials in areas where the company wanted to win lucrative cable TV franchises. The FCC agreed that such bias would be grounds to revoke Chronicle Broadcasting's licenses. Specifically, it held a hearing to determine "Whether the licensee has used the facilities of Stations KRON-FM and KRON-TV to 'manage' or slant the news and public affairs for the purpose of advancing the interests of the Chronicle Publishing Co."[106] With tens of millions of dollars at stake, Chronicle Broadcasting vigorously disputed the case and even hired private detectives to track the two reporters and find evidence to discredit their testimony. After four years of legal maneuverings, including some 40 boxes of documents, an FCC Examiner ruled in favor of the Chronicle Publishing Company on May 3, 1973.[107] In the end, it was decided that there was no smoking gun to prove the allegation. The senior executives of Chronicle had put nothing in writing and made no public statements, so the reporters had no verifiable evidence to back their claims.[108]

The Chronicle Broadcasting case marks perhaps the acme of aggressive FCC enforcement of the Fairness Doctrine and broadcast policy media objectivity. Local TV broadcasters were given reason to fear that they could lose

---

[106] Chronicle Broadcasting Co., 40 F.C.C.2d, Docket 18500, 3 May 1973, p. 776.

[107] Ibid.

[108] A similar incident occurred in 2000 when *San Francisco Examiner* Timothy White offered San Francisco Mayor Willie Brown favorable editorial coverage in return for his support of the proposed merger of the *Examiner* and *Chronicle*. The two newspapers had a joint newspaper operating agreement, and Hearst wanted to buy out the larger newspaper. Thomas Leonard, "San Francisco Fiasco is a Textbook Case," *Columbia Journalism Review*, July 2000, p. 54. Rem Reider, "Hearst's Pursuit of Chronicle Takes Some Decidedly Unlovely Turns," *American Journalism Review*, June 2000, p. 6.

This incident, in turn, was similar to a letter a Hearst publisher wrote to President Nixon in 1971 seeking his support of the Newspaper Preservation Act (which made possible the Joint Operating Agreement between the *Examiner* and *Chronicle*) in return for endorsing his re-election bid. Both newspapers were owned by companies with broadcast properties. See Radio-TV Gallery, "Rules for Electronic Media Coverage of Congress," p. 13. Tim Redmond, "Tim White Takes the Fall," *San Francisco Bay Guardian*, 3 May 2000.

their licenses if they pursued ownership interests at the expense of the public. But by 1987, when the FCC revoked most provisions of the "Fairness Doctrine," this fear had all but disappeared. Today's FCC would never dream of conducting such an investigation; it treats a broadcast license as all-but-irrevocable. No financially solvent local TV broadcaster has lost his license for decades. For all practical purposes, government penalties for broadcast industry media bias no longer exist. The only relevant sanctions for this type of bias stem from the marketplace.

One additional type of penalty that I've never seen mentioned but is worthy of note are the rules of the Radio-TV Gallery in the House and Senate. Congress grants Radio and TV reporters many perks, including free office space and support staff on Capitol Hill. In return, they're supposed to act as reporters, not lobbyists. This is manifested in the Radio-TV Gallery rules, which state: "Rules of Congress prohibit Gallery members from engaging in lobbying, advertising, publicity, or promotion work for any individual, corporation, organization, or government."[109] One might therefore reasonably infer that lobbying on behalf of media organizations would warrant expulsion from the Radio-TV Gallery. But I don't believe that such an inference has ever been made. *Communicator* reports, for example, that RTNDA President Barbara Cochran "implores journalists to lobby against paparazzi legislation that could impede everyday newsgathering efforts."[110] Elsewhere, *Communicator* advises news directors to guard the electronic newsgathering spectrum, and closes with these words of wisdom: "A Congressional staffer has this advice for news directors and others in broadcasting who want to protect the ENG spectrum: 'Stay vigilant, do not let the matter rest,' he said. 'Keep on them like white on rice.'"[111] An aide to Representative Chris Shays, sponsor of a bill requiring broadcasters to provide free airtime to Congressional candidates, reports that "a local TV reporter was parked outside the office" during the peak of the battle with the broadcasters.[112] This was interpreted by the office as a form of lobbying. But it would be hard to disprove the local station's likely retort that the reporter was investigating a bona fide news story.

Marketplace Penalties. Broadcasters ceaselessly repeat the mantra that good journalism is good business, so there is no conflict between ethics and

---

[109] Kovach and Rosenstiel, *The Elements of Journalism.*

[110] "President's Column," *Communicator,* August 1998, p. 4.

[111] "Guarding the ENG Spectrum," *Communicator,* September 1997, p. 12.

[112] Interview with Diana Dwyer, 1 September 1998. See also David DuBuisson, "Editors as Lobbyists: Is it ethical to twist arms of legislators to win votes for a press bill?" *Nieman Reports,* Spring 1994, p. 92.

business. In the words of Barbara Cochran, President of RTNDA: "The most precious commodity any station or network has is its credibility with the public."[113]

TV broadcasters and other agents do indeed have a strong economic incentive to *appear* impartial. But it's a lot less clear that they always have a strong economic incentive to actually *be* impartial.

The public seeks to acquire news from sources it trusts. In our media system, this trust comes from being perceived as an impartial, balanced news source.[114] The appearance of bias, therefore, leads to reduced audiences and profits. As the *New York Times'* Craig Whitney explains, if you force an opinion on the pubic, "you risk losing the trust of people who hold differing views. We sell a million copies of this paper every day. You want people on both sides of the question to keep reading you and not feel that you're shading information one way or another."[115]

However, the most profitable situation would occur if an agent such as a broadcaster could appear to be impartial while in fact pursuing bias.[116] Thus, to the extent that the public cannot detect opportunistic behavior, we should doubt the assertion that good business leads to good journalistic ethics. But even if the public could easily detect such behavior, we may still doubt the claimed linkage between the pursuit of profits and ethical behavior. That is because deterring opportunistic behavior is a function of both disclosure and penalties. If the penalties of opportunistic behavior are sufficiently small and the benefits—such as rights to spectrum worth tens of billions of dollars—sufficiently large, then opportunistic behavior can be rational even when disclosed and penalized.

What type of marketplace penalty might a broadcaster expect for being caught engaging in industry policy media bias? A broadcaster's relationship with viewers is multi-faceted. The primary service broadcasters provide to viewers is entertainment programming. Of the various types of news provided

---

[113] Lou Prato, "Punishing the Ethically Challenged," *American Journalism Review*, September 1999, p. 86.

[114] Black et al., *Doing Ethics in Journalism*, Kovach and Rosenstiel, *The Elements of Journalism*, Schudson, *Discovering the News*.

[115] Quoted in Sparrow, *Uncertain Guardians: The News Media as a Political Institution*, p. 83.

[116] Recall that in our definition of bias what counts is not what the broadcaster may or may not think is the public interest; it's what the public (its audience) thinks. This addresses the methodological problem that a rational agent will never acknowledge that his and his principals' interests aren't identical.

by broadcasters, including weather, sports, crime, education, and politics, it is doubtful that information about broadcast policy or Congressional accountability is very important to most viewers. If broadcasters provide appealing entertainment programming and provide credible news 99.9% of the time, it would not be rational for a viewer to exact much of a penalty for imperfections in the remaining .1%. Given the multi-billion dollar subsidies and rights broadcasters secure from government, a little loss of credibility could be a reasonable tradeoff.

This loss of credibility takes two forms, depending on whether the loss of credibility is a "pooling" or "separating equilibrium." In a pooling equilibrium, the viewer knows that a fraction of information about something is biased but doesn't know which. The result is that the credibility of the source is averaged across all the information it provides. This averaging may pertain to a large category such as "all news" or it may refer to a smaller but still expansive category such as "coverage of candidates for federal office."

In a "separating equilibrium," the audience can detect the specific bias and ignore that particular information while accepting the rest. We should expect separating equilibrium to be rare because there is no point in trying to exert bias if it can be detected. So through a sort of natural selection, this equilibrium should be eliminated. Nevertheless, for argument's sake, let's suppose the public detects a specific case of industry policy media bias. Unless it has good reason to believe that the bias is just the tip of the iceberg—and we have argued in Chapter 2 that that would be a faulty inference because the incentives for industry bias are much greater than for cross-industry bias—it should rationally just discard the narrow type of news involved and accept the rest. In other words, the market penalty for industry policy media bias should be slight.

People, of course, make these rational decisions all the time. No relationship with an individual or organization is perfect. No friend is perfect. No spouse is perfect. No employer is perfect. And the defects in these intimate relationships are often perfectly clear. Nevertheless, people make a decision that the good outweighs the bad. In the case of the broadcasters, the bad from an individual viewer's standpoint is not that the broadcasters may be getting a huge public windfall and greatly damaging the information economy; it is simply that a tiny (and probably boring)[117] fraction of media content may not consist of completely reliable information.

---

[117] Audience surveys indicate that the public appetite for public policy and candidate information is negligible, which is reflected in the negligible amount of time most local TV stations devote to it. See Barry Cole and Mal Oettinger, "Covering the Politics of Broadcasting," *Columbia Journalism Review*, April 1977, p. 60.

The 1990s Russian media offer a vivid example of the small penalties pragmatic audiences exert for narrow types of media bias. During the 1990s, the so-called business oligarchs provided more credible news in Russia than their competition, the media outlets still under state control. The Russian public widely understood that the oligarchs would and did slant the news in favor of their individual company business interests. But this involved only a tiny percentage of the news, and it was a small price to pay for the generally superior news coverage compared to the state controlled media.

Strong evidence of widespread pooling mechanisms in the U.S. are the surveys of public opinion that indicate the public believes broadcast programming is frequently influenced by advertisers. According to a survey sponsored by the Radio-Television News Directors Foundation, a large majority (84%) of the public believes that advertisers often (51%) or sometimes (33%) improperly influence the news.[118] The problem for the public is that it can much more readily intuit improper influence than know exactly when it occurs. And when specific evidence does become public, such as news media reports that a TV station in Chattanooga offered local businesses favorable news coverage in exchange for a fee, the offenders quickly proclaim that the specific activity will never happen again.[119]

To the extent that the type of bias an audience detects is wide ranging, the analysis above does not apply. A broadcaster with a reputation for being an ultraconservative or liberal, for example, would probably alienate a large fraction of the audience it could have otherwise attracted. But our analysis of the marketplace penalty of bias strictly relates to a narrow form of bias—industry policy media bias.

Conclusion

An astute legislator who grasps the incentives facing local TV stations could reasonably infer that the probability is slight of both 1) widespread disclosure of a given case of industry media bias, and 2) a substantial penalty for such disclosure. When the costs of such bias are matched against a prospective multibillion dollar payoff, a reasonable legislator might anticipate that the probability of at least one broadcaster in his political district exercising such bias is not only greater than zero but potentially much greater than zero.

---

[118] Barbara Cochran, "Not For Sale at Any Price," *Communicator*, September 1999, p. 31.
[119] Ibid.

Considering the political resources available to local broadcasters, this would be a daunting prospect.

CHAPTER 14:

The Argument From Example:
The Cable Act of 1992

"When it came to donating to Congressional campaigns, NAB Executive Vice President Jim May said broadcasters had long viewed themselves in the same league as newspapers. 'That somehow we were above it.' But faced with cable's growth and its significant capture of advertising revenues, the broadcasters became more sophisticated in lobbying Congress—and more generous with candidates."

—Mike Mills, *Congressional Quarterly Weekly Report*, 1992[1]

"[NAB has an] active membership, unlike that enjoyed by any other industry."

—NAB President Eddie Fritts to NAB Board, 1994[2]

The broadcasters' two largest grassroots political campaigns during the first half of the 1990s involved the legislation leading up to the Cable Television Consumer Protection and Competition Act of 1992 (P.L. 102-385; "Cable Act of 1992") and the Telecommunications Act of 1996 (P.L. 104-104; "Telecom Act of 1996"). Both cases illustrate broadcasters' willingness to use all the resources at their disposal, including media resources, to engage in information bias when given a sufficiently strong economic incentive to do so.

---

[1] Mike Mills, "Media Groups Try Paying Way to a Favorable Cable Bill," *Congressional Quarterly Weekly Report*, 30 May 1992.
[2] Cited in"NAB Board Hits GATT Spectrum Fee," *Television Digest*, 13 June 1994, p. 4. In the same article, NAB Joint Board Chairman Wayne Vriesman, from Tribune Broadcasting, described the NAB's role as to "lead the charge to fire the passion in the industry to become involved in the political process." See also Bill McConnell, "The Fritts Years," *Broadcasting & Cable*, 21 March 2005, pp. 32-41.

In the Cable Act of 1992, broadcasters won rights to cable must-carry, retransmission consent, and preferred channel positioning—rights worth billions of dollars—that forced competing telecommunications providers to give up substantial negotiating power in transactions with broadcasters. Must-carry requires competing broadband telecommunications providers to carry all local TV broadcast channels at no charge. Retransmission consent requires these competitors to pay the market rate for broadcast programming. The combination of must-carry and retransmission consent allows broadcasters to get free carriage of unpopular channels and compensated coverage of popular channels. Preferred channel positioning requires competitors to give broadcast stations preferred locations on the TV dial. Regulations also mandate that cable TV providers require viewers to purchase broadcast programming (the "basic" tier of services) before they can purchase any other competing programming. It is illegal in the United States, for example, to purchase C-SPAN or the Discovery Channel without having first purchased every local broadcast TV channel, including local broadcast TV home shopping and religious channels.

As described in Chapters 8 and 12, in the Telecom Act of 1996, broadcasters won spectrum flexibility on their permanent 6 MHz channel and an additional 6 MHz of spectrum to complement their existing 6 MHz. Spectrum flexibility allowed broadcasters to replace their single standard definition analog programming stream with as many digital programming streams and other data that can be fit into a 19.4 mbps data stream. With mid-1990s digital technology, 4 to 5 standard definition or 1 high definition program streams could fit in that 19.4 mbps data stream. With 2004 video technology, three to four times that number of standard or high definition program streams could fit in that same 6 MHz channel. The "loan" of a second 6 MHz of spectrum to facilitate the broadcasters' DTV transition included no interest payment, fixed date of return, or clear specification of what exactly would be returned.

Broadcasters were also essentially allowed to abandon the free TV business, which had always been bedrock to their public interest claims. As long as they provided one ad-supported ("free") standard definition TV channel, broadcasters could use their remaining spectrum for whatever they wanted, including fee-based information services.

Perhaps the major political difference between the Cable Act and the Telecom Act was their level of visibility prior to passage. The Cable Act involved the broadcasters publicly fighting with the cable TV industry prior to passage, whereas the Telecom Act involved the broadcasters negotiating with their competitors out of the public eye. With the Cable Act, the broadcasters could piggyback on a highly popular issue: the cable monopoly's rapidly rising prices and poor service. With the Telecom Act, piggybacking on its theme of deregulation and competition was much harder because the leading intellectuals favoring telecom deregulation and competition wanted spectrum auctions, not a give-away of spectrum to broadcasters. The Republicans who controlled the House and Senate were selling the Telecom Act as a way to rid the country of just the type of industrial policy the broadcasters were seeking. Consistent with this publicly espoused agenda, the Act's first sentence stated its purpose as "To promote competition and reduce regulation in order to secure lower prices and higher quality services for American telecommunications consumers and encourage the rapid deployment of new telecommunications technologies" (P.L. 104-104).

The Timing of the Cable Act of 1992

The timing of the broadcasters' lobbying over the Cable Act of 1992 is note-worthy in part because it was the broadcasters' first major political campaign after the FCC's 1987 repeal of the Fairness Doctrine, including the Cullman Doctrine. Many of the actions local broadcasters took, such as running count-less one-sided public service announcements in favor of free TV, would have been unthinkable under the Fairness Doctrine.[3]

The Fairness Doctrine required broadcasters to present programming on "controversial issues of public importance" in their communities, and to provide reasonable opportunity for presentation of contrasting views. The Fairness Doctrine also included the Cullman Doctrine, which applied the Fairness Doctrine to issue advertising (such as ads for or against free TV).

The Cable Act of 1992 was the first massive political campaign under the auspices of NAB President Eddie Fritts and Government Affairs Chief Jim May. In the late 1970s and early 1980s, the broadcast industry suffered a series of political and economic setbacks in relation to the rapidly growing cable industry. Previously, TV broadcasters had a monopoly on TV. Now, for the first

---

[3] In 1973, during the Congressional hearings over whether cable TV would be allowed to compete with local broadcasters, a local broadcaster publicly complained about the "meek silence" of the TV networks that cover national news for the local stations. NBC President Julian Goodman explained the silence: "Most issues of concern about TV are controversial, in the sense that there are opposing views about them. To the extent that we used our facil-ities to argue our own case, we would be required under the fairness doctrine to give a free national platform to our detractors—one they would certainly exploit—and I don't think that would advance the cause in which we all believe...." See Norman Black, "Senator Abandoning Amendment Effort," *Associated Press*, 13 April 1983.

time in their history, they faced what was perceived as life-or-death competition from another type of TV provider.

In response, broadcast leaders wanted the NAB to orchestrate a much more aggressive lobbying strategy and hired Eddie Fritts as president in 1982 to pursue that mission. When Bob Packwood, Chair of the Senate Commerce Committee told broadcast industry leaders that they couldn't lobby their way out of "a wet paper bag,"[4] this became the lobbying cry of the NAB Board: to "begin our fight out of 'a wet paper bag.'"[5] In 1988, after longtime NAB government affairs chief John Summers retired, Fritts hired Jim May to carry out this agenda. The Cable Act of 1992 was the bill on which Jim May made his formidable reputation within the broadcasting community.

As late as December 1987, Representative Tom Tauke, a member of the House Telecommunications Committee with jurisdiction over broadcasting issues, could write to NAB members:

> [T]he typical broadcaster does not communicate with members of Congress. A random sample of my colleagues confirms my own experience with broadcasters. First, members of Congress know the news personnel who work for broadcast outlets in their districts, but they do not know the station owners or managers. Second, members receive very little, if any, communication from their own broadcasters on legislative issues.
>
> As a member of the Telecommunications Subcommittee and a "friend" of the broadcast industry, most observers assume that I hear often from the broadcasters in my district. In fact, our records show that I have received oral or written communications on broadcast issues from only three station owners and managers in my district throughout all of 1987. And although there are 22 broadcast stations in the district, I know only five station owners or managers on a first-name basis.
>
> In contrast with insurance agents, hospital administrators, physicians, bankers, outdoor advertisers, truckers, manufacturers, farmers,

---

[4] "Groups That Don't Cut the Mustard in the Washington Lobbying World," *National Journal*, 4 July 1987.

[5] Summary of June 2003 NAB Board Meeting from NAB's 1984 TARPAC kit.

or newspaper publishers—broadcasters simply do not participate effectively in the legislative process.[6]

The Cable Act was also the broadcasters' last major grassroots lobbying campaign prior to their other life-or-death struggle, which began in earnest in 1994, over the spectrum clauses that would be included in the Telecom Act of 1996. Lobbying over the Cable Act demonstrated to members of Congress what the broadcasters were capable of, and they could expect a repeat performance if they didn't give the broadcasters what they wanted.

Chronology of Key Events

In the following chronological account of the grassroots lobbying leading up to the Cable Act of 1992, I generally try to let the documents speak for themselves and leave their interpretation to the reader. Most of the documents come from internal NAB correspondence to its member local TV stations. There is a presumption here that those exhortations had an effect and were in fact stimulated and authorized by the local broadcasters who dominate the NAB board of directors and are periodically elected by NAB members as their representatives.

I have included two types of information: First, any broadcaster lobbying activity that involved the use of the airwaves as a resource. Use of the airwaves includes hard news, soft news, ads, and public service announcements. Second, I describe conventional lobbying behavior that provides information about a broadcaster's motivation, knowledge, and propensity to engage in opportunistic behavior. Politicians and TV viewing audiences may not be as fastidious as political communication scholars in drawing distinctions between media and non-media lobbying.

I have highlighted certain passages by putting them in **bold type**. Comments in *italics* provide context for the chronological entries. All capitalized text, as in "FREE TELEVISION," is copied exactly as found in the original documents.

---

[6] Tom Tauke, "Congressmen Don't Get Smarter on Election Day, You Know," December 1987. Tom Tauke is currently the head of Government Relations for Verizon Communications, the largest telecommunications company in the United States. He was a member of the U.S. House of Representatives from 1979 to 1991, when he unsuccessfully ran for the U.S. Senate.

August 4, 1987. The FCC revokes the Fairness Doctrine. The Fairness Doctrine provided legal grounds for the FCC to terminate a broadcaster's license if it used the public airwaves to pursue ownership interests at the expense of the public. The importance of the Fairness Doctrine to members of Congress is illustrated by the fact that both the House and Senate voted overwhelmingly in both 1987 and 1989 to overturn the FCC decision and codify the Fairness Doctrine in legislation. Only two presidential vetoes prevented Congress from reinstating the Fairness Doctrine.[7]

December 11, 1987. The U.S. Appeals Court in Washington D.C. unanimously rules that the FCC's must-carry rules are unconstitutional and refuses to remand the issue back to the FCC. Broadcasters perceive this to be a major economic blow and consider a Congressional remedy.

March 14, 1988. NAB President/CEO Eddie Fritts hires Jim May as Executive Vice President/Government Relations. A former marine captain and son of a six-term Congresswoman, May previously held senior government affairs positions at Coca Cola, Pepsi, and the Grocery Manufacturers of America.[8] May's department will prod local TV station managers to pursue much more aggressive lobbying tactics. In reading hundreds of pages of written marching orders from NAB to local TV station managers alerting them to this new, more aggressive lobbying style, I am unable to find any advice that lobbying activities should be tempered by "journalistic ethics." When May leaves the NAB in 2003, Eddie Fritts congratulates him with the following words: "Under Jim's leadership, NAB government relations became a catalyst for energizing our grassroots membership, and NAB is regarded as one of the most effective lobbying operations in Washington."[9] Well-trained by the marines, May is a master of psychological warfare. One local TV station manager described the NAB's tactics under Fritts and May as akin to Lawrence of Arabia's military tactics. Lawrence of Arabia frequently used surprise and deception to attack the Ottomans in ways that left the Ottomans practically

---

[7] The NAB continued to lobby against reinstatement of the Fairness Doctrine through the 104th Congress. For example, see NAB Legislative Issue Papers, August 1992, February 1994, and April 1996. The grassroots talking points in the April 1996 issue of NAB's Legislative Issue Papers, asserts: "The experience of the past six years since the doctrine was lifted also shows that broadcasters do provide coverage of both sides of controversial issues, and the doctrine is not needed."

[8] "Jim May: NAB's Washington Insider," *Broadcasting & Cable*, 1 May 1989, p. 159.

[9] Bill McConnell, "NAB Seeks New Lobbyist as May Flies to ATA, "*Broadcasting & Cable*, 15 January 2003, p. 14.

defenseless. An example would be anonymously cutting vital supply lines (train tracks) at night or in the middle of a desert.

Consider how *National Journal*, a highly respected magazine of Washington, DC politics, changed its coverage of the NAB between 1987, when May took over, to 2003, when May left. In a 1987 article with the title "Groups That Don't Cut the Mustard in the Washington Lobbying World," it wrote:

> **National Association of Broadcasters (NAB).** If you've been pervasively regulated, "you tend to be a wimp." That's a telecommunications consultant's explanation of why the American Newspaper Publishers Association lobbies effectively and the NAB doesn't; broadcasters, unlike publishers, don't menace Members with the prospect of nasty editorials. They negotiate badly—they give too much away—and have proved "woefully poor in meeting [the industry's legislative; *sic*] objectives," the consultant said.
>
> They're held in low repute on Capitol Hill.... "They don't seem to be around much," said a Democratic Member from a committee that handles NAB issues. A Republican aide added, "For people who do 30-second editorials, they don't get their point across very well."[10]

By 2003, *National Journal*'s description of the NAB had changed dramatically:

> In the Washington lobbying world, the NAB's roll call of victories is legendary.... Part of the NAB's clout stems from money.... Another key to success is Fritts, who receives just over $1 million a year in salary and compensation.... By themselves, these factors don't explain the NAB's clout. In fact, according to PoliticalMoneyLine, the NAB ranked only 155th on the 2002 list of biggest PACs.... Rather, the NAB's biggest asset over the years has been the individual sway that its local broadcasting executives have over members of Congress. The NAB works overtime to bring station executives to Washington, and then it makes sure they meet up again when members of Congress return home. "Obviously, the broadcasters report the news, so I think most people in elective politics listen to them," said former Rep. Henson Moore, R-La., who's now president and CEO of the American Forest & Paper Association.[11]

---

[10] Louis Jacobson and Bara Vaida, "Lobbying—Broadcast Blues," *National Journal*, 9 August 2003.

[11] Sue Gorisek, "The Forbes Four Hundred: The up & Comers," *Forbes*, 28 October 1985.

April 11, 1988. At NAB's annual convention, broadcast industry leaders gather under the auspices of Milton Maltz to discuss developing a campaign to promote Free TV. Maltz, ranked by *Forbes* magazine as one of the wealthiest men in America,[12] is appointed chair of the Free TV task force. In addition to a large group of radio stations, Maltz owns four TV stations whose value has been greatly diminished by the court's must-carry ruling. The free television task force will eventually include representatives from the leading TV groups, including ABC, CBS, NBC, Fox, Post-Newsweek Stations, Group W, and Tribune Broadcasting. Maltz, a former employee of the National Security Agency, is a highly secretive man, and will later found the International Spy Museum in Washington, DC,[13] which markets itself with the phrase "All is not what it seems."[14] His small, private TV station group, excluding his chain of radio stations, will sell in 1998 for an undisclosed amount but estimated by *Broadcasting & Cable* magazine to be "as much as $1 billion."[15]

April 29, 1988. Representative Ed Markey, Chair of the House Telecommunications Subcommittee, writes a letter to the General Accounting Office (GAO) requesting it conduct a nationwide survey of cable television rates and services.

May 11, 1988. NAB President/CEO Eddie Fritts testifies before the House Telecommunications Subcommittee that must-carry is vital to consumers. He contends that it is possible to implement constitutionally sound must-carry rules.[16]

May 16, 1988. NAB releases a study prepared for NAB by University of Denver's Dr. Michael Wirth. According to NAB TV Board Chairman Ben McKeel, "This report conclusively shows that without federal regulation, cable TV is well on its way to becoming a monopoly and will have free reign to determine what the nation's viewers will be allowed to see."[17]

---

[12] "High Priced Malrite," *Broadcasting & Cable*, 13 April 1998.

[13] Manny Fernandez, "For New Museum, A Covert Crowd," *Washington Post*, 20 July 2002, p. B5.

[14] Animated introduction to the website at http://www.spymuseum.org on 21 January 2005.

[15]Cynthia Littleton, "Raycom Lands Malrite," *Daily Variety*, 7 April 1998. Another trade publication estimated a minimum of $500 million. See Roberto Santiago, "Malrite/Shamrock Update," *Plain Dealer*, 6 May 1993. His radio station group, 14th largest in the country, sold for close to $200 million in 1993. See Shepard, "Take the Money and Talk," p. 18.

[16] *TV Today*, 16 May 1988.

[17] *Ibid.*.

June 6, 1988. The U.S. Supreme Court decides not to review the appeals court's December 1987 ruling that the FCC's must-carry rules are unconstitutional. According to *TV Today*, "NAB immediately expressed 'disappointment' at the High Court action, but pledged to seek restoration of must-carry through Congress."[18]

June 8, 1988. At the monthly meeting of the broadcast industry's Washington lobbyists, Representative Markey, Chair of the House Telecommunications Subcommittee, expresses sympathy for the broadcasters' must-carry agenda.[19]

Week of July 11, 1988. NAB files comments with the FCC alleging abuses by cable companies in the absence of must-carry.[20]

October 25, 1988. NAB President Fritts tells his members that next year's top legislative priority for TV broadcasters will be "must-carry rules." He continues: "However, top priority for Congress will be fairness doctrine codification."[21]

December 5, 1988. NAB reminds general managers that cable TV rate hikes are boosting inflation as measured by the Consumer Price Index: "Big increases in cable TV fees and other commodities helped push the Consumer Price Index (CPI) up .4% in October. It was the 7th consecutive month the CPI rose by at least .3%."[22] *The NAB, like national political candidates, often conducts research to determine the best way to frame issues for political campaigns. TV managers had no intrinsic interest in cable rates, but over the next 34 months the charge that cable rate hikes were increasing faster than the rate of inflation— and indeed were contributing to inflation—will become a centerpiece of the broadcasters' political campaign, including news reports.*

April 29, 1989. At the NAB's 1989 annual convention, NAB Joint Board Chairman Wally Jorgenson says that "To meet the Association's goal of 'making NAB's Government Relations Department the best in Washington,' NAB has made sweeping changes, including: new leadership, staff additions, a doubling of the government relations budget, and an increased commitment to lobbying."[23]

April 30, 1989. At the same convention, Milton Maltz, Chair of the NAB's free television task force, officially announces NAB's plans for a national

---

[18] *TV Today*, 6 June 1988.

[19] *TV Today*, 13 Jun 1988.

[20] *TV Today*, 18 July 1988.

[21] *TV Today*, 31 October 1988.

[22] *TV Today*, 5 December 1988

[23] *TV Today*, 1 May 1989.

campaign to promote free-over-the-air television. At the TV luncheon announcing the launch, Maltz says:

> Increasingly, cable and VCR's are siphoning programming away from FREE TELEVISION; other technologies threaten to accelerate the trend. The ultimate result is not more choice or variety for the American people. Instead, they will be expected to pay for what they once got for free through the American system of broadcast television....
>
> FREE TELEVISION lights up the hearts and minds of millions of Americans every day. FREE TV lightens the burdens of millions of our citizens with the best in entertainment. FREE TV enlightens the minds of Americans with information and news....
>
> We must act now...before the course of events overtakes us. Broadcasters must make the American public aware of the danger facing our institution of FREE TV. It is time for the greatest marketers in the world—TV broadcasters...to start telling this story...selling the benefits of FREE TELEVISION.[24]

May 22, 1989. NAB sends to all TV station general managers an 8-page brochure on its upcoming "Free TV" campaign (*TV Today*, May 22, 1989).

June 5, 1989. NAB sends a startup kit of Free TV campaign materials to every TV station general manager in the country. The kit includes an 11-page local marketing plan; 2 story boards for "Free TV" public service announcements (PSAs), sample print ads, press clips, and other miscellaneous items. The marketing plan includes the following on-air tips:

> Produce :10, :30, :60 image/awareness **spots for radio and television**....
>
> .... Spokespersons from the **public service campaigns served by your station** will be glad to lend their endorsements....
>
> ...the kick-off of your campaign and other special events are all **opportunities for editorializing** during the campaign....
>
> .... Don't forget to **have your anchors close your evening news with:** "This is WXXX, Your Free Television Station, saying Good Evening."
>
> **Produce news stories** that historically show the significant role FREE TELEVISION has played in your community....

---

[24] Included in "The Free Television Campaign Kit," 5 June 1989.

July 3, 1989. New NAB TV Board Chairman Tom Goodgame says that must-carry and retransmission consent are NAB's top legislative/regulatory priority. NAB President/CEO Eddie Fritts explains to members: "If we are to see [local broadcast stations] offer continually expanded services, Congress must take steps to ensure that cable operators carry local broadcast signals on acceptable channels. If not, viewers will be unfairly steered from 'free TV' to 'fee TV.'"[25] Stations are asked to provide local support and join with other stations in their markets to set up local TV associations in a unified effort. NAB is coordinating the campaign, which is joined by the TV networks, the Association of Local Television Stations (then called INTV), and the Television Bureau of Advertising. The campaign is designed to alert Americans to the fact that free TV is being eroded by cable and other pay TV interests.[26]

July 8, 1989. NBC President Robert Wright blasts a Congressional proposal to reallocate some of the broadcasters' spectrum for mobile telephone service instead of HDTV. In a brilliant twist of logic, he manages to use the charge of broadcaster bias as an attack against incumbent members of Congress. The comment is intended to characterize the general political relationship between Congress and broadcasters.

> As National Broadcasting Co. president Robert C. Wright sees it, Congress has a love-hate relationship with the broadcast industry. "They like the fact that there are broadcast newscasts around the country which give Congress tremendous exposure and favor incumbents," he observed.... But they hate that families or groups got spectrum [licenses] years ago for free and then built up wealth and power through this government gift."[27]

July 17, 1989. This day marks the public launch date for the TV Industry's 'Free TV' Campaign. At the start of their prime time schedule, **local TV stations air a special 30-second message by Walter Cronkite, often hailed as** America's most trusted TV news reporter:

> What you are watching is called Free Television. It's part of a system—born 50 years ago—that is unlike any other in the world. Through your Free TV window, you've been witness to triumph and tragedy...to love, and laughter, learning life. It's offered free to all,

---

[25] *TV Today*, 3 July 1989.

[26] Ibid.

[27] Margaret E. Kriz, "The Fight for Access," *National Journal*, 8 July 1989, p. 1732.

even the cable systems that carry it. Imagine the impact if it were gone. Join us in the coming months, as we celebrate and stand watch, over Free TV.[28]

TV Today later reports: "Virtually all of the nation's 1,071 commercial TV stations joined together last Monday [July 17th] to launch a national campaign to promote free, over-the-air television with a prime time announcement featuring Walter Cronkite. Based on Nielsen's national overnight ratings, approximately 54 million viewers saw the launch spot."[29] **NAB describes the Cronkite spot as "a national prime-time roadblock."[30]** *This is a remarkable development because in 1986, only three years earlier, the NAB surveyed TV stations and found that only 20.5% ran political issue ads.[31] Either TV stations were now making an exception for their own political issue ads, or their policies had rapidly changed with the decline of the Fairness Doctrine and the new lobbying regime promoted by Fritts and May.*

NAB sends a "FREE TV Packet" to every member of Congress telling them about the FREE TELEVISION industry-wide campaign and the importance of FREE TELEVISION to American society.[32] Members are asked to watch the Cronkite spot and to expect additional information throughout the year. The packet includes statistics gathered by Roper (and paid for by NAB) on "how FREE TELEVISION continues to help shape American public opinion and provide fast-breaking news."[33] NAB *lobbying campaigns in the early 1980s for broadcast deregulation and in 1995 for spectrum flexibility included statistics reminding members of Congress that local broadcasters are not only local news providers, but also the country's most influential local news providers. This was a subtle reminder of broadcasters' potential political power, should they choose to use it.*

NAB also sends *Free Television Monitor*'s "Stage 1—Beginning a Local Campaign" to all TV station general managers." The checklist for developing a free television task force includes the following items: "Be prepared to offer the use of your facility," and "**Make sure your staff understands your local campaign and the overall industry-wide effort.**"[34] On-air suggestions include:

---

[28] *TV Today*, 24 July 1989.

[29] *Ibid*.

[30] *Free Television Monitor*, 31 July 1989.

[31] National Research Inc., "Political Airtime '86" (Washington, DC: NAB, 1987).

[32] The use of all capital letters for "FREE TV" and other words the NAB sought to emphasize are copied here exactly as in the original cited documents.

[33] *Free Television Monitor*, 31 July 1989.

[34] *Free Television Monitor*, 24 July 1989.

"**Produce an image spot** which reflects how well your station has served the American public over the years," and "Don't forget to **close your evening news with,** "This is WXXX, your FREE TELEVISION station." A testimonial from Robert F. Kalthoff, President of Granite Broadcasting, says: "The FREE TELE-VISION Campaign is something we must do to secure our future. **We're devoting 100+ efforts during the local evening news** and will run the spots multiple times daily."[35]

July 31, 1989. "Stage II—Campaign Implementation," includes the following advice:[36]

> "Produce local man-on-the-street testimonials. Use this same concept with school, government and civic leaders. Spokespersons from **the public service campaigns served by your station** will be glad to lend their endorsements."

> "**Air news stories** which reflect the significant role FREE TELEVI-SION has played in your community."

> "Request a local business club to host a "TV Day" Luncheon...."

> "Ask your mayor to declare a 'City TV Day.' Join forces with the other stations in your community to organize a special community event.... Create a festive occasion by bringing in sports and entertainment celebrities.... Invite the mayor to present the City Free Television Day Proclamation. **Remember to tape this event for the evening news.**"

> "Be visible in all walks of your community. Community outreach is as important as the air time devoted to your campaign. **Your staff and talent should be involved and committed to this industry endeavor.**"

August 3, 1989. The U.S. General Accounting Office releases its first survey of cable television rates and services. The survey, requested by Representative Markey, shows that the cost of cable is increasing faster than the inflation rate.

August 7, 1989. "Stage III—Campaign Implementation," includes the following advice: "Write letters to your members of Congress about the importance of FREE TELEVISION to your viewing area...and urge them to support legislation which can benefit the FREE TELEVISION industry.... **If any of your members serve on key Congressional committees which address broad-**

---

[35] *Ibid.*
[36] *Free Television Monitor,* 31 July 1989.

casting issues, do a special interview program with them about some of the issues facing the industry."[37]

John Spinola, the general manager of WBZ-TV in Boston, Massachusetts, offers this testimonial: "The FREE TELEVISION Campaign is long overdue. Up until now, our industry has gone about our business too quietly. We haven't taken advantage of our own media to tell the public about what we do."[38]

August 14, 1989. NAB distributes the following broadcaster testimonials:

> John Shine, General Manager of KIMT-TV, Mason City, Iowa: "All three television stations in this market (Rochester, Austin, Mason City) jumped right into this very important campaign. We have **produced spots** together **using local anchors**, network programs." *During the Iowa Caucuses in the 1996 presidential election, Shine will deliver a crucial threat to Senator Bob Dole, described in the next chapter, which helps the broadcasters secure tens of billions of dollars worth of spectrum rights.*

> LeBon Abercrombie, General Manager of KMPH-TV, Fresno, California: "**If we can get our viewers to understand** and appreciate that the availability of FREE TELEVISION is a social issue, as well as an economic benefit, we will have accomplished the most important goal of this campaign."

> Brady Dreasler, Operations Manager of WGEM-TV, Quincy, Illinois: "As part of its effort to **saturate the market with the concept of FREE TELEVISION**, WGEM will use the free television music and logo in all local PSAs."

> Jim Girodo, VP of KUSA-TV, Denver, Colorado: "The Free TV Campaign is very important.... **To support this initiative, KUSA has committed a minimum of 100 GRP's per week** since the campaign's kickoff (July 17). This fall, we will create several commercials supporting FREE TV by **utilizing local news and station personalities.**"

> Janet Anderson, KAAL-TV, Austin, Minnesota: "KAAL-TV is airing two :30 FREE TELEVISION spots which were produced in cooperation with KTTC-TV and KIMI-TV. In addition, we are utilizing the Walter Cronkite :30 announcement. **We anticipate producing a news**

---

[37] *Free Television Monitor,* 7 August 1989.
[38] *Ibid.*

series which will explain the campaign in greater detail to our viewers."

John Radeck, Owner of KTVH-TV, Helena, Montana: "KTVH-TV produced FREE TELEVISION spots which feature our news personalities. This creative approach allows our news talent to highlight special events and stories. The spots are changed monthly to keep the campaign fresh and alive. These spots, along with the Walter Cronkite spot, air in all day parts approximately 10 times per day. We also anticipate producing testimonial spots which feature our community's civic leaders."

Gene Hines, Promotions Manager of WREX-TV, Rockford, Illinois: "WREX-TV is airing seven FREE TELEVISION :30 spots, including the Cronkite spot which kicked off the campaign. Using the FREE TELEVISION logo package, spots feature WREX's current program lineup and news anchors."

September 11, 1989. An NAB survey finds that "nearly 70% of responding stations initiated local on-air 'Free TV' campaigns."[39] In other news, the NAB tells its members that the "Community Antenna Television Association (CATA) will launch a grassroots campaign opposing NAB's 'Free TV' Campaign. The CATA campaign will dispute the fact that broadcast television is really 'free,' while claiming that it 'costs consumers' an average of $297 per year in built-in advertising costs.... According to CATA, the campaign is designed to 'inform' editors and publishers of cable's side of the issue."[40] *CATA represents only small cable TV operators whose interests sometimes differ from the large cable TV operators. The National Cable Television Association (NCTA) is the umbrella trade association representing the common interests of both small and large cable TV operators.*

October 2, 1989. An NAB telephone survey of 100 randomly selected general managers finds that 68% of those responding have initiated "local, on-air campaigns to promote free over-the-air television.... On-air examples included: incorporating the free TV logo with station IDs; discussing cable versus free TV on talk shows; news coverage; and news interviews." The survey was conducted for NAB by National Research, Inc. of Chevy Chase, Maryland. Sample comments from general managers include:

---

[39] *TV Today*, 11 September 1989.
[40] Ibid.

"We have committed a fixed schedule to run and air the spots for the next five weeks—all local spots."

"A regular station promo each day. We'll localize some footage using the free TV logo and use it with Oprah, sports, movies and news."

"We're currently promoting free TV locally. When we ID our station we're saying, 'Support free TV.'"

"We are a small station in a rural area. We have taken a very tenacious position in support of the free TV campaign."[41]

October 25, 1989. Testifying before the Senate Communications Subcommittee, NAB President Fritts says: "Under no circumstances should the 101st Congress adjourn without passage of must-carry and channel positioning legislation."[42]

First week of December, 1989. The Free TV Task Force sends an information kit about the planned January 1990 FREE TELEVISION MONTH. The kit includes: the FREE TELEVISION MONTH Action Plan, a two-page free television brochure, and the story boards for three free TV PSAs called "Rabbit Ears," "Spelling Bee," and "Gramma's House." In the personal letter accompanying the kit, Milton Maltz starts: "Dear Fellow Broadcaster: January has been designated as FREE TELEVISION MONTH. Our objective is clear cut: establish the difference between FREE TELEVISION and cable."

The action plan includes the following general instructions:

Air PSAs…that focus on the benefits of free, over-the-air television.

Distribute the Free Television Brochure…. Make sure all staff members are familiar with the brochure.

Contact your member of Congress. FREE TELEVISION MONTH provides an excellent opportunity to lobby your Members of Congress about the importance of over-the-air television to their constituents.

Plan a Community Outreach Activity. Community outreach is as important as the air time. Your staff and talent should be involved and committed to FREE TELEVISION MONTH.

The advice for contacting your member of Congress includes the following specific instructions:

---

[41] *Free Television Monitor,* 2 October 1989.
[42] *TV Today,* 30 October 1989.

Send the sample letter enclosed in the kit to your Congressional delegation.[43]

Ask local officials to send similar notes to these same Members, reinforcing the important role over-the-air television has played in your local community.

[I]nvite Members of Congress for a tour of your station.... **Find out how you can help on issues confronting your community. Likewise, urge them to support legislation which can benefit the FREE TELEVISION industry.**

While members are touring, also **offer the opportunity to cut a PSA** for a favorite community organization. Make the job easy by preparing the script and following up with the appropriate organization.

The community outreach advice includes the following specific instructions:

Request a local business club to host a Television Day Luncheon.

Ask your **Mayor or Governor** to declare a FREE TELEVISION DAY. **The signing of such a proclamation will make a great photo opportunity.**

Co-host a special FREE TELEVISION event with the other over-the-air broadcasters in your community. Create a festive occasion by giving away FREE TELEVISION gifts. Be sure to include local civic and government leaders as well as sports and entertainment celebrities. Double the impact by arranging to place the enclosed Op-Ed article in your hometown paper on the day of the event.

Sponsor a Freedom of Speech Contest. Get students involved by asking them to write an essay which depicts life without this privilege. **Have the winning essay read on the air.** This is a worthwhile project that could be jointly shared with your city newspaper.

---

[43] Note the meaning of "your Congressional delegation" is ambiguous. Is it any member of Congress in the TV market area, any member of Congress in the Congressional district in which the station resides, or any member of Congress for whom the station manager or a station employee is a constituent? To the extent broadcasters lobby by media market rather than constituent district, this is striking because of the norm in grassroots politics to lobby with constituents. In general, local broadcasters lobby all Representatives in their media market, not just to the Representatives in the district(s) in which the station resides and its employees vote.

Whatever outreach activities you develop, make sure you distribute the FREE TELEVISION brochure. **Remember to document your activities for the nightly news.**

Support materials for Free Television month include sample **on-air editorials**, letters to members of Congress, an Op-ed article for the local newspaper, and a community speech. The on-air editorials come in thirty and sixty second versions. The transcript of the thirty second version reads:

> For 50 years Americans have watched television for free. Commercial Over-the-air TV stations have provided the nation a wide variety of entertainment, sports, public affairs programs, as well as national and local news.
>
> Today, changes threaten to divide the nation's TV viewers into an audience of haves and have-nots. With each season, viewers must pay to watch more programs on other channels, including sports, that they once saw free on commercial stations.
>
> Free TV is America's tradition. Without it, what you see is only what you pay for.

An NAB survey of 284 commercial TV station promotion directors conducted in March 1990 will find that **41% of TV stations participated in January's Free TV Campaign.** "Most of the participating stations ran an average of five spots per day."[44]

December 6, 1989. Four PSAs are satellite-fed to TV stations for Free TV Month in January 1990.[45]

December 11, 1989. A *TV Today* article entitled "Congress Is Home for the Holidays...Now's Your Chance—Nab 'Em!" says: "NAB's Legislative Liaison Committee (LLC) members are reminded to keep NAB Government Relations fully informed of any contacts they have with Members of Congress.... [W]hether the contact is in person, by phone or mail, the LLC should let NAB Government Relations know what the representative or senator said on any legislative issues as soon as possible."[46]

January 1, 1990. "'Free Television Month,' a continuation of the Free TV campaign, officially begins today, January 1."[47]

---

[44] *TV Today*, 14 May 1990.

[45] *TV Today*, 11 December 1989.

[46] *Ibid.*

[47] *TV Today*, 1 January 1990.

January 30, 1990. A guest editorial by Milton Maltz runs in *U.S.A. Today*: "[Cable operators] are moving up fast to shake down the USA's TV viewers. Their plan: charging you tomorrow for free TV you watch today..."[48] *U.S.A. Today is a subsidiary of Gannett, which has substantial broadcast interests.*

February 12, 1990. The National Advertising Division of the Better Business Bureaus (BBB) dismisses the Community Antenna Television Association's charge that "Free TV" does not accurately describe over-the-air broadcast TV.[49]

March 1990. NAB launches *Congressional Contact*, a special monthly newsletter for its 1,200 strong legislative liaison committee members (LLCs[50] NAB Executive Vice President for Government Relations, Jim May, boasts to his LLCs: "We think we have the best legislative team in town." In his lobbying tip of the month, he advises: "don't take 'no' for an answer.... As in any activity, persistence is the key." He describes how an NAB board member used this technique to win over his member of Congress.[51]

March 19, 1990. House Telecommunications Chairman Ed Markey (D-MA) tells broadcasters at their State Leadership Conference that "Complaints with cable service...are now reaching him from consumers, constituents and his colleagues on Capitol Hill."[52] *NAB's PR campaign is beginning to show results.*

March 29, 1990. NAB President Eddie Fritts and NAB TV Board Chairman Tom Goodgame, Westinghouse Broadcasting, testify before the Senate Communications Subcommittee on cable regulation.

March 31, 1990. At the National Association of Broadcasters annual convention, ABC Reporter Jeff Greenfield moderates a panel with the chief executives of ABC, CBS, and NBC on the future of the broadcast TV industry. *It is common for top TV journalists to not only attend but also moderate meetings where public policy regarding broadcasting is considered. In April 1994, Greenfield earned $12,000 from the NAB as a speaking fee. It would be a violation*

---

[48] Milton Maltz, "Don't Let Cable Undermine Free TV," *U.S.A. Today*, 30 January 1990, p. 10A.

[49] *TV Today*, 12 February 1990.

[50] A previous version of *Congressional Contact*, with a total of 16 issues, was published from June 1985 through March 1988. The earlier version focused on LLC social/lobbying events, a feature dropped from the revised version. The LLC social/lobbying events are now primarily covered in the state broadcast association newsletters.

[51] *Congressional Contact*, March 1990.

[52] *TV Today*, 19 March 1990.

of ABC's ethics code for Greenfield to take a similar speaking fee from a corporation he might cover. But for the NAB, ABC makes an exception.[53]

April 6, 1990. NAB files comments with the FCC on cable regulation: "The absence of rate regulation has allowed the cable industry to earn monopoly profits—profits it uses to compete unfairly against broadcasters for programming and advertising dollars."[54]

May 14, 1990. NAB encourages TV stations to continue running free TV ads through the summer of 1990. A decision is made to conduct a second "Free TV Month" in January 1991.[55]

May 16, 1990. NAB TV Board Chairman Tom Goodgame, Westinghouse Broadcasting, testifies before the House Telecommunications Subcommittee on cable re-regulation.

June 13, 1990. The U.S. General Accounting Office releases its second survey of cable television rates and services. The survey shows that the cost of cable is increasing faster than the inflation rate.

June 15, 1990 & July 20, 1990. To commemorate the first anniversary (July 17) of the Free Television campaign, NAB sends out announcements and award-winning Free TV public service announcements (from KSL-TV and WAFB-TV) for local stations to run.

July 20, 1990. NAB releases an issue paper entitled "Will Telcos Replace Broadcasters in the Video Marketplace?" The broadcasters are conducting a two-front war, one against the cable industry, the other against the telco industry. The broadcasting and cable industries share a common interest in keeping telcos out of television:

> Telephone companies reportedly are spending $24 million on a public relations, advertising and lobbying campaign to convince Congress and the FCC they should be allowed to provide television packaging and programming via fiber to the home. That's a lot of money, but it appears the telcos feel their rate-payers can afford it.... If Congress lets them provide television and programming services via fiber optics, the telcos have the economic power to swallow up both broadcasting and cable, creating the largest monopoly the nation has ever seen."[56]

---

[53] John Lippman, "Airwaves Sizzle over Bill to Regulate Cable TV Rates," *Los Angeles Times,* 12 September 1992, p. 1.

[54] *TV Today,* 16 April 1990.

[55] *TV Today,* 14 May 1990.

[56] "Will Telcos Replace Broadcasters in the Video Marketplace?" NAB Issue Paper, 20 July 1990.

Fourth week in July, 1990. *TV Today* reports that "In a major victory for television broadcasters, the House Energy and Commerce Committee last week approved H.R. 5267, legislation which will provide modest re-regulation of cable rates, along with important must-carry and channel positioning protections for broadcasters. In doing so, the committee also turned away from a potential amendment which would have allowed telephone company entry into the video programming business."[57]

September 24, 1990. *TV Today* reports that "Top-level Bush Administration officials advised NAB last Thursday they will do everything they can to kill the cable re-regulation bill.... If Congress passes the bill anyway, top White House officials said they will strongly recommend to the President that he veto the bill...."[58]

September 28, 1990. The Administration releases its policy:

> The Administration strongly opposes re-regulation of the cable television industry.... The Administration believes that 'must carry' requirements would raise most serious constitutional questions under the First Amendment.... The Administration continues to believe that competition, rather than regulation, creates both the most substantial benefits for consumers and the greatest opportunities for American industry.... [59]

January 1991. The second FREE TELEVISION Month.[60]

January 28–31, 1991. The NAB Board meets for its annual meeting and spends five hours discussing cable re-regulation. The Board makes "the strongest possible commitment to work for enactment of cable legislation in this Congress."[61]

March 2–5, 1991. The 1991 NAB State Leadership Conference is attended by 150 broadcasters. *Until 1986, the State Leadership Conference was restricted to State Association Presidents and Executives Directors. In 1986, as part of NAB's effort to strengthen its grassroots lobbying operation, presidents-elect, state LLC chairmen, and NAB Executive Committee members were added.* NAB

---

[57] *TV Today*, 30 July 1990.

[58] *TV Today*, 24 September 1990.

[59] Statement of the Executive Office of the President, Office of Management and Budget, 28 September 1990.

[60] I was unable to get a copy of the action plan for the January 1991 Free Television Month.

[61] *TV Today*, 29 April 1991.

VP/Government Relations Jim May sums up the highlights of the 1991 NAB State Leadership Conference:

> [W]e put a major emphasis on thinking about lobbying as a natural part of doing the business of broadcasting. My favorite session by far was that led by Michael Dunn, a grass roots lobbying expert.... Dunn's major theme was simply that only those interests willing to compete in Washington have the power to make things happen. 'Either you're a player or a victim' was how he phrased it, and he couldn't have been more accurate.
>
> He reminded all of us about the importance of cultivating a personal relationship with our members of Congress. Keep introducing yourself to lawmakers until they realize that you've decided to be a player and they'd better take notice.... Thanks to the lessons learned at this year's State Leadership Conference, I hope we have some more soldiers better able to go into battle for broadcasting.

Note Jim May's use of military language. Soldiers are taught to value secrecy and victory, even if this entails misleading an enemy.

On the last day of the conference, March 5, the broadcasters "blitz the Hill" and visit all 535 members of Congress. The briefing book for the NAB's 1991 State Leadership Conference includes an agenda for these calls on Congress. The verbatim text reads:

Agenda for Calls on Congress[62]

1. Introduction

Glad to be here.... appreciate your time with us....

2. Broadcasting Issues in the 102nd Congress.

NAB provides a summary of broadcast issues before Congress. The history of the issues and broadcaster positions are outlined.

3. What Can Broadcasters Do for the Senator/Representative?

News event coverage in the state

Publicity on special project or interest of the Member of Congress

---

[62] This "Agenda for Calls on Congress" would continue to be distributed to broadcaster state leadership through the fight for the "spectrum flexibility" clause contained in the Telecom Act of 1996.

Breakfast with civic leaders

Arranging speaking engagements

Arranging fund raisers

4. After Your Visit

Send an acknowledgement "thank you" letter that reminds the Representative/Senator about the topics you discussed.

Fill out the LLC Contact sheet provided by NAB and send a copy of your letter to NAB.

Although the "what can broadcasters do for the Senator/Representative" part of the agenda is cryptic, other NAB documents make it readily apparent what the intention is. An accompanying sheet to the "Agenda for Calls on Congress" is "Personal Visits to Capitol Hill." Among its eight points are the following two:

#6) Be Political: members of Congress want to be known for representing the best interests of their district or state. Whenever possible, show the connection between what you are requesting and the interests of your member's constituency, and describe to your member how you or your group can be of assistance. Ask for a commitment and **hold your representative accountable.**

#8) What Can We Do For You? Don't forget that broadcasters have a unique relationship with Congress. You have access to their constituents. You have relationships in the communities you serve with people important to that member. **Don't rule out helping the member get reelected. Ask if there is anything you can do for them.**

The five line items under "what can broadcasters do for the Senator/Representative" can be grouped into three clusters. The following advice from NAB government relations clarifies their intent:

1. News Event Coverage in the State/Publicity on special project or interest of the Member of Congress: "Become politically involved with your Member's campaign. A Member always remembers his political supporters. You can assist tremendously by keeping him/her up-to-date on local activities; providing the use of your facilities to exchange information with constituents; and publicly acknowledge his/her contribution to the community when they occur."[63]

---

[63] LLC State Chairperson's Workshop, 8 March 1992.

2. Arranging speaking engagements/Breakfast with civic leaders: Jim May: "Invite your lawmaker to speak at a local function. Rotary, Chamber of Commerce, or Kiwanis meetings are excellent forums for lawmakers."[64]

3. Arranging fund raisers: Jim May: "Remember that the 1992 elections are just around the corner. The best way to develop or enhance a relationship is to involve yourself in a member's campaign by contributing your money and/or your time. Campaign workers and benefactors are always guaranteed an audience with a member of Congress."[65]

The last line of the agenda that specifies "Fill out the LLC Contact sheet provided by NAB and send a copy of your letter to NAB" is an extremely important part of the agenda. The results are entered into a computerized legislative database, which helps identify broadcaster friends and foes. The key part of the contact report is a list of bills/issues and the LLC's evaluation of a Member's attitude toward each bill/issue: "Against," "Lean Against," "Uncommitted," "Lean For," or "For." This categorization corresponds to the Congressional whip system. Filling out these contact sheets is akin to religion for broadcasters: LLCs are reminded a dozen or more times a year to do this. An 800 number is also available to call in the results of contacts.[66] Few broadcasters move into positions of state and national leadership without a solid track record of not only filling out lots of these forms but also doing so in a way that demonstrates political acumen.

March 25, 1991. Jim May urges "broadcasters to remind their legislators of the many ways stations serve their local community through news, public affairs programming, public service projects, charity work and other activities."[67]

April 15, 1991. A 27-member delegation of senators and representatives attend the NAB convention in Las Vegas, Nevada. At the Congressional Breakfast and other events, members of Congress get to pitch stories to their local broadcasters. No other telecommunications trade association can boast as large a Congressional turnout.

April 29, 1991. *TV Today* reports that "Senate Communications Subcommittee Chairman Daniel Inouye (D-HI) has announced he will offer an amendment to the cable carriage provisions of S.12, the 'Cable Television Consumer Protection Act of 1991....'" The Senator's amendment proposes a

---

[64] *Congressional Contact*, October 1991.

[65] Ibid.

[66] Nowadays broadcasters often use a special password protected website to fill out these contact sheets and get the results to NAB government relations instantaneously. An advantage of web-based contact sheets is that they can easily be customized to specific issues.

[67] *TV Today*, 25 March 1991.

plan under which television broadcasters could opt for must-carry and channel positioning protections with cable, or could utilize new retransmission consent rights to negotiate with their local cable systems over the terms and conditions of cable carriage....'" Fritts comments, "'If ever there were a time for broadcasters to put their shoulders to the wheel to help pass legislation, it is now.'"[68]

May 6, 1991. NAB and the Network Television Association (NTA) release the most current edition of "America's Watching: Public Attitudes Toward Television," a study conducted by the Roper Organization, Inc. Among its findings: "98% of Americans watch television regularly—at least once a week.... 58% of persons polled cited TV as the most believable source of news; following television were newspapers (20%), magazines (6%), and radio (5%)."[69]

May 15, 1991. The House Telecommunications Subcommittee holds hearings on the public service obligations of broadcasters. *TV Today* reports that "NAB submitted to lawmakers summaries of more than 22,000 letters thanking broadcasters for their public service contributions...." NAB Research contends that in 1990 broadcasters donated $1.5 billion worth of air time for public service announcements (PSAs). The average TV station also raised $286,000 to help charities.[70]

Week of May 13, 1991. The Senate Commerce Committee approves legislation (16-3) including retransmission consent and must-carry provisions supported by broadcasters.

June 17, 1991. At the semi-annual NAB Board meeting, NAB President/CEO Eddie Fritts delivers the following comments to the Board:

> We have made powerful strides in government relations activities. Within the Administration and on Capitol Hill, there is a distinct difference in attitude and approach on issues of concern to us. Administration and Hill officials are coming to NAB to consult in advance about new proposals.... They have seen that unless broadcasters' concerns are addressed, they are asking for trouble.
>
> Jim May has revitalized our grassroots program. He and I were recently told by a prominent Senator to 'call off the dogs.' This member of Congress had heard from every broadcaster in his State about NAB's position on a particular piece of legislation. He not

---

[68] *TV Today*, 29 April 1991.

[69] *TV Today*, 6 May 1991.

[70] *TV Today*, 20 May 1991

only committed his vote, but asked how he could help keep his broadcasters happy in the future. Grassroots power at its best.

Within the public policy arena, in a not-so-subtle way, NAB is now a force to be reckoned with—on Capitol Hill, at the FCC, with cable and the telephone companies. We have earned their respect. No question about it, Senator Packwood's paper bag is gone.

One of the more visible demonstrations of NAB's strength was on Capitol Hill last month. You will recall that last January we asked the Board what they wanted for television. You said must carry and retransmission consent. We went to the Senate advocating both. We had cable, the phone companies and the Administration lobbying against us. We anticipated it would take two years to advance the issue.

But within two months, we had legislation introduced in the Senate Commerce Committee containing both must carry and retransmission consent. The final vote, in committee last month, was 16-3 in our favor. It was a major accomplishment against overwhelming odds. We will keep fighting just as hard as we work to move this legislation through Congress....

These changes do not happen by chance. They are the result of extraordinarily hard work on the part of you, your staff and local broadcasters. They are indicative of a new era of activism and a new era of respect for the broadcast industry in Washington...much of which is the result of progressive actions by this Board.

June 18, 1991. At the semi-annual NAB Board meeting, Joint Board Chairman Elect Gary R. Chapman states: "A decade ago the issues that the NAB Board were discussing, to a large part, were not life or death issues....Our ability to control our destiny is the real question and challenge we face today. If we are successful, our industry will still be facing many of the challenges of today.... But it will be an industry that has a stable future and we will occupy a prominent position in the American telecommunication landscape." In his conclusion, he brags that S.12 "represents 95% of the January Board policy and position, and this is what we charged our fine staff to make happen."[71]

June 24, 1991. NAB President Eddie Fritts testifies before the Senate Communications Subcommittee: "Broadcasters reach out to our communities

---

[71] Statement to the Joint Board by Joint Board Chairman Elect Gary R. Chapman, 18 June 1991.

on a daily basis…and provide a level of public service beyond anything our competitors can even comprehend doing." NAB submits to lawmakers "more than 22,000 letters thanking broadcasters for their public service efforts."[72]

June 25, 1991. The National Cable Television Association launches Phase I of its "Free TV Surcharge" Campaign. The press release accompanying the campaign is entitled "NCTA Blasts Broadcasters' Duplicitous Campaign to Use Regulation to Stifle Cable Competition." The text begins:

> The history of the broadcast television industry is one of broadcasters trying to use the political and regulatory processes of government to stifle competition from cable television, while at the same time working to free themselves of any meaningful public interest obligations, according to three documents released today by the National Cable Television Association.
>
> Referring to broadcast industry support for cable regulation, NCTA President James P. Mooney said, "somebody has got to call the broadcasters' game for what it is: a duplicitous, anticonsumer effort to use the government to hobble cable's ability to compete."

The NCTA campaign includes the following elements: 1) PR kit (letters to the editor, press release, talking points, letters to members of Congress). 2) Billstuffer (to all cable TV subscribers), 3) Newspaper Ads, and 4) Video Ads (to be run on member cable TV channels). In a later phase of the campaign, one member of the House of Representatives, Dan Glickman (D-KA), will reportedly have hundreds of local cable TV ad spots specifically directed against him.

July 1991. In his July column for *Congressional Contact*, "Summertime—and The Lobbying is Easy," Jim May provides the following advice:

> With the arrival of summer, congressmen and senators will be spending more time back home in their states and districts—meeting with voters, speaking to various civic groups, and just relaxing.
>
> But with all the issues broadcasters have before us in Washington, summer also means 'prime time' for lobbying your elected representatives….
>
> Is your senator a golf or tennis buff? How about inviting him or her to your club outing? Having a company picnic? **Pitch a drop-by visit**

---

[72] *TV Today*, 24 June 1991.

for your lawmaker—including a chance to meet your employees, who are both constituents and advocates for your business.

Many members of the House will use summer weekends and recess periods to hold town meetings in their district. This gives you an excellent opportunity to **tag along with your news reporter** and attend the meeting in your community....

From August 5 through September 10, the House and Senate will be off, with most members of Congress spending much of that time back home. Here's a great opportunity to schedule a meeting between local broadcasters in your region and your senator or representative.... Get your 'battle plan' ready at a pre-meeting, where you and the other broadcasters lay out who'll say what and what to ask for. Then be sure to listen to your legislator's concerns—**what can you do to help him or her?**

July 1, 1991. According to *TV Today*, the cable industry has launched "an all-out campaign...desperately seeking to derail cable re-regulation legislation now pending in the Senate (S.12). Spearheaded by NCTA, the campaign appears to focus on generating a flood of mail from consumers to senators in opposition to the bill.... With a $10-million PR budget obtained largely from an 80% dues surcharge on its members, NCTA can be expected to launch a costly advertising and publicity campaign nationwide to press its case." In a separate article in the same issue, *TV Today* admonishes: "With Congress in recess this week (July 1-7), broadcasters should look for opportunities to meet with their members.... NAB VP/Broadcaster Congressional Relations John David said **GMs should make sure they talk to their representatives or senators whenever those legislators drop by the station's newsroom.**"[73]

July 9, 1991. NCTA takes quarter page ads in the *New York Times* and *Washington Post* attacking the must-carry/retransmission consent provisions of S.12, the cable re-regulation bill awaiting Senate floor action. *TV Today* explains: "With its massive public relations budget, NCTA is attempting to position the provision as anti-consumer and to convince Congress that broadcasters' right to control the destiny of their signals will increase cable bills, in order to draw attention away from the rate regulation aspects of the bill. To counter this well-funded attack, NAB Government Relations says broadcasters will have to become very involved in telling the broadcasters' side of the story to the Congress, the press and the public."[74] *NAB retains Bozell Sawyer Miller*

---

[73] *TV Today*, 1 July 1991.
[74] *TV Today*, 15 July 1991.

Group (BSMG; then known as Sawyer Miller and now part of Interpublic Group)
to test different ways to frame the retransmission consent issue with the general
public. The testing involves polling and brainstorming with focus groups.

July 17, 1991. The U.S. General Accounting Office releases its third survey
of cable television rates and services. The report shows that the cost of cable is
increasing faster than the inflation rate. Members of Congress often request
GAO reports at the request of powerful interest groups such as the NAB.
Representative Ed Markey, Chairman of the House Subcommittee on
Telecommunications, requested the report.

August 8, 1991. The NAB sends out a 12 page August Action Plan Kit.
Accompanying the kit is a joint letter signed by NAB's President, Joint Board
Chairman, and TV Board Chairman, which includes the following message:

> If you are not concerned about your future as a broadcaster, then this
> kit is not for you. But if you realize that without fundamental
> changes, the video marketplace will slide further and further towards
> cable…then you must act…. Time is of the essence. The cable indus-
> try is spending millions of dollars to defeat this legislation and keep
> you and other broadcasters under its thumb. If broadcasters do their
> part, we can win this issue and gain the economic fairness we need to
> compete in an increasingly competitive marketplace. Do it now—for
> your station, for yourself, and for your community. The future of tel-
> evision is at stake.

The kit starts with an "Action Checklist" and asks "Have you done the following:" with a check box next to each item below:

> written letters to both your U.S. Senators, urging them to support
> S.12, the Senate cable bill, when it comes up for a vote?….
>
> **met with your employees** to talk about how important this legisla-
> tion is to their future…?
>
> sought an appointment with each of your Senators and local
> Representatives, to discuss with them your personal interest in this
> legislation and the need to pass the cable bill?…*Note the plural on*
> *representatives. As noted previously, Broadcasters lobby by media mar-*
> *ket, not Congressional district. Usually, members of Congress are only*
> *interested in seeing constituents. But for members of the local press,*
> *including station managers, they make an exception.*

assigned your Public Service Director to communicate with other organizations in your community, to explain the importance of this legislation to the future of your station, and to urge them to write your lawmakers?

talked with the mayor or others involved in the local cable franchise authority about the need to pass S.12 or similar legislation in order to give them the ability to control the cable monopoly and preserve over-the-air television?

reported to NAB any ads in your local paper being run by the cable systems in your area against retransmission consent? any "bill stuffers" in cable bills? any local cable spots urging citizens to write Congress in opposition to retransmission consent?

suggested to your news department that they look at the ad campaign as a local news story, including a look at the truthfulness of the claims made by the cable industry?

talked to other local news media about this issue, including the TV critic at your local paper?

considered other ways to reach the public with your point of view on this issue (op-ed pieces, **radio talk shows**, etc.)?

assigned an employee of your station to be the contact with NAB on this issue, to report back all contacts and any activity by the cable industry in your community?

Section 4 of the kit, "Public Relations Ideas for General Managers," includes the following text:

One way to create more support for cable legislation is to **use the news media to reach your local constituents.** Here are some ideas:

- Several TV stations have done **interview programs** on the issue of cable legislation....

- Attached are some quotes from those supporting S.12. Feel free to incorporate them into **interviews** you do **with local reporters.**...[75]

---

[75] Some examples, with NAB's exact wording:
Electronic Media, 22 July 1991: "Cable TV systems have jacked up rates for their most popular basic cable services by 61 percent since the industry was deregulated 4 ½ years ago."

- Do an op-ed piece which could run in local papers, using the information we've provided in this kit.
- Send any copies of newspaper articles or broadcast news stories which you see or hear on this issue to NAB's Public Affairs Department....

Section 5 of the kit, "A Grassroots Reply to the Cable Industry," includes the following text:

The cable industry recently launched a false and misleading advertising campaign in major newspapers across the country to derail retransmission/must-carry legislation.

The campaign's goal is to frighten consumers by alleging that cable rates will rise if legislation is passed. The cable industry hopes that if consumers are scared, so too will be members of the U.S. Senate and House of Representatives. You can play a critical role in blunting these false charges, as well as promoting your station's valuable community service activities. Congress must be made aware that it is the broadcasters who are on the side of consumers and that if the industry is threatened, their constituents will also lose.

We suggest you activate a plan to address the cable industry's deceptive ads. Here's what we recommend:

Rep. Ed Markey (D-MA), Chairman House Telecommunications Subcommittee, commenting on 1991 GAO report on cable rates, showing an average 61 percent increase over the past four years: "Prior to the release of these survey results, there was a widespread sense that the report would provide ammunition to critics of cable. In fact, it provides an arsenal."

Gene Kimmelman, Legislsative Director, Consumer Federation of America, 14 March 1991: "...studies show that, if cable companies were subject to the pricing pressure of a fully competitive market, cable rates would be about 50 percent lower and consumers would save approximately $6 billion a year.... S.12 would put an end to monopolistic cable practices, open the door to competition, promote improved cable service and help reduce rates."

National League of Cities and U.S. Conference of Mayors, testimony before the Senate Commerce Committee, 14 March 1991: "Actions by cable operators since 1989 only demonstrate the arrogant disregard cable operators have of efforts to regulate the industry. In the past year alone—a year that cable operators should have been expected to minimize rate increases...cable rates increased at more than twice the rate of inflation."

1) Catalog your community service activities

Make a list of all the community service activities your station has sponsored during the last twelve months. Also include a list of PSAs you've aired during this same time frame. Then write your Senators and Congressman using the enclosed sample letter as a guide. The thrust of the letter is to remind them that unlike cable, broadcasting is a truly local service with deep roots in the community.

2) Call your Senators and Congressmen

Tell them **you are angry** about the cable industry distorting the facts concerning retransmission/must-carry legislation. Point out that the legislation is designed to keep a lid on cable rates, and that retransmission/must-carry simply puts broadcasters on an equal competitive footing. **Remind them that your station's local news coverage is one of the most important means for communicating with their constituents. If the cable industry succeeds in destroying local broadcasters, that source of information will be lost or seriously compromised.**

3) Activate your Public Service Directors (PSDs)

Ask your PSD to personally contact 5-10 community organizations your station actively promotes. **PSDs are the ideal choice since they are the 'gate keepers' for your station's free air time.** The PSDs should explain to the local directors of these organizations that their help is needed to insure that your station can continue to provide the kind of community support they have come to expect (see enclosed "Talking Points"). As a personal favor, your PSDs should ask the local director to place a call to the same Members of Congress mentioned above to express their support for the continued community service activities of local broadcasters....

We recognize that these suggested action steps are time-consuming. However, we ask that you consider the alternatives to allowing the cable industry's charges to go unanswered. Cable operators around the country are already mobilizing to lobby each and every Member of Congress. Our stations must do the same....

Suggested Talking Points for Public Service Directors

For years, we have provided your organization with countless hours of free air time and indirect support.

We do these things because we want to do them, and because we think it is an important part of our community responsibility.

We never ask your organization for anything in return. But now, I must ask you for a personal favor.

We in the broadcast industry are fighting for our survival. Cable has grown enormously in recent years....

If the situation continues, we can no longer afford the luxury of providing the amount of community service your organization has come to expect....

What we need you to do is contact Senators _____ and Congressman _____ and let them know the kind of community service activities we have provided for you. Tell them that you think it is important to preserve the integrity of free, local broadcast television. For Senators, the message is support S.12. For Congressmen, the message is support retransmission/must-carry legislation.

Let me emphasize that we don't want or expect you to get an official board position on this legislation. This is a personal call from you to your representatives.

I would also like you to send a follow-up letter to the Congressman/Senator with a blind copy to me. *Note how local stations keep close tabs on the PSA recipients who have reciprocated politically for their free or discounted airtime.*

This is a favor to me and the station. And we won't forget your help.

August 9, 1991. NAB sends an information kit to all members of the House, except those on the Energy and Commerce Committee, to help them respond to constituent mail generated by the "misinformation campaign" of the cable industry. The kit contains three items. One item is called "How to Respond to Cable's Attacks on Retransmission Consent," and deals directly with the charges made in the cable advertisements. The second is called "A Primer on Retransmission Consent," which explains how this provision would work and how it will not raise consumers' cable rates. The third is a sample letter to use in responding to constituent mail on this issue.[76]

August 15, 1991. The CBS Television Network Affiliates Association sends an information package to its more than 200 affiliate stations. As part of this

---

[76] Letter from Eddie Fritts to House Members, 9 August 1991.

package, the CBS Affiliates Association resends the "NAB August Checklist" described above and calls it, in an accompanying letter, "a great how to."

A second item in the package is a position paper for CBS affiliates. Affiliates are encouraged to "**send a letter on your letterhead to all of the House Members in your market** telling them why retransmission consent is important to you and enclose the CBS Affiliate position paper. *Again, broadcasters lobby by media market, not district.*

A third item is a letter signed by top executives from 40 different Texas TV stations. The letter, sent to both Texas Senators, asks them to "end cable's extraordinary status as an unregulated monopoly." It also calls on them to support must-carry, preferred channel positioning, and retransmission consent.[77] The CBS Affiliates Association extols the letter:

> Our colleagues in Texas have put together a great letter to their Senators, and we enclose it and strongly urge you to copy the idea. Don't you think Senators Bentsen and Gramm will pay pretty close attention to a letter from almost every television station in Texas? Do the same in your state or market. Call your friends and competitors. Get help from your state association. But everyone who has seen this letter thinks it will have a powerful impact. There is no pride of authorship, so copy it at will! And send it to Members of the House as well![78]

Finally, the CBS Affiliates Assocation gives this piece of advice: "Keep up the pressure on your Senators. Write, call, schedule a personal meeting. Don't settle for a waffling answer. Pin them down."[79]

August 19, 1991. *TV Today* profiles Gene Kimmelman, the legislative director of the Consumer Federation of America.[80] Kimmelman is a passionate advocate of cable re-regulation but is at best a lukewarm advocate of cable must-carry with retransmission consent.[81] In exchange for NAB's support,

---

[77] Letter from Texas Association of Broadcasters to Senators Bentsen and Gramm, 25 July 1991.

[78] Letter to CBS Affiliates, 15 August 1991.

[79] Ibid.

[80] *TV Today*, 19 August 1991.

[81] On a panel discussion at the annual Western Cable Show entitled "Cable is Televisionary: Its Effects on our Publics," 11 November 1991, Steve Effros, President of CATA, asks Kimmelman why he supports S.12. Kimmelman replies: "[W]e only support cable rate regulation and service.... The cable industry made must-carry and retransmission consent

Kimmelman agrees to keep silent on must-carry with retransmission consent. Others, such as Ralph Nader, who only agree with the NAB's cable re-regulation agenda, are marginalized. *By October 1992, the broadcasters will have dozens of consumer, labor, and senior citizen group allies, but Kimmelman will become the most frequently cited consumer advocate in the national print and TV press[82]. One national publication will come to describe him as "the ubiquitous Gene Kimmelman."[83] He will become, in effect, NAB's dominant public face and spokesperson. One NAB employee describes Kimmelman as practically living at the NAB during this period. Few stories on the cable bill will be complete without Kimmelman's attack of the cable industry's price gauging of consumers.*

TV Today quotes Jim May regarding the August Action Plan Kit: "The intensity of the feelings by broadcasters is high, and it gets higher every time they see the falsehoods cable operators are spreading in their disinformation campaign.... **I urge broadcasters to** make this effort a high priority for the next three weeks, and to **involve their employees** and local community groups in this campaign."[84]

August 26, 1991. NAB feeds TV spots via satellite to combat cable. *TV Today* reports: "Designed to counter the grossly misleading cable campaign, the three 30-second spots supplement print material that has already been mailed to stations." The feed also includes "**background video** of recent cable

---

an issue by opposing any compromises in the Senate.... **We understand the realities of politics, which indicate that if you want to do something and you're not powerful enough yourself, you need allies politically.** I think retransmission consent has a lot of problems, predominantly because of broadcasters lack of vision on this issue.... **I don't think broadcasters know where they are going in the 21st century, and I feel a little bit sorry for them.** On this point [retransmission consent] I don't understand quite how this will help them." Steve Effros continues: "The moving force behind this bill, I think even you will concede, has not been the customer service and rate regulation this year. It has been that you found an ally to push it. And that ally was the broadcasting industry." Kimmelman replies: "It's taken a little bit of scratching below the surface to get people to understand that they might be able to do something about their complaints with cable. That is where our allegiance with the broadcasters has come in."

[82] E.g., "Consumer Federation, National Association of Broadcasters, Update Status of Cable Bill," press releases distributed on U.S. Newswire 16 October1992 and 2 October1992, listing as contacts Gene Kimmelman (Consumer Federation), Eddie Fritts/Lynn McReynolds (NAB), and Bob Chlopak (no affiliation given, but Chlopak orchestrated NAB's PR campaign).

[83] Kirk Victor, "Down to the Wire," *National Journal*, 16 May 1992, p. 1177.

[84] *TV Today*, 19 August 1991.

issue interviews **for possible use in your local news and public affairs programs.**"[85] The video news releases of broadcaster allies include footage of news conferences held by Senators Daniel Inouye (D-HI), John Danforth (R-MO), Al Gore (D-TN) and Slade Gorton (R-WA) on S.12, and by Representatives Jack Fields (R-TX) and Dennis Eckart (D-OH) on H.R. 3380.[86]

In a separate article, *TV Today* reports: "The battle against the cable disinformation campaign continues…. We know that cable is working hard on its disinformation advertising campaign. They have distributed flyers in subscriber cable bills and have produced newspaper advertisements, with some ads appearing on cable channels. If you have received one of these flyers, seen an advertisement in your local paper or, if you have received an ad on a cable channel, please let us know by calling our toll-free hotline at (800)424-8806.[87]

September 9, 1991. NAB Executive VP/Government Relations Jim May says "Broadcasters are reaching every U.S. senator between now and the end of September, when the cable bill may come up for consideration on the Senate floor…. We are continuing our public relations effort, and we are seeing progress there as well…. Let's keep the heat on our lawmakers during the next few weeks…. We can never have too much communication between broadcasters and their members of Congress on this issue."[88]

September 19, 1991. Jack Valenti, President of The Motion Picture Association of America (MPAA), which represents Hollywood, announces MPAA's opposition to S.12: "elimination of the compulsory license, not the introduction of retransmission consent, is the proper remedy to deal with the cable industry."[89] *In subsequent years, as the TV networks and Hollywood studios acquired each other, the MPAA would drop its opposition. By 2004, all four major TV networks would own major Hollywood studios, thus securing de facto control of the MPAA.*

September 20, 1991. *Telejournal* features an interview with Consumer Federation of America Legislative Director Gene Kimmelman.[90]

September 23, 1991. NAB's Jim May praises stations for running TV spots that are helping viewers clarify the real issues involved in S.12, the Senate Cable bill: "These spots have pointed out how cable has used its monopoly powers to

---

85 *TV Today*, 26 August 1991.

86 *TV Today*, 23 December 1991.

87 *TV Today*, 26 August 1991.

88 *TV Today*, 9 September 1991.

89 *TV Today*, 23 September 1991.

90 *TV Today*, 9 September 1991.

crush its competition and to rip off the American people," he said. "They are an excellent counter to the cable ads and bill stuffers that have been circulating around the nation."[91]

September 25, 1991. NAB distributes its Congressional Spouse PSAs. This year's spouses feature Second Lady Marilyn Quayle and Debbie Dingell, wife of House Commerce Committee Chair John Dingell (D-MI). During 1991, NAB will produce more than 400 PSAs featuring the spouses and families of members of Congress and the Administration. Approximately 100 Congressional spouses will participate.[92] *In conjunction with the Congressional Club (a group representing Congressional, administrative, and Supreme Court spouses) the NAB periodically makes public service announcements that feature the spouses and teenage children of prominent politicians. The tapings began in 1985 and are repeated for every new Congress during off-election years. The spouses are typically given a range of feel-good, non-controversial topics from which to choose (e.g., breast cancer awareness, under-age drinking, drug abuse, drinking during pregnancy, education, and driving while intoxicated). The spots help broadcasters cultivate goodwill and personal relationships with Congressional families.*

September 25, 1991. The House Telecommunications Subcommittee introduces H.R. 3380. The bill includes must-carry and retransmission consent.[93]

October 1991. In his October column for *Congressional Contact*, Jim May exhorts: "Would your lawmaker know you by first name if he or she saw you on the street? If the answer is yes, you're doing your job right...."

October 3, 1991. NAB sends a personally addressed letter to all Members of the House explaining to them why they should support H.R. 3380, the Fair Competition and Broadcasting Act. At the bottom of the letter is a notice stating that the letter is being copied to their local broadcasters.[94] *Again, a Member's local broadcaster is defined by media market, not Congressional district.*

October 17, 1991. The National Cable Television Association launches Phase II of its "Free TV Surcharge" Campaign. Phase II and Phase I have the same elements: PR Kit, Billstuffer, Newspaper Ad, and Video Ad.

November 4, 1991. *TV Today* reports: "The NAB TV Board and broadcasters from across the nation will be descending on Washington, DC this week for what NAB President/CEO Eddie Fritts is calling a 'final push' on Senate cable legislation.... 'We're in a sprint to the finish,' said Fritts. 'This is the most

---

[91] *TV Today*, 23 September 1991.

[92] *TV Today*, 23 December 1991.

[93] *TV Today*, 30 September 1991.

[94] Letter from Eddie Fritts to House Members, 3 October 1991.

important TV bill we've ever worked on, backed by the biggest grassroots effort we've ever undertaken.' Fritts said broadcasters need to 'keep pressure' on their senators, particularly those who are uncommitted on S.12. 'This bill is perhaps our last, best hope of gaining an equal foothold with cable,' he added."[95]

November 7, 1991. Jim May sends a legislative alert to all NAB TV GMs, all NAB TV group heads, all state association executive directors, and all NAB board members. The alert is titled "IMPENDING VOTE ON SENATE CABLE BILL—CONTACT YOUR SENATORS THIS WEEKEND." The alert includes the following text:

> ...Now is the hour of our greatest need for grass roots efforts.... Call each of your Senators' Washington office today....I also urge you to have **all your station employees** make similar calls to the Senators' offices. They do not need to speak to the Senators directly. They simply need to inform the Senators' Washington offices that they, as employees of a TV station in your state, believe **their jobs are on the line** and are asking the Senators to vote for S.12 and its broadcast provisions....

November 7, 1991. Four senators on the Senate Commerce Committee hold a news conference in support of S.12. Senator Danforth, Chair of the Senate Commerce Committee, reports: "This has been called the most important consumer legislation of the year, and it's not just the pundits or the experts in Washington who would call it that. When I am back in my state, there are certain communities...where I know that within five minutes of landing in town I am going to be asked about cable television. It is an issue which is very much on the minds of people in many communities." At the same meeting, Senator Inouye, Chair of the Senate Communications Subcommittee, reports that more than 120 national organizations back the cable bill. *None of the senators mention must-carry, retransmission consent, or the other broadcaster provisions in explaining their support for S.12. The themes that are repeatedly focused on are high cable rate increases and poor cable service.*

November 8, 1991. The NAB provides stations with new anti-cable TV ads designed to generate angry consumers. The ads give viewers an 800 number they can call toll-free to voice their support for S.12. The call-in responses will be transcribed into letters, which will then be sent to U.S. senators in support of

---

[95] *TV Today,* 4 November 1991.

S.12.[96] The ads highlight Gene Kimmelman, representing the Consumer Federation of America, attacking the cable TV industry. The ads "talk about the huge rate increases which cable TV subscribers have seen in recent years and the need to protect consumers from further rate hikes by the cable monopoly."[97]

The letter to Members of Congress begins: "I/We am/are among thousands of residents in your state that are fed up with skyrocketing cable rates. In fact, the situation is so bad that I/we called a special number to send this letter to you about it. Without passage of S.12, the Cable TV Consumer Protection Act, more and more people will be ripped off by the cable monopoly...."[98]

November 16, 1991. Ed Markey, Chairman of the House Telecommunications Subcommittee and sponsor of three much-quoted GAO reports on cable rates and services, writes an op-ed for the *Boston Globe* in favor of his cable legislation. It starts: "Across the nation, consumers are angry about rate-gouging by cable companies." It concludes: "It is time to rein in the cable renegades.... The public has every right to expect that Congress will pass a bill to regulate Cable TV by this spring."[99]

November 18, 1991. *TV Today* reports that Senate leaders "will begin floor debate of the cable reregulation bill (S.12) late in January, immediately after Congress returns from its holiday recess." NAB President/CEO Eddie Fritts is quoted saying: "Congress is hearing consumers loud and clear. Senate support for S.12 is growing, thanks to airing of the TV spots and direct broadcaster lobbying."[100]

November 25, 1991. *TV Today* instructs: "Many thanks to all TV broadcasters who ran the recent NAB cable spot. The PSA had tremendous impact on consumers and, in turn, generated thousands of letters to senators in support of S.12, the Senate cable bill. With Congress preparing to adjourn for the year, and with the date of January 27 now locked in for consideration of the bill on the Senate floor, NAB asks that stations put the spot on hold for now. You will be asked to resume airing the spot sometime during the second week of January. We will, however, keep the 800-number active between now and January 27 so that consumers or others who call during the next six weeks will be able to trigger letters to their senators in support of the bill."[101] *The NAB calls the local ads "public service announcements (PSAs)" rather than political*

---

[96] *NAB Legislative Alert*, 7 November 1991.

[97] Background information for NAB's 800 telephone operators, November 1991.

[98] Ibid.

[99] Eddie J. Markey, "Reining in the Cable TV Renegades," *Boston Globe*, 16 November 1991.

[100] *TV Today*, 19 November 1991.

[101] *TV Today*, 25 November 1991.

ads. They view the ads, like their public affairs programming, as a public service to the country. When broadcasters tally the value of public service announcements for their lobbying campaigns demonstrating public service, these spots are included. To my knowledge, only political ads by broadcasters are labeled PSAs. Many stations have a blanket policy of not running issue ads—except when they are their own and labeled PSAs.

December 27, 1991. On joint CFA/NAB stationary, CFA and NAB write to the local officials who regulate cable TV all over the country asking for their support on S.12. In addition to asking them to "write and call your state's two U.S. Senators between now and January 27," they suggest you "may want to **communicate with your local media.**"[102] *Some of those local media are local TV stations.*

January 3, 1992. The NAB sends a personally addressed letter to all members of the House Energy and Commerce Committee in support of H.R. 3380. Fritts signs the letter "Eddie." The letter includes a cover story from *U.S.A Today* entitled "Layoffs ravage local TV stations." The story makes no mention of the fact that Gannett, publisher of *U.S.A. Today*, is a major owner of TV stations and is, in effect, asking for a subsidy for itself. The story is used to bolster the central argument of the letter: "As this bill moves through the legislative process, you will hear from people representing both sides of this issue. The central issue, however, is whether we can be expected to continue to provide service to our local communities when we cannot effectively compete in the marketplace."

January 27, 1992. The Senate votes in favor of S.12, the Cable TV Consumer Protection Act. *TV Today* cites Jim May: "The Senate vote was one of the biggest victories in NAB history."[103]

March 30, 1992. *TV Today* reports that House Telecommunications Subcommittee Chairman Ed Markey (D-MA) unveiled his comprehensive cable legislation, HR 4850, last week. "Markey's bill is similar to the Senate's S.12, passed in late January." Jim May is cited as saying: "We must quickly build the support needed to pass this bill out of the subcommittee and on to the full Energy and Commerce committee. **All TV broadcasters** who have members of the Telecommunications Subcommittee **should pull out all the stops** to secure those members' support for the Markey bill and their opposition to any attempts to delete the retransmission consent/must-carry option."[104]

---

[102] Letter from Gene Kimmelman and Edward Fritts to Cable Administrators, 27 December 1991.

[103] *TV Today*, 10 February 1992.

[104] *TV Today*, 30 March 1992.

April 8, 1992. The House Telecommunications Subcommittee approves Markey's cable bill, 17-7.

May 1992. NAB sends out a 14 page grassroots lobbying kit to push for passage of S.12 and H.R. 4850.

June 17, 1992. The House Energy and Commerce Committee votes 31-12 to approve cable legislation H.R. 4850.

July 17, 1992. The CFA and NAB send a letter to all members of the House of Representatives to support H.R. 4850, the House cable bill. NAB also sends to many members an individualized report showing cable rate increases in their state. For example, the report to Washington State representatives lists the cable rate increases from 1986 through 1991 for four large cable systems in Washington State: Seattle (TCI), Tacoma (TCI), Spokane (Cox), and Pullman (Cablevision). The NAB includes with the report a sample weekly column/press release to be sent to local newspapers.

August 24, 1992. *TV Today* reports: "With cable sending its customers bill stuffers and running ads on their cable systems, NAB is urging broadcasters to maintain their strong grassroots efforts on cable legislation as well. NAB Executive VP/Government Relations Jim May said cable is in 'an all-out war' to defeat the bill or sustain a veto by the President. 'I again urge all stations to run the new cable spots we've provided to you,' said May. 'These spots will help energize our grassroots and will maintain the momentum we've built up with our victories in the House and Senate."[106]

September 3, 1992. Mike Waring, NAB's Director of Political Communications, writes to all Congressional press secretaries advising them how they can respond to the cable industry's misinformation campaign. *As noted in Chapter 7, the NAB has a very unusual relationship with press secretaries. Usually, legislative aids or legislative directors staff meetings between a member of Congress and an important interest group. For broadcasters, however, press secretaries often staff the meetings. When NAB wants to get a favorable story out, it sometimes plants it with a friendly press secretary. The basic strategy is to refer a reporter's query to a Member of Congress. The reporter calls the Member's press secretary, and the press secretary gives out the NAB line in the name of the Member. During the lobbying battles leading up to the Cable Act of 1992 and Telecom Act of 1996, Mike Waring, a former Senate press secretary, had close relationships with many top press secretaries and often attended their monthly social gatherings of the Senate press secretaries association. The NAB, via Mike Waring,*

---

[105] To date, President Clinton has not spoken at an NAB convention, but Vice President Al Gore has.

[106] *TV Today*, 24 August 1992.

also provided most of the staffing for the Senate Press Secretaries Association. For example, every fall Mike Waring organized a weekend trip to New York for the press secretaries. They took the train from Washington to New York, and when in New York, Mike Waring arranged for them to get advice on how to get on the air. The press secretaries typically met the top news reporters and anchors in the country, including Peter Jennings, Dan Rather, and Tom Brokaw.

September 3, 1992. Six senior NAB board members send a memo to NAB members urging them to use their news departments to produce on-air stories 'that give the lie' to cable's claims. 'Tell it like it is!' the memo says. 'Generate the news stories!'"[107] A briefing paper to be distributed as a handout to the news departments accompanies the memo. "Despite the strong wording," reports *Los Angeles Times* reporter John Lippman, the NAB "denies that the memo pressures TV journalists to take a partisan stand."[108] The NAB also notes that it routinely sends similar briefing papers "to more than 200 print journalists" (who are presumably its business competitors). *The NAB does not mention that many or most of these newspapers may be owned by companies with significant broadcast interests. The NAB also doesn't mention that television general managers are routinely asked to distribute NAB briefing papers and video clips to news directors.* Adds NAB spokeswoman Lynn McReynolds, "We're asking (TV journalists) to cover both sides of the story…. Broadcasters have traditionally shied away from covering stories that affect them."[109]

Robert Kalthoff, government relations chair for NBC, explains that he signed the memo because broadcasters are fighting a hard-ball public relations campaign against the well-heeled cable TV industry. Nevertheless, he says, "In hindsight, I wish it had been written a different way."[110] *This is the first report in major media suggesting that there might be a link between the broadcasters' lobbying on the cable bill and their news coverage of it. The reports provide no evidence of a pattern. Scholarly accounts, which relied on news reports, also treat this as an isolated event.*[111]

September 17, 1992. The House votes 280-128 to approve the conference report on S.12, the Cable TV Consumer Protection Act.

---

[107] Cited in Lippman, "Airwaves Sizzle over Bill to Regulate Cable TV Rates."

[108] Ibid.

[109] Ibid.

[110] Bruce C. Wolpe, Bertram J. Levine, and Congressional Quarterly inc., *Lobbying Congress: How the System Works*, 2nd ed. (Washington, D.C.: Congressional Quarterly, 1996), p. 142.; see also Mike Mills, "Scarred by Media War, Cable Bill Wins Solid Vote From House," *Congressional Quarterly Weekly Report*," 19 September 1992, pp. 2796, 2797, 2801.

[111] Rowse, "A Lobby the Media Won't Touch," p. 9.

September 19, 1992. *Congressional Quarterly Weekly Report* describes the battle over the cable bill as "the year's fiercest lobbying war." The same article notes that the cable industry sent fliers in cable bills to more than 35 million members and aired television spots on more than a dozen national cable channels.[112]

September 22, 1992. With a vote of 74-25, the U.S. Senate joins the House in approving the final version of S.12. The *Washington Post* reports: "For weeks now, the broadcast lobby has aired TV spots on stations around the country that argue the bill will lower cable rates; meanwhile, cable companies have flooded cable stations with exactly the opposite message." The article then adds: **"Broadcasters and cable stations have refused to run their rivals' ads."**[113]

September 28, 1992. NAB's Mike Waring sends another letter to Congressional press secretaries. The purpose of the letter is "To help prepare you for press opportunities which will emerge as Congress makes the final decision on the bill...." The letter includes a "Draft Weekly Column" for the Member to send to a local newspaper.

October 3, 1992. President Bush vetoes the cable bill.

October 5, 1992. Congress overrides President Bush's veto by a vote of 74-25 in the Senate and 308-114 in the House. Of Bush's 36 vetoes during his Administration, this is the only one Congress has successfully overridden. A *Washington Post* article estimates that opponents of the bill outspent supporters by nearly 3.5 times in terms of campaign contributions to Congress.[114]

October 12, 1992. *TV Today* reminds broadcasters "to thank their House and Senate members who voted to override the veto. Vote tally lists have been provided by fax to all stations, and copies may be obtained from NAB Government Relations."[115]

Cable Act Addendum

Broadcasters and their political allies promoted the Cable Act of 1992 to the public primarily as a way to reign in increasing cable TV rates and inflation. Broadcasters' elevation of Gene Kimmelman as the spokesperson for consumers

---

[112] Mike Mills, "Scarred by Media War, Cable Bill Wins Solid Vote From House," 19 September 1992, pp. 2796, 2797, 2801.

[113] Paul Farhi, "Foes of Cable Bill Outspend Its Supporters," 22 September 1992, p. D6.

[114] Ibid., p. D1. *Television Digest* puts the figure of broadcaster contributions at 27% of what cable and Hollywood spent. See "Senate Hands Cable Bill Backers Big Victory," *Television Digest*, 28 September 1992.

[115] *TV Today*, 12 October 1992.

is a manifestation of this strategy. The NAB's correspondence with its members clearly indicates that rate regulation wasn't the broadcasters' primary motivation for the Cable Act, merely one that sounded less self-serving for broadcasters and their news departments to promote than must-carry and retransmission consent. The subsequent course of events lends additional credence to the argument that broadcasters promoted rate regulation as political cover for must-carry and retransmission consent.

February 1, 1996. Congress passes the Telecom Act of 1996. The Telecom Act overturns the cable rate regulation portion of the Cable Act of 1992 with virtually no public or broadcaster opposition. The main pro-broadcaster provisions of the Cable Act of 1992, including must-carry and retransmission consent, are retained. Gene Kimmelman again tries to rally the public around cable rate regulation, but this time he doesn't have the NAB behind him, and the broadcasters don't cover him.[116]

November 29, 1999. Congress passes the Satellite Home Viewer Improvement Act (17 U.S.C. §119), making it legal for satellite carriers to provide local TV channels while giving broadcasters must-carry and retransmission consent rights on satellite TV. The law creates a new, market-by-market variant of must-carry rights called "carry one, carry all." It specifies that if a satellite operator wants to provide even one local broadcast TV channel into a TV market, it must do so for all local broadcast TV channels in that market. A major justification for the bill is that it's unfair to require cable companies to carry local broadcasting channel when satellite companies are under no such obligation. Former FCC Chair Reed Hundt argues that Congress would have done more to encourage cable consumer protection and competition in 1992 by passing this Act rather than the Cable Television Consumer Protection and Competition Act.[117]

---

[116] E.g., Mark Landler, "FCC is Urged to Keep Close Eye on Cable Rates," *New York Times*, 24 September 1997, p. C1. Kimmelman is quoted as saying: "The F.C.C.'s current regulation of the cable industry conceals pricing that is every bit as monopolistic as it was during the deregulatory heyday of the 1980s."

[117] Interview with former FCC Chair Reed Hundt, "Weathering the Telecom Storm," *McKinsey Quarterly*, Fall 2001. In Hundt's words:

If I had been the "master of all," I would have passed the Satellite Home Viewer Act in 1992 instead of the 1992 Cable Consumer Protection Act. When the satellite act was passed in 1998, it allowed, in effect, satellite companies like EchoStar and DirecTV to include local broadcast stations and to compete more effectively with cable. It would have been good in the beginning of the '90s to say that "we want satellite to compete with cable" and "we want the satellite firms to have all the content they need to compete." That would have made

February 10, 2005. The FCC votes against multicasting must-carry, which would give broadcasters must-carry and retransmission rights on cable TV for their entire 19.4 mbps digital programming stream. Current DTV must-carry rights limit broadcasters to mandatory cable TV carriage of only one programming stream. Speaking to the trade press, Eddie Fritts characterizes the defeat as a minor speed bump on the way to Congressional victory: "Bring it on. All along we've thought our best chances were in Congress."[118] In 2000, the NAB suffered a similar defeat on Low Power FM at the FCC, and then went on to win the issue in Congress.

Conclusion

The Cable Act of 1992 marked the flowering of the new NAB under President Eddie Fritts and Executive VP of Government Affairs Jim May. Never before had broadcasters run such a massive grassroots operation—including exploitation of their airwaves for political purposes. This aggressive and effective grass roots operation helped establish the conventional wisdom on Capitol Hill that, as Newt Gingrich put it in 1995, "nobody takes on the broadcasters."

---

home-TV access prices lower through competition, not through regulation. We've never found anything that works better than competition to set prices.

[118] Bill McConnell, "Enemies Sharpen Their Knives: NAB's power is seen to be waning," *Broadcasting & Cable*, 21 February 2005, p. 9.

CHAPTER 15:

The Argument From Example: Telecom Act of 1996

"'Giving digital channels to broadcasters is 'the biggest single gift of public property to any industry in this century.'"

—Reed Hundt, FCC Chair[1]

"TV broadcasters have rightly kept a watchful eye on a bloated government. Whether it was $600 toilet seats or $7000 coffee pots, they have always helped us quickly identify waste. But they have been strangely silent on this issue. In contrast, story after story, and editorial after editorial, protested this give-away in the print media. In fact, I have a whole bookful here."

—Bob Dole, Senate Majority Leader[2]

From my dozens of conversations with Congressional staff and lobbyists, I never developed the sense that the power of broadcasters stemmed from their ability to slant coverage of telecommunications policy. It wasn't that the broadcasters might not have the motive and means to slant such coverage. It was that whether they did or did not was not of much concern to legislators because telecommunications policy sways the vote of few voters. And if voters don't care, politicians don't much care either. In contrast, politicians do care deeply about whether their local TV stations seem to be giving them access to the airwaves and favorable coverage.

Chapters 4 and 5 introduced the distinction between candidate and issue centered bias. To recap that discussion, let us assume that the purpose of broadcaster bias is to influence the actions of Policymaker-Candidate P with respect to issue X. Even though the goal is to influence Policymaker-Candidate

---

[1] "FCC Begins Digital TV Channel Allocations," *Television Digest*, 29 July 1996, p. 2.
[2] US. Senate floor speech by Senator Bob Dole, 17 April 1996.

P with respect to issue X, pressure can be exerted on Policymaker-Candidate P via issues A, B, and C. Moreover, there is no a priori reason to believe that influencing Policymaker-Candidate P with respect to issue X is more effectively done by changing information incentives regarding X than A, B, or C. Power, like money, is fungible. Providing information that Policymaker-Candidate P is disloyal to his wife or in the pocket of a special interest might have a far greater electoral impact than providing information that Policymaker-Candidate P voted a certain way on an obscure provision of great importance only to a broadcaster. Moreover, presenting information about a broadcast policy issue immediately raises suspicion within the viewing public because a potential conflict of interest is obvious. But slamming an unsympathetic politician on just about any other issue can be applauded as broadcasters performing their highest journalistic function—serving as a watchdog.

Issue-Centered Bias

In this chapter, we'll look at both issue- and candidate-centered bias. Candidate-centered bias may be what candidates most fear or hope for, as the case may be, but issue-centered bias is what gets the lion's share of attention in the political communication literature. For our purposes, we shall divide issue-centered bias into editorial bias and news bias.

Editorials

The evidence is clear that the editorials the broadcasters ran strongly favored the broadcasters' lobbying position. In early 1996, the NAB launched a grass-roots campaign to apply pressure on members of Congress to support the spectrum clauses in the Telecom Act of 1996. As part of the campaign, NAB sent pre-packaged "public service announcements" as well as scripts for on-air "editorials." The pre-packaged PSAs were sent via *Telejournal*, NAB's monthly members-only TV broadcast to member stations. Every month NAB distributes PSAs to local TV stations via *Telejournal*. Most PSAs have nothing to do with telecommunications policy and encourage good behavior such as voting and not driving while drunk. Unlike ads, PSAs are run free of charge by local TV stations.

Here's the transcribed text from one of these PSAs sent out in January 1996:

> Air is a wonderful thing.
> Birds use it.

Kids use it.

We all breath it.

And it's free.

We use the air, too—we, your local TV broadcaster.

And free air let's us send you all the shows you love, plus local news, sports and weather.

Now Congress has a new idea.

They tax everything else—why not the airwaves?

You'll have to pay more to watch your favorite shows.

And we could lose them altogether.

Call toll free and tell Congress not to tax the airwaves.

[on-screen text: Call Toll-Free 888-No-TV-Tax]

Tell them to go fly a kite instead.

The background images evolve from pictures of clouds and a flying kite to snippets of popular TV programming, and back to the kite flying in the air.[3]

According to one public affairs journal, the value of the airtime provided by local TV stations for the PSAs was $9.5 million.[4] Although the NAB in press releases and reports frequently touts the value of the broadcast industry's public service announcements, it provided no public figures on the value of this particular PSA campaign. When I called NAB spokeswoman Lynn McReynolds, who had subsequently taken a position at Discovery Communications, Inc., and asked her about various valuations for the campaign that I had heard, she said I was wrong but refused to provide what she claimed was the correct figure.

The NAB also sent out a "Spectrum Auction Action Tool Kit," which included three scripts to be read as on-air editorials by local station management. One of the scripts started as follows:

---

[3] A great irony of this ad is that broadcasters had actually lobbied aggressively to abandon their free TV (ad-supported) business model. They did this most notably by inserting a clause in the Telecommunications Act of 1996 only requiring them to provide one ad-supported TV programming stream at standard definition quality; the balance could be used as they wanted. With today's technology, that implies that less than 10% of their spectrum is legally allocated for the purpose of providing ad-supported TV.

[4] Paul Farhi, "TV Claims Congress Could Steal the Show: Digital-Auction Advocates Dispute Ads' Scare Tactics," *Washington Post*, 20 March 1996, p. D1.

Hello, I'm _____, W_ _ _'s station manager. We've been bringing you free news, weather, sports, entertainment, and public service programming since 19_ _. That may all change.

There are factions in Washington that want to take local free TV away. They say that the airwaves that broadcasters have used in exchange for public interest programming since 1934 can no longer be given to broadcasters. They want to auction the airwaves off to the highest bidder. They say they can raise up to $100 billion dollars. I'm no mathematician. I'm a small local businessman, but the only way for me to be able to pay EVEN a share of the money Washington wants to take is to win the lottery. I don't want to take that chance....

The on-air editorials were clearly directed to influence members of Congress. The Spectrum Auction Action Tool Kit, for example, highlighted the following advice concerning customizing the on-air editorials: "The language should be made to conform to your local political environment, particularly what you may already know about the positions taken by the Members of Congress in your viewing area."

Editorials usually ran shortly after the early and late evening news, but often also ran during prime-time shows such as The Simpsons. The spokesperson in the editorials was usually affiliated with the business side of the local TV station. The *Charleston Daily Mail* reported:

> In an unprecedented move, four local stations combined to air messages alerting viewers to HDTV proposals now pending in Congress.... The four stations aired the same message to viewers. At 6:27 p.m. and 11:32 p.m., each station aired a brief message explaining what may be in the future for free over-the-air TV and asking viewers to contact their congressman to oppose parts of the HDTV plan.[5]

Some of the spots were presented by evening news anchors. The NAB urged its member stations to "run the spots as often as possible," and encouraged them to use local TV personalities to "educate viewers" about the issue.[6] The *Portland Press Herald* reported:

---

[5] Ron Hutchison, "Local Stations Unite Against Federal Bill," *Charleston Daily Mail*, 5 March 1996, p. A2.

[6] Ahrens, "FCC Sees Local Gain to Age of Max Media," p. E1, Alger, *Megamedia*, p. 110, Jube Shiver Jr., "Focus of Media Debate Turns to Congress," Business Section, p. 1, Rowse, "A Lobby the Media Won't Touch," p. 9.

Doug Rafferty, news anchor at WGME-TV, has been warning viewers that free television as we know it could disappear. Channel 13's Rafferty has been urging viewers to join a campaign against a plan threatening the free airwaves by contacting legislators or by calling 1-800-No-TV-Tax to voice their opposition.... Rafferty's appeal, aired most days, comes from a script developed by the National Association of Broadcasters. WGME shows the appeal at the end of the local newscast, after a commercial.[7]

Both the PSAs and editorials clearly take a hard line position in support of the broadcasters' lobbying agenda. There is no attempt to provide balance. However, the Spectrum Auction Action Tool Kit includes the following caveat. "Opposing views should be accommodated in the form of equal time for a response." But this instruction is not highlighted, and searches of various databases, including NEXIS and Dow Jones Interactive (now called "Factiva") produced no cases in which broadcasters presented opposing points of view.

On April 12, 1996, the Media Access Project (MAP) filed a suit against a California TV station, KNBC-TV, alleging a violation of the Fairness Doctrine. MAP said that KNBC-TV aired "no TV tax" spots but failed to provide opposing views on the issue of assigning licenses for advanced television.[8] This was arguably a publicity gambit because the political editorial principle of the Fairness Doctrine, which required presentation of competing views on controversial issues of public importance, was already defunct. On the other hand, MAP has frequently argued that the Fairness Doctrine is an inherent attribute of the Communications Act mandating that the FCC regulate broadcasting in the public interest.

Another category of broadcaster editorial is in local newspapers. Approximately half of the top 100 newspapers in the U.S. have substantial broadcast TV holdings.[9] A content analysis of daily newspaper editorials revealed that coverage of the spectrum giveaway was highly correlated with substantial ownership of local TV broadcasting stations.[10] See Table 15-1.

---

[7] Jeff Smith, "Stations Join Battle Against License Sales: WGME-TV Enlists Anchor to Fight the Plan, But Other Stations Steer Clear of Broadcast Journalists," *Portland Press Herald*, 9 April 1996, p. B7.

[8] Chris McConnell, "Federal Case Over Spectrum Ads," *Broadcasting & Cable*, 15 April 1996, p. 12.

[9] See Appendix B for data from 2002.

[10] This study has been widely cited. See Rifka Rosenwein, "Why Media Mergers Matter," *Brill's Content*, December 1999/January 2000, p. 94.

Table 15-1. Editorials

| | | | % of Revenue from TV Broadcasting | | |
			Low	High	Total
Favor granting broadcasters free spectrum?	Yes	Count		3	3
		%		100.0%	16.7%
	No	Count	15		15
		%	100.0%		83.3%
Total		Count	15	3	18
		%	100.0%	100.0%	100.0%

Difference significant at P < .001 by Chi-Square and by Fisher's Exact Test.
Gamma = -1.00.

Data for the editorial content analysis were derived from a Nexis search on daily newspapers for dates covering the first four months of 1996, the period of peak newspaper coverage of the spectrum issue.

I hypothesized a significant difference in incentive between editorial writers from media companies such as Dow Jones, publisher of the *Wall Street Journal*, with less than 1% of its revenue coming from TV broadcast stations, and A.H. Belo, publisher of the *Dallas Morning News*, with over 50% of its revenue coming from TV broadcast stations.[11] Accordingly, I gathered data on the extent of newspaper owners' TV interests, as measured by the percentage of their total revenue coming from TV broadcasting. For the cutoff point for high TV ownership, I used 20%.

The findings in Table 1 show that local TV broadcast ownership predicts editorial stands on the spectrum issue. The results on editorials are very strong and highly significant; in fact, among newspapers that editorialized on the subject, every one with high TV revenues editorialized in favor of the spectrum "giveaway," whereas the rest unanimously editorialized against it.

Another striking fact was that although 15 newspapers editorialized against the giveaway, only three favored it. Two of the three—the *Dallas Morning News* and the *Columbus Dispatch*—are noteworthy not only because of their large local TV broadcast interests but also because of their extensive involvement in grassroots NAB lobbying and testifying at public hearings in Congress on

[11]In 1995, 44% of A.H. Belo's revenue and 64% of its profits came from TV broadcasting. In September 1996 A.H. Belo acquired the Providence Journal Company, including 10 TV stations, for $1.5 billion, bringing its percentage of TV revenue from broadcasting to well over 50%.

behalf of broadcasters.[12] The chairman of Belo Corporation, parent of the *Dallas Morning News*, was Robert Decherd, an NAB TV Board member. Another senior Belo executive, Michael McCarthy, was Chair of the NAB's digital television task force and a board member of MSTV, another broadcast lobbying organization. The senior VP of Dispatch, parent of the *Columbus Dispatch*, was Michael Fiorile, later to become an NAB Executive Committee member who would testify before Congress on behalf of NAB.[13]

The finding of newspaper editorial bias is especially significant because use of newspapers rather than local TV stations to test for ownership bias allows for a more rigorous research design. That is because the influence of TV ownership on media content can be isolated.

Still, the findings are not entirely conclusive.[14] Reverse causation can reasonably be ruled out: it makes little sense to conceive of newsapers buying TV

---

[12] The third newspaper was the *Tampa Tribune*, owned by Media General. One unusual feature of the *Tampa Tribune* is that it is located in one of the few TV markets in the U.S. where the daily newspaper also owns a network affiliated local TV broadcast station. Another odd fact is that two of the three parent companies, Media General and Belo, not only are family-owned newspaper chains but also are run by a family member as CEO, an uncommon situation in today's media landscape. This might invite irrational economic behavior, such as the *Dallas Morning News* and *Tampa Tribune* openly advocating a highly controversial policy that obviously benefits their parent companies. In 1999, Media General acquired Spartan Communications, a company that will play an important role in the last half of this chapter.

[13] For another instance of the Dispatch using its newspapers to pursue its information policy agenda, see Deborah D. McAdams, "TV Retrans Squabble: Time Warner asks court to rule in dispute with Dispatch," *Broadcasting & Cable*, 15 November 1999, p. 56.

[14] Only publications that took a stand were included in the sample. The percentage of TV ownership can be hard to determine when ownership is scattered among different corporate entitities. For example, some wealthy individuals such as Mort Zuckerman, owner of the *New York Daily News* and *U.S. News & World Report*, hold multiple media properties but incorporate each of them separately. They are run as single companies, but the common ownership does not show up in the corporate books. Similarly, some media corporations either own or are partially owned by other media corporations. Ownership can also change. For example, Gannett bought 6 TV stations during 1995 and 1996, A.H. Belo bought 10 TV stations, and Capital Cities/ABC was bought by Disney (thus significantly diluting the % of TV ownership figure for Cap/ABC newspapers such as the *Kansas City Star*). These complexities were not incorporated into the figures for percentage of TV ownership. Figures were gathered from a diverse array of sources including Standard & Poor's, Compact Disclosures, Dun & Bradstreet's America's Corporate Families, and Hoover's

broadcast properties in anticipation of taking stands favorable to their interests. Omitted variables may be more of a problem. Notably, editors and journalists at elite newspapers such as the *New York Times*, *Wall Street Journal*, and *Washington Post* may be more sensitive to journalism norms of autonomy than their local, less scrutinized colleagues. All the elite media in the sample fit in the category of less than 20% TV ownership.[15] The one exception, the *Chicago Tribune* (with 37% TV ownership), ran no editorials on the spectrum issue. Being a member of the elite, heavily scrutinized print media could be a better predictor of stands on the spectrum issue than TV ownership. The sample of newspapers chosen may also have been biased. Nexis only includes a fraction of the top 100 daily newspapers in the United States. If that sample was systematically skewed, the results could be biased.[16]

One 20 year veteran editorial writer observed: "an editorial writer won't survive many big disagreements with a publisher."[17] Stated this way, my results seem obvious. But if, in a highly visible public forum, you asked an editorial page editor—the same person who endorses candidates—whether he editorializes on behalf of his publishers or readers, I'd wager a bet he'd say the latter or at least claim that the interests of readers and publisher are identical.

Guide to Private Companies. All figures were for 1995 or, if 1995 figures were not yet available, for 1994. In one case, the *Columbus Dispatch*, exact figures were not possible to get, yet it seemed reasonable to infer that the owners of the *Columbus Dispatch*, the Wolfe family, received more than 20% of their revenue from TV stations. In addition to their single newspaper, the Wolfe family owned two TV stations and and two radio stations. A telephone call to the assistant treasurer of the *Columbus Dispatch*, E.D. Goodyear, was not returned. The unit of analysis was the publication. Publications which ran multiple editorials on the spectrum issue were treated as a single case.

[15]The *Washington Post*, with 18% of its parent company's 1995 revenue from TV stations, was close. The moderate *Washington Post* was noteworthy among elite media because during the first four months of 1996 it ran no editorials on the subject. In contrast, the liberal *New York Times* ran two editorials (both opposed) and the conservative *Wall Street Journal* three editorials (all opposed).

[16] Nexis only includes abstracts of the *Wall Street Journal*. The Nexis full text result were supplemented by an independent search in Dow Jones Interactive of the full text of the *Wall Street Journal*.

[17] Stephen Burgaard, "More Than A Mouthpiece," *Columbia Journalism Review*, March/April 2003, p. 61.

News

Perhaps the most striking feature of the TV news coverage of the spectrum issue was the absence of coverage ("bias by omission"). This was noted by many commentators. Dole featured this observation in his April 17, 1996 speech with the title "Broadcast Blackout." In it he argued that "You never hear about it on television" and explained why he thought it a significant issue. On the Floor of the Senate, Senator McCain said: "You will not see this story on any television or hear it on any radio broadcast because it directly affects [broadcasters].[18] Nationally syndicated columnists William Safire and Molly Ivins made similar points (each mentioned the spectrum issue more than 5 times in their columns). The *Wall Street Journal* ran a news story entitled "Television News Tunes Out Airwaves-Auction Battle."[19] The *Columbia Journalism Review* ran a long article on the spectrum issue, a major theme of which was an alleged broadcasters' blackout.[20] The Associated Press ran a story, carried in dozens of newspapers across the United States, which quoted a 43 page report by Common Cause: "This $70 billion giveaway to broadcasters has avoided virtually all detection on the radar screens of TV's watchful reporters."[21]

Pat Mitchell, President of the Public Broadcasting System (PBS), delivered a speech to England's parliament where she stated: "I'm pleased to report to you that PBS was an exception to the news 'blackout'…just as we had been in 1996 when the Telecommunications Bill was voted into law, a law that resulted in the great spectrum giveaway. As we did then, PBS did report the story, did attempt to connect the issues to the democratic values potentially threatened.[22]

---

[18] Cited in: "National Press Club Luncheon with Journalist Bill Moyers" (Washington, DC, 22 March 2001). McCain said: "The average American does not know what digital spectrum is. They just don't know. But here in Washington, their assets that they owned were being given away, and the coverage was minuscule. You will not see this story on any television or hear it on any broadcast because it directly affects them." Cited in Albert R. Karr, "Television News Tunes out Airwaves-Auction Battle," *Wall Street Journal*, 1 May 1996, p. B1.

[19] Hickey, "What's at Stake in the Spectrum War?."

[20] Jeannine Aversa, "Study: Broadcasters Shape Policy," *Associated Press*, 2 April 1997.

[21] "Channeling Influence," p. 27. Moore, "Free Speech Is Fine, but Bill Moyers Wonders: Can You Afford It?."

[22] Testimony of Pat Mitchell before the House of Lords, London, England, June 26, 2003, p. 8.

Ironically, PBS, to the best of my knowledge, did not actually run any stories on the spectrum giveaway until it was a fait accompli, after which PBS gave it substantial coverage.[23] This suggests that the story was a case of PBS having its cake and eating it, too. PBS wanted the benefits of the digital giveaway while also claiming the high moral ground.

On June 8, 1999, journalist Bill Moyers devoted the better part of a PBS special, Free Speech for Sale, to the failure of commercial TV to cover the spectrum giveaway, and then delivered a speech at the National Press Club on the same subject, observing: "[T]he Telecommunications Act was introduced around May of 1995 and was finally passed in early February of 1996. During those nine months, the three major network news shows aired a sum total of only 19 minutes about the legislation, and none of the 19 minutes included a single mention of the debate over whether the broadcasters should pay for the digital spectrum."[24] Free Speech for Sale was then featured at local station fundraisers as a reason why public TV was different from commercial TV.

Another ironic twist is that Bill Moyers' staff and then Bill Moyers himself called me to get a copy of the Nick Evans letter featured later in this chapter. I told Bill I'd be happy to send it but needed some information in return: public television's lobbying toolkit from fall 1995. He replied: "I don't have it and cannot get it."[25] And I replied that all he had to do was walk down the hall from his office at WNET-TV and ask for it from such and such a person. In the end, there was no deal and Moyers didn't use the Evans letter.

To be fair, Moyers' report was, in my judgment, by far the best report on the spectrum giveaway that ever aired on an FCC licensed television station. But Moyers seemed to be acting exactly opposite the journalistic philosophy he was expounding. His program was advocating for commercial TV to have a higher journalistic standard than he was willing to apply to public TV, including himself. And getting lobbying documents from public as well as private television stations was immensely time consuming and difficult, so I thought this a fair trade for information he would most likely have pawned off as his own. (I had already learned from previous encounters with prestige journalists that they will call grad students for information but not credit them.)

Michael Eisner, CEO of Disney, which owns ABC News, explained the existence of a news blackout as a matter of corporate policy:

---

[23] "National Press Club Luncheon with Journalist Bill Moyers".

[24] Moore, "Free Speech Is Fine, but Bill Moyers Wonders: Can You Afford It?." See also Rosenwein, "Why Media Mergers Matter," p. 94.

[25] Telephone interview with Bill Moyers on 3 February 1999.

> I would prefer ABC not to cover Disney.... I think it's inappropriate
> for Disney to be covered by Disney.... [B]y and large, the way you
> avoid conflict of interest is to, as best you can, not cover yourself.[26]

My own research confirms the observation of minimal news coverage. Between mid-1994, when broadcasters got their desired "giveaway" clause inserted into the proposed telecommunications bill,[27] and February 1, 1996, when the bill actually passed, I was unable to find[28] even a single instance of a national TV network covering the controversy of whether to auction the spectrum or "loan" it to the broadcasters for free. Even when Dole held up the telecommunications bill—after it had already passed the House and Senate—solely on the basis of what he described as a spectrum "giveaway," the TV broadcasters remained silent. By contrast, the *Wall Street Journal*, the *New York Times*, and the *Washington Post*, gave the story extensive coverage. On February 1, 1996, ABC and CBS briefly mentioned the issue of the giveaway vs. spectrum auctions. On March 20, 1996 CBS Evening News aired a three-minute report that touched on the controversy.[29] On April 12, 1996 the NBC affiliate in

---

[26] Stevens, "Mouse-Ke-Fear," p. 97. This would seem to conflict with ABC News Senior Vice-President Richard Wald's statement that "There will be no instance in which we will [avoid reporting on Disney]. We do not play around with the integrity of the central question of our lives, which is to report fully and fairly what we know." Karr, "Television News Tunes out Airwaves-Auction Battle."

[27] Mid-1994 is also an important date because the first spectrum auctions took place in July 1994.

[28] From NEXIS search on ABC news transcripts, Dow Jones Interactive (now Factiva) searches on CBS and NBC transcripts, conversations with senior Congressional telecom aides, and various articles including: Hickey, "What's at Stake in the Spectrum War?." Farhi, "TV Claims Congress Could Steal the Show."

[29] The March 20, 1996 CBS report was the only substantial TV network report on the spectrum debate until the spectrum licenses were granted by the FCC on April 3, 1997. The report is of special interest because of the circumstances surrounding it. By mid-March many opponents of the broadcasters had begun commenting on the lack of TV coverage of the spectrum debate. On March 20, 1996 the *Washington Post* ran a story by Paul Farhi entitled "TV Claims Congress Could Steal the Show: Digital-Auction Advocates Dispute Ads' Scare Tactics." Farhi said that Senator John McCain, a senior member of the Senate Commerce Committee, "chided broadcasters for using the airwaves to advance their own political agenda. Saying that the auction issue has received little attention on network or local station news shows, he suggested that broadcasters haven't covered the story because 'exposure would be detrimental to their arguments.'" Farhi went on to say that the NAB's vice president for government affairs, Jim May, "said that one network is preparing a news

Washington DC ran a five minute segment on the issue on its Sunday, local public affairs program. By April 1996, when *Broadcasting & Cable* declared victory for the broadcasters, not a single national network TV newsmagazine or public affairs program had covered the issue.

At least one local TV news public affairs program covered the issue as a one-sided commentary. Reports the *Columbia Journalism Review* its DARTs and LAURELs column:

> DART to WPTA-TV, in Fort Wayne, Indiana, for forgetting that public interest and self-interest aren't quite the same thing. Apparently not convinced that all those commercials put out by the National Association of Broadcasters would sufficiently alert viewers to the deadly consequences that would befall their favorite programs if Uncle Sam did not hand over freely to the stations the highly lucrative waves of the high-definition spectrum, WPTA saw no conflict in being true to its very own self. In its Sunday morning 'public affairs program' Impact following the David Brinkley show, the ABC affiliate featured a panel discussion, hosted by anchor Victor Locke and featuring officials from three local stations, on 'how the transition to HDTV could end up taking away what we know as free TV.' Jammed with clips of NAB commercials, financial forecasts, predictions of TV stations 'going black,' and quotes from politicians who are 'in our

---

report and that a number of local stations have reported on the the issue." I was unable to confirm May's comment about local station news, but it is interesting that the NAB would know of network intentions at least a day before the CBS story was run. The CBS broadcast also came the evening before the crucial March 21, 1996 hearing of the House Commerce subcommittee. At that meeting the broadcasters' ad campaign came under attack by Representatives Fields, a strong broadcaster supporter, and Representative Oxley, also a broadcaster supporter. Oxley made the following comment: "I want to also comment on the ads from the broadcasters.... There is nothing necessarily wrong with the broadcasters protecting their particular turf and their interest, but there is something wrong, however, if, indeed, certain segments of the broadcasting industry don't present an objective, a view of this very complicated subject. And they have every right to run these types of ads, but I think also the obligation is very clear from the news portion of the broadcasting industry to present an objective analysis of this very complicated issue. So far, I have seen little, if any effort by the news departments to present this position.... [I]t seems to me that we ought to have more objective analysis in the news. I await that objective analyis, but so far we haven't seen much."

camp,' the 'community affairs presentation' concluded by urging viewers to contact their representatives in Washington."[30]

Whether or not the TV news blackout was as severe as described above is hard to nail down. The spectrum issue was a national issue as evidenced by the way newspapers covered the story out of their Washington bureaus. Since transcripts of the major national TV networks were easy to search in Nexis and Dow Jones Interactive (now called "Factiva"), I was able to confirm the newspaper, Congressional, and media critic accounts above. But local broadcast TV had no comparable online transcripts, so this type of more rigorous confirmation by looking at primary sources wasn't possible.

The argument of a local TV news blackout begins to break down on April 3, 1997, the day the FCC granted the broadcasters their digital license. On that day, the Associated Press asked about the blackout assertion and got the following response:

> NAB spokesman Dennis Wharton called the assertion "bogus," pointing out that two networks and a public TV news show have stories in the works. "So the notion that broadcasters are not covering the story is ludicrous," he said.
>
> NBC spokeswoman Lela Cocoros agreed, adding "our News Division deems what is newsworthy."[31]

Wharton's prediction about broadcast news coverage proved accurate. In fact, the previous night ABC World News Tonight ran a story mentioning the allegation of a spectrum giveaway,[32] and in the next few days the allegations of a spectrum giveaway was reported on many local broadcast TV news outlets.[33]

---

[30] Gloria Cooper, "Darts and Laurels," *Columbia Journalism Review*, November-December 1996, p. 23.

[31] Aversa, "Study.", Farhi, "TV Claims Congress Could Steal the Show.", Karr, "Television News Tunes out Airwaves-Auction Battle."

[32] ABC World News Tonight, 2 April 1997.

[33] E.g., KTBC-TV ("Fox 7 News Morning Report"), 4 April 1997; WAND-TV ("Good Morning Central Illinois"), 4 April 1997; WLWT-TV ("News 5 Today"), 4 April 1997; WRIC-TV ("8 News At Noon"), 4 April 1997; KTVI-TV ("2 News At Five"), 3 April 1997; PBS Network Programming ("The Newshour with Jim Lehrer"), 3 April 1997; NBC Nightly News, 3 April 1997.

However, in politics, timing is everything. The broadcasters only ran the story after the giveaway was for all practical purposes a fait accompli. That's a bit like only covering a presidential campaign after the election has taken place; it's an abdication of the media's democratic responsibility. Moreover, the TV media assigned no political responsibility for the spectrum giveaway; it was presented as a virgin political birth. So the report entailed no political consequences for policymakers who supported it. The report on ABC World News Tonight was typical. NAB President Eddie Fritts defended the new digital licenses, and Senator McCain attacked them as a giveaway:

> Reporter John Martin (voice-over):...TV broadcasters say they have already invested a lot of money in the old systems and in moving to the new, as required by the government, they will need to make additional heavy investments. They say "a deal is a deal."

> Fritts: The government said, "We will provide to you the frequencies if you will operate in the public interest." And broadcasters are doing that, and we're living up to our end of the compact.

> Reporter John Martin (voice-over): Senator John McCain of Arizona says the industry has already won the battle by convincing most of his colleagues to side with the broadcasters.

> McCain: If I were them, I would want to get it for free as well. But I don't think they should, and—but the reality is they will.[34]

A more balanced report would have pitted McCain against one of the great behind-the-scenes champions of the giveaway such as Senators Lott or Hollings, or Representatives Tauzin or Dingell.

The Question of Newsworthiness

Network TV's general response to the charge of a blackout was that the spectrum story was not newsworthy.[35] One way to evaluate this response is to determine whether the networks' actions were internally consistent. Did the networks follow standard journalistic methods or did they allow economic self-interest to influence story selection? This question cannot be answered definitively, but evidence points strongly in the direction of a blackout.

---

[34] ABC World News Tonight, 2 April 1997.

[35] E.g., Gans, *Deciding What's News*, pp. 9-10.

First, network executives themselves made frequent comments that this was an extraordinarily important issue for the future of America. In his keynote address to the broadcasters' 1996 annual national convention, Robert Wright, President of NBC, described the broadcasters as "in the fight of our lives."[36] A spectrum auction would destroy the wondrous public service benefits broadcasters bring to the American public. The entire American way of life would be changed, including the way people connect to their local communities, the way they watch sports, the way poor people can participate in democracy, and the way people spend their leisure time watching TV entertainment. The wrong outcome of the fight would also render "tens of millions of TV sets useless overnight" and require "consumers to spend billions for converter boxes or new sets."[37] Wright's comments were not isolated. The lobbying record is full of such comments, and the NAB made this a central talking point for communications between local station managers and members of Congress. Clearly, the broadcasters' own arguments would suggest that the spectrum issue (a.k.a. "the future of TV") was not only extraordinarily important, but also likely to be of interest to all TV watching Americans.

Second, journalists are often dependent on official sources for their news. According to Herbert Gans and other political communication scholars, the incumbent president is considered the most newsworthy individual in the country.[38] Almost everything the president says or does is considered newsworthy just because of who the president is. "News about leading presidential candidates ranks next; in presidential election years it often outnumbers stories about the president."[39] As a major presidential contender, Dole's repeated speeches about the issue on the Senate floor would seem to qualify for a high level of newsworthiness. Accordingly, elite newspapers such as the *New York Times* and *Wall Street Journal* gave the story prominent coverage. But the TV networks did not. Ironically for a national story, it was local TV stations in obscure markets that gave this story the most coverage, albeit one-sided and self-serving.

Third, the TV networks provided ample coverage of the high definition TV policy issues when it favored their interests to do so. Between 1987 and

---

[36] Robert Wright, Keynote speech delivered at NAB's annual convention in Las Vegas, Nevada, 15 April 1996.

[37] Ibid.

[38] Graber, *Mass Media and American Politics*, p. 129.

[39] Brinkley, *Defining Vision*.

mid-1994, the three TV networks repeatedly covered the developing HDTV story.[40] Although the broadcasters' main goal was to preserve and increase the value of their spectrum rights,[41] the issue was framed to the public as largely one of a Japanese threat to U.S. competitiveness. During the early years of the Clinton Administration, the issue was framed as broadcasters' contribution to the national information infrastructure and technological convergence.[42] But TV networks lost interest in the story when the dollar magnitude of what was being given to them came into clear focus (helped by the multi-billion dollar spectrum auctions beginning in late 1994).

Fourth, on December 20, 1995 the House and Senate conferees came to an agreement on the Telecommunications Act. That night CBS and NBC ran a story on the event, including the historic importance of the Telecommunications Act.[43] However, when Dole torpedoed the agreement several weeks later, all on the grounds of a "spectrum giveaway," the TV networks ignored the story. Its newsworthiness can be judged by the fact that the

---

[40] NEXIS search with the word "HDTV" on ABC transcripts beginning in January, 1990. Burrelle's search with the word "HDTV" on NBC Nightly New transcripts back to November, 1989, and CBS Evening News transcripts back to February, 1990. Between November 1989 and mid-1994, NBC mentioned HDTV in 18 stories; between February 1990 and mid-1994 CBS mentioned HDTV in 11 stories; between January 1990 and June 1994 ABC mentioned HDTV in 8 stories.

[41] Dupagne and Seel, *High-Definition Television*, chapter 6, Jeffrey A. Hart, *Technology, Television and Competition: The Politics of Digital TV* (New York: Cambridge University Press, 2004), chapter 5, John F. Rice, *HDTV: The Politics, Policies, and Economics of Tomorrow's Television*, 1st ed. (New York: Union Square Press, 1990), chapters 6 to 19.

[42] "Channeling Influence," p. 27.

[43] The transcript of the CBS report: "Vice President Gore called tonight to say there has been a bipartisan breakthrough in the telecommunications bill which will rewrite the rules on telephones, broadcasting, and other new forms of communication. It will also include the V-chip on television sets so parents can more easily control what their children watch. This breakthrough comes as a surprise. A vote could come before the weekend." CBS News immediately followed with this segment: "When we come back, NBC NEWS IN DEPTH tonight: THE FLEECING OF AMERICA. Ethanol, miracle fuel or taxpayer rip-off?" After the commercial: "Do subsidies for ethanol go against the grain of good sense? Some tough questions tonight." This sequence is ironic because opponents of the so-called "spectrum giveaway" in the Telecommunications Act considered it one of the largest "corporate welfare" subsidies in U.S. history. The story is also interesting because Bob Dole, soon to be the most visible opponent of the "spectrum giveaway," received large contributions from the ethanol industry and was one of their strongest supporters in Congress.

New York Times, Wall Street Journal, and *Washington Post* gave it prominent coverage.

Fifth, TV newsmagazines such as 60 Minutes, Dateline NBC, and PrimeTime Live routinely do stories on what many consider to be lesser examples of corporate welfare and lobbying excess. Common Cause made this point when it observed:

> The network nightly news programs are in love with stories on government boondoggles, and two of them even have regularly scheduled features to highlight the worst examples of government waste and corporate welfare like ABC's 'It's Your Money' and NBC's 'Fleecing of America.' But this $70-billion giveaway to broadcasters has avoided virtually all detection on the radar screens of TV's watchful reporters."[44]

Sixth, the broadcasters argued that the spectrum debate was not newsworthy because it "is too complicated and boring for the viewing public."[45] "But if that is the case," as Dole argued, "why did the National Association of Broadcasters vote to go on the offensive and launch a multi-million-dollar ad campaign to preserve, as they spin it, free, over-the-air broadcasting?"[46] The huge number of 30 second spots underscores that the broadcasters thought the spectrum debate (albeit framed as a tax on an existing service rather than a subsidy for a new service) could be framed in soundbites when it suited their interests to do so. Also noteworthy is that, thanks in part to years of broadcaster efforts, public awareness of HDTV was already very high. The spectrum debate could have been viewed simply as a new twist in the old and familiar story of HDTV.[47]

Seventh, the spectrum debate was linked politically to other issues, such as the v-chip. When those other issues were covered on broadcast TV, the linkage could have been noted. The v-chip was a device that would allow parents to screen unwanted programming from their children's eyes. The v-chip was closely linked to the White House because Vice President Gore was its greatest champion. The broadcasters opposed the v-chip. But they opposed the v-chip much less than spectrum auctions. Many insiders viewed broadcasters' ultimate

---

[44] Karr, "Television News Tunes out Airwaves-Auction Battle." See also the Dole quote opening this chapter.

[45] Dan Carney, "Industry Agrees to TV Ratings," *CQ*, 2 March 1996.

[46] 104th Congress, 2nd Session, *Congressional Record*, 17 April 1996, p. S3443.

[47] A 1992 Roper poll found that 28% of Americans had already heard of HDTV. See "Top Ten New Technologies," *The Public Pulse*, August 1992, p. 8.

acceptance of the v-chip as part of a quid pro quo with the White House in return for not supporting the auction of broadcasters' spectrum.[48]

The v-chip was the most widely reported provision affecting broadcasters in the Telecom Act of 1996.[49] Between December 20, 1995 and April 1, 1996 NBC, CBS, and ABC mentioned the v-chip on 37 different news programs. But never in their coverage was a link drawn between the v-chip and spectrum auctions. It is also interesting that the v-chip was the provision of the Telecommunications Act that received virtually all the TV coverage despite being considered a minor issue by the broadcasters themselves. Although the broadcasters had long opposed v-chip-like devices, they devoted an over-whelming share of their attention and lobbying resources to fighting spectrum auctions, not the v-chip.[50]

Eighth, there seems to be a discrepancy between prominent TV journalists criteria of newsworthiness and their reporting. Consider David Brinkley, host of ABC's top-rated Sunday morning public affairs show, This Week With David Brinkley. From 1993 to 1996 David Brinkley's son, Pulitzer prize winning *New York Times* journalist Joel Brinkley, researched a book that included damning accounts of the broadcasters' lobbying tactics regarding the spectrum giveaway.[51] On April 9, 1997, at a luncheon in front of several thousand broadcasters, David Brinkley said that the advent of digital TV was "the most interesting and important development in communications in my lifetime," and went on to praise his son's work. But if digital TV was so important, why didn't he cover the issue on his TV program? On December 30, 1990, his show discussed the HDTV issue in the context of the Japanese industrial threat. And on August 6, 1995 and February 4, 1996 his show covered the Telecom

---

[48] Graeme Browning, "No Oscar for Jack," *National Journal*, 23 August 1997, p. 1691. Brinkley, *Defining Vision*. Bryan Gruley, "Gingrich Seeks Credit for Limiting TV Sex, Violence," *Wall Street Journal*, 27 February 1996, p. B7. Kathleen Kirby, "The V-Chip Nonbattle," *Communicator*, May 1996, p. 38.

[49] Cindy Price, "Does Power Change the News? A Content Analysis of Network News Coverage of the Telecommunications Act of 1996," paper presented in the News Division at the Broadcast Education Association meeting, Las Vegas, Nevada, April 1998.Jim Naureckas, "Info-bandits," *In These Times*, 4 March 1996, p. 17.

[50] E.g., *NAB Legislative Issue Papers* for 1995 include extensive discussion of spectrum issues but devote only one sentence each to noting that the NAB opposes v-chip legislation. See *NAB Legislative Issue Papers* for May 1995 and October 1995.

[51] "NBC News Has No 'Shyness': Telecom Fight in Congress Is 'Messy Deal,'" *Communications Daily*, 19 January 1996, p. 5.

Act. The digital TV and spectrum provisions of that Act clearly must have been at the forefront of his mind, but he chose not to mention them.

Another interesting case, noted in Chapter 13, is Barbara Walters, host of 20/20 and an intermittent show called "Barbara Walter Specials." On March 19, 1997 she won an award from Harvard Kennedy School of Government's Joan Shorenstein Center on the Press, Politics, and Public Policy for outstanding contributions to journalism. During the question and answer time, she was asked about the spectrum issue and replied that she knew absolutely nothing about it. Less than three weeks later—on April 7, 1997 at NAB's annual convention—she received NAB's Distinguished Service Award and gave a major speech in front of several thousand broadcasters, mostly senior management at local stations. At this and at least several previous NAB conventions, the spectrum issue was the hottest policy issue on the agenda. Walters started her speech by thanking them for airing and running promotions supporting her programs over the years.[52] Local stations choose not only whether to run a program, but also whether to promote it with enthusiasm and schedule it at desirable times. Was Walters really ignorant of the spectrum issue? Does that explain why she ran no expose of it on 20/20? Or was she simply playing good politics with the people who justify her $10 million/year salary[53] by choosing day-in and day-out whether to run and promote her programs?

Ninth, it may be argued that broadcasters were appropriately reluctant to cover their own industry. But broadcasters have shown little reticence in covering their own industry when it has served their interests to do so. For example, ABC News featured the kick-off of Walt Disney World's 25th anniversary celebration,[54] a story ignored by NBC and CBS. Walt Disney is ABC's parent company.

One telling incident was the refusal of the top TV lobbyists to accept an invitation to stand next to President Clinton during the signing of the Telecom Act. This was striking for a number of reasons. First, these lobbyists had been thoroughly consumed with the issue for the prior several weeks. Second, they

---

[52] Keynote speakers at NAB shows usually make their text available in the press room or at least available to senior NAB staff prior to the show. Joel Brinkley, for example, gave a copy of his speech to NAB prior to delivering it. Shortly after Walters' speech, I called her assistant to ask for a copy of it. I was told that no written version of it existed.

[53] "1999 Salary Report," *Brill's Content*, May 1999, p. 86.

[54] Andie Tucher, "The Real Dangers of Conglomerate Control; A Columbia Journalism Review forum looks at the bad news about corporate synergy," *Columbia Journalism Review*, March/April 1997, p. 46.

were widely hailed as being victorious. Third, the other major telecom industries were present at the signing. Fourth, most people are flattered to stand next to a president of the United States, especially in front of national TV cameras. The simplest explanation of this omission is that the TV networks had nothing to gain by revealing to the public that they were a self-interested and major player in this story.

In contrast to the general blackout of broadcast TV coverage of the spectrum giveaway, daily newspapers generally covered it, regardless of whether the newspaper was owned by a broadcast company or not. I went to the Library of Congress and got copies of stories on the February 1, 1996 passage of the Telecommunications Act for the top 100 U.S. Daily newspapers. Most of the papers mentioned both that Senator Dole had held up passage of the Telecommunicatiosn Act and explained why. I could detect no pronounced difference either in balance or story placement in daily newspapers regardless of whether or not they had substantial local TV broadcast interests. One explanation of this finding is that even at the top 100 largest daily newspapers in the U.S. (where size is measured by circulation), most national news comes from a few sources, notably the Associated Press and the Washington news bureaus of the handful of major newspaper groups. A local editor's choice, therefore, largely comes down to whether or not to run a pre-written national story. Since passage of the Telecom Act was a must-carry story—usually on the front page—a local editor's discretion could be viewed as slight. In contrast, the editorial page is usually written locally, so it tends to be subject to a lot more discretion on the part of the local editor.

At least one prominent broadcaster, NBC News President Andrew Lack, acknowledged both the public interest in covering the telecom issue and his network's failure to do so:

> NBC News Pres. Andrew Lack said his division will show "absolutely [no] shyness" in going after big companies, including NBC parent GE. He said "landscape has changed in terms of pressure on news organizations to take on…the tough stories and the big corporations that are somewhat involved…We're going to do it…There's no shrinking from it…anywhere at NBC News. We're not going to be chilled."[55]

But then he acknowledges that was exactly what happened with the Telecom Act.

---

[55] "NBC News Has No 'Shyness': Telecom Fight in Congress Is 'Messy Deal.'"

He admitted networks haven't done a good job of covering telecom issues "because we're shy about the conflict-of-interest issue," but that's going to change: "It's a huge issue. It's terribly important to viewers…Up until now, I think we have done a lousy job." Question, he said, is "how will you cover that without looking like propagandists for your own good?"[56]

A reasonable interpretation of Lack's overall statement is that NBC made an error and will attempt to correct it in the future. But why should a politician necessarily trust a mere promise—and a vague one to boot?

Candidate-Centered Bias

My evidence for candidate-centered bias focuses on a threatening letter (the "Threat") received by Senator Bob Dole on January 23, 1996 from a local TV broadcaster who was in a position to do Dole significant political harm. Dole was the Senate Majority Leader, presumptive Republican presidential nominee, and leading Congressional opponent of the spectrum giveaway contained in the Telecommunications bill that would become the Telecom Act of 1996. For close to a month in early 1996, Dole held up passage of the Telecom Act because of objections to its giveaway of spectrum to the broadcasters. Several days after he received the Threat, Dole backed down and allowed the Telecom Act of 1996 to pass.

The Buildup to the Threat

May 8, 1992—The FCC outlines a proposed transition to HDTV. Existing broadcasters are to be given an additional channel to ease the transition from today's low definition to tomorrow's high-definition TV. Broadcasters must simulcast the same programming on both channels.

March 16, 1994—To the bill that is the precursor to the Telecom Act of 1996, Broadcasters win an amendment giving them "spectrum flexibility." Instead of using the additional 6MHz of spectrum granted by the FCC only for simulcasting HDTV, the broadcasters will be allowed to use it for a broad array of digital services.

April 18, 1994. NAB hosts a press secretaries reception for 150 Capitol Hill press secretaries. The purpose of the reception is to explain why auctioning

---

[56] William Safire, "The Greatest Auction Ever," *New York Times*, 16 March 1995.

broadcast spectrum is not in the public interest. Huge consumer benefits from HDTV and "free" TV are claimed, and pictures of blacks, elderly, and rural Americans benefiting from broadcast TV are shown.

March 16, 1995—William Safire lambastes the spectrum giveaway in a syndicated *New York Times* column:

> Even if accompanied by payment of rent to the Government, the exclusive arrangement sought by broadcasters would be an outrageous taxpayer ripoff.
>
> What is the digitized, divisible channel worth?.... Based only on current uses, which are primitive, the market value of the VHF, UHF, cellular, broadband and narrowband spectrum ranges around $120 billion.
>
> But in the near future, your television set will combine with your computers and telephone and fax machine into a single unit you can hang on the wall or fold up in your pocket. That's soon—possibly in the next Presidential term.
>
> I've seen not-for-attribution estimates that the market value of the digitized spectrum in that onrushing era will be—hold your breath—a half-trillion dollars, give or take a hundred billion.[57]

March 27, 1995. The White House releases a press release touting the results of its PCS spectrum auction: "The right to broadcast certain frequencies is worth a fortune, and the federal government shouldn't just give it away. But that's exactly what the government used to do until this Administration did something about it."[58]

April 3, 1995. *Electronic Media* reports that Dole is complaining about the giveaway, calling it a "spectrum grab."[59]

April 14, 1995. In the *Washington Post* and *Los Angeles Times*, columnist Michael Schrage ridicules the giveaway with as much intensity as William Safire

---

[57] Safire, "Stop the Giveaway." FCC Chair Reed Hundt asked Safire to write the column.

[58] "President Announces $7.7 Billion in Savings From FCC Auctions," press release from the White House Office of the Press Secretary, 27 March 1995.

[59] Jenny Hontz and Doug Halonen, "Battle brewing over advanced TV," *Electronic Media*, 3 April 1995, pp. 55-56.

...even the godfather of communism would have been impressed by the grasping entitlement and shameless chutzpah of broadcast socialists dressed up in multimedia capitalist's clothing. Comrade, can you spare a megahertz...

In essence, America's television broadcasters are taking a hideously botched technology policy and attempting to turn it into a multibillion-dollar government giveaway. Of course, if television broadcasters could program half as creatively as they lobby Congress for taxpayer subsidies, they wouldn't have to worry about competition from cable TV or the Baby Bells....

[T]he appropriate public policy isn't to give TV broadcasters more spectrum—it should be to start taking away the spectrum they already have. They don't even make full use of their existing allocations....[60]

May 5, 1995—At the request of four senators,[61] The FCC values broadcasters' currently licensed analog spectrum, if repackaged and sold by auction, at between $20 and $132 billion. It values the additional spectrum it proposes to license to broadcasters at between $11 billion and $70 billion. The $70 billion figure, which will become the most quoted valuation for the spectrum, is derived from the high bid for spectrum in a March 1995 auction for mobile telephone spectrum.[62]

September 6, 1995—The FCC offers a revised estimate of the value of the broadcasters' spectrum. The previous lower bound, $11 billion, was based on the anticipated sale value of a New York City UHF TV license with no tangible assets or goodwill as an ongoing concern. When the sale was shortly thereafter made, it generated much more than had initially been expected, so the valuation based on actual results was increased to $37 billion.

December 20, 1995—Capping a decade-long effort to overhaul United States telecommunications law, top Senate-House conferees reach a compromise on the last remaining issues. While the Republican leadership is briefing other conferees, Vice President Gore telephones newspapers and TV networks to proclaim the good news and boast that the Clinton administration got all it

---

[60] Michael Schrage, "HDTV's Policy and Technology Aren't Tuned to the Same Wavelength," *Washington Post*, 14 April 1995.

[61] Letter to FCC from Senators Joseph Lieberman (D-CT), Bob Kerrey (D-NE), Patrick Leahy (D-VT), and Kent Conrad (D-ND), 7 April 1995.

[62] Letter from Robert Pepper, Chair, FCC Office of Plans & Policies, to Senator Lieberman, 5 May 1995.

wanted: "There is not a single provision of the bill we're not happy about."[63] In the midst of their meeting, the Republican conferees are told that Gore is on NBC TV's evening news being interviewed by anchorman Tom Brokaw. They are enraged. Some publications later suggest that this episode causes Dole, who was running for president against the presidential ticket of Gore and Clinton, to change his position on the telecommunications bill.[64] In the words of Senator Larry Pressler, chair of the Senate Commerce Committee, "It may well be that Dole wanted to say, "Hey, I can stop this thing. I'm in charge here."[65]

December 28, 1995—Senate Majority Leader Bob Dole, a leading presidential contender, publicly says there are "a number of problems in the bill that could have been resolved in a different way," including a spectrum "giveaway." Dole's comment raises no new issues; for many months think tanks, interest groups, newspaper columnists, and even an occasional member of Congress (most notably Senator McCain) have attacked the "giveaway." The significance of Dole's comment lies not in its content but in the position of the person saying it. By virtue of his position, Dole can not only bring the issue to the forefront of the national agenda, but also stop the telecommunications bill from coming to a Senate vote.

December 29, 1995—The government is in the midst of a highly controversial and unpopular shutdown due to disagreement over the budget between the Republican-controlled Congress and President Clinton. In addition to blaming each other for the shutdown, both sides are desperate to come up with new ideas to resolve the impasse and balance the budget. A front-page story in the *New York Times* ties Dole's statement on the spectrum "giveaway" to the battle over the budget.[66] It's clear from the context and the Democratic response in the *New York Times* a week later (see January 9 letter below), that Dole is seeking to turn the issue into a partisan and thus highly visible issue.

January 3, 1996—Dole brings up the spectrum issue during budget negotiations with the White House.[67]

---

[63] Kirk Victor, "How the Gang of five Fared," *National Journal*, 20 January 1996, p. 145.

[64] Bryan Gruley, "Bill's Passage Represents Will of Both Parties," *Wall Street Journal*, 2 February 1996, p. B1; Dennis Wharton, "Telco dereg gets Gored," *Variety*, 1 January 1996, p. 59.

[65] Mike Mills, "A 'Camelot Moment' on Communications," *Washington Post*, 4 February 1996, p. H1.

[66] Jerry Gray. "Battle Over the Budget." *New York Times*, 29 December 1995, p. A1.

[67] Brooks Boliek, "Telcom bill sitting out while Congress dances budget," *Hollywood Reporter*, 8 January 1996.

January 4, 1996—Nationally syndicated *New York Times* columnist William Safire again attacks the spectrum giveaway. He quotes a January 3 interview with Dole: "This is a big big corporate welfare project. Here we're cutting Medicaid and doing all the painful things while we lend them the spectrum for 12 years. Why shouldn't they pay for it?" Safire himself calls the bill's spectrum clause a "ripoff...on a scale vaster than dreamed of by yesteryear's robber barons. It's as if each American family is to be taxed $1,000 to enrich the stockholders of Disney, G.E., and Westinghouse."[68] NAB spokesperson Walt Wurfel responds that it's "pretty clear" Dole is waging war against the broadcasters.[69] Between January 4 and January 23, the great majority of newspaper editorials across the country will support Dole's position. No nationally syndicated columnist will support the broadcasters.

January 4, 1996—Within hours of the Safire editorial, the President of the NAB sends a two page alert to "All NAB TV Group Heads." The fact that the alert comes from Eddie Fritts rather than Jim May, the VP of Government Relations and the usual author of such alerts, signals its importance. The memo includes the following text. Capitols and underlines are from the original.

IMMEDIATE ACTION NEEDED THIS MORNING
URGE ALL REPUBLICAN SENATORS TO CONTACT SEN. BOB DOLE AND VOICE THEIR OPPOSITION TO DIGITAL TV SPECTRUM AUCTIONS AS PART OF THE BUDGET PACKAGE.

1. Contact any and all Republican Senators in states where you have stations....

2. Ask to speak to the Senator directly. If he or she is not in Washington, ask how you can reach him or her....

3. ASK FOR THE ORDER. Ask your Senator to urge Bob Dole to drop his attempt to auction the spectrum TV broadcasters will need for the transition to digital....

4. Let us know what response you get by calling the Government Relations hotline at 1-800-424-8806.

---

[68] Reed E. Hundt, *You Say You Want a Revolution: A Story of Information Age Politics* (New Haven: Yale University Press, 2000), pp. 100-01, 70.

[69] Dennis Wharton, "Dole Demands Toll on Infopike Dereg Bill," *Variety*, 8 January 1996, p. 61.

TIME IS OF THE ESSENCE. YOU MUST MAKE THESE
CALLS TODAY. A FINAL BUDGET DEAL COULD BE
STRUCK AT ANY TIME.

January 5, 1996—NAB President Fritts writes a two page letter to Joseph Lelyveld, Executive Editor of the *New York Times*, attacking the Safire piece. The letter reads, in part:

> William Safire's column yesterday claiming that the assignment of spectrum for digital television to broadcasters is a "giveaway" suffers from an excess of misinformation and a shortage of facts.... Mr. Safire's estimates of the value that these channels could bring at auction are equally fantastic.... Rather than a "giveaway," the FCC would allow stations to borrow otherwise useless spectrum for a short period, at the end of which their existing channels will be returned to the government to be sold at far higher prices than any auction could bring today.[70]

The same day Fritts also writes a letter to all members of Congress, and includes the letter to the *New York Times* as an enclosure. The letter to Congress reads:

> You may have seen the op-ed piece in yesterday's <u>New York Times</u>, written by William Safire, which totally misrepresents the issue of spectrum auctions for digital TV spectrum which are being discussed within the budget negotiations now underway between the White House and the Congress.

> I am attaching a copy of a letter I sent to the <u>Times</u>, point out the many factual errors which Mr. Safire raises in his column.

> The facts are simple and straightforward. Unless broadcasters are allowed to use the spectrum which has been designated for their use to transition to digital, there will be no free, over-the-air digital television for the American public. We believe that requiring local TV stations to bid at auction for the spectrum they need would be an extremely short-sighted and disastrous public policy decision, and we urge you to encourage the budget negotiators to reject such an approach in their deliberations.

---

[70] Letter from Eddie Fritts to Joesph Lelyveld, 5 January 1996.

January 8, 1996—The *New York Times* prints an edited and slightly abbreviated version of the above letter attacking the Safire column. The same day, *Broadcasting & Cable* quotes Fritts as saying Dole's proposal could drive a "stake into the heart of the television industry."[71] Also on the same day, NAB's member-only weekly newsletter, *TV Today*, reports that Dole's budget package would be "a disaster for the TV industry."

January 8, 1996, *Daily Variety*, a major trade organ with impeccable ties to broadcasting lobbyists, reports: "Sources said broadcasters are preparing a grass-roots lobbying campaign to torpedo Dole's digital TV plans. One not-so-subtle strategy calls for TV station execs in key presidential primary states such as New Hampshire to remind the GOP presidential front-runner of the importance of passing the telecom bill."[72] The author of this article, Dennis Wharton, will shortly thereafter leave *Variety* to become an NAB senior Vice President and spokesperson.

January 9, 1996—The *New York Times* prints a letter from Senator Bob Kerrey saying "Democrats Don't Want To Give Away Airwaves." Kerrey argues that the Safire column mischaracterized the Democratic position as hiding on this issue when in fact Democrats "have worked to insure that taxpayers are compensated for the transfer of this national asset to private use." Kerrey's letter appears to be an effort to eliminate the spectrum giveaway as a partisan issue for Dole.[73] After the broadcasters' passionate blitz on Capitol Hill during the next few weeks, only two members of the Senate, Republicans Bob Dole and John McCain, and one member of the House, Democrat Barney Frank, will publicly advocate for removing the spectrum giveaway clause from the Telecom Act of 1996.

January 10, 1996—The CEOs of the three largest TV networks and a half dozen other prominent broadcasters write President Clinton a four-page letter opposing plans for a digital auction.[74]

---

[71] Christopher Stern, "Dole puts auction on table," *Broadcasting & Cable*, 8 January 1996, p. 4.

[72] Dennis Wharton, "Dole Demands Infopike Toll," *Daily Variety*, 8 January 1996, p. 5.

[73] Until Dole's December 28th statement, the broadcasters' nemesis was arguably FCC chairman Reed Hundt. Hundt sought to make the broadcasters pay for their new spectrum with greater public interest obligations. Broadcasters were furious with his valuation of the spectrum in May 1995 and accused him of encouraging competing interest groups to oppose broadcaster interests. See NBC, "The Case against Broadcast Spectrum Auctions."

[74] Snider, "Senate Hypocrisy over "Hot" Testimony." Also reported in Brooks Boliek, Turning Purple on Spectrum: Sale would doom free TV, execs lament in letter to Clinton," *Hollywood Reporter*, 12 January 1996, p. 1.

January 10, 1996—The *New York Times* reports: "Today both sides turned to an all-out battle for the public's support, with the Democrats attacking the Republicans' tax cut proposal and the Republicans questioning Mr. Clinton's sincerity in wanting a balanced budget at all."[75] On the Senate floor, Dole denounces the giveaway as a "giant" corporate welfare program: "Let me get this straight. America lends the broadcasters a national resource so they can increase their profit margins, but they do not think it's fair to pay rent." He concludes, "Let's, for the sake of taxpayers and for the sake of the American consumers, fix this one corporate welfare provision before we have to vote on it."[76] The *New York Times, Washington Post,* and *Wall Street Journal* report this speech, with the *Wall Street Journal* running its story on page 1. *Vital Speeches* reprints the speech as one of the most important speeches of January 1996. It is one of the few times in Dole's career that he receives this honor.[77]

January 11, 1996—Nationally syndicated liberal columnist Molly Ivins supports conservatives Dole and Safire in a column entitled "Greed Stampede; Airwaves giveaway will cheat the public."[78]

January 12, 1996—The *Washington Post* reports on Dole's November 30, 1995 meeting with the CEOs of the four major TV networks. One of the broadcasters present appears to have leaked the story. Dole is accused of using the spectrum issue to seek retribution for their coverage of the budget issue. Dole is quoted as saying: "Why should I give you a $40 billion giveaway when you're driving my [approval rating] numbers through the floor on Medicare?"[79] Three days later, *Variety* reports: "One attendee said Dole 'definitely had an agenda' going into the meeting.... Dole, however, was 'too smart' to make an explicit link between news coverage and whether broadcasters will get free spectrum."[80] News Corporation CEO Rupert Murdoch later writes to

---

[75] Alison Mitchell, "Budget Foes See Fight Continuing Till the Election," *New York Times,* 11 January 1996, p. A1.

[76] Edmund L. Andrews, "Dole Steps Up Criticism Of Telecommunications Bill," *New York Times,* 11 January 1996, p. D2.

[77] Bob Dole, "Telecommunications Reform: Should Broadcasters Get Something for Nothing?" *Vital Speeches,* 1 February 1996.

[78] Molly Ivins, "Greed Stampede: Airwaves giveaway will cheat the public," *Austin-American Statesman,* 14 January 1996, p. H3. The commentary first ran in the *Fort Worth Star-Telegram* on 11 January 1996.

[79] Paul Farhi, "Broadcast Executives Say Dole Vented Anger at Them; Senator Denies Linking Licenses to Coverage," *Washington Post,* 12 January 1996, p. F1.

[80] Dennis Wharton, "Dole's Political Spectrum," *Variety,* 15 January 1996, p. 140.

Dole apologizing for the behavior of his fellow CEO who apparently leaked this story to the press.

One potential interpretation of this accusation is that it could reflect the common psychological tendency to project one's own motivations onto others. It could also have been a self-conscious tactic of political hardball. A classic technique of hardball politics is to inoculate oneself from opponent accusations by first anticipating them and then firing a low-key warning shot accusing the opponent of exactly the same malfeasance. This serves to confuse the public, thus minimizing the political gain from an accusation that will now be reported as controversial and cutting both ways.

January 16, 1996—Democratic Senator Exon, a senior member of the Commerce Committee, appears to switch to Dole's side, saying: "we're very likely to expect more from the broadcasters from some kind of auction of the spectrum, more in billions than we had earlier anticipated."[81]

January 16, 1996—The Associated Press reports: "Some telecommunication lobbyists, including those representing TV broadcasters, said Dole was striking back at threats by unidentified broadcasters to restrain coverage of his campaign in the primaries if he pushed the channel payment issue."

January 17, 1996—Democratic Senators Kerrey and Lieberman write to President Clinton:

> We wanted to set the record straight on a matter that has come before the budget negotiators: television spectrum auctions. In the course of an otherwise sound critique of Congressional plans to give broadcasters billions of publically-owned airwaves for digital television at no charge, *New York Times* columnist William Safire incorrectly wrote on January 4th that, "Democrats are hiding" on the issue.
>
> Obviously, he did not take into account the fact that the Administration has made a major spectrum auction proposal, which is included in its latest January 10th budget proposal. We wanted you to know, too, that there is support for this initiative on the Democratic Congressional side…. The simple principle at stake, as you recognize, is whether a government going through such convulsions to climb out of debt should relinquish, without compensation, public resources worth many billions of dollars to private owners who stand to profit handsomely from them.

---

[81] "Bipartisan Spectrum Debate Flares," *Television Digest*, 22 January 1996, p. 3.

While members of Congress stand on both sides of this issue, they are not divided by partisan lines. We wanted you to know, as you press forward with auction proposals to ensure there is no spectrum giveaway, that there will be Congressional Democrats who will support this policy.[82]

January 17, 1996—*Daily Variety* reports that the 4,000 member Radio-Television News Director Association (RTNDA) "has criticized Sen. Robert Dole (R-Kan) over allegations that the Senate majority leader is blocking broadcasters' free transition to digital TV because he believes network TV coverage of GOP plans to curb Medicare growth has been biased." David Bartlett, president of RTNDA, is quoted as saying: "Sen. Dole's threats are another good example of why government regulation of the media is dangerous."[83]

January 13–17, 1996—NAB's TV Board meets at the La Quinta Resort & Club in La Quinta, California, and the spectrum threat tops its agenda.[84] *Television Digest* reports that the "NAB will fight Dole to bitter end on auctions."[85] The TV Board announces a grassroots lobbying and media campaign to educate the public and legislators about the value of Free TV. The campaign includes sending a grassroots lobbying kit to all local station general managers. Nick Evans, who would deliver a written threat to Dole one week later, is a member of the TV Board. At the end of the Board meeting, *Telejournal* tapes several statements for a private satellite broadcast delivered on January 19 to local TV station managers and lobbyists. Chuck Sherman, NAB's senior VP of Television, sets the stage:

My association with NAB goes back 30 years.... And I cannot recall a time during those 30 years, when I have ever seen the Television Board of NAB more unified behind an action than it is today, because the Board took a very decisive action today to provide for

---

[82] "Bipartisan Spectrum Debate Flares," *Television Digest*, 22 January 1996, p. 3.

[83] Dennis Wharton, "RTNDA Lambastes Dole," *Daily Variety*, 17 January 1996, p. 27. RTNDA, under Bartlett's leadership, lobbied with NAB and MSTV to preserve broadcasters' free access to tens of billions of dollars worth of spectrum for electronic news gathering. See Chris McConnell, "MSTV, NAB Ponder Court Fight Over 4 GHz," *Broadcasting & Cable*, 14 August 1995, p. 37.

[84] Kim McAvoy, "Digital TV tops NAB board's agenda," *Broadcasting & Cable*, 15 January 1995, p. 10; "Winter Board Meeting: Board Acts On Spectrum Threat, Key Issues," *TV Today*, 22 January 1996, p. 1.

[85] "NAB Sets Goals," *Television Digest*, 15 January 1996, p. 4.

the survival of this industry. Yes, the survival, because that is what we're talking about when we talk about the issue of broadcast spectrum. Spectrum is our lifeblood....

The Television Board took very decisive action to make sure that our survival is addressed. To give you a very clear, concise outline, I'm pleased to introduce NAB Executive VP for Government Relations, Jim May.

Jim May then outlines the plan:

This morning we had a very full discussion of the telecom bill, spectrum, and the challenges facing our industry. And I think it is fair to say that the Board recognizes, we all recognize, that never in the history of the business of television has there been a greater challenge to our future than the one presented now by Senator Dole and others who are trying to take away the very spectrum necessary for us to compete into the future.

[cut to Dole's unedited January 10th speech on the floor of the U.S. Senate.]

Let me review with you the elements of the policy adopted by the board. First and foremost, we have fully united in support of the telecommunications legislation pending before Congress and we are going to encourage you to encourage every member of Congress, as we will, that they expeditiously press this legislation through both the House and the Senate and send it along to the President for his signature.

Second, we recognize that we have a very serious challenge to the long-standing bipartisan plan by the FCC, which permits us to adopt a new digital technology moving us into the next century....

We do not accept this charge of corporate welfare, and we think that now is the time for us to fight fully for our right to convert to digital and to our future as broadcasters in the local markets....

We're going to send full information to you over the next few days to help further explain this issue.... But I want you to know that the people out there challenging us are challenging the very ability of this industry to go forward in the digital age....

If you are forced to buy that spectrum upfront, you simply aren't going to be able to afford the transition. So we are coming out opposed to accelerated or upfront auctions....

So, as a result of that background, the TV Board—and we anticipate the full, joint NAB board [which is made of the TV and Radio Boards]—on behalf of the entire industry, has directed NAB to immediately pursue an aggressive strategy to preserve this industry's ability to invest in the technological changes required by the future. The Board further assured us that NAB will have the full and complete support in this effort of all affiliate organizations, networks, independent stations, groups, and related industry associations. As you are well aware, all of those organizations are represented by the Board. They have in an incredibly unified way joined the NAB effort.

We will be out to you within the week with full blown information.... **We encourage you to use literally every resource at your command, including your own air, to prepare to fight what will be one of the major battles this industry has ever engaged in....**

One visual item is noteworthy. The floor speech from Senator Dole does not include the C-SPAN bubble indicating it came from a C-SPAN broadcast. Since the only outsiders with access to Senate floor coverage are C-SPAN and bona fide TV news media, it means that a TV news department provided NAB with the footage.[86] An irony here is that it is illegal for members of the public to use C-SPAN footage for political purposes.[87] The electronic media are exempt from that requirement because they are presumed to be impartial. But the use of this video is clearly self-interested and political, although not in a partisan way.

Stylistically, note the use of military terminology: "command," "fight," and "battles." Such language is not unusual in Washington DC lobbying circles. But coming from a former marine captain, they have additional resonance. As noted in the previous chapter, military tactics, like high-stakes political strategy, does not place a high value on revealing secrets or telling the truth to enemies.

January 18, 1996—Republican Senator McCain writes to Dole that Congress now "may be able to prevent a valuable public resource from being given away at no cost to corporate interests."[88]

---

[86] Note that committee hearing rooms are under different video recording rules. Some committee chairs let NAB cameramen into their committee room to tape hearings.

[87] Alliance for Better Campaigns, "Profiteering on Democracy."

[88] "Bipartisan Spectrum Debate Flares," *Television Digest*, 22 January 1996, p. 3.

January 18, 1996—*Daily Variety* reports that "[NBC president Robert] Wright and other broadcasters have grown apoplectic amid threats from Dole...."[89] *Broadcasting & Cable* asks Wright why he objects to auctions, and he replies: "The big guys will survive and the little guys will get hurt."[90] The reply is ironic because NBC is a division of General Electric, the largest company in the WORLD.

January 19, 1996—the *New York Times* runs an editorial in support of Dole: "Mr Dole Fights a Big Giveaway."

January 22, 1996—*Television Digest* reports that NAB's major PR campaign to sell story of free TV and get support for free spectrum "starts today" and industry will spend "whatever it takes."[91]

January 22, 1996—Speculation is rampant that President Clinton may side with or move closer to Dole on the spectrum issue.[92] This would be consistent

---

[89] Dennis Wharton, "NAB Fights Spectrum Sale," *Daily Variety*, 18 January 1996, p. 1.

[90] Don West, "Drawing the Line on Digital," *Broadcasting & Cable*, 22 January 1996, p. 3.

[91] "Fritts Seeks Unity," *Television Digest*, 22 January 1996, p. 1

[92] The Clinton administration's clever but cynical strategy was to defer the return of the spectrum to a later date. By projecting a sale of the spectrum in 2002, Clinton realized two great political benefits. First, he was able to project a seven-year balanced budget, a politically important goal in late 1995 and early 1996. The cleverness of this strategy was that Clinton got the budget benefit without actually having to take on the broadcasters. Second, he was able to make Dole look bad. The fixed return date lent credence to the argument that the broadcasters were only receiving a short-term loan. Moreover, he was able to argue that his approach would bring in more money for the treasury than Dole's approach, because the spectrum that would be sold at the end of the seven years would be more valuable, thanks to "repacking," than the spectrum in Dole's plan.

To no one's surprise, the 2002 auction date was later indefinitely postponed. The Clinton strategy wouldn't have been cynical if the Clinton administration had followed its original plan and insisted on providing vouchers (from the spectrum auction proceeds) for all Americans who couldn't afford to buy converters to receive digital TV. But once that provision was dropped—albeit under broadcaster pressure—the return policy became merely a budgetary gimmick. The broadcasters had little fear of the Clinton plan because they knew few politicians in their right mind would ever implement a government mandate to force millions of low-income Americans to throw away their old analog TV sets. Meanwhile, the broadcasters could make the politically useful claim that the spectrum they were getting was a short-term loan, not a giveaway. Nevertheless, it still was a multibillion-dollar interest-free loan. And, under the glare of sustained public scrutiny, would have put the Clinton administration in the awkward position of supporting one of the largest corporate welfare programs in United States history.

with Clinton's overall campaign strategy of narrowing the distance between himself and his opposition. It would also be consistent with his aversion to picking public fights on issues that give every sign of being unwinnable in the court of public opinion. Larry Irving, the top telecommunications advisor to the White House, tells broadcasters "there is no way anyone in Congress will let people keep (both digital and analog) spectrum for 15 years."[93] He says they are "dreaming" if they think otherwise.[94]

January 23, 1996—Senator Larry Pressler (R-SD), chair of the Senate Commerce Committee, tells reporters "We need a national debate on this."

The Threat

On January 23, John Shine,[95] the general manager of the CBS affiliate in Mason City, Iowa, personally hands the following letter to Robert Dole, the key opponent of the spectrum giveaway. With the make-or-break Iowa Caucuses less than three weeks away, Dole is campaigning for the Republican presidential nomination in Iowa. The two-page single-spaced letter is dated January 22 and written by Nick Evans, Shine's boss. Evans is the president of Spartan Communications, a television group with 13 stations (including one LMA station), consisting of eleven CBS and two ABC affiliates. According to a 1999 analysis by *Broadcasting & Cable*, all of Spartan's stations are ranked number 1 or 2 in their markets.[96] Evans is on NAB's TV board. His company also owns four TV stations in Dole's home state of Kansas.

Evans starts his letter by saying it is not a threat.

> I hope you take this letter in the spirit for which it is written. It is in no way intended to be disrespectful of you or your position as one of our nation's leaders, and it is not a threat. I simply want to bring a very important issue to light and inform you of our position and intentions if forced to defend what I believe to be the survival and livelihood of free over-the-air television. Personally, I want to support you and vote for you for President. However, my support is waning.

---

[93] Martin Peers, "Clinton May Side With Dole, *Daily Variety*, 23 January 1996, p. 1.

[94] Dennis Wharton, "Dole Presses Digital Bid," *Daily Variety*, 26 January 1996, p. 3.

[95] Shine also shows up in lobbying over the Cable Act of 1992. See 14 August 1989 entry on John Shine in the previous chapter.

[96] Elizabeth Rathbun, "Media General Doubles Its TVs in $605 Million Merger," *Broadcasting & Cable*, 13 December 1999, p. 10.

He continues by stating that Dole's position on spectrum auctions will kill him and that he won't go down without swinging.

> Your current stance and talk of auctioning spectrum will destroy free over-the-air television and America's local television stations. I cannot—and will not—sit on the sidelines and allow this to happen. My American and Southern heritage will force me to fight for victory or go down swinging.

Evans reminds Dole that "Our company owns television stations in Kansas, Iowa, South Carolina, Georgia, and Florida." The order in which Evans lists the states, starting with Kansas and Iowa, is a good approximation of the political importance to Dole of the various stations he owns. After explaining that Dole's auction proposal is prohibitively expensive and will destroy his company, Evans expresses his Republican sympathies and natural inclination to support Dole:

> Senator Dole, I am a registered Republican and have wanted to vote for you for President since I met you at Senator Strom Thurmond's 90th birthday celebration in Washington. I met Mrs. Dole a few years earlier at a dinner in Charlotte, North Carolina, and believe she would be one of the all-time great First Ladies.

Note the social intimacy between local broadcasters and members of Congress. Evans describes two social settings where he met with two high-powered politicians from states where he had local TV stations. The mindset reflected by Evans helps explain why local Southern broadcasters never exposed Senator Lott's sympathies for white supremacist groups and Senator Thurmond's hypocrisy in preaching white purity while having an out-of-wedlock daughter with a black maid servant. Both stories came to public attention—with consequent local coverage—only as a result of the efforts of the national press.

Next comes Evans' key paragraph, his threat to use his most potent weapon, his control over the media, to hurt Dole. Note Evans' assertion that his sentiments are representative of the larger broadcasting community. Given his national and local leadership positions within the broadcasting community, his threat that his 13 TV stations will not be alone in seeking retribution comes across as credible. Note also that the Iowa caucuses, a major hurdle in Dole's campaign for the Republican nomination, will be held on February 12.

Winning the Iowa caucuses, not fighting for spectrum reform, is clearly Dole's top priority.

> This is where the hard part comes into play. If over the next few days your position on spectrum has not changed and been made public, you will have lost my support. **I will be forced to use our resources to tell the viewers in all of our markets** of your plan to destroy free over-the-air television. I will be forced to tell the over 700 employees of our company of your plan and encourage their support of another Presidential candidate. **I have spoken with many other broadcasters who feel the same as I do.** Without speaking for them, I know that they are making the same plans that I am, while wishing and hoping that they can support your race for the Presidency.

In other words, Evans appears to be following through on what Jim May asked broadcasters like Evans to do several days earlier at NAB's January TV Board meeting, which was then broadcast to local station management. Admittedly, neither Evans nor May explicitly state that slanted public affairs coverage will be one of the employed resources. But it's a reasonable inference for a politician like Dole to make for three reasons. First, it's the broadcasters' most potent political resource. Slanted local TV coverage is a U.S. Senator's worst nightmare; no legislators spend proportionately more of their resources seeking positive TV coverage (mostly paid political ads but also PR for free news coverage) than U.S. Senators.[97] Second, like an elephant in a small room, broadcasters such as Evans and May, and politicians such as Dole, are extremely well aware of this potential resource. That, of course, is why broadcasters' public codes of ethics explicitly state and their public appearances insistently suggest that they would never allow bias to creep into their programming. Yet, ominously, Evans and May, in their private correspondence, don't bother to repeat the public claim that there are some resources a broadcaster can never use. Third, Evans and May make it very clear that broadcasters have a life-or-death incentive to use the most potent resources at their disposal. Broadcasters may truly be altruists—perhaps even masochists. But it's reasonable to believe that few successful politicians operate on such an assumption.

In a long paragraph, Evans elaborates on all the good things broadcasters do for their local communities. But the only charity he mentions by name is the

---

[97] See NAB, "A National Report on Local Broadcasters' Community Service," (Washington, DC: NAB, April 2000).

American Red Cross. This is noteworthy because Elizabeth Dole, Dole's wife, is the president of the Red Cross, and the Red Cross is heavily dependent on the free PR and fundraising support from the broadcasting community.[98] One reasonable interpretation is that this is a veiled threat that Dole might not be the only person in his family to lose the valuable support of local TV stations.

Then Evans summarizes his argument and warns Dole that if he doesn't change his position, Evans (and his fellow broadcasters) will begin a campaign against Dole in Iowa and elsewhere during the week preceding the Iowa caucuses.

> I believe the spectrum issue is important to the American people. I hope you will reconsider your views and position. Providing broadcasters a smooth transition to digital is not "corporate welfare." It is good business and a necessity for the American consumer and local broadcasters. My plan is to start our campaign against spectrum auctions and its supporters in the next ten days.

Evans concludes: "I hope that you will find a way to be with us so that we can be with you. My best wishes to you and your family for a safe and healthy 1996." By January 23, it's a little late to be offering New Years greetings. But given that 1996 represents the likely culmination of Dole's political career, it is a singularly apt allusion to what is at stake for Dole if he doesn't resolve this issue with Evans to mutual advantage.

On January 26, another Evans employee, Ron Collins, the General Manager of its CBS affiliate in Wichita, Kansas, conveyed the following threat to Dole's telecom legislative aide. The threat was then passed on to Senator Dole:

> In a conversation this afternoon with Ron Collins, General Manager of the CBS affiliate in Wichita, he…said his owner, who has stations in Iowa and South Carolina [two early presidential nominating states], will start running "editorials" in two weeks about how Congress/Senator Dole will kill free, over-the-air broadcasting if resolution is not reached. I "recommended" they reconsider as…what his boss intends to do is extortion. I assume NAB put them up to this and has ginned up other owners to run similar, self-serving editorials.[99]

---

[98] E.g., see the cover picture of Bob Dole, "Giving Away the Airwaves; Industry Should Pay for Licenses for Digital TV," *New York Times*, 27 March 1997, p. A29.

[99] Memo from David Wilson to Senator Dole, 26 January 1996.

Interpretation of the Threat

The type of media use implied in Evans' threat was not unambiguously clear. Was it just editorials or was it also news and public affairs coverage? Similarly, the scope of issues covered was also not unambiguous. Was it just coverage of telecom issues or was it coverage of any issue that might harm Dole?

Clearly, the threat covered broadcast editorials against spectrum auctions. Collins explicitly qualifies his threat with the word "editorial." But Collins' boss, Evans, doesn't make that qualification clear. Evans says: "I will be forced to use our resources to tell the viewers in all of our markets of your plan to destroy free over-the-air television." But he doesn't qualify resources to include only editorials.

Politically far more important is the question whether the threat covered not only telecom issues but also any issue that might make Dole look bad. The latter would have been a far more potent political threat because, as argued earlier, politicians generally care little about how the media does or does not cover telecom issues because it's not an issue that affects how the average citizen votes. The latter is also a far more damaging allegation against a TV broadcaster because of the widely held norm that each issue should be evaluated on its own merits. In public debates and courts of law, advocates for a policy position don't attack opponents based on unrelated policy positions. Doing otherwise is known as playing dirty and is publicly scorned.

Evans doesn't explicitly say he's going to run bad news and withhold good news about Dole. But it would certainly be a reasonable inference from the rest of his letter. He clearly states that this is a life-or-death issue for his company: "Your current stance and talk of auctioning spectrum will destroy free over-the-air television and America's local television stations." Then he says he will respond in proportion to this danger to his livelihood: "I cannot—and will not—sit on the sidelines and allow this to happen. My American and Southern heritage will force me to fight for victory or go down swinging."

Any journalist covering a presidential election who made such a statement publicly would be immediately fired because station management would contend that the journalist had forfeited his credibility in covering that politician with station audiences. Why shouldn't it be reasonable for a politician such as Dole to make the same inference?

Moreover, it is reasonable to assume that Evans intuitively knew that Dole would make such an inference. In politics, both threats and promises are rarely made explicitly, if only because exchanging resources (including both cash and media coverage) in return for Congressional favors (most notably votes on legislation) is widely perceived of as bribery. When such bribery is definitively documented, both the politician and interest group lose political support from the public at large.

Evans' willingness to use his airwaves to seek revenge may best be revealed by an incident having nothing to do with politics and mostly to do with wounded honor. During the summer of 1998, Evans had trouble getting his friends tickets to attend The Late Show with David Letterman. The Late Show had a policy of not providing its CBS affiliates with tickets during the summer months when popular demand by tourists reaches its peak. Evans, with 7 CBS affiliates, was incensed, and in retaliation took The Late Show off the air for a week.[100]

Aftermath of the Threat

Within one week of the Evans letter, Dole did almost everything Evans asked for, including keeping the spectrum issue out of the presidential campaign and letting the telecommunications bill pass with the spectrum clause intact. Was the Evans letter and its threat of using the media even partially the cause of Dole's change of heart? No definitive answer can be given. The Evans letter was just one of many pressures influencing Dole and may, singly, have been an insignificant one. Surely, however, Evans (with the NAB TV Board's backing?) would not invest his time in writing such a potentially compromising letter—and also have one of his managers personally deliver it in the most politically potent setting imaginable—if he didn't think it could be influential. Of course, Dole may have changed his mind about the telecommunications bill and kept the spectrum issue out of the presidential campaign for reasons wholly or largely independent of the forces the Evans letter represented. But Dole was a practical politician. It is reasonable to think that he took the Evans letter seriously and recognized that spectrum policy was not an issue for which he would risk sacrificing the Iowa caucus, the Republican nomination, and his life's ambition, the presidency. If Dole did come to conclude that pursuit of the spectrum issue would bias coverage against him by the Iowa TV stations and perhaps TV stations in other primary states, then his choice of action seems obvious.

---

[100] Bauder, David, "Station Owner Pulls Letterman Show," *Associated Press Online*, 15 July 1998. Hofbauer, Lisa, "Owner Pulls Own Stupid Human Trick," *Post and Courier*, 19 July 1998, p. F1. Barnhart, Aaron, *Late Show News*, Number 211, 21 July 1998, http://www.tvbarn.com/lsn-archive/lsn-072198.text

Late on the afternoon of January 26, three days after the Evans letter and ten days after the NAB's grassroots lobbying campaign went into high gear, Dole surprised nearly everyone by saying that he would let the telecommunications bill proceed.

The sense of surprise is captured by the alert that Jim May sent just the day before to ALL NAB TELEVISION MEMBERS. The Alert includes the following text, which suggests the NAB believed the auction proposal was still very much in play. Capitols and underlines are in the original.

HOUSE MAY MOVE ON SPECTRUM AUCTIONS AS EARLY AS NEXT WEEK

When legislation to extend the debt ceiling is considered next week, there is a great likelihood that a "mini-budget" agreement will be included in that legislation. Our sources tell us that House and Senate leadership in concert with the Administration are approaching agreement to include $25 TO $30 BILLION IN REVENUE FROM SPECTRUM AUCTIONS IN THE PACKAGE....

The stark reality is that we are now directly facing a Congressional initiative to auction off our future to our competitors. If you don't forcefully contact your Congressional delegation in the next few days and urge them not to auction off the future of free, over-the-air broadcasting, it may well be too late.[101]

Given that Dole had held up the telecommunications bill for close to a month with the goal of getting the spectrum giveaway clause either altered or removed, his release of the bill was a significant defeat. All he was able to get in the subsequent days before he brought the bill to a vote were three letters. The first, signed by the Congressional leadership, promised Dole that "we share your determination to protect America's taxpayers" and "agree that the FCC should not issue any initial licenses or construction permits for Advanced Television Services until Congress sets policy in this area."[102] The second letter, also signed by the Congressional leadership, was to FCC Chair Reed Hundt requesting that until Congress moves "legislation to overhaul our nation's policies governing the electromagnetic spectrum," the "Commission not issue

---

[101] Memo from Jim May to All NAB Television Members, 25 January 1996.

[102] Letter to Senate Majority Leader Dole from House Commerce Committee Chair Tom Bliley, Speaker of the House Newt Gingrich, Senate Commerce Committee Chair Larry Pressler, and Senate Majority Whip (2nd in command after Majority Leader Dole) Trent Lott, 31 January 1996.

any initial licenses or construction permits for Advanced Television Services...."[103] The third letter was a joint letter signed by all five FCC Commissioners responding to the Congressional leadership letter and promising to accede to their wishes.[104]

Some industry observers described this compromise as a "public relations ploy intended to save face for Senator Dole."[105] A less cynical explanation is that Dole simply tried to salvage what he could. In any case, the letters would not achieve their stated purpose of getting Congress to introduce spectrum legislation, and the FCC would go ahead and issue digital TV licenses in April 1997. The Telecom Act had not explicitly directed the FCC to issue such licenses but also had left the FCC no other option if it wanted to license the spectrum.

Perhaps most important for the broadcasters, Dole kept the issue out of the subsequent presidential campaign. When Dole, the presumptive Republican presidential nominee, publicly raised the spectrum issue on December 29, 1995, it was widely perceived as an attack on the Clinton administration, which had publicly endorsed and taken credit for the telecommunications bill. The position was intended to show that the Republicans, unlike the Democratic administration, were serious about attacking corporate welfare and balancing the budget. However, in the aftermath of the Evans letter and passage of the telecommunications bill, Dole kept the spectrum issue out of the presidential primary, not raising it again publicly until April 17, 1996, a date by which he had for all practical purposes secured the Republican nomination.

On April 17, Dole delivered a blistering attack on the Senate floor against the broadcasters. During that speech he for the first and only time publicly alluded to the Evans letter, which he ridiculed and implied could not intimidate him. The gist of Dole's speech attacked the broadcasters for their blackout

---

[103] Letter to FCC Chair Reed Hundt from House Commerce Committee Chair Tom Bliley, Speaker of the House Newt Gingrich, Senate Commerce Committee Chair Larry Pressler, and Senate Majority Leader Trent Lott, 31 January 1996. A copy of the letter can be found at 104th Congress, 2nd Session, *Congressional Record*, 24 July 1996, 142(110), p. H8272.

[104] A copy of the letter and Dole's discussion of it can be found at 104th Congress, 2nd Session, *Congressional Record*, 1 February 1996, 142(14), p. S719. A discussion can also be found in"Doubleheader—Both Houses Vote; Telecom Bill Sweeps Through Congress," *Communications Daily*, 2 February 1996, p. 1.

[105] Doug Halonen, "Historic Industry Rewrite Finally Passes," *Electronic Media*, 5 February 1996, p. 1.

of opposing views on the spectrum issue and their use of the airwaves to intimidate Congress.

The April 17th speech may be interpreted as Dole's last attempt to make this an issue in the general election. Perhaps not coincidentally, the previous day, April 16, Vice President Gore delivered a major address at the broadcasters' major annual convention. In it, Gore attacked the "Gingrich-Dole" plan to immediately auction digital TV spectrum.[106] Since Gingrich was a strong supporter of the broadcasters and would later overturn the letter Dole secured from the FCC, this accusation would appear to lack merit. Neither the broadcast TV networks nor their station affiliates covered these conflicting speeches.

Not until after the general election would Dole again speak publicly about the spectrum giveaway. On March 27, 1997, one week before the FCC handed out digital licenses to the broadcasters, Dole wrote an op-ed for the *New York Times* entitled "Giving Away the Airwaves; Industry should pay for licenses for digital TV."[107] Dole pointedly noted that the Republican Congressional leadership and the five FCC commissioners were about to violate their letters of agreement with him signed a year earlier.

Not until March 12, 1997—after the presidential election—would the Clinton administration publicly state that there should be a quid pro quo for the granting of additional spectrum to the broadcasters. Previously, the Clinton administration had called for increased public interest obligations for broadcasters, including the v-chip and more children's TV, but had kept the issues separate.

In an ironic twist, after the election Dole took a job at Verner, Lipfert, Bernhard, McPherson and Hand, a high-profile lobbying firm one of whose clients is the NAB. One of Dole's aides also took a job in NAB's government affairs department.

To be fair, the letters of commitment Dole got before the Telecom Act passed were interpreted as a significant threat by the broadcast industry leadership and led the NAB to orchestrate a massive grassroots campaign by its members stations, including the media campaign described in the first part of this chapter.

---

[106] Remarks of Vice President Al Gore before the National Association of Broadcasters' Annual Convention, Las Vegas, Nevada, 16 April 1996. The precise quote is: "[W]e have opposed every suggestion from the Gingrich-Dole Congress that we should just immediately auction the digital spectrum and let the winners tdo whatever they want with it." Alternatively, see Dennis Wharton, *Daily Variety*, Gore Cheers Kidvid Quotas at NAB," 17 April 1996, p. 8.

[107] Layton, "Lobbying Juggernaut."

Without that lobbying pressure (and Dole's loss in the presidential election), it's likely that the Republican Congressional leaders would have adhered to their promises.

In 1999, Media General purchased the 13 local TV stations of Evans' Spartan Communications Inc. for $605 million.[108]

Did Evans Act with The Approval of the NAB?

Did Evans act as a loner or with the approval of broadcast industry leaders? One plausible possibility is that he was acting with the awareness and support of the NAB TV Board. The 24 members of the NAB TV Board collectively control a large fraction, probably a majority, of the TV stations in the United States. As we have seen, the NAB TV Board met one week before the Evans letter was sent, with Jim May coming out of that meeting with arms swinging at Dole and asserting that all means were fair game in the coming attack.

Knowing how the NAB and Washington lobbying works, it is inconceivable that at some point during the TV Board meeting all eyes didn't turn to Nick Evans with a request to apply pressure on Dole. The well-established pattern at the NAB is to use local broadcasters to apply pressure on members of Congress. Washington broadcast lobbyists often visit members of Congress with local broadcasters in tow for just this reason. And local broadcasters are often chosen to testify before Congressional committees with a keen sensitivity to which members of Congress on the committee might need persuading. Heartland broadcasters like Evans are the heart and soul of the NAB.

With four TV stations in Dole's home sate of Kansas and a TV station in Iowa where Dole was campaigning, Evans was the logical go-to person on the NAB TV Board. Evans himself makes the claim that his threat is not an isolated one: "I have spoken with many other broadcasters who feel the same as I do." Some of those, surely, were on the NAB TV Board.

It's also reasonable to believe that NAB's governmental affairs department was aware of the Evans letter both before and after it was sent out. A central mandate of NAB's government affairs department is to orchestrate broadcasters' lobbying of Congress, especially Congressional leaders with control of broadcasting legislation. As part of that mandate, it maintains constant contact with members of the legislative liaison committees in each state, especially members in states with key lawmakers. To facilitate this exchange of

---

[108] Elizabeth Rathbun, "Media General Doubles Its TVs in $605 Million Merger," *Broadcasting & Cable*, 13 December 1999, p. 10.

information, it maintains a toll-free hotline just for Congressional contacts. It also regularly requests of all station members that copies of all Congressional correspondence be sent to NAB headquarters. For this purpose, it maintains a large cabinet filled with thousands of letters. Given Evans' position in the NAB, it seems unlikely that he would have flouted NAB protocol.

Assuming NAB did know, it is noteworthy that the NAB neither acknowledged nor denounced the Evans letter when journalists asked for reactions to allegations that fear of retribution was a major source of the NAB's power.[109]

Whether or not TV broadcasting managers knew the details of Evans' behavior, they bear some responsibility for choosing him as a leader. Approximately half the seats on the NAB TV board are chosen by ballot, and Evans holds one of those seats.[110] Almost every TV station in the United States had the opportunity to vote on Evans both before and after his letter dated January 22, 1996. In February 1997 Evans was reelected to the NAB TV Board in a highly competitive election in which 16 senior TV executives ran for only six open slots on the NAB TV board.[111] His victory can at least partly be attributed to the NAB leadership's appreciation for his good service to the broadcasting community. During 1999 and 2000, Evans chaired the Television Operators Caucus, an NAB-affiliated lobbying group of about a dozen of the nation's largest and most prestigious network affiliated TV operating groups, including Cox Broadcasting, Hearst-Argyle, and Post-Newsweek.[112]

In the final analysis, the evidence tying Evans' letter to the broader broadcasting community is circumstantial. Moreover, it is not clear that Evans or any other broadcaster would have carried out their threats of retribution.

---

[109] This is consistent with the observation that in thousands of pages of NAB correspondence with TV station general managers, the NAB has constantly exhorted station managers to lobby more aggressively, but never exhorted them not to breach the divide between the news and business sides of their companies. This point is all the more telling because in the past the NAB has encouraged its station managers to alert their news directors of information favorable to the broadcasters.

[110] The TV networks and representatives from other broadcasting organizations have standing seats on the board.

[111] After re-election, Nick Evans, apparently speaking for the NAB TV board, said of Congress: "Broadcasters are tired of being bullied." See Paige Albiniak, "NAB Board Focusing on Content, Spectrum," *Broadcasting & Cable*, 23 June 1997, p. 20. The statement is ironic not only because of Evans' own behavior and earlier victories, but because it came after the NAB had just used Congress to overturn the FCC and Clinton administration plan to force broadcasters to return their spectrum by 2006.

[112] "Personals," *Television Digest*, 10 April 2000.

However, what counts politically is not reality but perception. If the goal of media owners was to exert influence, all that matters is that Dole had reasonable grounds to believe that Evans was not a loner and was perhaps reflective of a significant fraction of the broadcasting community. Given this reality, the fact that the leadership of the broadcasting community has never exposed and punished the type of behavior exhibited by Evans makes them guilty not only of hypocrisy but of knowingly aiding and abetting a form of media bias that, even if rarely exercised and only by a small minority, greatly enhances their own political power as an industry.

In 2004, *American Journalism Review* writer Charles Layton interviewed Nick Evans about this letter and reported:

> He repeated the claim in his letter that he thought other broadcasters felt as he did. "I know that I had spoken with others and that others felt similar to what I was stating there. Whether or not they would have followed through was not my goal...I could only speak for myself." When asked what other broadcasters had thought of his letter, Evans said, "Most everybody I heard from was supportive."[113]

Retribution Against Interest Groups

The Nick Evans letter represents a case of potential media retribution against an elected official. But media retribution can also be used against competing interest groups.

The cellular telephone industry was the main competitor for the spectrum granted to the broadcasters.[114] The mobile telephone industry not only wanted the spectrum the broadcasters had; it also was outraged that whereas it had to pay tens of billions of dollars to get its sliver of spectrum, the broadcasters were getting theirs without paying a dime.

On September 6, 1995 the Campaign for Broadcast Competition (CBC) was announced. CBC opposed the broadcast giveaway and the largest share of its funding came from the Cellular Telecommunications Industry Association (CTIA). On October 18, 1995, ABC's PrimeTime Live ran an expose on CTIA's

---

[113] Brinkley, *Defining Vision*.

[114] Chris Stern, "The Cellular Telecommunications Industry Association Accuses ABC of Retaliating for Ctia's Complaints About the Radio Spectrum Auction in Which ABC Took Part with Other Broadcasters," *Broadcasting & Cable*, 23 October 1995, p. 22.

Congressional junkets.[115] The CTIA accused ABC of retaliation for the group's effort to oppose "the $37 billion spectrum rip-off of America's taxpayers by CapCities/ABC and other broadcasters."[116] In a letter to ABC News President Roone Arledge, the CTIA stated: "Your use of PrimeTime Live to attack CTIA for hosting an education forum and working session—which people had to give up their weekend to attend—can only be explained as reprisal for CTIA's willingness to stand up and blow the whistle on the broadcast giveaway."[117]

Given that the NAB is one of the kings of Congressional junkets to warm sunny climates for its annual meetings[118] and that the broadcast networks are famous for putting on great Congressional social events at inaugurals, national

---

[115] ABC Primetime, Transcript #424, 18 October 1995. ABC News Reporter Chris Wallace begins the segment on the CTIA junket: "[voice-over] In July, the Senate voted 98 to nothing effectively to ban corporate-sponsored trips, even so-called 'charity' events. But it doesn't take effect until next year and the House is still arguing about it.... But none of this stopped a trip to Lake Tahoe, Nevada, in June hosted by the Cellular Telecommunications Industry Association just as Congress was rewriting the telecommunications law. Steve Buyer, a second-term Republican from Indiana, was the lone Congressman on the trip along with six Congressional staffers. They stayed at Harrah's Casino and Hotel where rooms cost $130 per night. They attended work-shops and played golf at a nearby course-greens fees: $125...."

[116] Stern, "The Cellular Telecommunications Industry Association Accuses ABC of Retaliating for Ctia's Complaints About the Radio Spectrum Auction in Which ABC Took Part with Other Broadcasters."

[117] Robert Wright, "Assault on the Broadcast Business: A Commentary from Bob Wright, President and CEO, NBC," *Broadcasting & Cable*, 11 September 1995, p. 6.

[118] In addition to the annual NAB show in Las Vegas, there is the annual January NAB board retreat that often attracts top Congressional leadership. In January 1996, the NAB Board destination, with members of Congress in tow, was the La Quinta Resort & Club in La Quinta, California. The resort, a favorite haunt of Hollywood and sports celebrities as well as boards of other well-heeled telecom trade organizations, boasts of itself as a "hide-away" with three golf courses, five restaurants, and a spa. At $550 per room, per day, it's a remarkable Congressional perk. For articles mentioning NAB's Congressional retreats, see Richard Wolf, "Congress Still Being Courted: Ethics review hasn't ended wining, dining," *USA Today*, 19 January 1990, p. 3A, Don West, "NAB in La Quinta: Way station to the future," *Broadcasting & Cable*, 20 January 1992, p. 4. "Turner Well Position: Broadcaster Must Go Interactive," *Communications Daily*, 19 January 1994, p. 7. In August 1995, NAB canceled its legislative forum preceding its annual January board meeting, so in that sense ABC Primetime was not hypocritical in covering the CTIA legislative forum. See "NAB Board Imbalance Addressed," *Television Digest*, 14 August 1995, p. 5.

political party conventions, football games, and Christmas Parties, ABC's PrimeTime can at a minimum be accused of having a double standard.

Regardless of the merits of CTIA's complaint, CTIA abandoned the Campaign for Broadcast Competition. Compared to other issues in the telecom bill, the broadcasters' spectrum clause was of relatively little importance.[119] As long as broadcasters weren't allowed to use their new spectrum to provide mobile telephone service, the spectrum giveaway was no direct threat to CTIA members' interests. The ABC program may be viewed as a signal that if the mobile telephone industry went after the broadcast industry, the broadcast industry would respond in kind.[120] It was therefore in their mutual interest to cooperate and prevent public displays of conflict that would alert the public to items in the Telecom Act not in their interest.

The widely reported CTIA incident may have served as a cautionary tale to other interest groups. As *Electronic Media* reported shortly after the telecom bill passed, "According to [one] analysis, the broadcast industry's competitors haven't been lobbying for auctions overtly thus far, for fear of broadcaster retaliation."[121]

---

[119] This was the era of the "cellular wars," when cell companies were putting up huge numbers of 150' high cell towers and local residents were screaming to their town trustees: "not in my backyard." The arguments were numerous—aesthetically unpleasant vistas, zoning ordinance violations, decreased property values, increased health risks, bribery of town officials, and democratic due process violations—resulting in delay and extra expense. The '96 Telecom Act took most of the power away from localities in tower placement decisions.

[120] A more direct signal was sent out in a commentary in *Broadcasting & Cable* in which NBC President Robert Wright threatened to go after the mobile telephone industry's already allocated spectrum: "As Congress moves closer to a decision, a new organization has joined the fray, advocating significant spectrum fees for broadcasters. Bankrolled in part by the Cellular Telecommunications Industry Association and other spectrum users, the so-called Campaign for Broadcast Competition is pointing at broadcasters in an apparent attempt to insure its members avoid paying their fair share of deficit reduction. It is not unusual for corporations to use front groups to advocate for or against legislative proposals. What is ironic here is that the members of this shell group want broadcasters to pay while they continue to use their spectrum for free." Robert Waterman McChesney, *Telecommunications, Mass Media, and Democracy: The Battle for the Control of U.S. Broadcasting, 1928–1935* (New York: Oxford University Press, 1993). Note that Wright is referring to the mobile telephone industry's *existing* licenses whereas the broadcasters were seeking *new* licenses.

[121] Douglas Halonen, "Historic Rewrite Finally Passes," *Electronic Media*, 5 February 1996, p. 1.

Public TV

For many decades, public and private broadcasting were in political conflict.[122] Private broadcasters didn't want to fund public broadcasting and didn't want to share spectrum with it. But in the last few decades, public broadcasting has developed a close alliance with the commercial broadcasters, acting according to the principle: "if you cannot beat 'em, join 'em."

During 1995, both commercial and non-commercial TV broadcasters lobbied together for spectrum rights. But non-commercial broadcasters also had a much more pressing concern: to prevent being zeroed out of the federal budget. With the Republican sweep of Congress in 1994, public TV faced the very real threat of losing its federal funding. In this struggle for survival, public broadcasters viewed their airwaves as a lobbying asset. Here is a brief chronology of this period:

On January 17, 1995, Senate Commerce Committee Chair Larry Pressler writes the first of several op-eds calling for a phase out of federal subsidies for public TV.[123] Soon thereafter, PBS provides the following guidance to its member stations on recruiting political support with on-air messages:

> Our air is our most valuable communications resource. We have been using it for years to tell our constituents why public TV deserves support through our institutional positioning efforts. Now we have the opportunity to use our air to inform viewers why federal support is an essential part of the public television funding mix. Through our air, we can make the strongest and most compelling case for continued federal funding for public TV.[124]

PBS then provides general advice on how to develop the spots:

> **Consider your community.** Each station should take into account its community's potential reaction when weighing the decision to schedule messages about the federal funding situation over the air.

---

[122] E.g., APTS, "Grassroots Action Handbook," (Washington, DC: Association of America's Public Television Stations, September 1995).

[123] Larry Pressler, "Spring Big Bird from Its Gilded Cage," *St. Louis Post-Dispatch*, 17 January 1995, p. 11B. See also Larry Pressler, "Reality-Based Broadcasting," *Washington Post*, 8 March 1995, p. A19.

[124] Guidelines sent from PBS to its member stations on "Federal Funding and On-Air Messages," January 1995.

Ask for Action! Ask those who value your services to call or write their senators and representatives to let them know how valuable public television is to them. Reinforce our message points.

Help them help you. Be sure to help viewers take action by providing them with their congresspersons' addresses and phone numbers on the air, or by giving them a station phone number to call for more information.

Retagged local spots. Your existing local positioning spots afford an opportunity to highlight your station's value and encourage your viewers to let Congress know how much they value public TV. Consider retagging your local spots with a call to action tag or a tag listing a number to call at your station for information on how to contact local Congressional representatives.[125]

PBS also draws a boundary on acceptable over-the-air lobbying:

Make it non-partisan. Public TV has always enjoyed bipartisan support. Messages should not be, or appear to be, partisan in nature, single out individuals or single out either political party. Rather, we must make the affirmative case for public television.[126]

In response to those who question whether the airwaves should be used as a lobbying resource, PBS suggests the following three responses:

1) We have always communicated with our viewers, both on-air and off-air, about the activities and value of public television. It's part of our obligation to them as a public servant.

2) Our own air is a logical venue for informing viewers, because it involves negligible expense to us and thus is a wise use of our scarce resources.

3) There is a huge amount of misinformation being circulated about public television, including frequent statements by public television opponents on national television and in national publications. We can't buy time on national television to correct this misinformation, but our viewers deserve to know the truth.[127]

---

[125] APTS, "Grassroots Action Handbook."
[126] Ibid.
[127] Ibid.

In September 1995, the Association of Public Television Stations (APTS), which lobbies on behalf of PBS and local public TV stations, sends to its members a Grassroots Action Handbook.[128] The 50+ page Handbook includes the PBS on-air lobbying guidelines as well as local public TV station case studies of "Grassroots Strategies That Work." Some of the case studies appear to hew closely to the PBS guidelines:

> **WTVS, Detroit.** WTVS uses many "new-fashioned" tools to heighten awareness of current concerns. GM Bob Larsen went on-air urging the public to communicate their views on funding issues.
>
> **WUSF, Tampa.** Jim [the general manager of WUSF] visits his Congressional representatives in Washington two or three times a year, sometimes more often....
>
> Jim also works the other side of the equation, doing all he can to keep viewers informed of what's going on in Washington. He puts letters in the monthly viewer guidelines when necessary and also makes on-air announcements.[129]

But other case studies hint at using local TV stations as a type of political contribution. The description of WLIW's on-air lobbying activities starts in the PBS mold:

> **WLIW, New York.** For a successful letter writing campaign, Laura [Director of WLIW's Community Relations] found she first had some educating to do...WLIW used on-air spots to urge viewers to write, and even set up a hotline with information about members' addresses.[130]

But then the case study appears to veer off into more controversial territory:

> Laura keeps in touch with her Congressional delegation. Members often appear on WLIW's program "Window on Washington." When Congressional members of the New York, New Jersey and Connecticut delegations might not be convinced of the value of public television, general manager Terrel Cass uses his own style of persuasion,...[131]

---

[128] One of the original reasons for separating PBS and APTS was to create a firewall between the programming and lobbying arm of public TV.

[129] APTS, "Grassroots Action Handbook."

[130] Ibid.

[131] Ibid.

The case study of WNPB raises even more red flags:

> **WNPB, West Virginia.** With a small staff and limited resources, it's all the more important to work together and effectively communicate. Carolyn Bailey [WNPB's general manager] believes in partnerships, both within and outside the building....
>
> Carolyn keeps in touch with her delegation and their aides. They're on all mailing lists, they get dubs of pertinent local programs and documentaries, and members are invited to be on WNPB's weekly viewer phone-in program "On the Line With..." Carolyn ensures members know the station is available to them....
>
> When there's an event in the area, WNPB makes a point to be there, especially when members of Congress are in attendance. Carolyn and her staff attend receptions, ground-breakings, meetings, dedications and more....[132]

Similar incentives to use media as a lobbying resource may apply when candidates run for state office. In 1998, for example, Minnesota Governor Jesse Ventura proposed phasing out state funding for public broadcasters. *Electronic Media* reported the following comment from the spokesperson for Minnesota Public Radio, which represents 24 stations.

> He said Gov. Ventura's proposals are ironic because the lawmaker attributed much of his success as a third party candidate to his inclusion in gubernatorial debates on public TV and radio. "He said he got elected because of Minnesota Public Radio. We have it on tape," the spokesman said.[133]

There is nothing explicit in this comment linking TV coverage to policy stands, and I have no evidence that Minnesota Public Radio ever exercised any bias against Governor Ventura. But the comment does raise alarm bells because it suggests that Minnesota Public Radio has the motive and means to influence an election to benefit its own narrow self interest.

---

[132] David Hatch, "Jesse Puts Move on Minnesota Pubcasters," *Electronic Media*, 8 February 1998, p. 4.

[133] Lizette Alvarez, "Testing of a President: The Defender; a Lawmaker Uses His Own Shame as a Guide," *New York Times*, 13 December 1998, p. A18, "Judging Barney Frank," *New York Times*, 25 July 1990.

The case of Alan Chartock, executive director of public radio station WAMC-FM and one of the largest public radio media moguls, with ten stations covering seven states from Vermont to Pennsylvania, may be even more chilling. For twelve years Chartock ran a weekly half hour public affairs interview show called "Capital Connection" with New York Governor Cuomo,[134] who had major responsibility for funding his stations and was personally solicited by Chartock for more funds.[135] Political connections may also be useful in winning new FM licenses or winning expanded geographic coverage for existing stations.[136]

Unbeknownst to Cuomo, Chartock secretly taped the before and after show conversations with Cuomo. Chartock hoped to write a book one day and thought the tapes would be useful. In October 1995, a disgruntled employee collected some of those tapes and distributed them to competitive commercial radio broadcasters. A *Times Union* reporter summarized the political portion of the tape:

> He gave Cuomo advice on speeches. He told the governor about ostensibly private conversations with lobbyists and offered advice on how to deal with the media. Once, Cuomo even suggested that Chartock call GOP gubernatorial contender Herb London and urge him to write an angry letter to the New York Post. Chartock told Cuomo he'd do that, but he told me that he didn't follow through.[137]

The tapes revealed that Chartock was a strong partisan for Cuomo, even though he had claimed to be non-partisan. In 1994, for example, Chartock personally moderated the first gubernatorial debate between Democratic incumbent Cuomo and his Republican challenger, George Pataki. The debate was broadcast on Chartook's upstate New York radio network, C-SPAN TV, New York City public TV station WNET-TV, and New York City public radio

---

[134] Kathleen Schenectady, "Cuomo, Chartock Talk a Service to State Residents," Times Union, 31 October 1995, p. A10.

[135] Sarah Metzgar, "Pataki Deals Chartock Unkind Cut," *Times Union*, 18 January 1996, p. B2.

[136] RTNDA posed this "tough call" for broadcast news directors: "Two candidates are running for the U.S. Senate. One of them has opposed some of the purchases of additional stations by the owners of your station group. Word comes down from on high that the name of that candidate is not to be mentioned in any of your news stories. What do you do?" "Tough Calls," *Communicator*, November 1998, p. 64.

[137] Dan Lynch, "Tale of the Tape Speaks Volumes about Friendship, Fairness and Betrayal," *Times Union*, 19 October 1995, p. B1.

station WNYC-AM.[138] When Pataki refused to participate, the debate was held with Cuomo and four minor party candidates, one of whom (called "New York's version of Ross Perot") the Cuomo campaign thought was in a good position to siphon off votes from the Pataki campaign.[139]

After Cuomo lost, Chartock announced that his program would alternate between Democrats and Republicans, saying: "That's what public radio is all about. Let people hear different points of view and decide for themselves."[140] He invited Pataki to appear on his station but Pataki refused.[141] Later, Pataki commented: "There is nothing wrong with a liberal commentator being a liberal commentator. But it is the ultimate hypocrisy to have partisan political figures pretending to be unbiased political analysts, and it is unacceptable."[142]

After his election, Pataki proposed a budget zeroing out WAMC's funding. Chartock replied: "One has to assume there's some political motivation. If in fact this is political retribution, what we're talking about is government putting its grubby hands on the press and trying to alter its message."[143] What Chartock didn't apparently consider is that political motivation could cut both ways.[144] Politicians may reward public broadcasters for favorable coverage just as they can punish them for unfavorable coverage.

Later, I happened to be at a casual lunch where Chartock lambasted FCC Chair William Kennard and the Clinton administration in visceral, contemptuous terms for proposing new low power FM stations in the empty FM guard bands.[145] He wanted that spectrum to expand the reach of his own FM chain.[146]

---

[138] Alison Mitchell, "The 1994 Campaign," *New York Times*, 14 October 1994, p. B5.

[139] Tom Precious and Jane Gottlieb, "Governor 'Debate' Produces Little Heat," *Times Union*, 15 October 1994, p. A1. See also: Alison Mitchell, "The 1994 Campaign," *New York Times*, 14 October 1994, p. B5.

[140] Keith Marder, "Chartock Fills Spots Left by Cuomo's Loss," *Times Union*, 30 November 1994, p. B2.

[141] Keith Marder, "Listeners Speak Up," *Times Union*, 20 March 1996, p. C6.

[142] Tom Precious, "Pataki Rules Out Chartock Interview," *Times Union*, 20 October 1995, p. B2.

[143] Sarah Metzgar, "Pataki Deals Chartock Unkind Cut," *Times Union*, 18 January 1996, p. B2.

[144] As the *Times Union* editorialized, "this is a classic case where two wrongs don't make a right. Alan Chartock presents himself as a walking conflict of interest." See "Mr. Chartock Protests," *Times Union*, 25 January 1996, p. A10.

[145] Comments by Alan Chartock at Suny, Albany, 27 April 2000.

[146] "Radio Broadcasters Line Up to Buy Signal 'Translators' from FCC," *Business Review*, 16 May 2003, p. 6. See also "New Area FM License Draws a Crowd," *Capital District Business Review*, 18 January 1988, p. 1.

Conclusion

The case of the Telecom Act of 1996 provides evidence of both issue- and candidate-centered bias. It also provides evidence, if only based on common sense inferences from broadcasters' interactions with politicians, that candidate-centered bias may have been politically more important.

Of the various types of issue-centered bias, bias by omission seems to have been more important than bias by commission, at least for news reporting. This is consistent with the literature on political communication that the media's greatest power is its agenda setting power. By not covering the issue, TV broadcasters helped keep it off the public agenda. They also helped avoid any appearance that they might be covering the issue in a self-serving way.

When it comes to other forms of media coverage, notably ads and editorials in secondary media markets,[147] bias by commission appears to have been more evident. In the case of local TV broadcasters, the ads were framed in such a way that only an extremely well informed viewer could have inferred that the broadcasters were talking about avoiding paying a fee for additional spectrum rights. The reason is that the ads were framed to suggest that Congress wanted to kill local ad-supported ("free") TV programming while simultaneously imposing a new tax on viewers.

I believe that most members of Congress interpreted these ads as a warning shot rather than an effective grass roots mobilization tool. They helped signal that the broadcasters not only cared immensely about this issue, but also that they would play dirty and use their control of media, if need be. Whereas with the Cable Act of 1992 there was a genuine grassroots outpouring of support for the broadcasters about rising cable rates, with the Telecom Act of 1996 I could find no evidence of such support. Even when the broadcasters framed the issue of their paying for additional spectrum rights as a potential viewer tax and prime time program killer, the public did not respond. The best explanation I have for this is that with the Cable Act of 1992 broadcasters were promising to deal with an existing problem, rising cable rates and poor cable service, whereas with the Telecom Act of 1996 they were trying to scare the public with a hypothetical problem.

The extent to which the letter sent to Dole was indicative of the experience both Dole and other legislators had with other local broadcasters is hard to say. For the most part, broadcasters did not have incentives to react harshly to

---

[147] I found no evidence that the TV spots ran in major media markets such as New York City, Washington, DC, and Los Angeles.

members of Congress because most members of Congress did not support Dole's position, let along speak out publicly against the broadcasters' interest or have a leadership position with the ability to be politically effective.

Still, the evidence indicates that Evans represented a significant segment within broadcast industry management. Where Evans most diverted from industry mores was in leaving a paper trail. The pragmatic ethic of broadcast industry leaders is that as long as a form of media bias is undetectable or at least unverifiable, it's fair game for the exercise of political power. Perhaps because Dole did not make himself available for a face-to-face meeting at a crucial legislative moment in late January 1995, Evans was forced to communicate in a verifiable way what a politically savvy broadcaster would have instinctively communicated in a way to create plausible deniability.

Does opposition to broadcasters always invite media retribution? The most obvious contrary example would appear to be Senator McCain. Senator McCain is the only member of Congress who has publicly and consistently spoken out strongly against the giveaway of free spectrum rights to the broadcasters, yet he was subsequently re-elected to office. Have broadcasters given Senator McCain a pass or is McCain, arguably the most famous and trusted member of the U.S. Senate, simply too hard for them to topple?

I believe it is a combination of both. McCain may not see eye-to-eye with broadcasters on their biggest pocketbook issue—DTV spectrum—but he has been a helpful ally of theirs on other pocketbook issues.[148] Broadcasters may also think McCain is too hard to topple, so they just try to render him ineffective. Part of this may be fear of taking on McCain whose fame as a former POW stems from his withstanding torture for many years without breaking. The personal chemistry between Jim May, NAB executive Vice President of Government Affairs, and Senator McCain, may also have been a factor. Both are veterans, and May, a former Marine captain, and McCain, a former Navy captain, both attained comparable military rank. McCain, an economic conservative and social moderate with a swashbuckling entrepreneurial streak, may also fit the ideological profile of the typical local broadcast owner and manager. In a straw poll conducted at the NAB's annual state leadership meeting in 2000, where about 300 leading grassroots broadcast lobbyists come to Washington from all 50 states, Senator McCain came out tops. Explained one

---

[148] NAB press release entitled: "Statement by NAB President and CEO Edward O. Fritts on Senate Commerce Action on Budget Package," 17 June 1997. Bill McConnell, "Maverick McCain Rides Again," *Broadcasting & Cable*, 11 November 2002, p. 7.

broadcaster, "I don't have a problem with McCain. I've got an ABG attitude: anybody but Gore."[149]

During his chairmanship of the Senate Commerce Committee from 1997 through 2004, McCain appears to have been outmaneuvered by the NAB. The NAB has been able to use the Senate Appropriations committee, headed by NAB loyalist Senator Ted Stevens (R-Alaska),[150] to pass legislation bottled up in McCain's committee.[151] Accordingly, McCain was not in a position to do imminent harm to broadcasters the way Dole was when, as Senate Majority Leader, he tried to excise the spectrum clause from the Telecom Act of 1996.

In the 1997–1998 election cycle, McCain received $5,000 in PAC contributions from the NAB, which put him in the top 5% of members of Congress.[152] This was undoubtedly not due to any love of McCain but probably a realization

---

[149] Brooks Boliek, "Broadcasters Wary of a Gore-McCain Contest: Both have a long history with TV industry," *Hollywood Reporter*, 6 March 2000. See also: Brooks Boliek, "B'casters on McCain Bandwagon: Senator to head of class in poll at NAB conference," *Hollywood Reporter*, 22 February 2000. It may also be noted that broadcasters had no love lost for presidential candidate George Bush's dad, who introduced budgets including spectrum fees on broadcasters' analog spectrum and strongly opposed the Cable Act of 1992, making it the only veto of his administration (see Chapter 14). An NAB press release reported that if Bush vetoed the Cable Act of 1992, it would be a "nail in this coffin." See "Consumer Federation, National Association of Broadcasters, Update Status of Cable Bill," *U.S. Newswire*, 2 October 1992.

[150] In part for his longtime service to the broadcast industry, Stevens is a recipient of the Alaska Broadcasters Association Hall of Fame Award and a recipient of the NAB's annual Grover Cobb Memorial Award. Through last minute riders and "manager's amendments" on huge appropriations bills, Stevens has been able to get controversial broadcaster legislation passed without public debate or Congressional votes. E.g., see Frank Ahrens, "Panel Fires Shot Across FCC's Bow: Stevens Amendment Maintains Cap on TV Networks' Size," *Washington Post*, 5 September 2003, p. C1. In 2004, Stevens won control of the Senate Commerce Committee, thanks to terms limits on committee chairs. To prevent McCain from getting control of the communications subcommittee (which he would otherwise have gotten as a result of his seniority), Stevens abolished it and announced he would deal with all communications issues at the full committee level.

[151] E.g., see Terry Lane, "Senate Could Vote Soon on 'Legislative Veto' of Media Rules," *Communications Daily*, 8 September 2003. "Low Power FM Radio Service," 106th Congress, 2nd Session, *Congressional Record*, 26 October 2000, p. S11100.

[152] There are a total of 535 members of Congress, of which NAB gave PAC contributions to 188. Of those, 21 received more than Senator McCain and 6 received the exact same amount. Even among PAC recipients, McCain was in the top 15%. For PAC contribution data, see the Center for Responsive Politics. http://www.opensecrets.org.

that as long as he was unbeatable, cordial relations with the Chair of the Senate Commerce Committee was good politics.

On the House side, by far the most forceful and public, albeit brief, opponent of the spectrum rights giveaway was liberal Representative Barney Frank.[153] Despite being at the opposite partisan extreme as McCain and Dole, all three had two important things in common. First, they were in safe districts, and second, they were already highly visible and well known to their constituents. As one of the great quote meisters in the history of Congress, Barney Frank's constituents knew him well. He was also notorious for being not only openly gay but also involved indirectly in a gay prostitution ring that had brought him one of the few reprimands in the history of Congress. Yet he had survived that scandal stronger than ever.[154]

One example where broadcaster media bias might have actually changed the outcome of an election rather than just a candidate's stand on an issue is Senator Pressler (R-SD). I put this forward merely as an intriguing possibility because I have no solid evidence to back this hunch. Senator Pressler was chair of the Senate Commerce Committee during the period leading up to passage of the Telecom Act of 1996 and lost in the subsequent November 1996 election. Pressler's defeat was curious for a number of reasons.

---

[153] On January 26, 1996, Barney Frank's office sent out a press release starting "Congressman Barney Frank today expressed his admiration and support for the position that Senator Dole has taken that the digital spectrum should be auctioned rather than given to the broadcasters free of charge." On February 1, 1996, Frank made a forceful statement against the giveaway on the Floor of the House. See 104th Congress 2nd Session, *Congressional Record*, 1 February 1996, 142(14), p. H1150. On July 22, 1996, Frank's office sent out another press release announcing he would soon introduce an amendment on an FCC funding bill to "bar the FCC from giving away licenses for digital television." Frank followed that with an eloquent statement opposing the giveaway on the Floor of the House. 104th Congress, 2nd Session, *Congressional Record*, 24 July 1996, 142(110), p. H8266. This was the only legislation introduced in either House of Congress to stop the giveaway. On June 26, 1996, Frank wrote a long letter to FCC Chair Reed Hundt asking him not to grant free licenses to broadcasters until Congress passed legislation directly bearing "on this important issue."

[154] Daniel Pearl, "Senate Republicans Mull Feasibility of Auction for Digital TV," *Wall Street Journal*, 12 September 1995, p. B6, Jeffrey Silva, "Pressler Seeks to Auction HDTV as Part of Effort to Raise $14b," *RCR*, 18 September 1995, p. 11, Dennis Wharton, "Pressler Spectrum Plan No Smash," *Variety*, 18 September 1995, p. 31.

As chair of the Senate Commerce Committee, Pressler had early and passionately opposed the spectrum giveaway to broadcasters, if only for a brief period. As early as July 31, 1995, NAB President Eddie Fritts wrote to Pressler:

> I read with some distress a report in today's <u>Wall Street Journal</u> that indicates the Senate Commerce Committee is seriously considering using spectrum auctions for assigning digital TV spectrum. Please tell me the article is incorrect.
>
> ...the imposition of a spectrum auction for the transitional digital channel we need would be tantamount to signing a death warrant on advanced television.

Nevertheless, Pressler went ahead with his legislation.[155] And Pressler was the only one of the four signers of the January 31, 1996 letters to Senator Dole and FCC Chair Reed Hundt that didn't sign the follow-up letter to Reed Hundt on June 19, 1996 breaking their promise to Bob Dole that digital licenses to broadcasters wouldn't be granted until Congress moved "legislation to overhaul our nation's policies governing the electromagnetic spectrum."[156]

Tellingly, Pressler's Commerce Committee aides (who were among the most useful early contributors to this book) were adamantly opposed to the giveaway as a violation of free market principles.[157] The intellectual hypocrisy of opposing public subsidies for public television while supporting public subsidies for commercial television jarred them, as did claiming the

---

[155] E.g., Dole, "Giving Away the Airwaves." Complicating the analysis is that for the many years when broadcasters pursued a deregulatory agenda, Pressler vigorously championed their cause.

[156] The June 19, 1996 letter was signed by the three three signatories of the January 31 letters—House Commerce Committee Chair Tom Bliley, Speaker of the House Newt Gingrich, and Senate Majority Leader Trent Lott—as well as two Democrats: House Commerce Committee ranking minority member John Dingell, and Senate Commerce Committee ranking minority member Ernest Hollings. Senator Larry Pressler, Chair of the Commerce Committee, conspicuously refused to sign it. The letter was orchestrated by Rep. Bliley (whose wife, incidentally, was a close friend of NAB president Fritts' wife). Bliley got Sen. Lott, Eddie Fritts' college roommate to sign on, and from there had relatively little trouble in getting the other signatories on board (letter from James Derderian, Majority Staff Director, House Commerce Committee, to the House and Senate leadership, June 1996). However, after he signed it, Lott claimed he was not aware of what he had signed.

[157] Interviews with Donald McClelland and Jamie Linen on 2 October 1996 and later.

Telecommunications Act of 1996 was deregulatory legislation when it featured such bipartisan Soviet style central planning.

Finally, Pressler planned to introduce in the next Congress a grand spectrum bill that would have included spectrum fees and overlays within the broadcast band, a position the broadcasters hated because it would have made them pay for what they were planning to get for free.[158]

In the November 1996 elections, Pressler was the only Republican senator defeated, despite the facts that his campaign war chest was among the largest in the nation and far larger than his opponent's, and that at the time the massive Telecommunications Act passed by his committee was widely considered one of the legislative triumphs of the decade. The defeat was so remarkable that his opponent's unknown campaign manager became a star within Democratic circles, quickly rose to become the field director for the Democratic Senatorial Campaign Committee, and then amassed what the *Washington Monthly* called "a lousy record."[159]

Some of the charges against Pressler, including that he was gay and that his campaign manager was caught driving while under the influence, were either unsubstantiated (the gay charge) or of dubious political relevance (the campaign manager's drunken driving).[160] Yet Pressler was not a widely respected senator and many people I spoke to, even from his own party, weren't surprised by his defeat. Unlike McCain or Frank, Pressler was clearly vulnerable to defeat. It's conceivable—although I want to reiterate I have no evidence to verify the hypothesis—that his local broadcasters' balanced but extensive coverage of his race gave his opponent the electoral advantage he needed. For a Senator Lott or Representative Tauzin, great champions of local broadcasters, one would not expect such extensive coverage of opponents.

U.S. Senate candidate Gloria Tristani also provides an interesting case study. In 2002, she ran for U.S. Senate against Senator Pete Domenici. But in contrast to Senator Pressler's opponent, she was unable to get any televised debate time. The case is interesting because, as FCC Commissioner in the years preceding

---

[158] "Pressler Unveils 'Grand Spectrum' Bill: Discussion Draft Sets Out New National Policy for Managing and Allocating Electro-Magnetic Spectrum," press release from the Senate Commerce, Science, and Transportation Committee, 9 May 1996. See also "Senator Pressler's Bold Proposal for Spectrum Freedom," Washington, DC: Heritage Foundation, 7 June 1996, pp. 6-7.

[159] Amy Sullivan, "Fire the Consultants: Why do Democrats promote campaign advisors who lose races?" *Washington Monthly*, January/February 2005, pp. 14-17.

[160] Christopher Stern, "Ethics Issues Have Pressler on the Run," *Variety*, 28 October 1996, p. 37.

her race, she strongly opposed broadcasters on economic issues that were important to them.[161] In particular, while an FCC Commissioner and widely expected to run for the U.S. Senate, she supported low power FM, which would grant unused FM channels to new competitors rather than save them for incumbent broadcasters' future use. Charles Layton reports in the *American Journalism Review*:

> [Tristani] told me that Jerry Danziger, vice chairman of Albuquerque's KOB-TV and a board member of the New Mexico Broadcasters Association, tried to use her Senate race as leverage. She said he told her, 'If you're coming back here to run for Congress, you'd better not vote for low power, because you won't get on a radio or TV station again.'
>
> Tristani said Danziger made the threat twice—once to a member of her staff and a second time to her personally. She voted for low power anyway...and lost the election. Tristani said she didn't know whether the dispute really did affect coverage, but 'it was always in the back of my head.'"
>
> Danziger says he doesn't recall making such a threat.... [Paula Maes, head of the New Mexico Broadcasters Association] confirms that the statement was made. But she says it 'was a statemennt that was made by one broadcaster'—she refused to name him—'and the statement was prefaced by 'This is my position, as an individual broadcaster. This is not the position of the New Mexico broadcasters.'"[162]

The evidence indicates, however, that contrary to Maes' implication, Danziger was no loose cannon. He had been a longtime president and general manager of KOB-TV, an NBC affiliate station located in Albuquerque, the largest TV market in New Mexico. He was the longtime legislative chair for the New Mexico Association of Broadcasters, with direct responsibility for coordinating broadcast lobbying throughout the state, and held that position during

---

[161] E.g., David Hatch, "NAB Has Stake in Tristani Contest: Supports Domenici for senator in N.W. race," *Electronic Media*, 20 May 2002, p. 2. Tristani was arguably more critical of broadcast industry lobbying arguments than any FCC Commissioner since Nicholas Johnson. See Layton, "Lobbying Juggernaut."

[162] McChesney, *The Problem of the Media: U.S. Communication Politics in the Twenty-First Century*, p. 11.

1999 and 2000, the peak of the debate over Low Power FM.[163] He made his threat while serving on an official delegation from the New Mexico Association of Broadcasters. He also had a national presence, routinely attending NAB events, lobbying members of Congress in Washington, DC, and testifying on behalf of broadcasters in Congress.[164]

Tristani confirmed Layton's account of the Danziger incident in an interview with me, commenting "I wasn't surprised that they would do that. But to tell me to my face? We didn't have to be told."[165]

The staffer referred to in the *American Journalism Review* article was Rick Chessen, formerly Tristani's senior legal advisor and now the FCC's DTV Task Force Chair and deputy chief of the FCC's Mass Media Bureau with responsibility for regulating broadcast licenses. Tristani says that after Chessen met with the New Mexico Broadcasters Association on her behalf, she made him put his account in writing and sign it.[166] But Tristani couldn't find the letter and Chessen says it happened so long ago he could not remember what was said or whether he signed such a letter.[167] All he would say is that he recalls the broadcasters were "very passionate" at that meeting and that he "might" have signed the letter and the New Mexico broadcaster "might" have said what was reported in the *American Journalism Review* article. One possible explanation for Chessen's poor memory is that a good memory might have angered a potential future employer. In the past, senior officials in the Mass Media Bureau who play ball with the broadcasters have gotten treated very well, sometimes parlaying their FCC stint into high paying and prestigious positions in the broadcast industry. David Donovan, for example, went from legal advisor to the Chief of the Mass Media Bureau to Vice President of ALTV and now President of MSTV.

Overall, it is a fair question whether the Telecom Act of 1996 was an anomaly. With tens of billions of dollars at stake and with the benefits primarily divvied up within the top 25 TV broadcast companies, broadcasters' incentives to engage in opportunistic behavior were far higher than for the typical legislative proposal. I do not have an answer to that question. The primary question

---

[163] Subsequent to his comment to Tristani, he was re-elected to that position in 2002.

[164] These are all duties of a state legislative chair. Jerry Danziger testified on tower fees on behalf of broadcasters using federal lands before the U.S. Senate Public Lands Subcommittee, 23 March 1993.

[165] Interview with Gloria Tristani on 25 June 2004.

[166] Interviews with Gloria Tristani on 25 June 2004 and 19 August 2004.

[167] Interview with Rick Chessen on 4 October 2004.

I have sought to answer in this second part of this book is whether it was reasonable for legislators to fear such behavior in the context of the spectrum clause in the Telecom Act of 1996. To that question, I believe the clear answer is "yes."

Part III:

Recommendations

CHAPTER 16:

Public Policy and Other Recommendations

Quis ipsos custodies custodiet?

—Latin for "Who Will Guard the Guardians?"[1]

"We need to think creatively, not be imprisoned by the myth that there can be no alternative to the status quo."

—Robert W. McChesney, The Problem of the Media[2]

In the first chapter, we began by observing that the wealth and progress of civilization depends on increasing productivity through the division of labor. But there is also a dark side to the growing division of labor. The delegation of authority by a principal to an agent creates the possibility that the agent will act opportunistically, thus reducing social welfare.

Well-designed economic and political systems allow principals to efficiently delegate tasks to agents. Since markets left to their own devices fail to do this, governments have historically played a critical role in creating systems to allow principals to efficiently find, monitor, and reward good agents. For example, through well-designed transportation and telecommunications infrastructure, governments reduce the cost of principals and agents meeting at a distance. Through well-designed consumer disclosure and campaign finance laws, governments reduce the cost of principals identifying agent conflicts of interest. And through well-designed judicial and electoral laws, governments reduce the cost of penalizing opportunistic agents.

---

[1] From the Roman poet Juvenal.
[2] McChesney, *The Problem of the Media: U.S. Communication Politics in the Twenty-First Century*, p. 11.

Market Failure in Democratic Delegation

The problem of market failure in delegation is especially acute for democracy. As many political scientists have observed, democratic participation, including the acquisition of political information, has the characteristics of a public good rather than a private good.[3] The crux of the problem is that principals (voters) lack adequate incentives to evaluate agents (elected representatives) because they cannot capture for themselves the full benefits of such actions. For example, when an individual plans a family vacation, the full value of the investment in information accrues to himself and his family. But when that same individual invests in information about a political candidate, many other individuals benefit as well because the benefits of a well-run government cannot be restricted to just that individual and his family.

Among all forms of market failure, candidate information is unique in the difficulty of having democratically elected government officials rectify the problem. That's because the purpose of providing political information is to make elected officials more accountable to the voters who would be receiving the information. But elected officials have a conflict of interest in doing that. Their goal is to be re-elected, not to make themselves more accountable to voters. The Founders recognized this conflict of interest when they added to the U.S. Constitution the First Amendment: "Congress shall make no law…abridging the freedom of speech, or of the press."

This explains why the SEC (financial information), FDA (health information), FTC (advertising information), and hundreds of local professional licensing boards heavily regulate commercial speech. But market failure in political speech must be ignored, or dealt with in highly indirect and inefficient ways (like providing tens of billions of dollars in subsidies for "free TV" and vague, unenforceable "public interest obligations") because the cure would do more damage than the problem.

---

[3] C. Edwin Baker, *Media, Markets, and Democracy, Communication, Society, and Politics* (Cambridge ; New York: Cambridge University Press, 2002), Downs, *An Economic Theory of Democracy,* Robert Entman, "A Free and Responsible Press," in *University of Chicago Legal Forum* (Chicago: University of Chicago, 1993), Ferejohn and Kuklinski, *Information and Democratic Processes,* Grofman, *Information, Participation, and Choice: An Economic Theory of Democracy in Perspective,* Olson, *The Logic of Collective Action,* Popkin, *The Reasoning Voter,* Commission on Freedom of the Press, *A Free and Responsible Press* (Chicago: University of Chicago Press, 1947), J.H. Snider, "Alleviating the Problem of Rational Voter Ignorance: A Proposal for a 'Ballot Portal,'" *National Civic Review* (Spring 2004), Cass R. Sunstein, *Democracy and the Problem of Free Speech* (New York: The Free Press, 1993).

The result would appear to be a damned-if-you-do, damned-if-you-don't dilemma. The current media system may be rife with market failure, but the alternative of having the foxes guarding the chicken coop would appear to be even worse. For example, local TV broadcasters might have strong incentives for opportunistic behavior, but we don't want elected representatives regulating the very entities that are supposed to hold them accountable. Should we conclude, then, that the problem of democratic information failure is insolvable?[4]

The Problem of Guardians Guarding Themselves

The inability of elected leaders to credibly enforce media accountability is part of a much larger problem: the conflict of interest these leaders have in making themselves more democratically accountable. The system of checks and balances was the Founders' brilliant solution to the problem of power corrupting and absolute power corrupting absolutely. Each branch of government could not get too powerful because the other branches would keep it in check. But this allowed for the possibility that within each branch of government the system could be stacked to favor incumbents—especially if the media system became too monopolistic, inefficient, and protective of the powerful.

Evidence that the current system of guardians guarding themselves is stacked in favor of the guardians and does not foster democratic accountability is abundant. According to the Center for Voting and Democracy, the 2004 election for the U.S. House of Representatives was the least competitive in history: 416 out of 435 seats (95.6%) were won by non-competitive victory margins of at least 10%; and 369 out of 435 seats (84.5%) were won by landslide margins of at least 20%. More than 99% of incumbents outside of Texas won

---

[4] The irony here is that Congress and broadcasters have clearly answered "no" to that question. In the name of preserving "free TV" at the behest of local TV broadcasters, members of Congress, as we saw in Chapter 3, have provided local TV broadcasters with vast subsidies and monopoly powers that have strongly worked against the First Amendment dream of having numerous diverse and antagonistic information sources. The current system that fosters monopoly local daily newspapers in each community—and, in fact, gives local newspapers a special anti-trust exemption—is equally troublesome. A more pointed question, therefore, is whether the current subsidy and regulatory scheme that favors incumbent media outlets is working the way it should or another system that favors competitive entry, new voices, and consumer rather than producer media subsidies, might be a better approach. For an outline of my own policy solution to this problem, see Snider, "Alleviating the Problem of Rational Voter Ignorance: A Proposal for a 'Ballot Portal.'"

(the average U.S. House incumbent re-election rate over the last decade has hovered around 98%). And the four incumbents losing in Texas (more incumbents lost in Texas than in the rest of the country combined) was the result of a notorious Republican party gerrymandering, organized by U.S. House Majority Leader Tom Delay, to bring four more seats into the Repblican majority (as planned, all four seats went to the Republicans).[5] And this was all the more remarkable because Texas was one of the least competitive states in the U.S., with only 39% of state legislative races even contested by candidates of the two major parties.[6]

In California, 100% of the incumbents won in the general election for both the Assembly and Senate. In state elections nationwide, only 61% of seats were even contested by both parties.[7]

Comments a *New York Times* editorial on the sad state of American democracy:

> Totalitarian nations hold elections, but what sets democracies apart is elections that offer a real choice. In recent years, contests for the House of representatives and state legislatures have looked more and more like the Iraqi election in 2002, in which Saddam Hussein claimed 100 percent of the vote for his re-election…. In New York, more than 98 percent of the state legislators who run for re-election win, usually overwhelmingly. Anyone who know anything about New York's state government knows that's not because the populace is thrilled with the job they're doing.[8]

Incumbents have many means to ensure their own re-election because they have control of many of the key variables of democratic elections: redistricting, lower and upper limits on campaign funding, public campaign funding, disclosure of campaign funding, legislative ethics standards and enforcement, tax incentives for political influence, disclosure of lobbying activities and expenditures, and disclosure of their own activities and voting.

---

[5] Robert Ritchie, "Election 2004 by the Numbers" (Takoma Park, Maryland: Center for Voting and Democracy, 5 November 2004).

[6] "Uncontested State Legislative Race 2002–2004" (Takoma Park, Maryland: Center for Voting and Democracy, October 2004)

[7] Michael Doyle Bee, "It's Assigned Seating, Political Style, Whether Democrat or Republican: Once you're in Congress, you tend to stay," *Sacramento Bee*, 7 November 2004, p. A3.

[8] "Elections With No Meaning," *New York Times*, 21 February 2004, p. A28.

Redistricting illustrates the intractable nature of the problem.[9] As the population changes, it is necessary for electoral districts to change. Otherwise, the basic principle of democracy—one person, one vote—would be violated. But how should the borders of the districts be set? Someone has to decide. In a democracy with representation exclusively through elected representatives, the elected representatives are, by definition, the only democratically valid place to locate the redistricting power. The elected representatives can set up independent non-partisan redistricting commissions, which create a buffer between themselves and the outcome. That may alleviate partisan redistricting, but it doesn't address pro-incumbent redistricting because the bipartisan commissioners are chosen by incumbent politicians whose first priority is to protect themselves. Redistricting bias can be challenged in the courts, but only in the most extreme cases of such bias have the courts stepped in to the correct the problem.[10] The Federal Election Commission, the Congressional ethics committees, and the various Congressional record keepers all suffer from the same intractable pro-incumbent bias.

In theory, an independent media is supposed to place the necessary check on incumbent political power. But, in practice, the evidence above suggest the current media is ill-suited to do this. The current government disclosure system makes it very costly for any but the largest local media to gather information about incumbents. These media are set up in such a way that the vast majority see very little profit in carefully and critically covering the vast majority of elections. And what little coverage there is tends to favor incumbents.

---

[9] E.g., Linda Greenhouse, "Justices Revive Texas Districting Challenge," *New York Times*, 19 October 2004, p. A13, David M. Halbfinger, "Across U.S., Redistricting as a Never-Ending Battle," *New York Times*, 1 July 2003, p. A1, Samuel Issacharoff, Pamela S. Karlan, and Richard H. Pildes, *The Law of Democracy: Legal Structure of the Political Process*, Rev. 2nd ed., *University Casebook Series* (New York: Foundation Press, 2002), Adam Nagourney, "States See Growing Campaign to Change Redistricting Laws," *New York Times*, 7 February 2004, p. A1, Dennis F. Thompson, "Election Time: Normative Implications of Temporal Properties of the Electoral Process in the United States," *American Political Science Review* 98, no. 1 (2004).

[10] David E. Rosenbaum, "Justices Bow to Legislators in Political Gerrymander Case," *New York Times*, 29 April 2004, p. A22. Another solution is multimember districts, but this only mitigates the problem, albeit potentially significantly. See John Anderson and Robert Ritchie, "A Better Way to Vote: Partisan gerrymanders, winner-take-all elections, and decisions like Vieth v. Jubilirer degrade our democracy," *Legal Times*, 17 May 2004, p. 68, Nathaniel Persily, "In Defense of Foxes Guarding Henhouses: The Case for Judicial Acquiescence to Incumbent-Protecting Gerrymanders," *Harvard Law Review* 116 (2002).

The reasons for this are varied. One major reason is that media want cheap access to news, and politicians control much of that access. If they alienate their sources of news for the sake of a brief and largely unprofitable period of election news, they hurt their bottom line.

This book suggests another possible reason. If the big profits for local TV stations in covering obscure Congressional elections comes from winning government subsidies (rather than from informing the public), then a pro-incumbent bias would be a rational course of action. Why risk making an enemy of a powerful politician as long as they are giving you what you want? As long as the government's spectrum and copyright policies have a direct impact on local broadcasters' bottom line, this political calculus will not disapper.

Policy Solution

The specific solution I propose is to create a new type of representative body, a "Citizens' Committee," made up of a random selection of voters. This is a variation of the proposal for a "deliberative jury" advocated by Dahl, Fishkin, and Ackerman.[11] Their ideas, in turn, hearken back to the ancient Athenian Council of 500 (also known as the "Boule") that was annually chosen randomly by lot and, like Congress, was designed to represent the general public.[12] Until modern times, selection by lot (i.e., randomly) was a common form of democratic representation.[13] Jury selection is its last important modern manifestation.

The closest precedent for the Citizens' Committee proposed here is the Citizens' Assembly on Electoral Reform in British Columbia, Canada. That body was launched in May 2003 by the government of British Columbia. It was comprised of 160 individuals (80 men and 80 women) selected randomly. It met over a period of 11 months (January through November 2004), and in December 2004 recommended a new system to elect representatives for the

---

[11] Robert Dahl, Democracy and its Critics, 1989; James Fishkin, Democracy and Deliberation: New Directions for Democratic Reform, Yale University Press, 1992; Ackerman and Fishkin, 2004.

[12] P. J. Rhodes, The Athenian Boule (Oxford [Oxfordshire]: Clarendon Press, 1985).

[13] Bernard Manin, The Principles of Representative Government, Themes in the Social Sciences (New York: Cambridge University Press, 1997).

[14] "Making Every Vote Count: The Case for Electoral Reform in British Columbia," (British Columbia, Canada: British Columbia Citizens' Assembly on Electoral Reform, December 2004). See www.citizensassembly.bc.ca.

province of British Columbia. The recommendation will be put directly to the voters in a referendum on May 17, 2005.[14]

Citizens' Committee Powers

The formal title of the Citizens' Committee would be the "Committee on Candidate Information and Elections," and its jurisdiction would cover issues on which elected officials have an inherent conflict of interest; namely, candidate information and elections. Candidate information includes funding and disclosing information about candidates' sources and use of campaign funds, sources of personal income, official votes, public statements, and influence by lobbyists. Elections include setting district boundaries, scheduling elections, and aggregating votes.

The most important power of the Citizens' Committee would be to propose legislation that would go directly to the floors of the House and Senate for a vote. The reason it is not practical to have a Citizens' Committee actually pass legislation is that it would require a Constitutional amendment for it to acquire that power. By restricting the power of the Citizens' Committee to merely getting a bill introduced to the House and Senate floors, that problem is overcome.

Although requiring Congressional approval is a significant check on the power of the Citizens' Committee, it does not render it irrelevant. The most difficult part of democratic reform legislation is usually getting it through committee for a floor vote. Once reform legislation reaches the floor, it often passes with an overwhelming majority. For example, lobbyist disclosure law took decades to reach the floors of the U.S. Senate and House of Representatives for a vote, but when it did in 1995, it passed the Senate 98-0 and the House 421-0. The paradox is explained by the fact that members of Congress are wary of casting an unpopular vote that becomes part of their public record. Congressional leadership can usually kill a bill, even a popular reform bill, without creating a roll call vote. But if a bill manages to get to the floor for a roll call vote, the political dynamic is very different, which explains the number of lopsided votes for reform bills that in some cases have taken decades to get to a floor vote.

Another power of the Citizens' Committee could be the ability to request roll call votes on bills it submitted to Congress. This right would include amendments brought in conference committee or on the Floor of the Senate or House. The advantage of roll call votes is that they allow the public to hold members of Congress accountable for their actions.

When Congress amended legislation introduced by the Citizens' Committee, the Citizens' Committee could vote on the amendment. Although the Citizens' Committee would have no formal veto power, its censure would be a powerful check on Congressional abuse of power because of the democratic legitimacy the Citizens' Committee would presumably have on matters within its jurisdiction. The practical consequence is that members of Congress would have strong incentives to make policy recommendations directly to the Citizens' Committee rather than risk a floor vote in Congress that the Citizens' Committee might later rebuke.

A Citizens' Committee could also have the power to approve presidential nominations for entities, such as the Federal Elections Commission, where members of Congress have an inherent conflict of interest. After passing through the Citizens' Committee, nominations would go on to the full Senate for approval. This would mimic the nominating powers of the other standing committees in the U.S. Senate.

Even better, the Citizens' Committee could make nominations itself, although they would still be subject to the approval of the full Senate and the veto of the President. Given the inherent limitations of a Citizens' Committee, the task of picking nominees would have to be contracted out to one or more professional search firm, just as school boards typically hire a search firm to identify prospective school superintendents. Only after the list of prospective nominees had been reduced to a manageable number would the Citizens' Committee vote on them.

Ultimately, the Citizens' Committee could seek a Constitutional Amendment for the legal right to propose its own legislation through a national referendum. I would suggest limiting the referendum power solely to raising funds for the operation of the Citizens' Committee. Every Congressional cycle any change in its funding level could be set this way, just as many towns and school districts must go directly to the voters to request tax increases.

Citizens' Committee Representation and Procedure

To be a truly representative sample of the general public, the Citizens' Committee would have to have at least several hundred members. At the federal level, I suggest a body of 500, about the same size as a typical randomly selected professional opinion poll. For small states such as Vermont and Alaska, a Citizens' Committee of a few hundred would probably be ample.

Given its large size and amateur composition, the Citizens' Committee would clearly have to act more like a traditional jury than a conventional state or federal legislative committee. Foundations, think tanks, legislators, and other experts would have to do the bulk of the effort developing legislation. The primary task of the Citizens' Committee would be to choose among alternatives, including amendments, presented by others.[15]

Unlike a traditional jury, Committee participation could be voluntary yet paid, limiting terms to two years and restricting eligibility to citizens 66 years of age or whatever age the government determines citizens are eligible for full social security benefits.

Any age restriction is controversial because it appears to create a body unrepresentative of the general public. However, it does not create a conflict of interest with the general public because seniors' issues wouldn't be within the committee's jurisdiction; they would be handled by conventional legislative committees.

The narrow age restriction, like the narrow age range in which the army recruits soldiers, is designed to pick an optimal age for the task at hand. The advantage of the high lower bound age restriction is that it brings the Committee a greater wealth of experience combined with, on average, fewer family and work commitments—which are serious problems for traditional juries, even with their less substantial commitment of time. The advantage of the upper bound age restriction is that serving on the Committee would require physical and mental vigor, both of which tend to decline after retirement, which is also the rationale for the social security system.

In addition to the age restriction, there are other ways to minimize the burden of serving on the Citizens' Committee. Paying Committee members a decent wage would be critical. The wage could be set based on the higher of: 1) previous reported compensation of a particular Committee member; for example, the average basis for determining social security payments during the previous 2 years, or 2) average U.S. compensation; for example, the U.S. median basis for social security payments.

New broadband Internet technology would allow members of the Citizens' Committee to do their deliberative work with powerful new tools and without necessarily traveling to Washington, DC (for a federal citizens' committee) or to state capitols (for state citizens' committees). Each member would have to

---

[15] Even in Congress, most of the legislation is proposed by interest groups. A major difference is that this influence process in the Citizens' Committee would be completely transparent.

be provided with a high speed broadband connection and accompanying computer.

The incentive to improperly influence Committee members would be huge. After all, they would control significant resources. Therefore, laws to insulate Committee members from improper influence should be strict. As a model, I suggest using the laws to insulate conventional judges and juries from improper influence. Lobbying a Committee member outside a public forum should be treated as a felony, and Committee members found accepting bribes or otherwise compromising their independence should be disqualified to be Committee members.

Committee member terms could be staggered on two month intervals, so every two months one-twelfth of the Committee members would turn over. Each incoming class would become a cohesive unit for its two year term and the primary unit of Committee deliberation.

The senior class of each Citizens' Committee could serve as its Agenda and Rules Subcommittee. This Subcommittee would determine which groups would have the opportunity to present their ideas to the entire Committee and the rules guiding those deliberations and subsequent voting. Each Agenda and Rules Subcommittee could elect a chair for its two month duration. The agenda could be for the next session of the Citizens' Committee, when the term of the current Agenda and Rules Subcommittee had already expired. The separation of the agenda right from the deliberation and voting right creates an additional check and balance within this democratic system.

The retiring chair of each senior class could then join a personnel committee with one function: to nominate a new executive director every four years. The personnel committee would presumably hire a search firm to narrow down the list of prospects and then present one to the entire Citizens' Committee for a vote. This is somewhat similar to the way the U.S. president nominates people to senior executive offices that the U.S. Senate must then approve.

Funding for the Citizens' Committee could come either from a legislative body or a non-profit Foundation. The executive director should accept no funds on behalf of the Citizens' Committee that come with strings attached. All contributions should be unrestricted, and contributions from diverse sources are generally better than contributions from a single source.

A citizens' committee could be implemented in an incremental fashion. Following the precedent of the British Columbia Citizens' Assembly on Electoral Reform, a citizens' committee could be set up for a narrow purpose and limited duration. At the national level, for example, a citizens' committee could be set up for a fixed duration of time to advise Congress (or the

President) on the best way to pick commissioners for the notoriously pro incumbent Federal Election Commission. After the citizens' committee concept was tested, refined, and legitimized in this more restricted fashion, it could be expanded into the more ambitious form proposed above.

A Citizens' Committee is no panacea. But compared to the current system of having our guardians guard themselves for mutual advantage, it would add a valuable check and balance.

Recommendations for Future Media Subsidies

The basic recommendations I have for media policy are to redirect subsidies from the old broadcast to the new Internet TV model, from producer to consumer subsidies, from areas without market failure (e.g., entertainment TV and home shopping) to areas with market failure (e.g., civic discourse and preschool education), and from wealthy consumers (e.g., the most desirable 18 to 34 year old advertising demographic) to needy consumers (e.g., low income consumers unappealing to advertisers). Currently, media subsidies are focused on propping up the industries of the past and are predominately allocated based on the political power of the incumbent media players. Perhaps no other government corporate welfare program in U.S. history has been both larger and more narrowly targeted to create billionaires (e.g., Milt Maltz, Lowry Mays, and Bud Paxson) and subsidize corporate behemoths (e.g., Walt Disney, General Electric, and the News Corporation). One alternative is to simply abandon media subsidies in disgust at the failures of our political system. Another alternative, the one proposed here, is to try to fix the system.

Recommendations To Eliminate The Spectrum Subsidy

I recommend discontinuing four types of broadcaster spectrum subsidies. These subsidies are inefficient because they prop up a horse & buggy industry when the automobile has already arrived. They are inequitable because they pick favorites among industries and subsidize a handfall of hugely profitable companies at the expense of millions of taxpayers. And they violate First Amendment values because they concentrate speech rights in a handful of

---

[16] See Lawrence K. Grossman, "Why Local TV News Is So Awful," *Columbia Journalism Review*, November/December 1997, p. 21.

powerful entitities that may or may not have interests corresponding to the rest of the public.

1) The federal government should have no right to regulate the underlay spectrum; as a corollary, the broadcasters should not be allowed to either warehouse or move into it.[17]

Spectrum usage rights can be divided into underlay ("whispering") and overlay ("shouting") rights. Underlay rights can coexist with overlay rights just as background music can co-exist with table conversation at a restaurant. The quest for underlay rights within the broadcast band is relatively new because only recently has the integration of inexpensive computer and radio technology made those rights very valuable. In the relatively near future, the average home or business could have hundreds of wireless devices, some no bigger than a speck of dust, communicating to each other via underlay rights. Potential applications seem endless. They could include replacing the communications wires linking home consumer electronics devices; replacing cumbersome physical products such as product manuals, warranty cards, ingredients lists, health disclosures, and bar codes that are already ubiquitous on products; and making possible new types of products for health, security, and environmental monitoring. These devices, linked together, could constitute a pervasive, ultrahighspeed, wireless broadband network on university and business campuses; public highways, along the median strip; public trains and subways, along the tracks; and public streets from lamp post to lamp post.

The FCC has yet to allocate underlay rights in the broadcast band to anyone, broadcaster or otherwise. The broadcasters are fiercely opposed to anyone else getting underlay rights. They recognize that underlay rights are becoming extremely valuable, and they want to keep them out of others' hands. But the fact that broadcasters have overlay rights in a band of spectrum does not necessarily imply that they should also get the underlay rights in the same band. To date, there has not been an FCC proceeding seeking to give the underlay rights to the broadcasters. But the broadcasters' fierce opposition to anyone else getting those rights in Dockets 04-186 ("Unlicensed Operation in the Broadcast Bands") and several other proceedeings, implies that, ultimately, the

---

[17] For additional information, see Comments of NAF et al. to FCC in the matter of Unlicensed Operation in the Broadcast Bands, Docket 04-186, 30 November 2004, Snider and Holmes, "The Cartoon Guide to Federal Spectrum Policy.", J.H. Snider and Max Vilimpoc, "Reclaiming the 'Vast Wasteland': Unlicensed Sharing of the Broadcast Spectrum," (Washington, DC: New America Foundation, July 2003).

only politically feasible course will be to give broadcasters the underlay rights.[18]

Underlay and overlay rights need fundamentally different regulatory regimes. Whereas it is appropriate for the federal government to allocate overlay rights, it is not appropriate for it to allocate underlay rights.

Underlay rights properly belong to neither the broadcasters nor the government. They belong to anyone with property rights at a particular point in space and time. In addition, since underlay rights involve speech, they are subject to First Amendment values. Thus, homeowners and businesses should have underlay/whispering rights on their own property, local governments should have these rights on their roads and other public rights of way, and airplanes, boats and cars should have these rights within their vehicles. For the federal government to give exclusive underlay rights to broadcasters or any other third party is an unacceptable taking of property.[19] The federal government has no more right to allocate such property than it has the right to appropriate private property on state and municipal public lands without just compensation. When spectrum first came into use, communications using it traveled hundreds, if not thousands of miles, and was inherently interstate in nature. This made the federal government its natural regulator under the Interstate Commerce Clause of the U.S. Constitution. But with property-based underlays typically running less than a few hundred feet in distance, justifying federal regulation of all spectrum rights based on the Interstate Commerce Clause is no longer reasonable.

However, traditional property rights must be constrained by First Amendment values of free speech. Since underlays involve a type of speech, First Amendment values of speech should apply to them, thus providing a very different and highly restricted Constitutional rationale for federal regulation of underlays. Just as a citizen has the right to speak in public places or on certain private property via the acoustic spectrum, a citizen should also have the right to speak using the electromagnetic spectrum, providing the citizen does not shout excessively loudly. In other words, no more First Amendment

---

[18] For example, see Comments of NAB and MSTV to FCC in the matter of *Unlicensed Operation in the Broadcast Bands*, Docket 04-186, 30 November 2004, and presentation of MSTV to FCC Responding to Media Access Project's Claims Regarding the FCC's Part 15 Authority, ET Dockets 03-108, 03-237, 04-151, and 04-186, 2 March 2005.

[19] J.H. Snider, "FCC Lets the Telecom Giants Steal from You," *Sacramento Bee*, 7 April 2002, Snider and Ziporyn, *Future Shop*, pp. 237-8.

exemptions to free speech should be given to broadcasters or any other FCC licensee unless there is a clear and present danger from doing otherwise.

What this means is that current FCC rules that make underlay rights secondary to overlay rights must be eliminated. Overlay devices should receive no preferred protection from underlay devices any more than my neighbor's property line should be more respected than my property line. If a consumer buys a TV set that is too dumb to coordinate sharing the broadcast band underlay with other devices within the home, the conflict is not for the FCC to decide by, as the broadcasters demand, banning anything but a TV set from using the broadcast band underlay within the home. It's for the homeowner to decide. If consumers can manage a gaggle of devices sharing the WiFi bands within their own homes, they can do the same with devices sharing the broadcast bands.[20]

Local governments will need to specify acceptable interference limits at property boundaries. But this is a highly restricted right and should not be too onerous. Consider widely accepted norms for regulating acoustic interference at property boundaries. It's not reasonable to ask your children to be silent when playing in your back yard even if your next door neighbor sitting on his porch can hear them. On the other hand, you don't have a right to blast a stereo so loud that it can be heard throughout the neighborhood. But you do have the right to blast the stereo within the confines of your home, as long as the walls confine the sound. The same commonsense regulations need to apply to spectrum underlays.

One of the major objections to such a vision today is the lack of a credible enforcement mechanism. But as new smart radios evolve over the coming generation, this concern should whither away. The great majority of acoustic spectrum interference enforcement is done without government involvement. The human ear can hear a wide variety of acoustic sounds and pinpoint the location of their source. It doesn't need separate ears for specialized acoustic communication needs such as telephone sound, stereo sound, one-way communications, and two way communications. As a consequence, neighbors know that if they send too much noise over their property lines, it will be detected and invite social opprobrium. Only as a last resort and in rare conditions will a neighbor call the local police to enforce a local statute banning noise above a certain decibel level beyond a property line. As radios become

---

[20] For a description of how broadcast receivers could become smart like almost every other wireless device available today, see Reply Comments to FCC of Timothy X. Brown in the matter of *Unlicensed Operation in the Broadcast Bands*, Docket 04-186, 31 January 2005.

ever smarter and more ubiquitous, the same type of enforcement mechanism will work for communication via spectrum underlays.

It is important to note that unlicensed spectrum need not come in the form of an underlay. It can also come in the form of an overlay. The designation of spectrum as "unlicensed" refers to spectrum over which the FCC does not grant exclusive rights to a third party such as a TV broadcaster. Since we are positing that all underlay spectrum be unlicensed and that the FCC only have control of overlay spectrum, it is possible that an entire band could be dedicated to unlicensed use depending on how the FCC allocates the overlay spectrum. Such dedicated unlicensed bands may be viewed as the public parks of the information age. Few would disagree that the few lower frequency dedicated unlicensed parks in the United States have been a boon to the public and spawned countless innovations.[21] The most notable recent band is 2.40 GHz to 2.48 GHz, where WiFi is located. A similar park should also be located below 800 MHz (where the broadcast band is located) so that longhaul wireless networks in rural areas and shorthaul wireless networks in urban areas (e.g., from street curb to home or from streetlight to streetlight) can send signals that easily pass through trees and other obstacles rather than have to navigate around them with line-of-sight links. Currently, only 1% of spectrum below 2 GHz and 2% of spectrum below 5 GHz is allocated for such spectrum public parks.[22]

2) **Broadcasters should return their loaned channel for the DTV transition at a fixed date 18 months from today, thus opening up TV channels 52-69 for state-of-the-art telecommunications services, including affordable Internet TV.**[23] In Berlin, Germany, the entire broadcast DTV transition took 18 months from start to completion, and with far fewer subsidies to broadcasters than in the U.S. The key to this achievement was a subsidy for low income consumers to purchase DTV to analog converter boxes so they could continue to receive over-the-air reception on their analog TV sets after analog broadcasts were turned off. The same strategy for a rapid turnoff should be applied in the U.S. More generally, the strategy of speeding the broadcast DTV transition by giving subsidies to the broadcasters should be brought to an end. Any future subsidy to speed the transition should go directly to consumers. Legislation to this

---

[21] E.g., Kevin Werbach, "Radio Revolution: The Coming Age of Unlicensed Wireless," (Washington, DC: New America Foundation, 2003).

[22] William Lehr, "The Economic Case for Dedicated Unlicensed Spectrum Below 3ghz," (Washington, DC: New America Foundation, 2004).

[23] For an indepth discussion of this proposal, see Snider and Calabrese, "Speeding the DTV Transition."

effect was introduced in the 108th Congress and this author testified at one House Commerce Committee in support of such a plan.[24] Similar legislation is planned for the 109th Congress and should be supported.

However, even if such legislation passes, it will only free up 108 MHz of the 402 MHz allocated for channels 2-69 and does nothing to address the unlicensed underlay issue.

3) As new digital technology allows the guard bands between channels 2 and 51 to come into productive use, broadcasters shouldn't be given or allowed to warehouse that spectrum.[25]

At the end of the DTV transition, channels 52-69 are supposed to be returned to the public. But the future of most of channels 2-51 has yet to be decided.

In any given TV market, most channels on the TV dial between channels 2 and 51 are unused and will continue to be unused at the end of the broadcasters' DTV transition even after the stations currently on channels 52-69 migrate to channels 2-51.

Local TV broadcasters are lobbying to acquire as much of this spectrum as possible (See Appendices C and D). Their strategies for doing this include expanding the power levels and thus geographic area of stations, changing the interference protection model by which station contour lines are drawn, and acquiring the right to build cell towers throughout their market area to cover places never viewable from a single tower. This spectrum lebensraum should be brought to an end.

4) Broadcasters should ultimately be forced to migrate off channels 2-51.[26] Conventional broadcast TV—whether analog or digital—is rapidly becoming an obsolete business model. Already, more than 85% of American receive their primary TV signal from a competing TV distribution platform.[27] They do this because those platforms offer better reception and more programming choice. The result is that most TV watching is no longer of FCC licensed over-the-air

---

[24] Testimony of J.H. Snider on "The Digital Television Transition: What We Can Learn From Berlin," before the U.S. House Telecommunications Subcommittee, 21 July 2004.

[25] For a detailed discussion of this argument, see NAF et al. Economic and Legal Reply Comments to FCC in the matter of *Unlicensed Operation in the Broadcast Bands*, Docket 04-186, 31 January 2005, available at www.spectrumpolicy.org.

[26] The literature on this is large. See Brand, *The Media Lab*, Gilder, *Life after Television*, Hazlett, "The U.S. Digital TV Transition.", Nicholas Negroponte, *Being Digital*, 1st ed. (New York: Knopf, 1995), Bruce M. Owen, *The Internet Challenge to Television* (Cambridge, Mass.: Harvard University Press, 1999).

[27] See FCC Notice of Inquiry in the matter of *Over-the-Air Broadcast Television Viewers*, MB Docket 04-210, 27 May 2004, and Hazlett, "The U.S. Digital TV Transition."

programming. When Internet TV finally becomes affordable and pervasive, local broadcast TV will decline further. That is because Internet TV will offer much greater viewing options in terms of what is watched, how it is watched, and when it is watched.

Tellingly, no one buys low frequency spectrum today to broadcast TV images to a fixed location in your home. When companies purchase low frequency spectrum in the market, they do so to provide mobile services, which have no close wired substitutes (e.g., you cannot plug your car into a wire while driving).

The future of TV is TV delivered over the Internet. People also want to be able to watch mobile TV for both news and videogame-like entertainment programming. That technological revolution will come to TV within the next five to ten years. As Microsoft's Chief Technology Officer for Internet TV has said: "2004 is the last year when people consider video an exotic application for broadband."[28]

However, broadcasters currently lack the flexible spectrum rights necessary to provide such service. They are allowed only to provide a single signal from a single spot to a service area often more than a thousand square miles in size and with no return path. Moreover, the broadcast DTV standard doesn't facilitate mobile use.

There are two public policy solutions to this dilemma: give the broadcasters flexible rights, or take the broadcasters' licenses back at the end of their term. This is analogous to the options of 1) letting a food concession license expire that had a fixed location (e.g., a public park) and duration (e.g., New Year's Eve), or 2) giving the concession licensee development rights to the entire park in perpetuity.

Clearly, the broadcast band should be governed under a regime of flexible rights so that users of the band can provide the type of services people in the early 21st century value most highly. But should broadcasters simply be given those rights, as they contend? Many telecom analysts who think of themselves as political realists believe that this is the only way to bring the broadcast bands into productive use. Let the broadcasters have their windfall because then at least a host of valued new services could be provided to the public. But it turns out that this isn't so easy politically. It is extremely embarrassing for Congress to give away billion of dollars of public property to a handful of large and highly profitable corporations. So the only way this can be done is below the public radar screen, which in practice means having the FCC do it gradually over many years. Thus, the only politically realistic giveaway strategy entails

---

[28] Jim Hu, "Video Gamble for the Bells," *New York Times*, 22 November 2004.

depriving American consumers of valuable services for many years simply to provide the broadcasters and Congress with political cover.

A second solution is not to renew broadcasters' licenses when they expire at the end of 8 years. Then the spectrum could be reallocated to flexible use, either in the form of unlicensed use or a license acquired through an open and competitive bid. Since the airwaves belong to the public, this would be legal, although surely subject to lawsuits for many years. But no serious telecom analyst I know believes this proposal is even remotely politically plausible: the broadcasters are too powerful and the public neither understands nor cares about the opportunity cost of spectrum.

I suggest a third and middle way, which, given the broadcasters' reputation for political power, most serious analysts will still dismiss out of hand. But if 1) the public came to take an interest in the use of spectrum resources, and 2) Internet TV eliminated the source of the broadcasters' political power, this solution might evolve into a politically feasible compromise.

I suggest granting every U.S. broadcaster 19.4 mbps of spectrum capacity (enough with today's video compression technology for four HDTV programming streams) via satellite delivery. For this purpose, I would allocate high frequency spectrum currently allocated for broadcast auxiliary services, notably 500 MHz of such auxiliary spectrum in the 13 GHz band, which is near the 12 GHz band used by satellite TV services Echostar and DirectTV. As broadcasters have noted in numerous filings concerning Echostar and DirectTV, this is ample spectrum to reproduce every broadcast digital TV station in the U.S.[29]

Broadcasters, as many other spectrum licensees have been required to do over the years, would have to relocate from their high value spectrum to this low value spectrum that is nevertheless equally well suited to provide HDTV or SDTV service. This would free up 294 MHz, worth about $150 billion at today's prices. Either the government or broadcasters could pay the cost for the satellites—less than a billion dollars in total—and the change would only affect the small fraction of Americans who rely on terrestrial, over-the-air reception. (Alternatively, space could be leased on satellite TV providers Echostar or DirectTV, which in a few years will already be providing local broadcast TV into all 210 TV markets.) In addition, the millions of neotropical birds killed each year by broadcast towers could be saved.[30]

---

[29] E.g., Comments to FCC of NAB in the matter of *Annual Assessment of the Status of Competition in the Market for the Delivery of Video Programming*, Docket 04-227, 25 August 2004.

[30] See Comments to FCC in the matter of *Effects of Communications Towers on Migratory Birds*, WT Docket 03-187.

Today, the more than 1,700 local TV broadcasters require their own land, towers, and equipment to transmit their programming over the air. Those assets, according to the broadcasters' own calculations, are worth billions of dollars, depreciate within a decade, and take a small fortune to maintain. In comparison, the cost to purchase and maintain a couple of small satellites would probably save broadcasters money. The energy savings alone might be in the vicinity of $100 million/year for the industry. Compared to satellite transmitters, broadcast tower transmitters are energy guzzlers.

Viewers would need a satellite dish, but the programming, like much of satellite service outside the U.S., would be an unencrypted signal and thus not only free but also not require a decoding box. The universal service fund could then be modified to allow low income consumers to receive a one-time voucher that could be used to purchase one of these satellite dishes or a comparable cable settop box. Alternatively, the voucher could be used to purchase a more flexible—but probably also more expensive—broadband Internet connection (for TV as well as all other types of information services).

When the opportunity cost of the 294 MHz of beachfront spectrum that would be returned with this proposal is compared to the cost of a satellite dish, this proposal, like the Berlin DTV model, represents a stupendous return on investment. Even if 10 million low income Americans qualified, and the dishes cost $300 to purchase and install, the total cost would be only $4 billion. To economize on satellite installation costs and reach homes otherwise blocked, the small dishes could be placed atop an apartment building or telephone pole and then rebroadcast to clusters of nearby homes or apartments via unlicensed spectrum. Indeed, the unlicensed spectrum could transmit in the broadcast band and in broadcast DTV format, so people with old-fashioned broadcast DTV tuners could choose to pick up the signal directly from a satellite dish on their roof or nearby telephone pole. Their viewing experience would be identical, but the same spectrum used for TV in one building could be freed up for countless other applications elsewhere. Moreover, for a few dollars extra, instead of retransmitting every TV channel available on the TV dial, the unlicensed device could transmit only the ones actually being watched in a given household.

Again, such a proposal is not politically realistic today. But if Internet TV moves faster than broadcasters' ability to win additional spectrum rights giveaways from the government, it's possible that the political calculus could change.

Of course, all this begs the question why Congress and the broadcasters consider a five year old $2,000 personal computer a junk heap but a $200 ten year old analog TV a sacred public trust. It also begs the question what to do with the early broadcast DTV adopters whose sets will be made obsolete by the rapidly evolving operating system and hardware in future broadcast DTV sets.

In addition to the substantive changes recommended above, I also recommend procedural change focused on creating a more transparent system of spectrum accounting, including the transfer of spectrum rights from the public to private sector. All FCC proceedings or case-by-case rule waivers should estimate the opportunity cost of any change that gives an incumbent licensee additional spectrum rights. Current FCC rulemakings do a stupendous job of describing any harm that might come to incumbent licensees as a result of a rule change. But they completely ignore the question of any opportunity cost to the rest of America's citizens of giving spectrum windfalls to incumbents. My estimate is that during the first four years of the Bush Administration the FCC transferred from $50 to $100 billion of the public's airwaves to private enterprise without any public compensation. But one would never know this from reading any of the dozens of FCC proceedings that orchestrated this wealth transfer.[31]

The simplest explanation I have for this is that the Communications Act explicitly bans the FCC from giving anybody a spectrum windfall, so as a statutory matter the FCC is obliged to pretend it isn't giving away public assets when in fact that is exactly what it is doing. The FCC has little choice in this matter because whenever it attempts to do otherwise Congress gives it grief: budgets for pet projects don't get approved, oversight hearings and burdensome paper requests increase, and commissioners don't get reappointed or rise to position of chairman, let alone get appointed in the first place.

The one legal loophole is that "minor modifications" to license rights are not viewed as windfalls. The trick for spectrum lobbyists is to pursue lots of "minor modifications." Cumulatively, these minor modifications may add up

---

[31] For a vivid illustration of the misleading language with which the FCC describes massive rights transfers, see the FCC's Notice of Proposed Rulemaking in the matter of *Amendment of Parts 1, 21, 73, 74 and 101 of the Commission's Rules to Facilitate the Provision of Fixed and Mobile Broadband Access, Educational and Other Advanced Services in the 2150–2162 and 2500–2690 MHz Bands*, WT Docket No. 03-66, released 13 March 2003. Some of this is critiqued in Comments and Reply Comments to FCC of NAF et al. in this proceeding, filed 8 September 2003 and 23 October 2003. In this proceeding, a coalition of incumbents, including the Catholic church with its substantial spectrum holdings, won spectrum flexibility on 190 MHz of second tier but still excellent spectrum from 2.5 GHz to 2.69 GHz. Some other spectrum giveaways in recent years are in rulemakings associated with FCC dockets 95-18, 99-325, 00-258, 01-185, 02-55, 03-15, and 03-185.

over decades to constitute a completely new service. But the law says nothing about such patterns of "minor modifications," even if they are absolutely obvious to everyone at the FCC. Fortunately for incumbents, too, the press cannot be bothered with such minor modifications and is absolutely blind to long term patterns of behavior scattered in dozens of arcane, hard to locate, FCC rulemakings and waivers.

One solution is to mandate that in every FCC proceeding proposing modifications to incumbents' license rights for a particular class of service, the FCC estimate the total opportunity cost of 1) the proposed minor modifications in the proceeding, and 2) the cumulative value, in present terms, of all the minor modifications since the class of service originated.

The FCC's economic analyses are unlikely to be accurate because incumbent license holders dominate the FCC rulemaking process for intractable and well known reasons; for example, many of the smart young lawyers who write the proceedings later go to work for the regulated companies, so alienating these companies is not a good career strategy.

Still, there is value in this exercise. It would force the FCC to frame issues in a way that the public and journalists could understand, thus bringing them into the debate. Whereas today anyone who raises windfall issues in an FCC proceeding tends to be ridiculed and viewed as off-topic, this would provide legitimacy to those who believe they are relevant and directly implicated by not only the Communications Act but also the need to be able to hold elected leaders accountable for their use of public assets. It would also force incumbent licensees to justify how they compensate the public for the use of its property. Amazingly, incumbents engage in virtually no serious consideration of such issues in the vast majority of FCC proceedings granting them "minor modifications."

Already, FCC rulemakings are required to have separate impact statements. The Paperwork Reduction Act requires that the FCC estimate the paperwork cost to businesses of complying with proposed rule changes. The Regulatory Flexibility Act requires that the FCC estimate the cost of proposed rule changes on small businesses. What is missing is an impact statement on the costs of license modifications to the general public.

More generally, Congress needs to keep a clear inventory of the public's spectrum assets. These assets are now probably worth upwards of $1 trillion. But the public accounting for them is an utter pigsty. Most spectrum assignments are controlled by the NTIA, not the FCC, and may not even be public. Used by federal agencies, such as the Defense Department and Interior Department, they are considered top secret and off limits to public scrutiny and accountability. But even at the FCC the whole system of spectrum accounting seems designed to obscure rather than clarify. For example, license databases are scattered in different places, unintegrated for easy search and comparison, sometimes administered by secretive third parties, and often inaccurate. In contrast, Congress keeps a detailed inventory and economic accounting of every chair and desk on Capitol Hill. And it is a felony if a member of the public walks out with a $5 chair.

Congresss needs a clear, integrated, comprehensive, easily accessible, and accurate inventory and public database of spectrum holdings. For every national 100 MHz block of spectrum from 0 to 300 GHz, it should attach a monetary valuation, excluding underlays, and then convert that into a $/MHz-person unit.[32] Underlay rights are excluded, as we have seen, because the Federal government should have no jurisdiction over them. When overlay rights to that spectrum are given away, the opportunity cost of those rights should be debited. If real estate appraisers can value both private and public property, including zoning changes, surely spectrum appraisers can value spectrum. The prime difference is political. Municipalities need the property valuations to assess taxes. But a spectrum valuation would only alienate the powerful licensees who currently dictate spectrum policy.

Recommendations for Media Owners

People in our business seem starved for assurances that sticking by their standards will work.

Barbara Cochran, President, RTNDA[33]

"While appearing to be honest is generally considered better than its opposite, this is hardly the same thing as actually being honest."

—Eric Alterman, When Presidents Lie[34]

---

[32] For example, let's assume that a 100 MHz band was worth $3 billion and there are 300 million people in the U.S. That would come to $1 MHz-person ($3 billion X 100 MHz/300 million). This is by no means a perfect metric (and probably should be supplemented by other metrics), but neither are many other valuation metrics the government uses, such as for real estate tax assessment.

[33] Barbara Cochran, "Setting the Standard," *Communicator*, June 1998, p. 18.

[34] Cited in John W. Dean, "The Post-Truth Presidency: The Unintended Consequences of Presidential Lying," *Washington Monthly*, 1 November 2004, p. 37.

Even without an additional role for government, the current batch of pious journalistic ethics claims can be given more credibility. When RTNDA Chair Robert Garcia states that RTNDA's "revised code is our message to the public that along with press freedoms come responsibility,"[35] RTNDA should provide evidence that that statement isn't a lobbying ploy to win government privileges without credible responsibilities, but the first step of a genuine, controversial, and difficult effort to make those code words costly.[36]

As I have argued, an agency/ethics statement isn't credible if it's of the form: "I am an agent and will always act in the interests of my primary principal." This type of statement is meaningless because every rational agent will claim to act on behalf of his primary principal regardless of whether it is true. The closely related statement that "I am an agent and will always act in the interests of both my primary and secondary principals" is equally meaningless because it's not possible to act in all their interests when those interests conflict. Hence, media claims to invariably act on behalf of both viewers and stockholders aren't credible.

Credible ethics claims are those that are costly when violated. Statements by agents that aren't costly may be viewed as attempts to take a principal's payment without rendering the services for which payment was offered. By "costly" I don't mean mere claims of costliness, which are almost as ubiquitous as claims of media ethical behavior. Thus, the claim that "good journalism is good business" is equally meaningless unless accompanied by compelling evidence that bias is easy to detect, and, if detected, punished severely.

Ethics claims may be costly but target the wrong person: low level corporate employees (e.g., TV reporters) instead of high level corporate managers (e.g., TV general managers). Ethics claims may also be costly but target obvious conflicts that are trivial when compared to less obvious conflicts. For example, ABC bans reporters from covering a politician on whom they have published a book[37] but sees no ethical conflict when its station general managers lobby the same politician. In such situations, ethics claims should be heavily discounted.

---

[35] Quoted in RTNDA news release, "RTNDA Revises Its Code of Ethics," 14 September 2000.

[36] For a remarkably brief and potent illustration of RTNDA cheap talk, see Barstow and Stein, "Under Bush, a New Age of Prepackaged News," p. A1.

[37] Explains David Westin, President of ABC News, to one of his reporters: "we cannot have a Washington correspondent writing a book about one of our national leaders whom that correspondent will undoubtedly have to cover." Otherwise, ABC News could be "held up to ridicule that our reporting is influenced by views you/we have formed about the individual involved." Cited in Bob Zelnick, "ABC: Anyone but Conservatives," *Wall Street Journal*, 24 February 1998, p. A22.

It is hard or even impossible to develop costly codes of ethics without some type of government enforcement. There are a number of such laws on the books. For example, the anti-payola laws make it illegal for local broadcasters to take payment for programming without dislosing that fact to audiences.[38] But on the assumption that government enforcement is not realistic or desirable, I am proposing some costly signals media agents could send that would help the public determine the extent to which an ethics code is serious and enforceable in the court of public opinion.

1) Is the ethics code made public and published on the web?[39]

2) Does the ethics code contain a clear description of a media company's principal-agent relationships and take steps to lower the principal's cost of monitoring the agent? (The principal in this case is the station audience and the agents the producers of station news and other programming.)

3) Does the ethics code acknowledge possible conflicts among major groups of principals, such as viewers and media owners? And if it does acknowledge such conflicts, does it state which interests will take priority when they conflict?

4) Does management sign the codes of ethics or only low level employees? Credible systems of public accountability must start at the top of an

---

[38] Even here, disclosures may be made to avoid legal liability but not inform anybody. A TV show that complies with the anti-payola laws by obscurely and quickly disclosing a payment for product placement within the show in the credits at the end of the show might fit in that category. With today's digital TV technology, programmers could give viewers control of how these disclosures show up during or after the show, but the show does not give the viewer control of such disclosure.

[39] Although many newspapers publish their codes of ethics online, I was not able to find a single TV network or local broadcast station that did so. A simple explanation might be that lawyers for broadcast companies don't want codes of ethics publicized because they might be used against them in court.

[40] In the words of Securities and Exchange Commissioner Cynthia Glassman: "An ethics code means little if the company's chief executive officer or its directors conduct themselves as if the ethics code's provisions do not apply to them." This, of course, is exactly how general managers at TV stations operate. See Susan Kavanagh, "SEC Commissioner and Chairman Stress Importance of Ethical Culture," *Federal Ethics Report*, April 2003, p. 1. A survey by the Ethics Officers Association found that 78.4% of their members "have made the same code of conduct for employees applicable for the CEO and financial officers." See "The Impact of Recent Legislation and Regulation on Ethics and Compliance Programs," Waltham, MA: Ethics Officer Association, November 2003, p. 2.

organization because that's where the power is.[40] The trickle up theory of journalistic ethics propagated by media management pretends that the actual power relationships within media organizations do not exist. Nothing is more banal than corporate management blaming ethical failures on their underlings. That's why the Sarbarnes-Oxley Act mandates that CEO's and other senior executives sign the accounting statements. That way they cannot blame underlings for their lapses.[41]

5) Does the ethics code clearly specify the location of the ethics firewall (e.g., between the news director and general manager) and the steps that are taken to prevent an ethics firewall from being transformed into its opposite, a secrecy firewall?

6) Does the ethics code clearly specify that all individuals outside of the ethics firewall will disclose their lobbying activities? Journalists have a good excuse for not disclosing their exchanges with policymakers and other sources of information. Without promising secrecy, they could not get the information necessary to inform the general public. But individuals on the business side of the ethics firewall lack that excuse.

7) Does the ethics code create a mechanism for third parties to monitor and audit claimed ethical practices? For example, do media make archived media content as accessible to credible outside auditors as it does to its own working staff?

8) Does the ethics code have a whistleblower clause that would give employees, such as journalists, an incentive to expose ethics violations?[42]

9) Does the ethics code clearly state that what the news organization really cares about is actual conduct, not mere appearances? Codes of Ethics routinely state that the appearance of unethical behavior is just as bad

---

[41] E.g., Susan Pulliam, "The 'It Wasn't Me' Defense: CEOs from Enron to Sotheby's blame scandals on underlings; Too busy for all the details?" *Wall Street Journal*, 9 July 2004, p. B1.
[42] The Sarbanes-Oxley corporate accounting whistle blower statutes, as implemented by public companies, provide a variety of examples of such a system. See "Phyllis Plitch, "Blowing the Whistle: Sarbanes-Oxley requires that companies treat internal complaints—and complainers—seriously," *Wall Street Journal*, 21 June 2004, p. R6. Where whistle blowers aren't protected, information dries up and retribution is exacted. See Lisa Guerney, "Where Tips Meet Truth (Sometimes): From Enron to terrorism, whistle-blower sites mine clues amid mountains of suspicion," *New York Times*, 21 February 2002, p. E1, and C. Fred Alford, *Whistleblowers: Broken Lives and Organizational Power* (Ithaca: Cornell University Press, 2001).

as actual unethical behavior because appearances can have the very tangible effect of reducing audience credibility. But they are strikingly quiet about the situation when it is easy for a news organization to violate its stated ethics code without any appearance of doing so.

10) Does the media organization belong to the Ethics Officers Association and voluntarily follow its guidelines, even though non-media companies tend to be subject to a higher standard of accountability than news media companies? For example, the United States Federal Sentencing Guidelines imposes lighter penalties on companies that have adopted a corporate ethics compliance plan.[43] But the news media have less reason to worry about such laws—and do not belong to the Ethics Officers Association—because of their government granted exemptions, often stemming from the First Amendment.

11) Does the ethics code call on journalists to disclose only obvious conflicts of interest or is the standard of disclosure based on the seriousness of the potential conflict? For example, most media outlets will note when reporting on a subsidiary owned by a parent company, even though this type of information is readily available in public databases and often widely known. There aren't many news junkies who don't know that Disney owns ABC News or that General Electric owns NBC News. In contrast, when that same outlet is reporting on a politician that its parent company has lobbied aggressively, it will provide no public acknowledgment of the conflict of interest, despite the fact that this type of conflict of interest may be of greater importance to the public and much harder for it to discover without the benefit of media disclosure.

12) Does the media organization take advantage of new disclosure technology to enhance its ethics? The Securities & Exchange Commission, for example, now requires online disclosure of great amounts of information that will enhance trust in financial agents and the markets they help create. But media have been very slow to adopt similar technology. For example, the new broadcast digital TV technology allows meta program data to accompany the main programming data stream a viewer sees. Meta data includes program names, schedules, ratings, closed captions, video descriptions, and other program-related information. Journalistic ethics disclosures that would otherwise be intrusive and tedious to view

---

[43] Michael J. McCarthy, "How One Firm Tracks Ethics Electronically," *Wall Street Journal*, 21 October 1999, p. B1, Amy Zipkin, "Getting Religion on Corporate Ethics," *New York Times*, 10 October 2000, p. C1.

as part of a program can now be included in the program metadata, giving viewers the option of viewing it how and when they want.[44]

Many media organizations, such as RTNDA, the National Press Club, and the Society of Professional Journalists, both tout journalistic codes of ethics and offer awards for outstanding journalistic accomplishment. Quite remarkably, however, the highest values in the codes of ethics are rarely recognized in journalistic awards. To enhance the credibility of their codes of ethics, these organizations could feature an award—call it the "whistle blowers award"—specifically for journalists who expose the ethics violations of their parent companies and by doing so endanger their own careers.

This award, like memorials for journalists who are murdered by politicians for upholding their journalistic watchdog function, deserves to be elevated above other journalism awards because of the huge career risks entailed by such journalism. In the media world, like in any other organization, the whistle blower takes on huge risks with very little prospect of reward. That is why so many government statutes encourage and protect whistleblowers. Without witness protection, many opportunistic behaviors, such as the Enron accounting scandals, would never be solved. The lack of professional recognition and appreciation for taking perhaps the most heroic action a journalist can take—risking one's career for the sake of the ideals of the news profession—seriously undercuts the media industry's ethics claims.

Recommendations for Scholars of Media Bias

A recommendation for scholars and others who study media bias is that bias should no longer be defined in relation to abstractions such as objectivity, fairness, or the truth, but in relation to concrete audience preferences. For example, the answer to the following type of questions could be used to formulate ethics guidelines:

---

[44] Current broadcast law requires paid advertising embedded within a TV program to be disclosed at the end of the end of the program. But the disclosures pass quickly and are out of context, so they are easily missed. A better disclosure system for this and other types of conflict of interest information would be to embed conflict of interest tags in the meta data accompanying a DTV program. When combined with a digital video recorder, a viewer would have the option of seeing conflict of interest information during or after the show, and get substantial control over how the information was displayed. Of course, there is no reason to restrict disclosure solely to hidden ads. Any conflict of interest covered in a journalistic ethics code should be fair game.

1) If the general manager of your local TV station lobbies a particular politician, should reporters disclose that fact when reporting on that politician?

2) If the general manager of your local TV station socializes with a particular politician, should reporters disclose that fact when reporting on that politician?

3) If the general manager of your local TV station contributes to the campaign of a particular politician, should reporters disclose that fact when reporting on that politician?

For those who study policy media bias, especially industry and company media bias, I recommend placing more emphasis on politicians' reasonable expectations of media bias rather than evidence of the media bias itself. When media have strong incentives to commit bias, the burden of proof should shift from scholars trying to prove the bias to media trying to prove their objectivity. Media owners have always imposed such an "appearance" standard of evidence on their news employees. It's time that they themselves be subject to the same standard.

Ultimately, the power of media bias on policy is measured by the actions of policymakers. So studying their reasonable expectations of media bias gets closer to the actual goal of media bias. However, this presents a special methodological problem because politicians will no more acknowledge being intimidated by the threat of media bias than they will acknowledge being intimidated by powerful interest groups. When this consideration is combined with the strong incentives media organizations have to hide verifiable evidence of bias, more indirect measurements of bias, such as media's motives to commit bias, may have to become a greater part of the researchers' methodological toolkit.

Recommendations for Interest Group Scholars

The methodological problems of studying media bias are similar to those for studying interest group bias. In both cases, the paradox of bias applies: agents will only engage in forms of bias that are hard to publicly detect and verify. This shifts the burden of proof away from those seeking to prove bias and toward those seeking to prove agency/ethical behavior.

More generally, media bias and interest group bias can be viewed as special cases of a larger theory of political bias. In this more general theory, the political arts of raising costs on unfavorable information should be given comparatively more attention. Too much attention has focused on the political arts of lowering costs on favorable information. The critical importance of the time dimension to political persuasion also needs to be given greater attention. Types of information that are undocumented and therefore unverifiable at a later time may be far more important to political actors than their verifiable counterparts. Similarly, types of information that could merely potentially become known to the general public may be far more politically important than information that is actually known.

Will the Power of Broadcast Industry Media Bias Wane?

It is possible that broadcasters' political power stemming from control of media is on the verge of precipitous decline. Other forms of one-to-many ("broadcast") TV, including cable TV and satellite TV, continue to gain market share from local TV broadcasters. And no one disputes that the local broadcasters' share of the primetime viewing audience has been in decline for decades. Even more important, the next generation of broadband Internet technology will support Internet TV, which will drastically reduce barriers to entry in the TV business. With the limitless video choice and greater viewer convenience made possible via Internet TV, the broadcast-cable-satellite bottleneck on local TV content will be broken. Already, tens of millions of Japanese and South Koreans have access to such video broadband services. In just a few years, millions of Americans will, too. As the cost of these services continues to rapidly decline, the traditional broadcast model—whether analog or digital—becomes doomed to ever declining influence.

The old political alliance between broadcast TV and radio may also be on the verge of breaking up. Traditionally, broadcast TV and broadcast radio competed indirectly. This allowed NAB to represent both broadcast groups with fairly modest internal conflict. But as TV broadcasters transition from analog to digital technologies, the broadcast TV and radio industries will converge. A bit is a bit whether it transmits TV or radio information. A single TV license could conceivably use its spectrum to broadcast more than a hundred FM-quality audio programming streams. Unlike the European broadcast DTV system, the first generation of the U.S. broadcast DTV system was designed to prevent competition between broadcast radio and TV. But future generations of the U.S. broadcast DTV system are unlikely to preserve such a limitation. This split in interests might break the NAB into two competing and weakened organizations. The NAB TV Board's forced retirement of NAB President Eddie Fritts, an old radio broadcaster most closely allied with the NAB Radio Board, may reflect a growing recognition of conflicting interests between these two bedrock and overlapping NAB membership groups.[45]

On the other hand, countervailing forces may be leading to an increase in the power of broadcast TV. One force is increasing ownership across different types of media. If all forms of media continue to merge, then the interests of non-broadcast companies will tend to merge with the interests of broadcast companies. Instead of different media providing a check on each other, they could come to constitute a common interest adverse to the public. The jury is still out on whether the natural force of the new information technology will lead to this type of media concentration or lead to a renaissance of new information sources. My guess is that the development of the Internet will eventually undermine the current economies of scale that dominate the media business and help justify giant media companies.

A second countervailing force is the tendency of Congress to protect telecommunications and media incumbents, thus slowing the day of competition. Charles Ferguson, for example, has argued that Congressional policy has hindered the development of broadband Internet networks that would support Internet TV.[46] Cable TV doesn't want Internet TV because its business model depends on charging TV program providers for the privilege of using its networks; Internet-based TV-on-demand would allow program providers to bypass cable operators. Broadcasters, in turn, don't want the open access created by Internet TV because they already receive free and mandatory must-carry on cable TV networks; Internet TV would break the broadcaster-cable duopoly and allow other TV providers to compete on an equal playing field.

A third countervailing force is broadcasters' effort to use their spectrum to enter new media and telecom businesses. This must be done quietly, behind the scenes, because it runs contrary to their current lobbying rationale for public subsidies, which is to preserve the current system of broadcast TV by

---

[45] Bill McConnell, "The Fritts Years," *Broadcasting & Cable*, 21 March 2005, pp. 32-41.

[46] Jackson and Haring, "Pitfalls in the Economic Valuation of the Electromagnetic Spectrum.", MSTV, "MSTV White Paper: ATV Channels, Flexibility, and the Public Interest," (Washington, DC: MSTV, 1995), NAB, "Digital Television Broadcasting.", Cindy J. Price, "Does Power Change the News? A Content Analysis of Network News Coverage of the Telecommunications Act of 1996," (Las Vegas, Nevada: 1998), Snider, *Explanation of the Citizen's Guide to the Airwaves*, Zaller, *The Nature and Origins of Mass Opinion*.

only slightly modifying it. This is a very delicate task. On the one hand, they must pretend that ad-supported ("free"), terrestrial, over-the-air, one-to-many broadcast TV covering thousands of square miles and polluting thousands more (due to needed guard bands between channels in neighboring markets) has a glorious future built on continued consumer demand. On the other hand, they are anything but idiots. They know that the traditional broadcasting model—whether analog or digital—is rapidly becoming obsolete. Although it is no mean trick to expand public subsidies while in fact abandoning the rationale justifying them, the broadcasters to date have paid no penalty for such inconsistency.

No one knows whether broadcasters will be able to use their still extraordinary political power to continue to both warehouse their underutilized spectrum and win spectrum rights windfalls. My best guess is that broadcasters will continue to receive substantial additional windfalls, even as their power wanes.

Morality vs. Institutional Design

Now that I have reached the end of this book, I must reiterate what I said at the beginning. Broadcasters have neither been good nor bad. They have just played the hand they were dealt exceptionally well. If dealt the same hand, I do not believe most other professional industry lobbyists would have behaved any differently. Surely, for example, the cable TV industry has not been immune to the same media strategies used by the local TV broadcasters.

In the moral ledger, it must also be remembered that local TV broadcasters have been trying to stave off decline and extinction. For all their short-term advantages, they are keenly aware that the tide of history is strongly running against them. That doesn't make them any worthier of government subsidies and monopoly protections than the horse and buggy industry. But it does cast their behavior in a more sympathetic light.

Again, my ultimate purpose in writing this book has not been to make a moral case for or against broadcasters or any other individual or group, although that makes for a good journalistic story peg and livelier reading. It has been quite the opposite: to make individual morality a non-issue in the design of democratic information and election systems. We should not be asking guardians to guard themselves. We should be designing institutions so they don't have to. If guardians have an intrinsic conflict of interest in guarding themselves and have the ability to rig information and election systems to that end, this should alarm us and lead us to look for creative solutions.

The most obvious solution is simply to seek more competition among the guardians. But experience has proven that without well-designed institutions, guardians can minimize the level of competition. The world is full of leaders elected by popular vote (even Saddam Hussein of Iraq was elected by popular vote) but minimal opportunity for challengers and differences of opinion to compete. Before competition can work its magic, the right institutions have to be in place to foster competition.

Conclusion

A democracy is strengthened when citizens know where power lies and understand how it is exercised. As this book has shown, however, this knowledge may not be easy for citizens to attain because, when asymmetric information is the source of power, it is in the interest of power to hide itself. The broadcast industry may be remarkably successful in implementing such a strategy, but the strategy itself is endemic to special interest politics.

Regardless of whether or not broadcasters remain potent political players, the fundamental strategies they have used to secure political power will not go away. Those strategies are endemic to politics. Whether political actors use airwaves or any other resource to pursue their interests, their fundamental strategies remain constant: they will always seek to create and exploit asymmetric information. When the political actor is a local TV broadcaster or an incumbent politician—both of which have extraordinary resources to give themselves an information advantage—this poses a great dilemma for democratic governance.

The task of political reform is to create institutions that minimize the opportunity to create and exploit such asymmetric information. This can be a daunting problem when the political actors who have the power to pass such reforms lack the incentive to do so and would not be trusted by the public to do so for that very reason. The proposal put forth here to create a Citizens' Committee on Candidate Information and Elections attempts to address that dilemma.

REFERENCES

Ahrens, Frank. "FCC Sees Local Gain to Age of Max Media." *Washington Post*, 16 May 2003, p. E1.

Akerlof, George A. *An Economic Theorist's Book of Tales: Essays That Entertain the Consequences of New Assumptions in Economic Theory*. Cambridge [Cambridgeshire]; New York: Cambridge University Press, 1984.

Akhavan-Majid, Roya, and Gary Wolf. "America Mass Media and the Myth of Libertarianism: Toward an 'Elite Power Group' Theory." *Critical Studies in Mass Communication* 8 (1991): 139-51.

Albiniak, Paige. "King of the Hill." *Broadcasting & Cable*, 22 December 1997.

———. "Stations 'Waiver' on DTV." *Broadcasting & Cable*, 20 August 2001, p. 6.

Alford, C. Fred. *Whistleblowers: Broken Lives and Organizational Power*. Ithaca: Cornell University Press, 2001.

Alger, Dean. *The Media and Politics*. 2nd [rev.] ed. Belmont: Wadsworth Pub. Co., 1996.

———. *Megamedia: How Giant Corporations Dominate Mass Media, Distort Competition, and Endanger Democracy*. Lanham: Rowman & Littlefield, 1998.

Alliance for Better Campaigns. "Profiteering on Democracy: How the Television Industry Gouged Candidates in Campaign '02." 58. Washington, DC: Alliance for Better Campaigns, 2002.

Alvarez, Lizette. "Testing of a President: The Defender; a Lawmaker Uses His Own Shame as a Guide." *New York Times*, 13 December 1998, A45.

Anderson, Jack, and Daryl Gibson. *Peace, War, and Politics: An Eyewitness Account*. 1st ed. New York: Forge, 1999.

Andrews, Edmund L. "Winners of Wireless Auction to Pay $7 Billion." *New York Times*, 14 March 1995, p. D1.

Ansolabehere, S., J. M. de Figueiredo, and J. M. Snyder. "Why Is There So Little Money in U.S. Politics?" *Journal of Economic Perspectives* 17, no. 1 (2003): 105-30.

APTS. "Grassroots Action Handbook." Washington, DC: Association of America's Public Television Stations, September 1995.

Armistead, Leigh, Joint Forces Staff College (U.S.), and United States. National Security Agency/Central Security Service. *Information Operations: Warfare and the Hard Reality of Soft Power*. 1st ed, *Issues in Twenty-First Century Warfare*. Dulles, Va.: Brassey's, 2004.

Arnold, R. Douglas. *Congress, the Press, and Political Accountability*. Princeton, N.J.: Princeton University Press, 2004.

————. *The Logic of Congressional Action*. New Haven: Yale University Press, 1990.

Austen-Smith, David, and Jeffrey S. Banks. *Positive Political Theory I: Collective Preference, Michigan Studies in Political Analysis*. Ann Arbor: University of Michigan Press, 1999.

Aversa, Jeannine. "FCC Oks Pricey Digital TV." *Associated Press*, 4 April 1997.

————. "Study: Broadcasters Shape Policy." *Associated Press*, 2 April 1997.

Bagdikian, Ben H. *The Media Monopoly*. 4th ed. Boston: Beacon Press, 1992.

Baker, C. Edwin. *Media, Markets, and Democracy, Communication, Society, and Politics*. Cambridge ; New York: Cambridge University Press, 2002.

Balko, Radley. "All Politics Is Local: How Broadcasters Want to Silence Satellite Radio, Issue #71." *Cato TechKnowledge*, 20 January 2004.

Banks, Jeffrey S. *Signaling Games in Political Science*. Chur, Switzerland ; New York: Harwood Academic, 1991.

Barnouw, Erik. *The Sponsor: Notes on a Modern Potentate*. New York: Oxford University Press, 1978.

Barrett, Marvin. *Moments of Truth?* New York: Crowell, 1975.

Barstow, David, and Robin Stein. "Under Bush, a New Age of Prepackaged News." *New York Times*, 13 March 2005, A1.

Bartels, Larry M. *Presidential Primaries and the Dynamics of Public Choice*. Princeton, N.J.: Princeton University Press, 1988.

Basheda, Valerie. "She's So Fine: Wall Street's Media Analysts Have an Impact on the Way Newspaper Companies Operate." *American Journalism Review*, July/August 2001.

Baughman, James L. *Television's Guardians: The FCC and the Politics of Programming, 1958–1967*. Knoxville: University of Tennessee Press, 1985.

Baumgartner, Frank R., and Beth L. Leech. *Basic Interests: The Importance of Groups in Politics and in Political Science*. Princeton, N.J.: Princeton University Press, 1998.

Bazelon, Coleman, Michael Rothkopf, and Troy Kravitz. "The Value of the Airwaves." In *Explanation of the Citizen's Guide to the Airwaves*, edited by J.H. Snider, 52 p. Washington, DC: New America Foundation, 2003.

Belson, Ken. "Verizon Moves to Head Off Nextel in a Spectrum Swap." *New York Times*, 9 April 2004, C4.

Bendor, J., A. Glazer, and T. Hammond. "Theories of Delegation." *Annual Review of Political Science* 4 (2001): 235-69.

Bennett, Ralph Kinney. "The Great Airwaves Giveaway." *Reader's Digest*, June 1996, 150.

Bennett, W. Lance. *News, the Politics of Illusion*. 2nd ed. New York: Longman, 1988.

Berkowitz, Bruce D. *The New Face of War : How War Will Be Fought in the 21st Century*. New York: Free Press, 2003.

Bernstein, Carl, and Bob Woodward. *All the President's Men*. New York,: Simon and Schuster, 1974.

Berry, Jeffrey M. *The Interest Group Society*. 3rd ed. New York: Longman, 1997.

Birnbaum, Jeffrey H. "Advocacy Groups Blur Media Lines: Some Push Agendas by Producing Movies, Owning Newspapers." *Washington Post*, 6 December 2004, p. A1.

Black, Jay, Bob Steele, Ralph D. Barney, and Society of Professional Journalists (U.S.). *Doing Ethics in Journalism: A Handbook with Case Studies*. 3rd ed. Boston: Allyn and Bacon, 1999.

Black, Norman. "Senator Abandoning Amendment Effort." *Associated Press*, 13 April 1983.

Bradlee, Benjamin C. *A Good Life: Newspapering and Other Adventures*. New York: Simon & Schuster, 1995.

Brand, Stewart. *The Media Lab: Inventing the Future at Mit*. New York, N.Y.: Viking, 1987.

Brian, Denis. *Pulitzer: A Life*. New York: J. Wiley, 2001.

Brinkley, Joel. *Defining Vision: The Battle for the Future of Television*. 1st U.S. ed. New York: Harcourt Brace, 1997.

———. "Microsoft Undercut in Effort to Depict Rival as Thriving: E-Mails Suggest a Selective Search for Data." *New York Times*, 5 June 1999, p. B4.

"Broadcast." *Communications Daily*, 3 March 2004.

"The Broadcast Lobby: Resistant to Change." In *The Washington Lobby*. Washington, DC: Congressional Quarterly, 1979.

"Broadcast Television in a Multichannel Marketplace." Washington, DC: FCC's Office of Plans and Policy, 1991.

"Broadcasters and Bucks." *Broadcasting & Cable*, 11 January 1999, 18.

"Broadcasters Fight for UHF Spectrum; State of the Art Technology." *Broadcasting*, 27 October 1986, p. 89.

Broadcasters, National Association of. "Legislative Issue Papers, 105th Congress, 1st Session." Washington, DC: National Association of Broadcasters, 1997.

———. "A Model State Marketing Plan: The Marketing of Broadcaster's Public Service Record." Washington, DC: National Association of Broadcasters, 1998.

Bunker, Robert J., and Institute of Land Warfare (Association of the United States Army). *Information Operations and the Conduct of Land Warfare, Land Warfare Papers ; No. 31*. Arlington, VA: Institute of Land Warfare, Association of the United States Army, 1998.

Campaign Legal Center. "The Campaign Media Guide." Washington, DC: Campaign Legal Center, 2004.

Cannon, Carl M. "Hooked on Polls." *National Journal*, 17 October 1998, 2438-41.

Carmines, E. G., and J. A. Stimson. "The 2 Faces of Issue Voting." *American Political Science Review* 74, no. 1 (1980): 78-91.

Carney, Dan. "Industry Agrees to TV Ratings." *CQ*, 2 March 1996, 554.

"Channeling Influence: The Broadcast Lobby and the $70 Billion Free Ride." Washington, DC: Common Cause, 2 April 1997.

Clements, Michael E., and Amy D. Abramowitz. "Ownership Affiliation and the Programming Decisions of Cable Operators." Paper presented at the Telecommunications Policy Research Conference, Arlington, Virginia, 2 October 2004.

Colamosca, Anne. "Who's Left Out: Small Markets, Small Paychecks." *Columbia Journalism Review*, July/August 1999.

Cole, Barry, and Mal Oettinger. "Covering the Politics of Broadcasting." *Columbia Journalism Review*, April 1977, 58-63.

Commerce, Department of. "The Emerging Digital Economy II." Washington, DC: U.S. Department of Commerce, Office of Policy Development, June 1999.

Connolly, Terry, Hal R. Arkes, and Kenneth R. Hammond. *Judgment and Decision Making: An Interdisciplinary Reader*. 2nd ed, Cambridge Series on Judgment and Decision Making. Cambridge, U.K. ; New York: Cambridge University Press, 2000.

Cook, Timothy E. *Governing with the News: The News Media as a Political Institution, Studies in Communication, Media, and Public Opinion*. Chicago: University of Chicago Press, 1998.

———. *Making Laws and Making News: Media Strategies in the U.S. House of Representatives*. Washington, D.C.: Brookings Institution, 1989.

Cooper, Mark N. *Media Ownership and Democracy in the Digital Information Age: Promoting Diversity with First Amendment Principles and Market Structure Analysis*. Stanford, Calif.: Center for Internet & Society, Stanford Law School, 2003.

Corrado, Anthony. *Campaign Finance Reform: A Sourcebook*. Washington, D.C.: Brookings Institution, 1997.

Creech, Kenneth. *Electronic Media Law and Regulation*. 3rd ed. Boston: Focal Press, 2000.

Cronkite, Walter. *A Reporter's Life*. 1st ed. New York: A.A. Knopf, 1996.

Dahl, Robert Alan. *Democracy and Its Critics*. New Haven: Yale University Press, 1989.

"Daily Press Galleries Information Guide." Washington, DC: U.S. Congress, 1999.

Davis, Paul. "Moving to Washington: Rtnda Is a Major Player in Washington in First Amendment and Foi Battles Because of the Vision and Bullheaded Persistence of Its Early Leaders." *Communicator*, September 1995, p. 113.

Dean, John W. "The Post-Truth Presidency: The Unintended Consequences of Presidential Lying." *Washington Monthly*, 1 November 2004, 47.

Delli Carpini, Michael X., and Scott Keeter. *What Americans Know About Politics and Why It Matters*. New Haven [Conn.]: Yale University Press, 1996.

Denison, Dave. "Don't Mess with Television." *American Prospect*, 5 June 2000, 34-8.

Denning, Dorothy Elizabeth Robling. *Information Warfare and Security*. New York: Addison-Wesley, 1999.

Dewar, Michael. *The Art of Deception in Warfare, A David & Charles Military Book*. New York: Sterling Publishing, 1989.

Dixit, Avinash K., and Barry Nalebuff. *Thinking Strategically: The Competitive Edge in Business, Politics, and Everyday Life.* 1st ed. New York: Norton, 1991.

Dole, Bob. "Giving Away the Airwaves; Industry Should Pay for Licenses for Digital TV." *New York Times*, 27 March 1997, p. A29.

Dotinga, Randy. "Latest Path around Soft-Money Ban: Buy a TV Station." *Christian Science Monitor*, 17 December 2003, 2.

Dowding, Keith M. *Power, Concepts in Social Thought.* Minneapolis: University of Minnesota Press, 1996.

Downs, Anthony. *An Economic Theory of Democracy.* New York,: Harper, 1957.

Drew, Elizabeth. *The Corruption of American Politics: What Went Wrong and Why.* Secaucus, N.J.: Carol Pub. Group, 1999.

Dubner, Stephen J., and Steven D. Levitt. "What the Bagel Man Saw." *New York Times Magazine*, 6 June 2004, 62-5.

Dunham, Corydon B. *Fighting for the First Amendment: Stanton of CBS Vs. Congress and the Nixon White House.* Westport, Conn.: Praeger, 1997.

Dupagne, Michael, and Peter B. Seel. *High-Definition Television: A Global Perspective.* 1st ed. Ames: Iowa State University Press, 1998.

Dutta, Prajit K. *Strategies and Games: Theory and Practice.* Cambridge, Mass.: MIT Press, 1999.

Enelow, James M., and Melvin J. Hinich. *Advances in the Spatial Theory of Voting.* Cambridge [England] ; New York: Cambridge University Press, 1990.

Entman, Robert. "A Free and Responsible Press." In *University of Chicago Legal Forum.* Chicago: University of Chicago, 1993.

Farhi, Paul. "TV Claims Congress Could Steal the Show: Digital-Auction Advocates Dispute Ads' Scare Tactics." *Washington Post*, 20 March 1996, p. D1.

FCC. "Annual Assessment of the Status of Competition in the Market for the Delivery of Video Programming: Tenth Annual Report." In *CS Docket 01-129.* Washington, DC: FCC, 28 January 2004.

———. "Report to the Congress on the Low Power Fm Interference Testing Program Pub. L. No. 106-553." Washington, DC: FCC, 19 February 2004.

Fenno, Richard F. *Home Style : House Members in Their Districts.* Boston: Little, Brown, 1978.

Ferejohn, John A., and James H. Kuklinski. *Information and Democratic Processes.* Urbana: University of Illinois Press, 1990.

Flaherty, Joseph. "ATV How to Do It Whatever It Is." Paper presented at the Bit by Bit into the Future, Hilton Head, South Carolina, 27 September 1994.

———. "High Definition TV: Transition Scenario for TV Stations." New York City: CBS, 23 October 1990.

Fleetwood, Blake. "The Broken Wall: How Newspapers Are Selling Their Credibility to Advertisers." *Washington Monthly*, September 1999.

Forno, Richard, and Ronald Baklarz. *The Art of Information Warfare: Insight into the Knowledge Warrior Philosophy*. 2nd pbk. ed. Boca Raton, Florida: Universal Publishers, 1999.

Fowler, Mark S., and Daniel L. Brenner. "A Marketplace Approach to Broadcast Regulation." *Texas Law Review* 60, no. 2 (1982): 207-57.

Frankenfield, Wayne C. "Broadcast Accounting: Are We Sitting on a Powder Keg?" *The Financial Manager* October/November 2000.

Galperin, Hernan. *New Television, Old Politics: The Transition to Digital TV in the United States and Britain, Communication, Society, and Politics*. New York: Cambridge, 2004.

Gans, Herbert J. *Deciding What's News: A Study of CBS Evening News, NBC Nightly News, Newsweek, and Time*. 1st Vintage Books ed. New York: Vintage Books, 1980.

Gilder, George F. *Life after Television*. Knoxville, Tenn.: Whittle Direct Books, 1990.

Gilens, Martin, and Craig Hertzman. "Corporate Ownership and News Bias: Newspaper Coverage of the 1996 Telecommunications Act." *Journal of Politics* 62, no. 2 (2000).

Godson, Roy, and James J. Wirtz. *Strategic Denial and Deception: The Twenty-First Century Challenge*. New Brunswick, N.J.: Transaction Publishers, 2002.

Goldberg, Bernard. *Bias: A CBS Insider Exposes How the Media Distorts the News*. New York: Perennial, 2002.

Goldenson, Alvin I. "Toward a Theory of Social Power." In *Power: Readings in Social and Political Theory*, edited by Steven Lukes, vi, 283. New York: New York University Press, 1986.

Goodman, Ellen P. "Digital Television and the Allure of Auctions: The Birth and Stillbirth of DTV Legislation." *Federal Communications Law Journal* 49, no. 3 (1997): pp, 517-49.

Gordon, Andrew. *Understanding Broadcast & Cable Finance: A Handbook for the Non-Financial Manager*. Des Plaines: BCFM Press, 1994.

Gorisek, Sue. "The Forbes Four Hundred: The up & Comers." *Forbes*, 28 October 1985, 348.

Graber, Doris A. *Mass Media and American Politics*. 4th ed. Washington, D.C.: CQ Press, 1992.

———. *Mass Media and American Politics*. 2nd ed. Washington, D.C.: CQ Press, 1984.

Gray, Virginia, and David Lowery. *The Population Ecology of Interest Representation : Lobbying Communities in the American States*. Ann Arbor: The University of Michigan Press, 1996.

Greenwald, Robert. "Outfoxed: Rupert Murdoch's War on Journalism." 77 minutes: Carolina Productions, 2004.

Greider, William. *Who Will Tell the People: The Betrayal of American Democracy*. New York: Simon & Schuster, 1992.

Grofman, Bernard. *Information, Participation, and Choice: An Economic Theory of Democracy in Perspective*. Ann Arbor: University of Michigan Press, 1993.

Group, Harwood. "Citizens and Politics: A View from Main Street America." Dayton, Ohio: Kettering Foundation, 1991.

"Groups That Don't Cut the Mustard in the Washington Lobbying World." *National Journal*, 4 July 1987, 1710.

Guensburg, Carol. "When the Story Is About the Owner." *American Journalism Review*, December 1998.

Hackett, Robert A. "Decline of a Paradigm? Bias and Objectivity in News Media Studies." *Critical Studies in Mass Communication* 1, no. 3 (1984): 229-59.

Hall, R. L., and F. W. Wayman. "Buying Time—Moneyed Interests and the Mobilization of Bias in Congressional Committees." *American Political Science Review* 84, no. 3 (1990): 797-820.

Halonen, Doug. "NAB Now Rides a Wave of Capitol Clout." *Electronic Media*, 14 December 1998.

Harsanyi, John C. "Measurement of Social Power, Opportunity Costs, and the Theory of Two-Person Bargaining Games." *Behaviorial Science* 7 (1962): 67-80.

Hart, Jeffrey A. *Technology, Television and Competition: The Politics of Digital TV*. New York: Cambridge University Press, 2004.

Hart, Peter D. "People Versus Politics: Citizens Discuss Politicians, Campaigns, and Political Reform." Washington, DC: Peter D. Hart Research Associates, 1991.

Hart, Roderick P., and Bartholomew H. Sparrow. *Politics, Discourse, and American Society: New Agendas*. Lanham, Md.: Rowman & Littlefield, 2001.

Hasen, Richard L. "Double Standard: Media Corporations Have the Power to Endorse Candidates, but Other Companies Don't." *Brill's Content*, February 1999.

Hatch, David. "Jesse Puts Move on Minnesota Pubcasters." *Electronic Media*, 8 February 1998, p. 4.

Hayes, Michael T. *Lobbyists and Legislators: A Theory of Political Markets*. New Brunswick, N.J.: Rutgers University Press, 1981.

Hazlett, Thomas. "Assigning Property Rights to Radio Spectrum Users: Why Did FCC License Auctions Take 67 Years?" *Journal of Law & Economics* 41, no. 2 (1998): 529-75.

———. "Why the FCC Should Scrap Its Absurd Rules for Satellite Radio." *Slate*, 16 March 2004.

Hazlett, Thomas W. "The U.S. Digital TV Transition: Time to Toss the Negroponte Switch." Washington, DC: AEI-Brookings Joint Center for Regulatory Studies, 2001.

———. "The Wireless Craze: An Essay on Airwave Allocation Policy." *Harvard Journal of Law and Technology* (Spring 2001).

Hazlett, Thomas W., and Matthew L. Spitzer. "Digital Television and the Quid Pro Quo." *Business and Politics* 2, no. 2 (2000): 115-59.

Herman, Edward S., and Noam Chomsky. *Manufacturing Consent: The Political Economy of the Mass Media.* 1st ed. New York: Pantheon Books, 1988.

Hess, Stephen. *The Ultimate Insiders : U.S. Senators in the National Media.* Washington, D.C.: Brookings Institution, 1986.

Hibbing, John R., and Elizabeth Theiss-Morse. *Congress as Public Enemy : Public Attitudes toward American Political Institutions, Cambridge Studies in Political Psychology and Public Opinion.* Cambridge ; New York: Cambridge University Press, 1995.

Hickey, Neil. "Revolution in Cyberia." *Columbia Journalism Review,* July/August 1995.

———. "So Big: The Telecommunications Act at Year One." *Columbia Journalism Review,* January/February 1997, pp. 23-8.

———. "TV's Big Stick: What the Broadcast Industry Gets What It Wants in Washington." *Columbia Journalism Review,* September/October 2002.

———. "What's at Stake in the Spectrum War? Only Billions of Dollars and the Future of Television." *Columbia Journalism Review,* July/August 1996, 39-43.

U.S. Congress. Telecommunications, Trade and Consumer Protection Subcommittee. *High Definition Television,* 2nd Session, 25 July 2000.

"High Priced Malrite." *Broadcasting & Cable,* 13 April 1998, 18.

Hundt, Reed E. *You Say You Want a Revolution: A Story of Information Age Politics.* New Haven: Yale University Press, 2000.

Hundt, Reed, and Blair Levin. "The Digital TV Shuffle: Now You See It, Now You Don't." *Brill's Content,* July/August 1998, pp. 76-7.

Issacharoff, Samuel, Pamela S. Karlan, and Richard H. Pildes. *The Law of Democracy: Legal Structure of the Political Process.* Rev. 2nd ed, *University Casebook Series.* New York: Foundation Press, 2002.

Iyengar, Shanto, and Donald R. Kinder. *News That Matters : Television and American Opinion, American Politics and Political Economy.* Chicago: University of Chicago Press, 1987.

Jackson, Brooks. *Honest Graft : Big Money and the American Political Process.* Rev. ed. Washington, D.C.: Farragut Pub. Co., 1990.

Jackson, Charles J., and John Haring. "Pitfalls in the Economic Valuation of the Electromagnetic Spectrum." Bethesda, Maryland: Strategic Policy Research, 1995.

Jacobs, Lawrence R., and Robert Y. Shapiro. *Politicians Don't Pander: Political Manipulation and the Loss of Democratic Responsiveness, Studies in Communication, Media, and Public Opinion.* Chicago, IL.: University of Chicago Press, 2000.

Jacobson, Louis, and Bara Vaida. "Lobbying—Broadcast Blues." *National Journal,* 9 August 2003.

Jamieson, Kathleen Hall. *Dirty Politics: Deception, Distraction, and Democracy.* New York: Oxford University Press, 1992.

Johnson, Nicholas. *How to Talk Back to Your Television Set*. [1st] ed. Boston: Little Brown, 1970.

Jr., Bill Heniff. "Off-Budget Status of Federal Entities: Background and Current Proposals." Washington, DC: Congressional Research Service, 1999.

———. "User Fees: Applicable Budget Enforcement Procedures." Washington, DC: Congressional Research Service, 2000.

Jube Shiver Jr. "Focus of Media Debate Turns to Congress." *Los Angeles Times*, 28 July 2003, Business Section, p. 1.

"Judging Barney Frank." *New York Times*, 25 July 1990, A18.

Just, Marion, and Rosalind Levine. "News for Sale: Half of Stations Report Sponsor Pressure on News Decisions." *Columbia Journalism Review*, November/December 2001, pp. 2-3.

Just, Marion R., W. Russell Neuman, and Ann Crigler. "An Economic Theory of Learning from News." Cambridge: Joan Shorenstein Barone Center, 1992.

Kalter, Joanmarie. "Burnout." *Columbia Journalism Review*, July/August 1999.

Kaplan, Sheila. "Payments to the Powerful." *Columbia Journalism Review*, September 1998.

Karr, Albert R. "Television News Tunes out Airwaves-Auction Battle." *Wall Street Journal*, 1 May 1996, p. B1, p. B1.

Kernell, Samuel. *Going Public : New Strategies of Presidential Leadership*. 2nd ed. [Washington, DC]: CQ Press, 1993.

Kiewiet, D. Roderick, and Mathew D. McCubbins. *The Logic of Delegation: Congressional Parties and the Appropriations Process*. Chicago: University of Chicago Press, 1991.

Klite, Paul. "Tabloid Fever." *Television Quarterly* 27, no. 4 (1996).

Kohut, Andrew. "Self-Censorship: Counting the Ways." *Columbia Journalism Review*, May/June 2000.

Kovach, Bill, and Tom Rosenstiel. *The Elements of Journalism: What Newspeople Should Know and the Public Should Expect*. 1st ed. New York: Crown Publishers, 2001.

Kranish, Michael. "Campaign Finance Bill Shows TV's Clout: Networks Help Scuttle Free Ads." *Boston Globe*, 25 December 1997, A1.

Krasnow, Erwin G., and Lawrence D. Longley. *The Politics of Broadcast Regulation*. New York,: St. Martin's Press, 1973.

Krehbiel, Keith. *Information and Legislative Organization, Michigan Studies in Political Analysis*. Ann Arbor: University of Michigan Press, 1991.

Kriz, Margaret E. "The Fight for Access." *National Journal*, 8 July 1989, p. 1732.

Kunkel, Thomas, and Gene Roberts. "The Age of Corporate Newspapering: Leaving Readers Behind." *American Journalism Review*, May 2001.

Kuntz, Clayton. "DARS Wars: The Government Strikes Back." *Via Satellite*, April 1997.

Kurtz, Howard. "Journalists Not Loath to Donate to Politicians: Media Companies' Policies Vary Widely." *Washington Post*, 18 January 2004.

Kutzner, James, and William Zou. "High Defiinition Television: Member/PBS Transition Planning." Alexandria, Virginia: PBS, March 1991.

Lamolinara, Guy. "Wired for the Future: President Clinton Signs Telecommunications Act of 1996." *Library of Congress Information Bulletin* 55, no. 3 (1996): 43-45.

Lasswell, H.D. "The Structure and Function of Communication in Society." In *The Communication of Ideas*, edited by Lyman Bryson, ix, 296 p. New York: Harper & Row, 1948.

Latimer, Jon. *Deception in War*. 1st ed. Woodstock, NY: Overlook Press, 2001.

Layton, Charles. "Lobbying Juggernaut." *American Journalism Review*, October/November 2004.

Lehr, William. "The Economic Case for Dedicated Unlicensed Spectrum Below 3ghz." Washington, DC: New America Foundation, 2004.

Leonard, Thomas C. *The Power of the Press: The Birth of American Political Reporting*. New York: Oxford University Press, 1986.

Lessig, Lawrence. "Copyrighting the President." *Wired*, August 2003, 94.

Levy, Jonathan, Marcelino Ford-Livene, and Anne Levine. "Broadcast Television: Survivor in a Sea of Competition." Washington, DC: FCC Office of Plans and Policies, September 2002.

Lewis, Charles. "Media Money." *Columbia Journalism Review*, September/October 2000.

Lichter, S. Robert, Stanley Rothman, and Linda S. Lichter. *The Media Elite*. 1st ed. Bethesda, Md.: Adler & Adler, 1986.

Lieberman, Jon. "Why I Stood up to Sinclair." *Broadcasting & Cable*, 25 October 2004.

Lincoln, Abraham, and Don Edward Fehrenbacher. *Speeches and Writings, The Library of America*. New York, N.Y.: Viking Press, 1989.

Lippman, John. "Airwaves Sizzle over Bill to Regulate Cable TV Rates." *Los Angeles Times*, 12 September 1992, p. 1.

Little, Arthur D. "Assessment of the Impact of DTV on the Cost of Consumer Television Receivers." Cambridge, MA: Arthur D. Little, 10 September 2001.

Littleton, Cynthia. "Raycom Lands Malrite." *Daily Variety*, 7 April 1998, 6.

Livermore, Seward W. "The American Navy as a Factor in World Politics, 1903–1913." *American Historical Review* 63, no. 4 (1958): 863-79.

Lowi, Theodore J. *The End of Liberalism: Ideology, Policy, and the Crisis of Public Authority*. [1st ed. New York,: Norton, 1969.

———. *The End of Liberalism: The Second Republic of the United States*. 2d ed. New York: Norton, 1979.

Lupia, Arthur, and Mathew D. McCubbins. *The Democratic Dilemma: Can Citizens Learn What They Need to Know?, Political Economy of Institutions and Decisions*. New York: Cambridge University Press, 1998.

Machiavelli, Niccoláo, Luigi Ricci, and Eric Reginald Pearce Vincent. *The Prince*. London,: Oxford university press, 1935.

Macho-Stadler, Inâes, and J. David Pâerez-Castrillo. *An Introduction to the Economics of Information: Incentives and Contracts*. 2nd ed. Oxford ; New York: Oxford University Press, 2001.

"Making Every Vote Count: The Case for Electoral Reform in British Columbia." British Columbia, Canada: British Columbia Citizens' Assembly on Electoral Reform, December 2004.

Malcolm, Janet. *The Journalist and the Murderer*. New York: Knopf, 1990.

Manin, Bernard. *The Principles of Representative Government, Themes in the Social Sciences*. New York: Cambridge University Press, 1997.

Marcus, David R. "Defer Taxes on FCC Licenses with Like-Kind Exchanges." *Financial Manager* June/July 2002.

Marks, Jeffrey. "Raising Ethical Issues." *Communicator*, February 1995, p. 19.

Matusow, Barbara. "Heeere's Brian." *Washingtonian*, December 1994.

Mayhew, David R. *Congress: The Electoral Connection, Yale Studies in Political Science ; 26*. New Haven: Yale University Press, 1974.

McChesney, Robert Waterman. *The Problem of the Media: U.S. Communication Politics in the Twenty-First Century*. New York: Monthly Review Press, 2004.

————. *Rich Media, Poor Democracy: Communication Politics in Dubious Times, The History of Communication*. Urbana: University of Illinois Press, 1999.

————. *Telecommunications, Mass Media, and Democracy: The Battle for the Control of U.S. Broadcasting, 1928–1935*. New York: Oxford University Press, 1993.

McCombs, Maxwell E., Donald Lewis Shaw, and David H. Weaver. *Communication and Democracy: Exploring the Intellectual Frontiers in Agenda-Setting Theory*. Mahwah, NJ: Lawrence Erlbaum Associates, 1997.

McConnell, Chris. "More Channels, More Power for DTV." *Broadcasting & Cable*, 23 February 1998, p. 6.

McManus, John H. *Market-Driven Journalism: Let the Citizen Beware?* Thousand Oaks, Calif.: Sage Publications, 1994.

Mindich, David T. Z. *Just the Facts : How "Objectivity" Came to Define American Journalism*. New York: New York University Press, 1998.

Mitre. "Experimental Measurements of the Third-Adjacent Channel Impacts of Low-Power Fm Stations." McClean, VA: Mitre, May 2003.

Molho, Ian. *The Economics of Information: Lying and Cheating in Markets and Organizations*. Malden, Massachusetts: Blackwell, 1997.

Moore, Frazier. "Free Speech Is Fine, but Bill Moyers Wonders: Can You Afford It?" *Associated Press*, 7 June 1999.

Moore, John Leo, Robert Healy, and Margaret Thompson. *The Washington Lobby*. 3d ed. Washington: Congressional Quarterly, 1979.

Morrow, James D. *Game Theory for Political Scientists*. Princeton, N.J.: Princeton University Press, 1994.

MSTV. "MSTV White Paper on Broadcaster Flexibility to Provide Additional Service Using New Technologies within Existing Spectrum Allocation." Washington, DC: Association for Maximum Service Television, 4 April 1994.

———. "MSTV White Paper: ATV Channels, Flexibility, and the Public Interest." Washington, DC: MSTV, 1995.

Mundy, Alicia. "HDTV or Else." *MediaWeek*, 6 April 1998.

———. "Jack Valenti's Last Stand." *Business Dateline*, January 1991, p. 28.

———. "Ness Brokers Digital Deal." *MediaWeek*, 7 April 1997.

———. "Washington: In Whose Interest?" *Media Week*, 8 December 1997.

———. "What Spectrum Issue?" *Mediaweek*, 15 April 1996, 24-28.

NAB. "Ad Tax Deductions." In *Legislative Issue Papers, 103rd Congress*. Washington, DC: NAB, February 1994.

———. "Advertising Restrictions." In *Legislative Issue Papers, 101st Congress*. Washington, DC: NAB, February 1989.

———. "Alcohol Ad Warnings." In *Legislative Issue Papers, 104th Congress*. Washington, DC: NAB, September 1995.

———. "Campaign Finance Reform." In *Legislative Issue Papers, 106th Congress*. Washington, DC: NAB, August 1999.

———. "Digital Television Broadcasting: A Status Report from NAB Science & Technology." Washington, DC: NAB, 29 January 1997.

———. "A Model State Marketing Plan: The Marketing of Broadcaster's Public Service Record." Washington, DC: NAB, 1998.

———. "Moral Rights." In *Legislative Issue Papers, 102nd Congress*. Washington, DC: NAB, August 1992.

———. "A National Report on Local Broadcasters' Community Service." Washington, DC: NAB, June 2004.

———. "A National Report on Local Broadcasters' Community Service." Washington, DC: NAB, April 2000.

———. "A National Report on Local Broadcasters' Community Service." Washington, DC: NAB, 1998.

———. "Spectrum Auction Action Tool Kit." Washington, DC: National Association of Broadcasters, 1996.

———. "Spectrum Auctions." In *Legislative Issue Papers, 104th Congress*. Washington, DC: NAB, October 1995.

————. "Talking Points." In *Spectrum Auction Action Tool Kit*. Washington, DC: NAB, January 1996.

Nagourney, Adam. "States See Growing Campaign to Change Redistricting Laws." *New York Times*, 7 February 2004.

Nagourney, Adam, and Adam Clymer. "Local Television Stations Become the New Arbiters of Political Fair Play." *New York Times*, 2 October 2002.

Napoli, Philip M. "A Principal-Agent Approach to the Study of Media Organizations: Toward a Theory of the Media Firm." *Political Communication* 14, no. 2 (1997): 207-19.

Nasaw, David. *The Chief: The Life of William Randolph Hearst*. Boston: Houghton Mifflin, 2000.

"National Press Club Luncheon with Journalist Bill Moyers." Washington, DC, 22 March 2001.

NBC. "The Case against Broadcast Spectrum Auctions." New York: NBC, March 1996.

"NBC News Has No 'Shyness': Telecom Fight in Congress Is 'Messy Deal'." *Communications Daily*, 19 January 1996, p. 5.

Negroponte, Nicholas. *Being Digital*. 1st ed. New York: Knopf, 1995.

Neilson, Robert E. *Sun Tzu and Information Warfare: A Collection of Winning Papers from the Sun Tzu Art of War in Information Warfare Competition*. Washington, DC: National Defense University Press, 1997.

Neuman, W. Russell. "The Mass Audience Looks at HDTV: An Early Experiment." Cambridge, Massachusetts: MIT, 11 April 1988.

Noll, Roger G., Merton J. Peck, and John J. McGowan. *Economic Aspects of Television Regulation, Studies in the Regulation of Economic Activity*. Washington,: Brookings Institution, 1973.

O'Brien, Timothy L. *Bad Bet: The inside Story of America's Gambling Industry*. 1st ed. New York: Times Business, 1998.

"Off the Record: What Media Corporations Don't Tell You About Their Legislative Agendas." Washington, DC: Center for Public Integrity, 2000.

Olson, Mancur. *The Logic of Collective Action: Public Goods and the Theory of Groups, Harvard Economic Studies, V. 124*. Cambridge: Harvard University Press, 1965.

Ostrom, Elinor. *Governing the Commons: The Evolution of Institutions for Collective Action, The Political Economy of Institutions and Decisions*. New York: Cambridge University Press, 1990.

Owen, Bruce M. *The Internet Challenge to Television*. Cambridge, Mass.: Harvard University Press, 1999.

Owen, Bruce M., and Steven S. Wildman. *Video Economics*. Cambridge, Mass.: Harvard University Press, 1992.

Page, Benjamin I. "The Mass Media as Political Actors." *PS: Political Science and Politics* 29, no. 1 (1996): pp. 20-24.

————. *Who Deliberates?: Mass Media in Modern Democracy, American Politics and Political Economy*. Chicago: University of Chicago Press, 1996.

Page, Benjamin I., and Robert Y. Shapiro. *The Rational Public : Fifty Years of Trends in Americans' Policy Preferences*. Chicago: University of Chicago Press, 1992.

Papper, Bob. "2003 Local Television News Study of News Directors and the American Public." Washington, DC: Radio Television News Directors Foundation, 2003.

Papper, Bob, and Michael Gerhard. "Radio and Television Salary Survey." *Communicator*, May 2000, pp. 31-4.

Parenti, Michael. *Inventing Reality : The Politics of the Mass Media*. New York: St. Martin's Press, 1986.

Patterson, Thomas E. "The News Media: An Effective Political Actor?" *Political Communication* 14, no. 4 (1997): 445-55.

————. *The Vanishing Voter: Public Involvement in an Age of Uncertainty*. 1st ed. New York: Alfred A. Knopf : Distributed by Random House, 2002.

Patterson, Thomas E., and Wolfgang Donsbach. "News Decisions: Journalists as Partisan Actors." *Political Communication* 13 (1996): 455-68.

Pearl, Daniel. "Senate Republicans Mull Feasibility of Auction for Digital TV." *Wall Street Journal*, 12 September 1995.

Persily, Nathaniel. "In Defense of Foxes Guarding Henhouses: The Case for Judicial Acquiescence to Incumbent-Protecting Gerrymanders." *Harvard Law Review* 116 (2002): 649-82.

Pew Research Center. "Bottom-Line Pressures Now Hurting Coverage, Say Journalists." Washington, DC: Pew Research Center for The People & The Press, 2004.

————. "Self Censorship: How Often and Why." Washington, DC: Pew Research Center, 2000.

Philanthropy, AAFRC Trust for. "Giving USA 1998." Sewickley, Pennsylvania: AAFRC Trust for Philanthropy, 1998.

Pitney, John J. *The Art of Political Warfare*. Norman, OK: University of Oklahoma Press, 2000.

Plato. *The Republic*. Translated by Benjamin Jowett: Vintage Books, 1991.

Popkin, Samuel L. *The Reasoning Voter: Communication and Persuasion in Presidential Campaigns*. Chicago: University of Chicago Press, 1991.

Porter, Michael E. *Competitive Advantage: Creating and Sustaining Superior Performance*. New York: Free Press, 1985.

Povich Elaine S. *Partners & Adversaries: The Contentious Connection between Congress & the Media*. Arlington, Va.: Freedom Forum, 1996.

Powe, Lucas A. *American Broadcasting and the First Amendment*. Berkeley: University of California Press, 1987.

Prager, Joshua Harris. "Was the '51 Giants Comeback a Miracle, or Did They Simply Steal the Pennant." *Wall Street Journal*, 31 January 2001, p. A1.

Pratt, John W., and Richard J. Zeckhauser. "Principals and Agents: An Overview." In *Principals and Agents: An Overview*, edited by John W. Pratt and Richard J. Zeckhauser, 1-36. Boston: Harvard Business School Press, 1985.

Pratte, Alf, and Gordon Whiting. "What Newspaper Editorials Have Said About Deregulation of Broadcasting." *Journalism Quarterly* 61 (1986): 56-65.

Press, Commission on Freedom of the. *A Free and Responsible Press*. Chicago: University of Chicago Press, 1947.

Price, Cindy J. "Does Power Change the News? A Content Analysis of Network News Coverage of the Telecommunications Act of 1996." Las Vegas, Nevada, 1998.

Protess, David, and Maxwell E. McCombs. *Agenda Setting : Readings on Media, Public Opinion, and Policymaking, Communication Textbook Series. Journalism*. Hillsdale, N.J.: Erlbaum, 1991.

Radio-TV Gallery. "Rules for Electronic Media Coverage of Congress." Washington, DC: Radio-TV Gallery, 1999.

Raiffa, Howard. *The Art and Science of Negotiation*. Cambridge, Mass.: Belknap Press of Harvard University Press, 1982.

Register of Copyrights. "Droit De Suite: The Artist's Resale Royalty." Washington, DC: United States Copyright Office, December 1992.

Rhodes, P. J. *The Athenian Boule*. Oxford [Oxfordshire]: Clarendon Press, 1985.

Rice, John F. *HDTV: The Politics, Policies, and Economics of Tomorrow's Television*. 1st ed. New York: Union Square Press, 1990.

RMS. "New HDTV Estimates: $12 Million or Less." *Broadcasting*, 29 October 1990, p. 33.

"The Role of Broadcasters in the Political Process." Washington, DC: National Association of Broadcasters, 1986.

Rooney, Emily. "Truth Can Be Trouble." *Communicator*, September 1995, 122-4.

Rosenthal, Alan. *The Third House: Lobbyists and Lobbying in the States*. Washington, D.C.: CQ Press, 1993.

Rosenwein, Rifka. "Why Media Mergers Matter." *Brill's Content*, December 1999/January 2000.

Ross, Robert J. "The Cost of Converting a Broadcast Facility to HDTV: An Update." Paper presented at the 1990 NAB Engineering Conference Proceedings, Philadelphia, Pennsylvania 1990.

Rothenberg, Randall. "The Boom in Political Consulting." *New York Times*, 24 May 1987.

Rowse, Arthur E. "A Lobby the Media Won't Touch." *Washington Monthly*, May 1998, p. 9.

[Rules of the House of Representatives for the Year 1997–1998]. House; No. 1001. Boston, MA: House of Representatives, 1997.

Safire, William. "The Greatest Auction Ever." *New York Times*, 16 March 1995.

————. "Stop the Giveaway." *New York Times*, 4 January 1996, A21.

Sanford, Bruce W. *Don't Shoot the Messenger: How Our Growing Hatred of the Media Threatens Free Speech for All of Us.* New York: Free Press, 1999.

Santayana, George. *The Life of Reason.* New York: Scribner, 1953.

Santiago, Roberto. "Malrite/Shamrock Update." *Plain Dealer*, 6 May 1993.

Schattschneider, E. E. *Party Government.* Westport, Conn.: Greenwood Press, 1977.

————. *Politics, Pressures and the Tariff; a Study of Free Private Enterprise in Pressure Politics, as Shown in the 1929–1930 Revision of the Tariff.* New York,: Prentice-Hall, inc., 1935.

————. *The Semisovereign People: A Realist's View of Democracy in America.* New York: Holt, Rinehart and Winston, 1960.

Scherer, F. M., and David Ross. *Industrial Market Structure and Economic Performance.* 3rd ed. Boston: Houghton Mifflin, 1990.

Schlozman, Kay Lehman, and John T. Tierney. *Organized Interests and American Democracy.* New York: Harper & Row, 1986.

Schorr, Daniel. *Clearing the Air.* Boston: Houghton Mifflin, 1977.

Schudson, Michael. *Discovering the News: A Social History of American Newspapers.* New York: Basic Books, 1978.

————. "In All Fairness: Definitions of Fair Journalism Have Changed over the Last Two Centuries." *Media Studies Journal*, no. Spring/Summer (1998).

Seldes, George. *Lords of the Press.* New York,: J. Messner, 1938.

Setzer, Florence, and Jonathan Levy. "Broadcast Television in a Multichannel Marketplace." Washington, DC: FCC Office of Plans and Policies, June 1991.

Shanker, Thom, and Eric Schmitt. "Firing Leaflets and Electrons, U.S. Wages Information War." *New York Times*, 24 February 2003.

Shaw, David. "Special Report: Crossing the Line." *Los Angeles Times*, 12 December 1999.

Shepard, Alicia C. "Take the Money and Talk." *American Journalism Review*, June 1995, 18.

Shepsle, Kenneth A., and Mark S. Bonchek. *Analyzing Politics : Rationality, Behavior, and Institutions.* 1st ed. New York: W.W. Norton, 1997.

Shimberg, Benjamin. *Occupational Licensing: A Public Perspective.* Princeton, N.J.: Center for Occupational and Professional Assessment, Educational Testing Service, 1982.

Shoemaker, Pamela J., and Stephen D. Reese. *Mediating the Message: Theories of Influences on Mass Media Content.* 2nd ed. White Plains, N.Y.: Longman, 1996.

Silva, Jeffrey. "Pressler Seeks to Auction HDTV as Part of Effort to Raise $14b." *RCR*, 18 September 1995.

Silverstein, Ken. "His Biggest Takeover Ever: How Murdoch Bought Washington." *Nation*, 8 June 1998, 18.

Simon, Paul. *P.S.: The Autobiography of Paul Simon.* 1st ed. Chicago, Ill.: Bonus Books, 1999.

Simpson, Alan K. *Right in the Old Gazoo: A Lifetime of Scrapping with the Press*. 1st ed. New York: W. Morrow, 1997.

Snider, J.H. "Alleviating the Problem of Rational Voter Ignorance: A Proposal for a 'Ballot Portal'." *National Civic Review* (Spring 2004).

————. "The Decline of Broadcasters' Public Interest Obligations." Washington, DC: New America Foundation, 2004.

————. *Explanation of the Citizen's Guide to the Airwaves*. Washington, DC: New America Foundation, 2003.

————. "FCC Lets the Telecom Giants Steal from You." *Sacramento Bee*, 7 April 2002.

————. "Is Multicasting Must-Carry a Must-Giveaway?" Washington, DC: New America Foundation, 2003.

————. "The Myth of Free TV." Washington, DC: New America Foundation, June 2002.

————. "Should DTV Must-Carry Be Expanded, Sunset, or Preserved as-Is?" Washington, DC: New America Foundation, March 2005.

————. "Should the Public Meeting Enter the Information Age?" *National Civic Review* 92, no. 3 (Fall 2003): 20-9.

————. "Who Owns the Airwaves? Four Theories of Spectrum Property Rights." Washington, DC: New America Foundation, April 2002.

Snider, J.H., and Michael Calabrese. "Speeding the DTV Transition: A Consumer Tax Credit Can Unplug Analog TV, Reduce the Deficit and Redeploy Low-Frequency Spectrum for Wireless Broadband." Washington, DC: New America Foundation, 2004.

Snider, J.H., and Nigel Holmes. "The Cartoon Guide to Federal Spectrum Policy: What If the Government Regulated Spoken Words the Way It Regulates the Airwaves?" Washington, DC: New America Foundation, 2004.

Snider, J.H., and Benjamin I. Page. "Does Media Ownership Affect Media Stands? The Case of the Telecommunications Act of 1996." Paper presented at the Annual Meeting of the Midwest Political Science Association, Palmer House Hilton, Chicago, Illinois, 10-12 April 1997.

Snider, James H. "Local TV News Archives as a Public Good." *The Harvard International Journal of Press/Politics* 5, no. 2 (2000): 111-17.

————. "Senate Hypocrisy over "Hot" Testimony." *Chicago Tribune*, 27 January 1999, 13.

Snider, Jim, and Terra Diane Ziporyn. *Future Shop: How New Technologies Will Change the Way We Shop and What We Buy*. 1st ed. New York: St. Martin's Press, 1992.

Sniderman, Paul M., Richard A. Brody, and Philip Tetlock. *Reasoning and Choice : Explorations in Political Psychology*. Cambridge [England] ; New York: Cambridge University Press, 1991.

Solomon, Burt. "Measuring Clout." *National Journal*, 4 July 1987, p. 1706.

Sonne, Marcia L. De. "Advanced Broadcast/Media Technologies: Market Developments and Impacts in the 90's and Beyond." 123. Washington, DC: National Association of Broadcasters, 1992.

Southwick, Thomas P. *Distant Signals: How Cable TV Changed the World of Telecommunications.* Overland Park, KS: Primedia Intertec, 1999.

Sparrow, Bartholomew H. *Uncertain Guardians: The News Media as a Political Institution, Interpreting American Politics.* Baltimore: Johns Hopkins University Press, 1999.

Sterling, Christopher H., and John M. Kittross. *Stay Tuned: A History of American Broadcasting.* 3rd ed, *Lea's Communication Series.* Mahwah, N.J.: Lawrence Erlbaum Associates, 2002.

Stern, Chris. "B'cast 'Loan' Has Xmas Wrapping." *Variety,* 7 August 1997.

———. "The Cellular Telecommunications Industry Association Accuses ABC of Retaliating for Ctia's Complaints About the Radio Spectum Auction in Which ABC Took Part with Other Broadcasters." *Broadcasting & Cable,* 23 October 1995, p. 22.

Stevens, Elizabeth Lesly. "Mouse-Ke-Fear." *Brill's Content,* December 1998/January 1999.

Stigler, George Joseph. "The Economics of Information." In *The Essence of Stigler,* edited by Kurt R. Leube and Thomas Gale Moore, xxviii, 377 p. Stanford, Calif.: Hoover Institution Press, Stanford University, 1986.

Sturm, John F. "Lobbying for More Than Just Assets: The Lobbyists Protect the Business Interests, Which Promote the Vitality of the News Media." *Media Studies Journal,* Fall 2000.

Sunstein, Cass R. *Democracy and the Problem of Free Speech.* New York: The Free Press, 1993.

Szabo Associates Inc. "Should Broadcasters Extend Credit to Political Candidates? Governmental Regulations Cause Confusion and Concern." *The Financial Manager,* August/September 1996.

Taylor, Paul. "Superhighway Robbery: America's Broadcasters V. The Public Good." *New Republic,* 5 May 1997.

Thierer, Adam. "The Great Taxpayer Rip-Off of 1995." *Regulation,* no. 4 (1995).

Thompson, Dennis F. "Election Time: Normative Implications of Temporal Properties of the Electoral Process in the United States." *American Political Science Review* 98, no. 1 (2004).

Thompson, Nicholas. "Snake Eyes: Even Education Programs Can't Redeem State Lotteries." *Nicholas Thompson,* December 1999.

Trigoboff, Dan. "Nds Thrive on Gm Track: News Directors Find Doors Open to General Management, with More Making the Jump." *Broadcasting & Cable,* 27 September 1999, p. 51.

Tuchman, Gaye. *Making News: A Study in the Construction of Reality.* New York: Free Press, 1978.

Tulis, Jeffrey. *The Rhetorical Presidency*. Princeton, N.J.: Princeton University Press, 1987.

Tumber, Howard. *Media Power, Professionals, and Policies*. London ; New York: Routledge, 2000.

Turner, Ted. "My Beef with Big Media." *Washington Monthly*, July/August 2004.

Tysver, Robynn. "TV Station Tax Break Considered." *World-Herald Bureau*, 9 March 2000.

Underwood, Doug. *When MBAs Rule the Newsroom: How the Marketers and Managers Are Reshaping Today's Media*. New York: Columbia University Press, 1993.

United States. Congress. House. Committee on Standards of Official Conduct. *Ethics Manual for Members, Officers, and Employees of the U.S. House of Representatives*. Washington: U.S. G.P.O., 1992.

United States. Congress. Senate. Select Committee on Ethics. *Senate Ethics Manual, S. Prt. ; 104-60*. Washington, DC: For sale by the U.S. G.P.O., Supt. of Docs., Congressional Sales Office, 1996.

Urban, Christine D. "Why Newspaper Credibility Has Been Dropping." Reston, Virginia: American Society of Newspaper Editors, 1998.

Vilimpoc, J.H. Snider and Max. "Reclaiming the 'Vast Wasteland': Unlicensed Sharing of the Broadcast Spectrum." Washington, DC: New America Foundation, July 2003.

Walker, Jack L. *Mobilizing Interest Groups in America: Patrons, Professions, and Social Movements*. Ann Arbor: University of Michigan Press, 1991.

Waltz, Edward. *Information Warfare: Principles and Operations*. Boston: Artech House, 1998.

Wang, Karissa S. "Editorials Help Stations Stand Out." *Electronic Media*, 26 March 2001, 23.

Wartzman, Rick, and Lisa Bannon. "A Media Mogul Who Steers Clear of Media? Publicity-Shy Univision Chief Captures a Huge Market in Spanish Language TV." *Wall Street Journal*, 13 August 1999, p. A1.

"We Love Our Jobs: B&C's Annual Survey Finds a High Degree of Job Satisfaction among News Directors, yet Many Have Eye on Boss' Office." *Broadcasting & Cable*, 11 September 2000.

Weaver, David H., and G. Cleveland Wilhoit. *The American Journalist : A Portrait of U.S. News People and Their Work*. Bloomington: Indiana University Press, 1986.

Weiss, S. Merrill, and Rupert L. Stow. "NAB 1993 Guide to HDTV Implementation Costs." Washington, DC: NAB, 1993.

Werbach, Kevin. "Radio Revolution: The Coming Age of Unlicensed Wireless." Washington, DC: New America Foundation, 2003.

West, Darrell M., and Burdett A. Loomis. *The Sound of Money: How Political Interests Get What They Want*. New York: W.W. Norton, 1998.

West, Don, and Kim McAvoy. "Staking a Claim on the Future: Interview with Eddie Fritts, President of National Association of Broadcasters." *Broadcasting & Cable*, 19 April 1993.

Wharton, Dennis. "Pressler Spectrum Plan No Smash." *Variety*, 18 September 1995.

Wheatley, Gary F., and Richard E. Hayes. *Information Warfare and Deterrence*. Washington, DC: Institute for National Strategic Studies, National Defense University, 1996.

Williams, Alex. "The Alchemy of a Political Slogan: In Focus Groups, Pollsters Test the Words That Shape the Issues." *New York Times*, 22 August 2004, section 9, p. 1.

Wolpe, Bruce C., Bertram J. Levine, and Congressional Quarterly inc. *Lobbying Congress: How the System Works*. 2nd ed. Washington, D.C.: Congressional Quarterly, 1996.

Wolzien, Tom. "Whose Bandwidth Is It Anyway." Paper presented at the National Association of Broadcasters Futures Summit, Monterrey, California, 25 March 2001.

Wright, John R. *Interest Groups and Congress : Lobbying, Contributions, and Influence, New Topics in Politics*. Boston: Allyn and Bacon, 1996.

Wright, Robert. "Assault on the Broadcast Business: A Commentary from Bob Wright, President and CEO, NBC." *Broadcasting & Cable*, 11 September 1995, p. 6.

Zaller, John. *The Nature and Origins of Mass Opinion*. Cambridge [England] ; New York, NY, USA: Cambridge University Press, 1992.

Zarefsky, David. *Argumentation: The Study of Effective Reasoning*. Chantilly, VA: Teaching Company, 2001. sound recording.

———. *Public Speaking : Strategies for Success*. 3rd ed. Boston: Allyn and Bacon, 2002.

Zou, William Y. "ATV Implementation Plan: A Cost Study." Alexandria, Virginia: PBS, January 1996.

APPENDICES

Appendix A:
NAB Lobbying Activities for 1996[1]

<u>House</u>

H.C.R. 67	Resolution Concerning the Congressional Budgets for Fiscal Years 1996 through 2002
H.C.R.178	Resolution Concerning the Congressional Budgets for Fiscal Years 1997 through 2002
H.R. 177	Diversity in Media Act of 1995
H.R. 181	Telecommunications Policy Coordination Act of 1995
H.R. 187	Communications Act of 1934, Amendment
H.R. 208	Statutory Authority for the Corporation of Public Broadcasting
H.R. 274	Federal Election Campaign Act of 1971, Amendment
H.R. 296	House of Representatives Election Campaign Reform Act of 1995
H.R. 327	State Lottery Advertisements Subject of Federal Trade Commission Regulation
H.R. 411	Antitrust and Communications Reform Act of 1995
H.R. 514	Restrictions on Foreign Ownership of Licensed Telecommunications Facilities
H.R. 525	Certain Provisions of Title VI of the Communications Act of 1934
H.R. 545	Airfare Advertising Reform Act of 1995
H.R. 732	Federal Election Campaign Act of 1971, Amendment
H.R. 789	Fairness in Musical Licensing Act of 1995
H.R. 804	Tobacco Consumption Reduction and Health Improvement Act
H.R. 935	Right to View Professional Sports Act of 1995
H.R. 963	Communications Act of 1934
H.R. 989	Copyrights Term Extension Act of 1995
H.R. 1004	Communications Decency Act of 1934
H.R. 1218	Authority for Competitive Bidding of Federal Communications Commission Licenses
H.R. 1244	Theatrical Motion Picture Authorship Act of 1995
H.R. 1248	Film Disclosure Act of 1995
H.R. 1295	Federal Trademark Dilution Act of 1995
H.R. 1390	Children's Media Protection Act of 1995
H.R. 1506	Digital Performance Right in Sound Recordings Act of 1995
H.R. 1540	Family Viewing Cable Television Act of 1995
H.R. 1555	Communications Act of 1995
H.R. 1556	Communications Act of 1934, Amendment
H.R. 1641	Antitrust Reform Act of 1995
H.R. 1649	Comprehensive Fetal Alcohol Syndrome Prevention Act
H.R. 1734	National Film Preservation Act of 1995
H.R. 1807	Children's Media Protection Act of 1995
H.R. 1861	Copyright Clarifications Act of 1996

---

[1] Sources: NAB 1996 Lobbyist Disclosure Report; Public submissions by NAB to various government agencies.NBC, "The Case against Broadcast Spectrum Auctions."

H.R. 1869	Federal Communications Commission Authorization Act of 1995
H.R. 2030	Parental Choice in Television Act of 1995
H.R. 2072	Clean Congress Act of 1995
H.R. 2271	Fairness in Political Advertising Act of 1995
H.R. 2441	NII Copyright Protection Act of 1995
H.R. 2491	Seven-Year Balanced Budget Reconciliation
H.R. 2830	Campaign Finance Reform, Fairness, and Citizens Involvement Act
H.R. 2962	Internal Revenue Code of 1986, Amendment
H.R. 2964	Parents Television Empowerment Act of 1996
H.R. 2979	Public Broadcasting Self-Sufficiency Act of 1996
H.R. 3010	Advertisement Standard for State Lotteries
H.R. 3073	Communications Act of 1934, Amendment
H.R. 3192	Satellite Home Viewer Protection Act of 1996
H.R. 3207	Amateur Radio Volunteer Services Act of 1996
H.R. 3208	Congressional Campaign Finance Reform Act
H.R. 3274	Federal Election Campaign Act of 1971, Amendment
H.R. 3472	End Taxpayer Promotion of Alcohol Overseas Act
H.R. 3473	Children's Protection from Alcohol Advertising Act of 1996
H.R. 3474	Sensible Advertising and Family Education Act
H.R. 3475	Alcohol Advertising Accountability Act of 1996
H.R. 3476	College Campus Alcohol Abuse Prevention and Education Act
H.R. 3478	Alcohol Promotion and Advertising Tax Fairness Act
H.R. 3479	Comprehensive Alcohol Abuse Prevention Act of 1996
H.R. 3505	American Political Reform Act
H.R. 3515	Consumer Automobile Leasing Act of 1996
H.R. 3553	Federal Trade Commission Reauthorization Act
H.R. 3588	Public Interest Campaign Reform Act of 1996
H.R. 3623	Federal Communications Commission Television Duopoly Rules
H.R. 3644	Just Say No Act
H.R. 3685	Communications Privacy and Consumer Empowerment Act
H.R. 3700	Internet Election Information Act of 1996
H.R. 3760	Campaign Finance Reform Act of 1971, Amendment
H.R. 3800	Federal Election Campaign Act of 1971, Amendment
H.R. 3814	Department of Commerce, Justice and State, the Judiciary, and Related Agencies Appropriations Act, 1997
H.R. 3945	Broadcasting Tower Facility Sharing
H.R. 3957	FCC Modernization Act of 1996
H.R. 3995	Truth in Political Advertising Act
H.Res.484	Resolution Regarding Television Network "Family Hour"
H.Res.541	Resolution Concerning Violence on Television

========

Total: 73 House Bills or Resolutions

<u>**Senate**</u>

S. 10	Congressional Accountability Act of 1995; Congressional Campaign Spending Limit and Election Reform Act of 1995
S. 46	Senate Campaign Financing and Spending Reform Act
S. 116	Senate Fair Elections and Grassroots Democracy Act of 1995
S. 170	Comprehensive Fetal Alcohol Syndrome Prevention Act
S. 226	Digital Performance Right in Sound Recordings Act of 1995
S. 306	Television Violence Reduction Through Parental Empowerment Act of 1995
S. 314	Communications Decency Act of 1995

S. 332	Children's Media Protection Act of 1995
S. 470	Children's Protection from Violent Programming Act of 1995
S. 559	Film Disclosure Act of 1995
S. 652	Telecommunications Act of 1996
S. 704	Gambling Impact Study Commission Act
S. 888	Spectrum Auction Act of 1995
S. 1116	Broadcast and Cable Voluntary Standards and Practice Act
S. 1137	Fairness in Musical Licensing Act of 1995
S. 1219	Senate Campaign Finance Reform Act of 1996
S. 1241	Public Broadcasting Financial Independence and Family Viewing Act of 1995
S. 1262	Tobacco Products Control Act of 1995
S. 1284	NII Copyright Protection Act of 1995
S. 1330	Spectrum Auctions Offsetting Collection Availability Act
S. 1357	Seven-Year Balanced Budget Reconciliation Act of 1995
S. 1389	Senate Campaign Spending Limit and Election Reform Act of 1995
S. 1528	Senate Campaign Finance Reform Act of 1996
S. 1551	Communications Act of 1934, Amendment
S. 1567	Communications Act of 1934, Amendment
S. 1619	Music Licensing Reform Act of 1996
S. 1723	Accountability of Campaign Advertising
S. 1857	Bipartisan Campaign Practices Commission Act of 1996
S. 1932	Federal Election Campaign Act of 1971, Amendment
S. 1953	Campaign Finance Reform and Disclosure Act of 1996
S. 2025	Communications Act of 1934, Amendment
S. Res.290	Resolution Calling for the Revival of "Family Hour" on Network Television

========

Total: 32 Senate bills or resolutions

FCC

CS Docket No. 95-178	Definition of Television Markets for Must Carry
CS Docket No. 96-46	Open Video Systems
CS Docket No. 96-83	Antenna Restrictions
ET Docket No. 93-62	RF Radiation
ET Docket No. 95-18	Broadcast Auxiliary Spectrum and Reallocated Government Spectrum
FO Docket No. 91-171	Emergency Alert System
FO Docket No. 91-301	Emergency Alert System
Gen Docket No. 83-484	Personal Attack/Political Editorial
Gen Docket No. 90-357	Digital Audio Broadcasting
MD Docket No. 95-176	Radio Regulatory Fees
MD Docket No. 96-186	Radio Regulatory Fees
MM Docket No. 87-15	Broadcast Ownership Rules
MM Docket No. 87-154	Broadcast Ownership Rules
MM Docket No. 87-268	High Definition Television/ATV
MM Docket No. 87-7	Broadcast Ownership Rules
MM Docket No. 87-8	Broadcast Ownership Rules
MM Docket No. 91-221	Broadcast Ownership Rules
MM Docket No. 93-143	Children's Television
MM Docket No. 94-150	Broadcast Ownership Rules
MM Docket No. 95-176	Closed Captioning
MM Docket No. 96-16	Equal Employment Opportunity
MM Docket No. 96-62	Broadcast Blanketing Regulations

MM Docket No. 96-90   Broadcast License Terms
========
Total: 23 FCC dockets

Other FCC
Radio Ownership
Pirate Radio
Data Broadcasting
Requests by Fox Broadcasting and others for declaratory rulings concerning the offers of time to presidential
    candidates
Fairness Doctrine
Low Power FM Radio

White House
TV Parental Guidelines
Children's Television

Department of Justice
Relevant product market, etc. regarding radio mergers
Procedures for Review under Hart-Scott-Rodino Act

Federal Trade Commission
Procedures for Review under Hart-Scott-Rodino Act

Patent & Trademark Office
Proceedings relating to a proposed protocol to the Berne Convention
Proceedings relating to a proposed new instrument for the protection of producers and performers of sound
    recordings

Environmental Protection Agency
RF Radiation Registration

Appendix B:
TV-Newspaper Cross-Ownership

(Top 100 Daily Newspapers for 2002; TV = Broadcast TV)

Rank	Top 100 Daily Newspapers	Owner	Broadcast Interests?	Description
1	USA Today	Gannett Co Inc.	Yes	21 TV stations
2	Wall Street Journal	Dow Jones and Company Inc	No	
3	New York Times	New York Times Company	Yes	14 TV stations
4	LA Times	Tribune Company	Yes	28 TV stations
5	Washington Post	Post-Newsweek	Yes	6 TV stations
6	New York Daily News	Daily News LP	No	
7	Chicago Tribune	Tribune Company	Yes	28 TV stations
8	New York Post	News Corporation	Yes	2 Radio/38 TV stations
9	Newsday (Long Island)	Tribune Company	Yes	28 TV stations
10	Houston Chronicle	Hearst Newspapers	Yes	2 Radio/36 TV stations
11	San Francisco Chronicle	Hearst Newspapers	Yes	2 Radio/36 TV stations
12	Dallas Morning News	Belo	Yes	20 TV stations
13	Chicago Sun-Times	Hollinger International Inc	No	
14	Boston Globe	New York Times Company	Yes	14 TV stations
15	Arizona Republic (Phoenix)	Gannett Co Inc	Yes	21 TV stations
16	Star-Ledger (Newark, NJ)	Advance Publications Inc	No	WB broadcast network*
17	Philadelphia Inquirer	Knight Ridder	No	
18	Atlanta Journal-Consitution	Cox Newspapers	Yes	76 Radio/16 TV stations
19	Detroit Free Press	Knight Ridder	No	
20	Cleveland Plain Dealer	Advance Publications Inc	No	WB broadcast network*
21	Portland Oregonian	Advance Publications Inc	No	WB broadcast network*
22	Minneapolis Star Tribune	The McClatchy Co	No	
23	San Diego Union Tribune	The Copely Press Inc	No	
24	St. Petersburg Times	Times Publishing Co	No	
25	Miami Herald	Knight Ridder	No	
26	Denver Post	MediaNews Group Inc	Yes	4 Radio/1 TV station
27	Denver Rocky Mountain News	EW Scripps	Yes	10 TV stations
28	Orange County Register	Freedom Communications Inc	Yes	1 TV station
29	Baltimore Sun	Tribune Company	Yes	28 TV stations
30	St Louis Post-Dispatch	Pulitzer Inc	No	
31	Sacramento Bee	The McClatchy Co	No	
32	San Jose Mercury News	Knight Ridder	No	
33	Kansas City Star	Knight Ridder	No	
34	LA Investor's Business Daily	Investor's Business Daily Co	No	
35	Orlando Sentinel	Tribune Company	Yes	28 TV stations
36	New Orleans Times-Picayune	Advance Publications Inc	No	WB broadcast network*
37	Indianapolis Star	Gannett Co Inc	Yes	21 TV stations
38	Columbus Dispatch	Dispatch Broadcast Group	Yes	3 Radio/4 TV stations
39	Pittsburgh Post-Gazette	Block Communications	No	
40	Boston Herald	Herald Media Inc	No	
41	Detroit News	Gannett Co Inc	Yes	21 TV stations
42	Milwaukee Journal Sentinel	Journal Communications Inc	Yes	36 Radio/5 TV stations
43	Fort Lauderdale Sun Sentinel	Tribune Company	Yes	28 TV stations
44	Charlotte Observer	Knight Ridder	No	
45	Seattle Times	Hearst Corp	Yes	2 Radio/36 TV stations
46	Buffalo News	Berkshire Hathaway	No	
47	San Antonio Express-News	Hearst Newspapers	Yes	2 Radio/36 TV stations
48	Fort Worth Star-Telegram	Knight Ridder	No	

Rank	Top 100 Daily Newspapers	Owner	Broadcast Interests?	Description
49	Louisville Courier Journal	Gannett Co Inc	Yes	21 TV stations
50	Tampa Tribune	Media General	Yes	26 TV stations
51	Oklahoma Oklahoman	Oklahoma Publishing Co	Yes	1 Radio/1 TV station**
52	Norfolk Virginian Pilot	Landmark Communications	No	
53	St Paul Pioneer Press	Knight Ridder	No	
54	Hartford Courant	Tribune Company	Yes	28 TV stations
55	Omaha World Herald	Omaha World-Herald Co	No	
56	Cincinnati Enquirer	Gannett Co Inc	Yes	21 TV stations
57	Richmond Times-Dispatch	Media General	Yes	26 TV stations
58	Little Rock Democrat-Gazette	Wehco Media Inc	No	
59	Nashville Tennessean	Gannett Co Inc	Yes	21 TV stations
60	Austin American-Statesman	Cox Newspapers	Yes	76 Radio/16 TV stations
61	Contra Costa Times (Ca)	Knight Ridder	No	
62	Riverside Press-Enterprise	Belo Corporation	Yes	20 TV stations
63	Bergen County Record	North Jersey Media Group Inc	No	
64	Los Angeles Daily News	MediaNews Group Inc	No	
65	Rochester Democrat & Chronicle	Gannett Co Inc	Yes	21 TV stations
66	Neptune Asbury Park Press	Gannett Co Inc	Yes	21 TV stations
67	Jacksonville Times-Union	Morris Communications Co	No	
68	W Palm Beach Post	Cox Newspapers	Yes	76 Radio/16 TV stations
69	Providence journal	Belo Corporation	Yes	20 TV stations
70	Las Vegas Review-Journal	Stephens Media Group	No	
71	Raleigh News and Observer	The McClatchy Co	No	
72	Fresno Bee	The McClatchy Co	No	
73	Seattle Post-Intelligencer	Hearst Newspapers	Yes	2 Radio/36 TV stations
74	Memphis Commercial Appeal	EW Scripps	Yes	10 TV stations
75	Des Moines Register	Gannett Co Inc	Yes	21 TV stations
76	Philadelphia Daily News	Knight Ridder	No	
77	Chicago Daily Herald	Paddock Publications Inc	No	
78	Birmingham News	Advance Publications Inc	No	WB broadcast network
79	Honolulu Advertiser	Gannett Co Inc	Yes	21 TV stations
80	Toledo Blade	Block Communications	No	
81	Grand Rapids Press	Advance Publications Inc	No	WB broadcast network*
82	Tulsa World	World Publishing Co	No	
83	Westchester Journal News	Gannett Co Inc	Yes	21 TV stations
84	Salt Lake City Tribune	Newspaper Agency Corp	No	
85	Akron Beacon Journal	Knight Ridder	No	
86	Dayton Daily News	Cox Newspapers	Yes	76 Radio/16 TV stations
87	Tacoma News Tribune	The McClatchy Co	No	
88	La Opinion (LA)	Tribune Company	Yes	28 TV stations
89	Syracuse Post-Standard	Advance Publications Inc	No	WB broadcast network*
90	Greensburg Tribune-Review	Tribune Company	Yes	28 TV stations
91	Wilmington News Journal	Gannett Co Inc	Yes	21 TV stations
92	Allentown Morning Call	Tribune Company	Yes	28 TV stations
93	Columbia (SC) State	Knight Ridder	No	
94	Knoxville News-Sentinel	EW Scripps	Yes	10 TV stations
95	Lexington Herald Leader	Knight Ridder	No	
96	Albuquerque Journal	EW Scripps	Yes	10 TV stations
97	Sarasota Herald Tribune	New York Times Company	Yes	14 Television stations
98	Worcester Telegram & Gazette	Daily Gazette Co Inc	No	
99	Spokane Spokesman-Review	Cowles Publishing Co	No	
100	Harrisburg Patriot News	Advance Publications Inc	No	WB broadcast network*
	Total with TV or Radio		51	

* Minority interest.
** The TV station was sold in 1997.
Source: *Editor & Publisher Yearbook 2003* plus SEC filings from 2003.

Appendix C:
Chronology of America's "Advanced TV"
Industrial Policy

We cannot approach HDTV by asking Uncle Sugar [the U.S. government]…to put up the money, tempting as that may be. In view of [the] huge budget deficit, there is no way the American public would support such a proposal.

—Robert Mosbacher, U.S. Secretary of Commerce, 1989[1]

What is interesting is, we are talking not simply about a loss of revenue to the Federal Government, estimated upwards of $11 billion, some estimates go as high as $70 billion, but what is particularly striking to me is the majority is apparently expressing its preference here for central planning over the free market. We are being told that a Federal agency, the Federal Communications Commission, should as a matter of fiat decide how to allocate this valuable resource, and that the free market will not work to do it.

—Representative Barney Frank, 1996[2]

For more than twenty years local TV broadcasters and their political allies in Congress and the FCC have argued that industrial policies are urgently needed to speed local TV broadcasters' transition to "advanced TV" technology. These industrial policies have included warehousing unused broadcast band spectrum, giving incumbent broadcasters rights to that spectrum, and then reacquiring that spectrum at public expense. This history can be divided into three distinct periods based on the type of rights local TV broadcasters have lobbied for in the name of speeding America's transition to advanced TV. The early periods do not come to a definitive end but are given an end point here simply to denote when a different type of industrial policy agenda has come to the fore.

In the first period, from 1983–1994, broadcasters seek to be loaned a second channel for HDTV. The meaning of "advanced TV" in this period evolves from

---

[1] "EIA Opposes TV Tax; Mosbacher opposes government financial aid for HDTV Development," *Communications Daily*, 19 May 1989, p. 1.

[2] 104th Congress, 2nd Session, *Congressional Record*, 24 July 1996, p. H8266.

analog HDTV to digital HDTV. The FCC calls this the "conversion channel" because it is used to help local TV broadcasters to convert from standard to high definition TV. The primary battleground is the FCC.

In the second period, from 1994–1996, broadcasters seek to change and expand the scope of their digital channel rights from providing one TV programming stream to providing 19.4 mbps of whatever type of bit they want, including as many SDTV programming streams as they can cram into that 19.4 mbps bit rate. The meaning of "advanced TV" becomes almost incoherent during this period, except to refer to the idea that if the broadcasters want to provide some type of advanced TV, they will have that option. The primary battleground is Congress.

The first two periods have been described in detail by Joel Brinkley,[3] Michel Dupagne and Peter B. Seel,[4] Ellen Goodman,[5] Reed Hundt,[6] and Hernan Galperin.[7]

In the third and present period, from 1997–2005, the battleground switches back to the FCC, where the broadcasters seek three distinct sets of rights:

a) to acquire additional unassigned spectrum rights in the broadcast band (i.e., rights not currently assigned to their original or loaned channels),

b) to warehouse the acquired rights, and

c) to leverage the acquired spectrum rights into non-spectrum rights.

---

[3] Brinkley, *Defining Vision*. Brinkley's book has been by far the most readable and most read book on the DTV transition but suffers from Brinkley's slavish loyalty to his sources, notably broadcast lobbyist Richard Wiley.

[4] Dupagne and Seel, *High-Definition Television*. Dupagne and Steel provide the most detailed and documented regulatory history of the DTV transition. But this is not bedtime reading.

[5] Ellen P. Goodman, "Digital Television and the Allure of Auctions: The Birth and Stillbirth of DTV Legislation," *Federal Communications Law Journal* 49, no. 3 (1997). Goodman provides a well documented legislative history but is framed in broadcast industry terms.

[6] Hundt, *You Say You Want a Revolution*. Hundt, the former FCC Chair, provides some colorful anecdotes about his battle to ensure that broadcasters fairly compensate the public for the use of public property.

[7] Galperin, *New Television, Old Politics*. Galperin's strength is the comparison of the U.S. and British DTV experiences. He also brings the regulatory history up to 2002. Another recent DTV history, with yet another theoretical perspective almost wholly unrelated to the concerns of this book, is Hart, *Technology, Television and Competition: The Politics of Digital TV*.

Period #1 (1983–1994): Acquiring Second Channel Rights

"Those who cannot remember the past are condemned to repeat it."

—George Santayana[8]

Broadcasters lobby the FCC to "loan" them a 2nd channel for simulcast HDTV. By promising the FCC they will return the second channel, they can claim they are receiving no new spectrum. By promising that they will simulcast on their two channels during the advanced TV transition and then end up with only an improvement from SDTV to HDTV, they can claim that they are receiving only a "minor" modification of their license. If they received a "major" modification, they would be accused of receiving a financial windfall and also expose themselves to lawsuits claiming that the second channel should have been awarded through a competitive process such as an auction or lottery.

Year	Month	Description
1981	February	Japan's NHK demonstrates its HDTV system at the annual meeting of the Society of Motion Picture and Television Engineers (SMPTE). It is the first major HDTV exhibition in the U.S. It requires 20 MHz for a single HDTV channel.
1981	December	CBS and the Association for Maximum Service Television (now "MSTV"; then "MST") testify before the U.S. Senate that U.S. broadcasters will need additional spectrum for HDTV.
1983	March	NAB, MSTV, and other broadcasters file comments opposing an FCC rulemaking to allow mobile telephone service into the unused portions of UHF TV channels 21-69.
1983	May	The U.S. broadcasting, cable, and electronics industries create the Advanced Television Systems Committee (ATSC) to develop an advanced television standard.

---

[8] George Santayana, *The Life of Reason* (New York: Scribner, 1953), volume 1, chapter 12.

Year	Month	Description
1986	May	Delegates from over 70 countries participate in the 26th CCIR Plenary Assembly to discuss the future of advanced TV. Renville McMann, CBS engineer and head of ATSC's HDTV group, urges the delegates to adopt an HDTV standard at *this* Plenary Assembly: "ATSC can't wait. We've already waited and studied and waited for 10 years."[9]
1986	July	Broadcasters file comments opposing the FCC's proposal to open up 28 UHF channels (168 MHz) for mobile telephone use. Reports *Broadcasting* magazine: "NAB is arguing that the UHF spectrum should be retained for enhanced broadcast signals.... One well-placed FCC skeptic said he had received assurances from the broadcasting industry since the early 1970's that HDTV was just around the corner. 'How many times do you have to hear the same thing?' this source asked...."[10]
1987	February 17	MSTV and 57 other broadcast organizations petition the FCC to initiate a Notice of Inquiry (NOI) to look at issues relating to advanced TV and in the meantime prevent any other industry from being allocated unused spectrum in the broadcast bands.
1987	July 20	The FCC issues the requested NOI and freezes the broadcast band in order to guarantee sufficient spectrum for advanced television. The new docket created for this NOI (Docket 87-268) will become one of the largest and longest lasting in FCC history.
1987	October 8	At a Congressional hearing on HDTV, the NAB distributes a press release claiming that "[The broadcast industry] is doing its utmost to bring HDTV to consumer reality." The press release includes the attached scenario:
		The year is 1991. You're at a neighbor's house watching television. The screen is huge and wondrously clear and crisp—like something you would see in your best, local movie theater, except it's television.

---

[9] Dupagne and Seel, *High-Definition Television*, p. 17.

[10] "Broadcasters Fight for UHF Spectrum; State of the Art Technology," *Broadcasting*, 27 October 1986.

Year	Month	Description
		As you move closer to the screen to check out the picture, it is even more defined and clear. Unlike your 1987 model television set at home, up close, you see no lines....
		The press release then explains the policy significance of the scenario: "This is a likely scenario for conversion of our current television system to high definition—the next generation of television which, simply stated, will upgrade the picture quality to that of a 35 mm movie. But, the future of HDTV may not be as bright as the picture it provides unless Washington policy makers allocate spectrum to make it a reality." In other words, allocating the broadcast industry more spectrum will result in the rapid rollout of broadcast HDTV.
1987	November	The FCC forms the Advisory Committee on Advanced Television Service (ACATS) and appoints broadcast lobbyist and former FCC Chair Richard Wiley to head it.
1988	March	Seven broadcast organizations, led by NAB, establish the Advanced Television Test Center (ATTC) to "conduct broad, thorough, and impartial tests on ATV systems."[11]
1988	September 1	In its Tentative Decision and Further Notice of Inquiry (Docket 87-268), the FCC tentatively rules that incumbent broadcasters should be loaned a second channel for HDTV. It justifies this decision based on the rapid rollout of advanced TV it will bring: "We tentatively conclude that the benefits of this technology can be realized by the public most quickly if existing broadcasters are permitted to implement ATV."[12]
1989	April 26	In the Second Interim Report of the FCC Advisory Committee on Advanced Television Service (ACATS), ACATS Chair Richard Wiley writes to the FCC making a formal request to renew the lifespan of ACATS, which was originally chartered by the FCC to terminate by November 1989. Wiley predicts the FCC's work picking an ATV standard will be done by 1992: "The Advisory Committee

[11] Dupagne and Seel, *High-Definition Television*, p. 23.

[12] FCC Tentative Decision and Further Notice of Inquiry in the matter of *Advanced Television and Their Impact on the Existing Television Broadcast Service*, MM Docket 87-268, released 1 September 1988, para. 4.

Year	Month	Description
		believes that this work (including testing of proponent systems, further spectrum analysis, and standard recommendation) can be completed by November 1991. Thus, by extending the life of the Committee, the FCC should be in a position to establish a single terrestrial ATV standard sometime in 1992...."[13]
1990	June 1	General Instruments announces it will design an all-digital HDTV system.
1990	September 21	In its First Report and Order (Docket 87-268), the FCC decides that ATV will be implemented on a second 6 MHz channel. It thus rules out a single channel transition by using empty space within a broadcaster's current 6 MHz. It also rules out a second channel using less than 6 MHz. It characterizes this decision as picking the "simulcast option," which it defines as "a contraction of 'simultaneous broadcast' and means the broadcast of one program over two channels to the same area at the same time."
1992	May 8	In its Second Report and Order/Further Notice of Proposed Rule Making (Docket 87-268), the FCC makes a final determination that incumbent broadcasters will get the 6 MHz channel set aside for HDTV and that they will have to simulcast 100% of the programming on their existing 6 MHz analog channel "at the earliest appropriate time." It is thus able to conclude that "ATV is an enhancement of existing service and not a new video service." It argues that the precedent of *Ashbacker Radio Corp. V. FCC*, 326 U.S. 327 (1945) doesn't apply because of the overwhelming public interest in loaning broadcasters the 2nd channel. It describes this "public interest" as follows: "[E]xisting broadcasters' continued involvement in ATV is the most practical, expeditious, and non-disruptive way to bring improved service to the American public. Existing broadcasters possess the know-how and experience necessary to implement ATV swiftly and efficiently."[14]

---

[13] Richard E. Wiley, "Second Interim Report of the FCC Advisory Committee on Advanced Television Service," 26 April 1989.

[14] FCC Second Report and Order/Further Notice of Proposed Rule Making in the matter of Advanced Television Systems and Their Impact upon the Existing Television Broadcast Service, MM Docket 87-268, released 8 May 1992, paras. 5, 6

Year	Month	Description
1993	May 24	ACATS Chair Richard Wiley announces the Digital HDTV Grand Alliance, which is supposed to combine the best components of the competing HDTV systems being tested by ATTC.
1997	June 19	Addendum Without any public debate or roll call vote, Congress passes a rider to the bill that will become the Balanced Budget Act of 1997 (Public Law 105-33, Section 3003). The rider rolls back the fixed deadline for the return of the broadcasters' "loaned" second channel. Only when three conditions are met, including when an ambiguously defined 85% of Americans have DTV sets, must the broadcasters return their loaned spectrum. CTIA President Tom Wheeler calls this "the loophole of the century" because it gives broadcasters de facto property rights to the second channel.
2004	September 7	In its Report and Order in the Second Periodic DTV Review (Docket 03-15), the FCC drops the simulcast requirement, arguing that the simulcast rule is not only not speeding up the DTV transition but may be impeding it by discouraging the showing of new, innovative content not available on the paired analog channel. But when the FCC mandated simulcast in 1992, it made the exact opposite assertion: "We intend to reclaim the reversion channel as soon as possible. Requiring simulcasting will help us to do so by minimizing broadcaster and consumer reliance on the ATV channel as a separately programmed service."[15]

---

[15] Second Report and Order/Further Notice of Proposed Rule Making, Docket 87-268, para. 59.

Period #2 (1994–1996): Acquiring "Spectrum Flexibility" Rights

"What has once happened, will invariably happen again, when the same circumstances which combined to produce it, shall again combine in the same way."

—Abraham Lincoln.

Broadcasters lobby Congress for spectrum flexibility on their digital channel. By having Congress approve spectrum flexibility, they eliminate the risk that the Communications Act's ban on spectrum windfalls could later be used against them in the courts.

Year	Month	Description
1994	March 4	As part of the broadcast industry's push for spectrum flexibility, Broadcast Caucus Chairman Michael Sherlock, NBC Executive VP-Technology, reports that there was "a consensus around the table" this week to go ahead with COFDM,[16] the technically superior broadcast DTV transmission standard that will be adopted in the rest of the world. COFDM would replace the 8-VSB system patented by Grand Alliance members, and it would allow TV broadcasters to provide mobile applications, thus allowing them to compete with FM radio (possibly splitting the NAB into warring factions) and mobile telephone service (resulting in the wrath of that industry).
1994	March 16	Representative Billy Tauzin introduces a broadcaster spectrum flexibility amendment in the bill that would become the Telecommunications Act of 1996. The bill passes without dissent on a *voice* vote.
1994	March 21	NAB President Edward Fritts starts the NAB convention with the following statement: "I predict that in tomorrow's race for the gold, Marconi will give Alexander Graham Bell a real run for his money."[17] As the implications of the March 16 giveaway become clear, NAB will have to backtrack from such statements.

---

[16] *Communications Daily*, 4 March 1994, p. 4.

[17] "Advice from Hill," *Communications Daily*, 22 March 1994, p. 1.

Year	Month	Description
1995	May 5	Robert Pepper, Chief of the FCC's Office of Plans and Policies, estimates the current market value of NTSC channels at $11 billion and potential value of the same channels with completely flexible rights at up to $70 billion.
1995	July 19	NAB releases a report disputing Pepper's $70 billion valuation. As part of its analysis claiming that $2-$3 billion is a more realistic valuation, the NAB claims that 200 MHz would be returned after the DTV transition, thus flooding the market with spectrum and depressing spectrum prices.[18]
1995	July 24	ACATS rejects COFDM.[19] Crippling the U.S. broadcast DTV system provides the broadcast industry with a short-term political gain but means it will gradually have to orphan the early broadcast DTV set purchasers as it migrates to an enhanced 8-VSB. This process is known euphemistically as "backward compatibility."
1996	January 17	Europe's DVB group, similar in function to the U.S.'s ATSC, adopts a broadcast DTV terrestrial standard (DVB-T) based on COFDM transmission.
1996	February 8	President Clinton signs the Telecommunications Act of 1996 into law. At the signing, President Clinton says: "Today, with the stroke of a pen, our laws will catch up with our future. We will help to create an open marketplace where competition and innovation can move as quick as light."[20]
1996	December 26	In its Fourth Report & Order (Docket 87-268), the FCC adopts the ATSC standard, including 8-VSB. The standard will be modified, albeit in minor ways, in the report and orders coming out of the first and second periodic reviews of the broadcast DTV transition. The second periodic review acknowledges that such updates are likely to become routine. Congress and the FCC express great concern that

---

[18] Jackson and Haring, "Pitfalls in the Economic Valuation of the Electromagnetic Spectrum."

[19] "Experts Reject COFDM," *Communications Daily*, 25 July 1995, p. 4.

[20] Dan Carney, "Indecency Provision Attacked As Clinton Signs Bill," 10 February 1996, p. 359.

Year	Month	Description
		some analog TV sets will lose functionality if broadcasters are required to give back their loaned channel. But they express no concern about the loss of functionality to early DTV adopters associated with continuous changes in the ATSC standard.[21] The first type of forced TV obsolescence harms broadcaster interests; the second type does the opposite.
1997	April 3	In its Fifth Report and Order and Sixth Report and Order (Docket 87-268), the FCC formally abandons HDTV as a required service. The FCC asserts that the "rapid introduction of digital television in the U.S. will facilitate its adoption abroad" and that the new DTV table of allotments "replicates existing service areas" for existing broadcasters.

Period #3 (1996–2005)[22]

1) Acquiring guard band rights

"Study the past if you would divine the future."

—Confucius

Broadcasters seek to expand their geographic contours beyond their original Grade B contours and seek to win rights to divide their license areas into cells so they can fill in geographic areas previously blocked by obstacles such as mountains and buildings. A cellular architecture also better positions broadcasters to one day reuse their spectrum the way mobile telephone providers do.

---

[21] E.g., comments of members of Congress at hearing of the House Subcommittee on Telecommunications and the Internet on "Preparing Consumers for the End of the Digital Television Transition," 10 March 2005. Representative Rick Boucher warns: "Television reception has become the new third rail of American public life."

[22] New America Foundation Research Associate Kartik Ramachandran compiled the data for parts 1 and 2 of this section.

Year	Month	Description
1996	August 14	In its Sixth Further Proposed Notice of Rulemaking in the DTV proceeding (Docket 87-268), the FCC proposes expanded geographic areas for TV stations.
1997	April 22	In its Sixth Report and Order in the DTV proceeding (Docket 87-268), the FCC implements the proposed expansion of geographic areas in its DTV allotments. It establishes the following important principles and technical specifications: 1. Maximization: Recommended by the NAB, MSTV and the Broadcast Caucus, the Commission adopted the principle of "maximization," which allows TV stations to both enlarge their service areas and to intensify coverage within their service areas 2. Power: Power levels for UHF DTV stations are set at a minimum of 50 kW and a maximum of 1000 kW; moreover, stations can increase their geographic area by increasing their power, up to the Grade B contour of the largest TV station in the market 3. Antenna Height: TV Stations are permitted to request increases in their antenna height so that they can provide greater service
1998	February 18	In its Memorandum Opinion and Order on Reconsideration of the Sixth Report and Order in the DTV proceeding (Docket 87-268), the FCC further expands the geographic areas for TV stations, especially UHF broadcasters, who receive a massive increase in acceptable power levels.
1999	November 29	Broadcasters block satellite companies from serving customers that receive their TV signal even beyond broadcasters' Grade B contours in the Satellite Home Viewer Improvement Act. Five years later, the National Translator Association, which represents many local TV broadcasters, will try to use this expanded notion of protected coverage to block citizens' access to new technologies.

Year	Month	Description
2000	June 12	In the FCC's Report and Order in the medical telemetry proceeding (Docket 99-255), broadcasters get to kick off the medical telemetry devices from the broadcast bands to make way for broadcasters' DTV channel. Medical telemetry devices are used to monitor the health of patients and relay to health professionals vital patient information.
2002	November 13	In the FCC's Report and Order in the broadcast auxiliary services proceeding (Docket 01-75), broadcasters and producers get a sweetheart deal to use wireless assist video devices (WAVDs) under Part 74. Broadcasters (along with cable and Hollywood producers) petition for, and win, the right to use the guard band space for WAVDs, including the right to rent this service out to third parties. WAVDs are used by production crews to transmit low resolution video images during movie or television production.
2004	August 3	The FCC freezes the filing of certain TV and DTV requests for allotment or service area changes.
2004	September 7	In its Report and Order of the second DTV periodic review (Docket 03-15), the FCC grants broadcasters the right to elect which channel they keep after the DTV transition. The FCC also tentatively grants broadcasters the right to set up distributed networks, thus dividing their areas of license into many cells. This allows broadcasters to reach many additional eyeballs while also positioning themselves to push for cellular reuse of spectrum. Superficially, this right is similar to the old right to create "booster" stations. But because those stations could only operate where no analog system was present, this right is in fact qualitatively different. Of all the broadcaster handouts since 1997, this is potentially the most significant precisely because it positions broadcasters to abandon the declining one-size-fits-all broadcasting business model and transition to the cellular, mobile networks of the broadband Internet future—which is the service their low frequency spectrum is ideally suited to provide. The right to set up distributed networks is only one piece in the long-term puzzle to convert to the network architecture of the future, but it is a very big piece.

Year	Month	Description
2004	September 30	In the FCC's Report and Order on digital service rules for LPTV and TV translator stations (Docket 03-185), TV translator stations get expanded rights that high power broadcasters gained in 1997, as well as additional rights. TV translators are owned by a diverse group of entities, including high-power local TV broadcasters. Some of the rights that high-power broadcasters got in 1997 that are extended to TV translators include: rights to a second channel; the right to increase their service levels by up to 20 times; the right to provide non-broadcast services on their existing channel; and the right to abandon the free TV business on the vast majority of their spectrum. TV translators also get new rights: no fixed deadline (at least as yet); the right to multiplex SDTV from single TV translators in a single market and use the balance of the channels for any type of non-broadcast service they want by converting to an "LPTV" station. LPTV and translator stations push to expand their coverage areas, in some cases by a factor of ten or more.
2004	December 21	The FCC publishes new station information data, including population and area covered by analog and digital TV stations, to assist broadcasters in choosing which station they would like to keep. The data reveal that local TV broadcasters have acquired approximately $6 billion worth of guard band spectrum since 1997. See Figures C-1, C-2, and C-3 below.
	February 10	Channel elections begin. Broadcasters with two channels within the 2-51 core elect which of the two they keep after the DTV transition.

2) Warehousing acquired spectrum rights

"What's past is prologue."

—William Shakespeare

Broadcasters seek to warehouse as much of their acquired spectrum as possible. Covering the full area of license makes no business sense because the energy cost to do so is high, the fixed cost for a high power transmitter is high, and the advertising revenue that can be brought in is minimal until viewers not only have DTV sets but also DTV sets that include broadcast DTV receivers to pick up over-the-air signals. The rational broadcast industry business strategy has been to act as DTV parasites, waiting for other industries such as satellite, cable, and DVD to deliver DTV programming and spur consumers to purchase DTV sets. But as consumers acquire broadcast DTV sets, broadcasters' incentive to warehouse diminishes.

Year	Month	Description
1997	April 7	Days after the FCC grants broadcasters their DTV licenses, FCC Commissioner Susan Ness speaks to the broadcast industry leadership at the annual NAB convention and makes the following prediction: "If I had my crystal ball, I would predict that the digital revolution will sweep through broadcasting far more rapidly than any of us would envision today."[23] She also predicts that government's role in fostering the transition is largely over and that now markets can carry the ball.
1997	April 21	In its Fifth Report and Order (Docket 87-268), the FCC establishes the following construction deadlines: • By May 1, 1999, network affiliates in the top 10 markets must complete construction; • By November 1, 1999, network affiliates in markets 11-30 must do so; • By May 1, 2002, all remaining commercial stations must complete construction; • By May 1, 2003, all noncommercial stations must do so.
1998	February 23	In its Memorandum Opinion and Order on Reconsideration of the Sixth Report and Order (Docket 87-268), the FCC makes three important findings regarding power levels: 1) it clarifies that 50 kW is not the minimum power level that broadcasters are required to operate on, but rather the minimum assigned power level (broadcasters are welcome to operate at levels below this, if they so choose), 2) UHF DTV stations can request

---

[23] Susan Ness keynote address at NAB's annual convention, Las Vegas, Nevada, 9 April 1997.

Year	Month	Description
		increases in their power levels up to 200 kW to "maximize" their service areas, and 3) UHF DTV stations can request increases in their power levels up to 1000 kW if they use beam-tilting techniques.
1998	December 18	In its Second Memorandum Opinion and Order on Reconsideration of the Fifth and Sixth Reports and Orders (Docket 87-268), the FCC allows UHF digital broadcasters to increase their power level up to 1000 kW so long as they meet the Commission's new 2% de minimis interference standard.
2001	November 15	Broadcasters succeed in their goal of warehousing unused spectrum, enabling them to reduce costs while holding out for a future windfall. In its Memorandum Opinion and Order on Reconsideration (Docket 00-39), the FCC:

1. allows broadcasters to operate at low power so that they serve only their "community of license," while maintaining their rights to the entire "maximization" service area, even if unserved.

2. delays two major deadlines until the next periodic review of the transition: first, the deadline by which broadcasters have to choose their digital channel; and second, the deadline by which broadcasters have to replicate their chosen service area. For broadcasters who cannot meet minimum operating requirements (which were also reduced in this order), they may seek further extensions of the deadline.

3. allows broadcasters to operate their digital stations only during prime time.

In other words, broadcasters pursue a simultaneous strategy of maximizing their future revenues by expanding their geographic rights, while minimizing their present costs by warehousing the spectrum until the broadcast DTV transition reaches takeoff.

Year	Month	Description
2002	April 23	In a report titled "Many Broadcasters Will Not Meet May 2002 Digital Television Deadline," the GAO finds that ten days before the digital facilities construction deadline, only 185 out of 1,121 stations are broadcasting in digital (GAO-02-466).
2003	February 6	More than three years after the deadline to construct digital facilities, network-affiliated broadcasters in the top ten markets continue to seek additional extensions to the construction deadline. (See FCC 03-22, Order, 6 February 2003.)
2003	October 17	A study conducted by BIA Financial Network for MSTV finds that over 80% of the 517 digital stations operating under Special Temporary Authorizations (STAs) are not broadcasting with sufficient signal strength to replicate their analog population coverage. By operating at lower power, broadcasters provide a fraction of the service they are supposed to, while claiming that they are "using" these channels.[24]
2003	December 31	Deadline for channel election established by the FCC's Report and Order in the First Periodic DTV Review (Docket 00-39) on January 18, 2001. This deadline was then postponed by a Memorandum Opinion and Order (see November 15, 2001), and set to begin in December 2004 by the FCC's Report and Order in the Second Periodic DTV Review (Docket 03-15) of September 7, 2004.
2004	May 25	In comments filed for the Notice of Inquiry on Unlicensed Operation in the Broadcast Bands in Docket No. 02-380, broadcasters push to warehouse currently unassigned underlay and guard band spectrum for their own future use by claiming that there are virtually no parts of the broadcast bands that are unused. Broadcasters recommend that the FCC delay allowing new technologies to use unused spectrum until after the DTV transition.

---

[24] Mark R. Fratnik, "Reaching the Audience: An Analysis of Digital Broadcast Power and Coverage," 17 October 2003.

Year	Month	Description
2004	July 28	In its Report and Order in the Second DTV Period Review (Docket 03-15), the FCC finds that as of this date—more than two years after the construction deadline—212 commercial television stations have yet to begin broadcasting in digital.
2004	December 31	Initial deadline by which broadcasters had to replicate the population covered by their analog stations, by order of the FCC's Report and Order in the First Periodic DTV Review (Docket 00-39) on January 18, 2001. This deadline was then postponed by a Memorandum Opinion and Order (see November 15, 2001), and set for July 1, 2005 for commercial broadcasters in the top 100 markets, and July 1, 2006 for all other stations, by the FCC's Report and Order in the Second Periodic DTV Review (Docket 03-15) of September 7, 2004.

3) Leveraging acquired spectrum rights into non-spectrum rights.

I have but one lamp by which my feet are guided; and that is the lamp of experience. I know of no way of judging the future but by the past.

—Patrick Henry

Until 85% of Americans have broadcast DTV receivers in their homes, broadcasters are under no obligation to return their loaned channel. Moreover, the accepted wisdom in Washington, DC is that it is politically impossible to end analog broadcasts even if 85% of American can receive digital broadcasts. Since without government intervention an 85% or higher penetration rate may take decades to achieve and the spectrum reclaimed at that time is worth tens of billions of dollars, broadcasters have tremendous negotiating leverage to seek additional subsidies/rights for returning their "loaned" channel in a timely way.

Year	Month	Description
2002	August 8	**Tuner Mandate.** In its Second Report and Order and Second Memorandum Opinion (Docket 00-39), the FCC rules that in a five year phased implementation, starting gradually on July 1, 2004 and ending with a big bang on July 1, 2007, all broadcast TV tuners sold in America, including those in TVs, VCRs, and DVD players/recorders, must contain a DTV tuner, even if the device is not used for broadcast DTV. The tuner mandate is strongly opposed by the Consumer Electronics Association (CEA), consumer groups, and anti-tax groups. The CEA argues that the mandate is a "multi-billion dollar TV tax on American consumers."[25] However, two foreign owned consumer electronics companies that own patent rights to the ATSC broadcast DTV standard, notably Zenith and Thomson, support the mandate. Assuming that the 280 million analog terrestrial TV sets are all replaced with digital terrestrial TV sets and that the average patent fee is $12/tuner, the tuner mandate will help transfer more than $3 billion dollars from American consumers to these consumer electronics companies.
2003	September 10	**Plug and Play.** In its Report and Order in the Matter of Compatibility Between Cable Systems and Consumer Electronics Equipment (Docket 00-67), the FCC rules that DTV television sets labeled "Digital Cable Ready" must include a broadcast DTV tuner. This is highly misleading because a TV set could pick up digital TV signals without having a broadcast DTV tuner. But it is consistent with the broadcasters' PR campaign to treat DTV and broadcast DTV as one and the same.
2003	November 4	**Broadcast Flag.** In its Report and Order and Further Notice of Proposed Rulemaking in the Matter of Digital Broadcast Content Protection (Docket 02-230), the FCC rules that by July 1, 2005 all TVs, VCRS, and other consumer electronic devices capable of receiving any type of broadcast DTV content must be manufactured to incorporate content protection technology that will allow broadcasters to control redistribution of their content. Like the tuner mandate, this raises the cost of consumer electronics equipment. Broadcasters argue that without

[25] Cited in Lennard G. Kruger, "Digital Television: An Overview," order code RL31260 (Washington, DC: Congressional Research Service, 7 October 2004)13, p. .

Year	Month	Description
		such a mandate, high-quality program won't be available to broadcast in DTV, which will slow down the broadcast DTV transition.
2004	September 28	**Consumer Education Campaign.** The FCC kicks off a public education campaign, including a website at www.dtv.gov, to highlight the importance of the transition to digital television. The event press release reads: "Over the last several years, the FCC has worked in a partnership with every sector of the television industry to bring the benefits of high-definition and digital television to millions of Americans. As the DTV transition begins to hit its stride, many Americans remain confused about the DTV transition and the capabilities of new digital television sets. The Chairman will outline some of the key components of this multi-year effort to educate the public about the DTV transition."

The education campaign is ironic because the FCC has been one of the major causes of the very consumer confusion it claims to seek to alleviate. The website is full of poorly defined concepts. For example, it still uses broadcast DTV and DTV interchangeably, a major source of consumer confusion. It also leads consumers to think that, in order to avoid purchasing a separate cable settop box to receive a basic digital cable TV signal, they must purchase a TV set labeled "cable ready." But that isn't true. Many new plug and play digital TV sets can receive a digital cable TV signal that aren't labeled "cable ready." All that the "cable ready" sets have is a broadcast DTV tuner that costs several hundred dollars extra and that most consumers who rely on cable, DVD, video game, or other DTV technology will not benefit from.

By highlighting all the positive and none of the negative features of broadcast DTV, the FCC's education campaign is actually a PR campaign to get consumers to go out and purchase a DTV set. But many consumers were wise not to purchase the first generation of broadcast DTV tuners (the industry now claims to be on its fifth generation) and many would be wise not to purchase now. Most don't even need broadcast DTV tuners to watch DTV. The broadcast DTV tuners now on

Year	Month	Description
		the market will soon be substantially obsolete by planned future enhancements, such as enhanced VSB. And the FCC's implementation of the broadcast flag means that the consumer's traditional ability to freely store and view broadcast programming may be radically curtailed in the digital world, so there is also a downside to the broadcast DTV transition.
2005	February 10	**Multicast Must-Carry Rights on Cable and Satellite TV.** The FCC rejects the broadcasters' request for multicast must-carry rights, which broadcasters claim will speed up the broadcast DTV transition. The broadcasters then shift their lobbying to Capitol Hill, seeking a deal for multicast must-carry rights in exchange for a fixed (but renegotiable) deadline to end the broadcast DTV transition.[26]

Conclusion

During the 1980s, it was widely claimed that the broadcast industry was deregulated and that henceforth market forces would determine its success. A similar deregulatory claim was made for the Telecommunications Act of 1996. But from the standpoint of 2005, we can clearly see that was not what actually happened. What happened was that the nature of government regulation changed. Previously, an attempt was made to balance the value of the special government privileges granted the broadcast industry with fees paid for those privileges.[27] After the early 1980s, any serious pretense of balance was abandoned. The fees were eliminated while the value of the privileges skyrocketed. Hence, in economic terms, the era from 1980 to the present can best be characterized as the heyday of broadcasting industrial policy—featuring massive government subsidies and anti-competitive regulations—rather than an era of deregulation and reliance on market forces. Alternatively, using the language of legal rights, the era before 1980 can be described as a time when broadcasters faced

---

[26] See Snider, "Should DTV Must-Carry Be Expanded, Sunset, or Preserved as-Is?."
[27] Mark S. Fowler and Daniel L. Brenner, "A Marketplace Approach to Broadcast Regulation," *Texas Law Review* 60, no. 2 (1982).

special First Amendment obligations,[28] whereas the period after 1980 can be thought of as a time when broadcasters were given special First Amendment privileges.

---

[28] Lucas A. Powe, *American Broadcasting and the First Amendment* (Berkeley: University of California Press, 1987).

Appendix D:
Valuation of Guard Band Spectrum Acquired by Broadcasters (1997–2004)

After 1996, broadcasters sought and received a host of "minor modifications" to their FCC licenses that allowed them to expand their geographic and population coverage.[1] Originally, broadcasters claimed the second channel would only replicate the coverage areas of their original channels. But DTV technology somehow or other freed up more of the empty space on the TV dial than originally claimed, with the result that the FCC allowed broadcasters to expand their coverage areas.

Figure D-1. Change in Total Population Covered by Analog and Digital TV Stations compared to Change in US Population (%)[2]

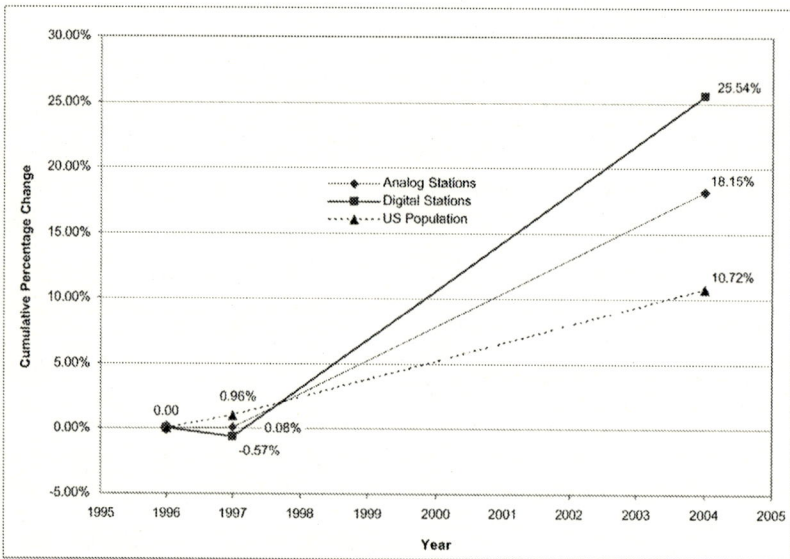

<u>Sources</u>

Population Covered by TV Stations, 2004: FCC, "Table of Station Assignment and Service Information," 21 December 2004; 1997: FCC, "DTV Table of Allotments," Sixth Report and Order, MM Docket No. 87-268, FCC 97-115, 21 April 1997; 1996: FCC,

---

[1] For a detailed discussion, see Technical and Legal Reply Comments of NAF et al. in the matter of Unlicensed Operation in the Broadcast Bands, Docket 04-186, 31 January 2005.

[2] New America Foundation Research Associate Kartik Ramachandran compiled this chart.

"Appendix B: Proposed DTV Table of Allotments," Sixth Further Notice of Proposed Rulemaking, MM Docket No. 87-268, FCC 96-317, 14 August 1996.

US Population, 2004: U.S. Census Bureau, "Table 1: Annual Estimate of the Population of the United States and States and Puerto Rico: April 1, 2000 to July 1, 2004," 22 December 2004, available at: http://www.census.gov/popest/states/tables/NST-EST2004-01.pdf; 1996 and 1997: U.S. Census Bureau, "Resident Population Estimates of the United States by Age and Sex: April 1, 1990 to July 1, 1999, with Short-Term Projection to November 1, 2000," 2 January 2001, available at: http://www.census.gov/popest/archives/1990s/nat-agesex.txt.

Figure D-2. Opportunity Cost of Broadcasters' Acquired Guard Space[3]

Digital Television Coverage Total Digital Population Coverage (2004, current)[1]		$3,457,371,605
Analog Television Coverage Total Analog Population Coverage (1996, baseline):		
1996 Total Population Coverage by Analog TV Stations[2]	$2,593,211,000	
Increase in Analog Population Coverage due to US Population Growth (1996–2004)	$277,992,219	
Total Analog Population Coverage Growth, (2004, adjusted for U.S. population)[4]	$2,871,203,219	-$2,871,203,219
Increase in Population Coverage from Analog to Digital in 2004		$586,168,386
# of MHz per Television Channel	6 MHz	
$ Value per MHz per Person[5]	$1.70	
$ Value per Channel per Person	$10.20	
Total Value of Increased Population Coverage from Analog to Digital ($ Value per Channel per Person x Increase in Population Coverage from Analog to Digital = $10.20 x 586,168,386)		$5,978,917,535

[3] New America Foundation Research Associate Kartik Ramachandran compiled this chart.

Notes

1. Sum of the population covered by all digital television stations (note: the large number is due to the presence of about 10 television stations in each market). (FCC, "Table of Station Assignment and Service Information," 21 December 2004, available at: http://hraunfoss.fcc.gov/edocs_public/attachmatch/DA-04-3922A2.pdf)

2. FCC, "Appendix B: Proposed DTV Table of Allotments," Sixth Further Notice of Proposed Rulemaking, MM Docket No. 87-268, FCC 96-317, 14 August 1996.

3. 2004: U.S. Census Bureau, "Table 1: Annual Estimate of the Population of the United States and States and Puerto Rico: April 1, 2000 to July 1, 2004," 22 December 2004, available at: http://www.census.gov/popest/states/tables/NST-EST2004-01.pdf; 1996: U.S. Census Bureau, "Resident Population Estimates of the United States by Age and Sex: April 1, 1990 to July 1, 1999, with Short-Term Projection to November 1, 2000," 2 January 2001, available at:
http://www.census.gov/popest/archives/1990s/nat-agesex.txt

4. 1996 analog television population coverage adjusted for population growth between 1996 and 2004. Actual analog television population coverage itself increased at a faster rate that US population growth (see Figure C-1).

5. This figure is based on a written commitment to the FCC by Verizon Wireless in April 2004 to start bidding for 10 MHz of spectrum at $5 billion, and the U.S. Census Bureau's estimate in July 2004 that US population was 293 million (Verizon Wireless, "Valuable Spectrum Auction Would Raise Minimum $5 Billion for U.S. Treasury," Press Release, April 8, 2004). Verizon Wireless made the offer in response to fears that the FCC might undervalue the spectrum that it would give Nextel in the 1.9 GHz band. A study completed for Verizon Wireless by Kane Reece Associates also found that the "fair market value" of those 10 MHz was $5.28 billion (*Communications Daily*, 28 October 2003, p. 5). The FCC eventually valued the spectrum at $4.8 billion (*Communications Daily*, "Nextel Gets 1.9 GHz Spectrum But Must Pay Billions," 9 July 2004).

Appendix E:
Adoption Rates for New Digital
Communication Devices

[To local TV broadcasters] "You are the cavalry on the forefront of digital technology."

—Michael Powell, then FCC Commissioner and now
FCC Chair, 6 April 1998[1]

In 1992, when the FCC "loaned" the 2nd channel to local TV broadcasters, it explained as its rationale that incumbent broadcasters deserved the channel because they would "undertake the business risks associated with being in the forefront of such new developments."[2] The notion that broadcasters were pioneers was also embedded in the terminology the FCC adopted to describe the broadcasters' transition to advanced television. It didn't speak of terrestrial broadcast HDTV or terrestrial broadcast DTV, but of HDTV and DTV. This was very different than the nomenclature used in Europe, where careful distinctions were made between terrestrial, satellite, cable, and other delivery vehicles for advanced television. The image of broadcasters as risk taking entrepreneurs rather than cautious monopolists was and still is deeply embedded in the discourse over DTV. Risk taking entrepreneurs evoke public sympathy for big returns because in our society returns are expected to be proportionate to risks taken. Cautious monopolists, in turn, evoke little sympathy for windfalls.

Michael Powell's speech to broadcast executives captures this economic and political logic when he instinctively flatters them: "You are the cavalry on the forefront of digital technology." The reality, which from the perspective of 2005 is now patently obvious, is that American broadcasters have been anything but at the forefront of digital technology (see Exhibits D-1 and D-2).

---

[1] Michael Powell keynote address at MSTV's annual membership meeting, Las Vegas, Nevada, 6 April 1998.

[2] Second Report and Order in the matter of Advanced Television, Docket 87-268, 8 May 1992, para. 6.

Figures E-1. Household Penetration of Major Consumer Digital Technologies, including Broadcast DTV Tuners (1994–2004)[3]

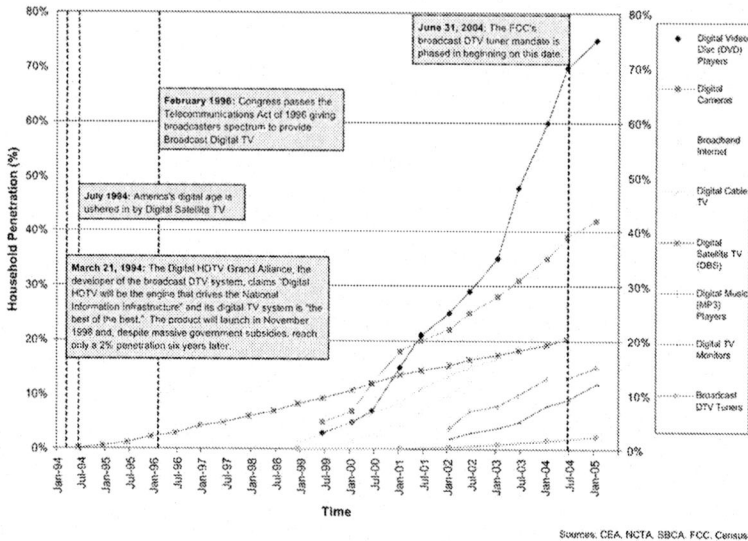

Sources: CEA, NCTA, SBCA, FCC, Census

Figures E-2. Adoption of Major Consumer Digital Technologies, including Broadcast DTV Tuners (June 2004)[4]

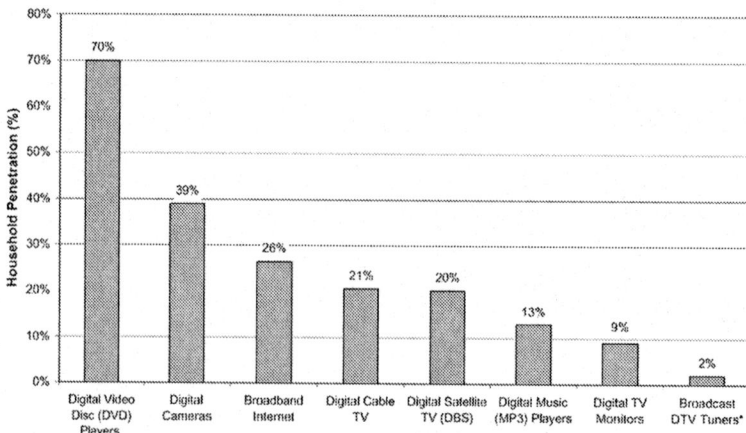

* As of January 2005
Sources: CEA, NCTA, SBCA, FCC, Census

---

[3] New America Foundation Research Associate Kartik Ramachandran compiled this chart.
[4] New America Foundation Research Associate Kartik Ramachandran compiled this chart.

INDEX

978-0-595-34704-9
0-595-34704-5

Printed in the United States
28260LVS00001B/154-171

9 780595 347049